PENGUIN BOOKS

CHARLOTTE BRONTË

'Affirmative, edifying, inspiring and humane – an admirable and appropriate tribute to its subject' *Sunday Express*

'Harman's sane, unshowy retelling is exactly right for the bicentenary. A retooled classic biographical narrative, shipshape and serviceable for the next two hundred years' Kathryn Hughes, *Guardian*

'Revelatory' Lucasta Miller, *Independent*

'Elegantly written, consistently perceptive, Harman succeeds in bringing Charlotte back to life in all her spiky vulnerability' *Daily Mail*

'A comprehensive biography to enjoy and admire. Harman writes well and she is a fine and sensitive critic' *The Times*

'[Harman] portrays Brontë's complexity and dark genius in elegant prose with deep human sympathy' *The Lady*

'Harman tells Charlotte's story with quick wit, a sharp sympathy, and a fire and fury of her own' Frances Wilson, *Evening Standard*

'Finely judged and authoritative' John Carey, *Sunday Times*

'Full of pleasing and piquant detail, scraps of passing recollection assembled from the various lives and letters in which the Brontës featured and from which we might reconstruct their world' *Financial Times*

'An excellent new bicentennial biography. Harman writes with warmth and a fine understanding of Ms Brontë's literary significance. Above all, she is a storyteller, with a sense of pace and timing, relish for a good scene and a wry sense of humour' *Economist*

'Vigorous, splendid' *Mail on Sunday*

'Immensely readable' *Woman and Home*

Charlotte Brontë

A Life

CLAIRE HARMAN

PENGUIN BOOKS

PENGUIN BOOKS

UK | USA | Canada | Ireland | Australia
India | New Zealand | South Africa

Penguin Books is part of the Penguin Random House group of companies
whose addresses can be found at global.penguinrandomhouse.com.

First published by Viking 2015
Published in Penguin Books 2016
002

Every effort has been made to trace copyright holders and to obtain their permission for the use
of copyright material. The publisher apologises for any errors or omissions and would be grateful to be
notified of any corrections that should be incorporated in future editions of this book.

Typeset in Bembo by Palimpsest Book Production Limited, Falkirk, Stirlingshire
Printed in Great Britain by Clays Ltd, St Ives plc

A CIP catalogue record for this book is available from the British Library

ISBN: 978-0-241-96366-1

www.greenpenguin.co.uk

MIX
Paper from
responsible sources
FSC® C018179

Penguin Random House is committed to a
sustainable future for our business, our readers
and our planet. This book is made from Forest
Stewardship Council® certified paper.

To Paul

. . . there's a fire and fury raging in that little woman a rage scorching her heart . . . She has had a story and a great grief that has gone badly with her

– William Makepeace Thackeray (1852)

. . . a tiny, delicate, little person, whose small hand nevertheless grasped a mighty lever which set all the literary world of that day vibrating

– Anne Thackeray Ritchie (1891)

. . . talented people almost always know full well the excellence that is in them

– Charlotte Brontë (1846)

Portrait of a young woman, by Charlotte Brontë; drawn in the copy of *Russell's General Atlas of Modern Geography* that she took with her to Brussels in 1842–3 (see p. 178). Copyright and photography: The Pierpont Morgan Library, New York, PML 129886.

Contents

List of Illustrations   xi

Prologue: 1 September 1843   1

1   Becoming Brontë   1777–1820   6

2   An Uncivilised Little Place   1820–25   23

3   The Genii of the Parsonage   1825–31   50

4   Among Schoolgirls   1831–5   64

5   The Double Life   1835–7   87

6   Labour in Vain   1837–41   105

7   In a Strange Land   1842   136

8   The Black Swan   1843   160

9   Long-looked-for Tidings   1844–5   182

10 Walking Invisible   1845–6   207

11 That Intensely Interesting Novel   1846–8   227

12 Across the Abyss   1848–9   258

13 Conquering the Big Babylon   1849–51   273

14 The Curate's Wife   1851–5   311

    Coda   351

Select Bibliography   361

Abbreviations   367

Notes   369

Acknowledgements   425

Index   429

Illustrations

1. Maria Branwell (1783–1821), copy of a miniature by J. Tonkin, 1799 (© Brontë Society)
2. Patrick Brontë (1777–1861), c. 1808 (© Brontë Society)
3. 26 Market Street, Thornton, c. 1904 (photograph by J. J. Stead, published in *The Bookman*, October 1904)
4. Haworth Parsonage, 1850s (© Brontë Society)
5. Map of Haworth, 1853, drawn up by the Board of Health (reproduced by permission of Bradford Libraries; photograph by Steven Wood)
6. Haworth – general view, a nineteenth-century engraving (© Brontë Society)
7. Interior of St Michael's Church, Haworth, c. 1865 (© Brontë Society)
8. Cowan Bridge School, engraving by O. Jewitt, 1824 (© Brontë Society)
9. Roe Head School, pencil drawing by Charlotte Brontë, c. 1831–2 (© Brontë Society)
10. Collection of juvenile manuscripts by Charlotte Brontë, 1826–30 (© Brontë Society)
11. Emily Jane Brontë, Diary Paper, 26 June 1837 (© Brontë Society)
12. Arthur Wellesley, pencil drawing by Charlotte Brontë, c. 1834 (© Brontë Society)
13. Branwell Brontë (1817–48), self-portrait in pencil (© Brontë Society)
14. Emily Brontë (1818–48), oil painting by Branwell Brontë, c. 1833–4 (© National Portrait Gallery, London)
15. Anne Brontë (1820–49), pencil drawing by Charlotte Brontë, 1833 (© Brontë Society)
16. Anne, Emily and Charlotte Brontë, oil painting by Branwell Brontë, c. 1833–4 (© National Portrait Gallery, London)
17. Interior of the Cathedral of SS-Michel-et-Gudule in Brussels, painting by T. Allom, engraved by T. Turnbull, 1840 (© Royal Library of Belgium, SIII 94143)
18. Rue d'Isabelle, Brussels, photograph by Victor Tahon, 1850s (© Archives of the City of Brussels, C-11525)
19. The Heger Family, oil painting by Ange François, 1846 (private collection)
20. Letter from Charlotte Brontë to Constantin Heger, 8 January 1845 (© The British Library Board, Add. 38732D)

21. Prospectus for the Misses Brontë's school, Haworth, 1844 (© Brontë Society)

22. Charlotte Brontë, chalk drawing by George Richmond, 1850 (© National Portrait Gallery, London)

23. Reverend William Weightman (1814–42), pencil drawing by Charlotte Brontë, *c*. 1840 (© Brontë Society)

24. Reverend Arthur Bell Nicholls (1819–1906), pencil sketch, probably by Charlotte Brontë, *c*. 1845–6 (© The Pierpont Morgan Library, New York, MA 2696.56)

25. Dining room, Haworth Parsonage (photograph by Simon Warner; © Brontë Society)

26. Title page of *Poems by Currer, Ellis and Acton Bell*, 1846

27. Autographs of Currer, Ellis and Acton Bell (© Brontë Society)

28. *A Parody*, drawing by Branwell Brontë, in a letter to J. B. Leyland (© Brontë Society)

29. George Smith (1824–1901), an anonymous portrait, *c*. 1848 (© Brontë Society)

30. William Smith Williams (1800–1875), photograph, *c*. 1860 (© Brontë Society)

31. Charlotte and Anne Brontë at the offices of Smith, Elder & Co. in July 1848, woodcut by Joan Hassall (from *The Brontë Story* by Margaret Lane)

32. William Makepeace Thackeray (1811–63), drawing by Francis Holl, after stipple engraving by Samuel Laurence, published 1853 (© National Portrait Gallery, London)

33. Harriet Martineau (1802–1876), chalk drawing by George Richmond, 1849 (© National Portrait Gallery, London)

34. Elizabeth Cleghorn Gaskell (1810–65), chalk drawing by George Richmond, 1851 (© National Portrait Gallery, London)

35. Ellen Nussey (1817–97), anonymous photograph, *c*. 1875 (reproduced by permission of Bradford Libraries)

36. Carte-de-visite photograph, probably of Ellen Nussey, *c*. 1855–6 (© Brontë Society)

37. Margaret Wooler (1792–1885), photograph, *c*. 1870 (© Brontë Society)

38. Mary Taylor (1817–93), photograph, *c*. 1870 (© Brontë Society)

39. Carte-de-visite photograph of Reverend Arthur Bell Nicholls (1819–1906), *c*. 1864 (© Brontë Society)

40. Patrick Brontë in old age (© Brontë Society)

41. Opening of Brontë Parsonage Museum, 1928 (© Brontë Society)

42. Charlotte Brontë, fair copy of *Jane Eyre*, 1847 (© The British Library Board, Add. 43474 f. 1)

Prologue

1 September 1843

It is 1 September 1843 and a 27-year-old Englishwoman is alone at the Pensionnat Heger in Brussels, a girls' school where she is an unpaid pupil-teacher. It is halfway through the long vacation and everyone else who has a home or family to go to left weeks ago: the proprietress, Madame Heger, is at the seaside with her husband and children; the other teachers are on holiday or travelling.

Miss Brontë's home is too far away to warrant a return for a mere two months. She can't afford the cost of the journey back to her father's Yorkshire parsonage, and, besides, arrangements should be kept to: Charlotte is a scrupulously dutiful person. But she is finding the empty dormitory oppressive, with all the beds covered in white cloths like a morgue; every meal is eaten alone, and the Pensionnat's beautiful garden, with its old fruit trees and *allée défendue* of limes, seems more of a prison than a refuge when the rest of the school is abandoned. To escape the heavy solitude, it is Miss Brontë's habit to go out and walk the city and the surrounding countryside for hours at a time. 'I should inevitably fall into the gulf of low spirits if I stayed always by myself here without a human being to speak to,' she writes to her sister Emily, who was her companion at the school the previous year and knows the place well. The truth is, although she doesn't tell Emily this, she is already in that gulf. She is desperately unhappy.

Her return to Brussels for a second year at the Pensionnat Heger Charlotte sees with hindsight to have been a terrible mistake, for she has fallen in love with someone who, it is painfully clear, will never see her in a romantic light. It is the headmistress's husband, Monsieur Constantin Heger, a man of impressive intellect and spirit, the first person outside her immediate family to take her seriously, the first man to treat her as a potential equal. But the thrill of having his attention in her first year, as a pupil, has been followed by misery in the second, as his junior colleague. The Hegers have become wary of Charlotte's ardour and eccentricities, and much more formal in their dealings with her. And now the man she considered her soul-mate is pretending that she is nothing special to him at all.

She looks in the mirror and sees, with ruthless clarity, a catalogue of defects; a huge brow, sallow complexion, prominent nose and a mouth that twists up slightly to the right, hiding missing and decayed teeth. She looks poor and ill-dressed, haunted and miserable, with none of the brilliant light from her 'great honest eyes' that other people sometimes saw, and marvelled at. '[I]t is an imbecility which I reject with contempt – for women who have neither fortune nor beauty . . . not to be able to convince themselves that they are unattractive.' That's what she had written six months earlier, when her friend Ellen, back home in Yorkshire, had ventured to suggest that there was some romantic motive for Charlotte's return abroad.

The pain of staying within doors is too much: she sets off along the length of the parc Royal to the porte de Louvain, through the gate and up the long hill heading eastwards away from the city. 'No inhabitant of Brussels need wander far to search for solitude,' she wrote later; 'let him but move half a league from his own city and he will find her brooding still and blank over the wide fields, so drear though so fertile, spread out treeless and trackless round the capital of Brabant.' Her destination is the Protestant Cemetery in Saint-Josse-ten-Noode, two miles beyond the walls of this predominantly Catholic city, a walk down into the hamlet of Evere, then up to the crest of a hill beyond. There is no church here, just a few dozen graves in a walled garden, heavily overgrown with cypress and yew, with inscriptions in English, French and German: the foreign tongues of alienated people dying far from home.

Charlotte has come to visit a particular grave, that of Martha Taylor, one of the West Riding family who had encouraged her to come out to Brussels in the first place and whose elder sister Mary had been Charlotte's most admired friend since girlhood. Charming, quirky Martha – a flirt and chatterbox – had been swept away by cholera: the last time Charlotte had been out to visit her grave was just two weeks after the funeral the previous October. Emily had been with her then, and Mary, and all three young women had gone back and spent a strange evening at the lodgings of another English family, the Dixons, in the rue Royale. But even that gloomy day seemed better than this utterly solitary one. The Dixons had all left Brussels now, as had Mary Taylor, and Emily was back home in Haworth.

From the cemetery Charlotte keeps walking away from the city, through valleys, farms and hamlets, to a hill where there is nothing but treeless fields as far as the eye can see. The furthest reach. She has to turn back, but coming into the city in the fading light she finds herself so desperately trying to put off returning to the Pensionnat that she ends up weaving around the surrounding streets to avoid it.

This unassuming-looking woman, tiny, unfashionable, darting out a look but not liking to hold one's eye, was *in extremis*.

Passing by the towering west front of the city's great cathedral, SS-Michel-et-Gudule, and hearing the bell calling the faithful to the evening service, Charlotte Brontë did something strange, unpredictable and entirely uncharacteristic: she followed the worshippers in. The prejudices that she had to overcome even to step inside the door of a Roman Catholic church were considerable; Charlotte, the daughter of an Irish Protestant minister, was, like all her family, ferociously anti-papist. She had been brought up to pity Catholics and to fear them – one of her great sources of discomfort in Belgium was the mere fact of being in a Catholic country, surrounded by a 'Romanism' that 'pervaded every arrangement'. Her letters from Brussels are full of remarks about the superstitious nature of her Catholic pupils and colleagues, their 'sensual indulgence' and the childishness of minds 'reared in slavery'. But, on that lonely September evening, she found herself wandering up and down the aisles of the venerable Gothic church and staying to hear the service. When it was over, she was still reluctant to leave and, gravitating towards a part of the cathedral where six or seven people were kneeling, she let herself be directed into a confessional. Explaining this queer whim to her sister the next day, she said, 'I felt as if I did not care what I did, provided it was not absolutely wrong, and that it served to vary my life and yield a moment's interest. I took a fancy to change myself into a Catholic and go and make a real confession to see what it was like.'

The ornate confessionals of Ste-Gudule are still there, guarded by massive wooden angels, with a central box for the priest and kneelers for penitents on either side. Charlotte had to wait at the grating for ten minutes while another confession proceeded in a barely audible whisper just a few feet away. It was a long interval for second and third thoughts to take hold, for the voice of her bigoted upbringing to shout down this strange 'fancy' – but she stayed put and eventually heard the communicating grille open and in the half-light saw the priest leaning her way – her cue to begin.

What did she say? In the letter she wrote about the episode to Emily the next day, Charlotte described everything but the substance of her confession: she described the difficulty she had explaining to the priest (in French, of course) what she, a Protestant, was doing in his church at all; she described the priest's surprise and alarm, and the news that her religion precluded her from enjoying 'le bonheur du sacrement'. '[B]ut I was determined to confess', Charlotte said, and the priest eventually agreed to hear her, reasoning that it might be the first step towards a conversion. Freed by this act of kindness, 'I actually did confess – a real confession.' Her sense of relief is palpable.

The object of Charlotte's unrequited love, Constantin Heger, was a difficult, mercurial character who haunted each of her later novels (as Rochester in *Jane Eyre*, Louis Moore in *Shirley*, Paul Emanuel in *Villette*), and he cost her two years of intense heartache, humiliation and futile hope. But Charlotte was also struggling with the larger issue of how she would ever accommodate her strong feelings – whether of love for Heger, or her intellectual passions, or her anger at circumstances and feelings of thwarted destiny – in the life that life seemed to have in store for her, one of patchy, unsatisfying employment, loneliness and hard work. What was someone like her, a plain, poor, clever, half-educated, dependent spinster daughter, to do with her own spiritual vitality and unfettered imagination? How could she live with the painful 'consciousness of faculties unexercised' that had moved her to go abroad in the first place, and that she recognised, from the example of her equally brilliant siblings, not as some sort of freakishness, but as an intimation of the sublime?

Coming away from the huge cathedral in the dark, Charlotte was already calculating how she would evade any consequences of the priest's interest in her situation, and she had no intention of ever repeating her experiment. But her moment of freedom in the confessional was a pivotal one. Far from home, speaking in a whisper in a foreign language to a priest of an utterly alien faith, she was able to express what had been an intolerable burden to contain. As Lucy Snowe in *Villette* says of her own confession, 'the mere relief of communication in an ear which was human and sentient, yet consecrated – the mere pouring out of some portion of long accumulating, long pent-up pain into a vessel whence it could not be again diffused – had done me good. I was already solaced.'

Charlotte Brontë's solace went further than the immediate comfort of confessional release. Her experience in Ste-Gudule gave her an idea not just of how to survive or override her most powerful feelings, but of how to transmute them into art. Within the year she was writing her first novel, *The Professor*, and, soon after that, sending out her poems to publishers with those of her sisters, under the pseudonyms Currer, Ellis and Acton Bell. The 'relief of communication' was in telling the truth: not to a stranger in the darkness in a whispered foreign tongue, but to readers, through her works.

Two weeks after Charlotte's visit to Ste-Gudule, the young Queen of England was in Brussels, on an official visit to her uncle Leopold, who, in 1831, had been made the first monarch of the new kingdom of Belgium. Victoria was an object of wonder across the globe – so young, so powerful, so female – and the sisters in Haworth had been fascinated by her ever since she came to the throne in 1837, a newly minted monarch of their own age and gender, ushering in a new age. Charlotte went out to see the royal party pass, and reported back to Emily, eager for any impressions. 'I saw her for an instant flashing through the Rue Royale in a carriage and six, surrounded by soldiers,' she wrote. 'She was laughing and talking, very gaily.'

Five years later, the insignificant little Englishwoman in the cheering crowd who had watched Victoria flash by would be keeping that queen and half the nation awake with the novel she had written.

Becoming Brontë

1777–1820

Charlotte Brontë's father was born on St Patrick's Day 1777, in a cottage in Emdale, County Down, in the last decades before the Act of Union with Great Britain. His father, Hugh Brunty, Prunty, O'Prunty or Branty – the name wasn't written down often enough to have a settled spelling – was a Protestant farm-hand and sometime lime-kiln worker, originally from the south of Ireland, who married a woman called Alice, or Eleanor, McClory. Facts about either parent are scarce. Was Alice a Catholic, as some traditions have it, snatched from a different bridegroom on her wedding day by the impetuous Hugh? Had Hugh run away from home as a boy? Was he, as some biographers claimed in the glory-days of Brontë myth-making, a famous local storyteller, a sort of peasant maker? Patrick Brontë himself shut down curiosity about them when he claimed his family history was so irrelevant that he hadn't ever bothered to find it out:

> My father's name was Hugh Brontë – He was a native of the South of Ireland, and was left an orphan at an early age – It was said that he was of an Ancient Family. Whether this was, or was not so, I never gave myself the trouble to inquire, since his lot in life, as well as mine, depended, under providence, not on family descent but our own exertions.

This was to Elizabeth Gaskell, the woman Patrick had appointed to write a memoir of his daughter Charlotte in the 1850s. Patrick Brontë is of course unlikely to have been such an innocent bystander of his own autobiography; on the contrary, he proved rather keen to control it. In his mind, though, the story only began with exertions which paid off.

The cottage where Patrick, the first of the Bruntys' ten children, is believed to have been born could not have been more modest: a two-roomed thatched cabin with a mud floor and rough-cast walls. The bedroom was in the back and the kitchen in the front, where Hugh is said to have earned a little extra money by roasting corn in a small kiln. This kind of primitive dwelling, typical of the time and place, is recalled in Patrick's poem 'The Irish Cabin', where he extols an ideal of simplicity and humility, a moral home:

> A neat Irish cabin, snowproof,
> Well thatched, had a good earthen floor,
> One chimney in midst of the roof,
> One window, and one latched door.

But it's not entirely certain that the Bruntys ever lived in such picturesque deprivation. The better documented home was the one where Hugh and Alice lived after 1781, a house in nearby Lisnacreevey, where in due course Patrick had some schooling and learnt to read and write. Both his parents were practically illiterate but fostered a respect for book-learning in their children and owned four books themselves: the Bible, a separate New Testament, *Pilgrim's Progress* and Robert Burns's *Poems*. Young Patrick Brunty would have been able to read many times Burns's account of how he was 'called' from the plough by his Muse, a story that galvanised a generation of romantics and dreamers. The triumph of native genius over poverty and obscurity could hardly have reached a more impressionable audience, or been passed on to great effect.

With the family growing at a steady rate of a baby almost every two years, the firstborn son of the Bruntys was never in any doubt of his duty to get out to work as soon as possible and make the most every opportunity to further both himself and the group at large. And was the age of twelve he was working part-time at the local blacks not cut later apprenticed to a linen-weaver and draper, but Padly, was of out to be a labourer or artisan; his work at the looms, like his poor standard because of his devotion to reading his task. The daughter Emily later, he had a book propped up memorised enormous amounts of verse, capturing in his m he couldn't own personally (*Paradise Lost* was a particular fa the local Presbyterian minister, Reverend Andrew Hardsha youth with scholarly habits and gave him free run of his own library. And after the boy turned sixteen, Hardshaw helped him to get a job teaching local children at the village school in Glascar.

Patrick Brunty's career as a teenaged schoolmaster was not very rewarding, as he had little empathy with children (despite coming from a large family) and was unwilling to stagnate at what seemed the furthest boundary of self-improvement. His wages were so small that in five or six years he managed to save only a few pounds and his future opportunities must have seemed rather bleak – worse than those of his siblings, who carried on the labouring life that was all his family had known thus far. But Patrick held out for something more cerebral.

This was a time of violence and upheaval in the country and abroad, of Levellers and small insurgent groups stalking the countryside at night with revolutionary hopes kindled by the dramatic example of what had just taken place in France. The Brunty family was divided dramatically on the issue of independence from English rule, and, one has to assume, along religious lines too, as Patrick's next youngest brother, William, was a United Irishman, one of Wolfe Tone's revolutionaries pressing violently for Catholic and Nonconformist emancipation. William fought at the Battle of Ballynahinch in 1798, which ended in a rout of Tone's supporters and marked the end of the ʳ⁻ellion in Ulster. No wonder Patrick kept his distance from this brᵒ⁻er; Catholic agitators were, in his view, 'insidious, And Malignanⁱ inhe emies' of the Protestant status quo, and mass movements politicᵃ dangerous. 'I am a true friend to liberty of conscience and most thᵃtty,' he once said, 'but . . . of all kinds of tyranny I dread Patrickʰᵉ multitude.'

reflected inᵗ sness and loneliness in these formative years might be cloud, havingʳʸ that he eventually left Glascar school under a ment with a ʰmplained of' for some sort of romantic entanglement twenties) he hadᵐer's daughter. But by that time (his early men in the district, the attention of one of the most influential of Ireland churchᵃᵗ Tighe, JP, vicar of the newly built Church as tutor to his two soⁿyroney. Tighe offered Patrick a position to a life in holy orders, ᵃⁿ to direct the young man's thoughts movement to regeneratⁱing him to participate in the powerful lished Church, spearheaded by John

Wesley and clerics such as Charles Simeon, Tighe's mentor at Cambridge. In return for tutoring the minister's sons, Patrick received lessons in Latin and Greek, the essential subjects for anyone aspiring to a university place, so that by the age of twenty-five – an advanced age, by any standards – and after years of dogged application and hard work, he was ready to apply for admission to Tighe's alma mater to study for the priesthood. Thus he left home and family ties behind him in 1802 and made his way across the Irish Sea, via the great and strange cities of Liverpool and London, to the cool splendour of Cambridge, the dizzying riches of the college libraries and the demanding company of a lot of clever, confident, privileged young men. It was a remarkable transition from one kind of life to another, the details of which Patrick never tired of relating and which never failed to impress.

Having no resources apart from a few pounds in his pocket, Patrick was admitted to St John's as a 'sizar', a student whose education was subsidised by domestic work, placing him in a distinctly different social stratum from the main body of commoners. His pride was in no way piqued by this lower status (unlike his daughter Charlotte when she found herself isolated socially as a governess), and he strove successfully for college prizes to help support himself, studying as hard as possible to justify the faith in him that Tighe and others had shown. In his second year Brunty received a grant of £20 from the Evangelical philanthropists William Wilberforce and Henry Thornton: a good use of funds, for the candidate was unusually frugal and focused, managing to live 'very genteelly' on a fraction of what the other undergraduates had, as fellow sizar Henry Kirke White noted with admiration when he arrived at the college three years later.

Patrick's time at Cambridge was marked by a very significant change. His first known signatures date from 1791, when he wrote his name five times over in a book, four times as 'Prunty' and once as 'Brunty', and when he matriculated at St John's, in 1802, it was under the name 'Patrick Branty', written down by a college official, and probably reflecting the new student's strong Irish accent. But the name he now wished to go by was Bronte, a more genteel and elegant rendition of his variable patronymic, with splendid associations ever since the award of the title Duke of Bronte to Rear-Admiral Horatio Nelson in 1799. Nelson's Bronte was a site on the slopes of Mount Etna in Sicily, divertingly exotic and un-Irish – the word is Greek, in fact, meaning 'thunder' (a pun Charlotte would later make hay with). Patrick tried out many variant spellings over the next few years – Bronté, Bronte, Brontë – eventually settling on the diaeresis and 'Brontë', probably to indicate how to pronounce it correctly. Nelson adopted the signature 'Bronte Nelson' or 'Nelson & Bronte', and in the years following the Battle of Trafalgar, in 1805, it can have done Patrick no harm to suggest a connection between himself and the demi-god who had saved the nation from invasion. Even in the 1840s his daughter Charlotte was assumed to be the hero's kin. Becoming 'Brontë' was a powerful act of refashioning on the part of Patrick Brunty, and, although his invented name sprang up and flourished for only one generation, it went far in fame.

A brief return to Drumballyroney in 1806 between graduation from Cambridge and taking holy orders seems to have been the last time Patrick Brontë set foot in his native land. He was there to secure the written proof of his birth, which was necessary for ordination, and during his visit preached his first sermon at Tighe's church, where his family worshipped, and where his parents and some of his siblings were later buried. He never went home again – despite an apparent disinclination 'to live & rot in old England'. In later life Patrick was surrounded by Irish clergymen in Yorkshire who thought nothing of travelling home once or twice a year, a journey that, after the establishment of the railways, was neither difficult nor prohibitively expensive. But Brontë stayed put. There seems to have been little love lost between him and his siblings, and he scarcely mentions his mother at all. He kept in touch with his family sporadically, mostly through the third eldest, Hugh, but his letters were not affectionate, and there's more than a touch of resentment in his reference, as late as 1855 (in his will), to having given them 'considerable sums in times past'.

Patrick took up his first curacy in Wethersfield, Essex, in the autumn of 1806 and was ordained priest the following year, at the age of thirty. At this point in his life he was more than ready to look for a wife, and thought he had found one in his landlady's niece, Mary Burder, an attractive nineteen-year-old who lived with her widowed mother and siblings. Patrick's ardent, eccentric manner and handsome person won Mary's heart, and he in turn seems to have been animated by her youthful simplicity and affection, sharing with her his hopes and ambitions for the future, and writing some wordy verses in her praise. By 1808 he had proposed and been accepted, albeit without her family's approval and possibly without their knowledge.

In the end, the engagement to Mary Burder foundered, it seems, because Brontë began to think he had 'violated both the dictates of my conscience and my judgment' by seeking to ally himself with a Nonconformist. If so, it shows him as both a reckless and rather chilly lover. After a brief time away in Leicestershire, assessing what his prospects for promotion there might be, he returned to Wethersfield in a mood of 'peace & contentment', as he reported complacently to a Cambridge friend. He fully expected Mary Burder to be equally mellow about their recent severance, and, even when she made a succession of trips away to avoid having to see him in the parish, the curate interpreted this as pragmatism rather than pique: 'The Lady I mentioned, is always in exile,' he wrote; 'her Guardians can scarcely believe me, that I have given the affair entirely up forever.'

Mary Burder was soon relieved of his presence. Patrick moved from Wethersfield to Wellington in Shropshire at the start of 1809 to take up a curacy under Reverend John Eyton, another of Charles Simeon's followers. Wellington was a growing centre of Methodism, and Brontë met a group of very like-minded men there, making lifelong friends with his fellow curate William Morgan, a strong-minded and talkative Welshman, and the local schoolmaster John Fennell. One of the areas being targeted by the movement was Yorkshire, so it was with the pleasure of champions entering the fray that all three young men, Brontë, Morgan and Fennell, found themselves posted to the West Riding. Morgan took a curacy, and Fennell was head of a new boarding school for the sons of Methodist preachers at Woodhouse Grove in Apperley Bridge near Leeds. Patrick himself went first to Dewsbury, where he was assistant to another inspirational vicar, John Buckworth, and in July 1810 took up his most responsible post to date, as perpetual curate of Hartshead-cum-Clifton, a village near Huddersfield.

Brontë's reputation for being an eccentric outsider seems to have originated in these early bachelor curacies. He is said not to have got on very well with his wealthier parishioners in Dewsbury, who cavilled at his Irish background and accent. Irishness also told against him at Hartshead, where he was called 'Old Staff' on account of the shillelagh that was his usual accessory and that he once used to drive some bell-ringers out of church when they broke the Sabbath by attempting a competition practice. There were other, more heroic stories about him too: rescuing a simpleton whom bullies had thrown into the flooded River Calder and fighting off a man threatening a parish school procession. His landlord's daughter later said that he was thought 'clever and good-hearted, but hot-tempered, and in fact, a little queer'.

One of the curate's reported peculiarities was that he had been seen pacing up and down the Dewsbury vicarage garden, pencil and paper in hand, writing. Patrick Brontë had in fact been composing poetry for at least three years and had high hopes for himself in the field, publishing, in 1810, at his own expense, a slim volume called *Winter-Evening Thoughts: A Miscellaneous Poem*. *Cottage Poems* followed the next year, a much longer production, with very fine paper, design and type for a volume, as the preface declared, aimed at 'the labouring poor'. What was the minister trying to achieve: literary fame, a novel way of spreading the gospel, or both? Or did he consider these self-published books as elaborate calling-cards, to advertise his talents abroad? The poems in his second publication were as undistinguished as the first; the rhymes and metres often risible (one poem, 'The Cottage Maid', sounding unfortunately like a series of limericks), his address to a highly sentimentalised common man doomed to miss its mark. And the message he wished to convey, in a period of extreme hardship and distress after fifteen years of war, was both anxiously reactionary and inhumanely pious: essentially, the poor should rejoice in their lot and not seek to change it. But the most revealing part of *Cottage Poems* is perhaps its introduction, in which Patrick Brontë admits, a little guiltily, how addictively enjoyable writing could be: 'from morning till noon, and from noon till night, [the author's] employment was full of real, indescribable pleasure, such as he could wish to taste as long as life lasts.'

Very few copies of this book survive, but one, in the Berg Collection of the New York Public Library, is bound in vellum and has a beautifully written inscription: 'To Miss Fennell,/By the Author,/as a Token of his/purest Friendship,/and Christian/Love'. The copy is missing its raciest page (a passage from 'Winter-Night Meditations' about rakes and prostitutes in 'sin-polluted' cities) and contains a number of corrections and annotations in ink that can have been made only by the author. Strangest of these is the adjustment of two lines in 'Verses Sent to a Lady on her Birth-Day', from 'Full soon your eyes of sparkling blue/And velvet lips of scarlet hue,/Discoloured, may decay' to 'Full soon your sparkling hazle eye/And velvet lips, of scarlet dye' etc. This was a poem written in the Mary Burder era, but in his adjustments it looks as if Patrick was customising his book for a new 'Lady', in a way that could seem familiar and jocular if the sentiments of the poems weren't so severe. 'But hark, fair maid! whate'er they say/You're but a breathing mass of clay/Fast ripening for the grave' are lines unlikely to delight a twenty-year-old girl, and if Brontë hoped they would draw Miss Fennell's hazel eye his way, he was mistaken. His friend William Morgan was about to take that prize.

Brontë had moved to Hartshead at a time of 'unhappy disturbance' in the West Riding, as more and more workers in the cloth industry were finding themselves replaced by machines, predominantly the cloth-dressers, or 'Croppers', who performed the most specialised and highly paid part of production, the trimming of wool fibres from finished material. The secret society known as the Luddites had formed in defence of the croppers and others like them, appearing under cover of darkness, armed, masked and, like their leader 'General Ludd', under false names. Hundreds of men, calling themselves armies, could be mustered in this way, their faces blackened, staves, pikes and hammers at the ready to damage or destroy the hated shearing-frames and gig-mills. In February 1812 there were nightly attacks of varying degrees of violence on mills in the West Riding and Spen Valley. Some owners were champing at the bit to fight back: William Horsfall of Ottiwells went as far as acquiring a cannon, while in Patrick Brontë's own parish William Cartwright of Rawfolds Mill armed his workmen with stones, guns and vitriol to protect his property at night.

Cartwright was ready and waiting for the Luddites when over a hundred of them mustered at a nearby inn on the night of 11 April 1812 and proceeded in silence to the mill. The attack on the building lasted twenty minutes, but, with so many guns and men on Cartwright's side, there was little doubt who would prevail, and the would-be machine-breakers had to retreat in disarray, leaving two of their number wounded. A detachment of the Queen's Bays arrived within the hour and the two captives were taken to an inn in nearby Roberttown and kept under arrest until they died, interrogated to the last by the vicar of Liversedge, Hammond Roberson, Patrick Brontë's predecessor at Hartshead.

Where was Patrick Brontë while the attack on Rawfolds Mill was going on? The rioters included many Hartshead parishioners, and there must have been widespread intelligence locally of the plan in preparation; even the sentinels at the mill were suspicious for the two preceding nights. As a clergyman of the Established Church, Patrick Brontë belonged ostensibly to the ruling class under attack, but he was conspicuously not of the group who helped Cartwright defend his property and if he signed the testimonial later condemning the action, we cannot know, as the ink has faded too much to read. None of the rioters was betrayed to the authorities, despite the presence of 4,000 troops in the region and many government spies, and despite the posting of vast rewards for information leading to the conviction of participants. Brontë's position was a difficult one: as a working cleric he fully understood the plight of his unemployed and desperate parishioners, but as a man, he had little confidence in his social power among his superiors. Legend has it that he secretly buried in unmarked graves at Hartshead fatally injured rioters, or some of the seventeen Luddites sentenced to death for their part in the Rawfolds attack following their show trial in York nine months later. Neither of these stories is likely to be true, but they reflect people's sense of where Patrick Brontë's sympathies lay and when she chose to set her third novel, *Shirley*, during the Luddite riots in the Spen Valley, Charlotte Brontë was in a way expressing her own, and her father's, delayed shock reactions to this bloody chapter in local and national history.

One of Patrick Brontë's responsibilities was to act as an examiner at Woodhouse Grove, and it was on a visit there in the summer of 1812 that he met Mrs Fennell's niece from Cornwall, 29-year-old Maria Branwell. Maria had come to help in the school, be a companion to her cousin Jane (an only child) and perhaps replace her in the Fennell household after Jane's marriage to William Morgan, planned for the end of the year.

The family Maria came from in Penzance was cultured and prosperous. Her father, Thomas Branwell, dead since 1808, had been an importer of luxury goods with a grocery shop in the Market Square; he had also had investments in a local brewery and bank, and had been a member of the town council. There was a sizeable family presence in the town, since Thomas had eleven children and his brother Richard, who was responsible for building the popular Assembly Rooms in the 1790s, was the father of ten, one of whom went on to have twelve children. They were a staunchly Methodist clan.

Maria was the eighth of her family, which was widely spread out in age (Mrs Branwell had been forty-seven when she had her last baby). A picture of Maria aged about fifteen shows a girl with a very lively and intelligent expression casting a quizzical look at the artist, a first and last glance from this enigmatic figure, since the only other images of her – an anonymous amateur profile and an enhanced copy of it lovingly made by Charlotte some years after her mother's death – show little more than a conventionally neat and modest matron. When Thomas Branwell died, he bequeathed each of his four daughters a £50 annuity, the generosity of which can be measured against the £20 a year that Charlotte Brontë earned as a governess thirty years later. This gave them a considerable degree of independence, and the three unmarried sisters, Elizabeth, Maria and Charlotte (aged thirty-two, twenty-five and seventeen respectively), stayed on at the family home with their mother, and then, after her death in 1809, on their own. 'For some years now I have been perfectly my own mistress,' Maria told Patrick Brontë when they were courting, 'subject to no *control* whatever – so far from it, that my sisters who are many years older than myself, and even my dear mother, used to consult me in every case of importance, and scarcely ever doubted the propriety of my opinions and actions.' Maria told her fiancé frankly that she felt she could have done with a little less of that freedom, and the responsibilities that went with it: 'I thank God, it never led me into error, yet, in circumstances of perplexity and doubt, I have deeply felt the want of a guide and instructor.' Her deference was conventional for a bride-to-be, but Maria was also communicating to Patrick a history of management and independence.

The death early in 1812 of their uncle Richard, who owned the house the sisters lived in, precipitated changes. Charlotte Branwell decided to stay in Penzance (she had fallen in love with her cousin Joseph and was engaged to marry him), as did Elizabeth, a confirmed spinster at thirty-six, but Maria made the bold move to join her aunt Jane and husband John Fennell in Yorkshire, and help them in the running of Woodhouse Grove. At twenty-nine, she seemed to have little intention of going back to a life of inaction, and while making herself useful at the school and offering herself as a future domestic substitute for her cousin Jane, she might also have been on the lookout for a mate herself.

She found one very quickly in the queer, talkative best friend of cousin Jane's fiancé. She and Patrick Brontë struck up an acquaintance on his visits to the school and soon were 'walking out' together to local beauty spots, where Patrick impressed her with his charm and qualities of mind and spirit. With his person too, no doubt. Patrick Brontë was tall and well-made, with dark red hair, piercing eyes, a 'nobly-shaped head, and erect carriage'. Mrs Gaskell, who met him when he was almost seventy years old, guessed immediately that 'in his youth he must have been unusually handsome'. Maria Branwell, on the other hand, was extremely small and 'not pretty, but very elegant', a description that passed without objection by Patrick Brontë, so must have truth in it and may have even originated with him. Very few other descriptions of her exist, but they indicate an amiable, wry and clever woman, 'possessing more than ordinary talents'.

We know about their courtship wholly from Maria's side, as nine remarkably frank and revealing letters she wrote to Patrick were preserved carefully by him. They contain almost all we know about the mother of the Brontës; the only other relic of her that has survived is a pious essay. That there are so few letters makes their thoughtful, soliloquising air all the more poignant, as Charlotte appreciated better than anybody when she read them forty years later: 'there is a rectitude, a refinement, a constancy, a modesty, a sense – a gentleness about them indescribable. I wished She had lived and that I had known her.' The first letter was written in August 1812, full of bemusement at the speed of events: 'If you knew what were my feelings whilst writing this you would pity me,' Maria said to the near-stranger she had fallen in love with. '[I] fear to go too far, and exceed the bounds of propriety.' The places they had known together had begun to seem insipid without 'your arm to assist me, and your conversation to shorten the walk'; she was thinking about her lover so much, in fact, that 'when I work, if I wish to get *forward* I may be glad that you are at a distance.' Somehow, she felt compelled to confess all this to Patrick: 'I have now written a pretty long letter without reserve or caution, and if all the sentiments of my heart are not laid open to you believe me it is not because I wish them to be concealed.'

By early September the couple were promised to each other in secret, Patrick having proposed, picturesquely, in the grounds of Kirkstall Abbey. Maria's cousin and family had formed 'a pretty correct notion' how matters stood, however, 'and as their hints, etc., meet with no contradiction from me, my silence passes for confirmation.' Maria had progressed from addressing Patrick as 'Dear Friend' to 'My dear Saucy Pat', but she was aware that every advance in intimacy left her more vulnerable. When there was a delay in getting a reply to her letters, or no answer at all, she was painfully disappointed, and Patrick's tendency to forget or mistake messages obviously disturbed her more scrupulous and dutiful nature. On one occasion, some visitors turned up at the Fennells' unannounced, Patrick having entirely forgotten to pass on their intention to call. Everyone put this down, good-humouredly, to the young minister's being 'mazed' with love: 'And even I begin to think that *this*, together with the *note*, bears some marks of *insanity*! However, I shall suspend my judgment until I hear what excuse you can make for yourself. I suppose you will be quite ready to make one of some kind or another.' This was an interesting tone to be adopting so early in their acquaintance: fond, indulgent, but consciously patient. Maria's expectation of happiness was great – 'the anticipation of sharing with you all the pleasures and pains, the cares and anxieties of life, of contributing to your comfort and becoming the companion of your pilgrimage, is more delightful to me than any other prospect which this world can possibly present' – but she also seems to have intuited that even requited love might not necessarily entail mental intimacy and that to some degree she would always be observing this unusual man and needing to accommodate his personality. No wonder that the letters resonated with Charlotte when she was shown them in 1850, who could herself have penned this frank, sensual, thoughtful declaration, written in fear of Patrick having cooled slightly in his responses, just three weeks before their wedding:

Real love is ever apt to suspect that it meets not with an equal return; you must not wonder then that my fears are sometimes excited. My pride cannot bear the idea of a diminution of your attachment, or to think that it is stronger on my side than on yours . . . I am certain no one ever loved you with an affection more pure, constant, tender, and ardent than that which I feel. Surely this is not saying too much; it is the truth, and I trust you are worthy to know it.

Charlotte's friend Ellen Nussey saw the letters in the 1850s too, and remembered 'a pathos of apprehension' in them from Maria's thoughtful, solitary musings about the man she was to marry. Impressive as Patrick Brontë was, and blessed with unflinching faith and an intellect that was all the stronger for its simplicity, Maria Branwell seems to have had the superior mind and finer sensibility, and the modesty to suppress that fact.

The summer and autumn of 1812 passed quickly for the lovers, snatching time to go on walks together, and for Patrick attending to the preparation of married quarters. Maria didn't go home to Cornwall to settle her affairs there, and just a few weeks before the wedding the trunk containing her possessions was involved in a shipwreck off the Devonshire coast. Everything was lost except 'a very few articles', including two very different kinds of reading matter, *The Imitation of Christ* and some copies of *The Lady's Magazine*. The shipwreck must have seemed strangely symbolic of the abrupt and final cutting off from home that her marriage effected, for, just as Patrick never returned to Ireland, there is no record of Maria ever going back to her beloved Cornwall after 1812. They were starting afresh, on their own voyage together.

The wedding – or weddings, rather – took place on 29 December 1812, for three were celebrated at the same time on the same day. While Charlotte Branwell and Joseph Branwell were exchanging vows in Cornwall, Patrick Brontë and Maria Branwell and William Morgan and Jane Fennell were doing so at Guiseley Church in North Yorkshire. In a charming, almost comical arrangement, Mr Fennell was to give both the Guiseley brides away and both couples interchanged roles in turn: first William performed the marriage ceremony for Patrick and Maria, with Jane acting as bridesmaid, then they all swapped round and Patrick was minister,

Maria the bridesmaid and Jane and William bride and groom. Meanwhile, Charlotte and Joseph were taking their vows 'on the same day and hour' in Madron Church, the very place where John Fennell and Jane Branwell had married twenty-two years earlier. Through these coincidences, the occasion enforced and celebrated all the connections between these very like-minded people, a little society in itself optimistically setting out to do good in the West Riding.

Patrick and Maria Brontë began their married life at Hartshead, in a rented house at the top of the hill. Patrick wasn't happy with the accommodation, especially after they knew that their first child was on the way, but his attempts to get a new parsonage built with money from the Church Commissioners led to disappointment and personal expense, and he seems to have been looking around almost immediately for a different parish. Maria gave birth to a daughter, named after her, early in 1814, and another daughter, Elizabeth, was born the following year. In the meantime, Patrick had come to a happy agreement with his friend Thomas Atkinson of Thornton (who was courting a young woman near Hartshead), and in May 1815 the two clerics swapped parishes and the Brontës moved with their two little girls to a square stone modern house on Market Street, just a few hundred yards from St James's Church and the main road into Bradford.

Patrick Brontë always spoke of his five years in Thornton as the best of his life. He and his wife were in their prime, their family was growing, and for the first and last time the Brontës made close and affectionate friendships in the village where they lived, most particularly with the local doctor, John Scholefield Firth and his eighteen-year-old daughter Elizabeth, who lived at Kipping House, a few minutes' walk down the road from the Brontës' modest parsonage. Elizabeth's mother had died the previous year in a riding accident, so Elizabeth, an only child, was running the household when the new curate's family moved in. She immediately warmed to Maria Brontë and her little girls and stood godmother to the younger one, Elizabeth, when she was baptised in August 1815.

There was 'constant friendly intercourse' between the two families and strong ties among their mutual friends, whose relationships were complex and close-knit. Thomas Atkinson, with whom Brontë had swapped livings (and who was a nephew of Hammond Roberson), married Dr Firth's niece Frances Walker soon after his move to Harts-head.★ Dr Firth's second wife, Anne, whom he married in 1815, had a twin sister, Mrs Frances Outhwaite, whose daughter Frances was a schoolfriend of Elizabeth Firth and became Anne Brontë's godmother. Her brother, John Outhwaite, a respected young physician in Brad-ford, became a friend of Patrick Brontë.† Between them, they made up a network of professional contacts, friends and godparents who stood the Brontës and their children in good stead their whole lives.

Maria's elder sister Elizabeth Branwell was also part of this friendly circle. She stayed with her sister and brother-in-law from the middle of 1815 (the time of her god-daughter Elizabeth Brontë's christening) until after the birth of the next baby in the summer of 1816, and became a good friend of Miss Firth. Bradford had a library and a literary society, of which Patrick Brontë was a member, and there were many musical events and lectures. They also enjoyed dinners, outings, countless tea-drinkings and long, ambitious walks – to the top of Allerton, to Swill Hill. Both these last were in July 1815, just before Maria Brontë found out she was expecting her third child. The Duke of Wellington's vic-tory at Waterloo was a cause of national rejoicing that summer, and at his church in Liversedge Hammond Roberson had just had a new set of bells fitted in time to celebrate, cast from cannon captured from the French at Genoa. In Thornton, the Firths and Brontës collected money for the widows and orphans of Waterloo and took part in a day of pub-lic thanksgiving in January 1816 for the restoration of peace, and it seemed a hopeful time when the new baby, a girl called Charlotte, was born on 21 April.

Elizabeth Branwell returned to Penzance soon after the baby's christening,‡ taking an affectionate leave of Miss Firth, who noted 'she kissed me and was much affected'. Patrick Brontë was also sorry to see her go, and inscribed a copy of *Cottage Poems* to his 'beloved sister' as a token of 'affection and esteem'. Aunt Branwell's later reputation was as

---

★ The Atkinsons became godparents to Charlotte Brontë and Mrs Atkinson was the aunt of Amelia Walker, one of Charlotte's later schoolfriends.

† The Outhwaites were a philanthropic family – John was well loved for not charg-ing the poorer patients at Bradford Infirmary, and Frances and her mother were patrons of the Bradford School of Industry.

‡ At which the godparents were Thomas and Frances Atkinson.

a bit of a dry old stick, but this shows that in 1816, aged thirty-nine, she was responsive, appreciative and very much part of the friendly Thornton group.

To help run the household, the Brontës got their first servant the same year, a twelve-year-old-girl called Nancy Garrs, who had been trained at Bradford School of Industry, a home for orphans and poor children of which Mrs Outhwaite was a patron. Nancy acted as cook, maid and nurse to the growing family. Mrs Brontë was soon pregnant again, and this time, much to everyone's delight, she gave birth to a son, Patrick Branwell Brontë, fourteen months after Charlotte, on 26 June 1817. Nancy's sister Sarah joined the household the following year, by which time another baby was on the way, a girl born on 30 July 1818 and christened Emily Jane. The comings and goings between the Firth and Brontë families were as frequent as ever, though Miss Firth's walks into Bradford were now mostly without Maria, so busy at home with her five young children, and tea parties were sometimes, charmingly, arranged for the older Brontë girls on their own. 'M. E. and C. Brontë to tea,' Miss Firth recorded in January 1819, and again, in October, 'The little Brontës called.'

The year 1819 was a troubled one in the north of England. The aftermath of the long war had brought widespread unemployment and new protectionist Corn Laws taxing imported grain led to distress from high bread prices. Tensions rose dramatically following the shocking slaughter in August of fifteen men and women attending a pro-reform rally in St Peter's Field, Manchester, bitterly dubbed 'Peterloo'. For some months that autumn and winter, the country seemed on the brink of armed rebellion, with uprisings uncomfortably close to Thornton, one as near as Huddersfield. On 29 September, Miss Firth noted: 'Came home in safety, thank God'; and on 31 March 1820, 'We sat up expecting the Radicals.' Her grandson later explained that Patrick Brontë had completely unnerved his old friends with tales of what he had witnessed in Ireland in 1798, and 'by his prophecies of what was coming in England, almost frightened Mr Firth to death, so that he had all his windows barred up in consequence'. Patrick's own habit of keeping loaded guns around the house, by his bed and even on his person (reported by various servants and visitors from the 1820s onwards) may well date from this time.

The anxious vigil at Kipping House took place just after the christening of Maria's sixth baby, Anne, to whom Elizabeth Firth and Fanny Outhwaite stood as godmothers. But the Brontës were not to be their neighbours much longer. The vicar of Bradford had nominated Patrick to the perpetual curacy of Haworth, a village only a few miles to the north-west of Thornton, but on high, windswept ground. The chapelry itself had a challengingly wide spread, taking in villages within a radius of almost eight miles, but it was the former parish of a famous evangelical preacher, William Grimshaw, and it possessed a good-sized, free-standing parsonage house, very suitable for the family, who by now must have struggled to fit into Market Street's modest rooms. They made plans to leave.

Patrick Brontë had published two more books in his years at Thornton, *The Maid of Killarney* (1818) and *The Cottage in the Wood; or, The Art of Becoming Rich and Happy* (1815), the latter a charming little production, 3 by 5 inches in size, with a beautifully executed frontispiece specially commissioned for the book, showing a pious cottager discovering a drunkard at his door. In later years the Brontë children must have been intensely interested in their father's little novel, scaled down to their size and with its fine illustration and neat print. Even the story would have enthralled them, with its taming of a rake by a good girl, and readers of Charlotte Brontë's novels might recognise some familiar themes – a man hoping he can bribe a girl into mistresshood or marriage, the girl's virtuous determination to support herself, whatever the difficulty, and her reward of a surprise bequest.

The author's preface marks a decided change from his confession in *Cottage Poems* of the thrill he got from writing; here, Patrick warns against developing an addiction to it that destroys the writer's contentment with the everyday:

> The sensual novelist and his admirer, are beings of depraved appetites and sickly imaginations, who having learnt the art of *self-tormenting*, are diligently and zealously employed in creating an imaginary world, which they can never inhabit, only to make the real world, with which they must necessarily be conversant, gloomy and insupportable.

Patrick Brontë's children had the run of his books and must have read these words often, but no group of young people ever took less heed of such a warning.

An Uncivilised Little Place

1820–25

Patrick Brontë's move to Haworth was fraught with vexations. The vicar of Bradford had made the appointment without seeking the opinion or approval of the church trustees, who did not take kindly to being ignored. Confusion reigned for a few weeks: Brontë resigned before he had even taken up residence, and his replacement, Samuel Redhead – also elected by the vicar without reference to the trustees – was given a potent demonstration of local discontent when the whole congregation walked out of his first service. In the wake of this decisive thumbs-down Patrick Brontë returned to the post, although he didn't move his family across to the village immediately. Haworth already seemed a contentious place in comparison with Thornton.

The parsonage the Brontës moved to in April 1820 was considerably bigger than the one they had left but stood at a remove, separated from the village by the church and from the church by the graveyard. The view that greeted them from their new front windows was of a small piece of scrubby garden, a low wall with a gate, then graves. At the back there were fewer windows, with mullions instead of wooden sashes, looking out on to the parson's field and beyond it to the moor.

The house itself had been built in the 1780s and had four main rooms on each of two floors and a small vaulted cellar. The front door opened into a wide hall with a dining room on the left, which became the family's chief reception room, and a parlour on the right, used by Patrick Brontë as his study. Behind that room was the main kitchen, the heart of the house, with a fire always burning in the range and a large table around which the children often gathered; and along a passageway was the back-kitchen, where the laundry was done in a copper and where tradesmen and parishioners who came on business were shown. There might also have been a scullery and peat store in this back part of the house, but it was demolished in the 1870s without any records being kept. The footprint of Haworth Parsonage can be seen in maps of the 1840s and 1850s, though, and it shows quite a large extension, connected to the house by a passage and forming a U-shape in the small backyard, in the south-west corner of which was a stone outbuilding housing a two-seater privy and in the north-west corner of which was a well.

On the first floor there were three main bedrooms and, over the front door, a small dressing-room that was used by the children as a playroom and occasional bedroom. How the family dispersed themselves upstairs is not entirely clear. Mrs Brontë occupied the bedroom to the left at the front, which had a fireplace in it, and the room on the other side of the landing later became Patrick Brontë's room. The girls – except for the baby, Anne – probably shared the bedroom at the back; Branwell slept on his own, presumably in the playroom; and the servants shared a room above the peat store that was accessible only by an external staircase. It must have made a chilly start to Nancy's and Sarah's day, dressing and descending to the kitchen via the yard.

Leaving the house on the short path down to the church, the Brontës passed the yard where the stonemason stored and worked his gravestones, the sexton's house on the left and then the backs of the houses and shops that clustered at the top of the steep Main Street. In front of the Black Bull and the steps leading up to St Michael's was an open area where hustings and meetings took place and that served as a sort of village square. In the Brontës' day, the view down into the valley from this spot was dominated by chimneys; the water power of the becks running off the moor into the River Worth had spawned no fewer than nineteen mills and most of the townspeople were employed in the textile industry, either in the mills themselves or doing piece-work at home, carding and weaving. The population was high, and sanitation and standards of housing were low but a handful of businessmen had made astonishing new wealth in the area, 'hundreds of thousands of pounds' by Mrs Gaskell's reckoning.

The church itself was entirely different in the 1820s, the current building having been erected by Patrick Brontë's successor, John Wade, fifty years later. The Brontës' St Michael's looked much more like a Low Church chapel, with plain windows, a modest altar, a gallery and a large triple-decker pulpit on the south aisle. Memories were still strong there of William Grimshaw, who was said to have rounded up malingerers at the pub with his horse-whip, nipping out of the church during the longer psalms to herd them in before the sermon. Grimshaw, a close friend of John Wesley and a pivotal figure in the Evangelical Revival, was revered in Haworth and beyond,* but his legacy proved troubling to Patrick Brontë, as Grimshaw had encouraged the local Methodists so effectively that they now had two chapels of their own. Though he had been nurtured by Simeonites and Wesleyans himself, Patrick Brontë saw the gradual detachment of Methodism from mainstream Anglicanism as a distinct threat, giving comfort to other Low Church and Nonconformist congregations – Baptists, Unitarians, Socinians, Ranters, Dissenters – and countenancing a rabble of doctrines that imperilled the very survival of the Established Church.

'A strange uncivilized little place' was how Charlotte apologised for her home town in the 1840s and how it struck many visitors. She did not blame readers of *Wuthering Heights* who expressed disbelief at the details of hill-farm life in Emily's book: 'the language, the manners, the very dwellings and household customs of the scattered inhabitants of those districts, must be to [genteel] readers in a great measure unintelligible, and – where intelligible – repulsive . . . [They] will hardly know what to make of the rough, strong utterance, the harshly manifested passions, the unbridled aversions, and headlong partialities of unlettered moorland hinds and rugged moorland squires, who have grown up untaught and unchecked, except by mentors as harsh as themselves.' In the 1820s the scattered homesteads on the moor – typically farms of between ten and twenty acres each, growing some oats or hay to feed a few cows – were places almost beyond the sight and reach of law. 'Brutal tendencies' characterised the life of the town, where bull-baiting, horse-racing, dog- and cock-fighting, and fist-fights between men were common sports.†

---

* Mary Burder admired him; see her letter to PB of 8 August 1823, *SHB* 1, 66.
† The women of Haworth were said to be as rough as the men: at bare-knuckle fights, the combatants' mothers often stood well to the front of the crowd, threatening a licking at home to anyone showing signs of weakness ('The Brontës and the Brontë Country: A Chat with One Who Knew Them', *The Bradford Observer*, 17 February 1894).

The moors around Haworth – stretching out for almost eight miles to the west, where they touch the Lancashire border near the Forest of Trawden, and five miles to the south, to Hebden Bridge – were not quite the semi-wildernesses of today, carefully preserved for walkers, shooting parties and the water industry; they were places of work for quarrymen and peat-cutters, hill farmers and smallholders. The route to what are now the isolated ruins of Top Withins Farm (popularly believed to occupy the position of Heathcliff's fictional home) passed by at least seven small homesteads in the Brontës' day, and walking on the moor would have had to take into account the dangers of trespassing, as well as large areas of permanently boggy and impassable terrain. Patrick Brontë was an exceptionally vigorous walker, and covered all his parish business on foot. He must often have been seen out in all weathers, with his staff in his hand and high top hat on his head. The children too became hardened walkers, as the nearest place to buy books, newspapers, stationery, dress or fine goods or to consult a lawyer or doctor was Keighley, four miles away. The Brontës never owned either horse or carriage.

The 'gentry' neighbours here were spread out, like everything in the chapelry: the Taylors at Stanbury Manor House; the Greenwoods at Spring Head (both Stephen Taylor and Joseph Greenwood were trustees of the church); the Heatons at Ponden Hall, a compact seventeenth-century house with a fine library.* In later years, the younger Brontës sometimes walked the two miles over Penistone Hill to borrow books from the Heatons but generally it was not a very sociable parish. The prevalence of 'the old hill spirit' struck Mrs Gaskell forcibly, coming as she did from a genteel Cheshire country town (immortalised in *Cranford*) and living as a minister's wife on the outskirts of Manchester in suburban comfort. 'I believe many of the Yorkshiremen would object to the system of parochial visiting,' she said; 'their surly independence would revolt from the idea of any one having a right, from his office, to inquire into their condition, to counsel, or to admonish them.' Patrick Brontë's habit as a minister was not to interfere with his parishioners' lives at all, unless they were sick, or came to him for help. Brontë made his views perfectly clear

* Which may have inspired Thrushcross Grange in *Wuthering Heights*.

every Sunday in robust sermons, but otherwise the family 'kept themselves very close' from the first.

What kind of a man was Patrick Brontë, and what was he like to be
married to, or to be the child of? Though he had plenty of natural wit,
he was far from light-hearted. His public manner was ponderous,
'Grandisonian', as one visitor remarked. He qualified everything he
said, 'indeed he was cautious to the last degree', and his many letters to
newspapers over the years – on subjects as diverse as parliamentary
reform, duelling and fire hazards – show a habit of making arguments
needlessly complicated. Perhaps this was to demonstrate his learning –
to himself as much as to others. Brontë's outstanding achievement in
getting from the cot in Emdale to St John's College had left him, in
many ways, a very anxious man.

Patrick had strategies for getting his own way that Maria had noticed
during their engagement (when the question of their future married
quarters arose): 'you have such a method of considering and digesting
a plan before you make it known to your friends', she had written to
him, 'that you run very little risk of incurring their disapprobations, or
of having your schemes frustrated. I greatly admire your talents this
way – may they never be perverted by being used in a bad cause!'

When Elizabeth Gaskell met Patrick Brontë in 1853, she found him
a model of old-fashioned manners and hostliness, but with a steely
edge that chilled her. 'I caught a glare of his stern eyes over his spectacles at Miss Brontë once or twice which made me know my man,' she
said, alert to the fact that a truly domineering character might take
pains to hide it; 'he talked *at* her sometimes.' Mrs Gaskell was intrigued
by her new friend's circumstances and had already heard all sorts of
stories about the incumbent of Haworth, which predisposed her to
think of him as a half-crazed domestic tyrant. Her main informant was
a notorious gossip, Janet Kay-Shuttleworth, who had got *her* information from a nurse who had looked after Maria Brontë, a woman who
certainly had plenty of opportunity to observe the Brontë family in
the months she lived with them in 1821, but whose dismissal (on
unspecified grounds) wasn't likely to have made her think or speak very
well of them afterwards.

Some picturesque stories about life at the Parsonage subsequently
emerged in Mrs Gaskell's book, which Patrick Brontë strenuously

refuted on publication and which had to be suppressed or modified in later editions (though privately Mrs Gaskell still clung to many of them). According to these, Patrick Brontë's quirks included denying his children meat – as part of a regime designed to discourage them from becoming comfort-loving – and having a 'volcanic' temper that he sometimes relieved by firing his pistols out of the back door 'in rapid succession'. There were several anecdotes about his burning things, which is odd, given Patrick's often-expressed fear of fire (he did not allow curtains or carpets in the Parsonage for years on account of the fire risk, and recommended only silk or wool clothes for his children, believing cotton to be more flammable). On one occasion he is said to have stuffed a hearthrug into the grate and watched, stifling, until it was all consumed; another time it was a set of coloured boots that met the flames, deemed too frivolous for his children's use. In a fit of sheer rage, Mrs Gaskell reported, he had once taken a saw to the chairs; and, most oddly of all, was said to have cut up one of his wife's dresses because 'either the make, the colour, or the material, was not according to his notions of consistent propriety'.

Patrick Brontë denied these stories when the *Life* was published, and Nancy Garrs, his servant for six years, backed him up, testifying to the exaggeration, or downright untruth, of Mrs Gaskell's portrait – with one exception, the dress incident. It is certainly a strange and persistent anecdote, with interesting variations. Elizabeth Gaskell said that Mrs Brontë never wore the offending article, but neither did she get rid of it, keeping it 'treasured up in her drawers, which were generally locked': 'One day, however, while in the kitchen, she remembered that she had left the key in her drawer, and, hearing Mr Brontë up-stairs, she augured some ill to her dress, and, running up in haste, she found it cut into shreds.' Nancy disagreed with the details of this account, though: what really happened, she said, was as follows: Mr Brontë noticed one morning that 'his Mrs' had put on a cotton print gown,

> in the fashion of that day, with a long waist and what he considered
> absurd-looking sleeves. In a pleasant humour he bantered her about the
> dress, and she went upstairs and laid it aside. Some time after, Mr Brontë
> entered her room, and cut off the sleeves. In the course of the day,
> Mrs Brontë found the sleeveless gown, and showed it me in the kitchen,

laughing heartily. Next day, however, he went to Keighley, and bought
the material for a silk gown, which was made to suit Mr Brontë's taste.

This version is every bit as suggestive as the one it displaces but sounds
more like a marital stand-off than a joke. Mrs Gaskell said that Charlotte herself was one of her sources for the dress-shredding story,
though she was only five when her mother died. Perhaps her elder sisters' or the servants' memories of it augmented her own. Charlotte
certainly passed it on to her friend Ellen Nussey as an illustration of her
father's iron will, specifically in relation to 'feminine temptations' to
vanity; Ellen herself added the detail that 'the obnoxious dress' had
been a present to Maria Brontë (not from her husband) and that by
destroying it he had put her out of vanity's way. 'There is not the
slightest doubt that he would have gained his object quite as surely by
kinder and wiser methods of action,' Ellen concluded reasonably, 'but
it was not his nature to woo obedience.' That said, Ellen testified that
this quick-tempered man '*did understand* his *own* idiosyncracy' and was
'always perfectly under control and quiescent' in company.

The dress incident, for all its difficulty to pin down, gives a glimpse
into the Brontës' marriage that perhaps tells us more about the wife
than about the husband. In one light, it shows Maria as a model man-
manager, enacting Thomas Greene's advice to wives that Patrick sent,
in a misremembered form, to Sarah Garrs on the eve of her wedding in
1829:

> They have their humors and their faults –
>   So mutable is man –
> Excuse his failings in your thought,
>   And hide them if you can.
>
> 'Tis not the way to scold at large,
>   To clamor, rage and boast,
> For wives their duties best discharge
>   Who condescend the most.

The absorption of male failings was a necessary skill in a society that
allowed little autonomy to women and in a culture that fetishised their
quietness. Maria Brontë loved her husband, had a philosophical temperament and an intelligence that rose above petty irritations; the last

thing she was going to do was scold him, however childishly or irrationally he behaved. Her daughters were brought up to placate him also, and to hide their opinion of his actions. Privately they would 'condescend', as their mother did, but in their writing they returned obsessively to just such scenes of questionable authority and exposed every nuance of injustice in them mercilessly.

Maria had been weak ever since the move to Haworth but developed sudden and serious new symptoms just a few months later and took to her bed at the end of January 1821. His wife's illness terrified Patrick: in the months that followed, he struggled to keep the household going, with the servants monitoring the children and a paid nurse to attend Maria, but he longed for the sort of friendly help and guidance that he would have got in Thornton from the generous Firths, or in Dewsbury from John Buckworth, to whom he lamented that he felt like 'a stranger in a strange land . . . left nearly quite alone, unless you suppose my six little children and the nurse and servants to have been company'. Doctors were called in, but Maria's painful ailment (which the nurse later described as 'an internal cancer') got steadily worse, and Patrick gave himself over to the gloomiest forebodings, expecting her to die 'almost every day' of that spring and summer. When all six children went down with scarlet fever at the same time and Maria's condition worsened too, he was virtually incapacitated with grief: 'an affectionate, agonising *something* sickened my whole frame, and which is I think of such a nature as cannot be described, and must be felt in order to be understood'. This insistence on his own suffering and sensibility cannot have been any comfort to the invalid, whose emotional withdrawal as she deteriorated was a further cause of distress to her husband: 'She was cold and silent and hardly seemed to notice what was passing around her.'

'The mother was not very anxious to see much of her children,' the nurse later told Elizabeth Gaskell; 'so the little things clung quietly together, for their father was busy in his study and in his parish, or with their mother.' It is striking that Maria kept her children at arm's length in these months; apart from trying to recruit her strength, this was not to be a season of tender advice-giving and farewell. Perhaps she thought she had a chance of getting better, or decided to behave as if she did. But these were lonely, painful and depressing months for Maria. A story survives from the sickbed of her asking to be raised up in bed so that she could see the grate of the fireplace being cleaned 'as it was done in Cornwall', a strange detail to fix on. Though much has changed at Haworth Parsonage since 1821, the same grate is still there, and it is sad to look at it today and feel Maria Brontë's private yearning for a touch of home.

For their part, the little Brontës crept round the house, keeping their voices to a whisper and trying to be as unobtrusive as possible. To the nurse, they seemed extremely well behaved but 'spiritless'; 'they were so different to any . . . I had ever seen.' Young Maria was in charge and read to her siblings or took them out on the moors in a straggling group of 'toddling wee things', as the nurse remembered them. It is possible they were rather strangely turned out: Maria herself, always described as an untidy child, was only seven years old that summer and the others were six, five, four and three respectively, with year-old baby Anne having to be carried and tended all day long.

With hope of a recovery dwindling, Elizabeth Branwell was called from Penzance to help run the household and support her ailing sister, and the two eldest girls were taken to Kipping House for a month by concerned Elizabeth Firth. Maria was in agonising pain, which could not be alleviated by any medicines: 'her constitution was enfeebled, and her frame wasted daily,' as Patrick wrote. The household was braced for death, and the nurse heard her patient crying 'oh God my poor children!' over and over.

Throughout their courtship, Maria had exulted in the faith that united her and Patrick, but this certainty forsook her towards the end. Patrick Brontë wrote, in obvious perturbation, to his friend John Buckworth: 'During many years she had walked with God, but the great enemy, envying her life of holiness, often disturbed her mind in the last conflict. Still, in general she had peace and joy in believing, and died, if not triumphantly, at least calmly, and with a holy yet humble confidence that Christ was her Saviour, and heaven her eternal home.' What a scene this evokes, of Maria Brontë not resigned to death at all, not cheered by the prospect of eternal salvation that had been her mainstay previously but 'disturbed' and conflicted in her final days and weeks. To any pious person attending the sickbed,

Maria's mental distress at the door of eternity must have been inexpressibly painful to witness.

On the morning of 15 September, Nancy Garrs related, Maria asked that 'all the dear faces should be about her', and the children were brought in to see their mother for the last time. Patrick Brontë stayed at the bedside and she died later that day, aged thirty-eight. After almost eight months of alternate dread and hope, and eight months of seclusion from their mother, this was a blow from which none of the family ever fully recovered. Charlotte's memories were very scant indeed: '[she] tried hard, in after years, to recall the remembrance of her mother,' Mrs Gaskell noted, 'and could bring back two or three pictures of her. One was when, sometime in the evening light, [Maria Brontë] had been playing with her little boy, Patrick Branwell, in the parlour of Haworth Parsonage.' How strange this fragmentary memory is (the only one of the promised 'two or three pictures' that Charlotte passed on, or Mrs Gaskell recorded) – the daughter looking into a room veiled in lambent light and seeing, like a tableau, mother and son playing together. But not part of that happy scene herself, nor having known anything like it.

Charlotte Brontë's heroines are all motherless, adrift and starving for parental love. The mere mention of the word 'mother', in *Shirley*, sets the orphaned Caroline Helstone thinking about her own, 'unknown, unloved, but not unlonged-for'. While her companion talks on about Nature, Caroline is lost in reverie:

> The longing of her childhood filled her soul again. The desire which many a night had kept her awake in her crib, and which fear of its fallacy had of late years almost extinguished, relit suddenly, and glowed warm in her heart: that her mother might come some happy day, and send for her to her presence – look upon her fondly with loving eyes, and say to her tenderly, in a sweet voice: -
>
>   'Caroline, my child, I have a home for you; you shall live with me. All the love you have needed, and not tasted, from infancy, I have saved for you carefully. Come! it shall cherish you now.'

In an exquisitely tender scene later in the book, Caroline and her mother are reunited. Her mother has, in fact, been there all along, undiscovered: 'The offspring nestled to the parent: that parent, feeling the endearment and hearing the appeal, gathered her closer still. She covered her with noiseless kisses: she murmured love over her, like a cushat fostering its young. There was silence in the room for a long while.' Caroline Helstone gets her dream-like, Shakespearian moment of restoration and restitution; but, for Charlotte Brontë, the only way to be reunited with her mother was in death.

Elizabeth Branwell stayed on at the Parsonage after her sister's death, though it isn't clear whether she went back to Penzance for a while after the initial period of mourning. The idea of her taking up the role of substitute mother to her nieces and nephews probably didn't arise immediately, as Patrick Brontë had a preferred solution to the family's predicament, which was to seek another wife. There is no doubt that he felt the loss of Maria with painful intensity, but he was also a practical man, and had six children to bring up as well as a large parish to run. He was forty-four years old, and such a move was to be expected in an age of high mortality among women of childbearing age. His friends Firth, Morgan, Dury and Fennell all remarried after their first wives' deaths.*

After a decent interval of mourning, Patrick set out for Kipping House, the scene of so many happy days in the past. Dr Firth had died in 1820, just after the Brontës' removal to Haworth, but Elizabeth lived on at the house with her stepmother. What sort of prospect the melancholic widower presented to lovely Miss Firth, who, in 1822, was still only twenty-five, can be guessed by her prompt refusal of him, but the fact that Elizabeth continued to do what she could for the Brontë children testifies to her kind heart and sincere affection for the family. And, though she had no intention of marrying Patrick Brontë, she must have continued to esteem him, as there is a family tradition that the letters he wrote to her were destroyed only years later, 'just before the Miss Brontës became famous'.

Patrick might then have approached Isabella Dury, the sister of his friend the curate of Keighley, as there was local gossip on the subject that Miss Dury responded to in lively tones in a letter of 1823: 'I heard before I left that I had quarrelled with my brother about Mr Brontë. I

---

* Firth in 1815, Morgan in 1836, Dury in 1822 and John Fennell in 1830.

beg if ever you hear such a report, you will contradict it as I can assure you it is perfectly unfounded. I think I should never be so very silly as to have the most distant idea of marrying anybody who has not some fortune and six children into the bargain. It is too ridiculous to imagine any truth in it.'

Patrick's last recorded attempt to find a new wife was even more ill-judged than these two, turning his attentions once more to Mary Burder. He hadn't seen her since leaving Wethersfield in 1809, but in April 1823 he wrote to her mother with an outline of his current situation, giving careful attention to salary and resources, asking after her children, 'whether they be married or single', and threatening to come down to visit the old neighbourhood. The gist of this was so obvious that no reply came for some months – the family must have been stunned at Brontë's re-emergence after fifteen years and at the gall of the man – but then at last Mrs Burder sent Mary's address. The old lover promptly revived his suit in a letter of quite remarkable crassness and egotism. He was glad to hear Mary was still single, he told her, suggesting that was very appropriate to the power of their former attachment: '*You* were the *first* whose hand I solicited, and no doubt I was the *first* to whom *you promised to give that hand* . . . However much you may dislike me now, I am sure you once loved me with an unaffected innocent love, and I feel confident that after all which you have seen and heard, you cannot doubt my love for you.' This claim sounded even more insulting in the context of his breezy assumption that not much could have happened to disturb Mary in the intervening period (not having married), whereas his harsh experience – including the death of his wife – had led him to believe 'this world to be but vanity, and . . . my heart's desire is to be found in the ways of divine Wisdom'. Then he got down to business, with suitable emphases: 'I have a *small* but *sweet* little family that often soothe my heart and afford me pleasure by their endearing little ways, and I have what I consider a competency of the good things of this life.' All he lacked was a 'dearly Beloved Friend' with whom to share this Elysium, which he was prepared to offer in apology for past wrongs: 'I cannot tell how *you* may feel on reading this,' he concluded, 'but I must say *my* ancient love is rekindled.' He was, in fact, rather moved.

Life rarely offers a slighted woman such a chance to disburden herself, and Mary Burder grasped it with relish. Far from awakening tender memories and kindling a new flame of love, Patrick's letter had prompted her to disinter and reread the ones he had sent before, during the three years of their former relationship, and to reflect on her lucky escape from 'one whom I cannot think was altogether clear of duplicity'. Paraphrasing the old love-notes in front of her (perhaps including one in which Patrick broke off communication), she satirises his hubris, then and now: 'Happily for me I have not been the ascribed cause of hindering your promotion, of preventing any brilliant alliance, nor have those great and affluent friends that you used to write and speak of withheld their patronage on my account, young, inexperienced, unsuspecting and ignorant as I then was of what I had a right to look forward to.' Her answer to his request for permission to visit was, unsurprisingly, 'a *decided* negative'.

Patrick Brontë's next move is a vivid example of his intransigence, pride and emotional blindness and gives some idea of what all of the women and some of the men in his life had to deal with. Instead of accepting Mary Burder's scorching reprimand in decent silence, he felt entitled, even obliged, to write back reprimanding *her* in turn for the 'many keen sarcasms' in her letter that 'surprised and grieved me'. He launches into an attack on her version of events fifteen years before and a defence of himself that is hectoring and wheedling by turns, but then his letter takes an astonishing turn: 'Once more let me ask you whether Mrs Burder and you would object to my calling on you at the Park some time during next spring or in the summer?' Mary Burder clearly did not answer this, but neither did she destroy these last salvos from her troublesome admirer. Perhaps they were kept as curiosities of human nature, and reminders of Divine Providence. She married the local Dissenting minister later the same year.

After the debacle with Mary Burder, Patrick Brontë seems to have accepted that his fate was to remain a widower. It is not clear who first suggested that Elizabeth Branwell should come and keep house at the Parsonage, but Elizabeth was clearly under no financial constraint to find a roof for her head, and proudly insisted on giving Patrick money for her upkeep all the years she lived with him. She must have been lonely or restless to have agreed to leave Cornwall permanently, for, like Maria, she found her home town vastly superior to Haworth, where the weather, the natives, the food, the flora and the poor social scene were just some of her categories for critique. This was not going to be a happy revival of Thornton days. Even before his wife's death, Patrick had adopted the practice of dining alone (for the sake of his digestion, it was said), and his habits of seclusion dictated the tone of the household. By 1823 he had settled for a pared-down, simplified existence: celibate, middle aged, eccentric, unpopular and burdened with melancholy.

Towards the children, Elizabeth Branwell seemed consciously to adopt an unsentimental, rather withholding demeanour, so as not to intrude too far on her dead sister's territory. She knew that she could never replace Maria in anyone's affections, but her constrained kind of love was not powerful enough to rouse much reciprocal feeling, not in Charlotte at any rate. The children Aunt Branwell were closest to were Anne, who did not remember her mother at all, and Branwell, who as the only boy seemed naturally preferable to his sisters.

Charlotte therefore found herself somewhat lost in the middle of her sibling group – not the paragon, Maria, not the reliable lieutenant Elizabeth, not the son and heir Branwell, not the endearing individual-ist Emily, not the baby Anne, who was most to be pitied, most motherless. A story she told to her schoolfriend Ellen Nussey in the 1830s poignantly illustrates her isolation at this time. Five-year-old Charlotte had heard the Garrs sisters describe the town of Bradford in such glowing terms that she imagined it must be the nearest thing to the Golden City in the Book of Revelation and the Celestial City of *The Pilgrim's Progress*, and that it was her duty to leave home to search for it, as Pilgrim did. But the little girl had hardly got a mile outside Haworth when a team of horses drawing a huge loaded wagon (the 1820s equivalent of a thundering juggernaut) bore past her with such noise, rush and darkness that she cowered at the roadside in fright, and stayed there until she was found by one of the servants who had noticed her absence and followed her. Filthy Bradford, the most rapidly indus-trialising city in the country, would have been a disappointing pilgrimage destination indeed, and Charlotte later joked about her mis-apprehension of it,* but the story shows Charlotte's essential solitude,

---

* Bradford was for a time the largest wool-processing town in the world. By 1841 it had thirty-eight worsted mills and by 1850 the population had soared to 100,000.

even at a time when all her siblings were still alive – a solitude of being and of mind, mulling over the powerful texts that spoke to her and feeling the urgency to act on them.

Charlotte's eldest sister, Maria, a precociously mature and intellectual child, was the children's emotional lynch-pin after their mother's death, 'a little mother among the rest', as Charlotte described her, 'superhuman in goodness and cleverness'. Maria was an avid reader of newspapers and periodicals, and her father later said she could converse 'on any of the leading topics of the day' just like an adult. She must also have been a deeply contemplative girl if it is true (as Charlotte insisted) that the character of Helen Burns in *Jane Eyre* was an exact, even under-stated, portrait of her. In the novel, Helen advises Jane not to let her grudges against Mrs Reed rankle, since other people's antipathies are beyond one's control; 'Would you not be happier if you tried to forget her severity, together with the passionate emotions it excited?' the young stoic counsels.

The 'plays' that Charlotte, Branwell, Emily and Anne later developed obsessively were already part of their private entertainment in their earliest childhood, and were presumably instigated by their eldest sister. Patrick Brontë told Mrs Gaskell that they made up such games 'as soon as they could read and write', and remembered sometimes having to step in when contentions between Hannibal, Caesar, Wellington and Bonaparte got too rowdy. Their father was often struck by 'signs of rising talent' in his offspring, but was somewhat mystified by its origins, and on one occasion devised a test of their opinions by assembling all six children in his study and giving them in turn a mask to wear from behind which they could 'speak boldly'.

I began with the youngest (Anne, afterwards Acton Bell), and asked what a child like her most wanted; she answered, 'Age and experience.' I asked the next (Emily, afterwards Ellis Bell), what I had best do with her brother Branwell, who was sometimes a naughty boy; she answered, 'Reason with him, and when he won't listen to reason, whip him.' I asked Branwell what was the best way of knowing the difference between the intellects of man and woman; he answered, 'By considering the difference between them as to their bodies.' I then asked Charlotte what was the best book in the world; she answered 'The Bible.' And what was the next best; she answered 'The Book of Nature.' I then asked the next what was the best mode of education for a woman; she answered, 'That which would make her rule her house well.' Lastly, I asked the oldest what was the best mode of spending time; she answered 'By laying it out in preparation for a happy eternity.'

Patrick was pleased with these responses, though even with the mask on, his children seem to have been in no doubt that this was a form of examination and they should say what was expected of them, with the exception perhaps of Emily, whose no-nonsense answer reflects a certain irritation at being asked a question about her brother instead of something more interesting. The two elder girls fell in with their Martha-and-Mary roles exactly and Charlotte's reply that the Bible was the best book in the world not satisfying her father, she had to answer figuratively the second time.

Patrick Brontë and his sister-in-law taught his children their first lessons, but, while Branwell could continue to be tutored by his father at home as he grew older, some formal schooling was clearly necessary to fit the girls for the only sort of work socially within their grasp: teaching or governessing. Maria and Elizabeth went briefly to a boarding school in Wakefield,* but early in 1824 a new establishment opened up near Kirkby Lonsdale, on the edge of the Lake District, which seemed like a direct answer to Patrick Brontë's prayers. The Clergy Daughters' School at Cowan Bridge — the first of its kind — had the backing of several leading evangelicals, including William Wilberforce, Hannah More and Charles Simeon and had been specifically set up to benefit 'the *really* necessitous clergy' by educating their children at a substantially subsidised rate. Patrick's old friends John Eyton (from Shropshire) and Theodore Dury from Keighley were among the trustees, and it was without difficulty that Maria and Elizabeth Brontë were accepted among the first pupils in the summer of 1824, for a fee of £14 each per annum. There was even a regular stagecoach service from Leeds to Kendal that passed along the high road right by the school and also

* Perhaps to Crofton Hall, which is where Elizabeth Firth had gone to school in 1812–13.

stopped in Keighley, making it a relatively easy journey for the time, albeit fifty miles across the Pennines from Haworth.

Maria and Elizabeth, who were both still convalescing from whooping cough, were taken to Cowan Bridge by their father on 21 July and Charlotte followed on 10 August. The school was in a picturesque situation, nestled in a wooded valley with a tributary of the River Lune running close by. Converted from a row of cottages, it had an expensive new wing containing a large schoolroom on the ground floor and four dormitories above. In the main section of the building was a dining room, the teachers' bedrooms and the superintendent's lodging, and the garden in front of the building, running down to the Leck Beck, was divided up into sections and little individual plots, with the idea that the pupils could learn to cultivate flowers and vegetables. There was a new covered walkway to one side of the garden, so that the girls could take some exercise whatever the weather, and just beyond that was the ancient bridge from which the hamlet gets its name.

The man behind the project was a powerful local landowner and philanthropist called William Carus Wilson, whose Cambridge-born evangelicism and circle of clerical acquaintance were very similar to Patrick Brontë's own, even if his Calvinistic views placed him on the outer margins of the Anglican spectrum. The regime he instigated at the school was a deliberately Spartan one of early rising, long prayers, spare facilities, plain food and outdoor exercise, based on familiar charity-school models. The curriculum was much more ambitious than that of a charity school, however, as befitted the daughters of clergymen: history, geography, 'the Use of Globes', grammar, writing and maths as well as needlework and 'the nicer kinds of household-work'. For those who might go on to be governesses or teachers, extras in French, music and drawing were offered at £3 a year each. Maria and Charlotte had extras, but Elizabeth did not, indicating that less was expected of her intellectually. In the admission register, compiled by the superintendent, Elizabeth was marked down as reading 'little', writing 'pretty well', but being poor in everything else. Maria didn't fare much better: she read 'tolerably', knew 'a little of Grammar' and French. Neither was much good with a needle. Charlotte was assessed as writing 'indifferently', 'Ciphers a little, and works neatly. Knows nothing of grammar, geography, history, or accomplishments. Altogether clever of her age, but knows nothing systematically.'

Wilson was an avid promoter of his own bracing brand of Christianity and published a magazine called *The Children's Friend*, full of hellfire and horror, in which God was quite likely to strike a child dead mid-tantrum to prove how high the stakes were, conduct-wise. In one of his stories a little girl applauds her teachers' habit of whipping the pupils: 'It is because they love us, and it is to make us remember what a sad thing sin is. God would be angry with them if they did not whip us.' *Child's First Tales* (1836) was another Wilson composition, written in monosyllables to help the very youngest readers, with stark woodcut illustrations: 'Look there! Do you not see a man hung by the neck? Oh! It is a sad sight. A rope is tied round his neck to what they call the gal-lows: and there he hangs till he is quite dead.' Other stories dealt with 'Mother's Sick-bed', 'Mother Dead' ('The big girl takes the sheet off the face, to have one more look') and 'Dead Boy', the story of a lad who died when he went skating on the Sabbath: 'He thought he should go to hell for all this. I fear he would go there. How sad it is to think of!'

This was standard fare in pious literature for children of the time, but must have appalled Charlotte Brontë almost as much as it does twenty-first-century readers, or she would not have satirised it so sharply in *Jane Eyre*. In the novel, *The Child's Guide* is the conduct book given to Jane by Mr Brocklehurst with the instruction to study 'an account of the awfully sudden death of Martha G——, a naughty child addicted to falsehood and deceit', but the fate of 'the Liar' seems to apply not to herself but to John and Mrs Reed, and provokes in the child not remorse for her own faults but 'a passion of resentment' at others'.

There were many things about the regime at Cowan Bridge that grated on Charlotte Brontë's nerves and tiny, skinny, eight-year-old body: the cold, the scant, bad food, the rote learning, the strict discipline, the soul-stifling air of Calvinism. Prayers and church services dominated the school week, and on Sundays, come rain or shine, the pupils had to walk to Wilson's church at Tunstall, two miles away across country. It was too far to walk back in the middle of the day for lunch, so the girls ate bread and cheese at the church before the afternoon service, and in the winter suffered a great deal from these long, cold, hungry Sundays, much like the Lowood girls in *Jane Eyre*. Although the Lune valley is outstandingly beautiful, Charlotte later blamed the school's low and damp position for the outbreaks of typhus, scrofula and consumption that periodically broke out, and just as culpable in her eyes was 'the diet, the discipline, the system of tuition' – everything about it, in other words, was hazardous to its 'ill-fated pupils'.

The picture of life at her fictional 'Lowood' in *Jane Eyre*, published twenty-two years after the author's own schooldays, reminded many readers of Charles Dickens's Dotheboys Hall in *Nicholas Nickleby* (1838–9). Already a by-word for grimness, it was based on first-hand research by Dickens in the 1830s into 'The Yorkshire schools'. These were no-torious north-country boarding establishments where boys of poor families (or poor relations, whom families wished to get rid of) could be roughly educated at the lowest possible price per capita. Dickens, with characteristic theatricality, had gone undercover in 1838 to see for himself the conditions at Bowes Academy, near Greta Bridge, and is said to have based Wackford Squeers, *Nickleby*'s infamous pedagogue sadist, on the headmaster, William Shaw. Shaw would almost cer-tainly have been known to the Brontës by repute, but it is interesting that there was an equally notorious local example of the type known to them personally: Hammond Roberson of Heald's Hall, whose name appears on a fragmentary list drawn up by Charlotte in the late 1830s with the words 'boy-destroyer' next to it, and followed by 'Mr. Squeers/Dotheboys-Hall/Greta-Bridge/Yorkshire. Favoured by Charles Dickens Esq.'* The conditions in these schools – one real and one fictional – clearly could be classed together in Charlotte's mind and seem to have contributed, along with her own memories of board-ing school, to her creation of Lowood and Mr Brocklehurst, *Jane Eyre*'s 'girl-destroyer'.† It was no surprise that when Elizabeth Gaskell drew

---

* The list, cut off at the top, is on the reverse of the autobiographical fragment known as 'Farewell to Angria', and obviously post-dates 1838/9, when *Nicholas Nickleby* was first published in serial form.

† Could it be that Branwell Brontë had some inside information about the local boarding establishments for boys? His friend Grundy later said that Branwell had had some brief and bad experience as 'an usher in a school' (*Interviews*, 47), though he could have been confused with Branwell's Sunday School teaching.

out the similarities in her *Life of Charlotte Brontë*, Cowan Bridge was widely assumed to have been *exactly* like Lowood, and as bad as 'a second Dotheboys' Hall' by inference.

Cowan Bridge remains hard to separate from its fictional counterpart. There's little information about the discipline at the school, but it is likely that the punishments meted out to Jane and Helen in *Jane Eyre* (being birched on the neck and having to endure public shaming) were similar to those the Brontë girls encountered, whether they experienced them or not. Every school had its 'scourgemistress', often worse than the novel's Miss Scatcherd,★ and it is perhaps notable that Charlotte allowed her heroine to be so outraged at such a very common practice. It implies that Patrick Brontë was not a very strict disciplinarian at home.

There is no record of Charlotte having been punished for anything at school. One former teacher, Miss Andrews, remembered her as 'a bright, clever, happy little girl never in disgrace'. But witnessing others being punished would have been almost more distressing to Charlotte; her own sorrows had made her, even at this age, profoundly sympathetic to anyone oppressed. Jane Eyre's fury on behalf of Helen Burns is an example of just such sympathetic outrage: Jane says she would take the rod and break it under Miss Scatcherd's nose, and when Helen is made to walk round wearing a sign saying 'Slattern', Jane takes the first opportunity to tear it off and throw it in the fire: 'the fury of which [Helen] was incapable had been burning in my soul all day, and tears, hot and large, had continually been scalding my cheek; for the spectacle of her sad resignation gave me an intolerable pain at the heart.'

The food at Cowan Bridge was, by every account, disgusting. One former pupil remembered grease swimming on top of the girls' warm milk from the dirty copper and seeing the housekeeper once pausing from cutting up raw meat to stir a teacher's tea with her finger. Mrs Gaskell heard numerous stories about the disgusting conditions under which the food at Cowan Bridge was kept and prepared. You wouldn't need to be a fussy eater to balk at tainted meat, rancid fat, burnt porridge, 'bingy' milk or anything cooked, as everything was, in

★ Corporal punishment was a common feature of British school life until at least the 1960s.

water from the rain-tub, full of dirt that had run off the roof. Another ex-pupil said that the paucity of edible food at school ruined her health for years.

Elizabeth Gaskell laid the blame for Charlotte's later ill-health and 'stunted' physique squarely at the door of Cowan Bridge, but, as Reverend Wilson's son pointed out in 1857, when moved to defend his father (who was still alive), the Brontë children were all 'naturally very delicate' to begin with and subject to a home regime every bit as influential as the school could have been, under an 'austere and peculiar' father; 'is it fair to trace all [Miss Brontë's] sufferings in after life, as Mrs Gaskell does, to the very short time she was at that establishment?' Miss Andrews backed him up vigorously, saying that Wilson senior was 'an excellent and eminently useful clergyman' whose school was of 'inestimable value' to poverty-stricken clergymen (with the implication that the Brontës might have been more grateful). When the two elder Brontë girls were presented in July 1824 they were 'so delicate that there were doubts whether they could be admitted into the school', but they *were* admitted and throve so much that Reverend Brontë brought 'two more' (Charlotte and Emily) later in the year: 'They all inherited consumption from their mother, and were taken home' – before, not after – 'any attack of fever', as she is careful to claim. Mrs Gaskell also heard that the elder Brontës were convalescent on arrival and that Maria's cough lingered. Could this have been the beginning of consumption? The poor girl was blistered on her side, presumably to treat chronic wheezing or coughing, and one of Mrs Gaskell's most painful stories (related to her by an unnamed pupil at the school) is of how Maria felt so ill after the treatment that her schoolfellows urged her to stay in bed, but she insisted on trying to get up to placate the teacher, only to be manhandled sadistically and shouted at for her trouble. It's not hard to see where Maria's reputation for saintliness came from, nor Charlotte's seething sense of injustice towards the staff bullies at Cowan Bridge.

The experiences Charlotte had at school were not extreme for the time, but they were extreme for her. She and her sisters were far away from home and unused to being with strangers under any circumstances: boarding school could not have been anything other than an ordeal. Charlotte tried to keep her head down, as she later told her publisher: 'My career was a very quiet one. I was plodding and industrious, perhaps I was very grave . . . but I think I was remarkable for nothing.' Interestingly, the kind teacher upon whom Miss Temple is based, Ann Evans (later Mrs Connor), remembered only one of the Brontës well, Elizabeth, and that was because the little girl had had such a severe cut to the head that for safety's sake, and 'for the sake of greater quiet', Miss Evans took her into her own room for a few days and nights. This is mirrored in *Jane Eyre* when Miss Temple nurses the dying Helen Burns in her room, which makes one think that Charlotte must have observed Elizabeth's removal to the haven of the teacher's room, or heard about it from her sister. Miss Evans herself seems to have literally not noticed Charlotte Brontë at all. 'Of the two younger ones (if two there were),' she told Mrs Gaskell, 'I have very slight recollections, save that one, a darling child, under five years of age, was quite the pet nursling of the school.' That was Emily, who was six before she went to Cowan Bridge, but still among the very youngest pupils. As the previous superintendent, Miss Andrews, remarked, when thinking of their case many years later, 'How far young and delicate children are able to contend with the necessary evils of a public school is, in my opinion, a very grave question.'

In September 1824, when they had been at school for just a few weeks, the Brontë girls had a visit on her wedding tour from Elizabeth Firth (now Mrs James Franks) and were given a half-crown each. Nothing at this point seemed amiss, nor when Patrick Brontë returned on 25 November, bringing Emily to join them. In the older girls' absence from home, on 2 September, an extraordinary thing had happened. Patrick had sent the three younger children out for an airing on the moor in the company of the servants, Sarah and Nancy Garrs. They had all been ill, he recorded (perhaps with the whooping cough that the elder three girls had just had), but it had been a fine day and Reverend Brontë didn't notice how long they had stayed out until about six o'clock, in itself a rather telling detail. When he began to be concerned and went to look for them from an upstairs window, he saw the sky darkening and heard the approach of a storm. 'My little family had escaped to a place of shelter, but I did not know it,' he related. 'I consequently watched every movement of the coming tempest with a painful degree of interest.' Then, to his great surprise, he heard an explosion and felt the room pulse with what he believed afterwards to have been an earthquake.

Out on the moor, as the storm broke violently, the children had taken shelter under Sarah Garrs' cloak and then the same explosion that their father heard back in the Parsonage shook the ground and a torrent of peat, rocks and water appeared from the direction of Crow Hill. A bog had burst, exploding under the pressure of methane building up during a long dry spell followed by this drenching. At the site, as crowds of curious tourists later discovered, tons of matter had been thrown into the air like an earthy volcano, leaving two huge craters, while waves of 'black moory substance' thirty to forty yards wide flowed downhill towards the town, uprooting trees and carrying boulders with it. As *The Leeds Mercury* reported later, 'The torrent was seen coming down the glen before it reached the hamlet, by a person who gave the alarm and thereby saved the lives of several children, who would otherwise have been swept away.' William Atkins speculates whether these children were Branwell, Emily and Anne Brontë, who were found, with Nancy and Sarah Garrs, cowering 'in a Porch' later, too terrified to proceed. The damage done by the eruption was indeed catastrophic, with fields and houses flooded by filthy debris, bridges broken, mills stopped and the River Aire polluted with mud as far as fifteen miles away. Though Maria, Elizabeth and Charlotte were away at Cowan Bridge when this drama was being played out on Crow Hill, they would surely have heard about it when their father and Emily joined them in November, and in later years Charlotte would have become familiar with the moralising poem Patrick published on the subject, 'The Phenomenon; or, An Account in Verse, of the Extraordinary Disruption of a Bog':

> . . . onward rolls the dark, resistless tide,
> Pale, trembling mortals flee on either side.
> The clanking engines, and the busy mill,
> In thick obstruction, deep immersed, stand still.

'Extraordinary Disruption' was certainly in store for the little family. Early in the new year of 1825 typhus fever broke out at Cowan Bridge. Wilson called in a professional nurse, ordered extra food and medicines and, on discovering the cook's filthy habits, sacked her, but his measures came too late to save several of the girls, two of whom died at the school and eleven of whom left because of ill-health before the end of the school year. The unnamed former pupil who remembered the dirty copper and greasy milk was saved from probable death, she believed, only by an accidental return home that alerted her parents to the seriousness of her own condition. The school had said nothing about her symptoms, and this lack of communication almost certainly harmed Maria and Elizabeth Brontë, for Maria had been ill for two months in the winter before her father went to fetch her home on St Valentine's Day 1825. She didn't have typhus, but pulmonary tuberculosis, probably masked in its earlier stages by the persistent cough that whooping cough leaves in its wake, and perhaps triggered by that virus. Eight-year-old Charlotte seems to have been painfully aware of the situation from day to day, but powerless to do anything about it, saying later, 'I suffered to see my sisters perishing', and one can only imagine how difficult it was for the older sisters to comfort her and six-year-old Emily. Patrick Brontë was slow to wake up to the dangers himself, leaving Elizabeth, Charlotte and Emily at the school when he removed Maria to Haworth, where she ailed for the next two and a half months and then, shockingly, died on 6 May.

While their elder sister was taken home and the next eldest lay ill at Cowan Bridge with a very similar cough, Charlotte and Emily were among a group of girls sent away from the school to Silverdale on the coast – in the wrong direction from home, with adults whose pre-occupation with the typhus crisis at the school must have been evident. It was a time of dread and confusion: news of Maria's death must have taken a long time to reach them and may even have been delayed until the end of May, when Patrick Brontë, now obviously very concerned that Elizabeth's lingering chest illness might, like Maria's, be consumption, arrived to gather up his daughters. He probably went on from Cowan Bridge to Silverdale to fetch the younger ones himself, since Elizabeth is known to have travelled back to Haworth with a school servant. The two younger girls got home (it was the midsummer holiday) just two weeks before Elizabeth also died.

The children were stunned and terrified at these two swift, devastating departures. Elizabeth had been only ten years old, Maria eleven.

Charlotte recalled the horror of Elizabeth's death in a fragmentary story of 1837, in which her heroine thinks of her elder sister's funeral-day, 'of the rigid & lengthened corpse laid in its coffin on the hall-table, of the servants pressing round to gaze on Miss Harriet for the last time, of the kiss that she herself was bidden to give the corpse, of the feeling which then first gushed into her childish & volatile heart that Harriet had left them for ever'. Branwell, who had seen both Maria and Elizabeth die, also retained his memories of it with hallucinatory vividness. In a poem he wrote in the 1830s, the narrator remembers being lifted up to see his dead sister in her coffin:

> And, to this moment, I can feel
> The voiceless gasp – the sickening chill –
> With which I hid my whitened face

One presumes that the children were spared Elizabeth's funeral itself, and the sight of the vault under the south aisle opened up again to receive a third coffin, when the lime mortar can have barely set from the previous occasion, only six weeks before. The officiator was, as it had been for Maria and her mother, William Morgan. Patrick Brontë could not be expected to oversee his own family's interments.

Very surprisingly, after this calamity, Patrick Brontë seems to have decided that it was in everyone's best interests to send Charlotte and Emily back to Cowan Bridge to see out the quarter's notice that each pupil was required to give of withdrawal. He had paid the tuition fees in advance, which may have influenced his decision. A tight ship was run at Haworth Parsonage: Patrick explained to his banker the previous winter that, although sending 'another of my little girls' (Emily) to school necessitated the withdrawal of £20 from his account, 'in the end I shall not loose [*sic*]', because his household would be reduced to just himself and the two remaining children, making it possible to replace Nancy and Sarah Garrs with 'one elderly woman', a 53-year-old local widow called Tabitha Aykroyd. Given that the fees at Cowan Bridge included board and lodging through the holidays, the arrangement seemed just worth stretching to meet.

On her return to Cowan Bridge, Charlotte found a protectress in one of the oldest pupils at the school, Mellaney Hayne, a seventeen-year-old orphan from Devon, whom Patrick Brontë remembered 'frequently espoused her cause against the encroachments of the elder girls'. Mrs Gaskell heard that Mellaney was 'a hungry, good-natured, ordinary girl', no substitute for Maria or Elizabeth, but a welcome companion for Charlotte, and the first person outside her own family to recognise her as an individual. She was likely the model for Mary Ann Wilson in *Jane Eyre*, the kindly older girl who shares 'racy and pungent gossip' with the young heroine, and with whom she spends long days of freedom out of doors while fever disrupts the usual school routine. Charlotte later told Mary Taylor that she used to go to stand on a stone alone in the middle of the burn and watch the water flow by, another very lonely image of the traumatised child.

Charlotte and Emily were only back at Cowan Bridge for a month, but it has been suggested that this return to the scene of disaster gave rise to Emily's later phobias about any removal from home and engendered the animus that Charlotte channelled into her portrait of Lowood School in *Jane Eyre*. There is indeed a special quality of loathing in the Lowood episodes of the novel that goes above and beyond a fictional exposé of a badly run institution. Lowood kills Helen Burns with its pestilential atmosphere, but its spirit-stifling dogmas are seen to be worse still, leading a saintly girl like her (or Maria Brontë) to believe that 'by dying young I shall escape great sufferings. I had not qualities or talents to make my way very well in the world. I should have been continually at fault.'

Charlotte Brontë's anger at the harm done to herself and her sisters bursts forth in her novel in Jane Eyre's outrage on her friend's behalf, all the more potent because articulated by a small girl. 'If people were always kind and obedient to those who are cruel and unjust,' Jane says, 'the wicked people would have it all their own way: they would never feel afraid, and so they would never alter, but would grow worse and worse. When we are struck at without a reason, we should strike back again very hard; I am sure we should – so hard as to teach the person who struck us never to do it again.'

The first readers of *Jane Eyre* were, understandably, bowled over by such passages. In 1847 nothing like it had been seen before. No one had ever dramatised the injustices of childhood so vividly; no one had thought to do so as 'an autobiography' (the novel's subtitle) – *Jane Eyre* was in fact the very first novel to use a first-person child narrator.

Jane's anger and bewilderment and pain therefore were like dispatches from a new frontier, a territory that everyone knew about but that until then had no maps or coordinates.

3

The Genii of the Parsonage

1825–31

The home that Charlotte and Emily came back to in 1825 had had a change of personnel. The Garrs sisters were both gone, and in their place was Tabitha Aykroyd – gruff, tender-hearted and 'very quaint in appearance'. 'Tabby' remained the only full-time servant at the Parsonage for many years, with occasional help with tasks like the washing from a number of local girls, all of whom were very young and very cheap hands. She was a native of the village and had known it long before any mill disturbed the beck in the valley or pavement 'causey' stretched across the fields to keep the factory workers out of the mud, and she had thrilling tales of the old days, of sprites and 'fairishes' that folk she knew had seen: 'It wur the factories as had driven 'em away,' she said. Tabby was no great cook and was later described by Charlotte as boiling the potatoes 'to a sort of vegetable glue', but the family valued her for qualities other than that. Her fund of local wisdom, her colourful dialect speech and her rough motherliness were balm to the little Brontës, and Emily's later teasing tone when she mimicked her – 'O Dear, O Dear, O Dear' – testifies to the deep affection they all came to feel for this rock-solid goddess of the Parsonage kitchen.

Elizabeth Branwell was still in charge of the housekeeping. The Garrs sisters hadn't liked her much, and called her 'a bit of a tyke' for keeping them strictly to only a half-pint of home-brewed beer each day, fetched herself from the cellar. She was generally thought rather narrow in her ideas and stiff in her beliefs, though 'kindly and con-scientious' at heart, 'with a good deal of character'. It is said that Aunt Branwell felt the cold through the Parsonage's stone flags so much that she took to wearing pattens – strap-on wooden platforms designed to keep one's feet above mud and puddles outdoors – *indoors*, a marked eccentricity, though one that the children might have appreciated, since it made her approach slow and audible. She was never seen outside the Parsonage anywhere other than at church, and, like Patrick Brontë, took most of her meals alone in her room, meaning that the children must have almost always eaten with the servants in the kitchen in that oddly compartmentalised household.

Habit was of the utmost importance to Patrick Brontë. He still had his coats made in Cambridge, though they were mended in Haworth. The neckcloth popular in his youth was also Mr Brontë's preferred style all his life, wound larger and larger under his chin, it seems, as the years went by. The local tailor's son retained for a long time the memory of having to broach this formidable personage in his study: 'there old Brontë, in accordance with his wont, was sitting in a plain, uncushioned chair, upright as a soldier.' Nine o'clock was his unchanging bed-time (even when attending a concert at the church or an evening gathering, he would leave at this time). As he went up to bed, he would always stop on the half-landing to wind the grandfather clock.

The children had chores to do in the house and study hours, and were encouraged to go out for walks as frequently as possible (always choosing the direction of the moor rather than the town), but most of the time they were left entirely on their own. There is no record of any one of them making friends with children from the village,* and, on one occasion, when they were invited to a party, they stood around like aliens, utterly at a loss as to what to do, as a local woman told Elizabeth Gaskell many years later. '[They] had no idea of ordinary games that any village child could play, such as "hunt the slipper" and "here we go round the gooseberry bush".'

So the family at the Parsonage lived in isolation, an odd household, certainly: at its head a solitary egotist, accustomed to being listened to but not seeking much by way of dialogue, with his somewhat agoraphobic maiden sister-in-law standing in as a pallid substitute for a wife and mother, and the four remaining children dependent on their own resources, with Charlotte thrown into the role left empty by the paragon Maria.

*

---

* Branwell is thought to have had most contact with the local children, but it wasn't very friendly.

After the disaster of Cowan Bridge, Patrick Brontë was in no hurry to send any of his children to school again. In Branwell's case, there was no need to: Patrick himself was an expert teacher, and the opportunity to shape his young son's wildly active mind gave him pride and pleasure. The saving of scant resources was of course one powerful motive, but Patrick must also have relished the home-schooling experiment as a way of proving the worth of both teacher and pupil. Branwell made impressive progress in the classics – prodigious, it seemed – under the demanding eye of his father; he had a phenomenal memory, was irrepressibly enthusiastic about history, geography and all manner of literature; he was also very musical and precociously good at art. No wonder he was treated as 'a sort of idol' at the Parsonage. But in other ways the intense tutelage Branwell had at home did him irreparable harm, depriving him of a peer group to measure himself against and engage with. The only person to be measured against was his awe-inspiring parent, and those long hours in the study alone with Papa must have been very quelling to Branwell's childish spirits.

Miss Branwell taught the girls in her room upstairs. Sewing and household skills took up a large amount of their time (all the basic shirt- and underclothes-making, and hemming of sheets and linen was done at home), and each girl passed the landmark of embroidering a sampler – a sort of textile certificate of dexterity and patience. These efforts hung on the wall next to those of their late sisters: Charlotte's was a text from Proverbs 22:4, 'My humility and the fear of the Lord are riches honour and life'. Aunt Branwell read to the girls and heard them read. She may have taught them French too, as Maria had known some before she went to Cowan Bridge. Though Charlotte protested as late as 1842 that her understanding of spoken French was rudimentary, she was so good at the language by the age of fourteen that she was able to translate the whole first volume of Voltaire's *La Henriade* – a rather spectacular proof of proficiency. Charlotte's efforts might have been in competition with Branwell's acquisition of Greek and Latin at the same time. Though the girls had some lessons with their father, intensive study of the classics was reserved for the boy, who could read parts of Homer and Virgil by the age of ten.

The children were all very familiar with *Aesop's Fables*, *Tales of the Genii*, *The Arabian Nights*, *The Pilgrim's Progress*, *Gulliver's Travels* and of course the Bible (Charlotte's favourite book was Revelation). They had the free run of their father's library, which included *Paradise Lost*, Samuel Johnson's *Lives of the Most Eminent English Poets*, James Thomson's *The Seasons*, Oliver Goldsmith's *History of Rome*, Reverend J. Goldsmith's *Grammar of General Geography* and David Hume's *History of England*. There were also editions of Shakespeare, Cowper, Southey and anthologies of contemporary poetry. When Charlotte went to school, aged fourteen, she amazed her classmates by already knowing by heart most of the pieces they were set to learn: '[she] would tell us the authors, the poems they were taken from, and sometimes repeat a page or two, and tell us the plot.' Most surprisingly, Patrick Brontë seems to have made no attempt to keep Byron away from his children, and the results were very marked. Charlotte was so familiar with the scandalous atheist's works by the age of ten that she quoted them freely in her own stories, and both she and Branwell came to admire him – for his style, bravado, wit and sensual excesses – more than any other contemporary writer.

The only reading material that Reverend Brontë is known to have censored was one equally to Charlotte's taste, the collection of old copies of *The Lady's Magazine* that had belonged to her mother and that were still stained with salt water from their survival of the shipwreck in 1812. Perhaps Patrick Brontë had not inspected these publications very closely until Charlotte took a fancy to them. 'One black day,' as she later recalled, he decided to burn them all for the very reason she valued them, 'because they contained foolish love-stories'. The aggression of this is notable – against the girl, obviously, but also against his late wife's taste and romance in general. And in burning them Patrick was destroying one of the few relics of Maria Branwell Brontë left in the house.

Once the hours of instruction were over, both adults in the family seemed best pleased to retreat into solitude. The tedium on winter's nights could be terrible, as Charlotte re-created vividly in her account of how the game 'The Islanders' began, in December 1827:

> One night, about the time when the cold sleet and dreary fogs of November are succeeded by the snowstorms, and high, piercing, night-winds of confirmed winter, we were all sitting round the warm blazing

kitchen fire, having just concluded a quarrel with Tabby concerning the propriety of lighting a candle, from which she came off victorious, no candle having been produced. A long pause succeeded, which was at last broken by Branwell saying, in a lazy manner, 'I don't know what to do.' This was re-echoed by Emily and Anne.

Tabby: Wha ya may go t'bed.

Branwell: I'd rather do anything [than] that.

and Charlotte: You're so glum tonight, Tabby. [? Well] suppose we had each an island.

Branwell: If we had I would choose the Island of Man.

Charlotte: And I would choose Isle of Wight.

Emily: The Isle of Arran for me.

Anne: And mine should be Guernsey.

This wasn't the children's first joint fantasy: imaginary games had been their main resource for years, though it was only in 1829 that Charlotte began to chronicle them. Branwell's toys had inspired earlier ones. He was given some wooden soldiers around the time of his seventh birthday, in the summer of 1824 (when his elder sisters had just gone away to Cowan Bridge), and received several more sets in the next two years, although the casualty rate was high: one whole boxful was 'maimed, lost, burned or destroyed'. Branwell augmented the soldiers with some Turkish musicians and later a band of Indians, and something of his loneliness can be caught from his careful account of the ebb and flow of these possessions: '[I had] a band of Turkish musicians which I continued to keep till the summer of AD 1825, when Charlotte and Emily returned from school, where they had been during the days of my former sets.' It sounds as if as soon as his sisters were home, they made free with his toys, knowing how much he valued *them* as playfellows. The date of this first sharing is significant, though: it was just after the deaths of Maria and Elizabeth.

In June of the following year, when Reverend Brontë came home one day from Leeds with gifts for everyone, Branwell allowed his twelve new soldiers, the most coveted present, to be treated as the children's common property, as Charlotte recalled:

it was night and we were in bed, so next morning Branwell came to our door with a box of soldiers. Emily and I jumped out of bed and I snatched up one and exclaimed, 'This is the Duke of Wellington! It shall be mine!' When I said this, Emily likewise took one and said it should be hers. When Anne came down she took one also. Mine was the prettiest of the whole and perfect in every part. Emilys was a grave-looking fellow. We called him Gravey. Anne's was a queer little thing, very much like herself. He was called Waiting Boy. Branwell chose Bonaparte.

In the vast, complex games that followed, the four children retained an Olympian manner, and Gulliver-like changes of scale and focus. They cast themselves in the roles of powerful genii called Tallii,* Branii, Emmii and Annii, or sometimes as the little King and Queens. As Charlotte recorded, the first three 'great plays' they devised in these years were 'The Young Men', based on the twelve wooden soldiers' travels and adventures, 'Our Fellows', which was based on characters from *Aesop's Fables* (and which melted into 'The O'Dears') and 'The Islanders', which featured the Duke of Wellington and his two sons Arthur Augustus Adrian Wellesley and Charles Wellesley – key figures in the mass of stories to come.

To chronicle the adventures of the 'Twelves' and the 'Genii', Branwell and Charlotte began to produce a series of tiny magazines for the toys, complete with editorials, advertising and publication details, stories, poems and histories for and about the characters who peopled 'Sneaky's Land', 'Parry's Land', 'Wellington's Land' and the 'Great Glass Town Confederacy'. In tiny writing, squared off to look as much as possible like print, and in booklets sometimes only an inch or so high,† bound with thread inside old sugar wrappers and scraps of wall-paper, the children laboured over the years to produce a wild, weird literature of their own.

Their making little books was not new. Charlotte's first surviving manuscript is just such a production for her youngest sister, an illus-trated story, 'There was once a little girl and her name was Ane', written when she was about ten. But the booklets connected with the 'Twelves'

---

* This genie name for Charlotte makes one wonder if she was known as 'Charlie' (pronounced 'Sharlie') by her siblings.
† Ann Dinsdale says the smallest is 36 × 55 mm (1.5 × 2.25 in.) (*The Brontës at Haworth*, 65).

soon evolved from props to something much more central, very consciously a way of bolstering the reality of the games they played, and making their everyday world a little less real, creating a zone where the two could coexist. The earliest stories of the 'Twelves' are often delightfully inconsequential and silly, with a large cast of characters behaving very much as if they were children. 'The Voyage of Discovery' describes their initial expedition:

> Thus having made everything ready we retired to the cabin, and everyone looked as sheepish as possible and no way inclined to meet our fate like men. Some of us began to cry, but we waited a long time and heard no sound of the wind, and the cloud did not increase in size.
>
> At last Marcus O'Donell exclaimed, 'I wish it would either go backward or forward.'
>
> At this Stewart reproved him, and Ferdinand gave him a box on the ear. O'Donell returned the compliment. But just then we heard the sound of the wind, and Ronald bawled out, 'The cloud is as big as me!'

Other early pieces show Charlotte's taste for the surreal and exotic, and her quick identification with the characters that were emerging. In 'Description of the Duke of W's small palace situated on the Banks of the Indirce', written in January 1830, her narrator, Charles Wellesley, is 'reclining under the shadow of an immense chestnut tree, playing upon a small Spanish guitar, with a nightingale perched upon his shoulder'. The song he sings is signed 'CB CW' – a collaboration between the author and her creature:

> Of College I am tired I wish to be at home
> Far from the pompous tutors voice & the hated schoolboys groan
>
> I wish that I had freedom to walk about at will
> That I no more was troubled with my Greek & slate & quill[.]

The books stayed tiny, no doubt both to save on material and to retain privacy. They looked childish, and would not prompt undue adult curiosity if found. Neither Papa nor Aunt Branwell had good enough eyesight to decipher the stories anyway.

By March 1829 the first games were sufficiently developed to warrant chronicling (in ordinary-sized writing), and Charlotte's 'History of the Year' gives a careful account of the daily life from which they had sprung. She wrote it sitting at the kitchen table with a book in front of her, an old atlas that used to belong to Maria and in which her dead elder sister had written 'Papa lent me this book'. Perhaps Charlotte was meant to be studying its maps and charts, but ended up reporting to posterity instead, in a manner that she and her sisters often repeated, a sort of log-book style rather than a diary, a taking of coordinates:

> I am in the kitchen of the parsonage house, Haworth. Tabby the servant is washing up after breakfast and Anne, my youngest sister (Maria was my eldest), is kneeling on a chair looking at some cakes which Tabby has been baking for us. Emily is in the parlour brushing it. Papa and Branwell are gone to Keighley. Aunt is up stairs in her room and I am sitting by the table writing this in the kitchin.

The twelve-year-old felt it was important to say exactly which papers Papa and Branwell had gone to fetch:

> We take 2 and see three newspapers a week. We take the Leeds Intelligencer, party Tory, and the Leeds Mercury, Whig, edited by Mr Baines and his brother, son in law and his 2 sons, Edward and Talbot. We see the John Bull; it is a High Tory, very violent. Mr Driver lends us it, as likewise Blackwood's Magazine, the most able periodical there is. The editor is Mr Christopher North, an old man, 74 years of age. The 1st of April is his birthday.

It is comical to think of Charlotte being so involved as to remember the (fictional) birthday of *Blackwood's* pseudonymous editor. *Blackwood's* was the leading Tory magazine of the day, published monthly and run from Edinburgh by John Wilson (aka Christopher North), John Gibson Lockhart and William Maginn. *Blackwood's* exactly suited the Brontë children's tastes, even while they could hardly define them; it was both conservative and satiric, mandarin and yet, in its promotion of Scott, Wordsworth, Coleridge and Shelley, deeply Romantic.

The whole family was passionately interested in news, and Patrick Brontë liked to read his children items from the papers and to air his uninflected views with an enthusiastic audience. Nothing pleased them all better than reports of a vigorous parliamentary debate. Charlotte

recalled their excitement in 1829 at the passage of the Catholic Emancipation Bill, a measure brought in by Peel and Wellington allowing
Catholics to hold public office that Patrick Brontë supported for the
same pragmatic reasons as the government's, that it was the lesser of
two evils. Charlotte showed genuine delight in following the twists
and turns of this contentious legislation:

> O those 3 months, from the time of the King's speech to the end!
> Nobody could think, speak or write on anything but the Catholic
> Question and the Duke of Wellington or Mr Peel. I remember the day
> when the Intelligence Extraordinary came with Mr Peel's speech in it,
> containing the terms on which the Catholics were to be let in. With
> what eagerness Papa tore off the cover, & how we all gathered round
> him, & with what breathless anxiety we listened, as one by one they
> were disclosed & explained & argued upon so ably & so well . . .

This was the world that absorbed her.

Charlotte also derived deep pleasure and imaginative stimulus from
whatever prints, pictures and even descriptions of art she had access to,
giving the evocations of grand buildings, 'high life' and exotic loca-
tions in her 'Glass Town' stories an eerie plausibility. Like Jane Eyre
when she reads Bewick's *History of British Birds* (a book owned by the
Brontës), Charlotte let her mind wander from pictures to the text and
back again, augmenting both from her own imagination on the way.
One of her favourite artists was John Martin, like Bewick a north-
country genius. She loved the grandeur of Martin's landscapes, the
dream-like, often nightmarish qualities of his vision and his taste for
apocalypse, with human figures appearing tiny, doomed and helpless
in the face of an evolving disaster. Martin was both a Romantic visionary and a man of the Brontës' very own time and place, putting visual
references to contemporary Newcastle and Edinburgh into his depictions of the New Jerusalem or Sodom and Gomorrah, a sublime
transfiguration of the industrialisation of both those cities. Patrick
Brontë owned several Martin prints, including the bestselling *Belshazzar's Feast*, *Joshua Commanding the Sun to Stand Still*, *The Deluge*, and
possibly others such as *St Paul Preaching at Athens*. The illustrated
Annuals, albums full of the most popular and interesting engravings of
the year, were also full of Martin's mesmerising canvases, alongside

fashionable portraitists such as Richard Westall, scenes from Scott and Byron, views of the Brighton Pavilion, or images of Arctic exploration. The Brontë children's profoundly visual imaginations fed avidly on them all, and by the age of thirteen Charlotte already had a very developed 'list of painters whose works I wish to see', which included 'Guido Reni, Julio Romano, Titian, Raphael, Michael Angelo, Correggio, Annibal Caracci, Leonardo da Vinci, Fra Bartolemeo, Carlo Cignani, Vandyke, Reubens, Bartolemeo Ramerghi'.

Branwell transported John Martin into the 'Glass Town' personnel in the character of an artist called Edward de Lisle, to live, breathe and paint among the other avatars. Charlotte had already established there the Duke of Wellington, her favourite, though he was more like a comic-book superhero than the retired general who in 1829 had just formed a government. 'His vision is uncommonly acute and his finely formed frame is so knit and moulded as to be equal to the greatest hardships of the most terrible campaigns,' Charlotte wrote, in 'Anecdotes of the Duke of Wellington'. 'His mind approaches as nearly to the perfection of greatness and wisdom as human fallibility will allow.' Perhaps because he wasn't quite fallible enough, Wellington's sons Arthur and Charles soon took over as the main characters in the 'Glass Town' saga (Arthur ennobled to the Marquis of Douro, on his way to greater honours).

'The History of the Year' doesn't make clear quite how much writing had been stimulated by the 'Twelves'. August and September of 1829 were particularly productive months; Charlotte wrote a number of long poems in collaboration with Branwell for his 'Blackwood's Young Men's Magazine' (which he had started in January 1829), many under the initials 'UT' or 'WT' for 'Us Two' and 'We Two'. She wrote 'Tales of the Islanders' (a founding text of the 'Glass Town' saga), 'An Adventure in Ireland' (a story full of ghosts, caves and fairies) and nine long poems that she made into a 'Book of Rhymes'. But this was nothing to the flood of writing the following year, staggering not just in its mass but in its rapidly increasing sophistication. Five months after her first collection of verse, she had written enough to fill another volume, called 'Miscellaneous Poems by C. Brontë'.

The physical size of the doll-books masked for years the scope of the compositions they contain. Mrs Gaskell was the first person outside the family to see the tiny manuscripts and was baffled at the sight of them, in 1856: 'an immense amount of manuscript, in an inconceivably small space; tales, dramas, poems, romances, written principally by Charlotte, in a hand which it is almost impossible to decipher without the aid of a magnifying glass'. The total length of the Brontë juvenilia, it has been calculated, considerably exceeds that of their published works. 'The Foundling', written by Charlotte in 1833, turned out to be 35,000 words long, as did 'The Green Dwarf', of the same year, and the four tales that Charlotte made into a booklet in 1834 – containing 'The Spell', 'High Life in Verdopolis' and 'The Scrap Book by Lord C. A. F. Wellesley' – come to around 62,000 words, a truly prodigious length.

There is something magical about the deceptive appearance of these compacted early works, a foiling of expectations, a withholding, and yet, like the genie in Aladdin's bottle, able under the right circumstances to be summoned forth to astonish and amaze. But even in their transcribed and printed versions, the juvenilia are hard to read, for several reasons. Prime among these is that they were clearly not *meant* to be read by outsiders and are unconcerned with providing narrative consistency or structure for any audience other than the Brontë siblings themselves. The plots, characterisations and time shifts are so fluid, the political and personal histories of the Angrians so volatile, that the stories are bound to confound and confuse the prying outsider. The essence of the saga is flux and freedom – to effect miraculous resuscitations and revivals if desired, changes of characters' names, careers, personalities even – oddly like a sort of compulsive 'gaming', two hundred years before the appropriate technology had been invented.

In August 1830 Charlotte drew up a catalogue of everything she had written in the previous sixteen months, 'Making in the whole 22 volumes', and the flood of writing continued all year: between 10 and 13 November 1830 alone, she composed 468 lines of polished, highly accomplished poetry. Her own production rate interested her intensely, and she was keen to log the details of what amounted to training sessions:

> I began this book on the 22 of February 1830, and finished it on the
> 23 of February 1830, doing 8 pages on the first day and 11 on the second.
> On the first day I wrote an hour and a half in the morning, and an hour
> and a half in the evening. On the third [*sic*] day I wrote a quarter of an
> hour in the morning, 2 hours in the afternoon and a quarter of an hour
> in the evening, making in the whole 5 hours and a half.

'I wrote this in 4 hours,' she notes on the manuscript of 'Albion and
Marina'. At the bottom of the poem 'Miss Hume's Dream' she records,
'I wrote this in half an hour'; it is sixty-four lines long.

Branwell was every bit as prolific, writing whole newspapers in the
mode of facsimiles,* and keen on mapping the territory of their imagined country (ostensibly located on the west coast of Africa, an area they
had read about in explorers' reports), providing details of mercantile life,
distances, produce, trade and population to match Charlotte's interest in
political intrigue and romance. He had a whole country's statistics in his
head. Their father was aware of these productions, 'little works of fiction, they call'd miniature novels', as he told Mrs Gaskell, and was content
that the children were harmlessly occupied. He must have taken fright,
though, at the shrinking of Charlotte's handwriting, for one of her notebooks, a good quality one, was a gift from him with the following
inscription: 'All that is written in this book must be in a good, plain, and
legible hand. – P. B.'

The content of the 'juvenilia' was never juvenile, the amount of it
was phenomenal, and the work continued well into adult life, composed concurrently, in Emily's and Anne's cases at least, with published
work, 'making subject matter rather than the authors' ages the most
useful basis for selection', as Christine Alexander has said. Perhaps the
distinction is also between private and public: the intended audiences.
There are self-conscious references all through Charlotte Brontë's early
works to the question of who might be reading them – for instance the
joke contained in the title of 'The Search after Happiness', 'A Tale by
Charlotte Brontë Printed by Herself and Sold by Nobody'. She and
Branwell wrote in collaboration, in competition, but not primarily for
each other. Aping the forms and styles of real books and magazines, the

---

* His 'Monthly Intelligencer', on display in the Brontë Parsonage Museum, is a
lovely example of this.

two elder Brontës both instinctively behaved like unpublished professional writers, trying things out on an endlessly indulgent ideal reader. Perhaps a more useful term for this massive body of writing, rather than 'juvenile' writing, would be 'hidden'.

In the summer and autumn of 1830, while Charlotte and Branwell were rapidly developing their intricate 'Glass Town' scenarios, Patrick Brontë became ill with a serious and lingering lung infection that he seems to have feared might be consumption. To his old friend Elizabeth Franks he confessed how feeble he had been in body and spirit for six months, hardly able to perform his clerical duties and worrying that he might never recover but 'fall into a decline'.

He didn't need such a prompt to consider his children's futures; it must have always been on his mind. In the event of his death, they would be not just orphaned but homeless, the Parsonage passing immediately to the next incumbent. Elizabeth Branwell's private income would not enable her to support any of her nieces and nephews: they would each have to earn their own livings. For the girls, this meant teaching or governessing, and for that they needed some documented, recognisable qualification. Not public exams, at that date, but a record of formal education.

During Patrick's long illness, his old friends from Thornton were enlisted into helping set up some provision against disaster. Charlotte's godparents, Thomas and Frances Atkinson, not only came up with a recommended school for her – run by a local woman known to them personally – but may have paid part of the fees. The place was Roe Head School, only a mile from their home in Mirfield in the Spen Valley; Charlotte was to be sent there in the new year, a couple of months before her fifteenth birthday.

What her feelings were at the prospect of going away from home alone, and at a time when her father's life seemed in danger, can be imagined. And the distress of being separated from her siblings was not much less than the constraints that boarding-school life would inevitably put on the imaginary games she relied on so much already, and the literature that was generated by them. Though Charlotte was a very insignificant-looking creature, so childlike in fact that one of Elizabeth Franks's friends took her on her knee and dandled her around like a baby ('[she] *would* nurse me', the teenager wrote in disgust), she was already the author of such poems as 'Reflections on the Fate of Neglected Genius' (1830):

> None can tell the bitter anguish
> Of those lofty souls that languish!
> With Grim Penury still dwelling
> Quenched by frowns their sacred fire,
> All their powers within them swelling
> Tortured by neglect to ire.

Her stories of this date contain passages that Charlotte hardly bettered, such as this description, from 'Strange Events', of Lord Charles Wellesley leafing through the pages of a book in the public library of Glass Town and falling into 'the strangest train of thought that ever visited even my mind, eccentric and unstable as it is said by some insolent puppies to be':

> It seemed as if I was a non-existent shadow, that I neither spoke, eat, imagined or lived of myself, but I was the mere idea of some other creatures brain. The Glass Town seemed so likewise. My father, Arthur and everyone with whom I am acquainted, passed into a state of annihilation: but suddenly I thought again that I and my relatives did exist, and yet not us but our minds and our bodies without ourselves. Then this supposition – the oddest of any – followed the former quickly, namely, that WE without US were shadows; also, but at the end of a long vista, as it were, appeared dimly and indistinctly, beings that really lived in a tangible shape, that were called by our names and were US from whom WE had been copied by something – I could not tell what.

She was fourteen years old when she wrote this astonishingly sophisticated passage, penetrating into the thought processes, dreams and fantasies of one of her own inventions, having this adult man in her mind muse on *her* when he senses the distant power or influence that has brought him into being, but that he can't imagine is simply a fourteen-year-old girl bending over a tiny scrap of paper in a cold room in Yorkshire.

4

Among Schoolgirls

1831–5

On 17 January 1831 Charlotte arrived at Roe Head, a handsome house on the old Leeds-to-Huddersfield road, recently converted into a school for about ten girls and run by Miss Margaret Wooler and three of her sisters. Roe Head was quite unlike Cowan Bridge, with its Calvinistic harshness and utilitarianism. Miss Wooler was, in her nephew's words, 'a keen-witted, ironical and very independent Yorkshire woman', sensible, even-tempered and sensitive to the needs of her charges, most of whom were the daughters of local businessmen and manufacturers. The school offered conventional girls' school fare: history, geography, literature, arithmetic and extras in French, music and drawing. Unlike Cowan Bridge, the new school was within hailing distance of home: Patrick Brontë was clearly not willing to take risks as he had before. But the outlay for this superior establishment was much greater than the subsidised clergy-daughters' rate, and Charlotte was left in no doubt about her responsibility to get on as fast and as successfully as she could in order to equip herself cost-efficiently for the best career open to her, that of governess.

The fourteen-year-old girl who got down from a covered cart on Roe Head's curving driveway that winter's day did not look like a particularly promising pupil. Undersized, undernourished, wearing an unflattering, old-fashioned dress and with her hair unkempt and frizzy, she was miserable and struggling with tears. The other girls must have watched her arrival from the schoolroom window, for when she joined them later, it was noted that 'her dress was changed, but just as old.' This was the observation of Mary Taylor, the attractive, energetic and outspoken elder daughter of a local cloth manufacturer, a natural leader and opinion-former among the little society of the school. Her first impressions of Charlotte were of a shy and nervous creature 'so short-sighted that she always appeared to be seeking something, and moving her head from side to side to catch a sight of it', a figure of fun for the way her nose was always almost touching her book, whether the book was lying flat or being held. Mary also noted another of the new girl's oddities: '[She] spoke with a strong Irish accent.'

Fortunately for Charlotte, another new pupil arrived the following week, Ellen Nussey, the daughter of a cloth merchant from nearby Birstall, who, when she was shown into the library by Miss Wooler, was surprised to discover she was not alone: 'there was a silent, weeping, dark little figure in the large bay-window; she must, I thought, have risen from the floor.' The shrinking girl wanted to hide, but when asked what the matter was, admitted she was homesick. Ellen's attempts to comfort her were not successful until she pointed out that they were both in the same boat, and that she, Ellen, might be even more to be pitied, having only just arrived. It was the magic formula that always worked with Charlotte – the call of sympathy. 'A faint quivering smile then lighted her face; the tear-drops fell', and the two girls held hands silently until the other pupils came in from outdoor play.

This was the beginning of a lifelong friendship, and one of great significance to Brontë studies because of Ellen's careful preservation of around 500 letters from Charlotte over the next twenty-four years. Only one of the many letters that Charlotte wrote to Mary Taylor has survived, a loss that severely unbalances the picture of Charlotte's life and opinions, since Mary was the more challenging friend, as ferociously and precociously interested in topical affairs as any Brontë. Ellen was a very conventional girl, mild and affectionate, while Mary seemed the opposite of Charlotte in every respect but intellectually – she might have proved a formidable enemy in such a small community as Roe Head, had she not recognised and responded to Charlotte's spirit. Between them, Mary and Ellen helped Charlotte to overcome her separation from home, becoming, indeed, almost substitute sisters.

Charlotte's abilities were evident from the outset; she shot from the bottom to the top of the class, staying there the whole of her eighteen-month school career. 'She was first in everything but play,' Ellen recalled later, 'yet never was a word heard of envy or jealousy from her companions; every one felt she had won her laurels by an amount of diligence and hard labor of which they were incapable.' Ellen later recalled that when the other girls were chatting round the fire or play-ing outside in their precious leisure hour, Charlotte 'would be kneeling close to the window busy with her studies', often so late into the gloam-ing that her friends joked she must be able to see in the dark. Such a girl could have been dreadfully unpopular, but Charlotte's decency and lack of pride endeared her to her classmates, who rather marvelled at the exotic nature of her knowledge and laughed affectionately at her oddities.

Ellen's reminiscences of Charlotte as a teenager stress her physical feebleness: her tiny appetite, terrible eyesight (which prevented her from reading music or learning any instrument), nervousness and lack of strength or spirit to join in the games that everyone else looked for-ward to with relish. During playtime at school, Charlotte always preferred to stand apart and watch, or read, and when Mary tried to get her to join in a ball game, she said she had never played and did not know how. 'We made her try, but soon found that she could not see the ball, so we put her out.'

'For years she had not tasted animal food,' Ellen said; 'she had the greatest dislike to it; she always had something specially provided for her at our midday repast.' Ellen thought it a triumph that at the end of the first term Charlotte had come round to trying a little gravy every now and then with her vegetables, and was consequently looking a bit livelier. Inadequate quantities of meat in his children's diet was one of Mrs Gaskell's later accusations against Patrick Brontë, but it's clear from Ellen's remarks that Charlotte was an infrequent meat-eater by inclination as much as by habit.*

Mary was particularly impressed by Charlotte's intense concentra-tion when examining any sort of picture, and her ability to explain what she thought about it: 'She made poetry and drawing . . . exceed-ingly interesting to me,' Mary recalled gratefully; 'and then I got the habit . . . of referring mentally to her opinion on all matters of that kind, along with many more.'

Not politics, however, as the Taylor family were vociferous Dissent-ers, and Charlotte was of course a rabid Tory. Nothing was more likely

---

* And the accusations were groundless anyway: according to the Garrs, and Patrick himself, the Brontës ate plenty of meat.

to rouse the inner spirit of the 'little old woman', as Mary called her, than a vigorous debate about the issues of the day, just the sort of talk she so missed from home. Mary was impressed at how much Charlotte knew in this field too:

> She knew the names of the two Ministries; the one that resigned, and the one that succeeded and passed the Reform Bill. She worshipped the Duke of Wellington, but said that Sir Robert Peel was not to be trusted; he did not act from principle, like the rest, but from expediency. I, being of the furious Radical party, told her, 'How could any of them trust one another? they were all of them rascals!' Then she would launch out into praises of the Duke of Wellington, referring to his actions; which I could not contradict, as I knew nothing about him. She said she had taken interest in politics ever since she was five years old. She did not get her opinions from her father – that is, not directly – but from the papers, etc., he preferred.

At Roe Head, Charlotte found, for the first and last time, happiness similar to that of home. Miss Wooler was thirty-nine when Charlotte arrived, and she proved a fine role model: maternal but not sentimental, and her unshowy neatness in dress and deportment was something that Charlotte emulated in adult life. Miss Wooler wore white at this date, and arranged her hair in a plaited coronet, like 'a lady abbess', as Ellen said. The girls enjoyed her company in the evenings when she relaxed and shared stories with them, some of the old days, when the area had been riven with strife over the march of the new technology in the mills (which Patrick Brontë had also experienced first-hand in nearby Hartshead) – the route of the attack on Rawfolds Mill had gone right past Roe Head. Her accounts of her travels on the Continent and the cities and art works she had seen would have particularly intrigued Charlotte, with her private wish-list of paintings she would one day like to view. When the weather did not allow these evening gatherings to take place outdoors, Miss Wooler would perambulate the long schoolroom instead, with the girls hanging about her 'delighted to listen to her, or have a chance of being nearest in the walk', another habit Charlotte was to make her own.

Having friends was a blessed novelty. Mary always spoke her mind, and countered Charlotte's tendency to brood with shafts of common sense. Her good intentions were always clear, however brusquely she sometimes expressed herself, and her affectionate interest broke down Charlotte's intense self-consciousness. Mary was perceptive about her friend: 'She took all our proceedings with pliable indifference,' she recalled of their schooldays, 'and always seemed to need a previous resolution to say "No" to anything' – the mark of a child over-anxious of authority. It was clear to Mary that Charlotte's upbringing had been odd and unhealthy, and that the make-believe powers that were so highly developed in her were the result of having insufficient other interests or stimulus. 'The whole family used to "make out" histories, and invent characters and events,' Mary told Mrs Gaskell later. 'I told her sometimes they were like growing potatoes in a cellar. She said, sadly, "Yes! I know we are!"' Charlotte had revealed to Mary the existence of 'The Young Men's Magazine': 'No one wrote in it, and no one read it, but herself, her brother, and two sisters. She promised to show me some of these magazines, but retracted it afterwards, and would never be persuaded to do so.' Charlotte must have had some of the tiny books with her at Roe Head and, in the warmth of her growing confidence in Mary, felt tempted – briefly – to share them. Interestingly, she never gave Ellen any hint of her private writing.

In the dormitory, the girls would lie in the dark, half hoping to hear the female ghost said to walk the attics,* or whisper long intimate conversations, risking a fine for 'late-talking' if discovered. Charlotte was often prevailed on to tell a story, and liked to oblige. The darkness was liberating, and the sense of an eager audience almost like home. She could extemporise with great ease and conviction, but on at least one occasion had too much success with the vividness of her invention and upset a girl who was meant to be convalescing. Characteristically, Charlotte felt conscience-stricken about this and didn't do it again.

But being at boarding school made her think of her dead sisters more than ever. 'Her love for them was most intense; a kind of adoration dwelt in her feelings,' Ellen perceived, astonished that Charlotte 'would still weep and suffer' when recalling Maria's last illness. Charlotte spoke of her eldest sister as 'superhuman in goodness and cleverness' and of

* Ellen Nussey, who tells this story in her 'Reminiscences of Charlotte Brontë' (*LCB* 1, 594), said that the tradition of the Roe Head ghost 'had a great charm for Charlotte'.

both as 'wonders of talent and kindness', but perhaps talking about them to strangers stirred her up in odd ways, for Charlotte told Mary about a disturbingly vivid dream she had around this time in which Maria and Elizabeth were waiting to see her in the Roe Head drawing room, but, when she went eagerly to meet them, they had changed into the type of fashionable young lady whom Charlotte loathed, vain and critical. '[T]hey had forgotten what they used to care for,' she said to Mary sadly. Her subconscious was perhaps telling her that continuing to grieve over her sisters' fates was useless – time had moved on.

But the griefs and fears expressed in Charlotte's dream touched a nerve that resonated painfully all her life: the understanding that there was a loss beyond loss, that bereavements might not only multiply but intensify. Such feelings torment the protagonist of *Villette* at the novel's crisis, the eye of suffering in that most suffering book: 'Methought the well-loved dead, who had loved me well in life, met me elsewhere, alienated: galled was my inmost spirit with an unutterable sense of despair.' Time does move on for the bereaved, but alarmingly. Healing, 'recovering', from a death is also a form of estrangement, a further loss.

The school's half-holidays were chances to play-act and revel, rare occurrences in Charlotte Brontë's life. Little performances were got up, with dancing to follow and a supper 'coaxed out of yielding mammas and elder sisters', as Ellen recalled. Charlotte was again the odd one out, not having any family near enough to take an interest in the junket, but she proved useful when the girls decided to stage a mock coronation (presumably around the time of the coronation of the new king, William IV, on 8 September 1831), making up aristocratic titles for her schoolfriends, writing speeches and directing the proceedings. Here was a glancing connection between real life and the courtly society of 'Glass Town' that must have struck a pleasurable chord in Charlotte's breast. Miss Wooler's sister Catherine acted as Queen, but the show was stolen by Mary Taylor's lively younger sister Martha, who threw herself into the role of mulatto servant and blacked up to serve at table.

In the shorter holidays from school, Charlotte did not go home, but to friends of the family nearer Roe Head. The school was only minutes away from the home of the Atkinsons and only four miles from the

Frankses in Huddersfield, where warm-hearted Elizabeth Franks was more than willing to keep an eye on her old friend's daughter, have her to stay at the vicarage and oversee her welfare.

Charlotte also visited Mary and Martha Taylor's home, the Red House in Gomersal, and met an eccentric and interesting family. The house had been built in the seventeenth century by one of their forebears and their prosperity came from a wool mill at Hunsworth established by their grandfather. Though the Taylors' fortunes were on the turn when Charlotte Brontë first met them in the early 1830s, that wasn't obvious from the look of their comfortable home, with its handsome family portraits in the hall, original artworks and a curious double-arched stained-glass window depicting Milton and Shakespeare in its central panels.* Nothing could have better expressed the Taylors' secular bent and their taste in books, art and culture: when Charlotte evoked their home in her novel *Shirley*, she called up images of candlelight, the sounds of lively debate and laughter, and the warmth of a coal fire, even in the summer. There was another kind of warmth too, a paterfamilias who ate and sat with his children, and liked to watch over them, 'naturally a social, hospitable man – an advocate for family unity'.

The air of comfort at the Red House was an eye-opener to Charlotte, a striking example of what a cultivated middle-class home looked like, compared with the windswept Parsonage with its unloved patch of thorns abutting graves. Mary was never complacent about her family's affluence, though; the necessity for girls as well as boys to earn their keep had been drummed into her from an early age. In the novel Mary wrote many years later, dealing with a set of young women of the 1830s trying to support themselves, the difficulties are starkly laid out: 'There's no decent way fit for you to take by which a woman can earn more than just a living. You must make up your mind to work close – all day, and every day, and all your life, and then, if you are sharp and thrifty, you may perhaps get bread.'

Charlotte and Mary got on so well at school that Miss Wooler ran out of things to teach them in the final term and set them both to commit to memory a book of *belles-lettres*. Mary protested against this

---

* This window is still at the Red House.

boring expedient and was sent supperless to bed for the last month of school, but Charlotte knuckled under, obedient to the last. Charlotte left with three prizes, and a silver medal for fulfilment of duties. Her intellectual powers were evident in her prodigious memory, analytic skill and avidity for learning, added to which she was a model of good conduct (only once incurring a fine, after telling those stories at night to the other girls) and not only 'very familiar with all the sublimest passages' in scripture, but genuinely pious. Miss Wooler could not have wished for a better pupil.

It only struck Charlotte on her last day at Roe Head that she had been such a diligent and obedient student that something had evaded her – the whole experience, in fact. Turning to Ellen, she said, 'I should for once like to feel *out and out* a school-girl; I wish something would happen! Let us run round the fruit garden; perhaps we shall meet some one, or we may have a fine for trespass.' Ellen was surprised at the suggestion, since she had never seen Charlotte run anywhere, or express an interest in livening things up. '[Charlotte] evidently was longing for some never-to-be-forgotten incident,' Ellen said. 'Nothing, however, arose from her little enterprise. She had to leave school as calmly and quietly as she had there lived.'

When Charlotte returned home from school in June 1832, having just turned sixteen, she was expected to share with Emily and Anne the schooling she had just received, taking charge of them every morning for three hours of lessons, including drawing. The sisters were delighted to be united again and soon settled down to a congenially unmonitored routine: lessons all morning, followed by a walk up on to the moors. One of their favourite destinations was a sheltered hollow under Round Hill now known as 'The Brontë Waterfall', where water from Oxenhope Edge runs down into South Dean Beck. Emily and Anne called this retreat 'The Meeting of the Waters' and led the way to it, fording the streams and putting down stepping stones for Charlotte if necessary: 'nothing appearing in view but miles and miles of heather: a glorious blue sky, and brightening sun . . . there was always a *lingering* delight in these spots, every moss, every flower, every tint and form, were noted and enjoyed.' They often stayed out until dinner time. '[A]fter dinner I sew till tea-time,' Charlotte told Ellen, who had not at this date ever visited Haworth, 'and after tea I either read, write, do a little fancy-work or draw, as I please. Thus in one delightful, though somewhat monotonous course my life is passed.'

What she wasn't mentioning to Ellen was the amount of writing that the siblings were doing, and their other lives in the 'Glass Town' stories that were the very opposite of monotonous. In her absence, 'Glass Town' itself had become the more classical-sounding 'Verdopolis', Wellington's son Arthur and his erstwhile friend Ellrington had acquired new titles – Duke of Zamorna and Earl of Northangerland respectively – and Zamorna had become king of the new country of Angria, formed after the latest Ashantee Wars in a manner rather like Napoleon's dealing out of kingdoms and honours to his sons and brothers in the years after 1802. Zamorna's rise to power stimulated Charlotte to write 'The Bridal', which summarised the existing narrative and restarted Charlotte's participation in it, and she added to the saga with 'The Green Dwarf', 'High Life in Verdopolis' and 'Arthuriana'. The content of the stories was moving on to reflect the siblings' charged adolescent preoccupations. The newly ennobled Duke of Zamorna became increasingly worldly, scandalous and ruthless, with dark secrets from his past suddenly revealed, mistresses and bastards discovered everywhere, and all this salacious detail relished by the young author. Meanwhile Branwell was developing Alexander Percy (aka Ellrington, aka Northangerland) into a fully fledged Byronic anti-hero, a sneering, black-clad atheist, with a wife called Augusta di Segovia who was the first really immoral female character in the tales.

Charlotte and Branwell's fight for imaginative space within their joint creations was competitive and stimulating, but their attitudes to their invented characters were markedly different. Branwell began to identify so closely with Northangerland that he published under that name from 1839 onwards and affected it in correspondence outside the family circle. Charlotte felt every bit as possessive and admiring of Zamorna, and knew his every thought, but retained an observer's view of him. This wasn't simply to do with gender: Charlotte was very much at ease in the skin of a male alter ego such as 'Charles Townshend', Zamorna's younger brother, whose name and initials she sometimes used in correspondence. Zamorna was beyond that sort of identification, though. Her intense feeling for him was more like a love affair.

Charlotte was a natural satirist and introduced a vulgar character called Wiggins into the stories who was a caricature of her cocky brother:

> His form was that of a lad of sixteen, his face that of a man of twenty-five, his hair red, his features not bad, for he had a Roman nose, small mouth and well-turned chin. His figure too though diminutive was perfectly symmetrical and of this he seemed not unconscious from the frequent and complacent looks he cast down on his nether man. A pair of spectacles garnished his nose and through these he was continually gazing at Flanigan [an Angrian boxing-master] whose breadth of shoulder appeared to attract his sincere admiration, as every now and then he touched his own with the tip of his forefinger and pushed out his small contracted chest to make it appear broader.

Wiggins had some embarrassing relations, as he told the Verdopolitan journalists:

> 'I've some people who call themselves akin to me in the shape of three girls, not that they are honoured by possessing me as a brother, but I deny that they're my sisters . . .'
> 'What are your sisters' names?'
> 'CHARLOTTE Wiggins, JANE Wiggins, and ANNE Wiggins.'
> 'Are they as queer as you?'
> 'Oh, they are miserable silly creatures not worth talking about. CHARLOTTE's eighteen years old, a broad dumpy thing, whose head does not come higher than my elbow. Emily's sixteen, lean and scant, with a face about the size of a penny, and Anne is nothing, absolutely nothing.'
> 'What! Is she an idiot?'
> 'Next door to it.'

Charlotte was very close to her brother at this time, and very proud of him; as Ellen Nussey said later, 'he was *then* . . . as dear to Charlotte as her own soul; they were in perfect accord of taste and feeling, it was mutual delight to be together.' When Charlotte paid her long-awaited first visit to Ellen's home, Rydings in Birstall, that September, Branwell (who had come along as escort) leapt round 'in wild ecstasy', delighted with the beautiful old house and gracious grounds. It belonged to Ellen's uncle (her father was dead) and housed many of the spread-out Nussey clan. Branwell said it was Paradise, and that if Charlotte was not happy there she never would be, but no doubt Charlotte enjoyed her recollections of Rydings much more than she did the experience of being there, and wished her brother had stayed, for she was as painfully shy as ever: Ellen recalled Charlotte being so nervous at being led into dinner by a stranger that 'she trembled and nearly burst into tears.'

When Ellen made her first visit to Haworth ten months later, it seemed 'wild and uncultivated' by comparison with the Spen Valley, though only twenty miles distant. The hill up to the church was so steep the horses' feet caught at the cobbles 'as if climbing'. Ellen noted Aunt Branwell and Reverend Brontë's formal manners and eccentricities; indeed everyone must have been on best behaviour, as it was so rare to have visitors to stay. It sounds as if Aunt Branwell opened up considerably to well-brought-up, pretty Ellen, who left a suggestive portrait of the lonely 56-year-old, stuck in the chilly town where she had come a dozen years earlier to nurse her sister, left to make the best of it as housekeeper to her queer brother-in-law. Ellen thought Miss Branwell very 'antiquated', with her big old-fashioned caps and false hairpiece of auburn curls; but she conceded that 'she probably had been pretty.' Having a teenaged visitor seems to have unleashed Aunt Branwell's memories of her own youth:

> She talked a great deal of her younger days, the gaities [*sic*] of her native town, Penzance in Cornwall, the soft warm climate &c . . . the social life of her younger days she appeared to recall with regret . . . In Summer she spent part of her afternoons in reading aloud to Mr Brontë, and in winter the evenings, she must have enjoyed this, for she and Mr Brontë had sometimes to finish their discussions on what she had read when we all met for tea, she would be very lively and intelligent 'in her talk', and tilted argument without fear against Mr Brontë.

This willingness to give as good as she got with her emphatic brother-in-law must have been a valuable example to her nieces. A wife would have had to be more circumspect. But Aunt Branwell had an independent streak and some unconventional habits, taking snuff out of a pretty little gold box, as Ellen noted, 'which she sometimes presented with a little laugh as if she enjoyed the slight shock and astonishment visible in your countenance'.

Ellen was similarly surprised by some of the stories that Charlotte's father chose to tell 'with great gusto' at the breakfast or tea-table, 'of some of the old inhabitants in out of [the] way places over the moors'. Ellen recognised some of the same rude material later in *Wuthering Heights*, but thought them strange tales to hear from the mouth of a clergyman when she was the only guest at tea, saying primly, 'I tried to hear as little as I could.'

There was a mood of optimism in the household in these years before any of the siblings left home to try their fortunes, fostered to a large extent by Charlotte's success at Roe Head. She had studied hard, won prizes and made friends (something they all found so hard to do) and expended a minimal amount of the family's resources. Best of all she had come home, and seemed likely to stay there. In her absence, Mr Brontë had succeeded in getting a new building erected in the lane between the Parsonage and the church for a Sunday School, using a grant from the National School Society. This was to be of benefit to the parishioners, of course, and was in itself a hopeful sign of better connections between the Established Church and the other denominations, and also between the Brontës and the town, standing as it did so close to the Parsonage (overlooking its small front garden in fact). Patrick Brontë must have had his eldest daughter in mind all along as the school's first superintendent, and she seems to have been content with having those duties on top of her sisters' schooling. The tiny sixteen-year-old coped with such responsibilities with less anxiety than at any other time of her life, telling Ellen about having the other teachers round to tea and themselves going to tea twice in the village – a previously unheard-of amount of local socialising. As a teacher, she was careful and diligent, and made a point of hearing every child read.

Branwell also taught at the Sunday School, though with less admired results. His lonely upbringing made him unfit to be in charge of boys who were just a year or two his junior and viewed him with hostility. One of them later remembered him as 'rapid and impulsive in his manner' and impatient with any slowness on the part of his charges. One day, when Branwell threatened to throw one of the bigger boys out of the class for struggling boringly with his reading, he got the defiant reply 'Tha' willn't, tha' old Irish —' as the boy got up to leave of his own accord. And when the recalcitrant scholars all trooped back into church to join the service, the vicar's son always took himself into a corner of the pew alone and read 'some book which was not the Prayer-book'. If disturbed by anyone, he would twist the miscreant's hair and give him 'a sharp rap with his knuckles'. And because they were in church, no one could cry out.

The tailor's son who remembered this also studied the other Brontës in church: Charlotte keeping out of sight in the Parsonage pew, Emily sitting bolt upright in a corner 'as motionless as a statue' with her eyelids half closed and mouth compressed. Their father would be preaching, extempore, with his watch laid on the cushion of the pulpit to keep exactly to half an hour. 'His discourses were characterised by a steady and continuous flow of language as pleasant as a gurgling rill,' the boy remembered, with obvious gratitude for the soporific qualities of Mr Brontë's voice and the utter predictability of the sermon's length.

Emily and Anne, who had become inseparable, 'like twins', as Ellen Nussey described them, had developed their own 'play' in Charlotte's absence, and the first mention of their breakaway invention, Gondal, is in a diary fragment written by Emily in November 1834, which, like Charlotte's 'History of the Year' and later autobiographical fragments, gives a vivid snapshot of a moment in the busy Brontë household:

> I fed Rainbow, Diamond, Snowflake Jasper [2 w. illeg.] this morning Branwell went down to Mr Drivers and brought news that Sir Robert peel was going to be invited to stand for Leeds Anne and I have been peeling Apples for Charlotte to make an apple pudding. Charlotte said she made puddings perfectly and she was of a quick but lim[i]ted intellect Taby said just now Come Anne pillopatata (ie pill a potato[)]. Aunt has come into the kitchen just now and said where are your feet Anne Anne answered on the floor Aunt papa opened the parlour Door and gave Branwell a Letter saying here Branwell read this and show it to your Aunt and Charlotte – The Gondals are discovering the interior of Gaaldine Sally mosley is washing in the back-kitchin
>
> It is past Twelve o'clock Anne and I have not tid[i]ed ourselves, done

our bed work or done our lessons and we want to go out to play We are
going to have for Dinner Boiled Beef Turnips potato's and applepud-
ding[.] the Kitchin is in avery untidy state Anne and I have not Done
our music excercise which consists of b majer Taby said on my putting
a pen in her face Ya pitter pottering there instead of pilling a potate[.] I
answered O Dear, O Dear, O Dear I will derictly[.] with that I get up,
take a Knife and begin pilling (finished pilling the potatos[)] papa going
to walk Mr Sunderland expected[.]

Six Diary Papers like this by Emily and Anne survive from the years
1834 to 1845. The sisters developed a plan to write brief accounts of
their lives every four years (around the date of Emily's birthday), read
the previous period's papers and seal up the new ones in a box or tin
until four more years had passed, like a time capsule. In 1834 the interval had not been decided yet, and Emily was looking forward a good
deal further than 1838:

Anne and I say I wonder what we shall be like and what we shall be and
where we shall be if all goes on well in the year 1874 – in which year I
shall be in my 57th year Anne will be going in her 55th year Branwell
will be going in his 58th year And Charlotte in her 59th year hoping we
shall all be well at that time We close our paper[.]

The two younger sisters seem to have expected life in their fifties to be
essentially a continuation of their current situation. No Papa and Aunt
around, of course, but no spouses or children either in that far-off time
of the 1870s.

Emily's terrible spelling and naive expression in this messily written
diary entry make one wonder what exactly the girls had been doing in
their lessons together since Charlotte returned from Roe Head. Nothing very difficult or disagreeable, one imagines. Emily's poor literacy
would seem amazing in any middle-class sixteen-year-old girl of the
time, but especially in one who within a few years would write a classic
novel and some of the most penetrating poetry of the age. Her mind,
always elusive and recalcitrant, seems particularly so here. Nor does
Anne Brontë seem destined for a literary career.

The problem of how to launch Branwell into the world had reached
a critical stage. With his own extraordinary leap from Drumballyroney

to St John's College as the only example on hand, Reverend Brontë was perhaps not very well qualified to advise his son on the best course of action. On one side, Patrick Brontë's experience had encouraged him to think that anything was possible when natural abilities, hard work and the will of God combined; on the other, his meteoric rise had left him with many social anxieties intact and much of his innate conservatism strengthened.

As the most intensively educated and apparently most promising of the Brontë children – and holding the trump card of maleness – Branwell might have been expected to blaze a trail for the others and raise them in the world together. Sacrifices had been made for his education (he had drawing lessons, boxing lessons, flute and possibly organ lessons from private teachers), allowances had been made for his temperament and volatility, and it is clear that great things were expected. Quite which great things, though? Branwell's talents seemed legion – that was part of the problem – but in order to develop them, money would be needed, and certain stages, such as a university education, were simply too expensive and too protracted to consider. The other traditional middle-class male professions of the law, medicine and the army were also dismissed, probably on grounds of expense. 'I once thought that he might get into the Mercantile line,' Patrick Brontë wrote a few years later, 'but there seem to be many and great difficulties in reference to this.' The Church also seems to have been ruled out early on, and Branwell was forthright about his complete lack of religious zeal, writing to his friend Grundy in 1842, 'I have not one mental qualification, save, perhaps, hypocrisy, which would make me cut a figure in its pulpits.' This brusque critique, and Branwell's frequent absence from church services, must have been extremely painful to his father.

But, for all his talk of prudence, planning and 'great precaution', Patrick Brontë ended up encouraging his only son to turn to a notoriously unstable profession, and one, moreover, in which Branwell's talents were far from outstanding: art. It was an especially rash strategy, given that Branwell had three unmarried sisters to be responsible for ultimately, and no family money to cushion him against failure.

All three sisters had had drawing lessons, from John Bradley, a founder member of Keighley Mechanics' Institute, one of many similar adult education establishments springing up in the industrialised towns.* An ability to sketch a landscape or take a likeness was a valuable accomplishment for middle-class girls (like being able to play the piano or sing), but no one expected them to take art seriously, or think of pursuing it professionally. The Brontë sisters had no interest in 'accomplishments', or living the sort of lives that included them, but latched on to art instruction eagerly and practised techniques from drawing manuals with obsessive dedication. Studying and copying pictures was for them a further route into worlds of the imagination, and away from society.

This is one of the reasons why Charlotte had become such an avid memoriser of art works, as if to capture them for future private use. Mary Taylor remembered that at school, whenever Charlotte had access to 'a picture or cut of any kind', 'she went over it piecemeal, with her eyes close to the paper, looking so long that we used to ask her "what she saw in it". She could always see plenty, and explained it very well.' Her own drawings had reached a high standard very early, and she had incredible dexterity on the most minute scales, rendering detail with obsessive care. On a highly finished drawing, such as one titled *St Martin's Parsonage, Birmingham* that she contributed to a schoolfriend's album, you need to use a magnifying glass to see that she has drawn each leaf of even the distant trees, a strange, secretive thoroughness.

Charlotte spent the three years after her return home from Roe Head in a frenzy of productivity, writing as much in 1833 as in any year of her life, according to her early editors Wise and Symington. But her main ambition at this date was, surprisingly, not to be a writer, but an artist: Branwell's friend Francis Leyland observed at the time that 'so strong was this intention, that she could scarcely be convinced that it was not her true vocation.' Clearly he did not think much of her chances. Charlotte came to agree with him, but only some fifteen years later, when, happening upon her old portfolio, she felt that 'some fairy had changed what I once thought sterling coin into dry leaves.' At that point she was 'much inclined to consign the whole collection of drawings to the fire'.

---

* Patrick Brontë was a member, and borrowed books for the whole family from its library.

Many drawings by Charlotte have survived, showing a high level of technical skill and a generally low level of originality. She always felt more comfortable copying the works of others, effectively taking possession of them, and her pictures drawn from life – of Anne, for example – do not seem very life-like. Flowers, birds and picturesque landscapes, copied from books, were her most frequent subjects and pencil her preferred medium, fitting her choice of miniature and highly detailed images. She could achieve a very convincing metallic finish with it, creating a look like the steel engravings she admired. Small scale suited her taste and her short-sight (she could get up close to a miniature and see what she was doing); it was also, of course, a lot cheaper to use only pencil, watercolour and small amounts of paper and board. It meant she could think of pursuing art as a career – perhaps as a book illustrator – without the need of a studio, a battery of equipment and oils, or a master.

Charlotte's most impressive pieces look as if they were made with one eye on compiling a professional portfolio and the other on making a lavish Angrian portrait gallery for purely personal consumption. She pored over prints in albums, picking out images that fitted scenarios or characters from 'Glass Town' and giving them tiny adjustments, as in *The Atheist Viewing the Dead Body of His Wife*, her appropriation of a lithograph by A. B. Clayton illustrating a poem by Robert Montgomery; she used this to show Zamorna contemplating the corpse of his mistress Mary Percy. Conversely, Branwell's paintings, also frequently copied from prints, tended to be in the sublime or heroic vein, such as his martial personification in *Terror* or his copy of John Martin's *Queen Esther*.

Charlotte's numerous drawings include three portraits of Anne (clearly a much more willing sitter than Emily, of whom no portrait by Charlotte exists), one in pencil, dated April 1833, and two watercolours, one undated but thought to be 1833 also, the other made in June 1834. Added to Branwell's portraits, this makes Anne the most-recorded of the Brontë siblings,* though placed together, one would not necessarily recognise the likenesses as of the same young girl: Charlotte's earliest picture has Anne posed elegantly in a veil, like a heroine of

---

* Their father, on the other hand, had several photographs taken in later life.

Gondal or Angria; the second is more animated, but oddly proportioned; and the latest seems rather formal for a fourteen-year-old, with her hair complexly curled. Charlotte's poor sight must have made life-drawing difficult, and every attempt partly imagined. Some features of her portraits of Anne, such as the neck and shoulders, seem so stylised or idealised as to be little help in picturing the subject herself.

The small mouth and set of the chin in Charlotte's 1833–4 portraits of Anne are reproduced (along with her hairstyle) in the clumsily naive painting Branwell made of all three sisters at about the same time, which, due to accidents of fame and fate, has become one of the most powerful author images ever created: *The Brontë Sisters*. When did he paint it? We have only Mrs Gaskell's remark to go on, when Charlotte showed her the picture on her first visit to Haworth in 1853: 'Miss Brontë brought down a rough, common-looking oil-painting, done by her brother, of herself, – a little, rather prim-looking girl of eighteen, – and the two other sisters, girls of 16 and 14, with cropped hair, and sad, dreamy-looking eyes.' Charlotte provided the information about her age and that of the 'two other sisters' – not known by name to Mrs Gaskell at this stage – and presumably the picture had been kept in its frame or on battens at this date, as, when Mrs Gaskell saw it, Charlotte was 'upholding the great frame of canvas, and consequently standing right behind it', which allowed the visitor to see a 'striking' resemblance, despite the passage of years.

If, as seems likely, the portrait was intended as a practice piece for Branwell, it could not have raised high hopes for his future professionally. Like all his pictures, it shows little sense of perspective or the relation of one object to another – even of one limb to another – and it would be hard to find a worse depiction anywhere of a hand under a book on a table. But, for all its technical shortcomings, Branwell has caught a potent stillness, a tension in his remarkable siblings, the 'sad dreamy-looking eyes' of all three: Charlotte's elder-sister apartness, Anne's abstracted air, Emily's penetrating, melancholy stare straight at her brother – and at us.

Mrs Gaskell describes 'a great pillar' in the centre of the picture, referring to the place where Branwell had originally included a self-portrait, later painted over (or scrubbed at with solvents), leaving a pale column and spectral form in the background. Branwell painted another group portrait of himself and his sisters – and left himself in the picture on this occasion – at about the same time, of which only the depiction of Emily survives, cut out from the larger canvas in an arch-topped shape.* The composition (as we know from a crude photograph that was taken before its destruction) showed the siblings as bookish gentry, standing around a table on which lay some books, papers and a dead game bird. Anne and Charlotte are to the left, Emily to the right and Branwell between them, holding a gun. The picture used to hang on the stairs at Haworth Parsonage, but perhaps only after the siblings were all dead. It was described in 1858 by a visitor as 'a shocking daub, not up to the rudest sign board style' and was still intact at Patrick Brontë's death in 1861, when it was inherited by Arthur Bell Nicholls and taken to Ireland the same year. At what date Nicholls cut out the picture of Emily and destroyed the rest is uncertain, but he clearly thought little of this and Branwell's other effort since *The Brontë Sisters* was found after his death stored negligently on the top of a wardrobe, unframed, folded, cracked, ruined. Perhaps the *Gun Group* was destroyed because it featured Branwell, whom Nicholls only knew from 1845 onwards and for whom he had no feelings other than disgust.†

The same 1858 visitor who was so unimpressed by the *Gun Group* quizzed the locals about the Brontës and was disappointed by hearing from all sides (except their loyal servant Martha Brown) that 'the girls were *so* plain. When I asked the old woman in the book shop which of them was the best looking, she shook her head and said there was not much to choose amongst them in that respect – The Sexton thought Anne the best looking, but indeed he could not say much for her looks.' Anne was always spoken of as the prettiest of the Brontë sisters, though none of them was ever called beautiful, in fact people seemed quite keen to make unpleasant remarks about their looks, even after they

---

* Now one of the treasures of the NPG.

† The *Gun Group* must have been considerably larger than *The Brontë Sisters*, as the Emily fragment is almost half the width, but takes up only a third of the lost original, judging from the evidence of the photograph. Tracings were also taken by John Greenwood, the Haworth stationer and friend of the family, which seem rather better than Branwell's original. See Juliet R. V. Barker, 'The Brontë Portraits: A Mystery Solved', *BST*, 20:1 (1990).

were famous and might have been awarded some retrospective idealisa-
tion. Benjamin Binns thought Emily looked ugly as well as haughty,
and that 'a large protruding tooth added to her peculiar aspect'; Charlotte was said to have 'many teeth gone' and to be 'extremely
insignificant and even displeasing' in appearance, 'not pleasant'. No
wonder she told Ellen she had made her mind up at the age of twelve
that she was 'doomed to be an old maid'. Branwell was, by Charlotte's
own account, better-looking than any of the girls – 'Nature had
favoured him with a fairer outside, as well as a finer constitution than
his Sisters' – but even Branwell was thought to be more charismatic
than handsome, with his wild red hair, long nose and receding chin.
The sense of not being attractive haunted Charlotte all her life, and was
a further goad to seeking a ruthless sort of independence.

In the summer of 1834, and presumably under the guidance of John
Bradley, Charlotte had a moment of triumph and deep gratification
when two of her pencil drawings were accepted by the Royal Northern Society for the Encouragement of the Fine Arts for their annual
summer exhibition in Leeds. Her subjects were Bolton Priory and
Kirkstall Abbey, neither done from nature, though both places were
close by and well known to Charlotte. She had a special fondness for
Kirkstall Abbey, as it was where her parents had become engaged, and
she had visited Bolton Abbey with Ellen only the previous summer;
but she still preferred to make copies from other people's work (*Bolton
Priory* is based on an engraving based on a drawing by Turner from
1809 – a very long way round from 'life'). The whole family went
proudly to see her drawings, displayed alongside a selection of old
masters from the county's private collections and new work by contemporaries of the very highest standard.

The exhibition in Leeds was the high point of Charlotte's artistic
career, for she never exhibited again, sold or attempted to sell any art-
work. Strangely, the very thing that she had once wished for – a
commission from a publisher to make illustrations for a book – came
in 1848 when her own publisher, having heard of her youthful ambition, suggested she should illustrate an edition of *Jane Eyre*. But it was
a suggestion she hastily refused. 'I have, in my day, wasted a certain
quantity of Bristol board and drawing-paper, crayons and cakes of
colour,' she told William Smith Williams, but 'I see they have no

value.' In the novel she wrote in 1852, her heroine also looks back with puzzlement at works she formerly laboured over: 'elaborate pencil-drawings finished like line-engravings; these, my very eyes ached at beholding again, recalling hours when they had followed, stroke by stroke and touch by touch, a tedious, feeble, finical, school-girl pencil.' It was a harsh judgement of her younger self, a bitter memory too of wasted time.

'We are all about to divide, break up, separate,' Charlotte told Ellen at the beginning of July 1835, contemplating the seismic change that faced her; 'Emily is going to school Branwell is going to London, and I am going to be a Governess.' 'Branwell is going to London' seems to have been a premature announcement: he had geared himself up to apply to the Royal Academy of Art as a student, and drafted a letter to the secretary, though whether it was ever sent is open to doubt.★ Instead of asking what the admission procedure might be, Branwell characteristically assumed an insider's tone:

> Where am I to present my drawing?
> At what time –?
> and especialy [*sic*]
> Can I do it in August or September?

Branwell's approach certainly lacked subtlety – is indeed like something his father might have written, with the father's bold disregard of obstacles. Perhaps the whole idea was more Patrick Brontë's pipedream than Branwell's. He was writing of it proudly to Mrs Franks in early July, as if nothing stood in the way: 'It is my design, to send my son . . . to the Royal Academy, for Artists, in London.'

Did the family truly think that Branwell could succeed as a painter? The results were never encouraging, yet Branwell was always encouraged, as if they all wished to corroborate any illusions he might have

★ Juliet Barker makes a strong counter-argument (in Barker, 226–32) to the assumption on many biographers' parts that Branwell not only sent the letter but presented himself at the Academy in London that autumn, faced a humiliating rejection and loss of confidence, and wasted on drink and dissipation the money he had been given to support himself, all as described in an Angrian story he wrote later, of which only 'incomplete and dismembered' fragments remain.

about his talents, nurture them assiduously. The project of Branwell seemed less to do with the only son making a living as making a name that the family could all take pride in.

Meanwhile, Charlotte was doing her father's job for him and pre-scribing a dutiful and self-sacrificial course of action for herself. The need to prepare for work was urgent, and work for the girls meant teaching in some form. After years of resistance to leaving home, and at the advanced age of seventeen, Emily was going to Roe Head to get some formal education, but how would the cost be met with the family's resources stretched to their limits launching Branwell? It so happened that the marriage of Miss Wooler's sister Marianne that sum-mer opened up a vacancy on the Roe Head staff, and the place was offered to Charlotte with the understanding that her wages would be withheld in lieu of Emily's fees. Charlotte saw her fate sealed. 'I should have to take the step sometime,' she told Ellen, announcing her immi-nent departure from home, 'and "better sune as syne"', adding that loath though she was to go, it was better to go somewhere that she knew, to an employer whom she liked and in the company of a sister whom she loved and was anxious to monitor, than to risk a worse situ-ation, which any other would be. Miss Wooler undoubtedly meant to do Charlotte a favour: she knew the family's circumstances and her former pupil's character and might well have intended this job as a chance for Charlotte to acquire, among friendly colleagues, some of the social and pedagogical skills she would need if she were ever to make a living as a teacher.

One of the things Charlotte tried to comfort herself with was the thought that, at Mirfield, she would be so close to Birstall and Gomer-sal – walking distance from Ellen and Mary – and that they would visit her occasionally. In her three tormentingly long years at Roe Head as a teacher, though, she saw less of these two friends than one would have thought possible. Ellen's brother George passed the school every week on his way to Huddersfield market, but scant use was made of this convenience to transport letters or messages from one girl to the other; and even when Charlotte begged for a note or signal from her friend – 'just a scrap . . . do – do it will cheer me. any-thing' – Ellen was neither speedy nor very ardent in her responses. The truth was that Charlotte's transition from young lady to working woman had degraded her socially, and Ellen was particularly sensitive to these striations, and how they might reflect on her own rather marginal position. As it turned out, Ellen never had to do a day's paid work in her life, but often talked about the prospect of needing to fend for herself, hoping perhaps to inspire in others the pity that this idea stirred in her own bosom.

Charlotte meanwhile was condemned to the retrograde step of returning to Roe Head as a teacher, which she did in late July 1835. 'Duty – Necessity – these are stern Misstresses [*sic*] who will not be disobeyed,' the nineteen-year-old reasoned. But it did not make her one jot happier.

5

The Double Life

1835–7

So, three years after leaving Roe Head as a schoolgirl, Charlotte went back there to teach, taking with her the reluctant Emily on the eve of her seventeenth birthday. It's a mark of how much more urgent the issue of income and self-sufficiency had become for all the siblings that the reclusive middle daughter could be prised away from Haworth at all. Though, like Branwell, all three sisters felt themselves to be poets and artists, unlike him, they had to face the prospect of spending their lives in drudgery instead of pursuing their vocations. They approached this doom with outer fatalism and inner disbelief, perhaps hoping that Branwell, their representative in the greater world, would become so successful that teaching and governessing would turn out to be merely temporary aberrations.

None of them seems to have expected or wanted to marry out of the dilemma; indeed marriage seems to have been almost literally the last thing on the Brontë sisters' minds. Spiritual communion, yes; love, sex, the sublime, yes; but the conventional female fate of marriage and motherhood does not appear either to have troubled or allured them much. Anne displayed a little wistfulness in her later teens, and her novels, like Charlotte's, reflect a yearning for companionate marriage to an idealised mate. But however loathsome the thought was of having to 'go out' into the harsh and humiliating working world, it was preferable to the state of feminine inertia – so consuming of the life of Ellen Nussey, for example – that overtook young women waiting to find someone to marry them.

The return to Roe Head was dismal from the start. This time there was no discovery or novelty to alleviate the pain of leaving home, and no optimism about the future. This time it was the beginning of a life sentence for Charlotte. Emily's position was also difficult because of her advanced age: at seventeen she was by far the oldest girl in a very small school, where some were as young as eight. Miss Wooler was in the habit of tutoring each new pupil separately before letting them join the general class, as a form of matriculation. This would have made Emily – tall, old and already painfully self-conscious and unhappy – feel particularly humiliated.

Emily made no friends and kept aloof from the other girls, though she had to share a bed with one of them. Charlotte and she were divided by their very different statuses, though so close in age and so clearly longing to be with each other rather than with anyone else. Charlotte was perhaps sitting with her 'at twilight, in the schoolroom' when Emily wrote the poems 'The Bluebell', 'A little while, a little while' and 'Loud without the wind was roaring', all of which Charlotte said dated from this year.

> Where wilt thou go, my harassed heart?
> Full many a land invites thee now;
> And places near, and far apart
> Have rest for thee, my weary brow –
>
> There is a spot, mid barren hills,
> Where winter howls and driving rain
> But if the dreary tempest chills
> There is a light that warms again

Emily lasted through only three months of school life. 'Nobody knew what ailed her but me – I knew only too well,' Charlotte recalled years later. 'The change from her own home to a school, and from her own very noiseless, very secluded, but unrestricted and in artificial [*sic*] mode of life, to one of disciplined routine (though under the kindliest auspices), was what she failed in enduring. Her nature proved here too strong for her fortitude. Every morning when she woke, the vision of home and the moors rushed on her, and darkened and saddened the day that lay before her.' Emily's mental strain soon showed in physical collapse: 'her white face, attenuated form, and failing strength threatened rapid decline.' It was like Cowan Bridge all over again.

Charlotte reacted accordingly. Convinced that Emily's life was in danger, she petitioned her father and Miss Wooler to let Emily go home immediately – and permanently. No doubt she made a very strong case for this course of action, since it was exactly what she wanted to do herself. But there was no one to oversee *her* case so closely, or petition for *her* release. Emily went home; Anne was sent in her place; and Charlotte was obliged to keep to her grindstone. Aunt Branwell and Patrick Brontë must have registered with some anxiety the general tendency of the children not to cope for long with the outside world, but Miss Wooler was not sorry to see Emily go: she had found her queer and non-compliant.

Back in Haworth, Emily recovered her spirits quickly and adopted a routine of helpful housekeeping (willingly taking on routine tasks such as baking and sweeping). She had only been allowed to go home on condition that she 'studied alone with diligence and perseverance', and so set about a course of self-education, making sure that she was seen learning her German vocabulary in public spaces like the kitchen (with her book propped up on the table as she kneaded dough) in order to leave her leisure hours as free as possible.

Emily's first job of every day was to feed the animals, and she saw no reason why they should not be treated every bit as well as their human companions. Better, in fact, if Charlotte's surmise was right and she was saving the best cuts of meat for the dogs. In 1835 they had a grizzled Irish terrier called Grasper, of whom Emily made a characterful portrait. He was replaced sometime after 1837 by Keeper, a part-mastiff who grew to impressive proportions, was a magnificently off-putting guard dog and became devoted to Emily. There were also, at various times during the 1830s, at least two cats in the household, Black Tom and Tiger, a canary called Dick (presumably kept in a cage) and three tame geese. There had been a wild goose, which escaped, and a fledgling hawk that Emily had found injured on the moor and brought home. 'Nero', as she called him, became the subject of another lovingly detailed portrait.

Branwell was in an optimistic mood that year. Royal Academy or no, he was pursuing his plan to become a portrait painter; indeed he was described as such by two local Freemasons, John Brown the sexton and Joseph Redman the parish clerk, when they sponsored him to join the Haworth Lodge the following spring. His hope was to travel abroad in 1836 'for the purpose of acquiring information or instruction', using the Masons as a networking aid. Quite how the family expected to fund his tour is not clear: perhaps that's why it never happened.

It must have been strange for Charlotte, returning home at Christmas with Anne, to find the household so absorbed in its own affairs, Branwell virtually having taken over Angria and Emily so happily tailoring her days to her own taste, writing and reading and taking long walks. Their father too was preoccupied, though in a less contented vein, being the object of a campaign against the church rate that had Haworth in an uproar, with the Dissenters challenging their obligation to pay anything towards the upkeep of a church that none of them attended.

Branwell's buoyancy about his prospects accentuated how poor Charlotte's own had become. When news reached them during the holiday of the death of James Hogg, the poet and essayist famous as 'The Ettrick Shepherd', Branwell became particularly animated. Hogg, the author of *The Private Memoirs and Confessions of a Justified Sinner* (1824), had been a star contributor to *Blackwood's Magazine* since its inception in the 1810s and his public profile – that of a self-taught 'natural' poet in the Burnsian (and Patrick Brontë) mould – was exactly as Branwell wished to present himself. Indeed Branwell was so struck by the similarities that he wrote to the magazine to point them out. That no one answered did not put Branwell off, and four months later he sent the editor some poetry, with the promise that he could also send prose, and would change either to order, so much in Blackwood's best interests it would be to take him on. He kept the letter relatively short, with 'Read now at least' along the top and 'CONDEMN NOT UNHEARD' at the bottom. That would surely do it. Branwell was nothing if not convinced of his own charm, and it certainly worked on friends such as John Brown, and the regulars at the Black Bull, who thought him one of the cleverest fellows alive.

None of Charlotte's letters survives from July 1835 to May 1836, but many must have been written to Ellen Nussey in that time, later lost or destroyed. From the sadly nervous, over-anxious tone of the correspondence when it picks up in 1836, nine months into Charlotte's hated new life, one can guess that Charlotte expressed a rawness and vulnerability in the intervening period that Ellen may have chosen to suppress.

It certainly came out in Charlotte's private writing, especially her poetry, which became her main solace.

In the Christmas holidays Charlotte finished writing a strange poem, known by its first line, 'We wove a web in childhood', which alludes to the secret growth of the siblings' sustaining fantasy, a process both surprising and subversive, in which a tiny spring has become 'An ocean with a thousand Isles/And scarce a glimpse of shore.' There are 185 lines of this poem, veering around formally, stylistically and conceptually in a way that is typical of Charlotte's writing in these years, when she releases herself into expression in a greedy, desperate manner. There is no time, no leisure, it seems, to refine her medium; it needs an outlet and must simply flow – which this poem does at length. It returns obsessively to images of imprisonment, desolation, exile and persecution, and there are abrupt changes of tempo and subject – a self-indulgence, a sort of bingeing, which was clearly the only way she felt she could proceed. She passes into the 'bright darling dream' herself and is transported to a former battlefield at night, where the poetry suddenly gives way to prose, as if what she had to relate was too urgent and had to be got down immediately:

> I now heard the far clatter of hoofs on the hard & milk-white road, the great highway that turns in a bend from Free-Town and stretches on to the West. two horsemen rode slowly up in the moonlight & leaving the path struck deep into the moor, galloping through heather to their Chargers breasts.

It was Zamorna, more real than life. The last paragraph is no longer poem or prose-poem, but diary, and the writer is setting it all down as she sits, apparently working, in front of a classful of students:

> Never shall I Charlotte Brontë forget what a voice of wild & wailing music now came thrillingly to my mind's almost to my body's ear, nor how distinctly I sitting in the school-room at Roe-head saw the Duke of Zamorna leaning against that obelisk with the mute marble Victory above him the fern waving at his feet his black horse turned loose grazing among the heather, the moonlight so mild & so exquisitely tranquil sleeping upon that vast & vacant road & the African sky quivering & shaking with stars expanded above all, I was quite gone I had really

utterly forgot where I was and all the gloom & cheerlessness of my situation I felt myself breathing quick & short as I beheld the Duke lifting up his sable crest which undulated as the plume of a hearse waves to the wind & knew that that music which seems as mournfully triumphant as the scriptural verse

> 'Oh Grave where is thy sting;
> Oh Death where is thy victory'

was exciting him & quickening his ever rapid pulse 'Miss Brontë what are you thinking about?' said a voice that dissipated all the charm & Miss Lister thrust her little rough black head into my face, 'Sic transit' &c.

Charlotte had been the girl who never misbehaved, who bore off the prizes and complied with every rule, but now, as a teacher, she was intransigent and uncooperative. She found herself prey to sudden, violent rages; fashionable young ladies irritated her and drew waspish remarks; her scorn for her 'oafish' pupils was obvious, 'boring me with their vulgar familiar trash all the time we were out. If those girls knew how I loathe their company, they would not seek mine so much as they do.' Even Miss Wooler had got on her wrong side, and must have been exercising great patience with her young colleague. An indication of how uncontrolled she must have been at this date comes from her comparison of a calmer period seven years later when she merely got 'red-in-the face with impatience' with her pupils, 'but don't think I ever scold or fly into a passion – if I spoke warmly, as warmly as I sometimes used to do at Roe-Head they would think me mad.' She knew it was irrational, that the things that rankled 'like venom' were 'things that nobody else cares for', but she felt powerless to control her feelings: 'I strive to conceal and suppress them as much as I can. but they burst out sometimes.'

Six partly autobiographical pieces of writing, now known as 'The Roe Head Journal', amply illustrate Charlotte's sense of alienation in these years. She fulfilled her duties with exceptionally bad grace and returned as frequently as possible to her 'ark' of make-believe. The recurring theme of the journal is the superior reality of her imagined world, and the pain of re-entering ordinary life at the end of each flight. Miss Wooler will come in with some butter, or Miss Lister will ask what she's thinking about, and their interruptions set Charlotte's nerves on edge and keep her not just from absorbing dreams (some distinctly erotic) but from what she imagines is a vital source of inspiration, rather like Samuel Taylor Coleridge being robbed of Kubla Khan by the oafish Person from Porlock. 'I felt as if I could have written gloriously – I longed to write,' she wrote one Friday in August, stuck in the classroom. 'The spirit of all Verdopolis, of all the mountainous North, of all the woodland West, of all the river-watered East came crowding into my mind. If I had had time to indulge it, I felt that the vague sensations of that moment would have settled down into some narrative better at least than any thing I ever produced before. But just then a dolt came up with a lesson. I thought I should have vomited.'

That class had not started well. Charlotte had spent nearly an hour trying to drum into three of her pupils the difference between an article and a substantive and sank 'into a kind of lethargy ... from irritation & weariness'. Irritation seemed to predominate:

> The thought came over me: am I to spend all the best part of my life in this wretched bondage, forcibly suppressing my rage at the idleness, the apathy and the hyperbolical & most asinine stupidity of those fat-headed oafs, and on compulsion assuming an air of kindness, patience & assiduity? Must I from day to day sit chained to this chair, prisoned within these four bare walls, while these glorious summer suns are burning in heaven & the year is revolving in its richest glow & declaring at the close of every summer day [that] the time I am losing will never come again?

She threw up the sash window on the glorious morning that was being sacrificed to fat-headed oafdom and heard the bells of Huddersfield Church 'full & liquid' in the distance: 'Huddersfield & the hills beyond it were all veiled in blue mist; the woods of Hopton & Heaton Lodge were clouding the water's-edge; & the Calder, silent but bright, was shooting among them like a silver arrow.' She shut the window on this idyllic scene – one imagines rather sharply – and went back to her seat.

Charlotte could dramatise and satirise the condition of living in two realities, but it became impossible to sustain. Her resentment and non-cooperation were glaringly obvious. Several of the Roe Head fragments were written during class, one while Miss Wooler was in the room and two pupils either side of Charlotte were silently 'staring, gaping' because their teacher was apparently writing something – in minuscule characters – *with her eyes shut.* 'Hang their astonishment!' Miss Brontë wrote, triumphant over circumstances she hated so much, and pleased to consternate the despised 'asses' around her: 'What in all this is there to remind me of the divine, silent, unseen land of thought, dim now & indefinite as the dream of a dream, the shadow of a shade?' The scene is peculiar, to say the least: the young teacher writing to herself in an unreadably tiny script, with her eyes closed, about an 'unseen land' – enough to make the girls gape indeed, as if she were hypnotised, or receiving spirit messages. The other fragments have the same wobbly and sometimes over-written lines, suggesting that she wrote them *all* with her eyes shut, a decisive removal from the distracting sight of Miss Lister and Miss Cook.

Charlotte's rage against her occupation, and the lifetime of drudgery it symbolised, might have blinded her to the ill-effects of retreating so often and so completely into the alternative reality of her Angrian fantasies. 'Phantasms' might be the better word, being the one that was commonly used to describe opium-induced reveries, so alluringly evoked by Thomas De Quincey in *Confessions of an English Opium-Eater*, a book that had fascinated all the young Brontës. Charlotte's Angrian writing, and her journal fragments of these years, are predominantly about 'altered states' of mind – but how had she got there? Opiates, usually in the form of laudanum drops, were a common tranquilliser in the Brontës' time, easily available over the druggist's counter. Alethea Hayter's description of the mental traits that predispose people to opium addiction fit Charlotte Brontë's condition at Roe Head with uncanny closeness: 'Men and women who feel all kinds of suffering keenly . . . who are unable to face and cope with painful situations, who are conscious of their own inadequacy and who resent the difficulties which have revealed it; who long for relief from tension, from the failures and disappointments of their everyday life, who yearn for something which will annihilate the gap between their idea of themselves and their actual selves'. Branwell, who also fits this description closely, later told a friend that he had experimented with 'opium-eating' after reading De Quincey. 'Opium-eating' was a practice that involved taking a lot more of the drug than was contained in ordinary analgesics, and, in Branwell's case, led to addiction in the 1840s, but it began at the time when he and Charlotte were still very close, and mutually engrossed by the 'world below' that they had created. It seems unlikely that, given the opportunity, Charlotte would not have joined him in some testing of the magical drug.*

But it remains that Charlotte denied using opium when Elizabeth Gaskell asked her outright, in 1853, about the very striking scenes in *Villette* where the streets of Brussels are seen through the drugged eyes of Lucy Snowe, under the influence of 'a strong opiate' administered surreptitiously to sedate her (but which has the opposite effect). Mrs Gaskell wanted to know if this was based on personal experience and was told that the author 'had never, to her knowledge, taken a grain of it in any shape'. Was Charlotte being evasive, making a rather specious distinction about the size of a dose, and, if so, why? It's hard to believe that she could have entirely avoided opiates in an age where laudanum was so widely used by children and adults alike. Mrs Gaskell had no reason to withhold her own usage of opium from the 1850s readers of her *Life of Charlotte Brontë*, describing the scenes in *Villette* as 'so exactly' like what she had experienced herself. Charlotte's denial leads, in the biography, to an explanation of how she writes about things she has not experienced: she would '[think] intently on it for many and many a night before falling to sleep, – wondering what it was like, or how it would be, – till at length, sometimes after the progress of her story had been arrested at this one point for weeks, she wakened up in the morning with all clear before her, as if she had in reality gone through the experience'. Mrs Gaskell clearly found this a strange claim, but, however Charlotte arrived at her visions, her 'world beneath' had much in common with what other people needed drugs to reach.

---

* Christine Alexander has brought readers' attention to an interesting passage in one of Charlotte's Angrian stories, written in the summer of 1838, in which the speaker, Macara Lofty, is discovered slumped in a chair, wreathed in smiles as he comes to from an opium-induced trance and explains that he took the drug to escape a feeling of unendurable despair. He has no qualms about it: 'Now, Townshend, so suffering, how far did I err when I had recourse to the sovereign specific which a simple narcotic drug offered me?' (Alexander, *The Early Writings of Charlotte Brontë*, 173).

Mrs Gaskell had not at that date seen 'The Roe Head Journal', with its much more protracted and explicit reveries. In one, Charlotte describes an August afternoon when she retreats to the dormitory alone at dusk and gives herself over to the bliss of solitude. 'The stream of thought, checked all day, came flowing free & calm along its channel . . . detached thoughts soothingly flitted round me, & unconnected scenes occurred and then vanished, producing an effect certainly strange but, to me, very pleasing.' The change 'acted on me like opium' and grew 'morbidly vivid'. 'I remember I quite seemed to see, with my bodily eyes, a lady standing in the hall of a gentleman's house.' The scene unfolded, with many sophistications; Charlotte knew that 'a thousand things' were connected to this vision that she did not have time to analyse, but meanwhile the sight of the doctor washing his bloody hands in the basin (she knew who he was – she had invented him – Dr Charles Brandon) and the woman (whom Charlotte did not recognise) holding the taper had acquired a solidity that Charlotte found disturbing and couldn't switch off: 'I grew frightened at the vivid glow of the candle, at the reality of the lady's erect & symmetrical figure, of her spirited & handsome face, of her anxious eye watching Brandon's & seeking out its meaning.'

The removal into this dream was so complete that she only gradually became aware of her real circumstances: 'a feeling like a heavy weight laid across me. I knew I was wide awake & that it was dark, & that, moreover, the ladies were now come into the room to get their curl-papers. They perceived me lying on the bed & I heard them talking about me. I wanted to speak, to rise – it was impossible. I felt that this was a frightful predicament – that it would not do. The weight pressed me as if some huge animal had flung itself across me. A horrid apprehension quickened every pulse I had. "I must get up", I thought, & I did so with a start . . . Tea's read[y]. Miss Wooler is impatient.'

So the banal world of Miss Wooler and tea again drew her back into the land of the living, but Charlotte became increasingly aware that 'It would not do.'

Feelings of guilt as well as deep pleasure attached to the ecstatic release of her visions, fantasies that made her pant and that were painful to have interrupted. Everything about Charlotte's willed removals into the 'bright dream' seems to have a sexual semblance, a masturbatory character and the ecstatic quality often associated with sexual or mystical experiences.

The pain of returning to ordinary life from the 'dream' found strikingly similar expression in a Gondal poem written by Emily a few years later:

> Oh, dreadful is the check – intense the agony –
> When the ear begins to hear, and the eye begins to see;
> When the pulse begins to throb, the brain to think again,
> The soul to feel the flesh, and the flesh to feel the chain.

Had these lines been known to Charlotte at Roe Head, she might have clung to her alternative world for much longer, but, as it was, experiences such as the 'frightful' incapacitation she felt in the dormitory had begun to alarm her. 'I have had enough of morbidly vivid realizations,' she wrote. 'Every advantage has its corresponding disadvantage.'

Ellen, stolidly reliable and consistent, unimpeachably unimaginative, became the person Charlotte fixed on as helpmeet in this crisis, but what started, in Charlotte's letters, as expressions of religious frailty kept reconstituting themselves quite differently. The widening gulf in their experience (and Ellen's limited understanding of what Charlotte suffered at this or at any other time) made Charlotte address her in an odd, pleading tone, in terms more appropriate for a doting lover than a spiritual companion:

> Don't deceive yourself by imagining that I have a bit of real goodness about me. My Darling if I were like you I should have my face Zionward . . . but I am *not like you*. If you knew my thoughts; the dreams that absorb me; and the fiery imagination that at times eats me up and makes me feel Society as it is, wretchedly insipid   you would pity and I dare say despise me.

Charlotte hinted darkly at what her faults might be: 'I have some qualities that make me very miserable some feelings that you can have no participation in – that few very few people in the world can at all understand', but there was no need for Ellen's mind to be contaminated with details: Ellen's presence and example, she felt sure, would be enough to effect a cure:

If I could always live with you, and daily read the bible with you, if your lips and mine could at the same time; drink the same draught from the same pure fountain of Mercy – I hope, I trust, I might one day become better, far better, than my evil wandering thoughts, my corrupt heart, cold to the spirit, and warm to the flesh will now permit me to be ... My eyes fill with tears when I contrast the bliss of such a state brightened by hopes of the future with the melancholy state I now live in, uncertain that I have ever felt true contrition, wandering in thought and deed, longing for holiness, which I shall *never*, *never* obtain.

Because Charlotte expressed the conflict she was feeling in terms of sin and guilt, her crisis at Roe Head has often been described as 'religious' – a sort of spiritual watershed – though it seems much more to do with self-doubt, and has as much suffocated erotic content as doctrinal. Charlotte had become alarmed by the possibility that she was temperamentally incapable of being contented, a sinful state, in effect, of resistance to God's will. The fear gripped her that she might be, in Calvinist terms, not one of the Elect at all, but damned. 'I know not how to pray – I cannot bend my life to the grand end of doing good,' she wrote to Ellen needily. 'I go on constantly seeking my own pleasure pursuing the Gratification of my own desires, I forget God and will not God forget me?'

This stark divide followed fairly easily from the polarising effects of her Angrian obsession, and its insidious, deeply pleasurable, interruptions of everyday duties. Her conscience plagued her, and yet: 'I keep trying to do right, checking wrong feelings, repressing wrong thoughts,' she told Ellen, 'but still – every instant I find – myself going astray ... I abhor myself – I despise myself – if the Doctrine of Calvin be true I am already an outcast – You cannot imagine how hard rebellious and intractable all my feelings are – When I begin to study on the subject I almost grow blasphemous, atheistical in my sentiments.'

Ellen did visit Charlotte at Roe Head that term, but very late and only after a barrage of pleading letters. Ellen's responses were full of platitudes – essentially that one must submit with resignation to the will of a higher power – and it shows what a low state Charlotte had reached that she clung to them for comfort. When Ellen cancelled a visit to Haworth at Christmas due to the weather, Charlotte felt the disappointment keenly, but no longer felt she really deserved such a treat: 'it seems as if some fatality stood between you and me, I am not good enough for you, and you must be kept from the contamination of too intimate society.' One time that autumn, Charlotte had admitted that she felt *too much* for Ellen, and was censoring her own post when it became too sentimental. 'I will not tell you all I think, and feel about you Ellen. I will preserve unbroken that reserve which alone enables me to maintain a decent character for judgment.' 'I am thine Charles Thunder,' she said in a moment of semi-levity, adopting one of her masculine personae from 'Glass Town'. 'I wish I could live with you always, I begin to cling to you more fondly than ever I did. If we had but a cottage and a competency of our own I do think we might live and love on till *Death* without being dependent on any third person for happiness'. Retreat, peace, safety; Ellen in a cottage – it was an alluring dream.

Charlotte's impotence affected even the sustaining dream world, for while she was isolated at Roe Head, Branwell had started a series of Angrian wars that threatened to destabilise the whole Verdopolitan Union: invasions, coups and turmoil ensued, to which Charlotte had little power to respond apart from a shift to trying to monopolise the romantic storylines and to dominate the invention and development of the female characters. She was delighted to receive, inside a letter from Branwell, a letter from Northangerland to his daughter, Mary Percy, Duchess of Zamorna, announcing an imminent return from exile. 'I lived on its contents for days,' Charlotte said, enthralled by the images it conjured of the Duchess reading and handling the very paper before her. But other bulletins from Branwell could be purely alarming. Had he really killed off the Duchess with whom she so strongly identified? 'Is she alone in the cold earth on this dreary night?' Charlotte asked herself, with no acknowledgement of how imaginary the deceased had been. 'I can't abide to think how hopelessly & cheerlessly she must have died.'

The power of her imaginary other-world was in proportion to its pleasure, and if she risked a sort of madness in its pursuit, Charlotte liked to play with that possibility. What else was as vivifying? As she sat at her desk in the classroom, eyes closed and feeling the edge of the paper for guidance, behind her eyelids Charles Thunder was carried away on the wings of a glorious, liberating storm:

There is a voice, there is an impulse that wakens up that dormant power, which in its torpidity I sometimes think dead. That wind, pouring in impetuous current through the air, sounding wildly, unremittingly from hour to hour, deepening its tone as the night advances, coming not in gusts but with a rapid gathering stormy swell. That wind I know is heard at this moment far away on the moors at Haworth. Branwell & Emily hear it, and as it sweeps over our house, down the church-yard & round the old church, they think perhaps of me & Anne.

Glorious! That blast was mighty. It reminded me of Northangerland. There was something so merciless in the heavier rush that made the very house groan as if it could scarce bear this acceleration of impetus. O, it has awakened a feeling that I cannot satisfy! A thousand wishes rose at its call which must die with me, for they will never be fulfilled. Now I should be agonized if I had not the dream to repose on. Its existences, its forms, its scenes do fill a little of the craving vacancy. Hohenlinden! Childe Harold! Flodden Field! The burial of Moore! Why cannot the blood rouse the heart, the heart wake the head, the head prompt the hand to do things like these?

Back home, during the Christmas holidays, Charlotte's anger and frustrations disappeared in the company of her siblings. Talking over their setbacks and plans, Charlotte and Branwell reached a crest of impatience about their chances of joining the world of letters and decided to take matters into their own hands with a series of bold initiatives, cheered on by Emily and Anne. Charlotte was going to solicit the opinion of the Poet Laureate himself, Robert Southey, and Branwell was going to approach Wordsworth. No one could accuse these two young people of thinking small.

Charlotte recalled her letter to Southey as a 'crude rhapsody' that caused her some embarrassment retrospectively. She sent him a poem (which one isn't known) and told the Laureate that she wanted nothing less than 'to be for ever known', asking him to stoop from his 'throne of light & glory' to tell her whether or not her aspirations were vain. She didn't withhold her name or gender, so was exposing herself and her ambitions fully, but her letter went beyond bounds in other ways too, with a description, obviously not essential to her purpose, of the state of heightened imagination she habitually lived in and the way in which the intensity of her ambition made the 'ordinary uses of the world' seem, to borrow Hamlet's words, 'flat & unprofitable'.

Charlotte returned to Roe Head with no answer from Southey, but her mind whirring with poetry. In January of 1837 alone, she wrote at least 700 lines of verse, much of it a continuation of her Angrian epic, as well as shorter poems and fragments that found their way into her first published collection almost a decade later. She was thinking on a grand scale and working with extreme focus and dedication; this was the discipline that might rescue her from the conventional world of oafs and asses.

Meanwhile, Branwell had written to the editor of *Blackwood's* again, taking him to task – in what he clearly thought was an engaging way – for never answering his letters: 'Is it pride which actuates you – or custom – or prejudice? – Be a man – Sir! and think no more of these things! *Write* to me.' A week later, and in much the same confident mood, he wrote directly to William Wordsworth at Rydal Mount, sending the opening passages from an (unfinished) poem called 'The Struggles of Flesh with Spirit' and pressing his credentials as a natural bard, brought up among 'secluded hills where I could neither know what I was or what I could do', a Wordsworthian character, in other words.

Not surprisingly, there was no answer from either *Blackwood's* or the bard, but we know of Wordsworth's reaction by chance, as Southey and he must have made the connection between their different correspondents in Haworth Parsonage. Southey told his friend Caroline Bowles (who had been with him when Charlotte's original 'flighty' letter arrived) that Wordsworth had been 'disgusted' by Branwell's petition, 'for it contained gross flattery to him, and plenty of abuse of other poets, including me'. Under the circumstances, it seems odd that Wordsworth bothered to complain about Branwell's letter, or even to preserve it – he must have received many such.* Charlotte's letter to Southey did receive a reply, though, forwarded from Haworth to Roe Head. That he answered at all is remarkable, as is his apology – a whole

---

* After the poet's death in 1850, it passed to his son-in-law Edward Quillinan. At that date the name Brontë was not yet famous (his sisters having published pseudonymously), but it seems a sad reflection on the thoroughness of Branwell's failure that his name has been glossed on the manuscript as '?Peter Bradwell – deceased – Bronte' (*LCB* 1, 161, textual note).

paragraph long – for the ten-week delay in doing so. Southey was obviously intrigued by both the letter and the verses Miss Brontë had sent, which 'bear the same stamp' as each other, expressing a state of mind that he could well understand, though didn't share. 'You live in a visionary world,' he said, with acuity.

His warning to his young correspondent was as much against this over-heated state of mind as anything else. Getting published was not in itself a worthwhile aim, he told her, and would not necessarily make her happy: 'Many volumes of poems are now published every year without attracting public attention, any one of wh, if it had appeared half a century ago, wd. have obtained a high reputation for its author. Whoever therefore is ambitious of distinction in this way, ought to be prepared for disappointment.' He advised her to write for its own sake: the less she aimed at celebrity, 'the more likely you will be to deserve, & finally to obtain it'. The Laureate makes it clear that he gives this advice to 'every young man who applies as an aspirant to me':

> You will say that a woman has no need of such a caution, there can be no peril in it for her: & in a certain sense this is true. But there is a danger of wh I wd with all kindness & all earnestness warn you. The daydreams in wh you habitually indulge are likely to induce a distempered state of mind, & in proportion as all the 'ordinary uses of the world' seem to you 'flat & unprofitable', you will be unfitted for them, without becoming fitted for anything else. Literature cannot be the business of a woman's life: & it ought not to be. The more she is engaged in her proper duties, the less leisure she will have for it, even as an accomplishment & a recreation. To those duties you have not yet been called, & when you are you will be less eager for celebrity.

The quelling phrase about literature not being the business of a woman's life has been held up, understandably, as an egregious example of unwarranted discouragement and prejudice, but in truth Southey's response, taken as a whole, was full of genuine kindness and interest in the unknown writer's work. He sensed (by the end of the letter) that what he was saying was unlikely to go down well with a young woman who possessed real gifts, and who displayed clear signs of the disturbance that goes with knowing it. 'It is not because I have forgotten that I once was young myself that I write to you in this strain – but because

I remember it,' he told her (note that the gender issue has been set aside here). 'You will neither doubt my sincerity, nor my good will . . . Tho' I may be but an ungracious adviser, you will allow me therefore to subscribe myself, With the best wishes for your happiness, here & here-after, Your true friend, Robert Southey.'

Charlotte opened this letter at Roe Head with the sort of fervid attention one would give to examination results or long-awaited life-changing news, a desire to know the contents instantly. As she took in the gist of it, her spirits plummeted: 'I felt a painful heat rise to my face, when I thought of the quires of paper I had covered with what once gave me so much delight, but which now was only a source of confusion.' On further perusal, though – and it's clear that she pored over it many times – she saw that there was food for encouragement, of a sort, and the reply she wrote Southey a few days later glossed his message thus: 'You do not forbid me to write; you do not say that what I write is utterly destitute of merit. You only warn me against the folly of neglecting real duties, for the sake of imaginative pleas-ures.'

In her reply, Charlotte protests how grateful she is for Southey's advice, but does so in a tone that rides the line between sarcasm and sincerity. She seems actually more piqued than advised: 'You kindly allow me to write poetry for its own sake,' she writes, 'provided I leave undone nothing which I ought to do, in order to pursue that single absorbing exquisite gratification.' But he was wrong to assume she was an 'idle dreaming being' who simply wanted permission to dabble and had been protected from life's buffets:

> My Father is a clergyman of limited, though competent, income, and I am the eldest of his children . . . I thought it therefore my duty, when I left school, to become a governess. In that capacity, I find enough to occupy my thoughts all day long, and my head & hands too, without having a moment's time for one dream of the imagination. In the even-ings, I confess, I do think, but I never trouble any one else with my thoughts. I carefully avoid any appearance of pre-occupation, and eccen-tricity, which might lead those I live amongst to suspect the nature of my pursuits . . . I have endeavoured not only attentively to observe all the duties a woman ought to fulfil, but to feel deeply interested in them.

I don't always succeed, for sometimes when I'm teaching or sewing I would rather be reading or writing; but I try to deny myself; and my Father's approbation amply rewarded me for the privation. Once more allow me to thank you with sincere gratitude. I trust I shall never more feel ambitious to see my name in print; if the wish should rise, I'll look at Southey's letter, and suppress it.

Southey wrote back a second time, a brief but sincere letter, obviously relieved that she had – as he thought – taken his advice so well, and regretting the dogmatic tone of his first communication. He regretted it so much, indeed, and was so cheered by her response, that he made an astonishing offer: 'Let me now request that if you ever should come to these Lakes while I am living here, you will let me see you. You will then think of me afterwards with more good will.' Southey was extending the hand of friendship!

Charlotte did not answer this for fear of imposing too far on his attention; nor was she ever able to act on the invitation to call on the Poet Laureate at home, not having the freedom or resources to do so. But his friendly gesture, offered in such a respectful way, as equals, was something to treasure and delight in. Her sly jibes in her second letter must have come to seem rather misdirected, given the almost naïve sincerity of his parting advice that she should 'Take care of over-excitement, & endeavour to keep a quiet mind; even for your health it is the best advice that can be given you. Your moral & spiritual improvement will then keep pace with the culture of your intellectual powers.' It was probably the heartfelt concern he expressed that caused her, alone at Roe Head on her twenty-first birthday, 21 April 1837, to write on the envelope: 'Southey's Advice/To be kept for ever', for of course she had no intention of giving up her ambition to be forever known.

6

Labour in Vain

1837–41

As the Brontë siblings grew to adulthood, they did not integrate successfully with their Haworth neighbours – or strive to. A notable example of their isolation was at the election in 1837, when the family found themselves in a decided Tory minority in the town, against the Whig candidate, Lord Morpeth, an old Etonian who had held a pre-Reform family seat. One of Haworth's traditions was open-air debate in the area in front of the Black Bull and the church at the top of Main Street, where 'many remarkable discussions' took place over the years, sometimes turning violent at sensitive times such as elections. The election of 1837 proved one such. The Whigs had a much larger turn-out than the Tories, the candidate having brought in supporters from the outskirts, and when Patrick Brontë tried to speak against him he was rudely shouted down. Branwell, in his impetuous way, 'rushed to the front crying, "If you won't let my father speak, you shan't speak"', and as a punishment for his presumption, an effigy of the parson's son was carried along Main Street later and burned, while Branwell watched aghast from inside a shop. It was made recognisable by the addition of a herring in one hand and a potato in the other – enough to signify an Irishman.

Feelings in the parish were running high over the issue of church tithes too. No one had really believed that Dissenters would be prosecuted for non-payment, but when the first cases were brought at the end of 1838, Patrick Brontë's unpopularity and the family's isolation reached new levels. This coincided with violent disturbances in the area in the first years of the Chartist movement, with 'ultra-Radicals' organising huge public gatherings such as the one in Manchester in September, when an estimated 300,000 people turned up to demand universal suffrage (for adult men) and a ballot vote, among other measures. The events were mirrored in Angria in Charlotte's story called 'Stancliffe's Hotel', in which the city of Zamorna (named after the Duke, and ostensibly an African location) seems to be taking on more and more of the attributes of a West Riding industrial town like Bradford or Leeds, and its citizens the aspects of the disaffected working men of 1838. In the story, an assemblage of 'mad mechanics and desperate operatives of Zamorna' are dispersed by sword-wielding cavalry in a scene reminiscent of the 1819 Peterloo Massacre, an event much referenced by the contemporary Chartists. Thus Charlotte and Branwell played out in 'the world below' the turbulence that surrounded them so uncontrollably day to day.

Charlotte's own inner turbulence and chronic dissatisfaction with her lot was leading inevitably towards a crisis at Roe Head. Just before Christmas 1837, Anne had been taken so severely ill at school that both she and Charlotte believed her life to be in danger, as did the Moravian minister, James La Trobe (later an influential bishop), who visited her sickbed several times to console her. His words were truly comforting to Anne, who was a deeply pious girl. Charlotte meanwhile was becoming frantic, just as she had been when Emily was ill at Roe Head two years before. The difficulty and pain Anne had breathing were inextricably linked in her mind with consumption. 'I cannot tell you what agony these symptoms give me,' she told Ellen when Mary Taylor suffered from similar shortness of breath and chest pains; 'they remind me so strongly of my two sisters whom no power of medicine could save.' But Miss Wooler did not share Charlotte's view of the seriousness of the situation and appeared 'hard and unfeeling' about it. Possibly she was rather tired of having to deal with her young colleague's hyper-sensitivity and was trying to encourage her to snap out of it; certainly Charlotte's implied criticism of her judgement and management – that she couldn't recognise a danger to one of her charges – was insulting.

What started as a difference of opinion about Anne's health rapidly escalated to a row, and after years of biting her tongue Charlotte suddenly let fly at Miss Wooler with bitter reproaches and 'one or two rather plain truths', as she reported to Ellen with pride. Miss Wooler was reduced to tears during the shocking scene, and unsurprisingly wrote to Patrick Brontë the next day, reporting his daughter's behaviour. The day after that Charlotte and Anne were called home. Charlotte, utterly unrepentant of her outburst and scornful of Miss Wooler's distress, had resolved to give in her notice, but in their parting interview agreed, rather loftily, to Miss Wooler's request that she should return after a break at home. She was determined that Anne was not going back, however.

For once Charlotte had asserted control over her situation, albeit violently, and when she returned a few weeks later, she was in a detached mood and disinclined to oblige anyone. She had spent her month's respite finishing a story called 'Mina Laury', her most ambitious fiction to date, depicting the slavish devotion of the heroine to the Duke of Zamorna. Sequestered and neglected in a country hideaway, Mina is poorly rewarded for her love by Zamorna's increasing disdain, and her obsessive focus on her cruel lover mirrors Charlotte's own feelings for this favourite product of her imagination: 'She had but one idea – Zamorna, Zamorna! . . . She could no more feel alienation from him than she could from herself.'

The school moved that winter from Roe Head to a smaller property on Dewsbury Moor, Heald's House, nearer Miss Wooler's ailing parents at Rouse Mill. Charlotte thought the situation damp and unhealthy, but one gets the impression that she had no intention of staying there long. The sole advantage of the move to Charlotte was that it was within easy walking distance of Brookroyd, the house in Birstall where Mrs Nussey and her family had moved after her brother-in-law's death, but, frustratingly, Ellen was away from home that spring on an extended visit to her brother John in London. Charlotte missed her terribly, worried about her health and that of all the Nusseys in the over-sensitive way that became characteristic of this period, and called on Ellen's mother and sisters whenever opportunity allowed. The family were having a dreadful year with William, Ellen's 31-year-old apothecary brother, suffering from a psychotic illness that led to his suicide in the summer. Ellen suppressed all references to William's death in her papers, as she did to her brother George's later mental breakdown, her brother Joseph's alcoholism and her sister Mercy's chronic nervous disorders. But, as Ellen's close friend and confidante, and friend to her sisters Mercy and Ann too, Charlotte was aware of the family's troubles, and agonised over them almost as much as she did her own.

By March, Charlotte was again sent home in a state of collapse, then returned in April to superintend the empty building at Heald's House during the holidays while Miss Wooler tended her father in his final illness. Sixteen days on her own in the school proved anything other than easy or restful, and an even more dramatic collapse followed. Term started again, but now that both Charlotte's sisters had gone home, her nerves gave way: 'she would turn sick and trembling at any sudden noise, and could hardly repress her screams when startled,' Mrs Gaskell heard. Miss Wooler clearly recognised that Charlotte's insurrectionary outburst at Christmas, released on Anne's behalf, had reflected her own chronic disturbance, and was genuinely concerned about Charlotte's mental state. She insisted that a doctor was called, and he, diagnosing the case as nervous, advised that Charlotte should also go home. She departed in May, on an indefinite sick leave, reinforcing the now familiar pattern of the Brontë siblings failing to thrive in any environment other than the Parsonage.

Miss Wooler had presented Charlotte with two books at her departure, inscribed with affection. Charlotte was by far the most remarkable student she had ever had, and Miss Wooler – who had no inkling of Charlotte's literary output and ambitions at this date – could not have imagined a more benign plan than for Charlotte to persevere with her career as a teacher. She was possibly already thinking ahead to her own retirement and who was to take over the running of the school – a subject she raised a few years later.

The severity of Charlotte's collapse can be gauged by the unusual treatment she received at home, where she was put to bed for a period of absolute rest and quiet. Who prescribed this? Patrick Brontë or Aunt Branwell? The doctor? The Brontës didn't always follow medical advice very closely, or seek it promptly, and Patrick's trusty reference work, Dr Thomas John Graham's *Modern Domestic Medicine*,★ had little to say on the subject of nervous disorders. Charlotte was kept alone and quiet for a full week, removed from all sources of excitement, including books and pictures. No doubt she was given a sedative, perhaps rather a heavy dose, to help her sleep and regain physical strength. The episode in *Jane*

★ A heavily annotated volume, now in the Brontë Parsonage Museum. It was Patrick Brontë's health-advice bible.

Eyre where Jane recovers from her collapse from hunger and exhaustion outside Moor House – and the similar scenes of extreme convalescence in *Shirley* and *Villette* – might well recall some of this time:

> I knew I was in a small room, and in a narrow bed. To that bed I seemed to have grown: I lay on it motionless as a stone; and to have torn me from it would have been almost to kill me. I took no note of the lapse of time – of the change from morning to noon, from noon to evening. I observed when any one entered or left the apartment; I could even tell who they were; I could understand what was said when the speaker stood near to me; but I could not answer: to open my lips or move my limbs was equally impossible.

Charlotte recovered in the warmth of her family's concern, and in the company of the Taylor sisters, who had been asked to come and cheer her up. The Parsonage brightened in the presence of these lively friends – Martha had been 'in a constant flow of good-humour during her stay here and has consequently been very fascinating', Charlotte reported to Ellen, who was still at her brother's house in London – and one can imagine the spirited discussions the group had over religion, literature and politics, Mary's forthright opinions voiced freely and Charlotte's mind expanding pleasurably after her lonely vigils at Heald's House. 'They are making such a noise about me I can not write any more,' she wrote happily; 'Mary is playing on the piano. Martha is chattering as fast as her little tongue can run and Branwell is standing before her laughing at her vivacity.'

No doubt the Taylors took a keen interest in the difficulties the Brontë girls were facing trying to establish themselves as wage-earners. Mary and Martha had been spared the same fate – so far – by a fairly narrow margin of privilege. Their large family was supported by ever-diminishing resources from Hunsworth Mill, and the two girls had been encouraged not to be complacent about their futures. Since leaving school, both had travelled and continued to study, but Mary was as unenthusiastic about teaching for a living as her friend. Mary's novel *Miss Miles* shows how engaged she became with the subject of women's self-sufficiency, and her later essays (published in the 1860s) insisted that women should be able to learn and earn enough to ensure they weren't 'driven into matrimony'.

In the next few years Charlotte and her siblings seem to have come to a form of compact between them that they would share the hated necessity of 'going out' to earn money, as long as they could also share times of respite, such as Charlotte greedily took advantage of in the summer of 1838. It's a measure of how reduced Charlotte was when she came home from Heald's House that Emily, the most ferocious hater of Elsewhere, attempted to do her bit and take a post at a school run by a Miss Elizabeth Patchett at Law Hill, on the hills outside Halifax.

Law Hill was large in comparison with Roe Head, having almost forty pupils, half of whom were boarders. Emily was kept at her work from the moment the girls woke up until after their bedtime, with, as Charlotte reported to Ellen, 'only one half hour of exercise between – this is slavery'. Emily responded with her own brand of non-compliance: one of the girls later recalled her as dreamy and untidy, a loner who at least once lashed out and told them that she preferred the house dog to any of her pupils. But privately she was studying and translating Virgil that year, writing a remarkable number of poems and storing up material. Law Hill had been built some fifty years earlier by a man called Jack Sharp, who had been adopted by John Walker of nearby Walterclough Hall, and was later ousted from the property by the rightful heir, his cousin. Law Hill was as near as Sharp could get to Walterclough, against which he conducted a cold-blooded campaign of revenge. This energetically malevolent man has so much in common with Heathcliff in *Wuthering Heights* that it is hard not to see him as a direct inspiration for the novel Emily would write in the next decade.

The Law Hill estate had a contemporary neighbour of equal notoriety and interest, the heiress Anne Lister, who lived at Shibden Hall with her lover Ann Walker in a lesbian relationship, the nature and ardour of which were only made widely known in the twentieth century when Lister's remarkable diaries were decoded and published. Local gossips would not have needed the evidence of a diary to confirm what was going on at Shibden Hall, though. Lister's masculine style was so pronounced that one of her lovers, Marianna Lawton, used to be ashamed to be seen in public with her, and her nickname in Halifax was 'Gentleman Jack'. 'You do not know what is said of your friend,' a tipsy well-wisher once warned Marianna, but she did, and Elizabeth Patchett surely did too. It would have been strange if Emily Brontë had not met

Anne Lister at some time in her seven-month soujourn next door, or heard the stories about her, and it is interesting that Emily's time at Law Hill, high on the moors, gave her both stories of bitter past rivalries prosecuted over generations, and understanding of a wild, passionate and very unconventional erotic force.

Anne Brontë went bravely off alone to her first governess post with a family called Ingham at Blake Hall, Mirfield, just a few weeks after Emily's return home. None of the sisters had any experience of governessing before, from either side of the divide, and her reports back must have been something of a shock. Anne was in charge of the elder two of five children, both 'desperate little dunces', as Charlotte told Ellen, whose bad behaviour Anne was not empowered to discipline: 'she is requested when they misbehave themselves to inform their Mamma – which she says is utterly out of the question as in that case she might be making complaints from morning until night.' This was the sort of difficulty that none of the sisters had imagined, and that they were all singularly ill-qualified to deal with, being so anxious socially. Anne had her extreme taciturnity to overcome too, and her stammer (the one probably exacerbated the other). She was the least complaining of all the siblings, the most long-suffering and the best employee among them by far. But she certainly found the life of a governess hard to bear, and missed home as much as any of them. Her survival strategy at Blake Hall, like Emily's in Halifax, was to collect her impressions for later use.

Presumably the techniques used to subdue her charges by Agnes Grey in Anne's novel were ones that Anne herself used, since they are presented as perfectly reasonable: shaking, pulling hair, holding down the child until she repeats part of the lesson correctly, pinning her in a corner with a chair. Just as surprising to twenty-first-century sensibilities is Agnes's solution to the discovery of little John's tormenting of a nest of baby birds – she finds a rock and smashes it down on the nest to put an end to the creatures' suffering. In the novel, this is proof of Agnes's tenderness as much as resolve, but is unquestionably severe. Anne was the sister who was least impatient with children, but even she found dealing with them more like battle than anything else: 'it was one struggle of life-wearing exertion' to keep the little Inghams 'in anything like decent order'.

Charlotte knew it would soon be her turn to rejoin 'that dreary Gin-horse round' and was due to go out herself as a governess that summer. But something happened in the spring of 1839 to remind her, if rather uncomfortingly, that there were other fates than work for a young woman in her position. Ellen's 27-year-old brother Henry, a recent graduate of Magdalene College Cambridge, had been aware of Charlotte's concern for their family during their crisis with William the previous year, and was probably much impressed by her fervent discussion of religious matters with Ellen around that time, for he was a rigidly pious man himself. He had had a personal crisis of his own in March 1838 (obliquely referred to a year later in his diary) and difficulties settling in to his first curacy at Earnley in Sussex. Charlotte undoubtedly heard about the latter through her friend; nevertheless, she was extremely surprised to get a letter from Henry Nussey, written on his birthday in February 1839 from Earnley, proposing marriage to her. Henry's diary shows that he was working his way methodically through a list of possible candidates, rather as Patrick Brontë had done in the early 1820s, and had just been turned down by a friend's sister: 'On Tuesday last received a decisive reply from M. A. L.'s papa. A loss, but I trust a providential one. Believe not her will, but her father's. All right. God knows best what is good for us, for his Church, & for his own Glory. This I humbly desire. And his Will be done, & not mine in this or in anything else . . . Wrote to a Yorke Friend, C. B.'

'C. B.' must have been more astonished by his proposal than flattered: it showed him to be so reckless. 'I have no personal repugnance to the idea of a union with you,' she wrote back to him, in a suitably matter-of-fact manner, 'but I feel convinced that mine is not the sort of disposition calculated to form the happiness of a man like you.' In describing what that might be, Charlotte gave an interesting self-portrait in the negative: '[Your future wife's] character should not be too marked, ardent and original – her temper should be mild, her piety undoubted, her spirits even and cheerful, and her *"personal attractions"* sufficient to please your eye and gratify your just pride.' She expressed herself grateful for his attention and for the suggestion that she could help him run a school in Sussex; but even with these incentives – and the alluring possibility that Ellen could come and live with them – Charlotte knew she could never marry for the sake of it, nor 'take a worthy man whom I am conscious I cannot render happy'. 'You do not know me,' she said truthfully. 'I am not the serious, grave, cool-headed individual you suppose.'

'Received an unfavourable report from C. B.,' Henry noted in his diary with barely perceptible disappointment. 'The will of the Lord be done.' Charlotte's wisdom in rejecting Henry's suit (if suit isn't too strong a word) seems obvious, and to Ellen, who had naturally been anxious to know the outcome, she was far more explicit about her reasons: 'I felt that though I esteemed Henry – though I had a kindly leaning towards him because he is an aimiable [*sic*] – well-disposed man Yet I had not, and never could have that intense attachment which would make me willing to die for him – and if ever I marry it must be in that light of adoration that I will regard my Husband.' One would expect no less from the creator of Mary Percy and Mina Laury, but it wasn't just 'intense attachment' and passionate love that Charlotte hoped for in a mate, but an all-encompassing familiarity, like that she had with her siblings: 'I was aware that Henry knew so little of me he could hardly be conscious to whom he was writing – why it would startle him to see me in my natural home-character he would think I was a wild, romantic enthusiast indeed – I could not sit all day long making a grave face before my husband – I would laugh and satirize and say whatever came into my head first – and if he were a clever man & loved me the whole world weighed in the balance against his smallest wish should be light as air –'

The proposal didn't put an end to the respectful friendship between Charlotte and Henry Nussey – if anything, it opened up their interest, or rather disinterest, in each other. Charlotte admired Henry's spiritual earnestness, but knew he was a prig at heart and she drew heavily on his characteristics for the worthy but priggish St John Rivers in *Jane Eyre*.

And, for all her talk of 'ten to one I shall never have the chance again' to consider a proposal, only five months later the former Haworth curate Mr Hodgson (who had moved away to Colne in 1837) came to tea with his subordinate, a 28-year-old Irishman, recently arrived from Dublin, called David Pryce. Pryce's manner was expansive and lively 'after the manner of his Countrymen', as Charlotte told Ellen later, and he caught Charlotte in the mood to enjoy and reciprocate. Most importantly, this first meeting took place at home: 'at home you know Ellen I talk with ease and am never shy – never weighed down & oppressed by the miserable mauvaise honte which torments & constrains me elsewhere – so I conversed with this Irishman & laughed at his jests.' The effect was remarkable: a few days later, she received a letter from him, asking for her hand. '[W]ell thought I – I've heard of love at first sight but this beats all.' She of course turned him down, but the episode was amusing and heartening.

Branwell's career was still undecided. His art master, William Robinson, died suddenly in 1838, leaving a wife and six children and at least one pupil without occupation. In February 1838 Patrick Brontë was applying to a Liverpool wine merchant he knew through a Haworth family (and also, evidently, through being the vintner's customer) for help in procuring Branwell 'an opening . . . as Clerk in some Respectable Bank. I know not what the usual terms, are, on which a Young man enters upon such a line of life, but I have heard, that they are comparatively easy, as far as money matters, are concerned.' The letter demonstrates again Patrick Brontë's ignorance of the usual procedure, and his touching trust in the likelihood of ability being recognised. It would do Branwell good, his father thought, to see a little of the world beyond Yorkshire and 'open a wider field, for talent, and suitable connexions'. His sights had been lowered from a possible move to London and the RA or a Continental tour; now the father was primarily interested in finding Branwell something respectable 'and in time, should he conduct himself well, sufficiently lucrative'.

Aunt Branwell and her savings came to the rescue when, in a bid to do something definite for his son, and with the help of his old friend William Morgan, Patrick Brontë decided to set Branwell up in business as a portrait painter in Bradford in the summer of 1838. A studio was rented, and lodgings found with a family called Kirby, on Fountain Street; the rest was meant to be up to Branwell. William Morgan proved an active patron, commissioning portraits of himself and his family; the Kirbys too provided their young tenant with work, but Branwell's talent was simply not up to the competition in his field, and he struggled from the first to find clients outside his immediate circle.

What Branwell enjoyed most about Bradford was the company of lively and intelligent friends who liked to congregate at the George

Hotel, including John Thompson, a former fellow pupil at William Robinson's studio, and the talented young sculptor Joseph Bentley Leyland. Leyland said later that Branwell was not a drunkard at this time (though he was no abstainer either). Under the eye of his god-father William Morgan, no doubt Branwell was on his best behaviour in public, but, as was to be expected from a 21-year-old youth set free for the first time, he was not immune to the temptations of the town and quickly got used to being in debt.

Portraits of local figures would have necessarily been Branwell's bread-and-butter work, had he ever developed his career as a professional artist, but ambitious, imaginary painting interested him far more, and the few of his works that survive, heavily indebted to the style of John Martin, are much more distinctive than his wooden portraiture. By May 1839 Branwell had had such little success in Bradford that there was no justifi-cation for keeping on the studio, and he came home again. Charlotte had visited her brother in Bradford once, apparently the only member of the family to do so. One wonders what she made of his bachelor quarters and workplace there. Did 'her sisterly ways', as the Kirbys' niece charac-terised them vaguely, include tidying up his canvases, brushes and paints, or did Charlotte and Branwell spend their time in discussion of their joint creations Wiggins, Townshend, Northangerland and mighty Zamorna? It would have been hard indeed for Charlotte not to run her eye over her brother's studio and wonder what she could have done with such a place to herself and such an opportunity.

Just as Branwell returned home, Charlotte had to leave for her first post as a governess, to the Sidgwick family at Stonegappe in Lothers-dale, only about twelve miles away. It was an appointment for less than two months (filling in for the regular governess), in a lovely place quite near home, among people of their acquaintance (the Sidgwicks were related to the Durys and Miss Wooler's sister was married to the local parson); nevertheless, Charlotte was in deep distress the whole time.

Her charges were seven-year-old Mathilda and her brother John, who was only three – both far too young to be able to benefit from Charlotte's teaching. Very young children did not interest her much, in fact she found them rather disgusting. Mrs Sidgwick was expecting her fifth baby in August. The only member of the family whom Charlotte considered interesting was the head of the household, Mr Sidgwick, who strolled the grounds at Stonegappe with a magnificent New-foundland dog at his heels, looking 'very like what a frank, wealthy, Conservative gentleman ought to be'.

When the family moved from one summer residence to another, where a large house-party gathered, Charlotte was very disturbed by being among so many strangers, writing to Emily (whose sympathy on this point could be guaranteed):

> I used to think I should like to be in the stir of grand folks' society but I have had enough of it – it is dreary work to look on and listen. I see now more clearly than I have ever done before that a private governess has no existence, is not considered as a living and rational being except as connected with the wearisome duties she has to fulfil. While she is teaching the children, working for them, amusing them, it is all right. If she steals a moment for herself she is a nuisance.

The similarities to Jane Eyre's feelings of being overlooked are striking. Charlotte's former dreams of being in 'grand folks' society' were really dreams of having her true worth recognised, but now that she was among 'grand folks', her employer – a woman whose lack of feeling and bourgeois complacency she scorned – refused to recognise anything about her at all, beyond her relation to the children. '[She] does not know my character & she does not wish to know it,' Charlotte complained to Ellen, 'I have never had five minutes conversation with her since I came – except while she was scolding me'. In a formulation much like that which Karl Marx was preparing to publish, she found Mrs Sidgwick exploitative, with her determination that 'the greatest possible quantity of labour may be squeezed out of me'. Not that labour repelled her; it was the loss of 'mental liberty' she raged against and that her position rendered her invisible, condemned to 'look on and listen' to fools, and then to wipe their children's noses, fetch and carry their things or sit hemming their sheets. It was far worse than Roe Head, and she was both miserable and surprisingly *angry*. 'At times I felt and I suppose seemed depressed,' she wrote to Ellen:

> to my astonishment I was taken to task on the subject by Mrs Sidgwick with a stern[n]ess of manner & a harshness of language scarcely credible – like a fool I cried most bitterly – I could not help it – my spirits quite

failed me at first   I thought I had done my best – strained every nerve
to please her – and to be treated in that way merely because I was shy
– and sometimes melancholy was too bad. at first I was for giving all up
and going home – But after a little reflection I determined – to summon
what energy I had and to weather the Storm –

The writer A. C. Benson was a nephew of her employers and recalled
them as 'extraordinarily benevolent people, much beloved, [who] would
not wittingly have given pain to any one connected with them'. Their
liberality was probably the problem, as far as Charlotte was concerned.
A. C. Benson heard that one of his cousins 'certainly on one occasion
threw a Bible at Miss Brontë', behaviour that she would have found intolerable, and yet was impotent to punish. This was her first experience of
having to deal with headstrong boys (there's no evidence that Branwell
ever behaved ill towards an adult in his childhood) and it appalled her. The
Sidgwicks' impression was that the temporary governess 'had no gifts for
the management of children' and was 'in a very morbid condition' all the
time she worked at Stonegappe: 'if she was invited to walk to church with
them, she thought she was being ordered about like a slave; if she was not
invited, she imagined she was excluded from the family circle.'

The bible that A. C. Benson heard about might be a confusion of
the story that has come down through the Benson and Sidgwick families of Charlotte Brontë being left in sole charge of John and his
ten-year-old brother William one day and their getting out of control. The elder brother egged on the younger, stones were lobbed at
the governess, and she was cut on the forehead. Quizzed the next day
by Mrs Sidgwick, she refused to tell on them, thereby earning a modicum of respect from her charges. But her antipathy towards Mrs
Sidgwick was confirmed when little John on one occasion at dinner
took Charlotte's hand and said 'I love 'ou, Miss Brontë', and his
mother reprimanded him: 'Love the *governess*, my dear!'★

The permanent governess returned to work in the middle of July, so

---

★ Ann Baer has brought to my attention her article in *Book Collector* ((Summer 2014),
281–2), 'Stoning Charlotte Brontë', in which she repeats her aunt Margie Sidgwick's
recollection of being visited in Oxford 'at some unknown date, but probably in the
1920s', by 'a very old man' called Benson Sidgwick, who claimed cousinship and told
Margie 'that he had once thrown a stone at Charlotte Brontë and hit her'.

Charlotte was free to go home, much to her employers' relief as well as her own. What is surprising, given her intense antipathy to the work, is that she ever considered doing it again.

Ellen's suggestion of a seaside holiday together could not have come at a better time for Charlotte, who felt that the prospect of weeks alone in Ellen's company was almost more fun than she deserved. The plan was in danger of frustration by Aunt Branwell's rival idea (much more boring, and not carried through) of taking the whole family to Liverpool for a holiday, and arrangements became so knotty that Ellen took the unusually firm step of simply turning up at Haworth one day in a carriage and forcing Aunt Branwell and Reverend Brontë to let Charlotte come away with her. Branwell provided comic commentary on this 'brave defeat' of the 'doubters' as his sister hurriedly packed for her five weeks away, so nearly missed because of dithering and second-guessing. As it was, Charlotte's visit to the north Yorkshire coast in 1839 was 'one of the green spots' of her life, recalled later with deep pleasure. She had taken her first ride on an amazing new railway train (from Leeds to York), she had stayed with strangers and not been too traumatised, and, at the age of twenty-three, she and Ellen had walked several miles from Easton to Bridlington to capture her first view of the sea. '[S]he was quite overpowered,' Ellen recalled; 'she could not speak till she had shed some tears . . . for the remainder of the day she was very quiet, subdued and exhausted.'

Between her release from Stonegappe and the end of the year, Charlotte was working on some much more ambitious stories, both in length and breadth, set ostensibly in Angria, but far from its 'African' original, and more like a parallel-universe version of the north of England, with some real names and places thrown in (such as Alnwick). 'Caroline Vernon' starts out in comic and domestic vein, with Northangerland grumpily back together with his wife and having to endure breakfast à deux, and Zamorna overseeing the harvest on his estates, like any complacent county landowner. Rather like Mr Sidgwick, in fact, whose Newfoundland dog also makes an appearance.*

* As he does in 'Ashworth' too, and most memorably in *Jane Eyre*, as Rochester's Pilot.

The character of Caroline Vernon is a remarkable study of adolescent sensibilities, quite unlike anything Charlotte had attempted before. Still writing in the tiny script, Brontë hit a subject that she could express with freshness and wit – the swooning and trembling delights of female adolescent sexuality:

> No doubt it is terrible to be looked fixedly at by a tall powerful man who knits his brows, & whose dark hair & whiskers & moustaches combine to shadow the eyes of a hawk & the features of a Roman statue. When such a man puts on an expression that you can't understand – stops suddenly as you are walking with him alone in a dim garden – removes your hand from his arm & places his hand on your shoulder – you are justified in feeling nervous & uneasy.

'Nervous & uneasy' – otherwise known as overpoweringly excited. Charlotte was cleverly capturing the mixture of flutter and focus that burgeoning sexual awareness excites in young girls. Asked (by a character called Hector Montmorency, who is deliberately trying to shock her) if she likes Zamorna (to whose mesmeric sexual attraction she is just awakening), Caroline answers 'No – yes – no – not much.' In fact, it is only this conversation, in which Montmorency reveals that Zamorna is a lifelong womaniser and that Mina Laury, whom Caroline thought a genteel recluse, is his mistress, that alerts Caroline to the nature of her own feelings about him, draws them into being, almost. 'The young lady's feelings were not exactly painful, they were strange, new & startling – she was getting to the bottom of an unsounded sea & lighting on rocks she had not guessed at.'

Caroline's awakening sensibilities are described as a stream of consciousness, many decades before such a term became commonplace: '"But how do I wish him to regard me? What terms should I like to be on with him? Really, I hardly know . . . I wonder whether I love him? O, I do! . . . I'm very wicked," she thought, shrinking again under the clothes.' The girl tries to account for her overpowering feelings, reasoning, 'She did not want him to love her in return . . . she only wanted him to be kind – to think well of her, to like to have her with him – nothing more.' Ultimately, Caroline runs away to be with Zamorna, and he quickly seduces her (in a scene of glances, touches and kisses that Brontë utterly relishes), but her statement of what she hoped from this mesmerising older man seems both comic and tragic: a wish for a guilt-free, sin-free love with a man whose primary attraction is sex — the idealised erotics of the adolescent finely identified and expressed by a woman of twenty-three.

The novelette is startlingly novel on other levels too, showing the same confident 'Postmodern' touches that Charlotte introduced into her work as early as 1830. The author draws attention to the fact that the action of the story shadows 'real time', pointing out that, far from being suspended in a narrative limbo, 'standing for upwards of a quarter of a year with her foot on the carriage-step', her heroine has got on very well without us in the space between chapters:

> No, be assured the young person sighed over Hawkscliffe but once, wept two tears on parting with a groom & a pony she had been on friendly terms with, wondered thrice what her dear mama would do without any-body to scold, for four minutes had a childish feeling of pity that she should be left behind, sat a quarter of an hour after the start in a fit of speechless thought she did not account for, & all the rest of the way was as merry as a grig.

With this complex comic snapshot, Charlotte Brontë has one hand stretched backwards towards Lawrence Sterne and one forwards towards Nabokov (whose *Pale Fire* has a passage using a very similar idea). What pleasure this must have given Charlotte to read to her siblings, and what a sophisticated comic writer this minuscule manuscript shows Charlotte Brontë could have been had she chosen that route.

In the autumn of 1839 Patrick Brontë secured a new curate, a keen 26-year-old fresh from Durham University, called William Weightman. Articulate and energetic, with views very much in harmony with the minister's own, he endeared himself immediately at the Parsonage and did a great deal to win over opinion in the town to Brontë's faction. Weightman became a good friend to Branwell too, and was a much better influence on him than John Brown, the sexton; he also managed what no outsider had yet with the girls, which was to break down their resistance to social charm. On hearing that none of the sisters had ever received a Valentine (aged twenty-three, twenty-one and twenty), he wrote them each some verses and walked ten miles to post them in a suitably incognito manner. Charlotte replied on behalf of them all in some deliberately plodding verses, reassuring the handsome curate that none of the girls read anything romantic into his gesture, a fairly sure sign that some of them did:

> A Rowland for your Oliver
>   We think you've justly earned;
> You sent us each a valentine,
>   Your gift is now returned.
>
> We cannot write or talk like you;
>   We're plain folks every one;
> You've played a clever jest on us,
>   We thank you for your fun.
>
> Believe us when we frankly say
>   (Our words, though blunt, are true),
> At home, abroad, by night or day,
>   We all wish well to you.

They considered him 'a pilgrim', she insisted, whose destiny is to meet a worthier fate (and mate) than Haworth could offer.

When Ellen came to visit, Weightman seemed to be singling her out for special attention, and even Mary Taylor was moved to banter with him over a chessboard. Only Emily remained immune, and she took up the role of protector, reportedly thwarting Weightman's attempts at lone walks on the moor with Ellen and earning the nickname 'The Major' for a 'swashing and martial' performance in mock (or not) aggression against him.

Weightman was a generous and thoughtful young man. When he gave a lecture at Keighley Mechanics' Institute in April 1840, he took pains to make it possible for the Brontë girls to attend, arranging for a married clergyman friend to offer to escort them to and from the venue. The plan passed muster with Aunt Branwell and Patrick Brontë (no small triumph), and the sisters were able to enjoy a rare evening of ordinary youthful fun, walking the eight miles to Keighley and back in a high-spirited party that also included Ellen Nussey. They got home at midnight, to find Aunt Branwell waiting unsmilingly with some stewed coffee and very much put out by having two more guests than she had bargained for. This was a dampener, but not a total quelling, of 'the great spirits of the walking party', as Ellen recalled, and though Charlotte felt embarrassed about her aunt's irritability, and guilty at having provoked it, Weightman seems to have understood all this and tried to make it into a joke, declaring himself 'very thirsty' for as much coffee as he could have. Thus he kept the young people's spirits up without malice – he does seem to have had an unusual capacity for doing the cheerful right thing.

Charlotte's fine pencil drawing of Weightman survives as a memento of lively days at the Parsonage, but also of her own persistent interest in the young curate. The sittings 'became alarming for length of time required', which Weightman was obviously happy to give her. They also allowed short-sighted Charlotte the opportunity to get up close and gaze for hours on end at this handsome, good-natured youth, with his carefully curled hair, genial smile and fine figure. No wonder she strung out the sittings. It's one of her best drawings.

But, at the same time, Charlotte was keen to tease Ellen about the new curate as often as possible, and at a later date – when nothing ignited there – she nurtured the idea that Weightman was smitten with Anne (who had been away from home at Blake Hall on his arrival in the parish): 'He sits opposite to Anne at Church sighing softly – & looking out of the corners of his eyes to win her attention . . . & Anne is so quiet, her look so downcast – they are a picture.' Anne certainly seems to have had tender feelings for Weightman, but can only have been made uncomfortable by Charlotte's showy teasing of everyone but herself over his interest.

There's another aspect to Weightman's presence that can't be over-looked, and that seems to have dawned on Charlotte gradually during 1840 and 1841. He was said to be attached to a girl back in Appleby, and carried on correspondences with a young woman in Swansea and another in Keighley, leading Charlotte to remark that 'the evident wandering instability of his mind is no favourable symptom at all.' She came to the conclusion that he was a 'thorough male-flirt', 'perfectly conscious of his irresistibleness & is as vain as a peacock on the subject'. The increasingly satirical edge to her remarks about Weightman indicate a developing theory, and Charlotte's repetition of her joke name for him, 'Miss Celia Amelia', and her use of the feminine pronoun when reciting his deeds become more pointed all the time. 'She thought you a fine-looking girl and a very good girl into the bargain,' Charlotte told Ellen, stoking Ellen's interest while warning her that 'Miss Celia Amelia' might be almost too good to be true. Her conclusion that he was a vain heartbreaker seems clouded here with other speculations or intuitions. When in the draft version of a letter Charlotte wrote the following winter, she joked about the modern confusability of gender – 'Several young gentlemen curl their hair and wear corsets – and several young ladies are excellent whips and by no means despicable jockies' – she may well have had in mind the confusing signals sent out by unconventional types such as Anne Lister, William Weightman or even her own sister Emily.

Emily's violently suppressed feelings and her strong personality were a source of awe to Charlotte, who later described her nature as 'standing alone' from all others. Keeper, with his intimidating bulk and strength, was her devoted familiar, and Ellen Nussey remembered how Emily used to agitate the dog on purpose to show off his ferocity, 'making him frantic in action and roaring with the voice of a lion' – a violent exhibition for a Victorian sitting room. Ellen passed the test of 'unresisting endurance' of Keeper's presence, was sat on and squashed by his considerable bulk on the sofa, and watched with interest as Emily and Anne ate their porridge with Keeper and Anne's spaniel Flossy at their sides, the two dogs waiting for the moment when the young women would hand down the bowls to be finished off.

But the incident that Charlotte witnessed (at an unspecified date) of Emily disciplining Keeper is the one that reflects her character most strangely. The dog had incurred her wrath by going upstairs once too often and dirtying the beds' clean counterpanes with his gigantic muddy footprints. When Tabby came in to report the crime, Emily's face whitened and her mouth set. The story was told later by Mrs Gaskell in her biography of Charlotte: '[Charlotte] dared not speak to interfere; no one dared when Emily's eyes glowed in that manner out of the paleness of her face, and when her lips were so compressed into stone.' She dragged the dog downstairs, he 'growling low and savagely all the time', and, having no stick to hand, set about him with her fists, punching him in the eyes before he could spring at her, until he was 'half-blind, stupefied' – at which point she took him off to his bed in the kitchen and bathed the injuries she had so brutally inflicted. Mrs Gaskell tells this story – as it had been told to her – as an example of Emily's noble strength of character. Its dreadful sadism is all that the modern reader sees – that, and the terror that Emily must have sometimes engendered in all members of the household.

Weightman's descent on Haworth highlighted the difficulties in love that beset Charlotte, her friends and sisters – prime among which was a notable absence of suitable men and the undignified frenzy around the available stock. Already the veteran of two proposals, Charlotte felt moved to advise Ellen in mock-comic mode 'as if it came from thy Grandmother' about how to conduct herself vis-à-vis Reverend Osman Parke Vincent, a friend of Henry Nussey, who seemed on the brink of proposing. His dithering, and his inappropriate discussions of his feelings with Henry rather than with Ellen, led Charlotte to suspect he was a fool, but she told her friend to weigh the case dispassionately and not 'have the romantic folly to wait for the awakening of what the French call "*Une grande passion*"'. Brave words, and very surprising ones from the part-time resident of a fantasy land ruled by erotic forces and the creator (unknown to Ellen) of so many torrid love scenes.

'Did you not once say to me in all childlike simplicity,' she recollected, '"I thought Charlotte – no young ladies should fall in love, till the offer was actually made."'

> I forget what answer I made at the time – but I now reply after due consideration – Right as a glove – the maxim is just – and I hope you will always attend to it – I will even extend and confirm it – no young lady should fall in love till the offer has been made, accepted – the marriage ceremony performed and the first half year of wedded life has passed away – a woman may then begin to love, but with great precaution – very coolly – very moderately – very rationally – If she ever loves so much that a harsh word or a cold look from her husband cuts her to the heart – she is a fool – if she ever loves so much that her husband's will is her law – and that she has got into a habit of watching his looks in order that she may anticipate his wishes she will soon be a neglected fool.

'On one hand don't accept if you are *certain* you cannot *tolerate* the man – on the other hand don't refuse because you cannot *adore* him.'

Though Charlotte said she was 'not quite in earnest' about parts of her letter, one wonders at the deep cynicism of her message here. Passion in women, the Grandmother concluded, renders them utterly vulnerable. Vividly in mind was a recent incident involving the most passionate female she knew, Mary Taylor, whose exceptional personality and high intelligence had roused Branwell's interest on the Taylors' visits to Haworth in 1839 and 1840. But as soon as Branwell had begun to realise that Mary might be just as interested in him as he was in her, he 'instantly conceived a sort of contempt for her', as Charlotte confided to Ellen. Charlotte was appalled and fascinated by Mary's predicament, 'the contempt, the remorse – the misconstruction which follow the development of feelings in themselves noble, warm – generous – devoted and profound – but which being too freely revealed – too frankly bestowed – are not estimated at their real value'. This tragic imbalance between what men and women could reveal of their feelings was to be one of Charlotte Brontë's most striking themes, her anger at it a call to arms.

One reason why Aunt Branwell might have been so put out about the midnight coffee episode, and all matters of household management, was that from the winter of 1839 the Brontës had to face the loss of Tabby. Her health had not recovered sufficiently after an accident in 1836, when she slipped on ice and dislocated her leg, and it was no longer possible for her to keep on working. Much to the sorrow of the family, it looked as if she would have to retire permanently to her sister's house in the village, and, though the girls insisted on maintaining the closest care of their old friend, the household was left with only John Brown's daughter Martha to serve it. Martha was strong, intelligent, able and loyal – as time amply showed – but she was only eleven years old. The Brontë sisters now had to perform the majority of the housework themselves.

Charlotte took over the cleaning and ironing, while Emily did the baking and managed the kitchen. Presumably, the family's diet became as simple as possible in this period: they were all fond of porridge, fortunately. 'We are such odd animals that we prefer this mode of contrivance to having a new face among us,' Charlotte told Ellen, and indeed it was rather peculiar for an ostensibly middle-class family to look after themselves so entirely. They didn't want Tabby 'supplanted by a stranger', who would break up the sacred ease of *home*: 'Human feelings are queer things,' Charlotte mused; 'I am much happier – black-leading the stoves – making the beds and sweeping the floors at home, than I should be living like a fine lady anywhere else.' That said, her first attempts at doing the ironing were dangerously unsuccessful and 'excited Aunt's wrath very much'. What is noteworthy here is that they were her first attempts.

On the first day of the new decade, Branwell went as a tutor to a family called Postlethwaite in Broughton-in-Furness. As his sisters busied themselves getting his linen ready for departure, making him shirts and collars, Charlotte contemplated how she would miss his enlivening presence, but was doubtful that his new position would suit, knowing his 'variable nature' and 'strong turn for active life'.

In the half-year he was in Broughton, Branwell lodged in a farmhouse outside town, the home of a surgeon called Fish. His charges at Broughton House were the eleven- and twelve-year-old sons of a local magistrate, but he spent most of his time in the Lake District working on his own poetry, walking, sketching and drinking. In a cheerful, bragging letter he wrote to his Haworth boon-companion John Brown, Branwell reported how he had taken part in a drunken brawl at an inn on his journey to the Lakes, but now in his post passed as 'A most calm, sedate, sober, abstemious, patient, mild-hearted, virtuous, gentlemanly philosopher, – the picture of good works, and the treasure-house of righteous thoughts'. At his landlord's house, they put away glasses and playing-cards when he entered the room, out of respect for his apparent temperance, and he was often to be found drinking tea with old ladies, a model of respectability. But 'as to the young ones!' he boasted, 'I have one sitting by me just now – fair-faced, blue-eyed, dark-haired, sweet eighteen – she little thinks the devil is so near her!'

Perhaps this young lady, or one like her, led to Branwell's dismissal in June following some scandalous, unrecorded revelation about his conduct. He had certainly been found by the Postlethwaites to be negligent of his duties and 'visibly the worst for drink' on more than one occasion, but Juliet Barker has made a strong case for Branwell having possibly fathered an illegitimate child during his Lancashire soujourn, based on Richard Monckton Milnes's note after talking to John Brown's family in 1859: '[Branwell] left Mr Postlethwaites with a natural child by one of the daughters or servants – which died.'

Branwell was not at all committed to a career as a tutor, and while in Broughton had written more soliciting letters, one to Thomas De Quincey and another to Hartley Coleridge, well known to the Brontës from his 1833 volume of poems and through his appearances in *Blackwood's Magazine* as 'The Old Bachelor'. Branwell's approach was much less brash and swaggering than in his letter to Wordsworth and paid off when Coleridge responded in a friendly manner, inviting Branwell to call on him in Rydal, just as Southey had invited Charlotte to Greta Bridge the previous year. Unlike Charlotte, it was easy and possible for Branwell to accept, and he set out from Broughton in the highest excitement on the first of May to meet the man he believed could be his conduit to 'that formidable personage, a London bookseller'. Branwell had originally sent Coleridge a long poem, 'At dead of midnight – drearily', and some versions of Horace's Odes. On the day they met, Coleridge encouraged him to continue with the latter, in which he found 'merit enough to commend without flattery'.

Branwell's dismissal in June cut short his chances to hob-nob with Coleridge again, but doesn't seem to have bothered him a bit. His sights were set on higher things now, and he returned home wiser but not sad at all. Whatever it was that he was accused of in Broughton, he concealed the worst of it and no one at home believed him to have been in the wrong. He was still 'my poor brother', an underappreciated golden boy, in Charlotte's eyes and in those of her sisters.

Branwell's successful connection with Hartley Coleridge encouraged Charlotte to solicit the writer's attention too, and she wrote to him sometime in late 1840, sending an early version of her attempted novel 'Ashworth' under the initials 'CT' – which fitted either her Angrian pseudonyms Captain Tree and Charles Townshend, or the persona of 'Charles Thunder' that she pursued with Ellen – and which concealed, most importantly, her sex, the issue that had distracted Southey so much. Coleridge sent CT's manuscript back with a note (now lost) that might have been brusquely candid, for Charlotte used the opportunity to reply in satirical vein, thanking him for having bothered to read her 'demi-semi novelette' but also suggesting that he had dismissed it too quickly: 'I do not think you would have hesitated to do the same to the immortal Sir Charles Grandison if Samuel Richardson Esqr. had sent you the first letters of Miss Harriet Byron – and Miss Lucy Selby for inspection.' His opinion left her little choice but to put the manuscript away 'till I get sense to produce something which shall at least *aim* at an object of some kind and meantime bind myself apprentice to a chemist and druggist if I am a young gentleman or to a Milliner and Dressmaker if I am a young lady'. She felt she had earned the right to tease him, and, under cover of CT's genderless initials, did so mercilessly. 'It is very pleasant to have something in one's power,' she wrote, refraining to divulge how she had got hold of his address (from Branwell, of course). To puzzle him further, she also seems to have introduced more special knowledge, not just of Hartley Coleridge's close relation to Wordsworth (which any fan might have found out) but of the complex imaginary kingdom that Coleridge had created for himself and retreated to obsessively as a child, called Ejuxria, so similar in kind to Angria and Gondal.

> It is very edifying and profitable to create a world out of one's own brain and people it with inhabitants who are like so many Melchisedecs – 'Without father, without mother, without descent, having neither beginning of days, nor end of life' . . . If you have ever been accustomed to such society Sir you will be aware how distinctly and vividly their forms and features fix themselves on the retina of that 'inward eye' which is said to be 'the bliss of solitude'

Coleridge might well have told Branwell about Ejuxria at their friendly meeting in May; its importance to him, just like Angria and Gondal to the Brontës, was a source both of comfort and of anxiety. It must have been odd to have this stranger, 'CT', hit on something so close to his own heart, and one can sense Charlotte relishing the power she had over him here, playful and mischievous, but also punishing him for his mistake in dismissing her.

Narratives like 'Ashworth', 'Caroline Vernon' and 'Henry Hastings' (jointly authored with Branwell) show Charlotte's strategic push away from the old Angrian tropes in the hope of breaking into the real world of letters with an acceptably realistic style of story. She made her intentions clear in a little manifesto, named by her later editors 'Fare-well to Angria', the survival of which seems amazing, given its insignificant look. It is written in faint pencil on a scrap of paper in size and type like the ones she used at Roe Head to write on surreptitiously during lessons, and the tiny writing floats off-line occasionally, as do the other manuscripts that were written with her eyes shut. She is addressing a 'Reader' who is familiar with the works she speaks of putting aside:

> It is no easy thing to dismiss from my imagination the images which have filled it so long. They were my friends & my intimate acquaintance & I could with little labour describe to you the faces, the voices, the actions, of those who peopled my thoughts by day & not seldom stole strangely even into my dreams by night. When I depart from these I feel almost as if I stood on the threshold of a home & were bidding farewell to its inmates. When I but strive to conjure up new inmates, I feel as if I had got into a distant country where every face was unknown & the character of all the population an enigma which it would take much study to comprehend & much talent to expound. Still, I long to quit for a while that burning clime where we have sojourned too long.

But it would take a while longer to put the shadow-world behind her and forgo the heat and excitement of that 'burning clime'.

Charlotte felt obliged to look for another job, but did so with obvious reluctance. 'I wish [the Misses Wooler] or somebody else would get me a Situation,' she complained to Ellen. 'I have answered advertise-ments without number – but my applications have met with no success.' She was looking for jobs near home and in small families, to avoid the difficulties of Stonegappe, for, as she told Henry Nussey the following year, 'it is indeed a hard thing for flesh and blood to leave home – especially a *good* home – not a wealthy or splendid one – my home is humble and unattractive to strangers but to me it contains what I shall find nowhere else in the world – [?the] profound, and intense affection which brothers and sisters feel for each other when their minds are cast in the same mould, their ideas drawn from the same source – when they have clung to each other from childhood and when family disputes have never sprung up to divide them.'

The post she went to in March 1841 was as governess to the White family of Upperwood House, Apperley Bridge. It was very near to Woodhouse Grove, where her mother Maria had been living with the Fennells in 1812 when she met Patrick Brontë, so the associations should have been comforting. Mr White was a merchant, and Charlotte liked him well enough (she did always have a tendency to judge men less harshly than their wives); Mrs White struck her as shallow and snobbish. Her charges were a girl of eight and a boy of six, but, again, it was the extra duties, and endless amounts of sewing, that annoyed the governess most, and that emphasised her servant status humiliatingly. Though she had hoped the Whites would be less condescending towards her than the Sidgwicks had been, she knew from the start she could not be comfortable under 'the heavy duty of endeavouring to seem always easy, cheerful & conversible with those whose ideas and feelings are nearly as incomprehensible to *me*, as probably mine (if I shewed them unreservedly) would be to *them*'.

It is doubtful that Charlotte *ever* seemed 'cheerful & conversible' in her governess work, for she knew that she lacked all the necessary qualities of temperament for it. Many years later, advising her friend W. S. Williams on careers for his daughters, she cautioned that a governess had to be 'Of pleasing exterior (that is always an advantage – children like it –) good sense, obliging disposition, cheerful, healthy, possessing a good average capacity, but no prominent master talent to make her miserable by its cravings for exercise by its mutiny under restraint'. Given those rather bland excellences, a governess could indeed be happy and successful, but Charlotte knew herself to be disqualified on several grounds.

A Mrs Slade recalled many years later (when Charlotte was dead, and famous as the author of *Jane Eyre*) that she had a vivid memory of the young governess 'sitting apart from the rest of the family, in a corner of the room, poring, in her short-sighted way, over a book'. Her impression was of a person ill at ease, 'who desired to escape notice and to avoid taking part in the general conversation' – exactly the character that Charlotte complained of being forced to assume, and that her heroine articulates so well. In the brief holiday she had at home, Charlotte planned avidly to get herself out of this obnoxious existence for good.

Branwell's next job after his dismissal from Broughton was in a totally new direction: he became a booking clerk at Sowerby Bridge Station

on the new Leeds-to-Manchester railway in September 1840. It was not quite the sort of transport that his admired Lake poets wrote about, but Branwell seemed happy with the move, as it allowed him time to write and draw. His spirits were buoyant, in fact, and when his friend Leyland's brother Francis met him for the first time, it was a young man on the way up, not the way down, who emerged from the office, laughing and talking, who 'seemed to be qualified for a much better position than the one he had chosen'. Branwell was perfectly cast in the part of undiscovered genius – as long as the discovery didn't take too long.

The recollections that Branwell's acquaintances left of him at this time give some idea of the rushes of energy that frequently possessed him and made him valued company, especially at convivial, all-male drinking sessions. One friend recalled how when Branwell was stirred by 'some topic that he was acquainted with, or some author he loved, he would rise from his seat, and, in beautiful language, describe the author's character, with a zeal and fluency I had never heard equalled'. Francis Leyland witnessed similar vatic outpourings when art and literature were being discussed: 'almost involuntarily, [he] would rise to his feet, and, with a beaming countenance, treat the subject with a vivid flow of imagination, displaying the rich stores of his information with wondrous and enthralling eloquence.' 'Almost involuntarily' recalls Charlotte's escapist removals into 'the world below', only here there was an audience, and alcohol. Branwell suffered none of the public shyness of his sisters, so his moments of imaginative flight in the company of others perhaps give us some idea of how the siblings *all* behaved, when they were together at home. Charlotte was known to have such capacities herself at school, and would very occasionally 'dramatise when her spirits rose to the necessary pitch of excitement'. Mary and Martha Taylor's brother Joe had heard such reports of Charlotte's flights that on one occasion he determined to orchestrate a demonstration, declaring he was going 'to stir Miss Brontë up to the exhibiting point' – but she was forewarned, and refused to oblige. It was exactly this potential to burst out of character that had provoked Mr Pryce into his proposal.

Emily was formidable both in her character of 'The Major' and socially, withering people with her silences and disapproval. Anne was perhaps the only true introvert in the family, having 'a remarkably

taciturn, still, thoughtful nature, reserved even with her nearest of kin', as Charlotte described it. This might have been provoked, and certainly not helped, by her speech defect, which would have made it difficult to get a word in edgeways with her excitable siblings. Emily's particular care of Anne, and sympathetic silence, shows a sensitivity to this issue.

Charlotte and Branwell were therefore a natural pair, rivals for the world's attention, though, as they grew up, Charlotte's opportunities to be stirred 'to the exhibiting point' shrank to almost none, while Branwell paraded a shabby version almost every night in the pub, a village Demosthenes presiding over homespun orations. But, underneath the bluster and egotism, Branwell was possibly more like his sisters than has been recognised and did not feel at home in his fate of having to go out into the world and make masculine noises. William Heaton saw a much quieter side to him: 'I shall never forget his love for the sublime and beautiful works of Nature, nor how he would tell of the lovely flowers and rare plants he had observed by the mountain stream and woodland rill.'

Branwell transferred from Sowerby Bridge to Luddenden Foot in March 1841, a new but insignificant station on the Manchester-to-Leeds line, housed in a temporary wooden hut, with little to do all day but read or write alone in his office, or go to the inn for society.* Emily's sardonic remark was that 'it *looks* like getting on at any rate.' Branwell recalled his year at Luddenden Foot as a 'nightmare' of 'malignant yet cold debauchery', and in a rare moment of self-knowledge said he had been 'lost . . . to all I really liked'. He was to surprise everyone, though, just a few weeks into his new post, when he became the first of the siblings to achieve their joint dream – publication – with the appearance in *The Halifax Guardian* of a poem called 'Heaven and Earth'. Branwell had used the pseudonym 'Northangerland', which must have been shocking for Charlotte to see in the local press, as if the personae

---

* The depths of Branwell's boredom might be suggested by a story John Brown told some visitors to Haworth in 1866: 'on one occasion when he was station master, being hurried over some necessary letter writing, two important letters remained to be written before the next train came in. The train was in sight, so Branwell, taking two sheets of paper and two pens, sat down and wrote two letters at the same time on two entirely different subjects' ('A Visit to Haworth in 1866', *BST*, 15:78 (1968)).

Maria Branwell in 1799, aged sixteen.

Patrick Brontë as a young man.

26 Market Street, Thornton, the house where Charlotte, Branwell, Emily and Anne Brontë were born.

The oldest known picture of Haworth Parsonage, an ambrotype taken from the church tower in the 1850s. It shows the building as the Brontës knew it, before the extension and alterations made by Reverend Brontë's successor, John Wade.

(*above*) 1853 plan of Haworth, drawn up by the Board of Health, showing the top of the town, and (*from left to right*) the Parsonage, the church school, the church, the post office and the Black Bull pub.

(*middle*) A view of Haworth in the early nineteenth century, showing Bridgehouse Beck and Ivy Bank Mill in the foreground and St Michael's Church and the Parsonage on the hill in the distance. A corner of the weaving shed at Bridgehouse Mill is visible at the bottom right.

(*left*) The interior of Haworth old church in the 1860s, much as the Brontës would have known it, showing the old gallery in the south-east corner, the organ loft suspended above the centre of the church and Reverend Brontë's pulpit along the south wall. The family's marble memorial stone (reinstated in the new church) can be seen in the distance, on the east wall.

Cowan Bridge School in its first year, 1824.

Charlotte's drawing of Roe Head School.

Four of Charlotte's minuscule manuscripts: her earliest surviving story, 'There was once a little girl and her name was Ane' (*top left*), and three issues of 'The Young Men's Magazine', from 1830.

Emily's Diary Paper for 26 June 1837, with a sketch of herself (*on the right*) and Anne writing at the dining table, with the tin box in which they kept the diaries at her elbow.

Arthur Wellesley, later Marquis of Douro, Duke of Zamorna and King of Angria, as drawn by Charlotte, *c.* 1834.

(*above*) Branwell Brontë, a self-portrait.
(*right*) Emily Jane Brontë, by Branwell Brontë
– the only surviving fragment of a larger
portrait known as *The Gun Group*.

Anne Brontë in 1833,
aged thirteen, drawn
by Charlotte.

The Brontë Sisters: Branwell's portrait of Anne, Emily and Charlotte, dating from about 1834, with his own image painted over in the centre. The damage to the canvas was done during decades of storage on the top of a wardrobe in Banagher, where the second Mrs Arthur Bell Nicholls found it after her husband's death in 1906.

The rue d'Isabelle, Brussels, in the 1850s, showing the Cathedral in the distance and the Pensionnat Heger, with its courtyard and tree-lined garden, on the left. Most of the street was destroyed in the early years of the twentieth century in a radical restructuring of roads in the quartier.

The interior of the Cathedral of SS-Michel-et-Gudule in Brussels in 1840, three years before Charlotte made her confession there.

The Heger Family, 1846, by Ange François, showing Constantin Heger in the background and Zoë Heger surrounded by her children.

(*above*) Part of Charlotte's letter to Constantin Heger, dated 8 January 1845, showing how the paper was torn up and then meticulously mended with thread.

(*left*) The prospectus that Charlotte and her sisters produced in 1844 for the school that never opened.

of her imagination were advancing across the borders of her two worlds.★

Branwell was sustained through his tedious work-days by this success and the promise of more to come (he placed another poem, this time a very topical one on the Afghan War, in *The Leeds Intelligencer* the next year). He had an indulgent circle of friends at Luddenden Foot, including Francis Grundy, a railway engineer working on the new lines in Yorkshire, through whom Branwell hoped for promotion. Grundy was one of few outsiders invited to visit the Parsonage, and he left a vividly unflattering description of its occupants: the father 'distantly courteous, white-haired, tall' greeted him with ponderous politeness, whereas the daughters said nothing, possibly because they sensed Grundy's judgement of their persons – 'distant and distrait, large of nose, small of figure, red of hair, prominent of spectacles'. Even Branwell, reputedly the best-looking of the young Brontës, he found 'the reverse of attractive at first sight'.

On her birthday in July 1841, Emily Brontë sat at home, writing her four-yearly Diary Paper, to be kept for comparison with her lot in 1837 and in 1845. 'A scheme is at present in agitation for setting us up in a school of our own,' she reported, with her characteristic tone of detached interest; 'as yet nothing is determined but I hope and trust it may go on and prosper and answer our highest expectations. This day 4-years I wonder whether we shall still be dragging on in our present condition or established to our heart's content Time will show –'

> I guess that at the time appointed for the opening of this paper – we (i.e.) Charlotte, Anne and I shall be all merrily seated in our own sitting-room in some pleasant and flourishing seminary having just gathered in for the midsummer holydays our debts will be paid off and we shall have cash in hand to a considerable amount. papa Aunt and Branwell will either have been – or be coming – to visit us – it will be a fine warm summery evening. very different from this bleak look-out Anne and I will perchance slip out into the garden a [illeg.] minutes to

★ The date of publication was 5 June 1841. I am assuming that his sisters *did* get to know of this feat, as Branwell would have been the least capable person on earth of keeping it to himself.

peruse our papers. I hope either this [o]r something better will be the
case —

Anne, writing her own Diary Paper on the same day, far away in Scarborough with the family called Robinson for whom she now worked, also mentioned the school plan, and how she hoped it would happen. She spoke as if it were not in her hands: 'nothing definite is settled about it yet, and we do not know whether we shall be able to or not.'

Charlotte was the one sister pressing to make the scheme succeed, and she found an ally in Aunt Branwell, who thought it a very reasonable solution to the problem of both living and working for three poor, possibly unmarriageable spinsters. The example of the Misses Wooler was encouraging, and the Brontë girls were intellectually so far above the average that there was no question of their capability. Aunt Branwell generously spoke of lending them £150 to get started, as long as they could get enough pupils to start up and find 'an eligible situation'. No one was thinking of siting the school in Haworth Parsonage at this point; Charlotte had a fancy to try Bridlington, where she had had such an enjoyable holiday with Ellen. Ellen herself featured in Charlotte's hopes for the plan – she wondered if her friend might be persuaded to join her, Emily and Anne. The sentence containing this suggestion was heavily scored through by Ellen later, who for some reason did not want the offer remembered.

The kind of establishment that Charlotte imagined might have been like the one her heroine Elizabeth envisions for herself in the story 'Henry Hastings', a school for older girls only (not the usual mix of all ages and abilities), 'those who had already mastered the elements of education – reading, commenting, explaining, leaving it to them to listen – if they failed, comfortably conscious that the blame would rest on her pupils, not herself'. Like Emily imagining herself debt-free and on permanent holiday, Charlotte's idea of running a school was not very realistic, but she saw it as the only way to secure a modicum of freedom. She understood by 1841 that she could not survive as a governess and she did not want to go back to teaching in someone else's school, even though Miss Wooler that year asked her to take over the running of Heald's House. The example that encouraged Charlotte most was that of Mary Taylor. For some years now, the well-travelled

Taylors had been sharing their French newspapers with Charlotte and sending her 'bales' of French books (one package contained about forty volumes – an education in itself). Mr Taylor was especially keen to have his girls finish their schooling abroad and acquire languages. But when he died early in 1841, the family began to break up quickly. Mary did not get on well with her mother and, with her brother Waring, was already thinking of emigrating to the other side of the world – New Zealand. Her brothers Joe and John were going to live at the cottage attached to Hunsworth Mill, and the girls were off to school in Brussels, where Martha had already spent a year.

Back with the White family at Upperwood House, Charlotte read a letter from Mary describing her travels in Belgium and Holland that summer that seemed to light a fuse in her heart:

> I hardly know what swelled to my throat as I read her letter – such a vehement impatience of restraint & steady work. such a strong wish for wings – wings such as wealth can furnish – such an urgent thirst to see – to know – to learn – something internal seemed to expand boldly for a minute – I was tantalized with the consciousness of faculties unexercised

The degradations she experienced as an employee and the stifling of potential that led to 'estrangement from one's real character', as she expressed it poignantly to Ellen, did not, surely, have to be tolerated for ever. The only reasonable escape route was to set up their own school, and the essential qualification to attract pupils would be languages, culture, 'finish'. An ardent correspondence with Mary and Martha followed, a careful appeal to Aunt Branwell for funds, an anxious wait before Aunt agreed to lend her two elder nieces the large sum, £150, necessary to cover their expenses for a year. Then, gloriously, Charlotte was able to hand in her notice to Mr and Mrs White and announce to them that she and her sister were going abroad, to study.

7

In a Strange Land

1842

As late as three weeks before they left for Brussels, Charlotte and Emily had been making plans to transfer to a school in Lille, but by the middle of January they had changed their minds again and come to an agreement with the proprietors of a highly recommended *pensionnat des demoiselles* within the city of Brussels that was almost within their budget. Charlotte had done the groundwork, and it was the 'simple earnest tone' of her letters, carefully inquiring about the costs and every aspect of the curriculum, that persuaded the owner, Madame Zoë Heger, to do what she could to encourage the prospective foreign students. 'These are the daughters of an English pastor, of moderate means, anxious to learn with an ulterior view of instructing others,' her husband remembered them saying to each other. 'Let us name a specific sum, within which all expenses shall be included.' Monsieur Heger proved a sensitive reader from the first.

So, on a cold February morning in 1842, Charlotte and Emily Brontë left Haworth with their father en route for Brussels, via London. They were accompanied by Mary Taylor and her brother Joe, old hands at the journey, whose experience helped the Brontës face some dizzying novelties: their first long-distance railway ride, their first journey by steamship, and not least (for the girls) their first sight of London. Patrick Brontë found them all accommodation at the Chapter Coffee House in Paternoster Row in the heart of the city, a tavern frequented by Dr Johnson and Thomas Chatterton in the previous century and still the haunt of literary hacks and booksellers; a very businesslike hostelry 'solely frequented by men', as far as Mrs Gaskell could tell when she went to see it in the 1850s. It was where Patrick had stayed in his student days travelling through London, and he was not the man to branch out unnecessarily, however inappropriate it might be as a place to lodge three young ladies.

The party arrived at night and had their first proper sight of London the next morning, an experience reflected in *Villette* when Lucy Snowe wakes in the capital for the first time and sees St Paul's and the City from her inn window: 'Above my head, above the house-tops, co-elevate almost with the clouds, I saw a solemn orbed mass, dark-blue and dim – THE DOME. While I looked, my inner self moved; my spirit shook its always-fettered wings half loose; I had a sudden feeling as if I, who had never yet truly lived, were at last about to taste life.' Mary Taylor, who, like Ellen Nussey, had visited the capital numerous times, was amused at Charlotte's determination to take in as much as she could of this precious treasure-store: 'she seemed to think our business was and ought to be, to see all the pictures and statues we could. She knew the artists, and knew where other productions of theirs were to be found.' After a couple of days of non-stop cultural bingeing, which included visits to Westminster Abbey, the British Museum and the National Gallery, everyone was exhausted. 'I don't remember what we saw except St Paul's,' Mary said later.*

Charlotte was sea-sick throughout the fourteen-hour crossing from London to Ostend and staggered ashore to face a long slow coach journey on to Brussels. But excitement trumped exhaustion, and to her hungry eye the flat, rainy, Flemish landscape they passed through was intensely interesting, just as it was for William Crimsworth, in her novel *The Professor*, when he makes the identical journey: 'not a beautiful, scarcely a picturesque object met my eye along the whole route, yet to me, all was beautiful, all was more than picturesque.' Patrick Brontë, as excited as any of them at his first trip to the Continent, had made himself a little phonetic phrasebook so that he could get by in French as the head of their party. The phrases, adapted to his accent, covered the usual travellers' concerns about accommodation and food, but also gave a little leeway for small talk, and one can imagine him sticking his head out of the window of the coach to ask 'Oo somay noo a prazong?' or to observe chattily 'La shaump-an-y me paray shaurmaung'. At the inns along the way, he was equipped to be 'tre caunetong'

---

* Charlotte complained many years later (when she was feeling out of sympathy with him) that Joe Taylor had dragged them from sight to sight exhaustingly, but at the time Mary said it was the other way round and that Charlotte was the relentless one.

with the beds, if appropriate, and able to ask for 'me soaliay' from the boot-boy, though one wonders if they had difficulty finding inns in the first place, if 'Maungtnaung indiqe moa un bong o'berzh sil voo play Mosyoo' is actually what he said to anyone in the street.

When they arrived in Brussels on the evening of 15 February, the Brontës were met by Reverend Evan Jenkins, chaplain to the British Embassy and the brother of an old friend of Patrick Brontë from Hartshead days. The Jenkinses were prominent members of a sizeable English colony in Brussels of about 2,000, many of whom had settled in the city after the victory at Waterloo in 1815. The English had their own newsletter, *The British and Continental Mercury*, published by an English bookseller whose shop made a natural meeting-place for the ex-pats (though the unsociable Brontës don't seem to have made much use of it). Anglican services in this thoroughly Catholic town were held in the Chapel Royal on an elegant *haute ville* square just a few minutes' walk from where the girls were going to be living, and an oddly dressed assortment of Englishers could be seen there every Sunday: army families, businessmen, widows – many of them in Brussels for the sake of economy, for it was a much cheaper place to live than England.

Patrick Brontë stayed a week with the Jenkinses to make sure that the girls were settled at their new school and to see the sights of Brussels, prime among which was the famous battlefield, only ten miles out of the city. Patrick was so enamoured of the Iron Duke ('the greatest man in the world', as he described him in a letter to the press the following year) that the proximity of Waterloo must have heavily influenced his decision to accompany the girls in the first place, might indeed have affected his acquiescence to the whole Brussels scheme. The battlefield had been a tourist draw while still strewn with the dead in 1815; by 1842 it was a vast memorial park, landscaped for ease of walking and embellished with a number of massy obelisks. In later life, Patrick Brontë needed little encouragement to reminisce about his visit and moralise about its significance, but his daughters had no time for sightseeing, so missed the excursion.

The city that the girls had come to live in had been substantially redesigned and reorganised since 1830, following its emergence as the capital of the newly created nation, Belgium. The old Brabantian medieval quarter was still a warren of narrow streets where buildings leant inwards and overshadowed the cobbles, and where guilds, trades and much humbler housing were all jumbled together, running down through all the mid-levels of society to the very lowest. High above these streets, like a three-dimensional model of the city's evolving social life, were the French-style *parcs* and *grands boulevards*, the creamy elegant villas of the rue Royale, and stately palace and government buildings – neither too obviously showy nor splendid, in keeping with a modern constitutional monarchy.

Access to the rue d'Isabelle from the direction of the Parc and place Royale was like a drop into the past, down a set of steps so long and steep that the top of them was higher than the Pensionnat's chimneys.* The street had been named after the Spanish Infanta and built as a short-cut from the old Palais de Coudenberg to the great cathedral of SS-Michel-et-Gudule, which stood only half a mile away and dominated the skyline. Another half-mile or so would take one to the Grand-Place and the place de la Monnaie, the city's most beautiful old squares. The cathedral bell was audible all day, calling the faithful to Matins, to Compline, to Mass. It was the voice of the quarter, just as its two towers dwarfed everything else on the skyline and drew one's eye and steps along the street towards it.

The Pensionnat Heger, where the Jenkinses escorted Patrick Brontë and his daughters on the morning after their arrival in Brussels, stood on the former exercise ground of an aristocratic guild of crossbowmen. Since then a hospice and a convent had both occupied the site, and the buildings where the school was set up in 1830 – the year of the revolution – were only a few decades old, with the exception of a quaintly decorated theatre at the end of the garden, dating from the seventeenth century and used as a recreation area and hall.

The owner of the school, Madame Zoë Heger, née Parent, was a

---

* Now that the old quarter has been largely obliterated by even more extensive remodelling in the late nineteenth and early twentieth centuries, the rue d'Isabelle exists only as a fragment of the medieval street that itself was unknown to the Brontës, buried in the foundations of the current Palais de Coudenberg. The whole area round where the Pensionnat used to stand is oddly jigsaw like and confusing, but the connections between the contemporary quarter and the one the Brontës knew have been brilliantly illustrated by Eric Ruijssenaars in *Charlotte Brontë's Promised Land* and *The Pensionnat Revisited*, with maps drawn by Selina Busch.

38-year-old Frenchwoman whose family had fled the revolution in 1789 and settled in Brussels. She had been brought up as a deeply pious and conservative Catholic, educated by an aunt who had formerly been a nun but started a school for girls after the religious order she had been a member of was disestablished. The school, which used to be housed in the Parent family home, was handed on to Zoë in the 1830s and moved to the premises in the rue d'Isabelle, where the enterprising young woman built up its academic reputation and also made it into a successful business, with about ninety pupils in 1842–3. She had married in 1836 and managed to combine her work with a full family life: when the Brontës arrived at her door, Madame Heger was already the mother of three small children and heavily pregnant with her fourth.

The neat, clean establishment she showed them round that February morning was set out around three sides of a square courtyard, one side of which fronted on the rue d'Isabelle and contained the living quarters of the directrice and her family. The ground floor of the school building housed three light and airy classrooms and a refectory that was also used as a general study area; upstairs was a dormitory and oratory, with a statue of the Virgin Mary under which a votive candle burned continually. One imagines the Brontës passed quickly by this evidence of the institution's religious affiliations. The school's reputation for educational excellence must have been very impressive indeed to overcome their deep antipathy to anything to do with Catholics.

Mr Brontë met the directrice one more time before he left for England later that week, but he did not meet her husband, who taught for the greater part of the day at the Athénée Royal, the most prestigious boys' school in Brussels, which stood immediately adjacent to the Pensionnat and was divided from it by a high wall. To discourage any impropriety, that part of the garden that could be seen from the windows of the boys' school, a shady walk of lime and laburnum, was out of bounds to the pupils and known as the 'alleé défendue'. The rest of the sizeable garden – quite a rarity in such a central city property – was one of the school's proudest features and a delightful pleasure-ground, beautifully laid out and maintained, with an arbour and a number of huge, venerable pear trees, famous for their yield and quality of fruit.

Patrick Brontë travelled home via Lille, Dunkirk and Calais, at a total cost, he was satisfied to note, of £23.10s. His three weeks away from parish duties was unprecedented, and this fascinating, if nerve-racking, expedition to the Continent was never repeated.

Charlotte and Emily were left on their own to adapt to a thoroughly novel environment, Charlotte, at least, relishing the change in the first stressful but stimulating months. To Ellen, she reported that 'the difference in Country & religion makes a broad line of demarcation between us & all the rest we are completely isolated in the midst of numbers – yet I think I am never unhappy – my present life is so delightful so congenial to my nature compared to that of a Governess – my time constantly occupied passes too rapidly.' Due to their foreignness and age, a corner of the dormitory was curtained off for the Brontë sisters, to allow a little privacy. They did not join the rest of the school for prayers, went alone to the Protestant Chapel Royal on Sundays and probably, like William Crimsworth in *The Professor*, said their own 'heretical' grace to themselves before meals.

For all its conventual background and structure, the Pensionnat was the home of a lively, formidably active and intellectual young couple with a growing family in the middle of a vibrant capital city, and the atmosphere was very different from that of any school Charlotte or Emily had formerly known. The effect of having both married women and men on the staff was not lost on Charlotte, who described Madame Heger with admiration as being 'of precisely the same cast of mind degree of cultivation & quality of character as Miss Catherine Wooler – I think the severe points are a little softened because she has not been disappointed & consequently soured – in a word – she is a married instead of a maiden lady.' Charlotte was less enthusiastic about the resident female staff – 'there are 3 teachers in the school Mademoiselle Blanche – mademoiselle Sophie & Mademoiselle Marie – The first two have no particular character – one is an old maid & the other will be one' – but she was impressed and perhaps slightly intimidated by the fact that 'no less than seven masters attend to teach the different branches of education – French drawing – music, singing, writing, arithmetic, and German.'

The most prominent of those masters and 'always an immense favourite' with the girls was the directrice's husband, a short, dark, cigar-smoking man who taught rhetoric and French literature. Constantin Georges Romain Heger was five years younger than his wife and had a more romantic and chequered background. His family were originally from the Palatinate (which today can be found in west Germany) and had once owned a jewellery business on the rue Royale, but a reversal of their fortunes in the 1820s had forced Constantin to move to Paris alone, at the incredibly young age of fourteen. He got a job as a legal secretary with a view to a career in the law, but struggled to support himself on a clerk's meagre wages and had to join the 'claque', or paid applauders, of a theatre to get access to the plays he adored but couldn't afford to see. By 1829 he was back in Brussels, where he got a job as a teacher of French and mathematics at the Athénée and met and married a girl called Marie-Josephine Noyer, with whom he had a child. He was still only twenty.

The next year he was involved in the revolution that founded the new Belgian nation, a revolt of the predominantly French-speaking, Catholic southern Netherlands provinces against their Dutch, Protestant, northern counterparts. In the four days of intense street fighting that took place in September 1830, Heger stood with the Nationalist rebels at the barricades and saw his young brother-in-law die there. Perhaps he resembled the young man at the top of the pyramidal form of triumphant citizens in Wappers's epic painting *Épisode des journées de septembre 1830 sur la place de l'Hôtel de Ville de Bruxelles*, whose finger is pointing at the proclamation that was the focus of the Nationalists' demands and that, by dint of this short but bloody action, shaped the new state. The picture expresses the energy and idealism of the revolutionary generation, and also its profound romanticism, all of which Heger personified.

In his private life, the young teacher was fated to suffer a terrible loss in the founding years of the new country, when both his wife and child died of cholera in 1833, a tragedy that later seemed to explain the fits of melancholy, moroseness and quick temper that were as much a part of his character as the outbursts of great tenderness and sympathy. By the time Charlotte Brontë met him, he had been married to his second wife, Zoë Parent, for six years and was thirty-three years old, only eight years Charlotte's senior.

The surprising pleasure Charlotte found in her new life had its source in the novelty of living at close quarters with this extremely interesting man. She introduced him in her letter to Ellen with studied casualness and satire:

> There is one individual of whom I have not yet spoken Monsieur Heger the husband of Madame – he is professor of Rhetoric a man of power as to mind but very choleric & irritable in temperament – a little, black, ugly being with a face that varies in expression, sometimes he borrows the lineaments of an insane Tom-cat – sometimes those of a delirious Hyena – occasionally – but very seldom he discards these perilous attractions and assumes an air not above a hundred degrees removed from what you would call mild & gentleman-like he is very angry with me just at present because I have written a translation which he chose to stigmatize as *peu correct* – not because it was particularly so in reality but because he happened to be in a bad humour when he read it.

There was an obvious difficulty, however, going back to being a school-girl after being a teacher and governess, and having to accept the same discipline as a teenager. Charlotte was so determined to prove herself a model pupil that she submitted to the situation uncomplainingly and took immense care over all her work, writing out her *devoirs* in the neat-est handwriting, on hand-drawn lines of perfect regularity. The titles were usually drawn like engraved lettering, and the margins elegantly double-ruled, ready to receive Monsieur's corrections. The content of these essays developed dramatically over the two years under his direc-tion, but the first, a retelling of a fable by La Fontaine,* seems like a very retrograde performance on the part of the 25-year-old, whose works – albeit unknown and unpublished – included the extraordinary sophistications of 'Caroline Vernon', 'Ashworth' and 'Henry Hastings', and whose knowledge of French, far from being rudimentary (like Emily's), had stretched to verse translation of Voltaire and prizes from Miss Wooler.

In the classroom, Charlotte's intellectual superiority was immedi-ately obvious. The Belgian girls were impressed, though not in a friendly way, and Charlotte did nothing to make herself agreeable to them. One day, their simmering mutual disdain came out when some of the class picked a fight with Charlotte on the subject of England's conduct towards Napoleon. Feelings about the late emperor had been

---

* CB's essay 'L'Ingratitude' came to light in 2012, having been lost for almost a hun-dred years. It is dated 16 March 1842. See *London Review of Books*, 8 March 2012, and Brian Bracken's notes.

revived by the long-delayed repatriation of his remains from St Helena to Paris in 1840, and no doubt Charlotte was fiery in the defence of her country and Wellington in particular. Louise de Bassompierre, a fellow classmate, intervened and appealed for calm, earning Charlotte's gratitude. Louise later wryly attributed to it the fact that the character given her surname in *Villette* was 'less disagreeable than some of the others'.

Some interesting reminiscences of the Brontës in Brussels were left by the family of a doctor called Wheelwright who had given up his practice in England because of failing sight and moved to Brussels to save money. All five Wheelwright girls arrived at the Pensionnat in 1842, and Frances remembered Charlotte as 'a diminutive, short-sighted, retiring personage, of remarkable talents and studious disposition, and very neat in appearance' – unlike her sister, who seemed of 'an unsociable, unattractive, unsympathetic disposition; lanky and untidy in person'. Emily's clothes caused widespread dismay: she had a leg-of-mutton sleeved dress, horribly out of fashion, but, worse still, she refused to display adequate shame about it. When challenged by the other girls, she simply replied that she was 'as God made her', and passed on. During the recreation periods in the garden, the Brontë sisters invariably kept apart from the other pupils, walking together in silence, 'Emily, though so much the taller, leaning on her sister. Charlotte would always answer when spoken to, taking the lead in replying to any remark addressed to both; Emily rarely spoke to any one.' Frances Wheelwright disliked the younger Brontë on sight, but thought she had even greater genius than her sister, and noted Charlotte's awed affection for her.

The Brontës didn't see much of their friends Mary and Martha Taylor, despite being only a few miles away from the school at Koekelberg. The establishments were quite different, and both sets of sisters were fully occupied. Mrs Jenkins had issued an open invitation to the Brontës to come to them on Sundays and holidays, but she soon let it lapse, as their company was simply too discomforting. Emily hardly ever opened her mouth, and Charlotte, though she could sometimes be persuaded to speak, and did so intelligently, had the utmost trouble making eye-contact and would wheel round on her chair to avoid it, ending up addressing the wall. The Jenkins' sons, John and Edward, never looked forward to escorting the Brontës home, as the walks would inevitably be conducted in a garroted silence. And this was among well-disposed English Protestants, friends at one remove from their father. With the girls at the Pensionnat, they must have appeared strange indeed.

Charlotte decided early on that it was easier to hate the Belgians than to worry about how uncomfortable they made her feel: 'If the national character of the Belgians is to be measured by the character of most of the girls in this school,' she wrote to Ellen, 'it is a character singularly cold, selfish, animal and inferior – they are besides very mutinous and difficult for the teachers to manage – and their principles are rotten to the core – we avoid them – which is not difficult to do – as we have the brand of Protestantism and Anglicism upon us.' She elaborated these views in *The Professor*, where the narrator, a young Englishman teaching in a Brussels pensionnat, gives a scorching critique of the schoolgirls in his care, whom he exposes as mendacious, self-interested, calculating and far from the angels of popular myth. National characteristics condemn some of them, such as the Flamandes, to 'deformity of person and imbecility of intellect', in his view; others have a propensity to malevolence and agitation. Crimsworth believes that the Roman Catholic faith may be held responsible for most of their vices and bad habits of mind, but even among the British Protestants he makes a distinction between the class of ex-pats – tainted by long exposure to Catholics – and the rarer 'British English' girl, the only kind worth anything.

It was a cause of envy that Monsieur Heger gave the Brontë sisters separate lessons, to take account of their mature age and foreignness. He didn't work them through the rudiments of the language, but started immediately on examples of classic French literature, and more recent works from his wide and avid reading. His taste was for the Romantics of his own language – Lamartine, Hugo, Chateaubriand and the essayists Mirabeau and Delavigne, all of whose works he could declaim in sonorous tones – and his teaching method was the same as he used with generations of his pupils: he would read aloud a carefully chosen passage and meticulously analyse its effects in discussion with the students. Then they would choose or be set a topic for composition 'attuned to the same key, either grave or gay, of the model of excellence he had given, but of a sufficiently different character to make anything resembling unintelligent imitation impossible'. At first, Emily strongly objected to being asked to do 'imitations' of any sort – she thought, with justification, it might stifle originality rather than help it – but Heger prevailed, and his method proved useful to both sisters. He was a stickler for revising and improving, and the girls soon got used to seeing the margins of their work dark with his commentaries. Rough copy, fair copy, corrected exercise: this was a discipline that neither Brontë had ever been required to think about. Charlotte had hitherto written whatever came into her head, and rarely shaped or revised it.

Charlotte was faced with a conflict of loyalties. She wanted, from a sense of duty, pride and growing personal inclination, to please Monsieur Heger, but the sister with whom she was so interdependent emotionally had an antipathy towards him, and an unsubmissive attitude to his pedagogy. Monsieur Heger and Emily 'don't draw well together at all', Charlotte reported in May, and though by July she was relieved to note that the Hegers were beginning to appreciate 'the valuable points of [Emily's] character under her singularities', one feels that their hosts were the ones making allowances, not the younger Brontë.

Emily clearly accentuated her 'singularities' to keep herself at a remove. A strange account of her reception in Brussels filtered through to Elizabeth Gaskell when she was writing Charlotte's biography that Emily had 'absolutely *repelled* people by her cold sullen manner'. It is clear from what Charlotte said later that Emily was struggling valiantly against feelings of profound homesickness. In February 1843 Mary Taylor wrote to Ellen from Germany, eager for gossip about how Emily's exposure to society (the most extended ordeal of the kind she ever underwent) had affected her. How could 'the newly acquired qualities . . . *fit* in, in the same head & heart that is occupied by the old ones'? Mary marvelled. 'Imagine Emily turning over prints or "taking wine" with any stupid fop & preserving her temper & politeness!'

The answer was, the newly acquired qualities didn't fit in at all, as Emily's *devoirs* for Monsieur Heger indicate. Asked to compose a letter of invitation and reply, Emily took the opportunity to write a letter from a piano teacher to her pupil, crying off a musical party and advising her pupil to 'choose a time when everyone is occupied with something other than music, for I fear that your performance will be a little too remarkable'. It's a joke as acidic as Mr Bennet's in *Pride and Prejudice* about his daughter Mary having 'delighted us long enough' (and makes one wonder if Emily had read Austen's novel – Charlotte had not at this date). Heger must have learnt to be on his mettle when he opened Emily's *cahiers*: given the subject of 'Filial Love', she handed in something like a harangue from a pulpit. God takes a dim view of human baseness, the schoolgirl argued, and knows that his command-ment 'Honour thy father and thy mother' can be enforced only through fear and threats.

When he was interviewed by Elizabeth Gaskell fifteen years later, Constantin Heger said he felt Emily to have been the more remarkable of the two Brontë sisters, with a head for logic and argument 'unusual in a man, and rare indeed in a woman'. 'She should have been a man – a great navigator,' he said. 'Her powerful reason would have deduced new spheres of discovery from the knowledge of the old; and her strong imperious will would never have been daunted by opposition or difficulty; never have given way but with life.' But, while this formid-able will that 'rendered her obtuse to all reasoning where her own wishes, or her own sense of right, was concerned' might have benefited a Magellan or a Drake, he acknowledged that it was hard to domesti-cate, and both he and his wife clearly found Emily an unsettling presence. Monsieur had also noticed how 'egotistical and exacting' she was compared with Charlotte and how 'in the anxiety of the elder to make her younger sister contented, she allowed [Emily] to exercise a kind of unconscious tyranny over her', an interesting insight both into the sisters' relationship and into Heger's keen observation of them.

Charlotte's essays, on the other hand, anticipated her teacher's responses in a much more collaborative way. She knew what would appeal to his sensibility and indulged it; she also delighted in his marks of approval – 'B' for 'Bon', 'Tr. B' for 'Très Bon'– which were as often about the content of her work as its correctness.

Charlotte's essays had none of Emily's bite, but showed an alertness to his suggestions that impressed Heger, as a pedagogue, very much indeed. At the end of an essay called 'Le Nid' ('The Nest'), which Char-lotte wrote for him in April, Heger – having extensively corrected and commented throughout – wrote the following pungent advice:

What importance should be given to details, in developing a subject? –

Remorselessly sacrifice everything that does not contribute to clarity, verisimilitude, and effect.

Accentuate everything that sets the main idea in relief, so that the impression be colourful, picturesque. It's sufficient that the rest be *in its proper place, but in half-tone*. That is what gives to style, as to painting, unity, perspective, and *effect*.

Read Harmony XIV of Lamartine, *The Infinite*: we will analyse it together, *from the point of view of the details*.

With what pleasure and interest Charlotte must have read this message from her master, and hastened to find Lamartine's poem. Her subsequent essay 'L'Immensité de Dieu' is heavily influenced by it, even down to Lamartine's imagery and language; traces of Bernardin de Saint-Pierre and Chateaubriand – two more of Monsieur's favourites – are also apparent. Monsieur's carefully chosen words had been heeded in every way, and were bearing remarkable fruit, albeit in a foreign language, now that she had a sufficiently demanding reader.

Heger's devotion to excellence was unusual in a teacher of young ladies. It could be thought of as educational idealism, or, in the economic theory of the day, perhaps as conspicuous waste: the most that any of his female pupils would be able or expected to do with their opened minds would be to teach in turn, in conditions of less promise, for salaries much lower than those of their male counterparts. The idea of nurturing in his bosom future *women of letters*, who could take their place on the bookshelf alongside the venerated writers and poets to whom he introduced them, would not have crossed Heger's mind at all. Yet he had two in the class before him: one taking notes assiduously, the other giving him an unsmiling stare.

With his natural acting ability and electrifying enthusiasms, it must have been an arresting experience to hear him read and comment on his favourite authors. When he was in 'insane Tom-cat' mode, however, he would shout and rage at his pupils, and deliver withering critiques. Emily sat through such performances stony-faced, but Charlotte was much more susceptible to criticism, though pleased to report to Ellen that if Monsieur ever reduced her to tears, his demeanour changed immediately, '& that sets all things straight'.

No one has left an account of how Constantin Heger behaved with a class of boys, who occupied by far the greater part of his teaching life. The ex-pupils who rallied to his defence in later years were all female, and Heger's power over girls seems to have pleased him particularly. Charlotte's depiction in *The Professor* of William Crimsworth's pleasure in domineering over a class of girls shows her complete awareness of the erotics of the classroom. Having deliberately dictated too fast, to discompose his new pupil, Crimsworth enjoys her confusion and anticipation of getting a bad mark, all the more to savour her relief at finding 'Bon' at the bottom of her returned book: 'she smiled, at first incredulously, then as if reassured, but did not lift her eyes; she could look at me, it seemed, when perplexed and bewildered, but not when gratified.'

Elsewhere, keen to scotch the idea that a classful of nubile females could be some sort of erotic free-for-all for a male teacher, Charlotte has Crimsworth explain how girls who in society might seem charming are revealed in their true colours in the schoolroom: 'sullen tempers are shewn, disfiguring frowns spoil the symmetry of the face, sometimes coarse gestures banish grace from the deportment while muttered expressions, redolent of native and ineradicable vulgarity, desecrate the sweetness of the voice.' They are Belgians, in other words. The conscientious tutor doesn't look for charm, beauty or flirtation in such a situation but 'glories chiefly in certain mental qualities; application, love of knowledge, natural capacity, docility, truthfulness, gratefulness . . . These he seeks but seldom meets; these if by chance he finds he would fain retain for ever, and when Separation deprives him of them, he feels as if some ruthless hand had snatched from him his only ewe-lamb.'

The Hegers' joint approach to the care of their charges was parental, attentive and, in many cases, affectionate. Writing to a favourite former pupil many years later, Madame reminded her of an incident when she was convalescent from an illness at school and Monsieur Heger had been so affected by her 'large languid eyes' that he kissed her and 'allowed himself to make a sort of discreet declaration. "Who", he asked the little invalid, "is my best girl?" "Your wife," said K— dryly, turning her face to the wall.' Madame was recalling this story fondly, as a joint possession of herself and her husband ('we do not separate what God has so happily joined' she told the same pupil on another occasion, 'and in our affection husband and wife are one'), but it evokes a way of dealing with pupils that the stiff-necked Brontës may well have found surprising. Monsieur's vulnerability to tears was well known, and the fact that he kept bon-bons in his pocket to hand out to the girls, and himself, whenever the mood took him. K's reminiscence of Monsieur at her sickbed makes one wonder about the inspiration behind Charlotte's poem 'I gave, at first, Attention close' (written in 1845–6). Was the tender scene it depicts between a teacher and student purely imaginary, or based on experience?

> One day when summoned to the bed
> > Where Pain and I did strive,
> I heard him, as he bent his head,
> > Say, 'God, she *must* revive!'
>
> I felt his hand, with gentle stress
> > A moment laid on mine,
> And wished to mark my consciousness
> > By some responsive sign.

There is a similar hint in Charlotte's poem 'Frances' (a poem spoken as by the heroine of *The Professor*) of 'a thrilling clasp' of the hand that persuaded the speaker that 'another heart esteemed [her's] dear'. If Constantin Heger made a habit of such gestures, it is not surprising that Charlotte, love-starved and sensual, did indeed feel the yearning to make 'some responsive sign'.

The summer vacation began on the Feast of the Assumption, 15 August, when the Heger family, with their three little girls, new baby son Prospère and English nanny Martha Trotman, departed for the seaside, and all the boarders except Emily and Charlotte Brontë went home. But before she left for her annual holiday, Madame made the sisters an offer that shows how pleased she was with their progress and keen to help them as well as herself. She proposed that they stay another half-year to continue their lessons in French and German, with free board, in exchange for Charlotte taking on all the teaching of English (Madame could then save quite a bit by dismissing the current English master) and Emily teaching music 'some part of each day'.

Mary Taylor, on the other hand (who had gone home to Yorkshire for the holidays with Martha), was ready to move on from Brussels to Germany, where she intended to live with a friend's family and look for work as a teacher of English. She wrote to Ellen, 'I am going to shut my eyes for a cold plunge – when I come up again I [will] tell you all what its like.' 'You all' included their mutual friends the Brontës, whom Mary reported 'well; not only in health but in mind & hope. They are content with their present position & even gay & I think they do quite right not to return to England though one of them at least could earn more at the beautiful town of Bradford than she is now doing' – that is, they'd be better off as mill-hands. '[I]f you can't see or rather feel why they are right,' she continued, in a mild reprimand to the only one of their circle who had yet to show a dash of independence, 'I could not make you understand them. It is a matter of taste & feeling, & I think you feel pent up enough where you are to see why they are right in staying outside the cage – though it is somewhat cold.'

Charlotte appreciated the goodwill behind Madame Heger's proposal, and was glad to accept – not least because they would be saving money (there was no extra charge for staying through the vacation) and generally furthering the school plan. Emily's feelings were very different: her views of what it meant to run a school must have been changing rapidly and 'the cage' is hardly how she thought of home – that description better fitted everywhere else, in her eyes. Only disgust at her own feebleness, as at Roe Head, kept her from giving up and begging to accompany the Taylors back to Yorkshire. Charlotte bore witness later to the struggle Emily went through in her ten months abroad: 'the same suffering and conflict ensued, heightened by the strong recoil of her upright, heretic and English spirit from the gentle Jesuitry of the foreign and Romish system', she wrote with heartfelt sympathy. 'Once more she seemed sinking, but this time she rallied through the mere force of resolution: with inward remorse and shame she looked back on her former failure, and resolved to conquer in this second ordeal.'

The summer heat was intense, and the Brontë sisters had the schoolrooms, and the beautiful garden, almost to themselves. They also had each other's company and the resources of the great city around them. They walked along the boulevards that followed the course of the old city walls, around the winding streets of the Basse-Ville and the tree-lined streets of the new *faubourgs*. They climbed the steep steps up to the Parc, and wandered along its pathways, between the bandstands and theatres, watching the *Bruxellois* promenading on foot or in carriages. They took excursions into the countryside to make sketches and spent much time and effort copying from printed sources, as before. A drawing by Charlotte known as *Watermill* dates from this time, almost certainly copied from an engraving and finished to an extremely high level: the tower, the mill, the water, every leaf on every tree and shrub have been rendered with stifling care. It is the opposite of lively, and represents days of effort.

During the holiday, the Brontës tutored the Wheelwright girls, whose parents had gone on a trip on the Rhine. Emily was meant to be teaching the three youngest ones piano, but she always arranged the lessons to suit her own convenience, and antagonised them as a result. It must have been clear to Charlotte, when revolving her own plans to start a school, that Emily was not likely to make a very promising member of staff.

There was bad news from Haworth: Branwell had yet again been dismissed from a job. Leaving the work of running the station at Lud-denden Foot to the porter, Branwell had been spending more and more time in the local inn, and when the station's accounts were investigated, and a significant shortfall detected (of £11.1s.6d.), he was naturally held responsible. Francis Grundy imagined the porter, not Branwell, had been the thief, but the outcome was the same.

Though it looked strange that the only son was back at home, un-employed, while his three sisters were all out in the world, struggling to pay their way, Branwell was still sustained by his dream of becoming known as a writer, and his success of the previous year was at last open-ing doors for him. Between leaving Luddenden Foot (where he had clearly been able to fit in quite a bit of scribbling between trains) and having to take up another post in January 1843, he published no fewer than nine poems, and articles too, all under his pseudonym 'Northang-erland'. And he was as assiduously as ever soliciting the attention of established writers – James Martineau and the current editor of *Black-wood's* – in the hope of getting published further afield.

Being at home alone with his disappointed elders made Branwell restless and uncomfortable, though: 'nothing to listen to except the wind moaning among old chimneys' (it was May) and 'nothing to look at except heathery hills walked over when life had all to hope for and nothing to regret with me'. His sisters' letters from Brussels and his father's recent journey abroad stung him with a craving to travel, perhaps get a job with a railway company on the Continent, where the system was just getting under way. He must have known his chances of employment in the same area at home were over, though he kept asking Grundy to look out for juicy vacancies.

Branwell had got to know William Weightman much better on his return to Haworth in the spring and found in the scholarly and charming curate a much more suitable companion than the town had offered him before, though one who stood so high in his father's opinion that it must have been hard for Branwell not to feel discomforted by comparisons. Weightman was never found lounging in the snug of the Black Bull or lying late in bed. Weightman hadn't been sent home time and again in defeat; he had used his talents and applied himself to work with ardour. God's work too. Branwell was hardly ever seen in church.

But Weightman's dedication to his duties had a tragic outcome in the autumn of 1842, when he contracted cholera while visiting the sick. It was then an incurable disease, and his death on 6 September, aged only twenty-eight, profoundly shocked the whole parish. Branwell, who had attended the curate's dying bed in distress for two weeks, felt he had lost 'one of my dearest friends'; Patrick Brontë mourned him as deeply, saying in a heartfelt funeral address, to a full congregation and to the accompaniment of Branwell's audible sobs, that he had considered Weightman as a son. But at least, for Patrick, there was real comfort in Weightman's exemplary deathbed, where the young man had 'expressed his entire dependence on the merits of the Saviour' and closed his eyes 'on this bustling, vain, selfish world . . . in tranquillity'.

Anne was away from home at her job with the Robinsons at Thorp Green Hall when Weightman died, and did not come home for the funeral, but the likelihood that she had been secretly in love with Weightman is strengthened by a poem she wrote that winter, 'I will not mourn thee, lovely one', which expressed much more than a general loss:

> I'll weep no more thine early doom
> But O I still must mourn –
> The pleasures buried in thy tomb
> For they will not return!

In Brussels, the two elder sisters were about to face another shock-ing and rapid death from cholera, that of Martha Taylor, the youngest of their little circle of expatriate Yorkshire friends. Martha was taken ill at the end of September, and, despite Mary's desperate efforts, 'watching – nursing – cherishing her – so tenderly, so unweariedly', she died on 12 October, aged twenty-three. Charlotte only heard that Martha was ill the day before, as she told Ellen: 'I hastened to Kokle-berg [*sic*] the next morning – unconscious that she was in great danger – and was told that it was finished, she had died in the night.' After so many alarms and vigils over her own and her family's feeble health over the years, Martha's swift removal by cholera, so prevalent in cities and areas of high population where water supplies could become quickly infected, was doubly shocking. Lively, flirtatious Miss Bois-terous, who had always prompted 'adventures' and jollity at Roe Head and Gomersal, had to be buried far from home, in the Protestant Cemetery of Saint-Josse-ten-Noode, two miles north-east of Brus-sels' city walls.

'Every trivial accident sad or pleasant reminds me of her & of what she went through,' Mary told Ellen three weeks later, when she went to visit the grave with the Brontës. But, battening down her terrible feelings of loss, she went ahead with her plan to move to Germany alone – an even colder plunge now than she had anticipated.

Just a few days later, on 2 November, a letter arrived for Charlotte and Emily from their father informing them that Aunt Branwell was seriously ill. The girls decided to go home immediately, but on the heels of the first letter came another telling them that Aunt Branwell was dead. However quickly they set off, it was clear they could not be in time for the funeral, but there was no question of staying in Brussels: the pull of home at this crisis was overpowering, and Emily, at least, was glad to be drawn back by *force majeure*. The interruption to their schooling would be considered later, as the Hegers made haste to re-assure them. The couple, always very sympathetic to matters of family duty, saw the Brontë sisters off with every kindness, and each of them wrote to Patrick Brontë offering sincere condolences and expressing the hope that his daughters' education could be resumed at an appropriate time.

On their hasty departure from the Pensionnat, and with the awful feeling that they might not be able to return, Charlotte gave Madame her fine drawing of the watermill, with a dedication written so small that it is barely visible, interwoven with the foliage – 'Madame Heger from one of her pupils' – to which the artist has added for clarification (but impossible to read with the naked eye), 'A token of affection and respect'. Emily gave her a watercolour, 'most spirited and beautiful', of a female figure arrested in flight. It was an adaptation of one of Richard Westall's illustrations to Thomas Moore's *Life of Byron* and perfectly expressed Emily's eagerness to depart.*

Emily and Charlotte travelled home by the next Sunday's steam packet from Antwerp to London, spent another full day travelling overland and reached Haworth on 8 October, five days after Elizabeth Branwell, 65-year-old spinster of a parish she had never wanted to live in, was buried, according to her wishes, 'as near as convenient to the remains of my dear sister'.

It was a sombre reunion of the siblings. Anne had not got home from Thorp Green in time to see her aunt alive, but Branwell had been there to witness 'such agonising suffering as I would not wish my worst enemy to endure', as he told his friend Francis Grundy, and spent many sleepless nights at his aunt's sickbed as she endured the rapid advance of what seems to have been a bowel or stomach cancer. Branwell had always been his aunt's favourite, and now felt that he had lost someone as dear as a mother to him, 'the guide and director of all the happy days connected with my childhood'. Already wrought up to a pitch of emotionalism by the death of William Weightman, he felt oppressed by 'gloomy visions either of this world or another' (casual wording that would have shocked his father to hear), and doubtless his pain over his

---

* Emily's picture is now lost, but a photograph of it remains (see *Art of the Brontës*, 385–7). It was in the Heger family until the 1880s, then given to a former pupil and bequeathed to her niece. It is known as *The North Wind*, though whether or not EJB gave it that title is uncertain. Charlotte's *Watermill* hangs at the Brontë Parsonage Museum; see *Art of the Brontës*, 260.

aunt's death was exacerbated by feelings of guilt that he had not managed to reward her faith in him with better results.

Branwell was presumably prepared for the contents of his aunt's will, since it did not consternate him. He was left a japanned dressing case as a personal memento and that was all. The four legatees were Charlotte, Emily, Anne and their cousin Eliza Kingston (the only child of Elizabeth's younger sister Jane Branwell, who had suffered an abusive marriage and returned to Penzance from America years before). The will had been drawn up in 1833, when Branwell was sixteen and had bright prospects ahead of him. Elizabeth Branwell clearly believed that a young man could make his own way, but girls without patrimony, like his sisters and Eliza, deserved to have family assets directed towards them, just as Elizabeth herself and her sister Maria had benefited significantly from the annuities left them by their father decades earlier. Not least, an inheritance would give the girls more choice over whether or not to marry.

Elizabeth Branwell had managed to put by quite a bit of money as well as pay her way at the Parsonage all the years she lived with her brother-in-law. Her independent, rigorously scrupulous behaviour had been a source of pride to her and a powerful example to her nieces. Though middle-class females of the period are so often thought of as having been financial burdens on their male relations, the stereotypes were reversed in the case of the Brontës; Patrick Brontë and his son were the ones needing to be subsidised by their womenfolk's frugality, hard work and careful stewardship of resources.

Aunt Branwell had invested over £1,000 in the York and North Midland Railway Company, promoted vigorously in the 1830s by 'The Railway King', George Hudson, as a portal to the future. The first part of the line from York to London opened in 1839 with huge success, and Aunt's investment was doing remarkably well, yielding around 10 per cent in each of the first four years. The Brontë sisters decided to hold on to the shares rather than cash them in – for the time being, at any rate – but the volatility of the railway business, requiring massive capitalisation as well as returns, unnerved Charlotte, who told Miss Wooler that 'any day a small share-holder may find his funds shrunk to their original dimensions'. Emily, on the other hand, was a risk-taker and found it extremely exciting to have a stake in the market. She took over the management of the investments on behalf of all three sisters and became obsessed with checking 'every paragraph & every advertisement in the news-papers that related to rail-roads'; not that she moved any of the stock in the years they owned it, but watching it rise so often as it did gave her deep pleasure. None of the sisters dwelt too long on the fate of Aunt's other speculation – in a Cornish tin-mining business that had collapsed entirely.★

Probate on Elizabeth Branwell's will was granted at the end of December, but in the weeks since their aunt's death the three sisters had taken stock of their changed situation and made some important decisions. They now each possessed a nest-egg worth about £300, the equivalent of twelve years' income at Anne's governess job. Patrick Brontë was ageing, his sight was deteriorating, and his spirits had been dashed by the recent bereavements; one of his daughters would be expected to stay at home and take their aunt's place as his companion and housekeeper. Anne was well established in her post with the Robinsons (and determined, moreover, to stick at it); she had also helped Branwell to get a job with the same family, starting in January 1843, as tutor to their twelve-year-old son, Edmund. Emily was the obvious candidate to stay at home. The only question was, would Charlotte stay with her?

The dash home in November had been a jarring interruption of the Brussels experiment, which Constantin Heger and his wife had regretted sincerely. Monsieur Heger had sent the sisters home with a letter addressed to their father, to make sure that there was some chance of a return: it was both a progress report and a suggested plan for the coming term. Heger paid tribute to the girls' 'love of work and their perseverance' – clearly learnt from home – and lamented that his own 'almost fatherly affection' was touched by their sudden departure: 'and our distress is increased by the realization that there are so many incomplete tasks, so many things which have been well begun, and which only need a little more time to be satisfactorily completed. In a year's time, each of your daughters would have been fully prepared for all

---

★ Elizabeth Branwell might also have owned some property in Cornwall, as CB makes a reference to rent paid in May 1846 by Eliza Kingston, the Cornish legatee, to Patrick Brontë, which seems to be connected to Miss Branwell's estate (*LCB* 1, 472).

future contingencies; each was both improving her knowledge and learning how to teach.' Emily had been about to have piano lessons 'from the best teacher we have in Belgium' (who happened to be Heger's first wife's brother-in-law); Charlotte had begun to give lessons in French 'and to gain the assurance and aplomb so essential in teaching'. A total interruption of their studies would be inadvisable, Heger felt, since they were within sight of reaping real rewards; one or other of them would be welcome as a full-time teacher in time. 'This is not a question of our personal advantage,' he wrote, 'but a question of affection; you must pardon me if we speak to you of your children and concern ourselves with their future as if they formed part of our family; their personal qualities, their good will, their extreme zeal are the only reasons leading us to venture in this way.'

The reference to 'one of them' possibly finding permanent employment at the Pensionnat was aimed of course at Charlotte, not Emily. She had a special place in Heger's affections, and knew it. His delight in her progress was heartfelt – she had been, in effect, his perfect pupil, clever, subordinate, vulnerable. He could see her intelligence and sense her genius, but it seemed his to awaken and, unlike Emily's, gratifyingly malleable. With this testimony to Heger's regard, and repeated encouragement from Madame, in kind and affectionate letters, to return and continue her studies, there was little doubt what Charlotte wanted to do. Three years later, she looked back on her decision with searing self-condemnation as 'selfish folly', indulged against the promptings of her conscience and punished 'by a total withdrawal for more than two year[s] of happiness and peace of mind'. But at the time the impulse to fly back to Brussels at the first opportunity was, as she admitted, 'irresistible'.

If Aunt Branwell had been alive, Charlotte would never have been allowed to undertake the journey as she did, completely alone. She left home on Friday, 27 January 1843, travelling from Leeds to London by train and arriving in the capital so late – ten o'clock at night – that she decided not to go as planned to the Chapter Coffee House but to take a cab and head straight for London Bridge wharf and try to board the steamship that she was booked on to leave the next morning. When the cabbie left her in an alarming scrum of foul-mouthed watermen, all jostling for custom, it dawned on Charlotte how dangerous her situation was, but she persisted in being rowed out to find the boat, a hard task in the inky darkness. They had to go from one vessel to another, holding up a lantern until the *Earl of Liverpool* was found. The crew were at first very dubious at the sight of a tiny young woman in heavy winter travelling dress standing in a rowing-boat among her valises and demanding to be let on board so many hours before time, but the 'quiet simple statement of her wish, and her reason for it' swayed the officer on duty, and she was hauled up and shown to a berth, where she collapsed in relief. 'I had no accident,' she told Ellen later, 'but of course some anxiety.' Any sense of danger had been eclipsed by a feverish and growing excitement. Elizabeth Gaskell later said that Charlotte's recollection of her journey back to Brussels was 'pretty much as she has since described it in "Villette"', but *Villette* offers no explanation for the heroine's sense of quiet exultation, which turns her apprehensions into a dark source of pleasure:

> Down the sable flood we glided; I thought of the Styx, and of Charon rowing some solitary soul to the Land of Shades. Amidst the strange scene, with a chilly wind blowing in my face, and midnight-clouds dropping rain above my head; with two rude rowers for companions, whose insane oaths still tortured my ear, I asked myself if I was wretched or terrified. I was neither. Often in my life have I been far more so under comparatively safe circumstances. 'How is this?' said I. 'Methinks I am animated and alert, instead of being depressed and apprehensive?' I could not tell how it was.

8

The Black Swan

1843

Charlotte returned to the Pensionnat as both student and teacher. She still took French classes with some of the pupils whom she now taught English, and they liked her no better than they had the previous year. As fellow student, they felt she was at an unfair advantage because of her age (twenty-six) and maturity – and because she was teacher's pet (Monsieur Heger often read her work aloud in class as an example). In classes such as dancing, she was ridiculed mercilessly for her ineptitude and lack of grace, and then these very same girls were presented at desks in front of her, to be taught English. Frederika Macdonald, interviewing some of the pupils who had been at the Pensionnat in 1842–3 many years later, found one 'Mlle C' who testified that the girls played up in Mademoiselle Brontë's class on purpose, because they scorned her lack of authority. One girl who was 'extremely difficult to manage' precipitated a crisis in an already rowdy class after throwing a knotted handkerchief across the room that hit Miss Brontë on the arm. 'Instead of showing anger or amusement, [she] appeared greatly distressed and embarrassed,' the former schoolgirl recalled, but Charlotte got her revenge at the next lesson when she brought in Monsieur Heger to reprimand the whole form, threaten the malefactors with expulsion if they did not improve their behaviour and exclude the ringleader from the English class.*

Another former pupil said that Miss Brontë 'was known to be very clever, but she had no sympathy with young people and no authority over them'. They despised her because she was ill-dressed, thin and sickly looking ('maigrelette' was the word), and also because she worked

---

* Charlotte would have been amused to learn that the teen troublemaker later became a nun (Frederika Macdonald, 'The Brontës at Brussels', 286).

so hard. Charlotte was learning German this year and making both English and French translations of Schiller.* She did a polished translation of 'Les Petits Orphelins' by Louis Belmontet, one of 'L'Idole' by Auguste Barbier and versions in French of her own old favourites Scott and Byron. 'L'Idole' (about Napoleon's ruthless pursuit of glory to his country's ruin) was an interesting choice, possibly Heger's. Charlotte and he were in friendly rivalry about the late emperor and his nemesis, Wellington, and when Charlotte came to write an essay 'The Death of Napoleon' later that spring, she made it into something of a partisan set-piece about the Duke. Heger was so pleased with it that he retained it for declamation at the school prize day.

On her return to Brussels, Charlotte made a valued new friend in Mary Dixon, the 34-year-old-cousin of Mary Taylor whom she had met after Martha's death the previous October. Mary, a mature and intelligent woman, in delicate health, lived on the rue de la Régence in a cheerful household headed by her father Abraham, a failed banker and former foreign commission agent who was trying to make a living in Brussels as an inventor. Charlotte took to spending Sundays with Mary, a substitute elder sister perhaps for the one she had lost so long ago.

Charlotte felt sufficiently at ease with Mary Dixon to submit to her request to sit for a portrait. 'I surrender my unfortunate head to you with resignation,' she wrote good-naturedly; 'the features thereof may yield good practice as they never yet submitted to any line of regularity – but have manifested each a spirit of independence, edifying to behold.' Charlotte advised her not to send any resulting portrait to Mary Taylor, however: 'she likes me well enough – but my face she can dispense with – and would tell you so in her own sincere and truthful language if you asked her.' This was all too true. Mary Taylor had been making rude remarks about Charlotte's appearance ever since they met at Roe Head, and later complained that George Richmond's 1850 portrait of Charlotte was far too flattering of 'an ugly woman'.

A small chalk, ink and wash drawing of a young woman wearing a bonnet came to light in the 1990s, formerly in the possession of William Law, an avid collector of Brontëana, who had bought it from the

---

* Her version of 'Der Taucher' ('The Diver') was the nearest thing she ever got to writing blank verse; an interesting experiment. See *PCB*, 357–61.

Brontës' servant Martha Brown some time before 1880. It has the words 'Portrait of Charlotte Brontë given to Martha Brown 1839' in pencil on the back and is assumed to be of Charlotte, assumed to be, in fact, the portrait by Mary Dixon that she agreed to sit for in 1843. Subsequently, its date has been adjusted to 'Brussels, *c.* 1843' in line with the letter quoted above. It seems much more likely that Mary Dixon's picture of Charlotte (if indeed she went ahead and made one) is now lost, and that the chalk drawing at the Parsonage is of Mary Dixon herself, executed at the same period and given to Charlotte as a memento. That Charlotte had such a memento is evident from the fact that she told Mary in October of 1843 (when Mary had left Brussels) that she had 'disinterred your portrait from the bottom of a trunk' because she was low-spirited and craved 'a little society': 'I was comforted by discovering a certain likeness – notwithstanding what yourself and William Henry affirmed to the contrary.' The 'William Henry' she refers to was William Henry Taylor, another cousin of the Dixons, fifteen years old, who was living with his Brussels relatives at the time. 'If it were a little slenderer and paler – it would be very much like.' Charlotte is clearly not talking about taking comfort from an image of herself.* The chalk drawing is rather sentimental, of a sweet, conventional-looking woman with extremely regular features – not fitting any description of Charlotte Brontë. Commentators have remarked that it makes 'Charlotte' look older and more matronly than one would expect of a 26-year-old, but Mary was seven years her senior.

Mary Taylor, now in Germany, was worried that Charlotte would not do well on her own in Brussels. '[S]he seems *content* at least but [I] fear her sister's absence [?will] have a bad effect,' she told Ellen; 'When people have so little amusement they cannot afford to lose *any*.' But, to begin with, Emily's absence freed Charlotte to concentrate entirely, exclusively and in a deeply pleasurable way on her admiration for Monsieur Heger. His generosity, his natural brilliance, his eloquence – even his charitable work, piety and expansive interest

---

* Since the chalk portrait was in Charlotte's possession in 1843, and presumably went back to Haworth with her the following year, its eventual home with Martha Brown, along with so many other items of Brontë memorabilia that ended up with her after Charlotte's death and Arthur Nicholls's removal to Ireland, is easily explicable.

in other people's welfare – all struck her afresh. Most of all, she loved the calibre of his mind. As Lucy Snowe says of Paul Emanuel in *Villette*, the character based on Constantin Heger, 'M. Emanuel was not a man to write books; but I have heard him lavish, with careless, unconscious prodigality, such mental wealth as books seldom boast; his mind was indeed my library, and whenever it was opened to me, I entered bliss.' And when Heger took Charlotte and another pupil into town to see the Mardi Gras carnival, though she dismissed the processions as 'nothing but masking and mummery', the thrill of being out in the evening with her beloved master, in the dark among a festive crowd, was a new sort of rapture.

The poem that she inserted into *The Professor* about the brief revelation of a gruff man's sympathetic nature might be illuminating here too. Though the teacher soon readopts his former distant manner, his pupil now understands it differently: 'I had learned to read/The secret meaning of his face,/And that was my best meed.' Reading 'secret meanings' in Heger's behaviour – which was, after all, very open to interpretation – became Charlotte's obsessive pleasure.

The development that most encouraged Charlotte's growing sense of intimacy with Heger was his request for her to give regular English lessons on Friday afternoons to him and his brother-in-law Monsieur Chapelle (the Conservatoire pianist with whom Emily had been hoping to study). This was a chance for Charlotte to assume authority at last, show her mettle as a teacher and engage with two adult male minds on terms of equality, a rare opportunity for any woman of the period. When Charlotte's social constraint was laid aside, the results were always formidable: Heger must have been very impressed, not only with her eloquence and erudition in her mother-tongue, but in her changed manner. Heger's ardent, anxious English student was transformed by the role-reversal into a woman of substance and seriousness, and Charlotte obviously relished the temporary power she had over her master, watching him struggle with vocabulary and pronunciation, as she reported amusedly to Ellen: 'they get on with wonderful rapidity – especially the first – he already begins to speak English very decently – if you could see and hear the efforts I make to teach them to pronounce like Englishmen and their unavailing attempts to imitate, you would laugh to all eternity.'

In French class, where the roles of teacher and pupil swapped round again, the growing sense of confidence continued and Charlotte's essays for Heger – less frequent, longer – became a form of colloquy. 'La Chute des Feuilles' ('The Fall of the Leaves'), written in March, was an attempt at analysing the style of Millevoye's poem, which, after a few pages of Charlotte posing questions about the nature and value of literary criticism, finds its way back to a subject always on her mind: the nature of genius. And at the point when she breaks cover and declares, 'I believe that all true poetry is but the faithful imprint of something that happens or has happened in the poet's soul,' Heger responds eagerly in the margin, 'Très bon, très juste.' 'I believe that genius, thus awakened, has no need to seek the details, that it scarcely pauses to reflect, that it never thinks of unity: I believe that details come quite naturally without the poet having to seek them, that inspiration takes the place of reflection.' 'Très bon . . . excellent.' Beneath this discussion of the balance between reason and inspiration, work and genius, analysis and production, another seems to be going on, about Charlotte's own desires to be an artist. In the increased intimacy she had briefly gained with Heger, she may well have told him about her own poetry, or even shown him some, for in his copious comments at the end of her essay – a set of thoughts and afterthoughts generously engaging with the issues raised – he encourages her to continue to study, analyse, reflect, *dissect* as well as practise her creative work.

> Without study, no art. Without art, no effect on humanity, because art epitomizes that which all the centuries bequeath to us, all that man has found *beautiful*, that which has had an effect on man, all that he has found worth saving from oblivion . . . *Poet* or *not*, then, study form. If a poet you will be more powerful & your works will live. If not, you will not create poetry, but you will savour its merits and its charms.

Heger's advice was practical, as Southey's had been, but lofty in spirit. He did not by any means rule out the possibility of Charlotte becoming – *being* – a poet, however little he thought she could or should do so professionally. And he didn't rule it out because he knew what a peculiarly sensitive and appreciative reader she was. 'His eyes pierced through the quartz and saw the diamond in the heart of it,' one acquaintance said in 1870 of the relationship between Heger and Charlotte; 'and he made much of her and drew her out.'

But it's clear from a letter as early as 6 March – only six weeks into her
new situation – that Charlotte was already beginning to feel dashed and
despondent. She told herself sternly that she could not be in love with
her teacher like any foolish schoolgirl; this wasn't a crush or a sexual fantasy, though the symptoms might be very similar – identical, indeed. As
she got to know Heger better and better, and felt his attraction more
powerfully, a concurrent awareness grew of the inappropriateness of
such feelings, and their essential futility. This could and did not stop her
from pursuing an intimacy that had an irresistible charm, mainly because
it took place largely in her own head and was powered by an extraordinary imagination.

The Hegers were sensitive to Charlotte's new status in the school
and had warmly encouraged her to make use of their sitting room as
her own; it was, in effect, a staff room during the day, where many
part-time employees, especially the music teachers, went to and fro and
waited for pupils. Charlotte found such lack of privacy upsetting and
avoided using the offered privilege during school hours, but it was even
more upsetting to her to go there in the evenings, when the sitting
room reverted to being the Hegers' family quarters. 'I will not and
ought not to intrude on Mr & Mde Heger & their children,' she told
Ellen in a homesick, lonely letter, but what she probably could not bear
was the sight of her master *en famille*, the devoted husband and father
relaxing with his little ones round the fire, his handsome wife, a baby
on her knee, regnant over all.

In the same letter to Ellen she said, 'if I could always keep up my
spirits – and never feel lonely or long for companionship or friendship
or *whatever they call it* [my italics], I should do very well.' Charlotte's
sense of isolation was less to do with her actual social life or opportunities (which had improved markedly) than with the quandary she was
in, having identified a way to happiness along an utterly inaccessible
path. It was the dilemma that caused her heroine Jane Eyre so much
mental pain – the ideal mate turns out to be the impossible mate –
though for Jane, Charlotte was able to adjust the outcome, and get rid
of the wife who stands in her way.

Ellen had passed on, in an arch manner, some Yorkshire gossip that infuriated Charlotte: that her return to Belgium at a rate of pay so inferior to what she could get at home could only have been because she had her eye on a future husband there. This was so close in spirit to the truth that Charlotte could only answer in a sort of false negative:

> These people are wiser than I am – They could not believe that I crossed the sea – merely to return as teacher to Mde Heger's – I must have some more powerful motive than respect for the character of my Master & Mistress, gratitude for their kindness to induce me to refuse a salary of 50£ in England and accept one of 16 in Belgium   I must forsooth have some remote hope of entrapping a husband somehow – somewhere – if these charitable people knew the total seclusion of the life I lead – that I never exchange a word with any other man than Monsieur Heger and seldom indeed with him – they would perhaps cease to suppose tha[t] any such chimerical & groundless notion has influenced my proceedings – Have I said enough to clear myself of so silly an imputation?

No, she hadn't. Ellen had visited Haworth in January, just before Charlotte's return, and must have been completely aware of, and surprised at, the intensity of her feelings for the Pensionnat and its charismatic *professeur*. Charlotte probably succumbed to the delicious temptation of talking far too much about Monsieur Heger all holiday, banking on the fact that, as a married man, he was securely off limits as a subject for romantic speculation. The girls were used to teasing and being teased over every bachelor of their acquaintance, eligible or not, and Ellen herself endured or enjoyed constant prods from Charlotte about the attentions of Mary Taylor's brothers Joe and John and others. The underlying message of the angry denial in her letter is the same: Ellen's choices are very different from hers: 'Not that it is a crime to marry – or a crime to wish to be married – but it is an imbecility which I reject with contempt – for women who have neither fortune nor beauty – to make marriage the principal object of their wishes & hopes & the aim of all their actions – not to be able to convince themselves that they are unattractive – and that they had better be quiet & think of other things than wedlock –'

The heightened state of excitement and expectation with which Charlotte had returned to the Pensionnat was evident to Madame

Heger from the start and soon aroused her concern privately. If Charlotte had become more outgoing and sociable as a result of her contact
with the family and the school, if she had lost some of her *mauvaise
honte*, Madame would have taken pride in the improvement (she made
repeated efforts to get Charlotte to socialise more and make friends).
But the English teacher's animation was obviously and exclusively generated by her contact with the directrice's husband, and he seemed to
have little idea of the effect he was having.

Charlotte professed amazement later at the construal of her feelings
towards Monsieur Heger being in any way romantic or erotic, but
Madame sensed trouble. Her whole family's livelihood depended on
the school's reputation, and it was her concern to monitor any sort of
behaviour – acknowledged or unacknowledged – that might threaten
it. She started to keep a close eye on Mademoiselle Brontë and probably asked one of the other young teachers, Mademoiselle Blanche, to
report back what was said in the staff dormitory and how Charlotte
used her spare time. Surveillance and discreet pre-emptive action were
Madame's preferred techniques – not confrontation. She may also have
had a word with her husband – 'crushes' on him must have occurred
frequently – for Charlotte became aware of a chill in the air and a
reduction in Monsieur's attention before anything else. The English
lessons stopped.

Charlotte at first couldn't quite believe what was going on, but
became increasingly unhappy and bitter. With Emily, she shared acid
commentary on the doings of the fellow teachers with whom she lived,
and aired her suspicions about Madame:

> I am convinced she does not like me – why, I can't tell, nor do I think
> she herself has any definite reason for the aversion; but for one thing,
> she cannot comprehend why I do not make intimate friends of Mes-
> dames Blanche, Sophie and Haussé. M. Heger is wondrously influenced
> by Madame, and I should not wonder if he disapproves very much of
> my unamiable want of sociability. He has already given me a brief lec-
> ture on universal *bienveillance*, and, perceiving that I don't improve in
> consequence, I fancy he has taken to considering me as a person to be let
> alone – left to the error of her ways; and consequently he has in a great
> measure withdrawn the light of his countenance, and I get on from day

to day in a very Robinson-Crusoe-like condition – very lonely. That
does not signify.

Of course it did signify, and Emily was the only person who would
truly understand.

Writing to Branwell, she reverted not just to childhood slang – 'the
people here are no go whatsoever' – but a torrent of abuse against Belgians who 'have not intellect or politeness or good-nature or
good-feeling . . . the phlegm that thickens their blood is too gluey to
boil.' The only exception – in the whole nation, she insinuates – is 'the
black Swan', Monsieur Heger, who, albeit less and less frequently, still
takes an interest in her, lends her books and is kindly disposed. Madame is already 'not quite an exception'.

Charlotte tried to joke with Branwell about growing 'misanthropic
and sour – you will say this is no news', but confessed that when she
was alone in the dormitory during the nightly Catholic prayers, she
retreated 'as fanatically as ever to the old ideas the old faces & the old
scenes in the world below', in other words, the trance-like escape into
Angrian fantasy that had almost taken over her life five years before. It
was a bad sign, and she knew it. What if she broke down again as she
had at Roe Head?

But, just as Charlotte was writing this anxious letter home, Monsieur Heger came in to the room and gave her a present, a little German
New Testament, kind encouragement and reward for her rapid mas-
tery of the new language. 'I was surprised for since a good many days
he has hardly spoken to me,' she told Branwell in a postscript; but how
foolish it was to have worried about any of that now – for here he was,
as animated and thoughtful as ever. The clouds rolled away.

Back in Haworth, 'these times, so critical and dangerous', were preying
on Patrick Brontë's mind continually. Keighley was a major centre of
Chartist activity, and the Working Men's Hall became their headquar-
ters. Brontë was also very agitated by dramatic proof of the growing
influence of the Dissenters, whose opposition to parts of the 1843 Factory Bill led to its significant amendment: all the clauses that pertained to
a new state school system had to be dropped because it had been proposed the Established Church should oversee it. He wrote an impassioned

letter on the subject to *The Leeds Intelligencer* and was no more calm the following week, when he addressed *The Halifax Guardian* about 'the Ominous and Dangerous Vagaries of the Times', among which he counted Irish agitation for Home Rule, Welsh protests against turnpike tolls ('the Rebecca riots') and the imminent separation from the Established Church of the United Free Church of Scotland. Everywhere was 'a restless disposition for change, an untoward ambition, a recklessness of consequences, and a struggle for power and predominance, like the hydrophobia of the canine race'. Presumably, Patrick's pistols were kept rigorously primed throughout this time.

Was rabies on his mind that summer because of an incident, undated in Elizabeth Gaskell's biography, when Emily saw a strange dog 'with hanging head and lolling tongue' in the lane outside the Parsonage one hot day and, taking pity on it as she did all animals in need, took it a drink of water, only to be bitten by it? The bite made Emily fear it could be rabid, so, with 'nobly stern presence of mind', she went straight to the kitchen and cauterised the wound herself with one of Tabby's smoothing irons, kept scorching hot on the stove, 'telling no one, till the danger was well-nigh over, for fear of the terrors that might beset their weaker minds'. The incident is almost as alarming as her battering of Keeper.

Anne had a dog too, a present from the Robinsons, in whose household she seemed firmly established; they had taken her on holiday with them to Scarborough that summer and given her a Blenheim spaniel called Flossy, soon to become a favourite at the Parsonage, where no creature so genteel had ever been known before. Fortunately Flossy got on well with Keeper, though, looking at the relative sizes of their metal collars (now on display at the Parsonage Museum), that was far from a certainty: Keeper's collar is almost eight inches in diameter, Flossy's four.

Charlotte had a 'general assurance' from Anne that Branwell was well settled at Thorp Green and satisfying his employers and their son, but Branwell himself proved a poor correspondent, and made excuses for the non-appearance of letters, which Charlotte clearly didn't quite believe. She was obviously concerned about him, and deeply sympathetic to his bouts of low spirits that so much resembled her own, but her awareness of his weaknesses also brought out a monitory tone that was gradually displacing their former intimacy.

Her family and friends must have puzzled over her insistence at stay-ing on in Brussels when she was so clearly unhappy. '[O]ne wear[ie]s from day to day of caring nothing, fearing nothing, liking nothing hating nothing – being nothing, doing nothing,' she wrote to Branwell uncompromisingly. In June she told Ellen that the reason for staying on, despite her depression (which she put down to loneliness and homesickness), was to learn more German, though of course she could have done that quite effectively by joining Mary Taylor in Iselholm. She had complained already of Madame Heger's 'mighty distance & reserve', but affected not to understand what could have caused it. 'I fancy I begin to perceive the reason,' she told Ellen; 'it sometimes makes me laugh & at other times nearly cry – When I am sure of it, I will tell it you.'

One Friday afternoon, eleven days before the end of term, Heger came into the classroom where Charlotte was teaching and handed her – silently, one imagines – a small object wrapped carefully in a piece of thin writing paper. She opened it as soon as he left: the girls must have been occupied in one of the tedious copying or memorising exercises that were so much a part of Charlotte's pedagogy. How did she hide her pleasure at the contents of the little package, a gift perfectly suited to her taste? Perhaps she could not, for inside the zig-zag wrapping was a small piece of pale wood, too thin to be anything other than crating, with the following written on it in ink: 'Je tiens ce morceau du cercueil de Ste Hélène du/prince Achille Murat qui le tenais du prince de Joinville./ Lebel.' It was a piece of 'Napoleon's coffin', or, rather, since Napoleon was famously coffined in tin within mahogany within lead, possibly a piece of the outer casings in which the great man's remains had been brought back to France three years earlier, under the command of his son, the Prince de Joinville, whose former secretary, Joachim-Joseph Lebel, was Heger's friend and principal of the Athénée. Out of the fog of disregard, Heger had reached out to her with his most personal and thoughtful gift yet, a relic at once to be revered for its connections and regarded with a touch of pleasant mutual cynicism, a continuation of their conversation about the emperor and his British nemesis, and a reminder of her triumphant essay on the subject; a small gift which could be slipped into her hand without fuss, which Madame Heger would never notice, and which, above all, was a token of her abiding place in his thoughts. While the girls were still busy, Charlotte wrote on the spread-out wrapper the exact co-ordinates of place and time of this precious new possession:

> August 4th 1843 – Brussels – Belgium
> 1 o'clock pm
> Monsieur Heger has just been into the 1st Class
> and given me this relic – he bought it from
> his intimate friend M. Lebel.
>
> C. Brontë

Charlotte must have got out this gift as a comfort and talisman many times in the dreary months that followed. The long vacation loomed ahead, but first Madame's feast day, the feast of Sainte Claire on 12 August, had to be endured, when the directrice appeared with her abundant hair beautifully dressed and in lovely clothes that showed 'the extreme whiteness and beauty' of her neck and arms, as one of the pupils recalled, and the swell of her belly, now just beginning to show another pregnancy.

Three days later was speech day, an extraordinary mixture for Charlotte of triumph and desolation. The triumph came when Monsieur Heger, in his most impressively oratorical mode and brimming with pride in himself and his pupil, declaimed Charlotte's essay on Napoleon to the assembled crowd of Belgian dumplings and their parents. The effect must have been electrifying for Charlotte: her speech for Wellington in Heger's mouth echoing round the little theatre.* On the same day, he presented her with the works of one of his favourite writers, Bernadin de Saint-Pierre, as a prize for her achievement, and in the evening they went out into the Parc and heard a concert at the bandstand, a 'wild Jäger chorus'.†

But speech day meant that term was over. The boarders left, the beds

---

* I am assuming that the year in which Charlotte's essay was read at the prize day was 1843, not 1842, as Heger himself assigned the date 1843 to the revised version (the one he read from), also the 'Mlle C' who gave her recollections of CB to Frederika Macdonald was recalling events almost exclusively from CB's year as a teacher.

† Winifred Gérin (*Charlotte Brontë*, 238) has shown that Charlotte must have attended the concert that she describes so specifically in *Villette*, as the programme of music at the bandstand on the evening of 15 August 1843 was the same.

were stripped and covered with dustcloths; the Hegers, with their delightful little brood, headed off to the seaside; an animated, noisy and cheerful departure. The only person left behind with Miss Brontë in the silence and emptiness of the abandoned school was the cook.

Mary Dixon had left Brussels at the end of June to travel to Spa for her health; the Wheelwrights left at the end of August. Charlotte begged Ellen for letters to see her through the gaping weeks of solitude ahead. 'It is the first time in my life that I have really dreaded the vacation,' she wrote pathetically. 'Alas I can hardly write, I have such a dreary weight at my heart.'

With so much time and solitude at her disposal, Charlotte found she could neither read nor write with pleasure. She wandered from room to room, unnerved by the silence. Walking the busy city streets was just as distressing: 'I know you, living in the country can hardly believe that it is possible life can be monotonous in the centre of a brilliant capital like Brussels,' she wrote to Ellen; 'but so it is.'

Charlotte dramatised her feelings of futility and loneliness in an essay – or story – called 'Le But de la Vie' ('The Aim of Life'), which she copied with great care and made into a little pamphlet, possibly as a gift for Monsieur's return. In it, she imagines a student rousing himself from a long period of solitary study to feel disgust at his own empty existence and waste of time. In his heart, he knows that the application that earns him praise from his peers and professors is a form of moral cowardice. The essay ends with the student resolving to dedicate himself to duty, guided by religion and reason alone, but what sticks with the reader is the uncompromising self-condemnation that precedes it: 'I flee the world because I do not have the qualities needed to shine in it. Vivacity, grace and liveliness I lack. The taciturn man is always a burden on society . . . hence he loves solitude because he is at ease in it, a base and contemptible motive that comes from selfishness and indolence.' Couched as a fiction, Charlotte was able to express exactly her own tormented feelings when she was alone at the Pensionnat that August and September, pacing the rooms and revolving constantly on what the aim of her own life could possibly be, and not loving solitude at all.

In the past, at home, Charlotte would have filled her days with writing. She had told Branwell, rather guiltily, of her continued recourse to 'the world below', for want of any other pleasure or distraction. Did she try to compose any more stories for the old heroes of her youth, neglected now for several years? Some of her Angrian texts were probably in her trunk at the Pensionnat – their portability was part of their value – and perhaps she read over them in these lonely weeks and lost herself in the parallel universe they revived. One of the Angrian booklets certainly ended up in Brussels with the Hegers, left behind by the author or, most likely, given as a present. It is a collection of stories written in 1834 and 1835, beginning with 'The Spell, An Extravaganza. By Lord Charles Albert Florian Wellesley' and containing 'High Life in Verdopolis' and Lord Charles's chatty 'Scrap Book'. Like all the Angrian manuscripts, it is a marvel of miniaturism and ink engineering, compressing into twenty-four of Charlotte's own small pages what appears in the modern printed edition in eighty-six. Monsieur Heger, if he was the recipient, is unlikely to have been able to decipher much of it, even with a magnifying glass, and, at more than 60,000 words, the length would have been baffling too.*

Did Charlotte begin to write a new kind of story in this long period of aimless solitude? She was thinking of doing so. Inside a German exercise book that year, she drew up a plan of a 'magazine tale', listing the elements she thought it should contain:

> Time – from 30 to 50 years ago
> Country – England
> Scene – rural
> Rank – middle
> Person – first
> Subject

Subject . . . there was a question! Charlotte wrote 'Certain remarkable occurrences' against this heading. Other categories were just as comically vague: the opening was to be 'cheerful or gloomy', the plot 'domestic – the romantic not excluded'. But by the end of the list, she had adopted the more businesslike tone of a memorandum and was warning herself to 'avoid Richardsonian multiplication' in the number

---

* In 1892 it was passing out of the hands of another Brussels resident, E. Nys, to a collector of Brontëana. See the coda for more on the fate of the Brontë papers and relics once in the Hegers' possession.

of characters (the besetting sin of the Angrian narratives) and to aim for 'as much compression – as little explanation as may be'.

> Mem. To be set about with proper spirit.
> To be carried out with the same.
> To be concluded idem.
> Observe – no grumbling allowed.

'The Master', a novel heavily based on her own experience in Brussels in 1842–3 and centring around the relationship between a teacher and his pupil, was completed three years later and could have been started at any time from 1842 onwards, though the final draft seems to follow a different set of objectives to the ones sketched out here: 'The Master' strives to be realistic rather than relying for drama on 'remarkable occurrences' and is full of what could be jokingly referred to as 'grumbling', the minute probing of injustices, great and small, that became characteristic of all Charlotte's novels. But the notebook contains an interesting fragment of a different story, at the back:

> There was once a large house called Gateshead stood not far from a [illeg.] high-road in the North of England – it is gone now every vestige of it, and the site is [replaced?] by a Railway Station. No great loss was the demolition of that said house for it was never a tasteful or picturesque building.

Charlotte Brontë later said that she always made two or three starts on her novels before settling down, and here we see a very early glimpse of her second novel, *Jane Eyre*, which opens at the home of Jane's aunt Reed, Gateshead Hall. It's odd to think Charlotte may have been hatching the story in the long lonely summer at the Pensionnat.

A cruel twist of fate was that Charlotte's solitude was broken only by the return at the end of August of the hated Mademoiselle Blanche from her holiday, after which they had to have meals together, conducted in rigid silence, so that Mademoiselle could be in no doubt of Miss Brontë's 'utter dislike'. '[She] never now speaks to me,' Charlotte reported to Emily with satisfaction; 'a great relief.' Charlotte took to walking the city streets to keep out of the way, and it was on one of these long days, 1 September, a Friday, that she went out to Saint-Josse-ten-Noode to visit Martha's grave. After visiting the cemetery,

Charlotte cast herself out further into the countryside, as far as she could go before the light began to fail. And that was the day when, coming back into the city at dusk, she let herself be drawn into the confessional at SS-Michel-et-Gudule.

'[W]hen people are by themselves they have singular fancies,' she told Emily, trying to relate this wholly uncharacteristic episode in a detached, almost anthropological manner, stressing novelties about the experience that she knew would interest her sister. 'They do not go into the sort of pew or cloister which the priest occupies, but kneel down on the steps and confess through a grating. Both the confessor and the penitent whisper very low, you can hardly hear their voices.' When her turn came, she explained, and the little wooden door behind the grating that separated her from the priest opened, Charlotte of course did not know what to do. 'It was a funny position,' she told Emily. 'I felt precisely as I did when alone on the Thames at midnight.' As on that strange, dark tide, Charlotte faced the unknown with an instinctive resolve to see it through, and though the priest, on hearing that she was a Protestant, at first refused to hear her confession, 'I was determined to confess.'

The corresponding scenes that form a crisis in *Villette*, the novel Charlotte wrote almost ten years later, could hardly be more different in tone. There is no joking or detachment here, though strung through the text are exact words and phrases from Charlotte's letter to Emily, and the movement of the narrative as the heroine is drawn into the *salut* by the bell as she passes the church, and joins the waiting penitents almost unawares, is identical. The incident in the novel is powered by the extraordinary force of mental horror that Lucy Snowe has experienced just before, alone in the Pensionnat:

> The solitude and the stillness of the long dormitory could not be borne any longer; the ghostly white beds were turning into spectres – the coronal of each became a death's head, huge and snow-bleached – dead dreams of an elder world and mightier race lay frozen in their wide gaping eye-holes.

This, from the perspective of 1852, has all the weight of the horrors Charlotte had lived through by that time, the devastating tragedies of her siblings' deaths. But her connection of that ravaged mental landscape with her time *in extremis* in Brussels is telling. These were consonant tides of suffering.

And Lucy's commerce with the priest in the confessional may give us a clue to what Charlotte Brontë said to the priest in the cathedral: not a confession of a sin or crime, not illicit love, but 'the mere outline of my experience'. Rather in the manner of unburdening oneself to a therapist or analyst, Lucy gains relief from 'pouring out of some portion of long accumulating, long pent-up pain into a vessel whence it could not be again diffused'.

When the Hegers returned from holiday and the school reassembled, Charlotte felt more homesick and isolated than ever. 'They are at their idolatrous "Messe",' she reported to Emily scornfully,

> and I am here, that is, in the Refectoire. I should like uncommonly to be in the dining-room at home, or in the kitchen, or in the back kitchen. I should like even to be cutting up the hash, with the clerk and some register-people at the other table, and you standing by, watching that I put enough flour, not too much pepper, and, above all, that I save the best pieces of the leg of mutton for Tiger and Keeper; the first of which personages would be jumping about the dish and carving-knife, and the latter standing like a devouring flame on the kitchen-floor ... How divine are these recollections to me at this moment!

But she felt that she lacked a 'pretext' for coming home: 'I have an idea that I should be of no use there; a sort of aged person upon the parish.'

Emily was clearly concerned about Charlotte's state of mind after receiving the letter about her confession and may have emphasised the severity of some news from home about the deterioration of their father's eyesight in order to sway Charlotte towards home and the call of duty; her father's condition certainly became Charlotte's presenting anxiety over the next few years. Emily might also have reported the gossip that was circulating in Haworth in October 1843 about the amount of alcohol the minister drank. Concern was such that the chairman of the Haworth Church Lands Trust and his wife had called at the Parsonage to assess the situation, after which Brontë issued a defiant denial, saying he would 'single out one or two of these slanderers and ... prosecute them, as the Law directs'. Perhaps some of his political enemies remarked that Brontë was both a founder member of the Haworth Temperance Society and a regular customer of James and Richard Thomas, wine merchants; someone had certainly complained that he smelt of alcohol. He had been using a lotion for his eyes, he explained, 'and they have ascribed the smell of that to a smell of a more exceptionable character'.

Patrick Brontë's behaviour was always sufficiently volatile to be interpreted as drunkenness, even when he was sober, and his eyesight was clouded by cataracts, so it is easy to see how he might have appeared drunk. But he became very defensive about the matter, preserving a copy of a letter to his old friend John Outhwaite of Bradford Infirmary in September 1844 with the words 'to be retained – semper', as if in expectation of having to produce evidence in his own defence. The letter signed off on their friendship in a stiff and proud way, and, though the editor of Brontë's letters speculates that this break might have been over politics (Outhwaite was always more rigidly conservative than Brontë), it smacks of something more personal and painful. Brontë had been sufficiently anxious about accusations of alcoholism to insist on getting his doctor's signature back in 1838 to a recommendation that, as a remedy for dyspepsia, he should take a glass of wine or spirits before dinner. And in 1841 one of his unsolicited letters of advice to *The Leeds Intelligencer* was on the medicinal value of a mixture of brandy and salt (proportions unstated), even to those not given to drink: 'Should any timid, over-scrupulous person imagine that this might lead to habits of intemperance, let him consider that such a melancholy result could never take place except where there was a previous bias, and that even where such a bias existed, the nauseous taste of the mixture I speak of would be far more likely to give a disrelish than an inclination for intoxicating liquors.'

Years later, Ellen Nussey claimed that Charlotte hurried home from Brussels on hearing that her father – in company with his curate Mr Smith – 'had fallen into habits of intemperance'. Ellen knew little, then or later, of Charlotte's racking misery over Constantin Heger, so may have misinterpreted some of the tensions in the household at the time, but insisted that she had been told about Reverend Brontë's problem 'by C. B. herself', who, she reported, 'remedied the evil . . . quietly and firmly' on arrival home.

*

In early October, Charlotte's nerve snapped and she went to Madame to give in her notice. The directrice, now just a few weeks away from the birth of her fourth daughter, accepted the resignation, probably with some relief, but when he was told about the move, her husband reacted very differently and called for Charlotte. His 'vehemence' against her decision surprised her and beat her down – 'I could not at that time have persevered in my intention without exciting him to passion' – but the scene was far from tender or gratifying, and since her departure was only delayed six weeks after this date, Heger's determination that she should stay till Christmas was probably prompted by reasons of orderliness and prior commitments, not least his wife's imminent confinement and the necessity of finding a replacement for the departing teacher.

The day after reporting this to Ellen, Charlotte sat at her desk on the *estrade* above the girls she was supervising, took her pen and wrote the following, neatly, inside the much-scribbled-on back boards of her copy of *Russell's General Atlas of Modern Geography*, brought from home:

> Brussels – Saturday Morning Octbr 14th 1843. – First Class – I am very
> cold – there is no Fire – I wish I were at home With Papa – Branwell
> Emily Anne & Tabby – I am tired of being amongst foreigners it is a
> dreary life – especially as there is only one person in this house worthy
> of being liked, also another who seems a rosy sugar-plum but I know
> her to be coloured chalk –

Charlotte used the unprinted backs of the maps in *Russell's General Atlas* as empty pages for doodling: she drew idealised heads, made lists and notes, and, very interestingly, totted up long calculations to do with lines and words, like the word count of a work in progress. Among the doodles is a romantic veiled female in three-quarter length, a bald man, a sharp-featured, frowning woman, a strange giant figure dancing among tiny ones, buildings, scribbles, eyes, mouths. There is also a queer little pencil drawing, on the reverse of the map of Australasia, of a young woman.* Her chin is resting on her right hand. She has hair parted in the middle and tied out of sight, a wide brow, prominent eyebrows and large, deep-set eyes, a long nose and a mouth that twists up at one side. An unflattering image, but one with the look of

---

* Reproduced at the front of this book.

having been observed from life rather than imagined. Could this be a self-portrait, made in Charlotte's long leisureless hours alone? In this season of miserable introspection, might she have done what Jane Eyre does as 'wholesome discipline': sit in front of a mirror and take her own likeness 'faithfully; without softening one defect: omit no harsh line, smooth away no displeasing irregularity; write under it, "Portrait of a Governess, disconnected, poor, and plain"'?* In the novel, the sketching of her own image is Jane's way of convincing herself that she must not interpret Rochester's behaviour towards her favourably. To do so is to court humiliation:

> '*You*,' I said, 'a favourite with Mr Rochester? *You* gifted with the power of pleasing him? *You* of importance to him in any way? Go! your folly sickens me. And you have derived pleasure from occasional tokens of preference – equivocal tokens, shown by a gentleman of family, and a man of the world, to a dependent and a novice. How dared you? Poor stupid dupe! – Could not even self-interest make you wiser? . . . It does good to no woman to be flattered by her superior, who cannot possibly intend to marry her; and it is madness in all women to let a secret love kindle within them, which, if unreturned and unknown, must devour the life that feeds it; and, if discovered and responded to, must lead, *ignis fatuus*-like, into miry wilds whence there is no extrication . . .'

A future as a teacher, not a poet, is what Constantin Heger imagined for his English pupil, and right up to the last Charlotte kept repeating the mantra of wanting to set up her own school. The Hegers were keen to encourage that idea and even suggested that they would send one of their own daughters to the Brontës as a pupil, though as the eldest, Pauline, was still only six, that was probably a gesture of goodwill rather than strong intent. Talking about thinking about running a school was one failsafe way to capture a little of Monsieur's attention, but throughout the whole two years of their acquaintance Charlotte had failed to make him understand that, bold though it might seem, her primary ambition lay quite beyond the classroom. One of her last *devoirs* for him, 'Lettre d'un pauvre Peintre à un grand Seigneur', tries to make it clear.

---

* To get the face turned aslant a self-portraitist would have to use two mirrors, no difficulty if the artist has access to a dressing table.

The letter is hardly at all about patronage, much about problems of artistic self-belief, as a young painter defiantly asserts his right to persevere in an artistic career despite the difficulties ahead: 'Do not be indignant at my presumption or accuse me of conceit; I do not know that feeble feeling, the child of vanity; but I know well another feeling, Respect for myself, a feeling born of independence and integrity. Milord, I believe I have Genius.'

'B', 'B', 'tr B', Heger wrote in the margins, lightly, in pencil. But there was no expansive commentary at the end of the paper, no engagement with the freighted content of this eloquent essay, which seems so directly addressed to him. Miss Brontë was preparing to leave the Pensionnat, and his work with her was 'done and well done', as one of his favourite phrases went.

By the middle of December, Charlotte's imminent departure was known all round the school and she was amazed to have pupils and fellow teachers express genuine sadness about it. 'I did not think it had been in their phlegmatic natures,' she said to Ellen, continuing an ungenerous habit of mind towards the Belgians she had lived with for two years. Mademoiselle Sophie was suddenly being nice to her and giving her souvenirs; the girls were relenting and wishing her well. On 10 December, a Sunday, she was taken to a concert at the Salle de la Grande Harmonie, an episode that she put into *Villette* in detail. One of the performers was Monsieur Chapelle, and perhaps he and his brother-in-law arranged the treat as a thank you to the departing assistant.

On 29 December, Monsieur Heger devised a little ceremonial that celebrated Charlotte's achievements at the Pensionnat, presenting her with a diploma, signed by himself and sealed with the seal of the Athénée Royal de Bruxelles, that certified her ability to teach French.* When she parted with him three days later, he gave her an anthology of sixteenth-century French verse, which she inscribed, with the same precision as usually accorded his presents: 'Given to me by Monsieur Heger on the 1st January 1844, the morning I left Brussels.' This last interview proved overwhelmingly emotional for Charlotte: 'I suffered much before I left Brussels – I think however long I live I shall not

---

* Only the envelope now remains (at BPM), but from what she says about it in *Life*, Mrs Gaskell must have seen the original in 1856–7.

forget what the parting with Monsr Heger cost me – It grieved me so much to grieve him who has been so true and kind and disinterested a friend.' *His* reciprocal sorrow at parting seems to explain a lot of Charlotte's subsequent anguish. It calls to mind the scene depicted in Charlotte's poem 'I gave, at first, Attention close' (later inserted into *The Professor*), where the teacher parting with his star pupil clasps her to his breast, a gesture that, if it happened in real life (as was likely – Heger was French, after all), would certainly have stoked Charlotte's already heated feelings. It also evokes the scene in *Jane Eyre* when Jane faces separation from Rochester just as her feelings for him have become clear: 'I have talked, face to face, with what I reverence; with what I delight in, – with an original, a vigorous, an expanded mind. I have known you, Mr. Rochester; and it strikes me with terror and anguish to feel I absolutely must be torn from you for ever. I see the necessity of departure; and it is like looking on the necessity of death.'

In the novel, the wrenching pain of separation is miraculously over-turned by Rochester's immediate declaration of love, proposal of marriage and rapturous embraces. In *Villette* too there is a parting scene that turns into a declaration of love: Paul Emanuel takes Lucy's hand and pushes back her bonnet to look into her face; later 'he gently raised his hand to stroke my hair; it touched my lips in passing; I pressed it close, I paid it tribute.' These tiny gestures, so minutely observed, are full of very obvious sexual meaning in Charlotte's fiction. In life, they caused her a great deal of anguish, but from this discrepancy – which was by no means a simple one, of an infatuated young woman on one side and a somewhat too demonstrative man on the other – the erotic charge of a classic novel was generated.

Madame Heger accompanied Charlotte to the packet boat at Ostend, on what must have been a dreadfully uncomfortable journey for both of them. There was a story that as they parted finally, Charlotte turned to her erstwhile employer and said, 'Je me vengerai!' – '*I will have my revenge!*' Such words are very unlikely to have been uttered. But the feelings were certainly there.

9

Long-looked-for Tidings

1844–5

On the morning that the packet steamer took Charlotte back across the Channel, 2 January 1844, the town she was coming home to was astir with excitement at the opening of a new day school in the Church Lane building. It was a proud if anxious occasion for Patrick Brontë, his latest move to fight back against the growing influence of Dissenters in the parish. In Charlotte's absence, he had secured a curate for Oxenhope and rented a room in which services could be held (to save parishioners the long walk to St Michael's). The day school was another attempt to nurture allegiance to the Established Church.

There was also a new curate in Haworth since Charlotte was last at home, an Irish graduate of Trinity College Dublin called James Smith, who had arrived in March 1843 (and whom the gossips had claimed was Patrick Brontë's secret drinking companion). Smith was energetic, but no substitute for William Weightman, and his temperament was too volatile to seem entirely trustworthy.* The incumbent was better pleased with his new schoolmaster, Ebenezer Rand, who was only twenty-three but learned and ambitious, and who managed to attract 170 pupils to the day school within the first six months. The usual excitement attending the arrival of a highly eligible young man in a small town was short-lived, for Rand seems to have come to Haworth already intending to marry a woman called Sarah Bacon, which he did that spring, and soon afterwards his reasonable request for an assistant at the school was answered by her appointment as schoolmistress at £20 per annum. Thus he both frustrated local spinsters by not being properly in want of a wife, and must have caused disappointment at the

---

* He was suspected of fiddling the accounts at his next parish, Keighley, and emigrated to North America in 1848 under a cloud.

Parsonage with the swift disposal of a job which any of the Brontë sisters would have been glad to take.

Charlotte was made very much aware of her father's increased agitation and distraction, and of the deterioration in his sight during her two years abroad, evident in the large, messy characters of his handwriting at this date. In February 1844 Reverend Brontë was putting off visiting the Taylors at the Manor House in Stanbury until there was a thaw, 'as my eyes, are very weak, I cannot, very well, go out whilst the snow, is on the ground.' His parish work fell largely on the shoulders of the curate, Mr Smith, and the household was left to Emily and Charlotte to run.

Charlotte sought to reassure him about her future by reviving the long-discussed plan for the girls to start up their own school at the Parsonage. She seemed newly motivated in that direction, and the diploma from Monsieur Heger could not have failed to impress her father. But privately Charlotte was terribly despondent and deflated after the heightened emotions of her departure from the rue d'Isabelle. '[T]here are times now when it appears to me as if all my ideas and feelings except a few friendships and affections are changed from what they used to be,' she wrote to Ellen three weeks after getting home; 'something in me which used to be enthusiasm is tamed down and broken – I have fewer illusions – what I wish for now is active exertion – a stake in life – Haworth seems such a lonely, quiet spot, buried away from the world – I no longer regard myself as young, indeed I shall soon be 28 – and it seems as if I ought to be working and braving the rough realities of the world as other people do.' *Ought to be working*, and could have been: Charlotte's return to Yorkshire, diplomaed and trilingual, had prompted interest in her as a teacher and soon after getting home she had received an invitation to run a large boarding school in Manchester for the impressive sum of £100 a year (which school and by whom is not known).* She dismissed the offer for what sounded like a rock-solid reason: her father needed her at home. But was that a valid explanation for passing up an opportunity like the one in Manchester, especially when Emily was at home now for good? Without

---

* The only reference to it is in CB's letter to Constantin Heger of 24 July 1844 (*LCB* 1, 358).

casting doubt on Charlotte's genuine concern for her father's welfare, she was very capable of overlooking it when she really wanted to do something (such as return to Brussels after Aunt Branwell's death) and capable also of using it as an excuse for inaction, as she did on many occasions over the next years.

She knew she could not bear to go back to being a governess again, and, although the practical difficulties of setting up her own establishment gave Charlotte many welcome reasons to stay in touch with Constantin Heger, in discussing them with her father, she saw only how unlikely it was that they could afford to convert the Parsonage into a school, or persuade anyone to send their children to it. She seemed in a state of suspended animation, waiting to be rescued by someone or something. And although she wrote to one of her former Belgian pupils (whom she now addressed fondly as 'My dear little Victoire') that she was 'not likely' ever to return to Brussels, she told Heger that as soon as she had the money, she would come back to see him, 'if it is only for a moment'. 'Oh it is certain that I shall see you again one day – it really has to be.'

She must have begun writing to him almost as soon as she was home, and he replied – not ardently, not quickly, but still, he replied. Perhaps this led Charlotte to think that the thing she wanted most – constant access to Heger's mind and possession of his attention – might be possible after all. 'I look on your letters as one of the greatest joys I know,' she told him unequivocally. 'I shall wait patiently to receive them until it pleases and suits you to send them.' By the time she wrote that, in July, she had already incurred Heger's displeasure for sending 'a letter which was hardly rational' (now lost). She swore such a performance would not be repeated (she lied), but at the rue d'Isabelle, Heger must have realised that all his worst fears about Charlotte were turning out to be true. She was obsessed with him, woefully dependent on his attention and behaving more like an incubus than a friend. He didn't answer.

None of Heger's letters to her and only four of Charlotte's to him survive from what must have been a fairly copious and almost entirely one-sided correspondence. These heartbreaking documents, three of which were torn up at some date and then very carefully mended, are possibly the most wrenching examples of unsolicited, unrequited love laments in our whole literature, 'a record of romantic love . . . that has never before been rivalled', as Frederika Macdonald described them soon after their publication in 1913. Except that, of course, they were not written *as literature*. Charlotte Brontë transferred much of the passion and yearning and heartbreak mapped out here into her novels, but she lived it first.

The first of the surviving letters, written on 24 July 1844, was already far into their correspondence and refers to Heger's request that she should not write to him again out of turn, a mild enough restriction, given that 'letter which was hardly rational' earlier in the year. By writing to him at all on 24 July, Charlotte was breaking the compact, but imagined there *had* to be some pressing professional reason for his uncommunicativeness – the end of term, the exams. Pathetically, she protested that she didn't want to 'add an atom to the burden . . . But all the same I can still write you a little letter from time to time – you have given me permission to do so.' It's clear that Charlotte can't believe Heger is deliberately ignoring her, can't believe that his feelings for her could have changed so significantly – or that she could have misinterpreted them in the first place.

There was indeed, she argued, a real *necessity* for her to keep in touch with him. She was anxious that she might forget French, she said, so was setting herself half a page a day to memorise and recite aloud, a process that let her imagine they were 'chatting' together. Keeping up her fluency was not just a matter of intellectual pride but had a poignant personal motive, which Heger can't have been comforted to hear: 'for I am quite convinced that I shall see you again one day – I don't know how or when – but it must happen since I so long for it, and then I would not like to stay silent in your presence – it would be too sad to see you and not be able to speak to you.' How like a ghost this makes her sound, a revenant appearing before him but condemned to silence.

What she really wanted to tell Heger was that she had not given up her true ambition:

I fear nothing so much as idleness – lack of employment – inertia – lethargy of the faculties – when the body is idle, the spirit suffers cruelly. I would not experience this lethargy if I could write – once upon a time I used to spend whole days, weeks, complete months in writing and not quite in vain since Southey and Coleridge – two of our

best authors, to whom I sent some manuscripts were pleased to express
their approval of them – but at present my sight is too weak for writing
– if I wrote a lot I would become blind.

Heger would of course have remembered the thick glasses from behind
which Miss Brontë's penetrating gaze was projected, her bent form
straining over a book, her uncertain apprehension of his approach, and
changed expression when she was sure of it. But this claim of incipient
blindness (in step, in sympathy, in competition, with her father?) must
have sounded neurotic, as it partly was.

> This weakness of sight is a terrible privation for me – without it, do you
> know what I would do, Monsieur? – I would write a book and I would
> dedicate it to my literature master – to the only master that I have ever
> had – to you Monsieur . . . That cannot be – it must not be thought of
> – a literary career is closed to me – only that of teaching is open to me
> – it does not offer the same attractions – never mind, I shall enter upon
> it and if I do not go far in it, it will not be for want of diligence.

Heger kept this very personal and confiding letter, talked to Elizabeth
Gaskell about it twelve years later and copied out this passage for use in
Gaskell's biography of Charlotte (where it was duly printed) – but he
did not answer it. Charlotte began to wonder – hope – if perhaps it had
gone astray, and on 24 October took advantage of Joe Taylor's return
to Brussels to send Heger another letter, deliberately simple and cheery,
to make sure of a reply this time and to present herself as busy, buoyant
and normal – not a postal stalker, in other words. Her artificial optimism is painful to read:

> I am not going to write a long letter – first of all I haven't the time – it
> has to go immediately – and then I am afraid of bothering you. I would
> just like to ask you whether you heard from me at the beginning of May
> and then in the month of August? For all those six months I have been
> expecting a letter from you, Monsieur – six months of waiting – is a
> very long time indeed! Nevertheless I am not complaining and I shall be
> richly recompensed for a little sadness – if you are now willing to write
> a letter and give it to this gentleman – or to his sister – who would
> deliver it to me without fail.

There was no reply to this letter either. Week after week went by in painful vigil, waiting for the post, which arrived at Haworth post office 'from all parts' at noon each day and was dispatched from there at three. Charlotte had written about such a situation in 'Passing Events' and in *Jane Eyre*, when 'the long-looked-for tidings' from Mr Rochester turn out to be a business note, but the strongest expression of this peculiarly female form of love-agony is expressed in *Villette*, and seems, like so much in that book, to reflect real experience:

> My hour of torment was the post-hour. Unfortunately I knew it too well, and tried as vainly as assiduously to cheat myself of that knowledge; dreading the rack of expectation, and the sick collapse of disappointment which daily preceded and followed upon that well-recognised ring.
>
> I suppose animals kept in cages, and so scantily fed as to be always upon the verge of famine, await their food as I awaited a letter . . . The well-beloved letter – would not come; and it was all of sweetness in life I had to look for.

Charlotte was expecting to see either Joe or Mary Taylor back from Brussels in November, but both postponed their returns for several weeks. Of course, Heger could have written at any time by post, but did not, and when Joe Taylor called at the Parsonage just after Christmas there was nothing by hand either. The disappointment felled Charlotte, but she hung on, waiting to see if Mary brought anything. A tender message, apologising for the silence and making amends, might have taken him longer to write . . . Mary might have been a more suitable emissary . . . there might even have been a gift to bring too, a token? But Mary, full of news, full of plans, full of advice as ever, arrived empty-handed. 'I did my utmost not to cry not to complain,' Charlotte wrote, but once Mary had left, her resolve crumbled. Given so many opportunities to communicate, and doing nothing, could be interpreted only as deliberate cruelty on Heger's part. She sat down to compose a searing, accusatory letter, letting him know what she was going through:

> – I said to myself, what I would say to someone else in such a case 'You will have to resign yourself to the fact, and above all, not distress yourself about a misfortune that you have not deserved.'

. . . But when one does not complain, and when one wants to master oneself with a tyrant's grip – one's faculties rise in revolt – and one pays for outward calm by an almost unbearable inner struggle.

Day and night I find neither rest nor peace – if I sleep I have tormenting dreams in which I see you always severe, always saturnine and angry with me –

Forgive me then Monsieur if I take the step of writing to you again – How can I bear my life unless I make an effort to alleviate its sufferings?

She had reached a point where there was nothing for it but to be explicit, even if, as she was aware, 'some cold and rational people' (i.e., his wife) 'would say on reading it – "she is raving"':

all I know – is that I cannot – that I will not resign myself to the total loss of my master's friendship – I would rather undergo the greatest bodily pains than have my heart constantly lacerated by searing regrets. If my master withdraws his friendship from me entirely I shall be absolutely without hope – if he gives me a little friendship – a very little – I shall be content – happy, I would have a motive for living – for working.

Monsieur, the poor do not need a great deal to live on – they ask only the crumbs of bread which fall from the rich men's table – but if they are refused these crumbs – they die of hunger – No more do I need a great deal of affection from those I love – I would not know what to do with a whole and complete friendship – I am not accustomed to it – but you showed a *little* interest in me in days gone by when I was your pupil in Brussels – and I cling to the preservation of this *little* interest – I cling to it as I would cling on to life.

'*Un peu* d'intérêt': sadly, it would indeed have sufficed Charlotte to have any word or friendly gesture from Heger at this stage, if only to perpetuate her hope in the recovery and regrowth of their relationship, but she deceived him, and herself, by suggesting that mere crumbs would suffice for long. She was right to say that she wouldn't really have known what to do with 'une amitié entière et complète': the union she craved with Heger was one of souls; a possession, a haunting, a living-through, a sharing of ideas, intensely verbal, profoundly silent, an enveloping warmth of love and shared awareness of power. Sex too, no doubt, if their charged beings had ever been in contact with each other again. But anything so paltry as a conventional friendship, anything as quotidian as adultery even, was clearly not in her mind.

She begged him to write, and to tell her candidly if he had entirely forgotten her. There was no reply.

Mary Taylor, who had come back to Yorkshire preparatory to her momentous move to New Zealand, was concerned at the state her friend was in, but clear about the solution. In her robust and far-sighted view, financial independence was the only way for women to avoid not simply poverty but the sort of 'self-suppression' that Charlotte was locked into. Such behaviour seemed perverse, as Mary told Mrs Gaskell years later:

> [S]he thought that there must be some possibility for some people of having a life of more variety and more communion with human kind, but she saw none for her. I told her very warmly that she ought not to stay at home ... Such a dark shadow came over her face when I said 'Think of what you'll be five years hence!' that I stopped, and said 'Don't cry, Charlotte!' She did not cry, but went on walking up and down the room, and said in a little while, 'But I intend to stay, Polly.'

Watching her friend pacing up and down like a caged animal (the image Charlotte herself used), Mary could only repeat that she should get away – and probably held out the offer of emigrating together, which would have suited Mary down to the ground. She had a low opinion of Reverend Brontë, describing him to Mrs Gaskell as a 'selfish old man', the recollection of whom filled her with 'gloomy anger'. Charlotte's grim determination to sacrifice herself to his needs at this point seemed inexplicable, but what Mary didn't understand (quite apart from Charlotte's extremely strong family loyalties) was the depth of Charlotte's misery about Monsieur Heger, or that, when she turned up at Haworth, Charlotte had been convinced Mary would have with her a letter from him.

By the time she saw Mary in late December 1844, Charlotte had been home almost a whole year, but had very little to report for it. She had taken over some of Aunt Branwell's functions, including the sort of civilities that Emily would *never* have willingly instigated or performed, such as entertaining Ebenezer Rand and his wife to tea; and trying to be polite to Mr Smith, who moved to Keighley that year, or to the new curate, Mr Grant, who replaced him temporarily in Haworth. But the adoption of this matronly mantle was clearly a bad sign, as Mary Taylor recognised. Aunt Branwell had herself been notably reclusive, and since none of the current generation of Brontës had married or spread out to their own households, the effects of isolation became more and more concentrated. The Brontë family saw less of their remaining relations than one would think possible, given that there was no known breach with any of them. Patrick Brontë never travelled back to the old country, or invited any of his brothers, sisters, nephews and nieces; until his death in 1841 they had kept in touch sporadically with (but rarely saw) great-uncle John Fennell, who had lived nearby in Todmorden since 1819; there was correspondence with Eliza Kingston in Cornwall following Aunt Branwell's death (prompted by business to do with Aunt's will); and in the 1850s they received a visit from two of the Branwell cousins (possibly drawn at that date by Charlotte's fame). That, as far as can be traced, was it, and that was obviously how it suited them.

With Emily, Charlotte walked on the moors until their shoes were worn almost out, talking over the school plan and their writing. Emily was enjoying an intensely productive period of poetry, and had begun copying her work into two separate notebooks – one called 'Gondal Poems' and the other 'E. J. B.', as if to make a clear separation at last between one side of her work and another. That Anne knew about Emily's surge in production and creativity is evident from her Diary Paper in 1845; Charlotte probably also knew by report – but she wasn't shown any of her sister's work.

Charlotte had got as far as having 'cards of terms' for their school printed in August 1844 and sent some to Ellen to pass round her acquaintance and canvass interest. The cards made the project sound almost real: 'The Misses Brontë's Establishment for the Board and Education of a limited number of Young Ladies, The Parsonage, Haworth, near Bradford' was to offer, for the sum of £35 a year, full board and tuition in writing, arithmetic, history, geography, grammar and needle-work. Extras in French, German, Latin, music and drawing would be available at a guinea a quarter each and laundry was extra too. None of this was cheap, by the lights of the day,★ and August was possibly not the best time of year to start looking for pupils. Forced to solicit for custom, Charlotte swallowed her disinclination to write to and call on suitable local families, but she hardly pursued the matter very far. Mrs Busfeild of Keighley regretted, as did others, that she had already placed her daughters elsewhere and hinted that the price was a bit high, given the 'retired situation' of Haworth (she didn't need to add anything about the town's lack of gentility). The Whites of Stonegappe, possibly rather surprised that Miss Brontë should be reviving their acquaintance, told her that if she had only written sooner, they might have sent their own daughter and recommended the school to Colonel Stott and his wife. As it was, those girls were all off to the Misses Cockills at Oakwell Hall in Birstall, an establishment whose success Charlotte had been watching carefully: Elizabeth Cockill had been one of her contemporaries at Roe Head.

Market forces were strongly at work in the burgeoning local school network. Patrick Brontë must have realised that it would be hard to keep a man of Ebenezer Rand's ability in a place with so few opportunities for advance (the Rands left in 1845), but he had hoped to be able at least to support the schoolmaster's post, and if possible to increase his salary, by voluntary subscriptions and the twopence per week fee that each pupil was charged. But when the new Wesleyan school in West Lane undercut the church school's fee, Reverend Brontë was forced to lower his prices and go cap-in-hand again to the National Society for a grant. And when only £20 was forthcoming from that quarter to help the school through its second year, he had to keep petitioning local worthies for donations to keep it afloat. All this would have been difficult and distasteful, even for robust business people, as the Brontës were certainly not.

By early October 1844 the sisters had given it all up. 'Every one wishes us well,' Charlotte told Ellen, 'but there are no pupils to be had.' This outcome seemed to be a relief to everyone. Patrick Brontë, a man who disliked dining with his own children, can never have relished the idea of sharing his home with five or six teenage strangers (his

---

★ And was £10 more than Charlotte had been considering only weeks before (see *LCB* 1, 363).

willingness to consider it at all was a powerful mark of his goodwill);
Emily had never been keen on teaching, or company – her vision had
been of holidays and money; Anne was inured to her position at Thorp
Green; and all three sisters wanted to write more than anything else.
'We have no present intention however of breaking our hearts on the
subject,' Charlotte concluded briskly.

When she came to write about it in 1857, Mrs Gaskell saw another
powerful impediment to the furtherance of the school plan – Branwell
Brontë, whose 'occasional home . . . could hardly be a fitting residence
for the children of strangers'. By 1845, Mrs Gaskell believed, his sisters
were 'silently aware that his habits were such as to render his society at
times most undesirable'. Bombarded with local gossip just eleven
years later, Mrs Gaskell came to the very reasonable conclusion that the
Brontë sisters had heard the same 'distressing rumours concerning
the cause of that remorse and agony of mind, which at times made
[Branwell] restless and unnaturally merry, at times rendered him
moody and irritable'. Opium-eating was one of his recreations, alcohol
another, poetry a third: between them, Branwell Brontë was prey to
powerful mood swings. When he was home from Thorp Green in the
summer of 1844, Charlotte had found his presence in the household
very disturbing, and to Heger she had described him as 'toujours malade'. 'Ill' became the family euphemism for 'drunk', but as yet none of
them apart from Anne had an inkling of what else Branwell was up to.
Patrick Brontë, forever wishing to see the proper start of his son's brilliant career, could only have been relieved that he had held down the
job at the Robinsons' for a whole eighteen months.

In fact, Branwell had been involved in a liaison with his employer's
wife almost from his arrival at Thorp Green, and the excitement and
melodrama of it worked on his flammable temperament to very ill-
effect. His success as a published poet in the local press had stoked his
ego and ambitions, and it was in the character of half-discovered genius
that he and Lydia Robinson began their affair. To his old friend Francis
Grundy, with whom he had been out of touch for two years, Branwell
described how it happened:

This lady [Lydia Robinson] (though her husband detested me) showed
me a degree of kindness which, when I was deeply grieved one day at

her husband's conduct, ripened into declarations of more than ordinary feeling. My admiration of her mental and personal attractions, my knowledge of her unselfish sincerity, her sweet temper and unwearied care for others, with but unrequited return where most should have been given . . . although she is seventeen years my senior, all combined to an attachment on my part, and led to reciprocations which I had little looked for.

Branwell's aggravation when he was at home in the summer of 1844 was at separation from this Sybil, with whom he was in constant correspondence – a fact that can't have escaped Charlotte's notice, nor Anne's. Anne is likely to have had suspicions about the relationship from the start, and must have had to endure many painful moments at Thorp Green resulting from it.

Anne gave in her notice in the middle of June 1845, just before the Robinson family were about to go on their annual seaside holiday. Her inability to explain fully why she was resigning must have perturbed both her employer and her family, and have alerted Mrs Robinson to the coming storm. She came home under this cloud, loyally silent, and didn't tell Charlotte what was going on until the latter's return from a holiday with Ellen in Derbyshire in July. By that time, Branwell had also arrived home, 'ill' ('he is so very often owing to his own fault,' Charlotte reported angrily to Ellen; 'I was not therefore shocked at first'). But this wasn't a holiday from work or a routine bender: Anne had to explain that Branwell had been sacked by Mr Robinson for 'proceedings which he characterised as bad beyond expression'.* The Thorp Green gardener had apparently alerted his employer after surprising Mrs Robinson and Branwell alone in a boathouse, and the tutor was dismissed at once in a furious letter from the injured spouse that charged him 'on pain of exposure' to break off all communication with every member of the family.

Lydia Robinson seems to have successfully represented herself to her husband as blameless after the exposure of her boathouse tryst, for the

---

* Some commentators have suggested that Branwell's 'proceedings . . . bad beyond expression' might have involved sexual offences against his pupil Edmund Robinson, then fourteen, though Juliet Barker has countered this theory convincingly (Barker, 456–64).

Robinsons continued their holiday in Scarborough after the crisis without undue disruption – Mr Robinson even bought his wife a necklace. Back at Haworth Parsonage, Branwell also claimed innocence, of a kind, and 'spoke freely' with his father on the subject, leaving the latter in no doubt that 'intimacy' had taken place, but also that the blame lay squarely with the matron, whom Reverend Brontë described to Elizabeth Gaskell as a 'diabolical seducer'. Whether the girls were as ready to exculpate Branwell was another matter: Anne was shocked and ashamed for her brother; Emily inclined to put the matter behind them all and move on. The person who felt most anger and mortification, and the one to whom Branwell felt the need to apologise by letter, was Charlotte, who was not just appalled by his behaviour but secretly furious at the ease with which he had been able to indulge his passions, while she was almost killing herself with the suppression of her own.

In the novel she finished the following year, Charlotte's violent feelings about Branwell's adultery are articulated in an extraordinary outburst by the protagonist William Crimsworth, who reflects on having observed close at hand an example of 'romantic domestic treachery': 'No golden halo of fiction was about this example, I saw it bare and real and it was very loathsome. I saw a mind degraded by the practice of mean subterfuge, by the habit of perfidious deception, and a body depraved by the infectious influence of the vice-polluted soul.' This, like the other eruptions of feeling in the book (and in Charlotte's later novels), has the quality of a hell-fire sermon. Crimsworth leaves his job because the woman who has been trying to engage his affections, Mademoiselle Reuter (a thinly disguised portrait of Zoë Heger), is about to marry his employer, and he imagines that if they live under one roof, adultery with her will follow inevitably. Charlotte is here both sympathising with young men who might find themselves targeted by vicious and predatory females and blaming those who don't take firm steps to avoid temptations in the first place. A young unmarried woman, by inference, has to be even more vigilant against her own passions. But that is not to say those passions, and adulterous impulses, don't exist.

The new curate who arrived in May 1845 was just in time to make the acquaintance of the Brontë family before they received the hammer-blow of Branwell's fresh disgrace. Arthur Bell Nicholls was a rather straight-laced 26-year-old Irishman, just out of Trinity College Dublin. He had been born near Belfast but had lived since the age of seven with a childless uncle and aunt in Banagher on the Shannon, a name which can't have failed to strike a chord with Charlotte, since she believed her hero Wellington (another Arthur) to have hailed from the same area. Nicholls's arrival was welcome and overdue for hard-pressed Patrick Brontë and immediately relieved him of many duties and services, including the management of the school. Charlotte was able to report to Mrs Rand after only a couple of weeks that Nicholls 'appears a respectable young man, reads well, and I hope will give satisfaction'. On the whole, though, she was extremely out of patience with the type. Before their visit to Hathersage in the summer, Ellen had been trying to interest her in one of Henry Nussey's clerical neighbours, a Mr Rooker, but Charlotte wrote back sharply that any visit to her brother's parish would not be on that account. '[He] must be like all the other curates I have seen,' she said, 'and they seem to me a self-seeking, vain, empty race.' The Haworth area seemed to be suddenly overrun with curates: Joseph Grant in Oxenhope (where he was in charge of the grammar school), James Bradley in Oakworth and now Arthur Nicholls in the home church. James Smith in Keighley was these young men's social leader and they could often be found together, in one another's lodgings, or descending *en masse* on the Parsonage unannounced, as they did one afternoon in June 1845. Perhaps this noisy group ate too much (in *Shirley*, Charlotte includes a very funny but feeling description of a curate's landlady being eaten out of house and home by him and his colleagues), they certainly *talked* too much – and Charlotte, seething over the teacups for a while at the presumption of these backwater boobies, suddenly let fly: 'I pronounced a few sentences sharply & rapidly which struck them all dumb,' she told Ellen, with evident satisfaction. 'Papa was greatly horrified also – I don't regret it.'

Charlotte's visit to Hathersage in July was an oblique reminder of what she had passed up in refusing Henry Nussey's proposal six years earlier, for she and Ellen stayed at the Vicarage to which he was about to bring his new bride, handsome and rich Miss Emily Prescott. Charlotte felt not a single pang of jealousy of the new Mrs Nussey; one feels she would always have much rather kept house with Ellen than with any man.

The holiday, which immediately preceded her hearing of Branwell's disgrace, was full of gentle pleasures, not least discovering the beauty of the Peak District, whose limestone dales, dramatic escarpments and caverns full of rare Blue John stone had been a draw for the romantic tourist for decades. The handsome Vicarage, nestled in a group of houses around the hilltop church in a beautiful prospect of rolling greenery, was like a Haworth enskied. Ellen and Charlotte went by pony and trap to Castleton and the ruins of Peveril Castle (whose associations with Walter Scott's novel *Peveril of the Peak* would have thrilled them) and a walk of about a mile through the fields outside Hathersage brought them to North Lees Hall, a small, battlemented stone house built in Elizabethan times. There the owner, a widow called Mary Eyre, told the young women of the ruined Catholic chapel nearby, showed them a tall cabinet decorated with heads of the twelve apostles and told them how a former mistress of the house had gone mad and been kept in a padded room on the top floor, where she died in a fire that had once damaged the house severely. In the parish church, they admired the ancient brasses of these Eyres, and the tomb of Damer de Rochester. Charlotte took it all in.

Back home, some decision had to be made about Branwell, who was keeping the household awake at night with his noisy despairing over Lydia Robinson. At the end of July he was sent to Liverpool and north Wales with his friend John Brown as minder, allowing the household at home a short respite. Emily was the only one to remain sanguine in the crisis, writing in her Diary Paper on her birthday, 'I am quite contented for myself . . . seldom or ever troubled with nothing to do . . . and merely desiring that every body could be as comfortable as myself and as undesponding and then we should have a very tolerable world of it.' Emily's contentment was partly to do with her continued pleasure in writing, which included her poems and 'a work on the First Wars' of Gondal, now lost. 'The Gondals still flo[u]rish bright as ever,' she reported to the little tin box, and it's odd to see her, at the age of twenty-seven, with an absolutely undiminished enthusiasm for role-playing. Her account of a two-day trip to York with Anne in June makes the undiscovered genius sound positively childlike, from the very fact that it was 'our first long Journey by ourselves' to the way they spent the excursion conspiratorially 'in character' as their Gondal avatars.

Anne was in a less equable mood as a result of her recent experiences at Thorp Green, as Charlotte acknowledged in 1850: 'hers was naturally a sensitive, reserved, and dejected nature; what she saw sank very deeply into her mind; it did her harm'. Having to resign her post after so many years of *being resigned* to it was less of an escape than a defeat; Branwell's transgressions had also lost Anne the friendship of the younger Robinson girls and affected her chances of getting a good 'character' from her former employers. Anne's Diary Paper is peppered with questions and uncertainty:

[Charlotte] is now sitting sewing in the Dining-Room Emily is ironing upstairs I am sitting in the Dining-Room in the Rocking chair before the fire with my feet on the fender Papa is in the parlour Tabby and Martha I think are in the Kitchen Keeper and Flossy are I do not know where little Dick [the canary] is hopping in his cage – When the last paper was written we were thinking of setting up a school – the scheem has been dropt and long after taken up again and dropt again because we could not get pupils – Charlotte is thinking about getting another situation – she wishes to go to Paris – Will she go? she has let Flossy in by the bye and he is now lying on the sopha – Emily is engeaged in writing the Emperor Julius's life she has read some of it and I very much want to hear the rest – she is writing some poetry too I wonder what it is about – I have begun the third volume of passages in the life of an Individual. I wish I had finished it – This afternoon I began to set about making my grey figured silk frock that was dyed at Keigthley – What sort of a hand shall I make of it? E. and I have a great deal of work to do – when shall we sensibly diminish it? I want to get a habit of early rising shall I succeed? . . . I wonder how we shall all be and where and how situated on the thirtyeth of July 1848 when if we are all alive Emily will be just 30 I shall be in my 29th year Charlotte in her 33rd and Branwell in his 32nd and what changes shall we have seen and known and shall we be much chan[g]ed ourselves? I hope not – for the worse [a]t least – I for my part cannot well b[e] *flatter* or older in mind than I am n[o]w – Hoping for the best I conclude Anne Brontë

Charlotte . . . wishes to go to Paris. This wish, clearly never put into action, shows Charlotte's restlessness after Branwell's return. 'My hopes ebb low indeed about Branwell,' she confided to Ellen, only a few weeks later. 'I sometimes fear he will never be fit for much – his bad habits seem more deeply rooted than I thought.' This is the first indication that Charlotte now understood her brother to be addicted to drink and, probably, opium as well. 'It is only absolute want of means that acts as any check to him,' she noted with disgust. Mrs Gaskell, relying on local sources other than Charlotte, one presumes, dated his full-blown addiction from this year: 'In procuring it he showed all the cunning of the opium-eater. He would steal out while the family were at church – to which he had professed himself too ill to go – and manage to cajole the village druggist out of a lump; or, it might be, the carrier had unsuspiciously brought him some in a packet from a distance.'

Getting away from home again, and getting nearer to Brussels, held out to Charlotte a glimmer of hope in this otherwise bleak time. On the way back from Hathersage, she had shared a railway carriage with a man who looked so French that she felt emboldened to address him in the language. 'He gave a start of surprise and answered immediately in his own tongue.' Hearing French again after so long 'sounded like music in my ears', as she confided to Heger a few months later. 'Every word was most precious to me because it reminded me of you.'

In an overlooked remark made to her publisher's editor two years later (in December 1847), Charlotte mentions 'a brief translation of some French verses sent anonymously to a Magazine', which was the only thing she had published by that date, besides her 'little book of rhymes' (*Poems*, 1846) and *Jane Eyre*. The magazine has never been identified, but the work could have been her translation of Auguste Barbier's poem about Napoleon, 'L'Idole', her only remaining attempt at 'some French verses' of the right date, and could have been worked on and submitted to a periodical at any time in 1844 or 1845. This unidentified and anonymous publication, now lost, was Charlotte Brontë's first appearance in print. It seems significant that after all her years of feverish ambition 'to be forever known' as a poet, her solicitations of notice from Southey, Coleridge and others, her authorship of hundreds of thousands of words of prose and verse of her own, she finally made her debut as a translator of poetry from the French. Attracting the attention of a magazine editor through the work of Barbier (or Belmontet, André Chénier, Millevoye – whichever poet it was: she was interested in them all) would have been easier than getting her own 'rhymes' published, but in 1844 and 1845 her priorities had shifted. Getting published was no longer a matter of lofty, distant personal ambition, but a way – perhaps the *only* way – to maintain communication with Constantin Heger. Sending him a magazine in which her translation appeared – undoubtedly of a text he had recommended to her in Brussels – would have made it almost impossible for him not to respond, surely? And the evidence of her intellectual and creative progress would have been a way of 'proving' that he, and Madame, had misjudged her frantic need to correspond. She wasn't a lovesick troublemaker, after all; she was a writer.

In their changed, unhappy household, each of the Brontë siblings was, separately and to a great extent privately, taking refuge in writing. They were all desperate for money and employment; indeed it is hard to see how Patrick Brontë could have afforded to have all four adult children back at home, not earning a penny. Writing, the old solace, now was also the only resource. Anne, as her diary makes clear, had almost finished a three-volume novel called 'Passages in the Life of an Individual' (almost certainly the work that appeared later as *Agnes Grey*), and Emily must have started her own novel around this time. Branwell was convinced that fiction writing was an easy road to riches and had drafted about forty pages of a story called 'And the Weary are at Rest', from which he hoped to earn at least £200. He also saw publication as a way to win back favour with Lydia Robinson, with whom he was more obsessed than ever. On 25 November he sent Leyland a very personal poem for *The Halifax Guardian* under his usual signature, 'Northangerland', telling his friend, 'I have no other way, not pregnant with danger, of communicating with one whom I cannot help loving.'

And, while Branwell's effusion about his 'Angel' appeared in the local paper, Charlotte was privately writing an early version of a poem just as personal and explicit about Constantin Heger, 'I gave, at first, Attention close', and working it into a novel of her own, called at this stage 'The Master' (later known as *The Professor*), a painfully obvious piece of wish-fulfilment in which an overlooked, misunderstood and dutiful young teacher in Brussels wins the affections of her demanding superior, and is found to be a poet of strength and seriousness.

The story must have been well under way by the end of 1845, as she finished it in June of the following year. In line with the notes she made in Brussels and with Heger's advice, she had decided to write a realistic story, putting aside 'ornamented and redundant' style and depicting a male protagonist who would 'work his way through life as I had seen real living men work theirs'. This immediately presented difficulties for someone who didn't in truth know much about men's working lives. Her Brussels experience could be adapted to fit, but more was needed, and her solution to the problem was to adapt some scenes and themes from her own stock of Angrian tales (notably 'Ashworth' and 'The Spell') along with material from Branwell's fraternal enemies story 'The Wool is Rising', which he had dashed off in a matter of days in the summer of 1834, at the very beginning of the Angrian chronicles. In it, Northangerland's rejected son Edward Percy progresses through the business world with ruthless single-mindedness to establish a huge mill empire, enter Parliament and marry a princess. His younger brother William, initially tyrannised by Edward, breaks free and joins the army, but it was only the early scenes, of William's oppression in his brother's counting house and the bitter sibling strife between them, that Charlotte recycled in her novel.

That Charlotte felt the need to use anything so old and odd, and *not of her invention*, is extraordinary. It's not as if she didn't have hundreds of thousands of written words of her own to draw on, or that she couldn't spin more at the drop of a hat. It's not that she was trying to pay tribute to Branwell's genius (his story doesn't show any) or involve him collaboratively in her venture. It's not likely that she even told him she was using it. What she seems to have been doing by grafting Branwell's mill scenes on to the start of her narrative was trying to establish a more vigorous, masculine tone in a novel that is desperately anxious not to look like a piece of woman's work and to distract attention from the story's starkly autobiographical core. She was intending to submit it anonymously.

At another level 'The Master' is a retelling, or correction, of what Charlotte felt had happened to her at the hands of Madame Heger. The plot and setting seem at many points like a literal transcription of Charlotte's Brussels experience, with an almost photographic return to the Pensionnat's airy salons, busy classrooms and shade-dappled garden, remembered lovingly shrub by shrub. But 'The Master' wasn't a simple form of revenge. Crimsworth is nothing like Monsieur Heger; he is like

Charlotte – English, Protestant, proud, angry, impoverished, even though his situation in the school is a fantasy version of Heger's before his marriage to Zoë Parent. Crimsworth is given the choice of two possible mates: the charming but guileful directrice, Mademoiselle Reuter, or the insignificant, independent, poor, plain Anglo-Swiss Protestant girl, Frances Henri, a person whom Crimsworth literally *doesn't see* in the classroom for some time, and then quickly comes to love. Frances is even more of a self-portrait of Charlotte than Crimsworth, from her unshowy looks to her poems straight out of the author's own notebooks. The resulting romance between these two authorial avatars is intense but hardly erotic.

'The Master' was a manuscript that Charlotte Brontë continued to work on for years, but that remained unpublished throughout her lifetime, much to her chagrin, as she felt, with justice, that parts of it were 'as good as I can write; it contains more pith, more substance, more reality, in my judgment, than much of "Jane Eyre"'. The love story may have been unconvincing, indeed a little dull, but as she was writing it, a lifetime's worth of unaired opinions, observations and grievances sprang to the tip of Charlotte's pen and found powerful expression. These are fascinating moments, when the narrator is diverted into some tirade or violent digression, against adulterers, against drunkards, against mill-owners' money-grubbing, like a bog bursting and bringing up 'black moory substance' from deep below the surface. In the year when Friedrich Engels, only forty miles away in Manchester, was writing his *Condition of the Working Class in England*, Charlotte Brontë was putting into the mouth of her character Hunsden some extraordinary speeches about the state of England. Hunsden's trajectory from rabble-rouser against Edward Crimsworth's despotism (bringing to mind the real-life West Riding protests of the early 1830s against conditions in the mills) to owner of a fine old Elizabethan home in an area 'whose verdure the smoke of mills has not yet sullied, whose waters still run pure' is narrated satirically by Crimsworth,* and the reader is not allowed to admire too much an undoubtedly *liberal* character, but Hunsden's eloquence on the evils of the times seems like a satire-free zone, and a release of sincere feeling. He protests that Frances

---

* Whose name is the same as a beck and dale near Hebden Bridge.

has no idea what England is really like and should test her idealism against facts:

> Come to England and see. Come to Birmingham and Manchester; come to St Giles in London and get a practical notion of how our system works. Examine the footprints of our august aristocracy see how they walk in blood, crushing hearts as they go. Just put your head in at English cottage doors, get a glimpse of Famine crouched torpid on black hearthstones; of Disease lying bare on beds without coverlets; of Infamy wantoning viciously with Ignorance, though indeed Luxury is her favourite paramour and princely halls are dearer to her than thatched hovels –

Just as striking is the way the novel deals with the subject of gender and the repression of women's opinions, even their voices, by speculating on what is left unsaid. When Crimsworth praises Frances's *devoir* and counsels her to cultivate her faculties, she replies not in words, but with a smile 'in her eyes . . . almost triumphant', which *seems* to mean the following: "'I am glad you have been forced to discover so much of my nature; you need not so carefully moderate your language. Do you think I am myself a stranger to myself? What you tell me in terms so qualified, I have known fully from a child.'" No words are uttered; that would be unseemly, and, the author implies, somewhat redundant. Brontë is depicting a very familiar scene – a silent, apparently submissive woman (like her mother) – and showing its double-sidedness. The convention of not answering back allows able women a scornful superiority, flashing out in looks, in suppression of comment, withheld speech; quellingly disdainful, devastatingly critical, but always held in check. This pent-up power, secretly triumphant because unrealised, is the incendiary device at the heart of *Jane Eyre*, and of all Charlotte Brontë's works. And through its identification and her precise observation of it, she presented something completely revolutionary.

At some point in May 1845 Charlotte's pulse had been set racing by the sight of Constantin Heger's writing on a letter for her, an electrifying pleasure, though the content was not intended to gratify her. None of his letters to her have survived, but from her references to this one in November that year, we have to deduce that Heger sent some form of reprimand (not surprising, given the intemperance of her outburst in January) and stipulated that in future she should not write more frequently than twice a year, limiting herself to matters of family news and health. She must have replied to him on 18 May (that letter is also now lost), for exactly six months later she felt free to write again. She had obviously been thinking about what to say to him and probably drafting the letter many times in the interim:

> The summer and autumn have seemed very long to me; to tell the truth I have had to make painful efforts to endure until now the privation I imposed upon myself: you, Monsieur – you cannot conceive what that means – but imagine for a moment that one of your children is separated from you by a distance of 160 leagues, and that you have to let six months go by without writing to him, without receiving news of him, without hearing him spoken of, without knowing how he is, then you will easily understand what hardship there is in such an obligation. I will tell you candidly that during this time of waiting I have tried to forget you, for the memory of a person one believes one is never to see again, and whom one nevertheless greatly respects, torments the mind exceedingly and when one has suffered this kind of anxiety for one or two years, one is ready to do anything to regain peace of mind. I have done everything, I have sought occupations, I have absolutely forbidden myself the pleasure of speaking about you – even to Emily, but I have not been able to overcome either my regrets or my impatience – and that is truly humiliating – not to know how to get the mastery over one's own thoughts, to be the slave of a regret, a memory, the slave of a dominant and fixed idea which has become a tyrant over one's mind. Why cannot I have for you exactly as much friendship as you have for me – neither more nor less? Then I would be so tranquil, so free – I could keep silence for ten years without effort.

Slave of a dominant and fixed idea which has become a tyrant over one's mind: this was a penetrating self-analysis, and a 'real confession' to make. How could Heger not have been arrested by it? Did he answer? Charlotte was expecting him to – the continuation of some kind of correspondence, however sporadic and circumscribed, seemed to be part of the compact. But what is also clear, as she draws towards the end

of this monologue and faces another half-year of torment, is that Charlotte's willingness to protract the agony was waning:

> Your last letter has sustained me – has nourished me for six months –
> now I need another and you will give it me – not because you have any
> friendship for me – you cannot have much – but because you have a
> compassionate soul and because you would not condemn anyone to
> undergo long suffering in order to spare yourself a few moments of
> tedium . . . [S]o long as I think you are fairly pleased with me, so long
> as I still have the hope of hearing from you, I can be tranquil and not
> too sad, but when a dreary and prolonged silence seems to warn me that
> my master is becoming estranged from me – when day after day I await
> a letter and day after day disappointment flings me down again into
> overwhelming misery, when the sweet delight of seeing your writing
> and reading your counsel flees from me like an empty vision – then I am
> in a fever – I lose my appetite and my sleep – I pine away.

All this was in French, but she added a postscript in English: 'I wish I
could write to you more cheerful letters, for when I read this over, I
find it to be somewhat gloomy – but forgive me my dear master – do
not be irritated at my sadness.' Perhaps the articulation of her sorrow
brought home to Charlotte the hopelessness of her situation, for the
way she signs off has a poignant sense of intuiting it is for the last time:
'Farewell my dear Master – may God protect you with special care and
crown you with peculiar blessings.'

When this heartbroken letter first came to public notice in 1913,
along with the other three remaining ones, they created a sensation
with their hints of hidden scandal in Brontë's life, or at the very least a
shamefully inappropriate unrequited love. The motivations of Monsieur Heger's children, who donated the letters to the British Library (it
was the Library that then publicised them, not the family), seem exemplary: they wanted the letters preserved for their literary and
biographical value. What happened to the letters between the dates of
arrival at the rue d'Isabelle in 1844–5 and their preservation under glass
in Bloomsbury sixty-nine years later is more difficult to piece together.
The story told by Madame Heger to her daughter Louise was that
Constantin tore up the letters after he had read them and threw them
away, whereupon Madame Heger retrieved them from the waste-paper

basket, mended them carefully – one with tiny gummed paper strips, two with thread – and preserved them in her jewel box for fifty years. Louise, who had been shown the letters by her mother, found them again after Madame's death in 1890 and gave them back to her father, who, apparently, tried to throw them away again.

This account implies that the tearing up of the letters happened on or near receipt, as did their rescue from the bin and preservation by Madame Heger. Her motives, if she did this, would seem clear: the letters were ample proof of Charlotte Brontë's irrationality, in case such was needed in future. But Heger showed or read the letters to Elizabeth Gaskell in 1856 when she interviewed him for her biography of Charlotte and copied out passages he felt happy for her to quote from. If they had been torn and mended at that date, Mrs Gaskell would have been the first to notice. Her remark to George Smith that she should 'deprecate anything leading to the publication of those letters' shows that she was conscious of the damage they could do to Charlotte's reputation.

The letters themselves hold a great deal of information in their very paper, in the way that three of them were torn and in the ways they were folded. The torn ones look as if they were 'in little pieces' before mending, but, in truth, they only needed two tears across from their original folded four-page form to make the correct number of fragments – casual disposal, in other words. The last one wasn't torn at all, but was obviously kept on Heger's desk for a while and used by him as a piece of rough paper. Next to Charlotte's pleas – 'I am in a fever – I lose my appetite and my sleep – I pine away' – he has noted the address of a cobbler.

Ignoring the tear marks and mending, something else is evident from the fold marks on the paper and signs of wear: these letters were folded again after they were read. They were stored somewhere, perhaps a pocket or drawer, that required them to be made smaller. They were not, in other words, torn up right away.

In the years after Charlotte became famous, Laetitia Wheelwright met her again in London and asked if she was still in correspondence with Monsieur Heger. Charlotte told her that she had ceased to write to him after Monsieur had mentioned in one letter that his wife didn't like it, 'and he asked her therefore to address her letters to the Royal

Athénée, where he gave lessons to the boys'. Could this be true? Did Heger, subsequent to Charlotte's last letter, really suggest that they could carry on a surreptitious correspondence, behind his wife's back and against her wishes? For him to have suggested it seems as extraordinary as Charlotte thinking it an appropriate thing to pass on to Laetitia Wheelwright; yet Laetitia had no doubt of Charlotte's veracity: 'She said [it] with the sincerity of manner which characterised her every utterance.'

And what happened to the letters he wrote to her, 'the only joy I have on earth'? Were they lost or destroyed in later years by Charlotte's widower? Did *she* destroy them before or after her marriage? Like so much in that novel that seems to be a transposition of her own life, one scene in *Villette* is heavily suggestive of what Charlotte Brontë herself might have done. When Lucy Snowe comes to the realisation that she will have no more letters from Dr John, she decides that they must be 'put away, out of sight: people who have undergone bereavement always jealously gather together and lock away mementos: it is not supportable to be stabbed to the heart each moment by sharp revival of regret'. She makes a little roll of the letters, wraps them in oiled silk and inserts them into a bottle, to be stoppered, sealed and rendered air-tight by an 'old Jew broker'. 'In all this I had a dreary something – not pleasure – but a sad, lonely satisfaction. The impulse under which I acted, the mood controlling me, were similar to the impulse and mood which had induced me to visit the confessional.' In the evening, Lucy steals out into the Pensionnat garden and buries the bottle in a hole under the oldest pear tree. 'I was not only going to hide a treasure – I meant also to bury a grief.'

10

Walking Invisible

1845–6

When Charlotte wrote a biographical preface in 1850 explaining the origins of her sisters' books, she made it clear that by 1845 they had fallen out of the habit of showing and sharing each other's work, 'hence it ensued, that we were mutually ignorant of the progress we might respectively have made.' Charlotte's surprise was all the greater, then, when in the autumn of 1845 she stumbled across a notebook in Emily's writing and found dozens of recent poems, including this:

> Riches I hold in light esteem
> And Love I laugh to scorn
> And Lust of Fame was but a dream
> That vanished with the morn –
>
> And if I pray – the only prayer
> That moves my lips for me
> Is – 'Leave the heart that now I bear
> 'And give me liberty' –
>
> Yes, as my swift days near their goal
> 'Tis all that I implore –
> In Life and death, a chainless soul,
> With courage to endure! –

'[The poems] stirred my heart like the sound of a trumpet when I read them alone and in secret,' Charlotte said, remembering this pivotal discovery. Here was evidence of astonishing development, maturity and power, 'not common effusions, nor at all like the poetry women generally write. I thought them condensed and terse, vigorous and genuine.' And this flowering of her sister's genius had taken place entirely out of her sight – indeed, privacy and secrecy had been essential to its production, just as one can say they were essential to Charlotte's reading – a reading that was surreptitious and unlicensed, and therefore unimpaired by the usual sisterly judgements and pecking orders. 'To my ear, they had also a peculiar music – wild, melancholy, and elevating,' she wrote later; 'no woman that ever lived – ever wrote such poetry before.'

If Charlotte had been any less astonished by Emily's poems, she is unlikely to have owned up to having snooped on them, for, as she said afterwards, her sister was not 'one, on the recesses of whose mind and feelings, even those nearest and dearest to her could, with impunity, intrude unlicensed'. Emily, in fact, was furious at the invasion of her privacy and property: 'it took hours to reconcile her to the discovery I had made, and days to persuade her that such poems merited publication.' No wonder that Emily resisted the idea of publication: many of the poems were intimately connected with her Gondal inventions, and even if they could be read or detached from their context (the poem above was eventually published under the title 'The Old Stoic'), they came from that most private world, not entirely shareable even with Anne.

As soon as the matter was out in the open, Anne produced a sheaf of her own, intimating (but not actually saying) that since Charlotte had enjoyed Emily's poems, she might like these too. Anne shows a certain flair here for making the most of a situation that could have otherwise remained intractable due to Emily's anger. Charlotte was turned to as judge and monitor, and the natural conclusion of this was that all three sisters decided to submit their work for publication together. Emily had one inflexible condition – that they remain strictly anonymous. They told neither their father nor their brother anything about the plan.

It was not perhaps how Charlotte had envisioned her first book, during so many years of restless composition, but the discovery of Emily's genius gave her a new focus and momentum. 'We had very early cherished the dream of one day becoming authors,' she wrote later. 'This dream, never relinquished even when distance divided and absorbing tasks occupied us, now suddenly acquired strength and consistency: it took the character of a resolve. We agreed to arrange a small selection of our poems, and, if possible, get them printed.'

'The bringing out of our little book was hard work,' she recalled with dry humour five years later. 'As was to be expected, neither we nor our poems were at all wanted; but for this we had been prepared at the outset.' The main difficulty was getting any answer at all from the publishers they approached, and, frustrated by this, Charlotte applied for guidance to Chambers of Edinburgh (the publishers of *Chambers' Edinburgh Journal*, a weekly whose aim was to 'instruct and elevate' the 'intelligent artisan'). She received 'a civil and sensible reply', and it was presumably on Chambers's advice that she approached the publisher Aylott and Jones, of Paternoster Row, asking if they would be prepared to publish 'a Collection of short poems in 1 vol. oct[avo]'.

That first letter to Aylott and Jones was characteristic of all Charlotte's correspondence with them: brief, businesslike and cautiously knowledgeable, suggesting that the author, if ignorant of certain 'insider' information, at least understood her position. She learnt something from every exchange, immediately deploying every piece of new knowledge: 'If you object to publishing at your own risk,' she asked the unknown young men in London, 'would you undertake it on the Author's account?' Aylott and Jones wrote back promptly, not out of interest in the text, which they had not yet laid eyes on, but because publishing 'at the author's risk' – vanity publishing, in essence – was, yes, very acceptable to them. They seemed, indeed, almost indifferent to what the contents of the proposed book might be, though had noticed the address of their correspondent, 'C Brontë', and wondered if the work was that of a clergyman. Charlotte wrote back saying no, nor were the poems 'exclusively of a religious character', adding, with a hint of irony, 'but I presume these circumstances will be immaterial'. In retrospect, describing Emily's heretical poetry as 'not exclusively of a religious character' seems rather an understatement.

The poems were to appear under pseudonyms, the choice of which 'yielded some harmless pleasure' to the sisters. In each case they kept their initials intact: Charlotte was to be 'Currer Bell', Emily 'Ellis Bell' and Anne 'Acton Bell',[*] deliberately androgynous-sounding names

---

[*] In her choice of name, Charlotte may have been remembering the 'Miss Currer' who was a trustee of Cowan Bridge School. If Emily Brontë was an admirer of Madame d'Arblay's innovative novel *The Wanderer* (1814), her choice of 'Ellis' might recall the shape-shifting, gender-indeterminate, homeless heroine of that book.

'dictated by a sort of conscientious scruple at assuming Christian names positively masculine, while we did not like to declare ourselves women, because – without at that time suspecting that our mode of writing and thinking was not what is called "feminine" – we had a vague impression that authoresses are liable to be looked on with prejudice'. The Brontë sisters understood a great deal about the print culture of their day and its misogynistic bias, but it was also gloriously true that they had read and written, up to this point, with minds free of 'what is called "feminine"'. At the point of publication, they instinctively moved to protect that freedom: 'we had noticed,' Charlotte concluded, 'how critics sometimes use for [women's] chastisement the weapon of personality, and for their reward, a flattery, which is not true praise.'

'C Brontë' gave no hint to Aylott and Jones of the multiple authorship of the work in question until the manuscript was submitted, with the names Currer, Ellis and Acton Bell appended; 'three persons – relatives', she told the publishers, without explaining her own connection to them, or their gender. An anxious nine days passed before the sisters heard that their manuscript had reached Paternoster Row safely and that production could go ahead once the authors had chosen a type size and face. Charlotte had considerably overestimated the size of the finished book (she had guessed 200–250 pages; it came out at 165 in the end) but could not possibly have predicted the costs for this slim volume: Aylott and Jones wanted £31.10s., with another £5 further down the line. This was an enormous sum: just slightly more than the whole of Anne's annual salary at Thorp Green, and a considerable bite out of each sister's careful savings. The edition was of 1,000 copies, far more than any untried poets were likely to sell, but Aylott and Jones kept their opinion on that matter to themselves, and the Bells were sufficiently optimistic about their first step into print to go ahead as suggested.

The book was made up of sixty-one poems, of almost an equal number from each writer, though Charlotte's contributions were notably longer than her sisters': 'Pilate's Wife's Dream', the ambitious monologue that opened the volume, with its carefully wrought effects, all lamps, glowings, glimmers and chiaroscuro, was 156 lines long and 'Mementos' 255 lines. Many of Charlotte's poems dated from her time at Roe Head and included former Angrian material; some, like 'Mementos', were essentially amalgamations of works with similar themes – grief, longing, lost love, loneliness. No part of the Byronic epic by which she had hoped 'to be forever known' was included.

Charlotte had one particular reader at the front of her mind as she made her selection: Constantin Heger. Though she could hardly send him a physical copy of the book without breaking her promise to Emily (whereas she could, and I am sure did, send him her earlier, solo, French translation), her expectations were of some modest success, and she meant to ensure that if *Poems by Currer, Ellis and Acton Bell* ever fell into Heger's hands, he would have little trouble guessing the authors. He would have had little trouble guessing too the impetus behind poems such as 'Frances', full of anguish at lost love, looking back to days of 'Eden sunshine' and a cup of joy that 'sank to dregs, all harsh and dim'. 'Gilbert' would have had similar resonances, with its characterisation of a married man who has toyed with the affections of an emotionally susceptible young woman. Gilbert's nature is not 'to linger o'er the past', so he remembers the name of his conquest with cold complacency rather than sorrow:

> He says, 'She loved me more than life;
>   And truly it was sweet
> To see so fair a woman kneel,
>   In bondage, at my feet.
>
> There was a sort of quiet bliss
>   To be so deeply loved,
> To gaze on trembling eagerness
>   And sit myself unmoved.
> And when it pleased my pride to grant,
>   At last some rare caress,
> To feel the fever of that hand
>   My fingers deigned to press.
>
> 'Twas sweet to see her strive to hide
>   What every glance revealed;
> Endowed, the while, with despot-might
>   Her destiny to wield.

But Gilbert's domestic contentment is broken by visions of the rejected girl drowning, and when her ghost appears, dripping, at his door, he is filled with remorse for his heartlessness and commits suicide. As a form of wish-fulfilment for Charlotte, it was a bleak and vengeful one. 'Frances' too indicates that her period of idealising Heger was over, and her former devotion was turning into anger. Frances has been the dupe of deferred hope as much as false love, as she realises at the end of the poem:

> And we might meet – time may have changed him;
> Chance may reveal the mystery,
> The secret influence which estranged him;
> Love may restore him yet to me.
>
> False thought – false hope – in scorn be banished!
> I am not loved – nor loved have been;
> Recall not, then, the dreams scarce vanished,
> Traitors! mislead me not again!

By the end of February, Charlotte felt it possible to take her first visit away from home in seven months, to Ellen at Birstall. Returning on the new train line to Keighley on 2 March, she walked the old road back to Haworth,★ thereby missing Emily and Anne, who had gone to meet her the other way. Perhaps they had wanted to prepare her for what she would find at home: Branwell silent and stupefied in bed. He had wheedled a sovereign out of their father in her absence on the pretense of needing to pay a debt and 'employed it as was to be expected'. '[It] was very forced work to address him,' Charlotte wrote bitterly to Ellen later. 'I might have spared myself the trouble as he took no notice & made no reply.' What a sad image this is of the siblings who were formerly so close, one coldly disapproving and the other locked in sullen defiant silence. When Emily and Anne got home, two hours later and soaked to the skin, Emily said she thought Branwell had become 'a hopeless being', a rare criticism from that quarter. Charlotte's response was less sorrowful than disgusted: 'In his present state,' she wrote to Ellen, 'it is scarcely possible to stay in the room where he is – what the future has in store – I do not know.'

★ Beatrice E. Stanley suggests this was via Hainworth Shay and Cradle Edge; see 'Changes at Haworth', *BST*, 10:5 (1944).

Given Branwell's hopelessness, the question of what to do in the event of their father losing his sight was more pressing than ever, and while she was away Charlotte had been canvassing medical opinion among the Nusseys' friends. She now tried to encourage him to submit to an eye operation, though Reverend Brontë was very fearful and glad to find excuses to defer any action as long as possible. His anxieties transmitted readily to his daughter, who told her cousin 'we shall be most thankful when it is well over for there is something formidable in the idea.' Meanwhile, Patrick needed to be led to the pulpit to preach, a sight full of pathos to parishioners no doubt, many of whom knew all about the trouble their vicar was having at home and how withdrawn the Brontë family had become. Fortunately, Mr Nicholls the curate was proving very kind and useful, took many of Reverend Brontë's services for him and provided a discreet buffer between the parish and the Parsonage. He lodged at the house of John Brown the sexton, so must have been well aware of everything going on there, but he was loyally silent on all delicate matters.

Thrown back on their resources, emotional and artistic, and desperately alert to the question of income, the sisters had made a bold decision while their poems were in production: not to wait for the reception of the book, but to press on immediately with trying to get their fiction before the public too. Charlotte was again the interlocutor for all three: the 'Bells' were prepared to shape their work, she told Aylott and Jones, 'three distinct and unconnected tales', in whatever format would be most likely to appeal. Charlotte was trying to guess what that might be: 'a work of 3 vols. of the ordinary novel-size, or separately as single vols.'. She stipulated that they did *not* wish to be published at their own expense this time, but at the publisher's risk. Clearly, the Bells expected Aylott and Jones to have been sufficiently impressed by their poems to be interested in a work of fiction from the same pens.

The sisters got a discouraging answer about their proposed novel, but this was hardly surprising: Aylott and Jones were known for their theological works, not 'light literature', and, much more importantly, the novel that was being proposed must have sounded – and *was* – far too 'unconnected' to be viable as a single publication. The three-volume model that was standard at the time was a substantial thing, typically of about 160,000 words. No one was likely to want to publish three much shorter books under one cover, nor publish them separately.

If Aylott and Jones had asked to see the 'three tales' they might well have been astonished, for volume one consisted of 'The Master', Charlotte's novel about Brussels (retitled, at an unknown date, *The Professor*); volume two was *Wuthering Heights*; and volume three *Agnes Grey*. How *Wuthering Heights* as we know it could ever have been sandwiched comfortably between any two other stories is a moot question; it seems a strange arrangement on grounds of length alone, and the scholars Tom Winnifrith and Edward Chitham are surely right to guess that Emily expanded her story later, and that the version proposed in 1846 was much shorter, possibly ending with the death of the elder Cathy.★ *The Professor* and *Agnes Grey* are both about the same length, approximately 70,000 to 80,000 words.

How long Emily had been preparing *Wuthering Heights*, and whether it was connected to any of her Gondal chronicles, is not known. The opening chapters are some of the most gripping ever written in English romance, and it is amazing to think they came from the pen of a young woman whose gaze had been turned inward for so long and who seemed to have so little concern for popular taste. The novel is nothing like a love story in any ordinary sense. The bond between Cathy and Heathcliff comes from the mutual recognition of like souls, a psychic identification that has little to do with their circumstances, and makes it almost redundant for the hero and heroine (if those words apply) to be paired off in the novel. Catherine tells the old housekeeper Nelly Dean, in a speech which has become one of the most famous and quoted in nineteenth-century literature, that she loves Heathcliff 'because he's more myself than I am . . . my love for Heathcliff resembles the eternal rocks beneath – a source of little visible delight, but necessary. Nelly, I *am* Heathcliff – he's always, always in my mind – not as a pleasure, any more than I am always a pleasure to myself – but, as my own being.' The reclusive and misanthropic second daughter of the

★ The latter two thirds of *Wuthering Heights* are notably reprise-like and cyclical, with their replaying of Heathcliff's old antagonisms and old love in and through the next generation. The end of volume one is, interestingly, the point at which the most famous film version – William Wyler's 1939 production starring Laurence Olivier and Merle Oberon – concludes the story.

Parsonage turned out to have a romantic vision more extravagant than any novelist before her. It was primal, visceral and decidedly heretical: 'heaven did not seem to be my home', Cathy says after she has dreamt of going there; 'and I broke my heart with weeping to come back to earth; and the angels were so angry that they flung me out, into the middle of the heath on the top of Wuthering Heights; where I woke sobbing for joy'.

In Charlotte's tribute to, and defence of, the book later, it was clear that, while she admired many things about her sister's novel, she also found it profoundly disturbing and difficult, as many other readers have too. Why was it so violent, so impious? Where had these brutish characters and coarse action come from? Charlotte discouraged the idea that Emily had had any personal experience similar to that in the book – Heathcliff's beatings and incarcerations of his family, the long attritions played out against Hindley and Linton and the younger Catherine, the brutalising of Hareton – but it was almost as alarming to think that Emily had spun such things out of her own head. Emily seemed to have no idea how unconventional her resulting portraits were: 'If the auditor of her work when read in manuscript, shuddered under the grinding influence of natures so relentless and implacable, of spirits so lost and fallen; if it was complained that the mere hearing of certain vivid and fearful scenes banished sleep by night, and disturbed mental peace by day, Ellis Bell would wonder what was meant, and suspect the complainant of affectation.' Even before it was published, there was a great deal about *Wuthering Heights* that made Charlotte uncomfortable.

Anne Brontë's contribution to the proposed three-decker made a jolting change of tone and style. *Agnes Grey* was a profoundly autobiographical account of the trials of a young governess, which she later claimed was 'carefully copied from the life, with a most scrupulous avoidance of all exaggeration'. It is hard to see where Anne Brontë got her reputation for being 'mild' and 'quiet'. Her novels, as the next one was to show even more explicitly, are seething with irritation, and their trapped heroines find only the bleakest and bitterest comfort from their superior morals and sensibilities. Agnes Grey's own impotence makes her a chilly and severe judge; her hope for her rival Rosalie's dangerous beauty is that it will eventually lead her into such folly that she will be 'incapacitated from deceiving and injuring others'. All Agnes's virtues are expressed in the negative, and act out in peculiar forms, none more so than in the disgusting scene in which she crushes a nest of baby birds. Her collusion with Rosalie's ruse to be alone with Mr Hatfield is deeply cynical, as is her conclusion that beautiful but heartless women might have been created by an omniscient deity as a 'useful' punishment for men, 'as vain, as selfish, and as heartless'.

The novel must have come as something of a revelation to Charlotte, who clearly saw in Anne's exposé of governess life potential for better use of her own autobiographical experiences. Agnes is at every sort of worldly disadvantage – impoverished, unbeautiful, insignificant – but insists on her essential worth and holds to the belief that she is at least the equal of 'her betters'. The happy ending, with marriage to the virtuous and delightful curate Weston (often imagined to be a portrait of William Weightman), triumphs over the tyranny of being judged on appearances, but the problem lingers in the reader's mind long after the happy ending has been arranged. Although Agnes knows that 'it is foolish to wish for beauty', nevertheless she can't help wishing she had some, if only to avoid the isolation or, worse, 'instinctive dislike' that unbeautiful women constantly encounter.

That Anne had experienced 'a passion of grief' was clear also from Agnes's heartfelt recollection of her own, when she feels that her love for Weston will never be recognised or reciprocated, a passage that would have provoked Charlotte's assent: 'Yes! at least, they could not deprive me of that; I could think of him day and night; and I could feel that he was worthy to be thought of. Nobody knew him as I did; nobody could appreciate him as I did; nobody could love him as I . . . could, if I might; but there was the evil. What business had I to think so much of one that never thought of me? Was it not foolish? . . . was it not wrong?'

Here, and in Emily's novel, was an emotional force that Charlotte had denied in her own first fiction in the effort to make it more acceptable, more 'realistic'. But her sisters showed her how to move forward. Charlotte was always learning, watching, turning the lock to find the right combination. Putting together Anne's autobiographical governess plot with her own story of Master and subordinate, and adding thrilling Gothic flights similar to those that made *Wuthering Heights* so electrifying, Charlotte began the process of creative amalgamation that would result in *Jane Eyre*.

All three novels, *The Professor*, *Wuthering Heights* and *Agnes Grey*, must have been well advanced by the date of Charlotte's letter to Aylott and Jones of April 1846, enquiring about possible publication; her own manuscript was completed on 27 June. The Haworth bookseller, John Greenwood, had begun to stock stationery in his shop and later told Mrs Gaskell how the demand for paper from the Brontë daughters at this time made him wonder what they were doing with so much of it. 'I sometimes thought they contributed to the Magazines. When I was out of stock, I was always afraid of their coming; they seemed so distressed about it, if I had none.' Greenwood was so eager to oblige the Misses Brontë, whom he always found 'much different to anybody else; so gentle and kind', that he would rather walk the eight or ten miles to Halifax to fetch a half-ream than have nothing to sell them.

Unknown to him, the dining room of the Parsonage had been turned into something like a book factory, as the sisters paced round the table, reading, listening and discussing each other's work, and sat bent over their portable desks for hours, writing. 'The sisters retained the old habit . . . of putting away their work at nine o'clock, and beginning their steady pacing up and down the sitting room,' Mrs Gaskell heard later from Charlotte. 'At this time, they talked over the stories they were engaged upon, and discussed their plots. Once or twice a week, each read to the others what she had written, and heard what they had to say about it.' Patrick Brontë never thought to inquire what they were doing. He was used to his children spending the greater part of their time together, his self-sufficiency being equal to their own. 'I never interfer'd with them at these times,' he told Mrs Gaskell. 'I judged it best to throw them upon their own responsibility.'

Charlotte admitted to Elizabeth Gaskell that she had rarely changed anything in her work because of her sisters' opinions; indeed, her creation of Jane Eyre as a plain and insignificant-seeming heroine, she said, was in direct defiance of them, though this is hard to square with Anne's characterisation of Agnes Grey, whom Jane resembles quite closely. Charlotte told fellow novelist Harriet Martineau that she had 'once told her sisters that they were wrong – even morally wrong – in making their heroines beautiful as a matter of course. They replied that it was impossible to make a heroine interesting on any other terms. Her answer was, "I will prove to you that you are wrong; I will show you a heroine as plain and as small as myself, who shall be as interesting as any of yours."' This sounds less like collaboration than invigorating competition. Emily had seen no reason for anyone to lose sleep over her depiction of Heathcliff, and had no intention of changing it accordingly. Charlotte was just as inflexible and 'possessed . . . with the feeling that she had described reality'. Nevertheless, the nocturnal readings in the Parsonage dining room were 'of great and stirring interest to all'.

All that year, the sisters had been hoping for some improvement in Branwell's situation, preferably his removal from the house: 'how can we be more comfortable so long as Branwell stays at home and degenerates instead of improving?' Charlotte wrote to Ellen. He had been offered his old job back on the railway, a rather remarkable break, which Charlotte of course expected him to seize on with gratitude, but Branwell was in no state to respond. 'He refuses to make an effort,' she wrote in disgust; 'he will not work – and at home he is a drain on every resource – an impediment to all happiness – But there's no use in complaining.'

Branwell felt equally affronted at 'the inability to make my family aware of the nature of most of my sufferings'. But while he lay in bed, planning an epic poem called 'Morley Hall', which kind Leyland had suggested and probably commissioned (it was to be based on a story in Leyland's own family history*), Charlotte continued as his secret scourge, punishing him for his own disabling vanity and pernicious addiction by keeping him entirely unaware of what his sisters were doing. He 'never knew', Charlotte said later, 'what his sisters had done in literature – he was not aware that they had ever published a line'. It was a most peculiar revenge, and one that, in the years following his death, she had no desire to recall. But in these months, while she was finishing *The Professor*, her feelings could not be entirely contained, as this outburst, utterly unrelated to the action of the novel, indicates:

---

* Ninety lines of the poem's prologue have survived.

if we rarely taste the fulness of joy in this life, we yet more rarely savour the acrid bitterness of hopeless anguish ... God, spirits, religion can have no place in our collapsed minds where linger only hideous and polluting recollections of vice; and Time brings us on to the brink of the grave and Dissolution flings us in – a rag eaten through and through with disease, wrung together with pain, stamped into the churchyard sod by the inexorable heel of Despair.

Patrick Brontë was also kept in the dark about the forthcoming book, but perhaps there were other people, in or around the Parsonage, who were suspicious of the sudden postal traffic between an address in London and 'C. Brontë Esq'. The 'Esquire' was an assumption on Aylott and Jones's part that Charlotte did nothing to correct until the proof sheets of the poems arrived in March and were somehow diverted, perhaps just momentarily, into the wrong hands, 'a little mistake', as Charlotte described it, that obviously threatened, but didn't break, their cover at home. Charlotte asked the publisher to address all further correspondence to 'Miss Brontë' – a declaration of her sex that she had hitherto avoided – but the interference with the post continued, and on receipt of the finished books in May, she reported back to Aylott and Jones that their last three letters and the parcel itself 'had all been opened – where or by whom, I cannot discover; the paper covering the parcel was torn in pieces and the books were brought in loose.' Was someone at the post office opening up her mail?

As production of the *Poems* progressed, Charlotte's opinion of Aylott and Jones diminished. Their main interest seemed to be in selling more services to the hopeful authors, but, having spent so much already, the sisters baulked at finding more money for advertising, and kept it to a minimum, £2.00.* If the review copies resulted in good notices, Charlotte was prepared to think again, but that moment never came. The little book arrived in May, bound in dark green cloth, with the words *Poems by Currer, Ellis and Acton Bell 4/–* embossed inside a geometrical design on the cover. The sisters' pleasure at handling their published work can be imagined: the solidity of the production, the excellence of the poems, the authority conferred by print – and anonymity.

---

* A typical outlay for book advertising at the time started at about ten times this much; see *LCB* 1, 474 n4.

The book was available to the public by the end of May, but the public did not seem to notice. Though *Poems by Currer, Ellis and Acton Bell* got three hearteningly affirmative reviews some time later – two on the same day in July and one in October – the sales were absurdly, extravagantly low – two copies, Charlotte believed: worse than nothing.

It was certainly an odd introduction to the world of letters. The elaborate defences of the pseudonyms now seemed hardly necessary, in fact quite an unwelcome distraction, since the first reviewer, in the *Critic*, used much of his wordage puzzling over the lack of editorial or biographical information about the Bells instead of doing what the authors had clearly intended: judging the poems 'upon their own merits alone, apart from all extraneous circumstances'. *The Dublin University Magazine* also wondered whether the Bells 'be in truth but one master spirit', and all three reviewers felt the compulsion to rank them, the *Athenaeum* placing Ellis firmly at the top, with this perceptive remark: 'a fine quaint spirit has the latter, which may have things to speak that men will be glad to hear, – and an evident power of wing that may reach heights not here attempted'. All three 'brothers' were included in the *Critic*'s equally warm praise for the originality and sincerity of their poetry, and 'the presence of more genius than it was supposed this utilitarian age had devoted to the loftier exercises of the intellect'.

The publication was a terrible anti-climax, though, and confirmed Emily in her belief that the whole thing had been a bad idea. She might well have taken secret pleasure in the fact that her contributions to the book garnered the most praise from the reviewers, but at home she referred to her work dismissively as 'rhymes' and by 1848 'never alludes to them', as Charlotte reported, 'or when she does – it is with scorn'. Charlotte was determined to make the best of the experience, however: they could at least now present themselves as 'published authors' to the publishers they hoped to interest in their novels. The strange package of stories went out in July to the publisher Henry Colburn, who refused it, but, undaunted, Charlotte sent it out again every time it came home.

And their book of poems was not entirely without readers: copy for copy, it had astonishing effect. A letter arrived at the Parsonage two months later from a nineteen-year-old called Frederick Enoch, of Warwick, who ought to go down in literary history as the John the Baptist of the Brontës' fame. He had not only bought the Bells' *Poems*, but was moved to write and praise them, and ask for the favour of the authors' autographs. The signatures that were sent him have now, by various by-ways, come back to Haworth Parsonage and are on exhibition in the Museum, the only examples of the sisters' writing together on one sheet. How novel it must have been for the girls to sign, for the first time, as their authorial alter egos – *Currer Bell, Ellis Bell, Acton Bell* – a lone but puissant contact with their tiny readership.

At exactly the time between the arrival of the printed *Poems* and the first reviews, in early June 1846, a bombshell hit the Parsonage in the form of an unexpected visitor from Thorp Green, the Robinsons' coachman, William Allison. What Branwell's thoughts could have been – or Anne's – at the sudden appearance of this former fellow employee, almost a year after their painful severance of communication with the family, can only be guessed. The very surprising news that Allison brought would certainly have given Branwell a momentary rush of almost unbearable hope – Edmund Robinson had died, aged forty-six, on 26 May, after a three-month illness. But in virtually the same breath, and clearly well rehearsed, Allison made it clear that this did not open the way to the new widow's arms: in fact no sort of approach to Mrs Robinson would be possible. She was in 'a dreadful state of health', Branwell related feelingly to Leyland the next day; 'the account which [Allison] gave of her sufferings was enough to burst my heart.' Apparently, Mrs Robinson was only able to kneel in her bedroom 'in bitter tears and prayers', following the final illness of her husband, 'worn . . . out in attendance on him'. Whether the coachman had provided these details or whether they sprang from Branwell's volatile imagination is hard to tell, but the message was clear: for the good of Lydia's health and mental equilibrium, Branwell must stay away from Thorp Green.★

Branwell seems to have believed what he told Leyland, which was that Edmund Robinson had changed his will, leaving his wife 'quite

---

★ Charlotte passed on to Ellen the news 'from all hands' that 'Mr Robinson had altered his will before he died and effectually prevented all chance of a marriage between his widow and Branwell by stipulating that she should not have a shilling if she ever ventured to reopen any communication with him' (CB to EN, 17 June 1846, *LCB* I, 477).

powerless' in the matter of further communication with her former lover. But Robinson's actual will, altered in January 1846, mentions nothing of the sort,★ so the widow may well have planted this misinformation on purpose to work on Branwell's feelings and keep him at bay. Unknown to Branwell, she had undergone a change of heart towards her husband now that he was dead, referring to him as 'my angel Edmund' in her account book (a suitable place, perhaps). It seems that in the months following the traumatic discovery of her adultery in the summer of 1845, Lydia Robinson had ceased to want to give up everything – or indeed *anything* – for love of Branwell Brontë.

Without any direct communication allowed between them, Branwell's delusions about his situation flourished. The new obstacles to his happiness gave him as much traction as had the old ones and he wrote to Leyland in a sort of wretched ecstasy, telling him that he was so much *persona non grata* at Thorp Green that one of Robinson's trustees had threatened to shoot him on sight, a remarkable claim given that one of the trustees was an archdeacon and the other an MP. Branwell couldn't eat or sleep but maintained a tortured watch over events. 'What I shall *do* I know not,' he wrote. 'I am too hard to die, and too wretched to live . . . my mind sees only a dreary future which I as little wish to enter on, as could a martyr to be bound to the stake' – an image he drew and sent to Leyland.

Branwell's letters to his friends seem confident of their interest in the continuing melodrama of his circumstances, but at home he had overplayed his hand long before, and he knew it. Charlotte was the most steely of all, believing him to be using the news from Thorp Green merely as a 'pretext to throw all about him into hubbub and confusion with his emotions – &c. &c.'. His distress, drinking, even his threats of suicide she interpreted as signs of hopelessly weakened character: '[he] declares now that he neither can nor will do anything for himself – good situations have been offered more than once – for which by a fortnight's work he might have qualified himself – but he will do nothing – except drink, and make us all wretched.'

The revulsion in Charlotte's tone is hardly surprising from one who

★ Though Robinson did disinherit his eldest daughter, Lydia Mary, who had run away to Gretna Green in October 1845 to marry an actor. The similarity of her name and her mother's might have led to some confusion once the story became known.

had striven so long to improve herself in the cause of earning an independence. The more hopeless Branwell became, the more stringently
Charlotte went about doing her duty. When, in the summer of 1846,
Ellen began to talk of having to earn a living herself (because of the
pressures on her family from her brother Joseph's dissipation and her
brother George's mental breakdown), Charlotte advised her categoric-
ally to do as she was doing: to put off thoughts of independence while
there was a pressing need for her to be at home. 'The right path is that
which necessitates the greatest sacrifice of self-interest,' Charlotte pronounced sternly, 'which implies the greatest good to others – and this
path steadily followed will lead *I believe* in time to prosperity and to
happiness though it may seem at the outset to tend quite in a contrary
direction.'

To the outside eye, it did look as if all three Brontë girls had given
up the idea of work, just when the family needed money most. Ellen
did not know about the Brontë sisters' poems, or their hopes of making money from writing (rather than losing it). And none of them
looked likely to marry, though Ellen had heard some juicy gossip –
from whom? Charlotte demanded – that 'Miss Brontë was . . . going to
be married to her papa's Curate.' The accusation earned a scornful
reply, which, when she saw the letter in 1856, Mrs Gaskell interpreted
as Charlotte really not having noticed Nicholls's growing devotion,
'though others had'. But to a suspicious nature (and to anyone aware
that Charlotte did eventually marry this man) Charlotte's protests
sound just a touch too much, rather like her denials of having any
romantic connection in Brussels:

> I scarcely need say that never was rumour more unfounded – it puzzles
> me to think how it could possibly have originated – A cold, far-away
> sort of civility are the only terms on which I have ever been with Mr
> Nicholls – I could by no means think of mentioning such a rumour to
> him even as a joke – it would make me the laughing-stock of himself
> and his fellow-curates for half a year to come – They regard me as an
> old maid, and I regard them, one and all, as highly uninteresting, nar-
> row and unattractive specimens of the 'coarser sex'.

Nicholls's feelings can be guessed from the fact that by June 1847, when
he had been at Haworth for two years and was ready for promotion to a

district, he stayed put – clearly from choice. He must have been aware of Patrick Brontë's reliance on him, aware too of Charlotte's anxiety on her father's behalf at the prospect of losing his curate, as she expressed in a letter to Ellen that summer. Given the intensity of his expressions of love for Charlotte later, he almost certainly was passing over preferment in order to stay near Miss Brontë and display his usefulness.

But, as the vehemence of her denial suggests, Charlotte's own feelings about Nicholls may not have been as cut and dried at this stage as she represented them to Ellen. A pencil drawing exists in the Bonnell Collection at the Pierpont Morgan Library* that was passed down in an envelope marked 'T̶h̶r̶e̶e̶ One pencil sketches by Charlotte Brontë, Signed, & 1 sketch of Mr Nicholls when he first went to Haworth'. The sketch is catalogued under 'dubious attributions' in *The Art of the Brontës*, presumably because of the distinction made on the envelope between items 'signed by Charlotte Brontë' and not. There is every reason to think that it *is* by Charlotte, though, signed or unsigned. It is very much in the style of her sketches and caricatures, and has been made on a corner of writing paper, probably surreptitiously – a rapid capturing of the new curate as he sits with his eyes cast downwards. It was bought by Bonnell from Mr Nicholls's niece and executrix, Violet Bolster, who had inherited it directly from Nicholls himself. Nicholls was not a vain man, and he is very unlikely to have agreed to sit to any sketcher willingly in his early days at the Parsonage. Nor would he have accepted or kept a drawing of himself unless he had strong reasons to do so. But he kept this one. I believe that either he found it in Charlotte's papers after her death, or he was given it by her. Her taking of his likeness is the most telling thing of all, however. It shows that Charlotte found him interesting and was observing Nicholls long before he guessed, or she was prepared to admit.

In the summer of 1846, and seemingly at their own instigation, Charlotte and Emily went to Manchester to 'search out an operator', that is, a surgeon, to treat their father's failing sight. The highly respected oculist they found, William Wilson, was a Leeds man and an old friend of John Outhwaite of Bradford, so perhaps the discovery was not accidental;

---

* Included in the second plate section.

naturally, though, Wilson could not give any diagnosis or promise any relief until he had seen the patient in person, so three weeks later Charlotte came back with her father, leaving Emily and Anne with the equally difficult task of monitoring Branwell in their absence.

After a consultation with Wilson, who told them that Patrick Brontë's cataracts were in a suitable state to be removed, Charlotte and her father prepared for a long stay in Manchester – they were told it would be a week before the operation could take place and then about a month of convalescence must follow. They took lodgings about two miles out of the city centre, at 83 Mount Pleasant, Boundary Street, a not-pleasant-at-all small brick house facing a timber yard, in the town's 'numerous similar streets of small monotonous-looking houses', as Mrs Gaskell described them, the Victorian terraces that later became so characteristic of the city. The house was kept by a Mr and Mrs Ball, known to Mr Wilson, but Mrs Ball was not at home all the time of the Brontës' residence, so they had to cater for themselves, a difficult task in a strange house, where the single servant was not at their command and a hired nurse had to be accommodated at the Brontës' responsibility. Charlotte wrote to Ellen for 'hints about how to manage': 'For ourselves I could contrive – papa's diet is so very simple – but there will be a nurse coming in a day or two – and I am afraid of not having things good enough for her – Papa requires nothing you know but plain beef & mutton, tea and bread and butter but a nurse will probably expect to live much better.' The weeks ahead looked bothersome and dreary, and there was no chance of diversion – even short outings – with no one to escort her through the built-up streets. And Charlotte was unsurprisingly struck by a 'feeling of strangeness . . . in this big town', with its widespread bustle of traffic, mills, wharfs, canals, the ever-expanding railway and population of hard-pressed and sometimes desperate refugees from the famine in Ireland.★

Patrick Brontë's nervous agitation increased as his operation loomed, and must have been difficult for Charlotte to witness. His description in a notebook of the procedure shows a nature inclined to dramatise his

★ Manchester's streets were described at the time as 'crowded with paupers, most of them Irish', hoping for work or access to emergency soup-kitchens (*The Times*, 17 February 1847).

own dangers, especially dangers passed: 'Belladonna, a virulent poison, prepared from deadly nightshade, was first applied, twice, to expand the pupil. This occasioned very acute pain for about five seconds.' But Wilson was an expert in his field and the procedure, on 25 August, a great success, eventually leading to a restoration of almost all Patrick Brontë's sight. For several days afterwards, however, he had to be kept in a darkened room with bandages over his eyes, and for weeks more was allowed only to sit in the dark with a screen between him and the fire. 'He is very patient but of course depressed and weary,' Charlotte reported. Charlotte, who was suffering terribly from tooth-ache all through the visit, was also tightly confined to the ugly little terrace on Boundary Street.

It was in these unpromising conditions that she began a new novel. On the very day of her father's operation, Charlotte had received a package in the post: it contained *The Professor*, back from its latest sojourn in a publisher's office, with a curt note of refusal. While not giving up her hopes that it would eventually find a home, Charlotte bravely put the parcel to one side, got out her pencil and little home-made paper notebooks, and in the dismal Manchester lodgings began something entirely different:

> *There was no possibility of taking a walk that day.*

That Intensely Interesting Novel

1846–8

Charlotte Brontë was not an artist who could command her muse at will. She was too much a prey to her feelings, to her state of body and mind, and to circumstances. She told Elizabeth Gaskell that she composed her books in fits and starts:

> it was not every day that she could write. Sometimes weeks or months elapsed before she felt she had anything to add to that portion of her story which was already written. Then, some morning she would waken up, and the progress of her tale lay clear and bright before her, in distinct vision. When this was the case, all her care was to discharge her household and filial duties, so as to obtain leisure to sit down and write out the incidents and consequent thoughts, which were, in fact, more present to her mind at such times than her actual life itself.

When Charlotte returned home from Manchester with her father at the end of September 1846, her new novel advanced in just that way, 'clear and bright before her'. Taking on board the lesson of *The Professor*'s rejection, she had decided on 'something more imaginative and poetical – something more consonant with a highly wrought fancy, with a native taste for pathos – with sentiments more tender – elevated – unworldly'. She went to the best source of strong feeling – her own – and in her story of an orphaned and unprotected girl made a return to her own childhood and its tragic losses, tapping into a vein of extraordinary power. Charlotte Brontë was essentially a poet of suffering; she understood every corner of it, dwelt both on and *in* it. In life, this propensity was a chronic burden; in her art, she let it speak to and comfort millions of others.

Not that *Jane Eyre* is a melancholy book. Its predominant emotion is anger, rushing through Jane's narrative of her life like the storm winds shaking the walls at Roe Head. It begins in the first pages, with Jane's resolve 'to go all lengths ... like any other rebel slave', continues through her defiance of the bullying teachers at Lowood School and propels her through her seemingly hopeless career with a belief that vengeance is due:

> Nobody knows how many rebellions besides political rebellions ferment in the masses of life which people earth. Women are supposed to be very calm generally: but women feel just as men feel; they need exercise for their faculties, and a field for their efforts as much as their brothers do; they suffer from too rigid a restraint, too absolute a stagnation, precisely as men would suffer; and it is narrow-minded in their more privileged fellow-creatures to say that they ought to confine themselves to making puddings and knitting stockings, to playing on the piano and embroidering bags.

Charlotte's return to her childhood and its tragic losses – that of Maria depicted so minutely in the death of Helen Burns – was a sort of exorcism, powered by strong feelings. This gave a peculiar momentum to the first weeks of writing that left her in a fever, and compelled to pause. The astonishing vividness of *Jane Eyre*, not least its personal address and energy, derives a great deal from this articulation of long-pent-up sorrows, and the author's identification with her unconventional heroine, a poor, plain, overlooked governess, licensed to speak for all underlings and trampled people. Jane was nothing like demure, correct, constrained Frances Henri in *The Professor*, with her meaningful silences and plan of gradual passive influence, but a girl pressed, like the author, into speaking her mind by ungovernable force: 'it seemed as if my tongue pronounced words without my will consenting to their utterance: something spoke out of me over which I had no control.' Jane's fear of transgressing is soon replaced by unbridled excitement, as she finds when she answers her manipulative and unloving aunt with a torrent of truth-telling:

> Ere I had finished this reply, my soul began to expand, to exult, with the strangest sense of freedom, of triumph, I ever felt. It seemed as if an invisible bond had burst, and that I had struggled out into unhoped-for liberty. Not without cause was this sentiment: Mrs Reed looked frightened; her

> work had slipped from her knee; she was lifting up her hands, rocking
> herself to and fro, and even twisting her face as if she would cry.

This could not have been more insurrectionary if it tried.

The appearance of her heroine, as previously announced to Emily and Anne, was deliberately unbeautiful, to emphasise her absolute right to love. '[A]t eighteen most people wish to please,' Jane says, with significant understatement, 'and the conviction that they have not an exterior likely to second that desire brings anything but gratification.' 'I sometimes regretted that I was not handsomer: I sometimes wished to have rosy cheeks, a straight nose, and small cherry mouth; I desired to be tall, stately, and finely developed in figure; I felt it a misfortune that I was so little, so pale, and had features so irregular and so marked.'

Her hero was meant to be imperfectly attractive too, though it is hard to keep that in mind as Edward Rochester rears into view through the mist on his black charger, a remarkable creation, combining Byronic cynicism, eloquence and wit with Zamorna's physical charisma, domineering nature and dark past. Rochester is passionate but never brutal, masterful but also vulnerable – helpless indeed at the end, when he is reduced to a blinded, maimed shadow of himself. He is the demon-lover domesticated and made humble, but not enfeebled: he never once in the book utters a piece of piety or cant.

With the massive literature of Angria and *The Professor* to her credit already, Charlotte had served as long and hard an apprenticeship as any writer could expect, but the perfection of *Jane Eyre* still takes one by surprise. The story itself is one of the most gripping ever written, and the telling of it effortlessly clever and assured: Adele's childish prattle as she introduces herself to Mademoiselle guilelessly exposes Rochester's chequered past; Mrs Fairfax is both friendly and secretive; the mystery of Grace Poole, introduced as a social puzzle, diverts attention away from the careful placing of observations in what is essentially a detective novel *avant la lettre*. And, although the novel is thoroughly Gothic in its use of dark stairways, mad women, mysterious laughter, fire, exile, near-starvation – the whole glorious gamut, in other words – Jane's resolute common sense, fatalism and instinct for the rational allow the enjoyment of all this 'burning clime' material without degenerating into the incredible.

Charlotte's ability to enter trance-like into her own imaginary world comes through in *Jane Eyre*'s intensely dramatic, *filmic* scenes, such as the preparation of Thornfield for the house party, the rescue of Rochester from his burning bed, the interrupted wedding ceremony, the revelation of Bertha, snarling in her attic corner. These superb visions come as from the author's mind straight to the reader's inner eye. She also slips into the present tense at moments, just for a half-page at a time, surreptitiously drawing us into the action, into Jane's thoughts. One such passage is when Jane returns to Thornfield after a month's absence, attending her dying aunt. The step-by-step approach to the house alerts us, as it dawns on Jane, that 'I have but a field or two to traverse, and then I shall cross the road and reach the gates. How full the hedges are of roses! But I have no time to gather any; I want to be at the house.' It is only when she catches sight of Rochester, whom she did not expect to meet, and 'every nerve I have is unstrung' that she begins to comprehend her own eagerness to be home.

There are other such strikingly modern touches, one as Proustian as Proust, when Jane re-enters the breakfast-room at Gateshead after ten years: 'There was every article of furniture looking just as it did on the morning I was first introduced to Mr Brocklehurst: the very rug he had stood upon still covered the hearth . . . The inanimate objects were not changed: but the living things had altered past recognition.' Elsewhere, Charlotte gives a brilliant description of a cognitive leap as Jane anticipates by a few seconds hearing the news that she and her beloved friends Diana and Mary Rivers (veiled portraits of Emily and Anne) are cousins:

> I stopped: I could not trust myself to entertain, much less to express, the thought that rushed upon me – that embodied itself, – that, in a second, stood out a strong, solid probability. Circumstances knit themselves, fitted themselves, shot into order: the chain that had been lying hitherto a formless lump of links, was drawn out straight, – every ring was perfect, the connection complete. I knew, by instinct, how the matter stood, before St John had said another word . . .

Not surprisingly, Monsieur Heger stalked the novel too, but obliquely. When Jane walks in the evening on the *parterre*, it is the scent of a cigar that announces the near presence of her dark-browed, choleric, volatile lover, and it is his wife (made over into an incarcerated fury, ready to kill for jealousy) who stands between Jane and her destined soul-mate. Rochester's feelings of soul-unity with Jane are akin to Cathy's with Heathcliff in *Wuthering Heights*, but much more gently expressed. His image of the communicating cord was indeed rather apposite in a decade when the first experimental telegraph cables were being laid under the English Channel:

> I sometimes have a queer feeling with regard to you – especially when you are near me, as now: it is as if I had a string somewhere under my left ribs, tightly and inextricably knotted to a similar string situated in the corresponding quarter of your little frame. And if that boisterous channel, and two hundred miles or so of land come broad between us, I am afraid that cord of communion will be snapt; and then I've a nervous notion I should take to bleeding inwardly.

Charlotte needed the comfort of her novel in hand to endure the difficulties of that winter. It's hard to see how the household carried on, hunkered down with only one income to support six adults (counting Tabby, as they always did) and no prospect of any improvement. In December the appearance of a sheriff's officer at the Parsonage, demanding payment of Branwell's debts or 'a trip to York', i.e., gaol, shamed and mortified the whole family, apart from the miscreant, who let his sisters and father stump up again. 'It is not agreeable to lose money time after time in this way,' Charlotte wrote grimly to Ellen, 'but it is ten times worse – to witness the shabbiness of his behaviour on such occasions.' Visitors had to be kept away from the Parsonage because of Branwell's volatility. On one occasion, it is said that he set his bed on fire, and was only rescued by Emily's prompt action, a story that, if true, seems to have gone straight into Charlotte's novel. In some remarks to J. A. Erskine Stuart many years later, Ellen Nussey implied that there was an unspoken point of no return that families recognised when dealing with their addict sons (hers had one, and so did the Taylors), and that she saw Branwell Brontë only once 'after he became an inebriate', 'and *then* he was full of the most intense egotism and vanity'.

The tailor's son, Benjamin Binns, remembered seeing Branwell around this time 'dragging his way home' of a night after leaving his boon companions at the Black Bull. Most of Branwell's time was spent in bed, writing poems about his misery and doodling bleak, black caricatures in his letters to Leyland and on the drafts of poems. One shows him lying like a figure on a tomb, draped classically in a robe; one is a Promethean figure in hell-fire, bound at the wrists with the word 'Myself' written beneath; one is a self-portrait as the convicted murderer Patrick Reid, with a noose around his neck, awaiting execution. His last sketch is called *A Parody* and shows him lying exhausted in bed, being summoned to a bout with a skeleton, who has readied his fists but also looks as if he is thumbing his nose while saying, 'The half minute time is up, so Come to the scratch; won't you?'*

Branwell had ceased to consider his family at all. He dreaded his father's death (which he presumed crassly would be fairly soon, due to age) because of the plunge into penury it would mean for himself, but he no longer felt capable of submitting to 'a new lifes battle [*sic*]', as he put it, one more time. It is clear at this point that he had never seriously intended to submit to it, always secretly hoping and expecting to make his name, and a living, through art, literature or personal charm. His dreams of marrying the Lady of Thorp Green were in tatters, but his self-interest in that scheme now became fully exposed. As her husband, he told Leyland, he had hoped, 'in more than competence' to 'live at leisure to try to make myself a name in the world of posterity, without being pestered by the small but countless botherments, which like mosquitoes sting us in the world of work-day toil'. With massive egotism, he persisted in thinking that the only thing that prevented this convenient arrangement from going ahead was the intimidation of Lydia Robinson by her trustees and by terrific deathbed vows that Branwell imagined her late husband had extracted from her with his 'ghastly dying eye'. The Robinson family doctor, on the other hand, was charged with returning Branwell's unopened letters and advised him to give up soliciting Mrs Robinson, 'cost what it may'. Charlotte was fairly sure, from the gossip that came their way, that Mrs Robinson now repented her 'errors' vis-à-vis Branwell. All three sisters strove carefully to hide from him that the younger daughters were back in touch with Anne, and the news that in March 1847 Mrs Robinson had moved away from Thorp Green to her cousin Lady Scott's commodious home at Great Barr in Birmingham.

*

* The picture is included in the second plate section.

By the summer of 1847 Currer, Ellis and Acton Bell's queer three-part novel had been out to numerous publishers – and had come back with a refusal every time. To cheer themselves, and perhaps rouse the interest of a champion, the sisters reverted to their old tactic of aggressive solicitation and posted out some copies of *Poems by Currer, Ellis and Acton Bell* to their most admired authors, Wordsworth, De Quincey, Hartley Coleridge, J. G. Lockhart and the coming man, Alfred Tennyson. The same very amusing covering letter, with minor variations, was sent to them all. This is the one to De Quincey:

Sir

My Relatives, Ellis and Acton Bell and myself, heedless of the repeated warnings of various respectable publishers, have committed the rash act of printing a volume of poems.

The consequences predicted have, of course, overtaken us; our book is found to be a drug; no man needs it or heeds it; in the space of a year our publisher has disposed but of two copies, and by what painful efforts he succeeded in getting rid of those two, himself only knows.

Before transferring the edition to the trunk-makers,* we have decided on distributing as presents a few copies of what we cannot sell – we beg to offer you one in acknowledgment of the pleasure and profit we have often and long derived from your works –

I am Sir
Yours very respectfully
Currer Bell.

Did they think to start at least a topic of conversation between the Lake Poets by sending out these packages simultaneously and making a virtue of their gad-fly status? And did Charlotte imagine that Hartley Coleridge had forgotten his former correspondence with 'CT' of Haworth, whose handwriting was identical to Currer Bell's, or with Patrick Branwell Brontë, who had hailed from the same village?

The sales of *Poems* crept with painful slowness from two copies in June 1846 to thirty-nine in September 1848, when the remaining stock

---

* Trunk-makers were known to use waste paper as lining material.

(of 961 copies) was bought by Charlotte's later publisher and reissued. It had more currency and influence than they ever knew, though. Among its early readers, unknown to the authors, was Richard Monckton Milnes, a well-connected amateur poet, bibliophile and MP for Pontefract, who took the book to Lea Hurst in Derbyshire in the autumn of 1846, and read some of it aloud to the young woman he was trying to woo, Florence Nightingale.* She was particularly struck by a poem she remembered as 'The Captive' ('The Prisoner'):

> He comes with western winds, with evening's wandering airs,
> With that clear dusk of heaven that brings the thickest stars.
> Winds take a pensive tone, and stars a tender fire,
> And visions rise, and change, that kill me with desire.

And, though the courtship of Milnes ended in a refusal of marriage, Florence Nightingale's intense interest in the 'Bells' and their clarion call to action and liberty had just begun.

And good news was on the way for Emily and Anne when they received a letter in July from Thomas Newby, of Cavendish Square, London, offering to publish *Wuthering Heights* and *Agnes Grey* together as a three-volume novel. Whether or not Newby saw and rejected *The Professor* at the same time is unclear, as the books might have been going around separately before this, in response to their frequent rejections. He proposed that *Wuthering Heights* should take up the first two volumes and *Agnes Grey* the third, and that they should publish on a shared-risk basis, the authors putting down a £50 deposit towards the costs of production, repayable on sufficient sales. Though they had taken such a hit the previous year with *Poems*, Emily and Anne felt sufficiently optimistic to pay up this large sum. From what reserves it is hard to tell, as they had not sold or transferred any of the railway stock they inherited from Aunt Branwell, and in 1847, the year of Railway Panic, there could have been little or no profits from the investment. But they accepted the terms, and by early August the first proofs of their book were ready.

Charlotte had by this time almost finished copying out her second

---

* Another owner of a first edition *Poems* was Charles Dodgson (later known to the public as Lewis Carroll, author of *Alice in Wonderland*). His copy of the book is now in the Berg Collection of the New York Public Library.

novel, *Jane Eyre*,★ but had still not found a home for *The Professor*. She sent it out yet again, with a note she must by this stage have tired of writing:

Gentlemen

I beg to submit to your consideration the accompanying Manuscript – I should be glad to learn whether it be such as you approve and would undertake to publish – at as early a period as possible.

The publisher George Smith remembered the arrival of this package at his Cornhill office, because the author had gauchely used as a wrapper the same paper it had been out in many times before, so he could see the whole history of the manuscript's rejection by fellow members of his trade. 'This was not calculated to prepossess us in favour of the MS,' Smith recalled drily, but the package was handed to his colleague, William Smith Williams, who wrote back to Mr Bell regretting that, though they didn't want to publish *The Professor*, the manuscript 'evinced great literary power', which convinced him that '[the writer] could produce a book which would command success.' Looking back three years later, Charlotte recalled the thrill of receiving this letter, the first to respond to her novel with intelligent interest; 'it declined, indeed, to publish that tale, for business reasons, but it discussed its merits and demerits so courteously, so considerately, in a spirit so rational, with a discrimination so enlightened, that this very refusal cheered the author better than a vulgarly expressed acceptance would have done.'

She wrote back promptly, eager to express her gratitude and respond to the suggestion that a future work of suitable length – three volumes – 'would meet with careful attention'. She had just such a work almost ready, which she told them could be sent in about a month (she actually managed to finish *Jane Eyre* in rather less time than that). But, even at this point, she couldn't help putting in another word – two more words – for the rejected Brussels novel. Why not publish *The Professor* anyway, she suggested, to 'accustom the public to the author's name'? She still felt strongly that having *The Professor* in print would make subsequent

★ The first leaf of the fair copy (see second plate section) bears the date 16 March [1847] and the copy was completed on 19 August.

success more probable. She even went as far as to suggest that she thought she might offer the books as a pair, a dangerous gamble to take at this juncture and one that Smith, Elder politely declined. Charlotte had no choice but to put aside her first novel and send off the second alone, walking to Keighley on 24 August to dispatch it by rail.

When Williams read *Jane Eyre*, he pressed it on Smith with an urgency that at first amused his employer, but that Smith understood when he settled down with the manuscript after breakfast on Sunday morning. He had been engaged to visit a friend at noon, but got so caught up in the story of the 'plain, insignificant governess' that when it was time to leave, he scribbled a note of apology to the friend, sent it off by his groom, and carried on reading. 'Presently the servant came to tell me that luncheon was ready; I asked him to bring me a sandwich and a glass of wine, and still went on with "Jane Eyre". Dinner came; for me the meal was a very hasty one, and before I went to bed that night I had finished reading the manuscript.'

The next day Smith wrote accepting the book for publication, although not without some 'advice' – now lost – to the author. From Currer Bell's response on 12 September it must have involved taming down the early chapters about Jane's treatment at the hands of her aunt and at Lowood School, and the death of Helen Burns. Currer Bell told Smith that he had already considerably softened the truth on which these episodes were based and could do no more without damaging the book's integrity: though they were strongly expressed, the harsher parts of *Jane Eyre* 'may suit the public taste better than you anticipate'.* Here, the debut novelist proved right. However, she – he – accepted the firm's other suggestion that the title could be changed, and 'Jane Eyre: a novel in three vols. By Currer Bell' became 'Jane Eyre: An

---

* Charlotte also mentions in this letter that the novel had been revised twice already and that she was unwilling to make any further large adjustments for fear of damaging what had already been difficult enough to shape. It makes one wonder whether she did not, in fact, write *Jane Eyre* in one glorious swoop of inspiration between August 1846 and August 1847, as is assumed, but rather incorporated some older material too (as she had in *The Professor*). The Gateshead and Lowood episodes, for all their extraordinary power, certainly relate to the main narrative rather oddly, and the jump of eight years after Helen Burns's death is very abrupt. And there was that paragraph in her 1843 notebook, beginning a story set in 'Gateshead Hall'.

Autobiography. Edited by Currer Bell'. Someone at Smith, Elder (and the manuscript had by this time been read by three of the staff, Williams, Smith and their young Scottish colleague James Taylor) had recognised the potential of making readers wonder – could this story actually *be true*? The tweak to the title created a fiction that made the heroine Jane less fictional, made her into an autobiographer, 'edited' – at some distance in time (for, as not many people notice, the action of the book starts in the 1810s) – by Currer Bell.

Smith was offering £100 for the copyright – an infinitely better deal than Emily and Anne's with Newby, which had amounted to little more than vanity publishing again. It was also considerably more than most women could ever dream of earning in a year, and one might have expected Charlotte to sound pleased when she wrote back to Smith, but she was in the character of Currer Bell, so made the dry observation that 'one hundred pounds is a small sum for a year's intellectual labour'. Part of the pleasure of being able 'to walk invisible' behind her male pseudonym was this new-found licence to answer as a man would – even if Smith didn't recognise it.

Charlotte also agreed to give Smith first refusal on her next two novels at the same rate, an astute move on the part of the publisher, whose hopes for *Jane Eyre* were high. Privately, though Currer Bell sniffed slightly at £100, Charlotte Brontë's relief was considerable, knowing that she had sold one book and had an interested market for others. In fact, she was so willing to do whatever was necessary to keep the door open (except revise *Jane Eyre*) that she asked Smith for specific advice 'as to choice of subject or style of treatment in my next effort – and if you can point out any works peculiarly remarkable for the qualities in which I am deficient, I would study them carefully and endeavour to remedy my errors.' Clearly, she did not want to lose Smith's patronage by starting off on another unsaleable work.

The progress of *Jane Eyre* through the press showed what safe hands Charlotte had fallen into at Smith, Elder by comparison with her sisters, whose dealings with Thomas Newby completely stalled in the autumn of 1847. Proofs came and went for Currer with no news at all for Ellis and Acton, and by the end of October *Jane Eyre* had sailed into print while *Wuthering Heights* and *Agnes Grey* still languished on Newby's desk.

Six sets of *Jane Eyre* arrived at the Parsonage on publication day, 19 October 1847, presumably much to the interest of the postmaster, Mr Hartley. Reviews began flooding in immediately, from the daily papers, religious journals, provincial gazettes, trade magazines, as well as from the expected literary organs such as the *Athenaeum*, *Critic* and *Literary Gazette*. Charlotte had been anxious about the critical reception of 'a mere domestic novel', hoping it would at least sell enough copies to justify her publisher's investment – in the event, it triumphed on both fronts. The response was powerful and immediate. Reviewers praised the unusual force of the writing: 'One of the freshest and most genuine books which we have read for a long time', 'far beyond the average', 'very clever and striking', with images 'like the Cartoons of Raphael . . . true, bold, well-defined'. 'This is not merely a work of great promise,' the *Atlas* said, 'it is one of absolute performance'; while the influential critic George Henry Lewes seemed spellbound by the book's 'psychological intuition': 'It reads like a page out of one's own life.' It sold in thousands and was reprinted within ten weeks; eventually, even Queen Victoria was arrested by 'that intensely interesting novel'. Only four days after publication, William Makepeace Thackeray, whose masterpiece *Vanity Fair* was unfolding before the public in serial form at exactly the same time, wrote to thank Williams for his complimentary copy of *Jane Eyre*. He had 'lost (or won if you like) a whole day in reading it'; in fact it had engrossed him so much that his own printers were kept waiting for the next instalment of Becky Sharp's adventures, and when the servant came in with the coals, he found Mr Thackeray weeping over Currer Bell's love scenes.

Who was Currer Bell? A man, obviously. This forthright tale of attempted bigamy and an unmarried woman's passion could have been written only by a man, thought Albany Fonblanque, the reviewer in John Forster's influential *Examiner*, who praised the book's thought and morals as 'true, sound, and original' and believed that 'Whatever faults may be urged against the book, no one can assert that it is weak or vapid. It is anything but a fashionable novel . . . as an analysis of a single mind . . . it may claim comparison with any work of the same species.'

Charlotte could hardly keep up with responding to the cuttings that Williams was sending on by every post, and even received a letter from George Henry Lewes while he was writing his review for *Fraser's*

Magazine, wanting to engage in a detailed analysis of the book. 'There are moments when I can hardly credit that anything I have done should be found worthy to give even transitory pleasure to such men as Mr. Thackeray, Sir John Herschel, Mr. Fonblanque, Leigh Hunt and Mr. Lewes,' Currer Bell told his publisher; 'that my humble efforts should have had such a result is a noble reward.' It must have been difficult for Emily and Anne to be wholly delighted for their sister, with their own books apparently forgotten, though when Newby saw the success of Currer Bell he suddenly moved back into action with the production of *Wuthering Heights and Agnes Grey*, hoping to cash in on the excitement.

In the middle of this storm of gratification, Charlotte wrote to Ellen as if literally nothing of note was happening in Haworth – 'heaven knows I have precious little to say' – but at home, the time had come to inform her father of the reason for the sudden flood of post from London, and his daughters' animation. Patrick Brontë told Mrs Gaskell later that he suspected all along that the girls were somehow trying to get published, 'but his suspicions could take no exact form, as all he was certain of was, that his children were perpetually writing – and not writing letters'. Sometime in November or early December 1847, between the publication of *Jane Eyre* and *Wuthering Heights and Agnes Grey*, Charlotte sought out her father in his study after his usual solitary dinner, with a copy of her novel to show him and two or three reviews, including one that was critical – a characteristic piece of scrupulousness. Mrs Gaskell wrote down, in the week she heard it, Charlotte's own report of the scene:

> 'Papa I've been writing a book.' 'Have you my dear?' and he went on reading. 'But Papa I want you to look at it.' 'I can't be troubled to read MS.' 'But it is printed.' 'I hope you have not been involving yourself in any such silly expense.' 'I think I shall gain some money by it. May I read you some reviews.' So she read them; and then she asked him if he would read the book. He said she might leave it, and he would see.

When he came in to tea some hours later it was with the announcement, 'Children, Charlotte has been writing a book – and I think it is a better one than I expected.' The scene made a pleasantly comical end to the secrecy that the girls had found obnoxious at home, however essential it seemed elsewhere, and Reverend Brontë's pride in his daughter's success became one of Charlotte's deepest pleasures in the following years. The old man began to take an intense interest in the review coverage (more than in the work, perhaps) and kept a cuttings book of everything that came his way, meticulously arranged and dated. Quite when he heard about Emily's and Anne's novels is unclear – presumably soon after their books were published in December 1847 – but he never esteemed their achievement as high as Charlotte's, and said that their works 'though clever in their kind, never reach'd the great celebrity of those works written by Charlotte, under the assum'd name of Currer Bell'. He seems to have been following exactly the drift of the critics, who heaped praise on Currer Bell's book but were troubled or even disgusted by Ellis's and not much impressed by Acton's. How the world viewed such public performances mattered to Patrick Brontë very much.

Emily and Anne were not well served by their publisher, and the copies of *Wuthering Heights and Agnes Grey* that arrived just before Christmas proved to be cheaply produced and full of errors uncorrected from the proofs. Worse still, Newby had indulged in some chicanery in his advertising of the book, suggesting that it was by the author of *Jane Eyre*. The reception was mixed, and the coverage far less extensive than that of Currer Bell's bestseller; reviewers seemed consternated by *Wuthering Heights*'s shocking violence and 'abominable paganism' – even the multiple narrators unsettled them. Not all the judgements were negative, however. The force and originality of Ellis Bell's book were indisputable, as was the mind behind it, 'of limited experience, but of original energy, and of a singular and distinctive cast', as the critic in *Britannia* said, while *Douglas Jerrold's Weekly* recognised that the author 'wants but the practised skill to make a great artist'. Emily was gratified by these few but potent marks of recognition and kept cuttings of five reviews in her writing desk, including one unidentified one, the best of all, which praised the novel's vital force and truth to 'all the emotions and passions which agitate the restless bosom of humanity' and 'talent of no common order'.

Appearing as an adjunct to such a strange and powerful story, *Agnes Grey* never had a chance of being judged on its own merits. The *Atlas*, crushingly, said that, unlike *Wuthering Heights*, *Agnes Grey* 'left no painful impression on the mind – some may think it leaves no impression at all'. It also looked pallid in comparison with Currer Bell's governess novel, which had in fact post-dated it.

But the appearance of two more novelists called Bell – one of whom was wickedly sensational – made a prime subject of gossip. Though none of the published works bore any biographical information about the authors, it became generally understood that the Bells were brothers, possibly through Charlotte's reference to them as 'relatives' in her correspondence with publishers, and with the writers to whom she had sent *Poems*. One of those writers, J. G. Lockhart, seemed much more interested in the gossip than in the work they had sent him and passed on to his friend Elizabeth Rigby the news that the Bells were 'brothers of the weaving order in some Lancashire town'. Another school of thought, fuelled by Newby's false advertising, favoured the idea that 'the Bells' were all one person.

Meanwhile, Charlotte remained modest and cautious about her overnight success – and considerably better off, receiving a further cheque for £100 in February when the third edition was in preparation. For the second edition, she had decided to add a dedication: not to her 'Master', as formerly imagined, but to Thackeray, in homage to his effectiveness as a 'social regenerator'. In a resounding preface, freighted with biblical allusions, she praised the dauntlessness and daring of the satirist who 'comes before the great ones of society, much as the son of Imlah came before the throned Kings of Judah and Israel; and who speaks truth as deep, with a power as prophet-like and as vital'. Thackeray was 'the very master of that working corps [in which she clearly hoped to be counted herself] who would restore to rectitude the warped system of things'.

Thackeray was of course 'a total stranger' to Currer Bell, as she was careful to make clear in her dedication, but that didn't prevent people wondering, when they read this very extravagant homage, if some more interesting relation was being concealed. Unknown to Charlotte, but known to many London literary people, Thackeray's wife had had a mental breakdown some years before, and was cared for in reclusion in Camberwell, having been previously in a French asylum. The similarity to the Rochester–Bertha plot was irresistible to rumour-mongers, who began to say that Currer Bell must once have been a governess in

Thackeray's household – with the implication that Currer Bell must also have been his 'chère amie'.

When Charlotte heard of Thackeray's circumstances, which she did from the man himself when he wrote to thank her for her dedication, she was completely mortified, and wrote to Williams of how '*very, very* sorry' she was for her 'inadvertent blunder'. She had apologised to Thackeray, she told Williams, but with full awareness of how futile apologies were when such damage had been done. The incident illustrated for her how much she needed advice and guidance to deal with literary life at a distance.

Her growing friendship with George Smith's second-in-command, William Smith Williams, was one of the great pleasures that came to Charlotte through publication, and for almost a year she conducted a very open and lively correspondence with him in the person of the androgynous 'Currer Bell', with no revelation of her real name, sex or circumstances. The freedom that this gave her was unique in her life: she wrote to Williams not as a man or a woman, but the free spirit, unsnared, that her heroine Jane had defined and defended. Williams was forty-seven at the time, married and the father of eight children, ranging in age from their early twenties to a toddler. He had had many friends in the literary world: in his youth he had known Keats and Hazlitt, and had nursed ambitions to be a poet; Leigh Hunt was a lifelong friend; and, since joining Smith, Elder as literary adviser in 1845, he had made friends with Thackeray, Lewes and Ruskin. Unlike his boss, Smith, Williams wasn't a particularly confident man, but discerning and sensitive, and with the time and inclination to correspond with Currer Bell on a range of topics that included contemporary politics, London literary life, ethics, female education and employment, industrialisation, religion and of course, predominantly, literature.

From the frankness with which Currer Bell tackles the question in one letter of what Williams's daughters might do to earn an independent living, it is clear that Williams had shared (in his missing side of the correspondence) many details of his family life and circumstances with his new correspondent, whoever 'Currer Bell' was. He could hardly have been in serious doubt that the author of *Jane Eyre* and of these letters was a woman, but the fiction of her non-womanness was maintained scrupulously in their early correspondence. It was in many respects the sort of relationship that Charlotte felt she ought to have had with Monsieur Heger, but which sexual attraction had fatally compromised in that instance. Williams had unbent so far as to share with Currer Bell his sense of failure and disappointment in his career – he was, in fact, a depressed and needy man under the skin, having worked for thirty-five years 'in a position where your tastes had no scope, and your faculties no exercise'. As Currer perceived, 'I feel that your cup of life must often have been a most bitter one – and I would fain say something consolatory without knowing very well how to express myself.' The simple sincerity of this must have endeared the writer to Williams very much indeed.

Of course, as the months passed after the publication of *Jane Eyre* (which went into its third edition in April 1848), Smith, Elder were keen to hear if Currer Bell had a new work in mind, but the reclusive author reported that none of the three attempts made so far (as early as December 1847) were any good. Showing something of the persistence that her father had displayed over his rejection by Mary Burder, Charlotte/Currer then proposed *yet again* to Smith that he might think of publishing *The Professor*, in an enlarged and 'recast' version. Looking over the manuscript, Bell had come to the conclusion that, although the beginning was feeble and the plot rather uneventful, the Belgian episodes were 'as good as I can write'.

Williams had to write back with the unenviable task of explaining once more to their new bestselling author that *The Professor* was not wanted, a judgement that puzzled Charlotte more and more, but that she had to accept. 'It is my wish to do my best in the career on which I have entered', she told her publisher, 'so I shall study and strive, and by dint of time, thought and effort, I hope yet to deserve in part the encouragement you and others have so generously accorded me. But *Time* will be necessary: that I feel more than ever.'

A pencilled draft of her brief letter to Williams about *The Professor* has survived because on the reverse of the paper is the draft of a poem, never published in Charlotte's lifetime, which shows what revisiting her Brussels novel had stirred up in her mind. It begins thus:

> He saw my heart's woe discovered my soul's anguish
> How in fever – in thirst, in atrophy it pined

Knew he could heal yet looked and let it languish
To its moans spirit-deaf, to its pangs spirit-blind

But once a year he heard a whisper low and dreary
Appealing for aid, entreating some reply
Only when sick soul-worn, and torture weary
Breathed I that prayer – heaved I that sigh

He was mute as is the grave – he stood stirless as a tower
At last I looked up and saw I prayed to stone
I asked help of that which to help had no power
I sought love where love was utterly unknown

By December 1847, this is where her thoughts of Heger had led her: to the image of him 'stirless as a tower', impenetrable, distant, cruelly unresponsive. Charlotte packed up copies of *Jane Eyre* and *Wuthering Heights and Agnes Grey* to send to Mary Taylor in Wellington; did she also send a copy to the rue d'Isabelle? It seems unlikely. *Jane Eyre* should have been the proof, spectacular and irrefutable, that she was worthy of her Master's continued attention, his love, esteem and recognition; instead the moment of its publication parted them even further. Charlotte had finally realised the futility of her suffering, though she stopped short of admitting that the love of an idol was idolatrous. A merciful God could not possibly condemn such a love, she felt:

He gave our hearts to love, he will not love despise
E'en if the gift be lost as mine was long ago
He will forgive the fault – will bid the offender rise
Wash out with dews of bliss the fiery brand of woe.

By the time *Agnes Grey* was published, Anne Brontë was well ahead with her second novel, *The Tenant of Wildfell Hall*, the story of an abused wife seeking refuge from her marriage, whose situation and attempts to earn her own living as an artist excite suspicion and scorn among her new neighbours. Just as Charlotte had learnt from *Wuthering Heights* to add passion and excitement to the plot of *Jane Eyre*, so Anne noted the pace and skilful handling of both her sisters' books, and brought those qualities to bear on her own, which has the feel of a mystery and thriller as much as of a morality tale. But the book obsessed the author

in ways that worried her eldest sister, who saw Anne continually
stooped over her work, writing for too many hours of each day. '[It] is
with difficulty one can prevail on her to take a walk or induce her to
converse,' Charlotte told Ellen. It was only later, when she understood
that the new novel depicted with painful verisimilitude the stages of a
long ruination through vice and drink, that Charlotte understood
Anne's grim determination over its composition. Much that was criticised (not least by Charlotte) as coarse and unpleasant in the book was
an unvarnished account of some aspects of life at Haworth Parsonage
in 1847–8: the daily ordeal of having to tolerate the violence and
degraded behaviour of a drunkard. 'The motives which dictated this
choice were pure, but, I think, slightly morbid,' Charlotte wrote later
in explanation of her sister's subject. 'She had, in the course of her life,
been called on to contemplate, near at hand and for a long time, the
terrible effects of talents misused and faculties abused; hers was naturally a sensitive, reserved, and dejected nature; what she saw sank very
deeply into her mind; it did her harm.' But in many ways Anne Brontë
showed considerable bravery in exposing the realities around her – not
least because of the resistance from her older sister. Perhaps the only
way she could cope with Branwell's dissolution was to hold it up to
others as a warning.

Emily was planning, and possibly writing, a second novel at the
beginning of 1848, as one can deduce from a remark in a letter to her
from Newby that he would have 'great pleasure in making arrangements' for it, and advised 'I would not hurry its completion, for I think
you are quite right not to let it go before the world until well satisfied
with it.' She composed very little poetry at this time: the reception of
Poems had not encouraged her at all. Charlotte was also thinking about
what to write next, intimidating though it was to bear in mind, as
Newby had told Emily, that 'much depends on your next work if it be
an improvement on your first you will have established yourself as a
first rate novelist, but if it fall short the Critics will be too apt to say
that you have expended your talent.' Forced to shelve *The Professor*,
Charlotte turned to something quite different from both it and *Jane
Eyre*, armed with her new knowledge of what real audiences, rather
than her imagined audience, might like or demand. The new novel,
called 'Hollows Mill' at this early stage, was going to reflect life and

society in her own corner of the world, the West Riding, a 'condition of England' novel that would also attempt a light, satirical tone, possibly in emulation of Thackeray, whose work she admired even more now that she knew he admired hers.

The authorial voice she adopted for the purpose seemed nervously aware of the pressure on her to satisfy an audience of eager *Jane Eyre* fans; on the first page she warned that this was to be a story as 'unromantic as Monday morning' — something 'real, cool, and solid', with very little 'taste of the exciting'. Brontë baulked, though, at a realistic *contemporary* setting, placing the action thirty years earlier, in the 1810s.

That she originally considered setting her new novel in the 1840s, and against the background of Chartism, was suggested by a local Chartist sympathiser called Francis Butterfield, who in old age published an account of how Charlotte Brontë had visited him one afternoon (in the spring or summer of 1848) to consult 'with respect to a proposed story on the Chartists' agitations'. Miss Brontë had walked over from Haworth to Butterfield's home in Wilsden, he said, accompanied by her dog Floss, and by the end of tea had been dissuaded from her plan, 'which at that time would only have added a flame to the still smouldering embers of discontent', as a chronicler of old Bingley retold the story. Though the meeting is not corroborated elsewhere, and seems socially strange (for example, in that Charlotte was unaccompanied, unless you count the spaniel), there are reasons to believe it. It shows the same concern with research and getting her facts right that Charlotte demonstrated later, when she had changed her subject from the Chartists to the Luddites and borrowed files from the archives of *The Leeds Mercury* to read contemporary accounts of the events of 1811–12. And she or one or both of her sisters were also admirers of another Chartist sympathiser, the Leeds poet Ebenezer Elliott, to whom they had sent a copy of the Bells' *Poems* in 1847.[*]

Her decision to avoid Chartism and the present day came from a rapid toning down of her enthusiasm for the revolutionary dramas being played out in Italy, Hungary, France and Germany in the spring

---

[*] His copy, in the BPM, is noticeably worn from much reading. Charlotte may well have had more than one reason to seek out Butterfield's advice: he was a leading light in the local Temperance Society and the biographer of temperance hero Thomas Worsnop. She might have spoken to him about her brother.

and summer of 1848. Her feelings at the beginning of the year were empathetic and engaged, partly because some of the figures connected with unfolding events in France were ones she knew of from her discussions of politics and literature with Constantin Heger. Charlotte had written a well-informed and discursive letter to Williams (man to man, as it were, as 'Currer Bell') about the promotion to government of men like Lamartine and Thiers, wondering what it would be like in Britain under similar circumstances, if Carlyle, Sir John Herschel, Tennyson and Thackeray were suddenly made into national legislators: 'do such men sway the public mind most effectually from their quiet studies or from a council-chamber?' This was in the same month – February – in which she had written her preface to the second edition of her genuinely inflammatory novel, *Jane Eyre*, with its praise of Thackeray as a leader who could 'restore to rectitude the warped system of things'. At this point Currer Bell could have been easily mistaken for a revolutionary sympathiser. Perhaps at heart she was. By March, she regretted that the wording of her preface had been so warm, given the proclamation of a republican government in France that was sparking Chartist celebrations in London and elsewhere. Her remarks about Thackeray as leading 'social regenerator' now seemed particularly impertinent. 'I wish I had written it in a cool moment,' she told Williams; 'I should have said the same things, but in a different manner.'

Though she sympathised with German states wanting constitutional reform in the wake of the French revolution – referring to 'their rational and justifiable efforts for liberty' – Charlotte's natural conservatism reasserted itself as soon as the contagion of revolt threatened her own shores. '[E]arthquakes roll lower than the ocean, and we know neither the day nor the hour when the tremor and heat, passing beneath our island, may unsettle and dissolve its foundations,' she told Williams. There had been a mass meeting of Chartists in Leeds on 10 March, and, though the group was keen to appear non-violent, and focused on the presentation of their 'monster petition' of more than a million signatories to Parliament (planned for the following month), many of the men at the Lees Moor muster were armed, some crudely with sharpened staves, and the flag they hoisted was that of the French republic. Charlotte used the earthquake image again in a letter of 31 March to Margaret Wooler:

I have still no doubt that the shock of moral earthquakes wakens a vivid sense of life both in Nations and individuals; that the fear of dangers on a broad national scale diverts men's minds momentarily from brooding over small private perils, and, for the time, gives them something like largeness of views; but – as little doubt have I that convulsive revolutions put back the world in all that is good, check civilisation, bring the dregs of society to its surface, in short, it appears to me that insurrections and battles are the acute diseases of nations, and that their tendency is to exhaust by their violence the vital energies of the countries where they occur. That England may be spared the spasms, cramps and frenzy-fits now contorting the Continent and threatening Ireland, I earnestly pray!

The transposition of her story back in time forty years was a way of writing about 1848 at one remove, identifying some of the early symptoms of the 'disease', but it created obvious difficulties. Charlotte had planned her story around local characters drawn from the life, but it was the life of the 1830s and 1840s, not the period just before her own birth. Emily Brontë was to be the model for Shirley herself, the Taylor family for the radical Yorkes, Hammond Roberson for Matthewson Helstone, Ellen may have contributed something to his niece Caroline, Miss Wooler to Mrs Pryor, Mademoiselle Haussé of the Pensionnat Heger to Hortense Gérard Moore, and Monsieur Heger was plundered for aspects of both the Belgian brothers, Robert and Louis Moore. This gave a strange anachronism to the novel's manners, though Charlotte managed (through careful research) to reconstruct the social moment skilfully.

Casting the issues of 1848 back on to this screen, Charlotte made some interesting observations about the impenetrability of class boundaries, which Will Farren, one of the mill-workers whose jobs are lost to Robert Moore's new machinery, complains cannot be crossed: 'I believe that "the people" will never have any true friends but theirsel'n, and them two or three good folk i' different stations, that is friends to all the world. Human natur', taking it i' th' lump, is naught but selfishness.' The comparable predicaments of workers and women are linked all through the novel in a very interesting meld of the personal with the political. In the same passage where she thinks about the unattractiveness of neediness, Caroline comes to some stark conclusions: 'old maids, like the houseless and the unemployed poor, should

not ask for a place and an occupation in the world: the demand disturbs
the happy and rich: it disturbs parents.' But this underemployment of
women makes them narrow-minded and fixated on capturing a husband, Caroline realises, and, since so many of them will never marry (it
is an 'overstocked market', she says, using an appropriately commercial
term), their futile coquetry only earns more male scorn, lowering the
stock even further.

For all the explicit political argument in the book, *Shirley* is directed
inwards more than outwards, and the most striking passages are to do
with the private and for the most part silent interior battles of an apparently subsidiary character, Caroline. Her quietness is a marked recession
from Jane Eyre's urge to speak; nor is it used strategically like Frances
Henri, but makes a study in impotence. When Robert Moore, the
brusque, domineering, sexy, half-Belgian owner of Hollow's Mill,
withdraws the light of his favour from the young woman whose love
he has carelessly engaged, Caroline realises that she cannot even seek an
explanation for his behaviour without incurring shame, for 'a lover
feminine can say nothing'. 'Take the matter as you find it,' the narrator
steps in bitterly to remark:

> ask no questions; utter no remonstrances: it is your best wisdom. You
> expected bread, and you have got a stone; break your teeth on it, and
> don't shriek because the nerves are martyrized . . . You held out your
> hand for an egg, and fate put into it a scorpion. Show no consternation:
> close your fingers firmly upon the gift; let it sting through your palm.
> Never mind: in time, after your hand and arm have swelled and quiv-
> ered long with torture, the squeezed scorpion will die, and you will
> have learned the great lesson how to endure without a sob.

The violence of expression here is striking. Charlotte knew that this
book would be published – and it was the first time she had been in
such a position. This wasn't, like *The Professor* or *Jane Eyre*, a shot in the
dark. But instead of tempering her voice (as she claims to be about to
do in the first chapter), she used this public space very personally and
very vehemently.

The novel is full of such interjections, all extremely disorienting, as
one supposes they were intended to be. The narrator addresses the
reader, apologises, directs attention to the fictional nature of the story,

glosses, jokes, but remains in an undeclared relation to the action she can't resist interrupting. One such moment, part-way through the first scene at Briarmains (the house based on the Taylors' Red House), takes a morbid detour into a vision of the family's future, rather like a dark version of Emily's and Anne's Diary Papers: Jessy Yorke will die young and be buried in a foreign grave, we are cruelly informed; her sister Rose will be a lonely emigrant 'in some region of the southern hemisphere'. One minute, we are being told about Shirley's plans to help the poor of the parish, and informed that her smile is not like the usual female downcast look, a veiled look, in other words. Then comes this most arbitrary and violent digression:

> I remember once seeing a pair of blue eyes, that were usually thought sleepy, secretly on the alert, and I knew by their expression – an expression which chilled my blood . . . that for years they had been accustomed to silent soul-reading. The world called the owner of these blue eyes 'bonne petite femme' (she was not an Englishwoman): I learned her nature afterwards – got it off by heart – studied it in its farthest, most hidden recesses – she was the finest, deepest, subtlest schemer in Europe.

What is this viciously exaggerated attack on Madame Heger doing here? The narrator recovers the thread of the story immediately afterwards, but there it sits, unwarranted on any grounds, artistic or personal. Another bog burst from Charlotte's seething substratum.

When *Jane Eyre* went into its third edition, in April, Charlotte provided yet another preface, short and to the point this time, stating that it was Currer Bell's sole work, and that 'If . . . the authorship of other works of fiction has been attributed to me, an honour is awarded where it is not merited.' This was an attempt to quell the increasingly annoying speculation that *Jane Eyre*, *Wuthering Heights* and *Agnes Grey* were all by the same author (quite an author!) 'insanely bent on severing himself into three', as Currer joked with Williams. Her correspondent kept her abreast of some of the follies committed in her name in 'your great world – your London', the worst of which was a dramatisation of her novel (done without any need to seek permission at that date) only two months after the book was published, in January 1848. Charlotte had been intrigued to hear of such a production, and even considered going down to the capital to sneak in and watch it incognito. That being impossible, she encouraged Williams to go on her behalf, but his subsequent description of the play was a horrible shock, 'a glimpse of what I might call *loathsome*, but which I prefer calling *strange*', with the introduction of some low-comedy characters, an extra mad person and a lot of physical violence. If such a spectacle was the result of fame, Emily must have seemed right to shun it.

Meanwhile, as if he sensed that he was being put into 'Hollow's Mill', Joe Taylor had turned up uninvited at the Parsonage one day in June with his cousin William Henry (whom Charlotte knew well from Brussels) and another cousin. Charlotte was suspicious of their motives for this 'capricious' visit (no Brontë liked or encouraged informal socialising), guessing it was 'prompted . . . by curiosity' and that Joe had indeed deduced the identity of 'Currer Bell'. Charlotte fended off the Taylors, as she did Ellen, who was in London that summer and aware of 'quite a *fureur*' about the Bells and the authorship of *Jane Eyre*. Ellen acquired the book, it seems, purely to test the theory of whether or not it had been written by her friend, and claimed many years later that, while reading it, it 'was as though Charlotte Brontë herself was present in every word, her voice and spirit thrilling through and through'. Charlotte had been correcting proof sheets when she was at Brookroyd the previous autumn, without explaining what she was doing, so Ellen didn't have much trouble putting two and two together. But when she wrote to Charlotte, coyly asking her opinion of the new bestseller, she got a sardonic answer: 'we do not subscribe to a circulating library at Haworth and consequently "new novels" rarely indeed come in our way, and consequently again we are not qualified to give opinions thereon.' That should have confirmed it pretty much beyond doubt.

For some time, Patrick Brontë had been keeping Branwell in his own room and sleeping on a cot at the foot of the bed, to have him under surveillance. The distraught father thus tried to absorb and contain some of the disturbance in the house, but, unlike the humble cottager in his own story, 'The Cottage in the Wood', whose fervent prayers reformed the dissolute young man found on the doorstep, he was unable to halt Branwell's decline. Patrick's faith in God's strength, and his own, made him look continually for hopeful signs; Charlotte, on the other hand, seems to have given up on her brother. In this and the other trials she was about to face, her prayers tended to be for strength to bear what God's inexorable will had in store for her; she had a Calvinistic aversion to the idea that personal intercession could change it.

Patrick Brontë was doling out only a shilling a day to his son, but that was no obstacle to Branwell, as a pathetic note attests, written to John Brown one Sunday when everyone else was in church, and sealed with wax for secrecy:

Dear John,

I shall feel very much obliged to you if can [*sic*] contrive to get me Five pence worth of Gin in a proper measure

Should it be speedily got I could perhaps take it from you or Billy at the lane top or what would be quite as well, sent out for, to you.

I anxiously ask the favour because I know the ~~favour~~ good it will do me.

Punctualy [*sic*] at Half past Nine in the morning you will be paid the 5d out of a shilling given me then.

Yours P. B. B.

Anne was not the only member of the household to have been affected 'very deeply' by the spectacle of Branwell's decline – the noise, the surges of energy, crazy determinations and unrestrainable force of the deteriorating addict. Patrick Brontë hardly slept. And, just as Branwell's setting fire to his bed curtains seems to have found its way quickly into *Jane Eyre*, other aspects of his behaviour linger in Charlotte's characterisation of Bertha in that novel, locked in the attic for fear of the havoc she might cause. The madwoman scenes had come in for some criticism when the book came out for being too 'horrid', but Charlotte defended herself by saying that such behaviour was 'but too natural'. 'There is a phase of insanity which may be called moral madness, in which all that is good or even human seems to disappear from the mind and a fiend-nature replaces it,' she told Williams. 'The sole aim and desire of the being thus possessed is to exasperate, to molest, to destroy, and preternatural ingenuity and energy are often exercised to that dreadful end.'

Francis Grundy had a more sympathetic view of his old friend's predicament (he didn't have to live with him) and gave it tender expression: Branwell was 'no domestic demon', he said; 'just a man moving in a mist, who lost his way'. Years later, he told a horrific story of Branwell's state in the last weeks of his life, of going to visit him in Haworth after Branwell had failed to keep an appointment in Skipton. Grundy ordered a dinner for two at the Black Bull and sent to the Parsonage for his friend, only to have Reverend Brontë appear, formally but sorrowfully explaining that his son had been very ill but would be arriving shortly. When Branwell did turn up, he was in a shocking state: spectrally thin, unkempt, 'the cheeks yellow and hollow, the mouth fallen . . . the sunken eyes, once small, now glaring with the light of madness' – all the marks of the hopeless opium-eater. Although he seemed to steady himself with brandy and some food, when Branwell was leaving he showed Grundy a carving-knife that he had been hiding in his sleeve all evening, having imagined that his summons to the inn had been from Satan, whom he was determined to stab. The familiarity of Grundy's voice had shaken him from this terrible delusion, but the incident (even if heightened for dramatic effect) gives some idea of the danger, as well as the utter misery, that the Parsonage household was being made to endure day and night through the summer of 1848.

The Tenant of Wildfell Hall was published in late June 1848, stoking press interest in 'all these Bells', as one paper called them, who suddenly seemed to be flooding the market with sensational novels – four in nine months. It encouraged the worst in Thomas Newby, who suggested to an American publisher that the Bells' works, including this new one, were all the product of a single pen, Currer's, and when *Tenant of Wildfell Hall* was advertised in this way – 'by the author of "Jane Eyre", "Wuthering Heights" and "Agnes Grey"' – the American firm Harper's, which had an agreement with Smith, Elder to publish Currer Bell's next book, was understandably offended. George Smith could only pass on his own sense of affront to his author in Haworth by post, and ask for an explanation.

This was a dreadful letter for Charlotte to receive, threatening to ruin her hitherto excellent relations with Smith, Elder and tainting her and her sisters with blame for what had been Newby's casual double-dealing. She was so mortified that only direct action seemed appropriate, and instead of getting out her desk to write a letter of explanation, she set about packing a small box instead and had it sent down to Keighley Station by carrier. After a heated discussion with Emily and a hurried meal, she and Anne set off on foot for four miles in pouring rain, caught the train to Leeds and from there took the night train to London. Emily was having no part in this rash adventure, and Patrick Brontë does not seem to have been either consulted or informed.

Telling Mary Taylor about these eventful few days, in a wonderfully comic letter, Charlotte described how on arrival in the capital early the next morning she and Anne made for the Chapter Coffee House, not knowing where else to go:

> We washed ourselves – had some breakfast – sat a few minutes and then set of[f] in queer, inward excitement, to 65. Cornhill. Neither Mr. Smith nor Mr. Williams knew we were coming   they had never seen us – they did not know whether we were men or women – but had always written to us as men.

No. 65 Cornhill, the magical address to which Charlotte had been writing for the past year, turned out to be a large bookseller's shop 'in a street almost as bustling as the Strand':

> – we went in – walked up to the counter – there were a great many young men and lads here and there – I said to the first I could accost –
>
> 'May I see Mr. Smith –?' he hesitated, looked a little surprised – but went to fetch him – We sat down and waited awhile – looking a[t] some books on the counter – publications of theirs well known to us – of many of which they had sent us copies as presents. At last somebody came up and said dubiously
>
> 'Do you wish to see me, Ma'am?'
>
> 'Is it Mr Smith?' I said looking up through my spectacles at a young, tall, gentlemanly man
>
> 'It is.'
>
> I then put his own letter into his hand directed to 'Currer Bell'. He looked at it – then at me – again – yet again – I laughed at his queer perplexity – A recognition took place –. I gave my real name – 'Miss Brontë –'

It is significant that Charlotte's personal acquaintance with her publisher began with a laugh and a double-take. He never quite got over his amazement at the incongruity of it, that this strange little woman in glasses and old-fashioned travelling clothes was *Currer Bell*. And she, given the advantage of surprise, was able to make this first scrutiny of him without self-consciousness. What she saw was a tall, charming man of twenty-four, elegantly dressed and brimming with excitement at meeting her. He hurried his visitors into an office, where rapid explanations were gone into on both sides, accompanied by strong mutual condemnation of the 'shuffling scamp', Newby. At the first opportunity Smith called in his colleague Williams to share the revelation of their best-selling author's identity, and now it was Charlotte's turn to be surprised, for Williams, her confidential correspondent of the past year, appeared in the guise of 'a pale, mild, stooping man of fifty', stammering and shy. The shock to both of them must have been profound, having communicated so freely and equally, to meet at last and have to fit their epistolary personalities into these unlikely casings – one of them female. There was 'a long, nervous shaking of hands – Then followed talk – talk – talk – Mr. Williams being silent – Mr. Smith loquacious.'

Smith was fully animated, and immediately had a dozen plans for the entertainment of the Misses Brontë and their introduction to London society. '[Y]ou must go to the Italian opera – you must see the Exhibition – Mr. Thackeray would be pleased to see you – If Mr. Lewes knew "Currer Bell" was in town – he would have to be shut up', et cetera, et cetera. Delightful though all these suggestions were, Charlotte cut him short with the warning that the sisters' incognito had to be strictly preserved. She and Acton Bell had only revealed themselves to him to prove their innocence in the matter of Newby's lies. '[T]o all the rest of the world we must be "gentlemen" as heretofore,' she told him.

Nevertheless, Smith was determined to fête them, offered them the hospitality of his own home and, when that was refused, came up with the idea of introducing the sisters not as authors but as his 'country cousins', the Misses Brown. 'The desire to see some of the personages whose names he mentioned – kindled in me very strongly,' Charlotte told Mary, 'but when I found on further examination that he could not venture to ask such men as Thackeray &c. at a short notice, without giving them a hint as to whom they were to meet, I declined even this – I felt it would have ended in our being made a show of – a thing I have ever resolved to avoid.' The sisters retired to the Coffee House, exhausted, where Charlotte took smelling salts – the conventional if rather potent remedy of the time against headache and pains – to prepare herself for a promised call later in the day from Smith and his sisters. But when the Smiths turned up, young and lovely in full evening dress (right down to white gloves), it was with the expectation that the Misses Brown would accompany them to the Opera – which Charlotte and Anne had 'by no means understood'. But, despite their unpreparedness, and the effects of the analgesic, Charlotte decided on the spur of the moment that it would be better to go along with the plan, so within minutes she and Anne were being helped into the Smiths' carriage, where Williams was also in full fig. 'They must have thought us queer, quizzical looking beings – especially me with my spectacles,' Charlotte related with deep amusement. 'I smiled inwardly at the contrast which must have been apparent between me and Mr. Smith as I walked with him up the crimson carpeted staircase of the Opera House and stood amongst a brilliant throng at the box-door which was not yet open. Fine ladies & gentlemen glanced at us with a slight, graceful supercili-ousness quite warranted by the circumstances – Still I felt pleasurably excited – in spite of headache sickness & conscious clownishness; and I saw Anne was calm and gentle which she always is –'

Also in the audience that night, watching the Royal Italian Opera Company perform *The Barber of Seville*, were the Earl and Countess of Desart, Viscount Lascelles, the author Lady Morgan and the philanthropist Angela Burdett-Coutts, a glamorous glimpse of real High Life for the two Brontës after all their years of imagining it in their writings. Charlotte was so impressed by the splendour of the Opera House building and company that she pressed Williams's arm and whispered, 'You know I am not accustomed to this sort of thing.' Making such an aside to a man she had only just met would have been unthinkable at home, but Charlotte found herself so far outside her milieu that night that she could behave naturally without impunity. And her authorial persona protected her further. It was not Miss Brown on the arm of dashing young George Smith, nor even Miss Brontë, but Currer Bell.

The next day the sisters were taken to church by Williams, and dined by Smith at his home in Westbourne Place, Paddington, an elegantly designed, mid-sized terraced house in the new streets surrounding the railway station, which he shared with his siblings and their widowed mother, a sensible, handsome woman of fifty-one. Charlotte admired Mrs Smith and her daughters' good manners, not being consternated by picking up 'a couple of odd-looking country-women' at a City tavern, though 'to see their elegant, handsome son & brother treating with scrupulous politeness these insignificant spinsters – must have puzzled them thoroughly'. The next day the 'Browns' were taken to the Royal Academy and the National Gallery, dined again at Smith's and took tea at Mr Williams's house, where one of the daughters of the poet and critic Leigh Hunt was visiting and sang charmingly at the piano.

'A more jaded wretch than I looked when I returned, it would be difficult to conceive,' Charlotte told Mary, but the outing had been a most remarkable success. They got home laden with books that Smith had given them, and more to tell Emily than could ever be exhausted. One unpleasant task had had to be performed, though, before the sisters boarded the train north at Euston on Tuesday, 11 July: to confront Thomas Newby. It was a risky thing to do, as Newby had no discretion and might have tried to exploit this proof that Currer and Acton Bell were women (he discovered Charlotte's real name, as she later lamented). No record of what was said has survived, but it seems reasonable to surmise that Charlotte and Anne gave him a piece of their minds. How the interview affected Emily's and Anne's future treatment by the firm is a moot point. Charlotte hoped that her sisters would move their business to Smith, and corresponded with him about it, but neither Emily nor Anne was willing to make the move. Neither liked to go back on an agreement, however badly it had been kept by the other party, and they probably also feared the loss of their £50 investment (with good reason). Smith's arrangement with Charlotte was far from perfectly fair,[*] but she had at least earned £250 already from sales of *Jane Eyre*, and was on her way to earning more with *Shirley*.

---

[*] He had somewhat underpaid her for the copyright, with the understanding that he would supplement that sum with occasional extra payments, at discretion, if the book did well. He kept to this promise, but never paid her at a rate that accurately reflected the profits made by the firm on *Jane Eyre*, or the later titles.

12

Across the Abyss

1848–9

Unknown to Charlotte, the trip to London with Anne was to be the last bright spot in her life for a very long time. Branwell was sinking rapidly, worn out by the physical toll of his addictions and 'intolerable mental wretchedness', as he told Leyland. He owed money in many local inns, one of which had sent a demand for payment to Reverend Brontë and threatened his son with an arrest warrant. Branwell begged his friend Leyland to go both to the Talbot and to the Old Cock in Halifax on his behalf and get him an extension on his debts while he waited for word from Dr Crosby, the Robinsons' surgeon, who seems to have been acting as a conduit for sporadic payments from Branwell's former mistress (either loans or a form of hush-money). Branwell had probably heard by the summer of 1848 that Lydia Robinson had moved to Birmingham, but had the gossip reached him (as it had Charlotte) that she was already the 'infatuated slave' of her ailing cousin's husband, Sir Edward, and hoped to marry him as soon as his wife died? The first Lady Scott obligingly passed away on 4 August 1848 and Lydia Robinson took her place just three months later, on 8 November, by special licence.

One can't avoid the suspicion that news of these unfolding events reached Branwell and precipitated his death in late September – that his death was in effect a form of suicide from self-neglect. The coincidence of the timing seems too much, as does the degree of his despair. Branwell's death certificate states the cause as 'Chronic bronchitis–Marasmus' (wasting away), and Charlotte later described him as 'latterly consumptive', but he was also clearly suffering from the effects of his addictions, including, from Grundy's description, delirium tremens.

That Branwell was infected with tuberculosis bacteria is almost certain, given the highly infectious nature of the disease (transmittable even through the ordinary breathing of an active sufferer), and given that all his siblings had it in one form or another – with the possible exception of Charlotte. Pulmonary tuberculosis (or consumption, or phsythis, as it was called in the Brontës' time) can lie dormant for years and is often activated or aggravated by other viral infections; hence Maria and Elizabeth Brontë's transition from whooping-cough to consumption in 1824–5 and the apparent triggering of Branwell's last illness through bronchitis. He had always been the strongest of Patrick Brontë's children but perhaps had come to over-rely on his superior powers of recovery. In January 1847 he even counted as a curse 'a constitution still so strong that it will keep me years in torture and despair when I should every hour pray that I might die'. By the autumn of 1848, it failed him.

Just a couple of days before Branwell's death, Tabitha Brown, Martha's younger sister, remembered seeing him struggle to mount the steps to the Parsonage's front door 'and . . . catch hold to the door side – it seemed such hard work for him'. It was the last time Branwell left the Parsonage. When the doctor was called, the family was told to prepare for the worst – an eventuality that seems to have taken them by surprise, worn down as they all were by the years of his degeneration.

On 24 September his stricken family gathered round Branwell's deathbed – the first, Charlotte told W. S. Williams, that she had ever attended.* Branwell's atheism, which had been a subject of such moment that it was never mentioned, now reared up as the killing, quelling fact – worse than his death, even, for nothing less than his eternal soul hung in the balance. 'The sting of death is sin' is the verse from Saint Paul on the Brontë memorial stone in Haworth Church; Patrick Brontë had preached on that text in his funeral sermon for William Weightman six years before, reminding the congregation that a good Christian should be ever ready for judgement at 'the bar of eternity'. Branwell seemed about to face that awful trial doomed to failure, a thought that sent his distraught father into a frenzy of prayer at the bedside, desperate for signs of repentance, and for signs of faith. Most fortunately, a change came over Branwell in his final days that gave his family some relief and hope: he seemed to be

---

* This statement implies that Charlotte saw her mother and her sister Elizabeth ill but not dying (somewhat contrary to what Sarah Garrs said about taking the children in to see Mrs Brontë on the morning of her death). Charlotte was not at home for the death of her sister Maria.

amenable to their prayers and spoke kindly to them at last. To his friend John Brown, who must have bitterly regretted his encouragement of Branwell's past extravagances, Branwell spoke of his family's love for him and 'the depth and tenderness of which affection he could find no language to express'. He didn't mention Lydia Robinson at all in this final interview but grabbed the sexton's hand and cried out, 'Oh, John, I am dying!' and 'In all my past life I have done nothing either great or good.'

Branwell did do one good thing, as he lay dying on the morning of 24 September, with his sisters and his father gathered round him: he was heard praying softly and when Patrick Brontë offered up a final prayer, replied 'Amen'. 'How unusual that word appeared from his lips – of course you who did not know him, cannot conceive,' Charlotte told Williams. But the 'painful, mournful joy' of hearing it was short-lived: Branwell died in his father's arms later that day, aged thirty-one. 'My Son! My Son!' Patrick cried out piteously, refusing to be comforted, alone in his room. He never thought that his remaining children might have needed his comfort in return after their ordeal. 'My poor Father naturally thought more of his *only* son than of his daughters,' Charlotte remarked sombrely.

The horror of Branwell's death struck in the succeeding days, felling Charlotte in a way very similar to her breakdown in 1838 on return from Roe Head. She took to her bed, incapable of even speaking, waking from fitful sleep into a renewed awareness of what had taken place, a nightmarish state with 'impressions experienced . . . such as we do not put into language.' Anne and Emily were left to support their father alone through the funeral service, which was again taken by William Morgan, Branwell's godfather.* John Brown did his sexton's offices: prepared the vault under the chancel floor and added Branwell's name under those of his mother and sisters on the memorial that stood on the east wall.

Charlotte's earliest letter about her brother's death, written a week later, shows how low her feelings for Branwell had sunk in the preceding four or five years, but from what a high platform. It reads more like an indictment than an obituary:

---

* Anne also kept an eye on Charlotte's business matters, writing on her behalf to Williams on the day of the funeral (*LCB* 2, 121).

I do not weep from a sense of bereavement – there is no prop with-drawn, no consolation torn away, no dear companion lost – but for the wreck of talent, the ruin of promise, the untimely, dreary extinction of what might have been a burning and a shining light. My brother was a year my junior; I had aspirations and ambitions for him once – long ago – they have perished mournfully – nothing remains of him but a mem-ory of errors and sufferings – There is such a bitterness of pity for his life and death – such a yearning for the emptiness of his whole existence as I cannot describe – I trust time will allay these feelings.

Time did begin to allay them, replacing her anger and resentment with a miserable vacancy. She tried to squeeze consolation from faith, but it did not console her in the way in which Patrick Brontë, for instance, stemmed his misery at the loss of his son and heir. Charlotte may have been much more like godless Branwell and heretic Emily in this regard, though she struggled so vehemently against it. 'When I looked on the noble face and forehead of my dead brother,' she wrote to Williams, 'and asked myself what had made him go ever wrong, tend ever down-wards, when he had so many gifts to induce to, and aid in an upward course – I seemed to receive an oppressive revelation of the feebleness of humanity; of the inadequacy of even genius to lead to true greatness if unaided by religion and principle.' To Ellen, she spoke more famil-iarly: 'The final separation – the spectacle of his pale corpse gave more acute, bitter pain than I could have imagined – Till the last hour comes we never know how much we can forgive, pity, regret a near relation – All his vices were and are nothing now – we remember only his woes.'

Charlotte answered her friend's concern about her state of mind and health with 'I feel much more uneasy about my sisters than myself just now.' Emily had caught a chill, it seemed, on the day of the funeral, and had a persistent, racking cough. Charlotte at first blamed the weather and the stress of Branwell's death, but the cough persisted, worsened, and she began to be deeply alarmed: 'Emily's cold and cough are very obstinate; I fear she has a pain in the chest – and I sometimes catch a shortness in her breathing when she has moved at all quickly – she looks very, very thin and pale.' But her sister was not a good patient – not *patient* at all. 'Her reserved nature occasions one great uneasiness of mind – it is useless to question her – you get no answers – it is still more useless to recommend remedies – they are never adopted.' By early November, when Anne and Tabby were also ill, Emily's harsh dry cough and breathlessness, and her frightening emaciation, were getting worse. '[M]y sister Emily has something like a slow inflammation of the lungs,' Charlotte told Williams on 2 November, apologising for her preoccupation with personal matters; 'I kept waiting for a cheerful day and mood in which to address you.'

Charlotte at first described Emily as 'a real stoic in illness', trying to see her intransigence in the best possible light, but the sick woman's refusal to accept any help or sympathy or to make any adjustments to her daily routine became increasingly distressing to her sisters: 'you must look on, and see her do what she is unfit to do, and not dare to say a word.' 'I have again and again incurred her displeasure by urging the necessity of seeking advice, and I fear I must yet incur it again and again.' This recalls 'the unconscious tyranny' that Constantin Heger observed in Emily's treatment of Charlotte that may not have been unconscious at all. 'When she is ill there seems to be no sunshine in the world for me,' Charlotte told Williams. 'I think a certain harshness in her powerful and peculiar character only makes one cling to her more.' Indeed, Emily seems to have fully understood her power over Charlotte – over the whole household – and been strangely determined to test it at this juncture, imposing on them what Charlotte later called 'forced, total neglect'. 'Stern selfishness' is how Mrs Gaskell described Emily's conduct during her last illness, then she had second thoughts and crossed the phrase out. But it remains a persuasive opinion.

Did Emily think she could *will* herself through a fatal illness, did will mean more to her than survival? Perhaps her grim, sardonic 'stoicism' was a form of rage against the disease which she fully understood was killing her, and against which her family's concern appeared to her futile, puny and insulting. When Charlotte passed on a book about homoeopathy, sent by Williams, Emily looked over it and denounced it as 'quackery'; conventional medics seemed to her no better than poisoners. And when Charlotte wrote in secret to a London doctor recommended by Williams, she told him that the patient 'has never consented to lie in bed for a single day' but rose at seven every morning, as usual, and went to bed at ten.

The weather that autumn was very wet and cold. There were hard frosts and snow by early November; 'a good deal of snow' in the middle of the month; and rain, snow and hoarfrost through December – with scarcely a day marked 'clear'. Emily's cough and fever did not subside; she had a pain in the chest and struggled to breathe, but, taking their cue from the patient's fierce refusal to see any 'poisoning doctor', her sisters continued to hope against hope for a recovery. Patrick Brontë, on the other hand, saw the similarities between Emily's symptoms and those of Maria and Elizabeth, and shook his head.

George Smith's gifts of books and periodicals diverted the household during these awful months, though the growing notoriety of the brothers Bell, the guessing games about their true identities and the temptation to rank them as competitors were signs of notice more agitating than gratifying. From her later remarks about *Wuthering Heights*, it is clear that Charlotte thought it an immature work that Ellis Bell would improve on, given time; the undervaluing of Ellis Bell's poetry, on the other hand, was a source of increasing annoyance to her. Smith had bought the unsold, unloved stock of the 1846 volume and reissued it in 1848 after the success of *Jane Eyre*. But still there was insufficient appreciation, in Charlotte's view, for the genius of Ellis Bell, especially now that Currer's novel, the most successful of the four by far, always seemed to dispose critics in his favour. It was hard to read aloud to her ailing sister notices that spoke of Ellis's and Acton's 'comparative inferiority . . . from the greater quietness of a small or the triteness of a common subject'. Charlotte thought such critics 'blind . . . as any bat – insensate as any stone'.★

Among the articles that Smith, Elder forwarded to Haworth was one from *North American Review*, considering all four of the Bell novels in the light of the 'Jane Eyre fever' currently sweeping the eastern United States. A feverish confusion certainly surrounded the authorship of

---

★ The outburst in *Jane Eyre* about contemporary poetry, completely unrelated to the action, seems to me a veiled reference to Emily's unrecognised genius. Jane has been given a copy of Walter Scott's *Marmion*, recently published (in 1808), prompting a lament by the narrator for that 'golden age of modern literature'. 'But, courage!' she continues. 'I know poetry is not dead, nor genius lost; nor has Mammon gained power over either, to bind or slay: they will both assert their existence, their presence, their liberty, and strength again one day' (*Jane Eyre*, 370).

each novel – the American editions attributed *Wuthering Heights* to 'the author of *Jane Eyre*' and *The Tenant of Wildfell Hall* to the 'author of *Wuthering Heights*' – and taken together, the Bells, powerfully clever though they were, seemed to embody all that was brutal and offensive. The reviewer deplored the fact that Heathcliff's creator 'seems to take a morose satisfaction in developing a full and complete science of human brutality', while Acton Bell succeeded in depicting profligacy without making virtue pleasing. Charlotte enjoyed describing to Williams the actual home life of this depraved crew:

> As I sat between them at our quiet but now somewhat melancholy fire-side, I studied the two ferocious authors. Ellis the 'man of uncommon talents but dogged, brutal and morose', sat leaning back in his easy chair drawing his impeded breath as he best could, and looking, alas! piteously pale and wasted – it is not his wont to laugh – but he smiled half-amused and half in scorn as he listened – Acton was sewing, no emotion ever stirs him to loquacity, so he only smiled too, dropping at the same time a single word of calm amazement to hear his character so darkly pourtrayed [*sic*].

Charlotte found particularly amusing the reviewer's suggestion that the Bells might be a brother-and-sister or husband-and-wife team (their work bearing 'the marks of more than one mind, and one sex'): 'Strange patch-work it must seem to them, this chapter being penned by Mr., and that by Miss or Mrs. Bell; that character or scene being delineated by the husband – that other by the wife! The gentleman of course doing the rough work – the lady getting up the finer parts.' But one can sympathise with the reviewer, trying to make sense of the new phenomenon represented by the Bells. No one had written novels like this before, with so much unaccountable power.

Charlotte wrote in wrenching anxiety to Ellen on 23 November that Emily's 'deep tight' cough had got worse, her pulse was racing, her form wasted. '[S]he is *very* ill: I believe if you were to see her your impression would be that there is no hope,' Charlotte said, incapable of expressing her own loss of hope directly. Emily still refused to see a doctor and did not want her illness even alluded to, insisted on attempting her usual chores, but collapsed in the cold passageway from the main kitchen to the back kitchen on her way to feed Flossy and Keeper. 'God only knows how all this is to terminate,' Charlotte wrote. 'More than once I have been forced boldly to regard the terrible event of her loss as possible and even probable. But Nature shrinks from such thoughts – I think Emily seems the nearest thing to my heart in this world.'

On the evening of 18 December, Charlotte read to Emily from one of Emerson's essays, that had arrived in the latest parcel from George Smith. Emily drifted off to sleep and Charlotte put the book down, thinking they would continue the next day. But the next day, 'the first glance at her face' assured Charlotte her sister was dying.

Martha Brown told Mrs Gaskell that on her last morning, Emily got up, 'dying all the time – the rattle in her throat while she *would* dress herself; & neither Miss Brontë nor I dared offer to help her'. Emily's violent display of denial went as far as trying to take up her *sewing*, though the servants saw that her eyes had already begun to glaze over. This was the fight that Charlotte described later to Williams, and that Emily forced her to witness, 'the conflict of the strangely strong spirit and the fragile frame . . . relentless conflict – once seen, never to be forgotten'.

Charlotte told Mrs Gaskell that she went out on to the moor on that bleak December day, desperate to find any small spray of heather to take to her dying sister, though the flowers were all brown and withered at that time of year. Emily did not recognise them. Two hours before she died, she said, 'If you will send for a doctor, I will see him now', but of course it was too late. Dr Wheelhouse may not even have got to the Parsonage in time to see Emily die 'in the arms of those who loved her'.★

She was buried three days later, on a clear, frosty morning. Arthur Nicholls took the service, and the chancel flagstones, hardly settled from Branwell's funeral less than three months earlier, were levered up again. The coffin was the narrowest that William Wood ever recalled making for a grown person. It measured five foot seven by only sixteen inches wide. Keeper, who had stayed by Emily's deathbed and followed her coffin to the church, now lay outside the bedroom door, howling.

★ There is a tradition that Emily died on the sofa in the dining room of the Parsonage, but, as Juliet Barker has pointed out, there are no contemporary sources for the story, first mentioned in A. M. F. Robinson's 1883 biography of EJB, and it is much more likely that she died upstairs. Charlotte refers to Keeper lying 'at the side of her dying-bed' (Barker, 576, and CB to WSW, 25 June 1849, *LCB* 2, 224).

Emily suffers no more either from pain or weakness now. She never will suffer more in this world – she is gone after a hard, short conflict . . . Yes – there is no Emily in Time or on Earth now – yesterday we put her poor, wasted mortal frame quietly under the Church pavement. We are very calm [a]t present, why should we be otherwise? – the anguish of seeing [he]r suffer is over, the spectacle of the pains of D[ea]th is gone by – the funeral day is past – we feel she is at peace – no need now to tremble for the hard frost and keen wind – Emily does not feel them.

Charlotte did not take to her bed as she had done after Branwell's death. Anne's cough, weakness and the pains in her side were all too clearly indicative of the same disease, though no one wanted to believe it possible. When Ellen Nussey came to visit at the turn of the new year, she found the family 'calm and sustained' but very anxious about Anne. Reverend Brontë had inquired after the best Leeds doctor, and a Mr Teale subsequently came to examine the invalid, whom Ellen thought was looking 'sweetly pretty and flushed and in capital spirits'. But when the doctor left and Patrick Brontë came into the room, it was clear that the news was bad. This most undemonstrative of fathers sat next to his youngest child on the sofa and drew her towards him, saying, 'My dear little Anne', as if they were already parting.

Charlotte tried to convince herself that the doctor could be wrong, but Anne's own terrors at the diagnosis were expressed with heartbreaking poignancy in the poem she wrote the following day:

> A dreadful darkness closes in
>   On my bewildered mind;
> O let me suffer and not sin,
>   Be tortured yet resigned.
>
> Through all this world of whelming mist
>   Still let me look to Thee,
> And give me courage to resist
>   The Tempter till he flee.
>
> Weary I am – O give me strength
>   And leave me not to faint;
> Say Thou wilt comfort me at length
>   And pity my complaint.

With her new understanding of consumption, Charlotte guessed rightly that the family had been harbouring it for years, 'unused any of us to the possession of robust health, we have not noticed the gradual approaches of decay; we did not know its symptoms; the little cough, the small appetite, the tendency to take cold at every variation of atmosphere have been regarded as things of course – I see them in another light now.' Anne submitted to all the treatments that Emily would never countenance: she was examined with a stethoscope, she used a respirator, she was blistered, she took cod-liver oil (that smelt 'like train oil') and iron tonics, she accepted help walking round the room, she rested (in what used to be Emily's chair), but still she did not improve. Charlotte's instinct was to take the patient somewhere warmer, but travel was not recommended by the doctor until the weather improved, so they waited out the coldest months of the year on the edge of the frozen moor, hoping to get to the seaside – Scarborough was Anne's longing – as soon as the weather improved. Charlotte probably had in mind somewhere more temperate than the bracing east coast resort; the place recommended for consumptives in Thomas John Graham's *Modern Domestic Medicine* was Penzance, the Branwells' soft, southern, sunny native town. 'It is well known that many persons far gone in consumption have perfectly recovered from a lengthened stay at Penzance,' the oracle by the sickbed said. It was queerly as if the ghosts of Anne's mother and aunt were calling her home.

Charlotte was almost paralysed with fear, waking at night to the renewed knowledge that Emily was dead and Anne dying. '[L]ife has become very void, and hope has proved a strange traitor,' she wrote to Williams, 'when I shall again be able to put confidence in her suggestions, I know not; she kept whispering that Emily would not – *could* not die – and where is she now? Out of my reach – out of my world, torn from me.' 'When we lost Emily I thought we had drained the very dregs of our cup of trial, but now when I hear Anne cough as Emily coughed, I tremble lest there should be exquisite bitterness yet to taste. However I must not look forwards, nor must I look backwards. Too often I feel like one crossing an abyss on a narrow plank – a glance round might quite unnerve.'

Work seemed out of the question, though Charlotte knew that Smith, Elder were keen for her to continue with the novel she had started the year before, and that they had originally suggested she might publish as a serial, as Dickens and Thackeray had done so successfully and lucratively. Smith had even suggested that Charlotte might be able, like Thackeray, to do her own illustrations to *Shirley* – an idea that she quickly declined. She had told Williams about her old ambition to be an illustrator, but, looking back on her portfolio of drawings, she couldn't imagine how she had ever thought such a thing possible.

'Currer Bell' was in abeyance, but to placate her publishers Charlotte asked them to look at the first volume of *Shirley* and give their opinion on its progress. It was a rather extraordinary, and desperate, act of submission. She had finished and copied the first volume and was working on the second before Branwell's death, but now had little hope of being able to take up the thread, and was plagued with doubts about its quality and novelty. Having just read *Mary Barton*, the first novel by a Unitarian minister's wife from Manchester, Elizabeth Gaskell, she felt dismayed at the similarity of that book to what she had in mind herself. When Williams wrote back, with the opinions of himself, George Smith and their colleague James Taylor on the beginning of *Shirley*, Charlotte was unwilling to do as they suggested – change the first chapter, with its boisterous comedy about the curates – because, like the Lowood scenes in *Jane Eyre*, Charlotte maintained '*it is true*': the curates, she insisted (totally missing the point, but using a surprisingly new image), 'are merely photographed from the life'.

A second opinion from a London doctor recommended by Smith warned Charlotte and her father not to entertain 'sanguine hopes' of Anne's recovery, but that, if her current regime were kept to, her life could be prolonged a year or even two. '[T]here have been hours – days – weeks of inexpressible anguish to undergo – and the cloud of impending distress still lowers dark and sullen above us,' Charlotte wrote to Laetitia Wheelwright, her acquaintance from Brussels days who had lately become a closer friend and correspondent. At the end of March, Charlotte asked Ellen if she would be willing to accompany Anne to the seaside, which she felt was the only thing that might do her good – or at least please her. Anne herself was acutely aware that the beneficial effects of any change of scene would be lost if they left it too long, but, unbelievably, Patrick Brontë's refusal to leave home himself made Charlotte feel 'consequently obliged' to stay with him. Both father and daughter seem to have become blinded to their priorities at this point, and it was left to the invalid herself to suggest that Ellen Nussey might consider accompanying her in Charlotte's stead. But weeks later they were still in Haworth, waiting for better weather, for a miraculous turnaround of the disease, for Patrick Brontë to agree to be left alone with the servants for a while. Mr Nicholls had offered to come and stay with him at the Parsonage, but he would not hear of it. The sisters tried to get outside together every day, for however short a time, but 'we creep rather than walk', Charlotte told Ellen. By the middle of May, Anne could hardly climb the stairs however slowly, spent the day 'in a semi-lethargic state' and was looking even thinner than Emily.

The trip to Scarborough finally went ahead at the end of that month, too late to be more than a distressing last wish, as Tabby and Martha, watching Anne being lifted into the chaise, saw too plainly. The journey, broken for a night in York, was arduous and the semblance of a holiday seemed to Charlotte like a 'dreary mockery'. 'Oh – if it would please God to strengthen and revive Anne how happy we might be together! His will – however – must be done.' Anne was a model patient, the opposite of Emily: she bore the discomforts and anxieties of the journey with what Ellen emotionally termed 'the pious courage and fortitude of a martyr' and, with heroic selflessness, tried to minimise the distress to her two companions. She was also doubtless trying to set an example to Charlotte, whose stricken face must have caused the dying girl deep pain.

Their lodgings on the front included a bedroom and sitting room overlooking the sea in one of the best properties in the town, known to Anne from her holidays with the Robinsons. Money was available to do the thing properly, as Anne had received a legacy of £200 from her godmother Frances Outhwaite just a few months before. On the Saturday, they went on to the sands and Anne had a ride in a donkey carriage, taking the reins from the boy driver so that the donkey would not be driven too hard, and advising him how to treat the animal in future. It was the last active thing she ever did. The next evening she was wheeled to the window to watch a spectacular sunset lighting the castle and distant ships at sea, and the day after that she died.

Ellen provided the details of Anne's death to Elizabeth Gaskell, but

added to them later in notes to her proposed edition of Charlotte's letters, relating a ghastly scene of disagreement and confusion on the last
morning, when Anne, proving too weak to get down the stairs to
breakfast, agreed to let Ellen carry her down 'baby fashion'. Charlotte
was 'nervously angry' at the proposal and her objections made Anne
demur, but Ellen argued to the contrary, having got it into her head
that this would be a good and useful thing to do. The scheme did not
go well, however. Ellen staggered at the bottom of the stairs and had to
drop the invalid into a nearby chair. One can well imagine Charlotte's
frantic reprimands, but Anne, whose head was lolling and arms stiffen-
ing, told Ellen not to worry: 'I am not hurt, you know you did your
best.'

They called the doctor out later that morning, as Anne asked if it
would be possible to get home in time if they set off immediately. She
sensed she was dying, and the doctor confirmed it, earning this brave
woman's gratitude for his honesty. Anne's last hours and actions were
all exemplary, 'deeply assured that a better existence lay before her –
she believed – she hoped'. She prayed for blessings on her sister and
friend, and tried to comfort them, saying, 'Take courage, Charlotte;
take courage', an echo of their old rallying cry. She was tranquil,
expectant even, and just before she died she told them she was very
happy. The door to the room was half open and, as Charlotte closed
her sister's eyes, they heard the dinner bell ring: life went on in the
lodging house. Unrestrained now, Charlotte gave herself over to grief,
which 'burst forth', as Ellen described it, 'in agonised strength'.

To spare her father the agony of burying a fifth child, Charlotte
waited until the following day to write home, hoping that his commitment to an annual church event would dissuade him from travelling to
the funeral, which took place two days later. Miss Wooler attended,
though; her friendship had proved more and more valuable in the years
since Charlotte returned from Brussels, with Roe Head eruptions quite
forgotten. Anne was buried in the hillside graveyard of the parish
church, overlooking the sea, the only member of the Brontë family not
to lie in Haworth.

'Anne, from her childhood seemed preparing for an early death,'
Charlotte told Williams, in a deeply personal and confiding letter written a few days later. If that is true, what a sad reflection on the tenor of

the household, the lack of health, joy and optimism out of which Anne Brontë's resignation grew. Charlotte tried to bear in mind the strength of Anne's faith and take some comfort from it, but, though she told herself that God was 'wise – perfect – merciful', the gap between his will and her happiness seemed stretched beyond bearing: 'Why life is so blank, brief and bitter I do not know – Why younger and far better than I are snatched from it with projects unfulfilled I cannot comprehend.' And Anne's calmness in the face of death 'but half consoles . . . there is piercing pain in it. Anne had had enough of life such as it was – in her twenty-eighth year she laid it down as a burden. I hardly know whether it is sadder to think of that than of Emily turning her dying eyes reluctantly from the pleasant sun.'

At her father's suggestion, Charlotte and Ellen did not come home immediately but left Scarborough and its tragic associations for Filey, then a quiet fishing-village seven miles to the south. The wild beauty and loneliness of the place was balm to Charlotte, who spent hours on the beach or at the window watching the sea, as the seagulls and cormorants skimmed the water between the shore and the ridge of black rocks that stretched outwards for half a mile. Her mind revolved on the difficulty of having to believe ever more strongly in something incredible, the mercy and wisdom of God. She wrote to Williams, 'There must be Heaven or we must despair',

> for life seems bitter, brief – blank. To me – these two [Emily and Anne] have left in their memories a noble legacy. Were I quite solitary in the world – bereft even of Papa – there is something in the past I can love intensely and honour deeply – and it is something which cannot change – which cannot decay – which immortality guarantees from corruption . . .
>
> A year ago – had a prophet warned me how I should stand in June 1849 – how stripped and bereaved – had he foretold the autumn – the winter, the spring of sickness and suffering to be gone through – I should have thought – this can never be endured. It is over. Branwell – Emily – Anne are gone like dreams – gone as Maria and Elizabeth went twenty years ago. One by one I have watched them fall asleep on my arm – and closed their glazed eyes – I have seen them buried one by one – and – thus far – God has upheld me. from my heart I thank Him.

When Charlotte returned to Haworth on Midsummer Day, to the sombre, affectionate embraces of her father, Tabby and Martha, there was little to say. But, heartbreakingly, Keeper and Flossy bounded around her 'in strange ecstasy', thinking that Emily and Anne must be coming home too. Keeper patrolled the little bedroom that Emily had latterly used, and Charlotte noticed that Flossy 'may look wistfully round' for Anne: 'they will never see them again – nor shall I – at least the human part of me.'

I left Papa soon and went into the dining room – I shut the door – I tried to be glad that I was come home – I have always been glad before – except once – even then I was cheered. but this time joy was not to be the sensation. I felt that the house was all silent – the rooms were all empty – I remembered where the three were laid – in what narrow dark dwellings – never were they to reappear on earth. So the sense of desolation and bitterness took possession of me – the agony that *was to be undergone* – and *was not* to be avoided came on – I underwent it & passed a dreary evening and night and a mournful morrow – to-day I am better.

I do not know how life will pass – but I certainly do feel confidence in Him who has upheld me hitherto. Solitude may be cheered and made endurable beyond what I can believe. The great trial is when evening closes and night approaches – At that hour we used to assemble in the dining-room – we used to talk – Now I sit by myself – necessarily I am silent. – I cannot help thinking of their last days – remembering their sufferings and what they said and did and how they looked in mortal affliction – perhaps all this will become less poignant in time. Let me thank you once more, dear Ellen, for your kindness to me which I do not mean to forget – How did they think you looking at home? – Papa thought me a little stronger – he said my eyes were not so sunken. I am glad to hear a good account of your Mother and a tolerable one of Mercy – I hope she will soon recover her health – Give my love to her and to all – Write again very soon and tell me how poor Miss Heald goes on –

Yours sincerely
C Brontë

13

Conquering the Big Babylon

1849–51

Charlotte had caught a cold at the coast that she couldn't shake off, and that, with the accompaniment of pains between her shoulders, of course filled her with dread, though she strove to hide any signs of ill-health from her father; 'his anxiety harasses me inexpressibly'. Looking back over the last year, with her siblings dying one after another in autumn, winter and spring, Charlotte could hardly have expected to survive them long. The infectious nature of consumption was not understood for another twenty years, with the development of germ theory, but the rapid decline of her more robust sister Emily, who had seemed to have 'spirit . . . strong enough to bear her to fulness of years', meant Charlotte felt the spectre of sudden decline and death hanging over her ever after.

Ellen Nussey wanted to come and stay at Haworth, but Charlotte turned down the offer, on the harsh principle of needing to endure the worst as soon as possible. Williams too, her most generously sympathetic friend and the recipient of her most heartbreaking letters, was moved by Charlotte's predicament to suggest she should have a companion come to live with her.* She declined this also, there being 'two persons whom it would not suit': primarily the young person condemned to share such a melancholy and uneventful existence, 'a church and stony churchyard for her prospect – the dead silence of a village parsonage . . . a grave, silent spinster for her companion. I should not like to see youth thus immured.' The other person whom the arrangement would not suit was of course Patrick Brontë. There was no change there, after the disastrous winnowing of his family; no adjustment to his habits of retirement and solitary meals, and no better tolerance of

---

* Possibly he was suggesting one of his own daughters, though this isn't clear from CB's side of the correspondence (CB to WSW, 26 July 1849, *LCB* 2, 232).

intrusions. The older he got, the more entirely Charlotte considered his wishes, however much against her own interests they were. A young female companion coming to live at the Parsonage in 1849 might indeed have been a real comfort to her.

Sitting in a house so silent that the tick of the clock on the landing was the only sign of life, Charlotte wrote to Williams that she knew work was the thing to sustain her: 'Lonely as I am – how should I be if Providence had never given me courage to adopt a career – perseverance to plead through two long, weary years with publishers till they admitted me?'

> hereafter I look for no great earthly comfort except what congenial occupation can give – For society – long seclusion has in great measure unfitted me – I doubt whether I should enjoy it if I might have it. Sometimes I think I should, and I thirst for it – but at other times I doubt my capability of pleasing or deriving pleasure. The prisoner in solitary confinement – the toad in the block of marble – all in time shape themselves to their lot.

In the long days alone Charlotte returned to the manuscript of 'Hollow's Mill', which she had struggled to continue writing the previous year and abandoned when Anne was dying. But what had started life as a conscious attempt at a realistic 'condition of England' novel, with strong dramatisations of social and religious questions and suppression of too much 'romance' in the love stories, had been overtaken by events. Charlotte's heart was no longer in it, except that there was a melancholy pleasure in making her dead sister Emily the model for the novel's heroine, Shirley Keeldar, and perhaps putting herself (combined with aspects of Anne) into the character of Caroline Helstone.* Charlotte told Elizabeth Gaskell that Shirley Keeldar was an attempt to depict 'what Emily Brontë would have been, had she been placed in health and prosperity' – a fantasy version of her sister, in other words. In August she wrote to Williams telling him that she was changing the name of the book to that of the character who had turned out to be 'the most prominent and peculiar'.

Rich, clever, carefree Shirley is a visionary, a philosopher, but passive

---

* Ellen Nussey's self-identification with Caroline Helstone is not very convincing.

and contemplative, for all her talk of wanting to do things in the world. She spends hours on the heath, lying in heather and staring at the sky, or at windows, looking out at stars; a poet in thought, but one who doesn't write. Charlotte gave her such a self-contented and philosophical disposition that the character ran the risk of seeming incredible (however true a reflection of Emily Brontë's inner calm it might have been): her prospective marriage to Louis Moore at the end of the story seems almost irrelevant to her happiness, as well as unlikely.

Shirley needs her counterpart, suffering and sensitive Caroline Helstone, to earth her, and Caroline's inactivity and repression are the most dynamic things in the book. Caroline is a creature of silences, concealing secret eloquence, a commentator who rarely gets to comment. One of her most rabble-rousing internal monologues culminates in something like a battle-cry: 'Men of England! look at your poor girls, many of them fading around you, dropping off in consumption or decline; or, what is worse, degenerating to sour old maids, – envious, backbiting, wretched, because life is a desert to them; or, what is worst of all, reduced to strive, by scarce modest coquetry and debasing artifice, to gain that position and consideration by marriage, which to celibacy is denied.' But all this is thought, not uttered, and melts seamlessly into the narrator's own commentary.

'What on earth is the matter with you?' Helstone asks his niece, anticipating Freud's question 'What do women want?' by some fifty years. Caroline tells him quite explicitly that she wants occupation – 'I feel weaker than formerly. I believe I should have more to do' – but her uncle chooses to hear this as a typical example of female irrationality, and the course of action he proposes is to buy her a new frock. This is mirrored in a scene where the workman Joe Scott questions what interest Shirley can possibly have in the newspapers, and when she replies, 'I read the leading articles, Joe, and the foreign intelligence, and I look over the market prices: in short, I read just what gentlemen read', he looks at her 'as if he thought this talk was like the chattering of a pie'.

Florence Nightingale, who had been impressed by the Bells' *Poems* and by *Jane Eyre*,[*] read Currer Bell's new novel as she was about to set

---

[*] She wrote of the heroine, 'we know her – we have lived with her, we shall meet her again' (letter to Julia Ward Howe, 28 July 1848, Laura E. Richards (ed.), 'Letters of Florence Nightingale', *Yale Review*, 24 (December 1934), 342–3).

off to study at the Institution of Deaconesses at Kaiserswerth in 1850, following a long and painful struggle with her family for permission to find '*necessary* occupation'. The message of both *Jane Eyre* and *Shirley* was reflected in her own first publication the following year, in which she made a passionate case for action: 'what are they to do with that thirst for action, useful action, which every woman feels who is not diseased in mind or body? God planted it there.' Shirley Keeldar was, like her, privileged, scholarly, strong-willed, and, like her, adopted a masculine outlook.* Currer Bell's latest heroine may have spoken even more powerfully to Nightingale than the first, and her words 'may well have been uppermost in Florence's mind' as the young deaconess set out on the career that would lead her, within four years, to hospitals at Scutari and in the Crimea.

Contrary to plan, Charlotte couldn't keep her Brussels experience out of the mix. It was still on her mind – perhaps more painfully than ever once bitterness and humiliation had replaced hope and waiting – and kept poking through into the text. Charlotte recast the rivalrous Crimsworth brothers of *The Professor* (with their long Angrian lineage) as Belgian immigrants in Yorkshire; Robert and Louis Gérard Moore – one of them a hard-nosed man of business, the other a sensitive scholar – along with their sister Hortense, retain many Continental habits and mannerisms. Robert likes to recite some of the poems that Monsieur Heger introduced to Charlotte back in 1842–3, while Louis, Shirley's former tutor and now her not-very-secret admirer, reminisces about her brilliance as a student and recites, incredibly enough from memory, a *devoir* she once wrote for him on the subject of female genius. '[W]hat were the faults of that devoir?' Shirley asks, looking at all her tutor's markings over her work. 'What else did they denote?' 'No matter now,' Louis replies meaningfully. Like Heger's animated commentary on Charlotte's essays, his marks obviously denote excitement, engagement and intellectual affinity, signs that Louis Moore sees retrospectively as evidence of love.

But more problematically, the novel bore the burden of Charlotte's agony of bereavement. When she returned to the manuscript after the

---

* Nightingale wanted to be thought of as her parents' 'vagabond son' (Bostridge, *Florence Nightingale*, 160).

deaths of Branwell, Emily and Anne, it was to the chapter that opens
the third volume, 'The Valley of the Shadow of Death', in which Caroline Helstone falls victim to an illness that is both a physical and a
mental fever, a collapse in the face of sorrow. Her sense of imminent
death makes her wonder what the departed soul will feel, if there is any
hope of communication between the dead and the living, perhaps
'electrical' influences in the atmosphere that can play 'over our nerves
like fingers on stringed instruments, and call forth now a sweet note,
and now a wail'. Charlotte's own wish to be haunted is clear, as are her
fears, intensified so many fold by absolute severance from her sisters
and brother:

> *Where is* the other world? In *what* will another life consist? Why do I
> ask? Have I not cause to think that the hour is hasting but too fast when
> the veil must be rent for me? . . . Great Spirit! in whose goodness I con-
> fide; whom, as my Father, I have petitioned night and morning from
> early infancy, help the weak creation of thy hands! Sustain me through
> the ordeal I dread and must undergo! Give me strength! Give me
> patience! Give me – oh! *give me* FAITH!'

In the novel, the heroine survives this crisis with the discovery that her
nurse, Mrs Pryor, is her mother, long thought dead, and the scene ends
in an exhausted and emotional silence as parent embraces child. But
there was no such return and no such comfort for Charlotte.

Almost two years after *Jane Eyre*'s first publication, criticism of it was
still appearing, and Charlotte still felt defensive about it. In August
1849 a review in the *North British Review* followed the by now common
presumption that the 'Bells' were one and the same, and concluded that
Currer Bell, if a woman, 'must be a woman pretty nearly unsexed'.
Charlotte deeply resented the implied double standard, which it had
been her objective to circumvent: 'To such critics I would say – "to you
I am neither Man nor Woman – I come before you as an Author only
– it is the sole standard by which you have a right to judge me – the sole
ground on which I accept your judgment."'

Worse than any remarks about her own work, though, were deni-
grations of her sisters': the reviewer said he could not finish *Wuthering
Heights*, he found it so disgusting, and *The Tenant of Wildfell Hall* was

not much better, with scenes of 'naked vice' that he refused to believe possible among the gentry. Such lashing rebukes were 'scarce supportable'; Charlotte was glad Emily and Anne weren't alive to read them, but her anger on their behalf grew.

In the long months of reclusion, Charlotte felt she had been insufficiently vigilant of her own and her sisters' reputations, and a notice in *The Quarterly Review* from December 1848, which had been perceived through the fog of Emily's death, now seemed to require an answer urgently. In a long article, which first heaped praise on Thackeray's *Vanity Fair*, the anonymous reviewer (Elizabeth Rigby, the friend with whom J. G. Lockhart had been exchanging gossip about the Bells) had lambasted Currer Bell for his vulgarity and, while admitting in passing many virtues of pace, style and feeling in the book, maintained a harsh and sarcastic attack on the debut novelist.

> Jane Eyre, in spite of some grand things about her, is a being totally uncongenial to our feelings from beginning to end . . . the impression she leaves on our mind is that of a decidedly vulgar-minded woman – one whom we should not care for as an acquaintance, whom we should not seek as a friend, whom we should not desire for a relation, and whom we should scrupulously avoid for a governess.

Jane Eyre was a dangerous, 'anti-Christian' book:

> There is throughout it a murmuring against the comforts of the rich and against the privations of the poor, which, as far as each individual is concerned, is a murmuring against God's appointment – there is a proud and perpetual assertion of the rights of man, for which we find no authority either in God's word or in God's providence – there is that pervading tone of ungodly discontent which is at once the most prominent and the most subtle evil which the law and the pulpit, which all civilized society in fact has at the present day to contend with. We do not hesitate to say that the tone of the mind and thought which has overthrown authority and violated every code human and divine abroad, and fostered Chartism and rebellion at home, is the same which has also written Jane Eyre.

However it was the passages that expressed disgust at Ellis Bell's novel – 'too odiously and abominably pagan to be palatable even to the most vitiated class of English readers' – that roused Charlotte to respond. Her anger on behalf of Emily was perfectly justified, but the nine-month delay in answering was not, nor was her idea – to address *The Quarterly* in a preface to her new book – a good one. The 'Word to *The Quarterly*' that she drafted had an uncomfortably flippant tone, and targeted the most minor points raised, such as whether Currer Bell had an adequate knowledge of ladies' fashion in the 1820s, which had convinced Rigby that the author of *Jane Eyre* was a man.

Smith and Williams did not like the piece at all and asked Charlotte to change it for something that would engage the public's sympathies rather than stir up an image of a disgruntled carper. They were much more aware than she of her fame, and how such a display could damage her reputation, things for which Charlotte cared little at this stage. Smith believed that a preface that alluded to her personal circumstances and the deaths of Ellis and Acton Bell might provide a useful context to *Shirley*, but Charlotte dismissed such an idea severely. 'What we deeply feel is our own – we must keep it to ourselves,' she told Williams. 'Ellis and Acton Bell were, for me, Emily and Anne; my sisters – to me intimately near, tenderly dear – to the public they were nothing – beings speculated upon, misunderstood, misrepresented. If I live, the hour may come when the spirit will move me to speak of them, but it is not come yet.' In the meantime, *Shirley* went into print in October with no preface at all.

Elizabeth Rigby was hardly wrong in noticing *Jane Eyre*'s revolutionary bent, however much Charlotte remained in denial about it. When the second edition of *Jane Eyre* appeared early in 1848 (just as revolution was breaking out in France, Germany and Italy), a reviewer in the ultra-respectable *Christian Remembrancer* had accused the book of 'moral Jacobinism' on every page. 'Never was there a better hater,' the author said of the novel's angry heroine; '"Unjust, unjust," is the burden of every reflection upon the things and powers that be. All virtue is but well masked vice, all religious profession and conduct is but the whitening of the sepulchre.' It is easy to see how a book like *Jane Eyre* could strike readers as all the more subversive because of its surface conventionality. 'To say that *Jane Eyre* is positively immoral or antichristian, would be to do its writer an injustice,' the *Remembrancer* concluded. 'Still it wears a questionable aspect.'

Such interpretations made Charlotte very uncomfortable. As with her initial response to the 1848 revolutions, she seemed to regret exposing the warmth of her political sympathies and feared seeing her principles put too literally into action. She was very pleased with a review of *Jane Eyre* in the October 1848 edition of *Revue des deux mondes*, written by the Anglophile, anti-socialist journalist Eugène Forçade, who praised the Anglo-Saxon spirit of the book, 'masculine, inured to suffering and hardship', and felt that it spoke for itself, without having explicitly to call down 'fiery judgment on society in a drama in which society nevertheless plays more or less the cruel and tyrannical role assigned to fate in the tragedies of antiquity'. For him, the novel was an interesting glimpse back at 'the old order', from the perspective of the fast-evolving nations of the Continent. It may have been a congenial order for many men, he said, but not for women, whom he compared as a class to the disaffected bourgeoisie: 'they have not the same means of winning a place in the sun'.

> Among the middle classes especially, how many girls belonging to the junior branch of the family, must decline through poverty to dependence and destitution! How often must one find, especially among these Englishwomen, that inner conflict, that fatality arising from their situation, so cruelly felt by our needy middle classes, and which grows out of a disharmony between birth, education and fortune.

Quite how he, or Currer Bell, felt that these insights would bolster 'the old order' is hard to imagine.

Charlotte had said back in July 1849 that, although she felt she might have lost any ability to enjoy society again, she did sometimes crave it, and a change of scene. Smith and Williams were keen to encourage her to come to London and engage with other writers; they understood how useful it might be to her critical reception as much as to her own well-being to emerge now and then from her Yorkshire fastness. Charlotte had no desire to go to parties and be lionised – in fact the idea filled her with revulsion – but being able to meet 'some of the truly great literary characters' of the day, Thackeray, Dickens, Harriet Martineau, tempted her strongly. 'However this is not to be yet – I cannot sacrifice my incognito – And let me be content with seclusion – it has its advantages. In general indeed I am tranquil – it is only now and then that a struggle disturbs me – that I wish for a wider world than Haworth.' Her isolation was problematic artistically, though, as she was aware on completion of *Shirley*. Until she heard from Williams that he liked the book, she had no confidence in it at all, not having been able to share it with her sisters, or with anybody.

Sometimes the gloom of home simply overwhelmed her, as on a day in September 1849 when both Tabby and Martha were ill, Tabby plagued with lameness again and Martha with an 'internal inflammation' that Patrick Brontë unhelpfully opined might be life-threatening. Just as he was saying this, Charlotte heard Tabby call from the kitchen and rushed in to find the old servant collapsed on the floor with her head under the grate. Charlotte, who had a headache and felt sick herself, 'fairly broke down for ten minutes – sat & cried like a fool', as she told Ellen.

The publication of *Shirley* also left her very vulnerable, not just from some of the reviews, which she knew she took too much to heart ('Were my Sisters now alive they and I would laugh over this notice,' she told Williams of one slightly bad one), but from the frenzy of interest locally in the identity of Currer Bell, hugely provoked by the appearance of a book that was all about the West Riding, albeit thirty years in the past. Charlotte already suspected that her post was being opened on purpose in Keighley, and that her retirement was resented there. '[T]he gossiping inquisitiveness of small towns is rife ... they are sadly puzzled to guess why I never visit, encourage no overtures to acquaintance, and always stay at home.' A visit to Ellen at Brookroyd that autumn alerted her, rather late in the day, to the fact that *Jane Eyre* 'has been read all over the district', and she was aware of people treating her differently. This was perturbing, as it meant she was losing her anonymity: 'I met sometimes with new deference, with augmented kindness – old schoolfellows and old teachers too, greeted me with generous warmth – and again – ecclesiastical brows lowered thunder on me [because of the depiction of Carus Wilson in *Jane Eyre*]. When I confronted one or two large-made priests I longed for the battle to come on.'

To the disappointment of no longer being able to 'walk invisible' was added the annoyance of Currer Bell's gender always being a matter of concern to readers and critics. 'Why can [the Press] not be content to take Currer Bell for a man?' she asked James Taylor, the editor at Smith, Elder with whom she had begun to correspond (and who had taken a special interest in *Shirley*, coming to the Parsonage in September to pick up the manuscript personally). 'I imagined – mistakenly it now appears – that "Shirley" bore fewer traces of a female hand than "Jane Eyre": that I have misjudged disappoints me a little – though I cannot exactly see where the error lies.' The most aggravating judgement had come from her former champion, G. H. Lewes, whose review of *Shirley* in *The Edinburgh Review* criticised the coarseness of the book, and the inferiority of female creativity in general, concluding (in a reprise of what Robert Southey had said in 1837) that 'the grand function of woman . . . is, and ever must be, Maternity.' Charlotte was so angry that she sent him a single sentence: 'I can be on my guard against my enemies, but God deliver me from my friends!'

Even if they hadn't read *Jane Eyre*, the reviewers all treated *Shirley* as a woman's work, and harped annoyingly on speculation about the authoress. Gossip about Currer Bell had spread wide by this date, and from her sofa in the Casa Guidi in Florence Elizabeth Barrett Browning wrote to thank her friend Mary Russell Mitford for the latest snippet – that *Jane Eyre* had been written by a governess from Cowan Bridge School: 'I certainly don't think that the qualities, half savage and & half freethinking, expressed in 'Jane Eyre', are likely to suit a model governess,' the poet observed wryly. 'Your account falls like dew upon the parched curiosity of some of our friends here, to whom (as mere gossip . . .) I couldn't resist the temptation of communicating it. People *are* so curious . . . about this particular authorship.'

A similarly avid interest in Currer Bell's identity was shown by Harriet Martineau, a novelist who had much in common with Charlotte. Martineau, who came from an intellectually distinguished Unitarian family, had come to notice in the 1830s with her essays on social reform, *Illustrations of Political Economy*, and her bestselling novel, *Deerbrook*. Charlotte was an admirer of the novel and in tribute sent Martineau a copy of *Shirley* on publication. Little did she imagine how closely the accompanying note would be examined by its recipient for clues as to Currer Bell's sex. 'The hand was a cramped and nervous one,' Martineau recalled in her autobiography, 'which might belong to any body who had written too much, or was in bad health, or who had been badly taught.' Martineau had noticed what might or might not have been a genuine slip of the pen when Currer Bell changed the pronoun 'she' to 'he' in his/her covering letter, but was convinced anyway, from some domestic details in *Jane Eyre*, that the author could only have been a woman. She therefore addressed her reply on the outside to 'Currer Bell Esqre' but began it 'Madam'.

There was no point struggling too long against this tide, especially when it brought with it very welcome messages such as the one that Smith, Elder forwarded in November from Elizabeth Gaskell, praising *Shirley* in such generous and sympathetic terms that it brought tears to Charlotte's eyes. 'She said I was not to answer it – but I cannot help doing so,' Charlotte told Williams. '[S]he is a good – she is a great woman – proud am I that I can touch a chord of sympathy in souls so noble. In Mrs Gaskell's nature – it mournfully pleases me to fancy a remote affinity to my Sister Emily – in Miss Martineau's mind I have always felt the same – though there are wide differences – Both these ladies are above me – certainly far my superiors in attainments and experience – I think I could look up to them if I knew them.' In her reply to Mrs Gaskell, Currer Bell used the female pronoun without demur.

Eagerness to know such people began to work on Charlotte in a beneficial way. She came to realise, gradually and imperfectly, the effect that her presence on the literary scene had been having ever since the publication of *Jane Eyre* – its effect on readers, writers and the culture generated between them. That world had its own life and momentum and would go on without her whether she joined it or not, though she began to think it time to assert herself. Just before she fell out with him over his disappointing review of *Shirley*, Charlotte had confessed to George Henry Lewes that during the previous year she had sometimes ceased 'to care about literature and critics and fame' altogether, that she had temporarily 'lost sight of whatever was prominent in my thoughts at the first publication of "Jane Eyre"'. '[B]ut now I want these things to come back – vividly – if possible.' Something else was also impelling her to find new distractions – the anniversary of Emily's death looming, memories of which were revived with intolerable poignancy by the returning season. By the middle of November, she told Williams that she had 'almost formed the resolution of coming to London', and then – nearly as abruptly as her trip to London with Anne in 1848 – she was packing her bags and heading for a fortnight's stay with George Smith and his family in the 'big Babylon'.

George Smith was very obviously delighted to be allowed to present Miss Brontë to his friends at last, however modestly she said she wished to be entertained. He had instructed his mother and sisters to treat their guest at their terraced townhouse in Paddington with special care; the first day or two were consequently rather constrained, as the Smiths ran around making sure there were enough candles and fire for their frail-looking visitor. When Mrs Smith relaxed from this sentinel posture, Charlotte began to like her a great deal. '[K]indness is a potent heart-winner,' Charlotte remarked to Ellen. She liked young Mr Smith much better than before too, having seen how good a son and brother he was.

The visit was a chance to make better acquaintance with W. S. Williams, although there was still constraint there, by comparison with the freedom of their letters: '[he] too is really most gentlemanly and well-informed – his weak points he certainly has – but these are not seen in society.' The third member of the Smith, Elder team, 'the little man', red-headed, 33-year-old James Taylor, was more difficult to assess. Taylor had a position of some responsibility, overseeing at least forty junior staff, whom he ruled, Charlotte heard, with an iron will. Taylor's striking resemblance to Branwell might have disturbed Charlotte; her father had noticed it when the young publisher called at the Parsonage in September to pick up the manuscript of *Shirley*. She found him both attractive and repulsive at once; reminiscent of 'the Helstone order of men' for his despotism and rigidity, but with intriguing flashes of sensitivity. 'He tries to be very kind and even to express sympathy sometimes,' Charlotte told Ellen, 'and he does not manage it – he has a determined, dreadful nose in the midd[l]e of his face which when poked into my countenance cuts into my soul like iron – Still he is horribly intelligent, quick, searching, sagacious – and with a memory of relentless tenacity: to turn to Williams after him or to Smith himself is to turn from granite to easy down or warm fur.'

Smith was keen to treat his guest to some stimulating outings: Charlotte saw Macready, the most famous actor of the day, both in *Macbeth* and in *Othello* (though she shocked a dinner party by being insufficiently impressed with him) and went to the National Gallery, where she was delighted with an exhibition of some of the paintings that Turner had bequeathed to the nation. If John Ruskin, whose *Modern Painters* Charlotte had admired very much, had not been out of the country, Smith would undoubtedly have arranged an introduction to him: Smith was Ruskin's friend and publisher. Smith had a whole list of people he wished Charlotte to meet: Lady Morgan (author of *The Wild Irish Girl*), Catherine Gore (one of the fashionable 'silver-fork' novelists), Anthony Trollope, Charles Dickens. As it was, he tested Miss Brontë's sociability to a new extreme by inviting two gentlemen to dinner one evening: Dr John Forbes, with whom Charlotte had been in correspondence during Anne's last illness, and William Makepeace Thackeray. Smith had forewarned the novelist not to upset Miss Brontë by indicating that he knew she was Currer Bell, but Thackeray couldn't resist making a remark about his cigar, quoting from *Jane Eyre*, when the gentlemen rejoined the ladies after dinner. Charlotte was discomposed (not surprisingly, since Rochester's cigar habit was one of Constantin Heger's bequests to her novel) and shut down the conversation 'in a chilly fashion', as Smith was sorry to see, but Thackeray apparently went off to his club none the worse for his reprimand, saying, 'Boys! I have been dining with "Jane Eyre".'

To her father, Charlotte described the great man, whom she knew had been assessing her from a distance all through dinner: 'He is a very tall man – above six feet high, with a peculiar face – not handsome – very ugly indeed – generally somewhat satirical and stern in expression, but capable also of a kind look . . . I should think to have him for a friend than an enemy – for he is a most formidable looking personage. I listened to him as he conversed with the other gentlemen – all he says is most simple but often cynical, harsh and contradictory.' For all its interest, Charlotte found the evening very taxing, and knew that nerves had made her 'painfully stupid' with the man whose works she so admired. She fared much better with an introduction she arranged herself, writing to Harriet Martineau as Currer Bell to ask if she could call. Martineau and her relations waited in suspense to see who would turn up at the appointed hour: 'whether a tall moustached man six feet high or an aged female, or a girl, or – altogether a ghost, a hoax or a swindler!' Miss Martineau needed the aid of an ear trumpet, so was hoping that the visitor's real name was properly announced; she told her cousins they were to shout it distinctly into the horn if not. When a carriage was heard at the door and the bell rung, 'in came a neat little woman, a *very* little sprite of a creature nicely dressed; & with nice tidy bright hair.' Charlotte did reveal her real name, but the Martineaus were sworn to keep it secret, and Charlotte must have been pleased with them and with the frisson her dramatic arrival caused, for she relaxed and was able to talk to them very naturally. '[S]he was so pleasant & so naive, that is to say so innocent and un Londony that we were quite charmed with her,' one of Martineau's cousins said.

When Charlotte got back to Haworth in the week before Christmas, exhausted, she wrote to Williams – now safely back in his epistolary sphere – that her time in London had furnished her with 'ideas, images, pleasant feelings – such as may perhaps cheer many a long winter evening', but that as soon as the routine of home closed round her again, the whole visit seemed as unreal as a dream. 'I think I should scarcely like to live in London,' she told Miss Wooler, 'and were I obliged to live there, I should certainly go little into company – especially I should eschew the literary coteries.'

Smith's generosity and thoughtfulness meant that more such visits occurred, though, and over the next four years Charlotte returned three times to Smith's home, attended exhibitions, plays, concerts, operas; heard famous preachers and the infamous Cardinal Wiseman; breakfasted with the poet Samuel Rogers; took tea with Miss Martineau; dined with Thackeray. If Smith had hoped that this injection of activity and interest into Miss Brontë's life would bring her out of her shell, he was wrong – she was and remained very self-conscious in company – but the closer contacts she made, with Elizabeth Gaskell particularly, fed her craving for intelligent discussion and a sympathetic audience.

Gaskell had been intrigued with Miss Brontë's story – such of it as she could find out – long before they met, which was not until the summer of 1850. In the spring of that year an active but interfering man called James Kay-Shuttleworth, a former physician and Poor Law commissioner who had acquired a title and a castellated mansion called Gawthorpe, in Lancashire, from his wife Lady Janet, drove over to

Haworth on a whim to be introduced to the famous Miss Brontë. Charlotte was far from pleased at the intrusion, but Patrick Brontë was strongly impressed by Sir James's title and confident manner, and urged his daughter to accept the invitation that had been held out to her, to visit the couple at Gawthorpe Hall. Mrs Gaskell had heard all about their meeting from her friend Lady Janet: it was through this channel that she picked up the first stories about Reverend Brontë's eccentricities that caused trouble later, in her biography. But in 1850 such anecdotes simply added to the romance around the author of *Jane Eyre*.

When the two novelists met at the Kay-Shuttleworths' house by Lake Windermere, Briery Close, in August, Gaskell was immediately impressed by Charlotte's modesty and retirement, 'a little lady in a black silk gown' who worked at her sewing and hardly spoke. '[B]ut I had time for a good look at her,' Gaskell told her correspondent, Catherine Winkworth (who was to become a friend of Charlotte's herself). 'She is, (as she calls herself) *undeveloped*; thin and more than ½ a head shorter than I, soft brown hair not so dark as mine; eyes (very good and expressive looking straight & open at you) of the same colour, a reddish face; large mouth & many teeth gone; altogether *plain*; the forehead square, broad and *rather* overhanging.' This unpromising description was mitigated by Mrs Gaskell's tribute to Miss Brontë's quiet charm and sincerity: 'She has a very sweet voice, rather hesitates in choosing her expressions, but when chosen they seem without an effort, *admirable* and *just* befitting the occasion. There is nothing overstrained but perfectly simple.'

Mrs Gaskell was intrigued by the long conversations she had during these three days with Miss Brontë, who told her the story of her life in some detail, including some amusingly narrated set-piece scenes, such as Charlotte going in to tell her father about the publication of *Jane Eyre* and his response at tea, 'Children, Charlotte has been writing a book.' It is notable that most of these anecdotes, clearly encouraged by Mrs Gaskell's eager appreciation of every detail, were ones relating to her father, and tended to illustrate the opposition Charlotte had encountered from him all her life. It was rather disloyal as well as confessional to be telling this stranger that 'At 19 I should have been thankful for an allowance of 1d a week. I asked my father, but he said What did women want with money.' No wonder, when Gaskell added this information to the garbled tales of parental tyranny she had heard elsewhere, that she produced such a negative portrait of Patrick Brontë in the biography she wrote seven years later. It had been dictated in part by his daughter.

Charlotte may have been encouraged by Elizabeth Gaskell's interest in her life, and her deeply sympathetic response to the story of her siblings' deaths from consumption (which Gaskell, incidentally, immediately assumed the emaciated Miss Brontë had also contracted), to consider doing what she had previously refused, and write something biographical about them. The adverse criticism that the works of Ellis and Acton Bell had attracted and the fading of interest in them since their deaths – which the public didn't know about, of course – hung on Charlotte's conscience. While she was fêted and rewarded, while she visited celebrities and banked large cheques from her publisher (£500 for the copyright of *Shirley*), her sisters were forgotten. Having asked George Smith to buy back the rights to *Wuthering Heights* and *Agnes Grey* from the recalcitrant Newby, Charlotte offered to write a biographical preface to a new edition, in line with what he and Williams had suggested in 1849. In prose of sombre power and beauty, she outlined her family's remote country upbringing, close sibling bonds and love of their moorland home, their delight in composition and – after Charlotte's chance discovery of Emily's poems – their efforts to get the poems, and then their novels, published and read. It made an irresistible narrative.

> [Their works] appeared at last. Critics failed to do them justice. The immature but very real powers revealed in *Wuthering Heights* were scarcely recognised; its import and nature were misunderstood; the identity of its author was misrepresented; it was said that this was an earlier and ruder attempt of the same pen which had produced *Jane Eyre*. Unjust and grievous error! We laughed at it at first, but I deeply lament it now. Hence, I fear, arose a prejudice against the book.

Emily's character comes strongly before the reader: proud, uncompromising, distant, stoical. Her death, and that of Anne, were told briefly, but from a depth of personal pain that made this one of the most moving memorials of the age, to two tragic young women whose real names were only just being revealed:

Never in all her life had [Emily] lingered over any task that lay before her, and she did not linger now. She sank rapidly. She made haste to leave us. Yet, while physically she perished, mentally she grew stronger than we had yet known her. Day by day, when I saw with what a front she met suffering, I looked on her with an anguish of love and awe. I have seen nothing like it; but indeed I have never seen her parallel in anything. Stronger than a man, simpler than a child, her nature stood alone.

'An interpreter ought always to have stood between her and the world,' Charlotte said, brilliantly fulfilling that role herself in this poignant tribute to doomed and unrecognised genius. Of Anne, whose personality was, as in life, eclipsed by the heroic Emily, Charlotte said, '[she was] long-suffering, self-denying, reflective, and intelligent', but that 'a constitutional reserve and taciturnity placed and kept her in the shade, and covered her mind, and especially her feelings, with a sort of nun-like veil, which was rarely lifted.' As character studies, these could hardly have been more suggestive and intriguing. The mystery of 'the Bells' was solved – the legend of 'the Brontës' begun.

In the months following her visit to London in December 1849, Charlotte felt much more intimate with her publisher George Smith, and his mother, and corresponded with both of them. Her second visit to their home, in the summer of 1850 (a new one – they had just moved to Gloucester Terrace), confirmed her increasing fondness for Smith, but also her vulnerability to his ebullient youthful charm. Defensively, she lampooned herself in advance as a dithery incompetent who would be 'thankful to subside into any quiet corner of your drawing-room, where I might find a chair of suitable height', perhaps hinting to him not to take her admiration the wrong way.

Charlotte was better prepared to meet the challenge of Smith's hospitality this time round, and did so with grateful enthusiasm. There were as many outings as Miss Brontë could cope with – to the Royal Academy, the Opera, the zoological gardens in Regent's Park (an amazing experience for Charlotte, seeing for the first time outside an engraved book lions, tigers, elephants, 'cameleopards' and the zoo's newly acquired hippopotamus) – and on the second Friday of her stay

Mrs Smith held a ball at Gloucester Terrace, to which both Dickens and Thackeray were invited. Thackeray's reply expressed his regret that he wouldn't be able to meet her on that occasion; Dickens, who was also unable to attend, cited 'other and less agreeable engagements', although his absence was of less moment to Charlotte. Williams and his family made a fine show: 'all five were remarkable – their dress – their appearance were a decoration to the rooms – as Mrs Smith afterwards remarked', and they were graceful and elegant dancers. Whether Charlotte danced is not recorded. Did she *ever* dance, after the sorry attempts at school in Brussels? She never mentions dancing anywhere in her letters or novels. Was it one of the things she simply wasn't interested in, or had somehow ruled out for herself?

G. H. Lewes wrote the party up (under a pseudonym) the following week in a piece jocularly complaining about how town was 'full of authoresses', prime among whom was 'the charming CURRER BELL' surrounded by enthusiasts of *Jane Eyre* affecting '"Rochester" airs'. This image of a fully social Charlotte, charmingly coping with a crowd of male admirers, is so wildly at variance with almost every other description of her 'company' manners (except the extraordinary, proposal-triggering charisma that so affected the curate David Pryce back in 1840) that one has to believe Lewes was smitten with her himself to some extent. Perhaps he picked up on a powerful signal from those brilliant and mesmerising eyes, for Charlotte fixed on him as soon as he entered the room and he spent most of the evening sitting next to her, 'greatly interested by her conversation'. Unknown to Lewes, Charlotte was staring ardently at a face other than his own: Emily's, which she saw in a ghostly way reflected there – '[Emily's] eyes, her features – the very nose, the somewhat prominent mouth, the forehead – even at moments the expression'. It was a very peculiar sensation to have this bewhiskered controversialist rouse feelings of such tenderness, but she felt that whatever differences she and Lewes might continue to have about books and writing, she could now never hate him.*

---

* There is a photograph of G. H. Lewes from almost this period that makes CB's ardent identification of his and Emily's features all the more interesting. Lewes was known as one of the ugliest men in London, it seems with justice, but there is something about his stare, and perhaps his defiant look, that could have spoken to Charlotte.

She had a similar experience of haunting the same week when she met the young Irish novelist Julia Kavanagh, a woman even smaller and more fragile-looking than herself, who nevertheless managed to support herself and her mother through writing, her father having abandoned them both. Kavanagh's circumstances roused Charlotte's compassion, but it was something else that made her want to go back and talk to her again – she resembled Martha Taylor 'in every lineament'.

Thackeray called a few days later with an invitation to dinner and sat talking for more than two hours with Charlotte and George Smith. She found the close attention of 'the giant' in a private conversation much less intimidating than having to speak to him in a general party – indeed she found on this occasion an ease of expression that showed her true sense of equality with such a man. This was nothing to do with vanity, though Thackeray had every reason to be surprised at her forthrightness. 'I was moved to speak to him of some of his short-comings (literary of course),' she reported in a letter to Ellen, who was presumably pretty surprised herself at this account of her friend's temerity; 'one by one the faults came into my mind and one by one I brought them out and sought some explanation or defence – He did defend himself like a great Turk and heathen – that is to say, the excuses were often worse than the crime itself. The matter ended in decent amity.'

Thackeray left his own accounts of their conversation: 'Twice I recollect she took me to task for what she held to be errors in doctrine . . . She spoke her mind out. She jumped too rapidly to conclusions . . . Often she seemed to me to be judging the London folk prematurely: but perhaps the city is rather angry at being judged. I fancied an austere little Joan of Arc marching in upon us, and rebuking our easy lives, our easy morals. She gave me the impression of being a very pure, and lofty, and high-minded person.'

Thackeray's admiration for 'Currer Bell' was less critical than hers for him, and his curiosity about her character and history was intense. Knowing hardly anything yet of Miss Brontë's circumstances and personal history, Thackeray brought his superb novelist's eye to bear on 'the trembling little frame, the little hand, the great honest eyes' that met his. 'An impetuous honesty' was his wonderful phrase to describe her presiding characteristic. He saw her ardour for the truth, however inconvenient or abruptly expressed it might be. 'New to the London world, she entered it with an independent, indomitable spirit of her own; and judged of contemporaries, and especially spied out arrogance or affectation, with extraordinary keenness of vision.'

Smith devised a treat entirely suited to her tastes when he took Charlotte the following Sunday to the Chapel Royal in St James's, where the Duke of Wellington was a regular attendant. The previous week she had been admiring Landseer's portrait of her hero on the field of Waterloo at the Royal Academy – here he was large as life, walking just a few yards in front of her after the service. 'I indulged Miss Brontë by so arranging our walk that she met him twice on his way to Apsley House,' Smith recalled later. For Charlotte, it was understandably one of the 'chief incidents' of her visit, and possibly of her life – a close encounter with the man she had idolised so intensely in her youth and whose Angrian avatar had been her earliest obsession. One senses Smith's pleasure in arranging such an event and *her* pleasure in it must have been palpable. 'I indulged Miss Brontë' could well have been his motto on these visits. He was treating her a little like an exotic pet, which responded only to the most expert handling.

Smith's esteem for Charlotte was deep, and his desire to please and praise her was of course a first for her, made so wary by experience. She had had recognition of her ability and intelligence before – from Constantin Heger – but she had never been really admired for them until now. Her peculiarities didn't bother Smith, because he had no interest in judging her socially (though he realised that his mother and sisters felt otherwise and found Miss Brontë 'a somewhat difficult guest', for her self-consciousness as much as anything). 'Strangers used to say that they were afraid of her,' Smith wrote many years later. 'For my own part, I found her conversation most interesting; her quick and clear intelligence was delightful. When she became excited on any subject she was really eloquent, and it was a pleasure to listen to her.'

After three weeks in his company and staying in his home, Charlotte had reached a state of intimacy with Smith that seems to have taken her somewhat by surprise. Her reason told her – severely – that there was no romantic content in his behaviour, but her heart responded warmly to the attention he lavished on her, his sincere admiration, his good looks and his 'buoyant animal spirits'. But when he began to talk, as if

it were simple and inevitable, of taking her with him on a trip to Edinburgh (where he was going, in the company of his sister Eliza, to fetch
his younger brother Alick home for the holidays), Charlotte sensed
that – whether he knew it or not – her publisher was crossing some line
into a different category of connection. Mrs Smith certainly thought
so: Charlotte could tell from her manner and her readiness to support
Charlotte's opposition to the plan. But the more the women objected,
the more Smith warmed to his own scheme and soon he wouldn't take
no for an answer.

Writing to warn Ellen not to read too much into the fact that she
was about to go travelling with her handsome young publisher, Charlotte made clear how significant, or tricky, she found the situation: 'I
believe that George and I understand each other very well,' she said,
surely making Ellen sit up at the use of Mr Smith's Christian name and
the great list of extenuating circumstances that followed – '[we] respect
each other very sincerely – we both know the wide breach time has
made between us – we do not embarrass each other, or very rarely – my
six or eight years of seniority, to say nothing of lack of all pretensions
to beauty &c. are a perfect safeguard – I should not in the least fear to
go with him to China – I like to see him pleased – I greatly *dis*like to
ruffle and disappoint him – so he shall have his mind.'

Her readiness to put herself in a category of absolute 'safety' due to
age and 'lack of all pretensions to beauty &c.' sounds rather abject,
until one reads what Smith said about her in a letter to Mrs Humphry
Ward many years later, a matter-of-fact judgement about Charlotte
Brontë's personal charms:

> No, I never was in the least bit in love with Charlotte Brontë. I am
> afraid that the confession will not raise me in your opinion, but the
> truth is, I never could have loved any woman who had not some charm
> or grace of person, and Charlotte Brontë had none – I liked her and was
> interested in her, and I admired her – especially when she was in York-
> shire and I was in London. I never was coxcomb enough to suppose that
> she was in love with me. But, I believe that my mother was at one time
> rather alarmed.

'Especially when she was in Yorkshire and I was in London' was an
ungallant way to admire a lady. In his memoirs, written forty years

later, he was equally forthright about his first impression of Charlotte
Brontë as being 'interesting rather than attractive':

> She was very small, and had a quaint old-fashioned look. Her head
> seemed too large for her body. She had fine eyes, but her face was
> marred by the shape of the mouth and by the complexion. There was
> but little feminine charm about her; and of this fact she herself was
> uneasily and perpetually conscious.

Charlotte must have been aware of Smith's judgement from the start,
at some level or other. His charming manner confused her, though, and
she accepted the invitation to go to Edinburgh with him at the end of
June not quite sure of his intentions.

One of the highlights of this trip to London in the summer of 1850
was meant to be the dinner that Thackeray held in Currer Bell's honour
at his home in Young Street, Kensington, but it turned out comically
badly. The family had been looking forward excitedly to meeting the
author of *Jane Eyre*, and on the evening in question Thackeray's elder
daughter Anny, her sister and governess, Miss Trulock, were lined up
ready for 'the great event': 'we all sat silent and expectant; my father,
who rarely waited, waiting with us.' The carriage arrived, Smith
jumped down, and in came Miss Brontë, 'in mittens, in silence, in seriousness'. 'This then is the authoress, the unknown power whose books
have set all London talking, reading, speculating', Anny recalled, in a
marvellous evocation of the sorceress's celebrity:

> To say that we little girls had been given *Jane Eyre* to read scarcely rep-
> resents the facts of the case; to say that we had taken it without leave,
> read bits here and read bits there, been carried away by an undreamed-
> of and hitherto unimagined whirlwind into things, times, places, all
> utterly absorbing and at the same time absolutely unintelligible to us,
> would more accurately describe our states of mind on that summer's
> evening as we look at Jane Eyre – the great Jane Eyre – the tiny little
> lady.

But the excitement dissipated quickly. Miss Brontë was stiff and formal
with everyone but the governess, and told Smith later that she found
the girls' manners too lively. At dinner, she listened intently to whatever her host said, but barely spoke or ate, and when the ladies all

retired to the drawing room a dreadful constraint descended: 'Every one waited for the brilliant conversation which never began at all . . . The room looked very dark, the lamp began to smoke a little, the conversation grew dimmer and more dim, the ladies sat round still expectant.' One guest bravely tried to open up a conversation by hoping that the famous authoress liked London, only to be told curtly, 'I do and I don't' – followed by silence. Another, Mrs Procter, thought her introduction to the great Currer Bell had been 'one of the dullest evenings she ever spent in her life', and Thackeray himself found it all such a strain that at the first opportunity he escaped to his club. Anny came upon him in the hall, with his hat on and a finger to his lips.

What did Charlotte feel about the evening? Oddly enough, for one so self-conscious, her own social shortcomings don't seem to have bothered her much. Perhaps she felt it absurd that anything might be expected of her, even at a reception given *for* her, when Thackeray was of the company. Perhaps it was her modesty as much as social ineptitude that made her such hard work to be seated next to at dinner. She certainly began to get a reputation, though, from occasions such as this for being chilly, possibly difficult and judgemental.

Smith was fully aware of what a failure the dinner had been, but in the carriage on the way back to Gloucester Terrace, Charlotte had something else entirely on her mind and startled Smith by leaning forward from her seat opposite him, putting her hands on his knees and saying, 'She would make you a very nice wife.' At first, he wasn't sure what she was talking about, but Charlotte replied, 'Oh! you know whom I mean', and Smith realised she was referring to Mrs Procter's charming and beautiful 25-year-old daughter Adelaide, the author of a book of poems. Smith had certainly admired Miss Procter that evening, but not in the pointed way Charlotte detected, and one can't help thinking she was presuming too much all round here and that her signalling of approval was impertinent. Touching him like that was a strangely inappropriate gesture. There seems something studied about it – as if she were staking a claim in an alternative kind of intimacy (like that of a sister or friend) to have when Miss Procter, or some other girl like her, finally did catch Smith's eye and whisk him away.

Charlotte's close observation of him cannot have been entirely pleasant for George Smith, who was no flirt. When he said that he found her 'uneasily and perpetually conscious' of her own looks, he seemed puzzled and sorry that his admired author was, in effect, *vain*, that 'the possession of genius did not lift her above the weakness of an excessive anxiety about her personal appearance. But I believe that she would have given all her genius and her fame to have been beautiful. Perhaps few women ever existed more anxious to be pretty than she, or more angrily conscious of the circumstance that she was *not* pretty.' One would like to hope this was not true for Charlotte, that the creator of Jane Eyre had more faith in herself, but the more she went into society, the more she was worn down by an extreme self-consciousness. Lucy Snowe in *Villette*, distracted by an awareness that she is not pleasing for Monsieur Paul to look at, seems to speak directly for the author when she says, 'I never remember the time when I had not a haunting dread of what might be the degree of my outward deficiency . . . Was it weak to lay so much stress on an opinion about appearance? I fear it might be – I fear it was; but in that case I must avow no light share of weakness. I must own a great fear of displeasing.'

Charlotte's awareness of her looks can hardly have been put under more strain on this eventful London visit than when Smith decided that she should sit for a portrait to the fashionable and expensive George Richmond, whom Smith knew through John Ruskin and whose chalk and crayon likenesses of writers and artists, including Martineau, Gaskell, Ruskin, Swinburne and Charlotte M. Yonge, were much admired. One can imagine Miss Brontë raised strong objections when this plan was first mooted, but Smith's stated intention – to make a present of the portrait to Charlotte's father – quickly trumped any of her personal misgivings.

She made three trips to Richmond's York Street studio for the sittings over a period of nine days in June. The artist's son later said that his father got the impression of 'some early hip trouble' from her slightly ungainly carriage, and that she was 'not remarkable in appearance except for having eyes of extraordinary brilliancy & penetration'. The sittings didn't start auspiciously when Richmond asked his subject to remove a wad of brown merino wool that had stayed on top of her head when she took her bonnet off and that he imagined was connected with it. This was a hairpiece bought in Leeds preparatory to her visit, not performing as hoped, and of course Charlotte was mortified (to the point of tears) to have attention drawn to it. Richmond said that it took until the last of the sittings to get her to relax, and then only through the accident of the Duke of Wellington's servant having left the house just as she arrived. The thought that she could have been introduced to the Duke himself fifteen minutes earlier enthralled Charlotte and distracted her from the ordeal of being scrutinised so that Richmond was able to catch the expression in the portrait. He shows her thoughtful and intense, animated not with high spirits, but with a brooding inner energy – an expression difficult for a society portraitist to flatter into pleasantness.

Richmond's portrait is of great importance as it is the only one of Charlotte Brontë taken from life by a professional artist and so our best guide to what she really looked like. Branwell's depiction of his sisters in *The Brontë Sisters* and the sketches remaining from the destroyed *Gun Group* have great iconic power but are hardly good records of the sitters' actual features: Branwell's Charlotte has the squareness of face described by Mary Taylor and the 'general impression of *chin*' that Anne Thackeray noticed, but the expression is stolid and dough-like, which even people who despised Charlotte's lack of beauty never accused her of. Richmond's portrait managed both to flatter his subject and to record the 'data' of her face, so to speak: his chalk highlights indicate the prominence of her noble brow, her large nose, the twist at the right side of her mouth and the length of her chin (minimised by the angle at which he posed her) – but his composition focuses attention on her large and luminous eyes, which he recognised as her outstanding feature, 'illuminating features that would have otherwise been plain'.

It wasn't Richmond's practice to allow sitters to view his work in progress, but on the last day he showed the picture to Miss Brontë and stood waiting for a verdict, only to find to his surprise that she was silently in tears. She turned to him 'half in apology' and explained that her emotional response was nothing to do with the likeness to herself but because the picture looked so much like her sister. Which sister is not clear, as two versions of the story exist, one citing Anne and the other Emily, but it was another incidence of Charlotte seeing ghost faces all around her in the new London scene she had entered, and when one stands in front of Richmond's portrait in the National

Portrait Gallery today, it is strange to think of the subject seeing dead Emily or dead Anne there, rather than herself.

George Smith's inspired generosity changed Charlotte Brontë's life in ways she had not imagined possible, but she retained a clear sense of her own social limitations, and fended off many of his initiatives on her behalf, knowing that they would exhaust her physically and mentally. The more she saw of the effects of fame (on Thackeray, for instance, whom she thought in danger of losing his head over it), the less she wanted it herself. She turned down invitations to meet Dickens socially, though the two seem to have been introduced, fleetingly, after a play that Smith took her to. In later life Smith said he had introduced them, and Charlotte told John Stores Smith, an early fan, that she had met Dickens but didn't like him (although she admired his books). The contact of their imaginations, however, went much deeper. Dickens's depiction of systematic negligence and cruelty in *Nicholas Nickleby* had impressed Charlotte and, as we have seen, probably contributed to her picture of Lowood School in *Jane Eyre*. Dickens told Lockhart that he had never read *Jane Eyre*, 'and never would', but he didn't need to read such a talked-about book in order to be influenced by it in turn. His friend Forster, who *had* read *Jane Eyre* and was struck by the astonishing power of the early chapters being told from the oppressed child's point of view, suggested to Dickens that it would be an interesting experiment to try the same thing, and Dickens, with his keen appetite for novelty, took up the idea immediately in the composition of *David Copperfield*. Between them, these two great novels marked a sea-change in how the developing consciousness was represented in art and how writers showed adult psychology being forged from childhood experience. We think nothing now of stories told from a child's point of view, but Charlotte Brontë was the first to do it, and Dickens the second.

Charlotte's friendships with fellow writers in these years gave her pleasure but did not make it easier for her to write – rather the contrary. She could not match the productivity of Martineau or Gaskell, and did not sufficiently trust her own ability to meet a deadline to accept the few offers she had to write for the commercial press. Her friendship with Martineau had started very promisingly with an invitation to her home in Ambleside in 1850; there Charlotte observed an enviably orderly and productive single writer's life. Miss Martineau rose early, took a cold bath, went for a walk, had breakfast and was at work by eight thirty. Guests were expected to amuse themselves until two, when they would 'meet, work, talk and walk together till 5'. Then dinner was followed by an evening of fluent and frank conversation, and after guests retired, Miss Martineau stayed up writing letters until midnight. 'She appears exhaustless in strength and spirits, and indefatigable in the faculty of labour,' Charlotte wrote to Ellen, clearly awed and envious of this smoothly satisfying routine. Harriet Martineau had health, energy and 'social cheerfulness' all far beyond Charlotte's capacities, and her strong intellect was a pleasure to engage. One evening she showed Charlotte the work she was writing on the Peninsular War for Charles Knight's *History of the Thirty Years' Peace* and was surprised at the emotional reaction she got to a passage about the Duke of Wellington. '[S]he looked up at me and stole her hand into mine, and, to my amazement, the tears were running down her cheeks,' she told Mrs Gaskell later. 'I saw at once there was a touch of idolatry in the case, but it was a charming enthusiasm.' Charlotte's impulse to take her hostess's hand also shows the demonstrative, tactile spirit that was so often held in check.

But when Martineau's jointly authored book, *Letters on the Laws of Man's Nature and Development*, was published the next year, Charlotte was painfully conflicted about her new friend. She had seen part of the book in proof at Ambleside, and gave Martineau the impression that, although she did not at all agree with its religious position (Martineau frankly admitted her agnosticism), 'this did not prevent her doing justice' to its social objectives. This led Martineau to suspect Charlotte of hypocrisy and double-dealing later, when she found that Charlotte was as horrified as many readers and reviewers at the aggressive secularism of her vision and had written expressing it to her publisher, saying that *Letters* gave 'a death-blow to [Martineau's] future usefulness'. 'Who can trust the word or rely on the judgment of an avowed Atheist?' Charlotte could not contemplate a life empty of faith; without it, the afterlife disappeared, and the hope of being reunited with her loved ones. If 'a better place' did not exist, how could anyone face the 'utter desolation' of this world?

*

Charlotte's two days in Edinburgh with Smith after her stay at his house in June 1850 and his equally extraordinary invitation to her the next spring to join him on a cruise down the Rhine (which she felt she had to refuse), created the impression, in everyone else's head but his own, that the handsome young publisher and Currer Bell were becoming significantly close. Ellen Nussey had seen with her own eyes how excited Charlotte was by her visit to London in June and the prospect of Edinburgh: Charlotte spent the week between these two trips at Brookroyd, not going home to Haworth. Even after her visit to Edinburgh (where Smith and his sister Eliza took her all round the capital, looking at sites connected with Walter Scott; they went out to Abbotsford to see the great man's house), she didn't go straight home but spent another few days with Ellen, exhausted by her travels and undoubtedly having one of her emotional collapses too. Being almost alone with charming 'George' for three days had given Charlotte 'some hours as happy almost as any I ever spent', and Ellen needed no more encouragement to hear the distant sound of wedding bells. Charlotte poo-pooed the idea, but clearly considered it a possibility, and Patrick Brontë had somehow picked up on the possibility too, though he knew Smith only by name and as the sender of well-chosen parcels of books to the Parsonage. While Charlotte was still at Brookroyd, Patrick began to get nervous about her protracted absence from home (six weeks by this time) and feared her 'somehow about to be married to somebody – having "received some overtures"'.

But at the same time that Smith was getting so friendly, Charlotte became aware of another possible admirer in the Cornhill office: Smith's intense young colleague James Taylor. Quite what Taylor felt for Miss Brontë was hard to gauge, as he never got round to articulating it clearly, but their correspondence in 1850 had become important to both parties (though not witty and bantering like Charlotte's letters to Smith), and when he announced that he would soon be leaving England to go to run a branch of the firm in Bombay – a post that necessitated at least five years' absence – Charlotte found herself surprisingly sad and perturbed. Her letter of farewell conveyed this, and next thing she knew Taylor was asking to pay her a call at the Parsonage – he would happen to be passing, he said.

Taylor had been to the Parsonage before – when he picked up the manuscript of *Shirley* in the autumn of 1849 – but this second visit was one of confused expectations and pregnant silences. Taylor looked older, stranger and very nervous – not surprisingly, perhaps, now that he was on the brink of declaring himself to the famous authoress. Quite what he said is unclear – even to Charlotte – but he seems to have suggested that on his return from India in five years he would like to marry her. His manner of expressing himself, however, was as repellent as ever, as Charlotte described to Ellen:

> each moment he came near me – and that I could see his eyes fastened on me – my veins ran ice. Now that he is away I feel far more gently towards him – it is only close by that I grow rigid – stiffening with a strange mixture of apprehension and anger – which nothing softens but his retreat and a perfect subduing of his manner. I did not want to be proud nor intend to be proud – but I was forced to be so.

One would think the matter decided by this powerful antipathy, but Charlotte brooded on it for weeks and resented Taylor's removal to the other side of the world, depriving her of a support in her solitude. More than his letters even, she felt she would regret 'the exclusion of his idea from my mind', showing a strange propensity to feel pain in almost abstract ways, like an old virus coming out in her nerve endings. She understood from hints Taylor had given that there had been some breach in relations between him and George Smith (who might have deliberately wanted him out of the London office for several reasons), and in her mind she couldn't help wondering if the two entertained some rivalry over her. This shows a certain blindness about the feelings of both men – Taylor's so strong (if unwanted); Smith's so careless (if desired).

Rather alarmingly, Taylor's motives seemed crystal clear to Patrick Brontë as soon as he heard that the visit was in the offing. He had taken a liking to 'the little man' as Charlotte called him, bade him the sort of formal farewell he reserved for approved persons and referred to him afterwards 'with significant eulogy', as Charlotte wryly noted. 'I have told him nothing – yet he seems to be au fait to the whole business – I could think at some moments – his guesses go farther than mine.' This penetration of the situation had made Patrick Brontë very disturbed on the day of the visit itself, and after Taylor had left, his smile collapsed and he was taken immediately ill in anticipation of an imminent proposal. The idea of Charlotte suddenly leaving him was his worst fear. But, over the succeeding weeks, Patrick Brontë quite made up his mind that a long engagement to James Taylor would be just the thing for his daughter; it meant he wouldn't have to face the prospect of losing her yet, but that she would be supported by a husband in a future he might not live to see. The fact that she didn't want to marry Taylor was not relevant as far as he was concerned and put him 'out of patience'.

Charlotte had tried to explain to her father that, despite Taylor's cleverness, she thought his mind essentially 'second-rate' and his character lacking an essential element, 'something of the gentleman', as she told Ellen in a characteristically candid letter. Ellen hardly needed her friend to explain that she meant 'the *natural* gentleman – you know I can dispense with acquired polish – and for looks – I know myself too well to think that I have any right to be exacting on that point.' But, regretfully, in Taylor she could not find 'one passing glimpse of true good-breeding . . . it is hard to say – but it is *true*'.

It is interesting that Charlotte spent so much emotional energy refusing a man she quite disliked when almost under her nose was one so naturally gentlemanly as to not have imposed his feelings for Miss Brontë on her at all. Arthur Bell Nicholls nurtured his devotion, with decreasing hope, one imagines, all through these years when Charlotte was becoming famous locally and going up and down to London with hairpieces and bonnets in her luggage. He would have noted as keenly as anyone the second visit to the Parsonage of the agitated red-haired Londoner, and no doubt spent some anxious weeks waiting to hear of an engagement. He carried on his duties with admirable efficiency, but he was not very much appreciated or admired by the parson and his daughter, nor by the parishioners; his campaign to get the local Haworth women to stop drying their laundry in the churchyard made some of them wish he would not come back from his annual holiday in Ireland.

Charlotte did begin to notice Nicholls, gradually. She found him 'good – mild and uncontentious' when invited to tea, and he had been surprisingly sporting about the caricature of him she had put into *Shirley*, along with (much worse) depictions of the other local curates. 'Mr Macarthey' in the novel labours faithfully in the Sunday School and day-school, and has only 'proper, steady-going, clerical faults'; 'finding himself invited to tea with a Dissenter would unhinge him for a week' and burying an unbaptised person 'could make strange havoc in [his] physical and mental economy; otherwise, he was sane and rational'. Nicholls found this so amusing (or so flattering) that his landlady, Martha's mother, heard him roaring with laughter as he read the book; 'he sat alone – clapping his hands and stamping on the floor' with pleasure at it.

Shirley's mixed reception in the winter of 1849/50 had been much as Charlotte feared: even the most well-disposed critics seemed disappointed not to have a suitably exciting sequel to *Jane Eyre*. One reviewer, in *Fraser's Magazine*, described how he expected to be kept awake all night, as he had been by Currer Bell's first novel, only to find that the new story had quite the opposite effect and sent him quickly to sleep; others complained bitterly about the 'cool and solid' realism that had been Charlotte's express aim to depict. One savage review in *The Times* appeared in December 1849, when Charlotte was staying at the Smiths'. George Smith had tried to hide the paper from his guest but failed, and when he saw her later with tears streaming down her face he knew she had seen its condemnation of her book as 'at once the most highflown and the stalest of fictions'.

Charlotte's confidence, shaky at the best of times ever since she had lost her armour of invisibility, took a battering from these salvos, and she struggled to find the will to start another book. Given the amount of writing she used to do in the years when she had no hope of an audience, this was ironic, to say the least. In her desire to have something to work on, she turned back to her manuscript of *The Professor*, regardless of Smith, Elder having rejected it so decisively just four years before. The fair copy, which has survived (a patchwork of different-aged papers and handwriting styles), presumably contains a set of significant further changes from this period, or she would not have dared to resubmit it to the firm in the spring of 1851. She may have cut the beginning of the book drastically, to reduce the rival-brothers plot that had owed so much to Branwell's recycled Angrian story. And she certainly at this date wrote a preface explaining what she had intended to do: show the real struggles of a protagonist who 'as Adam's son . . . should share

Adam's doom – Labour throughout life and a mixed and moderate cup of enjoyment'. Williams felt the changes had some merit, but he may have exaggerated this to compensate for the fact that George Smith still very much thought otherwise. The upshot was that *The Professor* was rejected for a ninth time overall, and Charlotte regretfully had to put it by – not in her desk, she told Smith, for she would see its unloved face peep out at her too often, but in a cupboard all by itself.

Charlotte was prepared to joke with Smith about her tenacious affection for her much-rejected book, saying 'my feelings towards it can only be paralleled by those of a doting parent towards an idiot child . . . You may allege that [its] merit is not visible to the naked eye. Granted; but the smaller the commodity – the more inestimable its value.' She locked it out of sight, but the themes of the book – and its dramatisation of so much of the Brussels experience that had changed the course of her life – had come fresh to her mind again. Instead of tinkering with *The Professor*, she began to think of writing an entirely new novel around some of the same material, a novel that would confound the admirers of *Jane Eyre* and the critics of *Shirley* alike by taking realistic eventlessness to a new extreme.

Charlotte made a number of starts at *Villette*, casting and recasting her net around all the things she still wished to say about Brussels, the Pensionnat, Catholicism and Monsieur Heger, adding to them impressions and incidents from her more recent experiences in London, and her close, admiring observation of George Smith. Madame Heger appeared as the subtle, scheming directrice of the school, Madame Beck, whose jealousy of her impoverished English underling, Lucy, blights Lucy's chances of love at every turn, but whose healthy egotism and instinct to dominate wins a grudging respect from her victim. George Smith appears as 'Dr John', an Englishman abroad, whose healing temperament is suggested by his profession, but who exists in a world of sunny fortune so alien to Lucy that they can never quite co-exist, and, in a book bizarrely full of scenes when people fail to recognise each other, mistake identity, veil themselves, forget, deceive and change beyond recall, these two potential lovers are fated to share one glance of mutual understanding (not a loving glance, but a penetrating stare) and then part.

Constantin Heger, who was only introduced into *The Professor* obliquely as Zoraïde Reuter's kinsman, appears in *Villette* in a startlingly literal portrait as Monsieur Paul Emanuel, the dark-haired, choleric, demanding but brilliant and charming teacher of French literature at Madame Beck's pensionnat. His mannerisms, his speeches, his bons-bons, paletot, Greek cap and cigars are set down with daring explicitness: no one reading the novel who knew anything about the Brontës' two years in Brussels would have had any trouble tracing the character back to its original. Charlotte's use of him – and of their relationship – was like a gauntlet thrown down. In life he had cut her off – it was as if they had never known each other. What secret, then, was there to keep? In the novel, she could answer his silence with scenes remembered and imagined, details invented and forensically re-created: he would know exactly what she meant, but now had forfeited the right to reply.

To begin with, Charlotte had intended her narrator to be a 'sensible, unimaginative' girl called Elizabeth Home, but this very un-Brontëish character soon departed, leaving in her place a disturbing, hypersensitive alter ego, a ticking bomb of emotions called Lucy Snowe. Lucy has suffered so much before the story even begins – in ways that are never specified – that she appears before us disinvested from life; orphaned, unloved, overlooked, her only objective is to subsist as best she can. She is a person without hope, without illusions and armoured against love; a soul, or a self, to use the coming term, pared back to essentials. She is a heroine who does not care what we think of her, who wants to be left alone, who stands by at the book's appalling ending and watches our response to reading it.

With James Taylor safely out of the way in India, Charlotte accepted another invitation from the Smiths, arriving at 112 Gloucester Terrace on 28 May 1851. Mrs Smith took her to one of Thackeray's lectures the next day, where Charlotte was alarmed to be not only an object of general interest in a very fashionable crowd, but singled out for notice by the lecturer at the end of his talk: he had been publicising the presence of 'Jane Eyre', and introduced her as such to one or two people, much to her discomfort. On the way out of the rooms, Charlotte had to pass through a bevy of admirers, whose deferential smiles made her tremble on her hostess's arm – but with what mixture of fear, anger and excitement it is not possible to say.

The next day she was taken to the season's unmissable wonder, the

Great Exhibition, brainchild of the Prince Consort. This brilliant showcase for British manufacturing, design and engineering drew enormous crowds to the jewel-like 'Crystal Palace' that had risen in the middle of Hyde Park; on the day that Charlotte first visited, she was awed to be among 'thirty thousand souls', a dreamlike swathe of humanity, among whom 'not one loud noise was to be heard – not one irregular movement seen – the living tide rolls on quietly – with a deep hum like the sea heard from a distance'. The Exhibition included items from all round the world and aspired to promote world peace – a consumerist answer to the spirit of 1848, perhaps – but the overall effect was triumphantly nationalistic and aggressively commercial, a mesmerising vision of the riches technology had already produced and the promise of more to come. 'The brightest colours blaze on all sides – and ware of all kinds – from diamonds to spinning jennies and Printing Presses are there to be seen,' Charlotte wrote home to her father. 'It was very fine – gorgeous – animated – bewildering':

> Whatever human industry has created – you find there – from the great compartments filled with Railway Engines and boilers, with Mill-machinery in full work – with splendid carriages of all kinds – with harness of every description – to the glass-covered and velvet spread stands loaded with the most gorgeous work of the goldsmith and silver-smith – and the carefully guarded caskets full of real diamonds and pearls worth hundreds of thousands of pounds.

Charlotte's protests that this sort of thing was 'not much in my way' seem surprising, not just because her description of its being 'a mixture of a Genii Palace and a mighty Bazaar' sounds so Angrian (Branwell Brontë would have been in heaven among the mixture of steam and gems) but also because she made five visits to the site during her three-week stay chez Smith. Was Charlotte thinking in terms of 'research' as much as of pleasure? The last of her visits was in the company of Sir David Brewster, the distinguished optics inventor* (and a friend of the Kay-Shuttleworths), who gave Charlotte a personal tour and explained the science behind many of the exhibits. She seems to have been enthralled (as well she might have been) by the lush beauty of many

---

* He had invented the kaleidoscope in 1816.

objects in Paxton's great glass halls: the fabrics, the silks, the Koh-i-noor diamond, the exiled French royal family (wandering around like any other bourgeois group there) and extraordinary novelties such as the bed that had an alarm fitted and tipped its occupant out at the appropriate hour – Thackeray should have one, she joked to George Smith, to help him finish *Henry Esmond*.

The idea of 'research' certainly seems to have been behind Charlotte's interest in gathering information in London that summer about the surge in popularity of Roman Catholicism (much promoted by the conversion of John Henry Newman in 1845 and the Oxford Movement to re-establish High Church traditions within the Church of England). Charlotte had seen and admired (while not agreeing wholeheartedly with her politics) the way in which Elizabeth Gaskell had addressed the plight of workers in the cotton trade in her first novel, *Mary Barton*, and she knew of Gaskell's work-in-progress, *Ruth*, which controversially dealt with the fate of 'fallen women' (among whom, as an urban minister's wife, Gaskell had done much charitable work). Dickens's effectiveness as a public educator was an even more impressive example, and perhaps Charlotte felt she too could use her position as a bestselling novelist to influence public opinion by featuring or dramatising the Catholic threat in her next book. On this 1851 visit to London, she attended a hardcore lecture on the subject by Jean-Henri Merle d'Aubigné, a French Protestant preacher; she also infiltrated a meeting of the Saint Vincent de Paul Society led by Cardinal Wiseman, of whom she sent a splenetic caricature to her father:

> he has not merely a double but a treble and quadruple chin; he has a very large mouth with oily lips, and looks as if he would relish a good dinner with a bottle of wine after it. He came swimming into the room smiling, simpering, and bowing like a fat old lady, and sat down very demure in his chair and looked the picture of a sleek hypocrite . . . All the speeches turned on the necessity of straining every nerve to make converts to popery. It is in such a scene that one feels what the Catholics are doing. Most perserving [*sic*] and enthusiastic are they in their work! Let Protestants look to it.

Charlotte was more of one mind (and voice) with her father here than over anything else in her life, and might well have thought it was an area in which she was qualified to speak. *Villette* didn't end up with much – or any – topical relevance, mostly because the action is set (as all Brontë's novels are) just out of range of the present day. But in the sheer amount of anti-Catholic polemic in the final volume of the novel, its hysterical nature (casting Madame Walravens, a grotesque dwarf, in the role of a papist witch) and its tenuous relevance to the plot one can perhaps see the relics of a different agenda.

That she was thinking about Constantin Heger in connection with her London excursions that summer is evident. It was 'strangely suggestive to hear the French language once more' at d'Aubigné's lecture, she told Ellen Nussey, and the very name of the Saint Vincent de Paul Society would have attracted her attention, since Monsieur Heger was a member of it.

George Smith was overworked and preoccupied during much of Charlotte's 1851 visit and left her to the care of his mother and sisters more than she would have chosen. As with James Taylor, she responded to signs of withdrawal with renewed tenacity, and as she sensed Smith treating her more and more like an aunt, so her spirits sank. Just as in *Villette*, when Lucy Snowe acknowledges the strength of her feelings for Dr John only when she feels them slipping away, Charlotte began both to mourn the loss of a never-realised love for George Smith and to cling to signs of what it had almost been. When they visited a phrenologist together in June (the interpretation of bumps on the skull being a highly fashionable pseudo-science of the day), it must have been hard not to bask in the conspiratorial closeness of everything to do with this lark, or to see significance not just in the 'readings' produced, but in the desire of Smith to have glimpses into the hidden depths of her character. They went to Dr Browne's studio on the Strand in the guise of a brother and sister, 'Mr and Miss Fraser'. Miss Fraser's head was 'very remarkable', the doctor's report concluded, exhibiting 'the presence of an intellect at once perspicacious and perspicuous'. Browne detected a nervous temperament and a warmly affectionate nature, but not a sentimental one. 'Her attachments are strong and enduring . . . Her sense of truth and justice would be offended by any dereliction of duty, and she would in such cases express her disapprobation with warmth and energy.'

Charlotte Brontë by George Richmond, 1850. The only professional image of Charlotte to have been done from life.

A faint pencil sketch of Arthur Bell Nicholls, 'when he first went to Haworth' (1845), very likely to have been made by Charlotte.

William Weightman, Reverend Brontë's charming curate, in about 1840. The drawing is attributed to Charlotte.

The dining room of Haworth Parsonage, where the Brontë sisters wrote their books, with the original table that they walked around while discussing their work together.

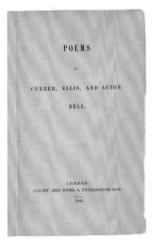

The autographs of Currer, Ellis and Acton Bell, provided for their first fan, Frederick Enoch of Warwick.

Title page of *Poems by Currer, Ellis and Acton Bell*, the sisters' spectacularly unsuccessful first book, published in 1846.

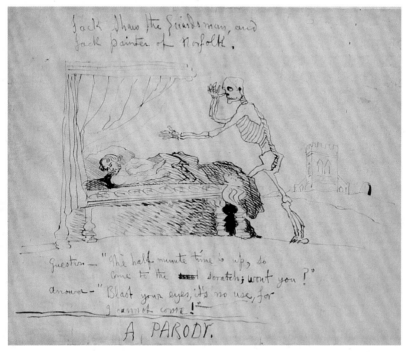

A Parody: Branwell's bleak cartoon showing himself being challenged by Death to a fight.

(*right*) Charlotte's charming young publisher, George Smith.

(*below*) William Smith Williams, Charlotte's valued editor and correspondent, *c.* 1860.

Charlotte and Anne reveal their identities to George Smith at his offices in Cornhill in July 1848, a scene imagined by Joan Hassall.

William Makepeace Thackeray.

Harriet Martineau.

Elizabeth Cleghorn
Gaskell, a chalk
drawing by George
Richmond, 1851.

Ellen Nussey in late middle age.

Carte-de-visite photograph dating from
1855–6, sometimes thought to be of Charlotte
Brontë, but more likely to be Ellen Nussey.

Margaret Wooler in her later years.

Mary Taylor in late middle age.

A carte-de-visite photograph of Arthur Bell Nicholls, *c.* 1864.

Patrick Brontë in old age, showing the steely regard Mrs Gaskell noted.

Crowds surging up Church Lane in Haworth on the day that the Parsonage opened as the Brontë Museum in 1928. The building in the background is the church school, erected in 1832.

Jane Eyre

by Currer Bell

~ol. 1 ~

Chap. 1ˢᵗ

There was no possibility of taking a walk that day.
We had been wandering indeed in the leafless shrubbery
an hour in the morning, but since dinner (Mrs Reed,
when there was no company, dined early) the cold winter
wind had brought with it clouds so sombre, a rain so penetrating that further out-door exercise was now out of the
question.

I was glad of it; I never liked long walks – especially
on chilly afternoons; dreadful to me was the coming home
in the raw twilight with nipped fingers and toes and a heart
saddened by the chidings of Bessie, the nurse, and humbled
by the consciousness of my physical inferiority to Eliza, John
and Georgiana Reed.

The said Eliza, John and Georgiana were now clustered
round their mamma in the Drawing-room; she lay reclin-

The first page of Charlotte's fair copy of *Jane Eyre*, 1847.

She is sensitive and is very anxious to succeed in her undertakings, but is not so sanguine as to the probability of success . . . [she] should guard against the effect of this where her affection is engaged, for her sense of her own importance is moderate and not strong enough to steel her heart against disappointment.

George Smith read this 'estimate' a short while later when Charlotte sent it on to him, but whatever he made of its revelations he kept to himself, and his benevolence, like that of Dr John in *Villette*, remained at one remove from its object. Charlotte adopted a much warmer tone in her correspondence with him in the autumn of 1851, but he did not respond in kind, just as, when he took Charlotte to see the great tragedian Rachel (the stage name of Eliza Félix) act in Scribe and Legouvé's *Adrienne Lecouvreur* and as Camille in Corneille's *Horace*, he seemed unwilling to submit to the power of the actress's art in the way that Charlotte did. It was as if he was consciously holding back from the meeting of minds and spirits that she sensed was possible and had begun to crave.

Charlotte's instinct was to proceed cautiously; she could of course not judge the validity of her own hopes and expectations. But it is strange to see her, in July 1851, imposing on herself exactly the sort of restrictions Constantin Heger had once demanded. 'Before I received your last,' she wrote to Smith, 'I had made up my mind to tell you that I should expect no letters from Cornhill for three months to come (intending afterwards to extend the abstinence to six months for I am jealous of becoming dependent on this indulgence – you – doubtless cannot see why, because you do not live my life.) – Nor shall I now *expect* a letter – but since you say that you would like to write now and then – I cannot say *never write*.'

She seems again to have been thinking of her experience with Heger when she made clear to Smith, later that autumn, that whatever else happened, she felt she had earned a permanent right to part of his attention. To Smith this can only have seemed inappropriately demanding, and he turned a blind eye to it, preferring a tacit continuation of business as usual with his intense and needy author. 'Can I help wishing you well when I owe you directly or indirectly most of the good moments I now enjoy?' she wrote to him in September, in apology for not feeling able to oblige him by writing her next novel in serial form:

You do not know – you *cannot* know how strongly [Currer Bell's] nature inclines him to adopt suggestions coming from so friendly a quarter; how he would like to take them up – cherish them – give them form – conduct them to a successful issue; and how sorrowfully he turns away feeling in his inmost heart that this work – this pleasure is not for him.

But though Currer Bell cannot do this – you are still to think him your friend – and you are still to be *his* friend. You are to keep a fraction of yourself – if it be only the end of your little finger – for *him*, and that fraction he will neither let gentleman or lady . . . take possession of – or so much as meddle with. He reduces his claim to a minute point – and that point he monopolises.

One 'minute point', under these terms, was of course a vast commitment. Well disposed as he was, generous, gregarious and gentlemanly to a fault, George Smith could never submit to it. By making this ostensibly minimal demand, Charlotte had unwittingly written the relationship's death sentence.

14

The Curate's Wife

1851–5

Charlotte's fast-growing friendship with Elizabeth Gaskell was the most rewarding of all she made in the years following her sisters' deaths, despite their difference in religion (an issue Gaskell, as a Dissenter, was always sensitive to). Charlotte's first visit to the Gaskells' home in the summer of 1851 was brief – just a couple of days on the way back to Haworth from London – but assured Charlotte of a warm welcome there in the future, and by 1853 the two women had come to a friendly understanding that whenever Charlotte craved society and Elizabeth quiet, they would know where to turn. The Gaskells' home at 42 Plymouth Grove was a large, airy villa in the Victoria Park area 'quite out of Manchester Smoke', with a large garden and orchard and French windows that were kept open all the long summer days (though it was one of William Gaskell's indulgences also to keep a fire blazing in his study whatever the weather). The Gaskells' four charming daughters, Marianne, Meta, Florence and Julia, flitted through the house; seven-year-old Julia Gaskell was Charlotte's particular favourite, and she observed the little girl's beauty and sprightliness with a strange awe – more like one child with a crush on another than an adult acquaintance (a covert doting very much like Lucy Snowe's attitude to Paulina in *Villette*). When she tried to explain this feeling to Elizabeth Gaskell a year or so later, she said the girls made her feel like 'a fond but bashful suitor who views at a distance the fair personage to whom – in his clownish awe – he dare not risk a near approach.' '[T]o what children am I not a stranger?' she said, as if she had never been one herself. 'They seem to me little wonders – their talk – their ways are all matter of half-admiring – half-puzzled speculation.'

Elizabeth Gaskell had written her first novel, *Mary Barton*, during 1846, at the same time as Charlotte had been staying in Manchester with her father for his eye operation. Her husband had suggested writing as a distraction after the death of their only son the previous year, and her subsequent career as a novelist had been conducted under the full demands of a very busy domestic life, extensive social work connected with William Gaskell's ministry (Cross Street Unitarian Chapel, in the centre of the city, was one of Manchester's most thriving churches) and an enthusiastic pursuit of literary friendships, which included Dickens, the Carlyles, the Arnolds and the Brownings. Gaskell was also a friend of the philanthropist Angela Burdett-Coutts, and of the Nightingale family, and was an indefatigable letter-writer to them all. Charlotte looked with amazement on her friend's life of activity; she could never match it, but it provided a valuable example of what was possible for a normally energetic and healthy woman to achieve and showed that a disciplined but lonely regime like Harriet Martineau's was not the only way to pursue a writing career.

The winter of 1851/2 was, however, spent more at home than away. Charlotte's health was very poor the whole season, with a long-lasting bilious condition that was made much worse by mercury poisoning from a medicine prescribed for it. Her spirits were also very low, not just because her book was progressing slowly and with difficulty, but because, for all the excitement of her new friendships, her essential loneliness seemed to have hardened and grown. She had invitations from the Gaskells, the Kay-Shuttleworths, Harriet Martineau and George Smith, but, in her depressed state, found the contrast between one mode of life and another too difficult to accommodate, as she tried to explain to Smith:

> What is it you say about my breaking the interval between this and Christmas by going from home for a week? No – if there were no other objection – (and there are many) there is the pain of that last bidding good-bye – that hopeless shaking hands – yet undulled – and unforgotten. I don't like it. I could not bear its frequent repetition. Do not recur to this plan. Going to London is a mere palliative and stimulant: reaction follows.

When the anniversary of Emily's death came round again, she made sure that Ellen Nussey came for a visit and that she could have the comfort of sharing a bed with someone, a reminder of her sisters' warmth and love, and the 'calm sleep' that went with it. Keeper had died that month, in enfeebled old age. People had suggested both to Charlotte and to her father that the blind old dog should be put down, but neither had the heart to hasten by a single minute the departure of this last link to Emily.

Charlotte was also disturbed by the breaking off of relations with James Taylor, who by May 1852 had been in India almost a year and had written to her only twice. Having applied confidentially to Williams for his opinion of the man's character, she had been unhappy to learn that Taylor was thought by his colleagues to be volatile and argumentative; her subsequent letters to him in Bombay were stiff and formal, almost guaranteeing an end to their friendship. 'I am not sure myself that any other termination would be better than lasting estrangement and unbroken silence,' she wrote to Ellen (who had tactfully stopped inquiring about this particular person of interest), 'yet a good deal of pain has been and must be gone through in that case.' She hated abandonment, even by a man to whom she was not very attached.

The painstaking return in memory to the sights, sounds and events of 1842–3 that Charlotte was living day to day in the composition of *Villette* also took its toll. The book – so different in mood from *The Professor* as to seem like the same story written by two entirely different people – was far more explicit, forensic even, about her feelings for Constantin Heger (and for George Smith). But it was the underlying feelings, the loveless condition from which Lucy emerges and lapses back into, that gave the book its grim power, the unexplained hopelessness at the base of her existence, so closely reflecting Charlotte's deprived and bereaved state since the deaths of Emily and Anne and her own fears of dying. All her life's suffering went into *Villette*, a cumulative account, as one of the reviewers, in *The Examiner*, later seemed to guess: 'we find it difficult to disconnect from [the book] a feeling of the bitterness of experience actually undergone, and that a real heart throbs at such times under the veil of Lucy Snowe.' Indeed, Lucy's tides of feeling flow as near to despair as a believer can go:

> A sorrowful indifference to existence often pressed on me – a despairing resignation to reach betimes the end of all things earthly. Alas! When I had full leisure to look on life as life must be looked on by such as me, I

found it but a hopeless desert: tawny sands, with no green field, no palm-tree, no well in view.

'[I]s there nothing more for me in life?' Lucy asks herself, when the hope of love has been indisputably removed, 'nothing to be dearer to me than myself?' 'Very good. I see a huge mass of my fellow-creatures in no better circumstances.' Her conclusion constitutes an alternative Creed: 'I believe in some blending of hope and sunshine sweetening the worst lots. I believe that this life is not all; neither the beginning nor the end. I believe while I tremble; I trust while I weep.'

Charlotte had given up the idea – obviously discussed with Smith and Williams at some point – of bringing explicit topical interest to the book; her great contemporaries in that field were too intimidatingly good. 'I cannot write books handling the topics of the day,' she warned her publisher, 'it is of no use trying. Nor can I write a book for its moral – Nor can I take up a philanthropic scheme though I honour Philanthropy – And voluntarily and sincerely veil my face before such a mighty subject as that handled in Mrs Beecher Stowe's work – "Uncle Tom's Cabin".'* *Villette* could never pretend to such seriousness, she felt; besides, the book had gathered its own peculiar momentum and unity of purpose. It travelled inward, not outward. But by choosing this unusual path, Charlotte Brontë ended up addressing public interest of a new sort and the preoccupations of the coming age. *Villette*, forged from such personal and painful material, reached psychological depths never attempted in fiction before and became, unwittingly, a landmark in the depiction of states of mind and self-perception, a thoroughly, peculiarly and disturbingly *Modernist* novel.

That summer Charlotte did not visit the Smiths in London but went on her own to the seaside instead, taking her unfinished manuscript with her. She felt guilty about not informing Ellen of her trip – or suggesting they went together – but there were private reasons for wanting to be alone. As well as working on her novel, Charlotte intended to

---

* Harriet Beecher Stowe's landmark novel, published in March 1852, was reputed to have sold more than a million copies in England that year, 'nearly all of them pirated'. CB had read the book by September, when she recommended it to EN (*LCB* 3, 67 and 68 n2).

make a pilgrimage to Anne's grave in Scarborough (coinciding with the anniversary of her death) and to inspect the stone that she had ordered in 1849 but never seen. There were five errors on it, a shameful mess in the sorrowing sister's eyes, almost like proofs from Newby. Stricken by feelings of negligence, she ordered the corrections to be made immediately.

Charlotte went on to Filey, to the same lodging house where she and Ellen had stayed after Anne's death, and spent a melancholy month there, going on coastal walks (or 'trudges', as she described them cheerlessly), bathing once in the sea and attempting to recruit her strength. 'The Sea is very grand,' she wrote to her father. 'Yesterday it was a somewhat unusually high tide – and I stood about an hour on the cliffs yesterday afternoon – watching the tumbling in of great tawny turbid waves – that made the whole shore white with foam and filled the air with a sound hollower and deeper than thunder.' It was cold and lonely, and her thoughts went back to Anne's death, and to anxieties about Martha and her father, both of whom had been ill. She also thought about Mr Nicholls: when she was at church in Filey, an absurd bit of shuffling about by the choir and congregation (when both ended up facing away from the pulpit during a hymn) had almost managed to amuse her, and she knew it would have amused him. '[H]ad Mr. Nicholls been there – he certainly would have laughed out,' she told her father, asking at the end of her letter to be remembered kindly to that person.

The autumn came and *Villette* was still unfinished. Aware of Smith's expectations to publish a new work by Currer Bell as soon as possible (it was three years since the appearance of *Shirley*), she sent him the first two volumes on their own, longing to know what he thought – 'not that I am likely to alter anything', she cautioned. Smith must have been consternated to find that the new novel returned so doggedly to the material of *The Professor*, and was a book of such sombreness and negativity. He had queries about the flow of the narrative and the consistency of the characterisation (as well he might have – both are extremely confusing) and can't have failed to recognise, and been perturbed by, the portraits of himself and his mother contained in Charlotte's characterisation of Dr John Graham Bretton and Mrs Bretton, and the inclusion of scenes (such as the fire in the theatre) lifted whole from his own experience. His curiosity about how the plot was going to end, therefore, had a very personal slant. Was his bestselling author about to publish a love story in which they were married off to each other at the end? Charlotte's précis of the third volume was a form of covert reassurance:

> Lucy must not marry Dr John; he is far too youthful, handsome, bright-spirited and sweet-tempered; he is a 'curled darling' of Nature and of Fortune; he must draw a prize in Life's Lottery; his wife must be young, rich and pretty; he must be made very happy indeed. If Lucy marries anybody – it must be the Professor – a man in whom there is much to forgive – much to 'put up with'. But I am not leniently disposed towards Miss Frost* – from the beginning I never intended to appoint her lines in pleasant places.

Smith would also have been troubled by Charlotte's hope that the new novel might be published anonymously, in an attempt to claw back the freedom she had felt when writing *Jane Eyre*. 'If the witholding of the author's name should tend materially to injure the publisher's interest – to interfere with booksellers' orders &c. I would not press the point; but if no such detriment is contingent – I should be most thankful for the sheltering shadow of an incognito,' she wrote to him when she sent the first two volumes. 'I seem to dread the advertisements – the large lettered "Currer Bell's New Novel" or "New Work by the Author of 'Jane Eyre'". These, however, I feel well enough are the transcendental-isms of a retired wretch.' This is the most explicit evidence of how Charlotte's fame had begun to oppress her, and of how much the tragic story of Emily's and Anne's short lives and early deaths, as revealed in her 1850 edition of their novels, had worked on public opinion. She did not wish to be 'consumed' by a public hungry for celebrities. But the name of 'Currer Bell' was too valuable for Smith to put by, and, unsurprisingly, he insisted on using it.

Had the hope that she would be allowed to 'walk invisible' again in *Villette* affected the way Charlotte wrote the book? It is certainly the

---

* CB changed the name of her protagonist from Lucy Snowe to Lucy Frost and back again while writing *Villette*.

most explicitly personal of all her works, laying out scenes and characters in direct imitation of real ones, which would be instantly
recognisable to anyone of her acquaintance. Her trips to the theatre, to
the Conservatoire concert, to the Salon Exhibition, the fête in the park,
and of course the whole layout and organisation of the Pensionnat are
put into the novel unedited and unabridged, with the flavour of meticulously recalled memories. Their artificiality in the novel would be truly
evident only to the novelist – her friends would of course mostly see a
peculiarly thorough form of self-exposure. Thackeray read it as straight
autobiography, writing to his young friend Lucy Baxter,

> it amuses me to read the author's naïve confession of being in love with
> 2 men at the same time; and her readiness to fall in love at *any* time. The
> poor little woman of genius! the fiery little eager brave tremulous
> homely-faced creature! I can read a great deal of her life as I fancy in her
> book, and see that rather than have fame rather than any other earthly
> good or mayhap heavenly one she wants some Tomkins or another to
> love her and be in love with. But you see she is a little bit of a creature
> without a penny worth of good looks, thirty years old I should think
> buried in the country, and eating up her own heart there, and no Tom-
> kins will come.

Unknown to him, of course, Charlotte Brontë had her very own Tom-
kins resident in Haworth – but whether she craved him as Thackeray
imagined was another matter.

Charlotte sent off the last volume of *Villette* to Cornhill on
20 November 1852, but then had to endure a long silence from Smith.
Did he hate the ending – did he hate the whole book? On 1 December
she could bear the wait no longer and wrote directly to ask him, only
to have several more days' anxiety before his reply finally arrived. He
had more cavils about the focus of the story, complaining about the
'transfer of interest' from one group of characters to another at the end
(and the introduction of the new romance with Monsieur Paul). Again
Charlotte said she agreed with him, but did nothing to change her
manuscript. Her only significant adjustment at this stage was to switch
the heroine's surname.

The most tangible sign of Smith's disappointment in the novel was
his offer of only £500 for the copyright, when Charlotte, and her

father, had expected an increase on that sum, the same as for *Jane Eyre* and *Shirley*. But Smith clearly did not expect a runaway success, either in terms of sales or of reviews. Currer Bell's public all longed for a reprise of the *Jane Eyre* thrill, and *Villette*, for all its power, was unable to supply that.

Released from the labour of finishing her book, Charlotte allowed herself to think of another trip to London of a few weeks, to coincide with the correction of proofs and to see the book through to publication. Not knowing she was about to be depicted in Charlotte's new novel, Mrs Smith had held open an invitation and a date was set for the new year. Charlotte prepared by buying new bonnets and dress materials in Leeds and having the errant 1850 hairpiece 'rearranged' – 'it is now a very different matter to the bushy, tasteless thing it was before.' But before the trip could go ahead, and two weeks before Christmas 1852, Charlotte was completely taken by surprise and the household thrown into turmoil by a drama unfolding rapidly at the Parsonage. She wrote to Ellen about it two days later, wondering if her friend had had any intimation that Arthur Bell Nicholls was in love with her, since she, not being able to *see* clearly, she said, had not understood the significance of his gestures and looks, beyond 'dim misgivings'. Papa, for all his physical blindness, seems to have picked up much more of what had been passing (as he had with James Taylor) and had noticed 'with little sympathy and much indirect sarcasm' the curate's recent low spirits and threats to leave Haworth.

On the evening of 13 December, the three of them had been taking tea in Reverend Brontë's study and Charlotte 'vaguely felt ... the meaning of [Nicholls's] constant looks – and strange, feverish restraint'. As usual, she left the two men alone after a while and retired to the dining room. Between eight and nine o'clock, she heard the study door open and expected it to be followed by the sound of the front door shutting, but instead there was a hesitation, the sound of a silent curate hovering in the hall, and then a gentle tap at the dining-room door.

> like lightning it flashed on me what was coming. He entered. He stood before me. What his words were – you can guess; his manner – you can hardly realize – nor can I forget it – Shaking from head to foot, looking

deadly pale, speaking low, vehemently yet with difficulty – he made me for the first time feel what it costs a man to declare affection when he doubts response . . . He spoke of sufferings he had borne for months – of sufferings he could endure no longer – and craved leave for some hope.

Nicholls was not just in love, but painfully so, and the spectacle of 'one ordinarily so statue-like – thus trembling, stirred, and overcome' was astonishing to Charlotte, who had no idea that he was capable of such passion. Her sympathy flared up at the thought of how he must have suffered in silence for so long; and it was as a fellow victim of a one-sided passion, rather than as someone in love *with her*, that her heart went out to him. But of course she did not encourage this sudden suit. Whatever her feelings for him at this point (and they were not ardent), the interview gave her 'a strange shock': 'I could only entreat him to leave me then and promise a reply on the morrow. I asked if he had spoken to Papa. He said – he dared not – I think I half-led, half put him out of the room.'

Nicholls's fear of speaking to Mr Brontë on this topic was fully justified, as Charlotte discovered when she went into the study as soon as Nicholls left and reported what had taken place:

Agitation and Anger disproportionate to the occasion ensued – if I had *loved* Mr. N— and had heard such epithets applied to him as were used – it would have transported me past my patience – as it was – my blood boiled with a sense of injustice – but Papa worked himself into a state not to be trifled with – the veins on his temples started up like whip-cord – and his eyes became suddenly blood-shot – I made haste to promise that Mr. Nicholls should on the morrow have a distinct refusal.

The symptoms of imminent apoplexy put an end to any debate. Charlotte had been told by the doctor just a few months earlier that her father's blood pressure was so high that any 'rush to the brain' would 'almost be to kill him at once'. But in her careful noting of Papa's symptoms, one senses Charlotte's shifting sympathies, away from his incontinent display of selfishness and towards her own feelings and judgements, which she had never abandoned of course, but which were so habitually subordinated to those of her parent.

There followed a period of dreadful turmoil in the Parsonage, with

Patrick Brontë fuming and furious on one side, Nicholls distraught and desperate on the other, and Charlotte stuck in the middle. As soon as he understood the strength of the vicar's disapproval, Nicholls resigned and promised to leave Haworth by the following May, but the amount of 'turbulence of feeling' produced in the interim consternated Charlotte, since it had so little to do with *her*. Meanwhile she was forced to listen to her father's constant outbursts of indignation against the curate: 'He just treats him with a hardness not to be bent – and a contempt not to be propitiated.'

When the cause of the trouble was known around the Parsonage, Charlotte was sorry to find that she was the only person to pity Mr Nicholls. Martha was 'bitter against him' (probably thinking no one was good enough for Miss Brontë), while Martha's father, John Brown the sexton, said he wanted to shoot him – uncomfortable for Nicholls, as Brown was his landlord. 'They don't understand the nature of his feelings,' Charlotte explained to Ellen, indicating the way her own were changing subtly as people around her ganged up. 'Mr. N is one of those who attach themselves to very few, whose sensations are close and deep – like an underground stream, running strong but in a narrow channel.'

Early in the new year Nicholls made an inquiry to the Society for the Propagation of the Gospel, offering his services abroad as a missionary. Any idea that this was a touch of melodrama on Nicholls's part is scotched by the degree of commitment such an application required, with a full account from the candidate of his qualifications and intentions and four testimonials witnessing to his character and achievements. One of these, unfortunately, had to be elicited from the man he had just incensed, who wrote a fair but tight-lipped letter, clearly intended to speed the removal of the offender to some remote part of the globe: 'He is very discreet, is under no pecuniary embarrassment, that I am aware of, nor is he, I think, likely to be so, since, in all pecuniary and other matters, as far as I have been able to discover, he is wary, and prudent.' The qualifications here seem as prominent as the statements.

Nicholls did rather better from his other referees, who all praised his exceptional zeal and ability, especially in the management of the school, and the vicar of Bradford added that Nicholls had worked wonders in a parish so full of 'a rude, and dissenting population' that his work 'has nearly approached that of a missionary' already.

Charlotte felt her father was glad for once to pack her off to London at the end of January, and the Smiths thought her more animated than usual, without knowing why. She asserted herself more too, asking not to go much into society or on pleasure trips to the theatre et cetera, but to be taken to places illustrating 'rather the *real* than the *decorative* side of Life' – Newgate and Pentonville prisons, the Bank of England, the Bethlehem Hospital (the asylum for the insane known as Bedlam), the Stock Exchange and the Foundling Hospital. 'Mrs S[mith] and her daughters are – I believe – a little amazed at my gloomy tastes, but I take no notice.' Having decided that she could not write on 'matters of public interest' without giving them proper study, and with *Villette* behind her, perhaps Charlotte was thinking of future material – if so, it seems as if it might have strayed over into Dickens's territory. At Newgate (a site that Dickens had used in *Sketches by Boz*, *Oliver Twist* and, most recently, *Barnaby Rudge*), George Smith recalled Miss Brontë quickly fixing her attention on an individual prisoner: 'There was a poor girl with an interesting face, and an expression of the deepest misery. She had, I believe, killed her illegitimate child. Miss Brontë walked up to her, took her hand, and began to talk to her. She was, of course, quickly interrupted by the prison warder with the formula "Visitors are not allowed to speak to the prisoners."'

Charlotte was in town when *Villette* was published on 28 January 1853, to widespread and for the most part very laudatory reviews. Charlotte reported to Ellen that she had received seven good notices on two consecutive days in February, enough 'to make my heart swell with thankfulness to Him who takes note both of suffering and work and motives – Papa is pleased too.' The reviewer in the *Literary Gazette* acknowledged the book's strange evanescent qualities, the trance-like movement between states of mind rather than scenes, by saying 'It must be read continuously, – we had almost said, studied, before its finest qualities can be appreciated', while G. H. Lewes brought weight to bear in the *Leader* with resounding praise that delighted the author: 'In Passion and Power – those noble twins of Genius – Currer Bell has no living rival, except George Sand. Hers is the passionate heart to feel, and the powerful brain to give feeling shape; and that is why she is so original, so fascinating.'

'Currer Bell might have called her new novel "Passages from the Life of a Teacher in a Girls' School at Brussels, written by herself"',' said the *Spectator*, drolly acknowledging the almost plodding drabness of the plot, and how little the plot mattered among so many 'violent emotions of the heart'. That Charlotte had wondered how the book would be received in Brussels is clear from the fact that she tried to retain control over any possible translation of it into French; but, while she waited to see if there was any response from the rue d'Isabelle, she became aware of the amusing effect her portrait of Monsieur Paul was having elsewhere. Several letters reached her, via Smith, Elder, from women wanting to know more about the fate of the harsh, demanding, secretly honourable and devoted Master. 'You see how much the ladies think of this little man whom none of you like,' she teased Williams. One correspondent who had previously determined to marry only the counterpart of Mr Knightley (from Jane Austen's *Emma*) 'now . . . vowed that she would either find the duplicate of Professor Emanuel or remain forever single!!!'

The focus on Lucy's hunger for sexual love, so desperately and unconventionally aimed first at Dr John and then at Monsieur Paul, did not escape notice or censure, most prominently from Harriet Martineau, whose review in the *Daily News* was one of the first to appear. She had written privately in advance to Charlotte, who, for all her talk of welcoming criticism of her novel, was upset that Martineau disliked the treatment of love in it, 'either the kind or the degree'. In her printed review, Martineau expanded this theme, pointing out, with some justice, the disservice it did to women to represent them as such abject slaves to one emotion. Charlotte reacted in her most high-falutin manner. Having made such a show of championing Miss Martineau against critics of her atheism, she felt she was owed more loyalty than this. Before the review even appeared, she remonstrated with Martineau: 'I know what love is as I understand it – & if man or woman shd. feel ashamed of feeling such love – then there is nothing right, noble, faithful, truthful, unselfish on this earth as I comprehend rectitude, nobleness, fidelity, truth & disinterestedness.' It is strange that Charlotte tried to represent in such a heroic light her anatomy of desire and not 'love' but love *sickness*, so brilliantly but unheroically depicted in Lucy Snowe's haunted, hungry soul.

There were other, fiercer, critics, whose opinions Charlotte never got to hear. Matthew Arnold hated the book because it dealt too clearly with a malaise among middle-class women – their frustrations and unanswered desires in both love and the world – which he did not like to contemplate: 'the writer's mind contains nothing but hunger, rebellion and rage, and therefore that is all she can, in fact put into her book.' But it was exactly this power to discomfit people that made Charlotte's work valuable to others. The very elements that made Arnold avert his eyes made George Eliot (yet to publish any novels herself) think *Villette* 'a still more wonderful book than *Jane Eyre*. There is something almost preternatural in its power.' '*Villette – Villette –*' she wrote a month later, 'have you read it?'

Arthur Bell Nicholls had chosen his time to declare himself shrewdly. No doubt he had waited deliberately until Charlotte's novel, so long in the making, was finished and sent off to London, knowing how preoccupied she would be until then and unreceptive to his suit. Not knowing the contents of the book, he could not have guessed how much it related to questions of choices in love, right and wrong desires and decisions. When she went down to London to oversee the correction of proofs and wait for the book's reception, Charlotte had plenty of time to think about Nicholls in this powerful new light and wonder what her experience of love had come to up to this point; where she should have been looking for it, and where she might have found it.

Her father's hysterical letters to her from home showed a bizarre assumption that, on the subject of her suitor, they thought as one. Nicholls, he felt sure, had exposed his 'dangerous designs' and was no longer to be trusted: 'His conduct might have been excus'd by the world, in a confirmed rake – or unprincipled army officer, but in a *Clergyman*, it is justly chargeable, with base design and inconsistency . . . [I] wish that every woman may avoid him, forever, unless she should be determined on her own misery.' In case Charlotte hadn't got the message, he wrote another horribly cloying letter, in the character of Flossy, reporting on the seducer's 'manoeuvres' witnessed from a doggy vantage point: 'I see people cheating one another, and yet appearing to be friends – many are the disagreeable discoveries, which I make . . . Ah! My dear Mistress, trust dogs rather than men – They are very selfish, and when they have the power, (which no wise person will readily give them) very tyrannical.' Patrick Brontë clearly thought this clever and charming and the warning about tyrannical men not in the least bit applicable to himself.

Nicholls had been making anxious inquiries to the Society for the Propagation of the Gospel about the progress of his application, but towards the end of February asked if they could suspend the process indefinitely, as 'some doubts have occurred to me as to the desirability of leaving the country at present'. He seems to have decided to stand his ground – though not ground in Haworth: he had applied for a separate curacy at Kirk Smeaton, about twelve miles away and was to move there in June. In the meantime, his increasingly melancholic and erratic behaviour was causing gossip in the village. He was said to sit in his rooms alone for hours, or take his long face on glum solitary walks. When forced into the company of Reverend Brontë, he was surly and snappish and had caused raised eyebrows by his withdrawn manner when the Bishop came to stay in March. Charlotte had begun to worry about 'that dark gloom of his' and that he had followed her along the lane after church, also stopped her in the passageway on the Bishop evening, forcing a strategic retreat upstairs. Martha had noted his 'flay-some' looks on that occasion, and developed a very unflattering view of Nicholls's character. The only person he saw was his friend Sutcliffe Sowden, curate of Oxenhope, but he had spread no stories about his rebuff at the Parsonage; 'I own I respect him for this', Charlotte told Ellen.

> I pity him inexpressibly. We never meet nor speak – nor dare I look at him – silent pity is just all I can give him – and as he knows nothing about that – it does not comfort . . . alas! I do not know him well enough to be sure that there is truth and true affection – or only rancour and corroding disappointment at the bottom of his chagrin. In this state of things I must be and I am – *entirely passive*. I may be losing the purest gem – and to me far the most precious – life can give – genuine attachment – or I may be escaping the yoke of a morose temper – In this doubt conscience will not suffer me to take one step in opposition to Papas will – blended as that will is with the most bitter and unreasonable prejudices. So I just leave the matter where we must leave all important matters.

Charlotte felt powerless, but was hardly as entirely passive as she claims. Warned by her father so melodramatically about Nicholls's malignant temper and dark designs, she was on the look-out constantly for evidence to the contrary and, all through these uncomfortable months while he was waiting to leave Haworth, took the opportunity to assess his demeanour. She soon had proof of his feelings (and felt 'punished' for her doubts of him), when, on Whit Sunday, taking the communion service for the last time in Haworth, Nicholls lost control of himself in church and began to shake and falter when he saw Charlotte at the rail. '[He] stood before my eyes and in the sight of all the communicants white, shaking, voiceless.' The parish clerk had to have a word with him, but Nicholls could only whisper the rest of the service. Several ladies in the congregation were moved to tears by this spectacle, and Charlotte herself was almost overcome, but when Reverend Brontë heard of these shameless displays of sentimentalism, his response was to call Nicholls an 'unmanly driveller'. 'Compassion or relenting is no more to be looked for than sap from firewood,' Charlotte remarked bitterly to Ellen. A further point in Nicholls's favour was his refusal to suggest any criticism of Patrick Brontë when quizzed by curious parishioners, though Charlotte couldn't help noticing his continued chilliness towards her father in person. A snub at the school's tea-drinking was the sort of public discourtesy that she knew Papa would 'never . . . forget or forgive'. 'I am afraid both are unchristian in their mutual feelings,' Charlotte wrote sadly to Ellen, stuck in the middle of this battle of wills. 'Nor do I know which of them is least accessible to reason or least likely to forgive. It is a dismal state of things.'

Nicholls left Haworth on 27 May, having received a handsome gold watch from the parish and Sunday School in recognition of his eight years of service. Not surprisingly, Patrick Brontë found himself indisposed on the day of the presentation and did not attend. Nicholls delivered the deeds of the school to Reverend Brontë on the evening before his departure, but his hopes of seeing Charlotte to say goodbye were thwarted by her sitting room being occupied by the servants, who were washing down the paintwork. Charlotte didn't want to see Nicholls in her father's presence, so said she was not available; however, when she surreptitiously watched him leave the house for what he imagined was the last time, she noticed that he lingered near the garden gate, in obvious distress. Her heart went out to him:

> remembering his long grief I took courage and went out trembling and miserable. I found him leaning again[st] the garden-door in a paroxysm of anguish – sobbing as women never sob. Of course I went straight to him. Very few words were interchanged – those few barely articulate: several things I should have liked to ask him were swept entirely from my memory. Poor fellow! but he wanted such hope and such encouragement as I *could* not give him. Still I trust he must know now tha[t] I am not cruelly blind and indifferent to his constancy and grief.

Though Charlotte believed she could and had not encouraged Nicholls at this tender moment, he was made of sterner stuff, and clearly stored the scene away with renewed hope, however small. Charlotte, on the other hand, felt much worse at their parting, waking up as she was to her own feelings. She did not even know where Nicholls's new curacy was going to be, and saw no chance of hearing anything more about him, except through second-hand sources and gossip, the worst possible channels. She had to revert to her lonely life with her father, and, worst of all, witness his voluble relief at having routed the interloper, for, as she told Ellen, Patrick Brontë remained 'implacable' on the subject of the wily curate.

Following Nicholls's departure, Charlotte became ill with influenza, exacerbated by a continued headache and other nervous symptoms that left her so 'weak and bewildered' that she had to put off a visit by Elizabeth Gaskell that she had been looking forward to. Her father was also ill, and, despite his late shameful behaviour in relation to her, Charlotte's compassion and anxiety for him were still intact. When one evening she heard him call her name, she rose from her sickbed and found him 'strangely arrested' on the stairs, holding a candle but saying that he could see nothing. The old terror of losing his sight gripped both of them, and, though Patrick began to recover the next day, saying 'it seemed as if a thick curtain was gradually drawn up', the incident served to make any travel away from home impossible.

Ellen filled the need for companionship by coming to stay at the Parsonage in late June, but the visit proved an unhappy one for their friendship. Charlotte had a great deal to share about the distressing events of the past few months, and Nicholls's departure from Haworth. Her letters to Ellen about the proposal and its aftermath had, as ever, been frank and vivid, but may have veiled the intensity of her feelings, and her growing regrets that the relationship seemed to be over. All this became evident to Ellen when she saw her friend face to face, and she took it as signs of weakness and defection. Perhaps Charlotte had already received one of the 'very miserable' letters she later told Catherine Winkworth that Nicholls had written to her from exile, which she had answered by saying he must submit to his lot as well as he could. Nicholls carefully kept this line of communication open.

Charlotte certainly seemed to be thinking more sympathetically than ever of the former curate now that he was gone, and Ellen didn't like it. Ellen's misgivings about him as a potential husband for her friend are understandable: she had known Nicholls for the past eight years and didn't find him at all exciting – more to the point, Charlotte had hardly had a good word to say for him all that time. Having been privy to so many intimate conversations over the years, and the recipient of so many confiding letters, Ellen might well have felt the full force of Charlotte's inconsistency and been piqued or disturbed by it. It downgraded her own consistency and fidelity. Whatever the exact grounds for their falling-out, it is clear that she and Charlotte quarrelled seriously for the first time ever, either during her visit to Haworth in July 1853 or soon after, and no letters exist from this time until eight months later.

Simple jealousy must have also played its part in the rift, as Ellen knew she would be significantly sidelined if Charlotte fell in love or got married. At the age of thirty-six (she was one year younger than Charlotte almost to the day) Ellen had got used to the idea of being an old maid and wrote complainingly to Mary Taylor about Charlotte abandoning their supposed joint fate, and how she would be best off 'bearing her position' and 'enduring to the end' without Mr Nicholls disturbing everything. It was a pity that Charlotte couldn't have seen Mary Taylor's sharp reply: 'You talk wonderful nonsense abt C. Brontë in yr letter,' Mary scolded.

If its C's lot to be married shd n't she bear that too? or does your strange morality mean that she shd refuse to ameliorate her lot when it lies in her power. How wd. she be inconsistent with herself in marrying?

Because she considers her own pleasure? If this is so new for her to do, it is high time she began to make it more common. It is an outrageous exaction to expect her to give up her choice in a matter so important, & I think her to blame in having been hitherto so yielding that her friends can think of making such an impudent demand.

By the time this reached Birstall, in the summer of 1854, much of its force would have been spent; Mary knew that she was essentially talking out loud in her home above the shop she was running in Wellington, New Zealand, on the other side of the world. But what she lost in dialogue, she made up for in truth-telling.

Back when Ellen wrote to Mary, though, in the summer of 1853, Charlotte was becoming increasingly isolated herself. Arthur Nicholls had removed to Kirk Smeaton, Ellen was estranged, she had broken friends with Harriet Martineau and felt so much that her influence over George Smith was on the wane that she wrote to chide him over his negligence of her, making clear her own upset and anger: 'when you turn with distaste from the task of answering a friendly letter . . . let me just say, though I say it not without pain, a correspondence which has not interest enough in itself to sustain life – *ought* to die.' Pressure of work was insufficient explanation for the falling-off of Smith's correspondence since the publication of *Villette*. Had she heard somehow, or sensed, that his thoughts were elsewhere – that he had in fact fallen madly in love? For, in the months since her visit to London (which turned out to be her last), Smith had met young, lovely Elizabeth Blakeway, the woman he would propose to later that year.

With all the time in the world to be writing, Charlotte was doing very little. In the spring of 1853, with *Villette* successfully published, she made the surprising announcement to Elizabeth Gaskell that she was 'not going to write again for some time', though the next month, she wrote the fragments now known as 'The Story of Willie Ellen', a return to the theme of two rival brothers. It did not, however, get far – just a dozen or so pages.

After reading Elizabeth Gaskell's sprightly *Cranford* in July 1853 (and now knowing what a frenetically busy home life Gaskell managed as well as writing) she asked, 'Do you . . . find it easy, when you sit down to write – to isolate yourself from all those ties and their sweet associations – [so] as to be quite *your own woman* – uninfluenced, unswayed by the consciousness of how your work may affect other minds – what blame, what sympathy it may call forth? Does no luminous cloud come between you and the severe Truth – as you know it in your own secret and clear-seeing Soul?'

Deprived of her usual resource in Ellen, Charlotte went to stay with Miss Wooler in Hornsea in October, and accompanied Joe Taylor, his wife Amelia and baby 'Tim' (the nickname for their daughter) on a trip to Cumberland. She clearly felt at home neither with undiluted maiden-ladyhood nor with the young parents, and remained a sarcastic observer of the Taylors' fussy modern manners: 'Papa and Mamma could only take their meals, rest and exercise at such times and in such measure as the despotic infant permitted. While Mrs J. eat her dinner, Mr J – relieved guard as nurse. A nominal nurse indeed accompanied the party, but her place was a sort of anxious, waiting sinecure, as the child did not fancy her attendance.'

Elizabeth Gaskell's deferred first visit to Haworth in September was much more to Charlotte's taste and an opportunity to release herself into intimacy, for however brief a time. Gaskell wrote one of her headlong letters to John Forster soon after she got home to Plymouth Grove, crammed with details of her week at Currer Bell's home, the wild situation, the 'pestiferous' churchyard, with the graves peering over the wall of the Parsonage garden and the wind that half blew her back from the door. Everything within doors was warm and welcoming, though, and scrupulously clean and tidy; Miss Brontë was clearly very particular, and anything out of place would have annoyed her sense of order.

The romance of the place, and of Miss Brontë's tragic life, struck Gaskell very forcibly and seems to have excited in her the possibility of writing about it all one day. The extraordinary detail of her letter to Forster, and of those to other friends such as Catherine Winkworth and Emma Shaen on the same subject, certainly looks like the salting-down of impressions, and Gaskell did in fact use parts of her own letters almost verbatim in the biography she eventually wrote three years later. The essence of that book is already present in her description to Forster of the wind 'piping & wailing and sobbing round the square unsheltered house in a very strange unearthly way', of Mr Brontë's queer formality and habit of dining alone '(fancy it! only they two left)', of his habit of putting a loaded pistol in his pocket 'just as regularly as he puts on his watch. There was this little deadly pistol sitting down to breakfast with us, kneeling down to prayers at night – to say nothing of a loaded gun hanging up on high ready to pop off on the slightest emergency.' There was the sensual appeal of the place too, so evocative of the sisters' untamed spirits. 'Before tea we had a long, delicious walk,' Gaskell reported,

> right against the wind on Penistone Moor which stretches directly behind the Parsonage going over the hill in brown & purple sweeps and falling softly down into a little upland valley through which a 'beck' ran; & beyond again was another great waving hill, – and in the dip of that might be seen another yet more distant, & beyond that she said Lancashire came; but the sinuous hills seemed to girdle the world like the great Norse serpent, & for my part I don't know if they don't stretch up to the North Pole.

Elizabeth Gaskell wasn't to know it at this point, but Charlotte had taken her to her sisters' favourite spot, 'The Meeting of the Waters'. Coming back across the moor, Charlotte showed her some of the desolate farms and told stories that thrilled her friend, 'such wild tales of the ungovernable families, who lived or had lived therein that Wuthering Heights even seemed tame comparatively'. She also pointed out several newly built churches in the distance, places 'which her Irish curates see after'.

Having such an eager, intelligent friend was remarkably like a return of sibling warmth and affection, and the two women stayed up late talking every night, for Charlotte's life-circumstances fascinated her guest. Elizabeth Gaskell saw the family graves in the church and spoke to Tabby and to Martha about Emily and Anne, whose portrait by Branwell she was shown.

> Tabby says since they were little bairns Miss Brontë & Miss Emily & Miss Anne used to put away their sewing after prayers, [']& walk all three one after the other round the table in the parlour till near eleven o'clock. Miss Emily walked as long as she could; & when she died Miss Anne &

Miss Brontë took it up, – and now my heart aches to hear Miss Brontë walking, walking on alone.' And on enquiring I found that after Miss Brontë had seen me to my room, she did come down every night, & begin that slow monotonous incessant walk in which I am sure I should fancy I heard the steps of the dead following me.

Charlotte must have found comfort in having these sad secret habits shared at last with an astute and loving friend.

Charlotte confided in Elizabeth Gaskell about Arthur Nicholls too, and must have told her that he had come back to Haworth earlier that month, hoping to revive his suit, and that he had been writing to her occasionally. Although it disturbed Charlotte to be withholding this news from her father, she clearly welcomed the return of interest from Nicholls, and the chance to make up for the pain of his departure in June. Elizabeth Gaskell felt emboldened to go behind her back, when she returned to Manchester, with an initiative to improve Nicholls's income and prospects, and make him more appealing to Patrick Brontë as a son-in-law. Swearing him to secrecy, she enlisted the help of her friend Richard Monckton Milnes, who, in January 1854, under the auspices of the Vicar of Leeds, travelled to Kirk Smeaton to offer the curate two posts, one in Scotland and one in Lancashire. Milnes reported back to Mrs Gaskell that Charlotte Brontë's would-be spouse was 'a strong-built, somewhat hard-featured man, with a good deal of Celtic sentiment about his manner & voice – quite of the type of the Northern Irishmen', but that he had seemed despondent, 'sadly broken in health & spirits', and had refused both the proffered jobs. Nicholls was privately puzzled by the visit, as he had no idea who Milnes was, or that strings were being pulled on his behalf. But, putting two and two together, he must have been encouraged by the idea that his situation had been noted, and that Charlotte was somehow involved. He lost no time in pressing to be allowed to visit her again.

Charlotte received this renewal of Nicholls's suit in a very different mood from that of the previous year. She had, in effect, decided to marry him. In the intervening months between Elizabeth Gaskell's visit and Monckton Milnes's visit to Kirk Smeaton, Charlotte's unhappiness about George Smith had come to a head. His (relative) neglect of her all through 1853 made her suspicious that someone had taken over his affections, and she may have heard rumours about Miss Blakeway, for when she was planning a business trip to London in the autumn – ostensibly to sort out her investments, but cancelled casually, so perhaps it was not very urgent – she pointedly let him know she expected to stay in rented accommodation this time. When this provoked an ambiguous response, written on mourning stationery, Charlotte wrote to his mother for an explanation, and was told that the mourning was for an elderly relation, but hinted that George had joyous news to impart and bright prospects: indeed, he was going to be married.

Charlotte's response was not to her credit, but shows the degree to which she had deluded herself, both about her real feelings for Smith (not sisterly at all) and about the reasonableness of being able to monopolise a part, however small, of his heart, as she had demanded. That she felt betrayed by his engagement is clear from the curt and ambiguously worded note that she sent: 'My dear Sir, In great happiness, as in great grief – words of sympathy should be few. Accept my meed of congratulation – and believe me Sincerely yours, C. Brontë .' Worse still, she felt impelled to send Williams an even more offensive message, sending back one of the firm's generous boxes of books with the wish that he not trouble to send any more. 'These courtesies must cease some day – and I would rather give them up than wear them out.' Smith of course understood the subtext of these letters very well: he made an acute reference to them fifty years later in his 'Recollections' when he said that Miss Brontë 'afterwards wrote more at length on the same subject, when informing me of her engagement to Mr Nicholls'.

So Charlotte's change of heart towards Nicholls, or rather towards marriage with him, had an air of calculation about it, of assessing what her options were in a changed landscape. Once she had made up her mind, the obstacles that seemed so insuperable before fell away with relative ease. The main one was of course Papa's consent, to which end Charlotte challenged him with quiet but irresistible force, as she recounted to Elizabeth Gaskell later, who found the imagined scene 'really fine': 'She said "Father I am not a young girl, not a young woman even – I never was pretty. I now am ugly. At your death I shall have 300£ besides the little I have earned myself – do you think there are many men who would serve seven years for me?' To his renewed objections about Nicholls's unworthiness and lack of status, she said, 'I must marry a curate if I marry at all; not merely a curate but *your* curate', adding that since she could never leave her father, they would all need to live together in one house. This was meant to be conciliatory, but Patrick Brontë's pride was stung to the quick. He refused point blank to consider having 'another man in this house', stalked out of the room and wouldn't talk to his daughter for a week. Only when poor old ill Tabby confronted him with the harm he was doing to Charlotte, and asked 'if he wished to kill his daughter?', did the intransigent old man begin to reconsider.

Nicholls had permission then to come to stay for ten days with his friend Sowden at Oxenhope and walk over every day to meet Charlotte. This was the first time, after almost nine years' acquaintance, that they had the opportunity to get to know each other closely. Nicholls's ardour and faithfulness were very touching, and his willingness to do whatever was necessary to consider the needs of Reverend Brontë won Charlotte's especial admiration. At times he must have wondered which of the two – father or daughter – was being courted. By early April 1854, Charlotte was able to tell Ellen, in the first letter since their quarrel the previous July, that her father's consent had at last been gained, and some degree of respect too: 'for Mr. Nicholls has in all things proved himself disinterested and forbearing. He has shewn too that while his feelings are exquisitely keen – he can freely forgive. Certainly I must respect him – nor can I withhold from him more than mere cool respect. In fact, dear Ellen, I am engaged.' The humorous throwaway is similar to Jane Eyre's famous announcement of her happy ending, *Reader, I married him*, but the degree of passion behind it startlingly different.

When Nicholls proposed the first time, it had only been the parallel with her own one-sided passion for Heger that shocked Charlotte into the recognition that his secret feelings might merit her attention. She remained quite detached and resolutely unsentimental (in accounts to friends at least) all through her engagement. When she went to visit Elizabeth Gaskell in May, Charlotte had a long intimate talk with Catherine Winkworth about her situation and told her, '[I]t has cost me a good deal to come to this . . . I cannot conceal from myself that he is *not* intellectual; there are many places into which he could not follow me intellectually.' Then when 'Lily' (Mrs Gaskell) came in, she said again that, though she felt very confident about Nicholls's reliability and love for her, she feared that 'such a character would be far less amusing and interesting than a more impulsive and fickle one; it might be dull!' The creator of Edward Rochester and Paul Emanuel might well say so. It made the two other women uncomfortable to hear Miss Brontë talk so baldly about her husband-to-be, and Catherine attempted to lighten the moment by saying that Charlotte would at least have the chance to 'do the fickleness' herself, which made them all laugh. Charlotte sounded even less enamoured when she explained her feelings to Ellen: 'I am still very calm – *very* – inexpectant,' she said, employing a suitably peculiar word. 'Providence offers me this destiny. Doubtless then it is the best for me.'

It is clear that Patrick Brontë must have pictured Nicholls as a sort of gold-digger, or Charlotte would not have made such careful provision in a marriage settlement dated 24 May 1854 to protect her assets from her husband. This pre-nuptial arrangement was devised to circumvent the normal fate of a married woman's property at that date, which was to fall to the husband's control; Charlotte's money – a tidy sum of £1,678.9s.9d., derived from her earnings as a writer and the residue of Aunt Branwell's legacies – was to be ring-fenced for her sole use during her lifetime and left to her father if she predeceased Nicholls without issue. This left Nicholls with no claim on her money whatever, and that he agreed to the scheme willingly proves how disinterested his motives in marrying Charlotte really were. One hopes Patrick Brontë felt uncomfortable at the sight. Joe Taylor was to be the sole trustee.

At home in Haworth, waiting to be married, Charlotte existed in a lonely, abstract state, just at a time when she might have hoped to be feeling happy and triumphant. Relief at placating her father and devising a plan that suited him seemed more dominant than her own feelings, so thoroughly had she interiorised his needs. But whose anger did she really dread more, one wonders, his or her own? When he had almost burst a blood vessel over Nicholls's decorous first approaches, Charlotte had rightly seen his reactions as ludicrous at some level. It had changed her course of action, but it hadn't changed her mind – if anything such displays gave her an insight into what she really wanted to do.

The wedding went ahead more quickly than Charlotte expected, or even wanted, partly due to the ill-will of the departing temporary curate, George de Renzy, who demanded an early release from duty. The ceremony was to be an exceptionally quiet affair. Charlotte had cards printed to send to a dozen or so close friends, but only two were invited to the wedding itself: Ellen and Miss Wooler. The latter proved her kindness and usefulness in a crisis when, at the last minute, Patrick Brontë announced that he was not going to be able to attend the service, or give the bride away as planned. A hurried consultation of the Prayer Book showed that 'a friend' could do that office, so Miss Wooler stepped in kindly and acted as parent in Reverend Brontë's stead.

So Charlotte rose early on 29 June, a Thursday, got dressed in her tiered, unshowy white muslin dress and delicately embroidered bonnet and veil,★ and went to her wedding at eight o'clock in the morning, looking 'like a snowdrop', as one of the few locals who saw her walk to the church remarked. Nicholls's friend Sutcliffe Sowden took the service, and the only other people present were Nicholls's friend Joseph Grant, the churchwarden Mr Redman and, presumably, Tabby and Martha. The event passed off every bit as quietly as the bride had wished.

The newly-weds left the Parsonage straight after the wedding breakfast, travelling by train from Keighley to Conwy in north Wales, where they spent their wedding night at an inn close to the spectacular ruins of the thirteenth-century castle. Their route along the north Wales coast to Holyhead during the next week took in some of the great picturesque sights: Snowdon, Conwy Bay, Penrhyn Castle and the grand sweep of the Menai Strait near Bangor, exactly the sort of views Charlotte had spent her youth and ruined her eyesight copying from engravings in books and periodicals – now they all sprang to life vividly before her. Nicholls had chosen their itinerary well, with a drive

---

★ On show at the Brontë Parsonage Museum – a charming, and expensive-looking, object.

around Snowdon along the Pass of Llanberis, which 'surpassed anything I remember of the English Lakes', as Charlotte wrote to Catherine Wooler. They almost certainly also saw Caernarfon on their way back from Beddgelert to cross the bridge over to Anglesey, and – from the Conwy-to-Bangor train – the mountain at Penmaenmawr that had inspired a melancholy poem by Branwell on his visit to north Wales in 1845.

Crossing by steamer from Holyhead to Dublin, they were met at the dock by Nicholls's elder brother Alan, an engineer in charge of the Grand Canal from Dublin to Banagher, and two of his cousins, Joseph Bell, a 23-year-old student at Trinity College, and Mary Anna Bell, 'a pretty lady-like girl with gentle English manners'. Charlotte's prejudices against Ireland and the Irish had to be rapidly abandoned: Arthur's relations made a charming group, refined and courteous, and almost everything about the country struck her with pleasant surprise. After two days in Dublin, seeing the university and its library, museums and churches, the party travelled together back to Banagher, home to the younger Bells and former home of the Nicholls brothers, both of whom had been adopted into their uncle's family in childhood. Cuba House, where the Royal School had been housed since 1818, was on the eastern edge of the town, the first property on the road as it came in from Parsonstown. A carriage had been sent out to the station to meet them – quite a step up in gentility from the rented fly or four-mile walk facing travellers to Haworth – and Charlotte was amazed by her husband's former home as it came into view up the tree-lined drive. Grey stone, four-square and handsomely pedimented, it looked remarkably 'like a gentleman's country-seat'.

Inside, the house was rather gaunt, in the provincial Irish manner: 'the passages look desolate and bare', Charlotte reported to Miss Wooler; 'our bed-room, a great room on the ground floor would have looked gloomy when we were shown into it but for the turf-fire that was burning in the wide old chimney.' But the reception rooms were spacious and comfortable, and the lady of the house, Arthur's aunt Harriette, a hostess exactly to Charlotte's taste, 'quiet, kind and well-bred ... like an English or Scotch Matron'. Again, Charlotte seemed unwilling to admit much Irishness here, or in the 'English order and repose' of the household arrangements: 'It seems [Mrs. Bell] was brought up in London.'*

The renowned Banagher Royal Free School, which must have been in recess during Charlotte's visit that July, was housed in buildings adjacent to Cuba House† and had been run by Mrs Bell's late husband, Dr Allan Bell, LLD, until his death in 1839, and latterly by her son James Adamson Bell. The Bells' own five sons and their nephews Alan and Arthur Nicholls had been educated there and all had gone on to Trinity College, making an impressively learned and cultivated group.

'I must say I like my new relations,' Charlotte reported to Miss Wooler. 'My dear husband too appears in a new light here in his own country. More than once I have had deep pleasure in hearing his praises on all sides. Some of the old servants and followers of the family tell me I am a most fortunate person for that I have got one of the best gentlemen in the country. His Aunt too speaks of him with a mixture of affection and respect most gratifying to hear.' Charlotte was seeing Nicholls's virtues complete for the first time, and was humbled by them: 'I pray to be enabled to repay as I ought the affectionate devotion of a truthful, honourable, unboastful man.' The degree to which her husband had been 'unboastful' was probably the most striking thing of all. Patrick Brontë's snobbery about Nicholls and mean-spirited antagonism seemed all the more outrageous in the context of Cuba House and its gentle denizens.

The couple stayed in Banagher for about a week, then moved on down the course of the Shannon to Limerick and on to Kilkee, a favoured bathing-spot on the west coast, 'such a wild, iron-bound coast – with such an ocean-view as I had not yet seen – and such battling of waves with rocks as I had never imagined'. Here, Nicholls passed another test, of great importance. When they went out on to the cliffs on their first morning, Charlotte was so enthralled by the view that she needed to be alone with it, to 'take the matter in my own way', as she expressed it in a letter to Catherine Winkworth: 'I did not want to talk – but I *did* want to look and be silent.' Nicholls intuited this, and left her alone, covering her lap with a rug against

* Mrs Bell had been to finishing school in London, for a few weeks only.

† Ruins of these buildings and the old coach house are still visible in the fields where Cuba House, now demolished, used to stand.

the spray. 'He only interrupted me when he thought I crept too near the edge of the cliff . . . this protection which does not interfere or pretend – is I believe a thousand times better than any half sort of pseudo sympathy.'

Their tour continued across the mouth of the Shannon to Tarbert, then inland to Killarney, where Charlotte had a near-miss with death in the Gap of Dunloe, a spectacular mountain path about six miles long that links five lakes along the River Loe. Arthur was on foot and Charlotte on a hired pony when they came to a rough and narrow part of the track, at which place their guide advised Charlotte to dismount. Uncharacteristically, Charlotte ignored the warning and had got past the difficult section when the pony became unnerved and suddenly 'seemed to go mad – reared, plunged'. Charlotte was thrown off, unnoticed by Nicholls, who was trying to lead the animal along. 'I saw and felt her kick, plunge, trample round me,' Charlotte recalled dramatically, seeing her own death swooping near. 'I had my thoughts about the moment – its consequences – my husband – my father.'

This vision of her own mortality jolted Charlotte more than the fall itself. It also released intense anxieties about her father, left alone in Haworth for a month by this point, and the very next day she persuaded Nicholls to cut short the rest of their honeymoon and start home. Perhaps there had been a letter from Patrick Brontë at one of their stops along the way, as Charlotte told Ellen 'Papa has not been well' and that she had started 'longing, *longing intensely*' to get back to him. Once she had begun to feel her familiar terrors about Papa's health and well-being, 'I could enjoy and rest no more.'

Her own cough, which was ostensibly one reason for going home, cleared up before they left Ireland, and soon after they got back to Haworth, on 1 August, Patrick Brontë became perfectly well too. 'The wish for his continued life – together with a certain solicitude for his happiness and health seems – I scarcely know why – stronger in me now than before I was married,' she told Miss Wooler.

The odd trio then settled down to life together at the Parsonage. Patrick Brontë rarely took services any more or emerged from his study. Mrs Gaskell asked what he could possibly have been doing in there all day, and it is a good question. Nicholls strove to spare him any exertion, much to his wife's approval. 'Each time I see Mr. Nicholls put on gown or surplice – I feel comforted to think that this marriage has secured Papa good aid in his old age.'

Papa had his study; Nicholls had a den made out of the former peat-room, given a coat of paint and a covering of sprigged wallpaper; and Charlotte, as before, had the dining room to work in. But the work she did in it was very different now that her circumstances had changed. As the wife of the curate, Charlotte knew a level of busyness unprecedented in her life: visiting parishioners and the sick, offering and receiving teas and suppers, writing letters on behalf of her husband and organising charitable initiatives. Britain entered the war against Russia in March of that year, when the combined British and French fleet had already been in the Black Sea for three months, and the hard campaign in the Crimean winter, military setbacks and disease were reported back to the British public in more graphic detail than ever before through William Howard Russell's famous dispatches to *The Times*, the first war reporting of its sort in the age of telegraphy. The effect on public opinion was immediate and profound, and Haworth followed much of the country in holding meetings to help the Patriotic Fund, set up to help the families of the many casualties. Charlotte's own response to the war showed how she had lost all her youthful zest for militarism: she told Margaret Wooler that she felt war was 'one of the greatest curses that can fall upon mankind . . . no glory to be gained can compensate for the sufferings which must be endured.'

Marriage certainly suited Nicholls. '[M]y husband flourishes,' she told Ellen; 'he begins indeed to express some slight alarm at the growing improvement in his condition. I think I am decent – better certainly than I was two months ago, but people don't compliment me as they do Arthur – excuse the name – it has grown natural to use it now.' 'People' would have been looking out for indicators of Charlotte's well-being, signs of bridal shock or pleasure, and of the early signs of pregnancy, so their lack of compliments seems significant.

There is a photograph that is supposed to illustrate Charlotte's married contentment, and that some people guess was taken on her honeymoon, but that cannot be of Charlotte Brontë. Two copies of this carte de visite exist, neither bearing any studio or production information. One is marked in ink on the reverse, in Ellen Nussey's hand, 'Within a year of C. B.'s death'; the other in pencil, in an unknown hand, 'Miss Ellen Nussey, friend of Charlotte Brontë, c. 1860'. This leaves little doubt that it is a picture of Ellen Nussey.★

Ellen herself said, when asked by T. Wemyss Reid if there was a photograph of Charlotte to use as a frontispiece for his projected biography, 'I am afraid there is not *any* portrait of Charlotte Brontë but the one by Richmond – I never heard or saw any other that I remember – There was a painting in oils of Emily & Anne by Branwell when a boy, but it was a very poor picture even as regarded [sic] *likeness*, which sometimes is good, when the painting is very bad.'

Though there may be no photographic evidence of Charlotte's contentment in these short months of marriage, her letters are full of it, and of her gratitude to 'dear Arthur' and pleasure in his companionship. 'I did not expect perfection,' she said with great philosophy, and as the months went by her feelings for Nicholls deepened and her appreciation of his character gave her unsought pleasure. Papa was 'settled and content' – which was half the battle won – and her own life too: 'May God make me thankful for it! I have a good, kind, attached husband, and every day makes my own attachment to him stronger.' It was hardly, though, the passionate meeting of 'true souls' that her novels – and her sisters' novels – blazoned as the highest goal of the emotional

---

★ Ellen Nussey lived long into the age of photography and became very keen on having her picture taken. Lined up next to later images (see the plate section for an example), it certainly looks like the same person: well-fed, healthy, genteel, complacent. The writing of 'Within a year of C. B.'s death' makes clear that the subject is *not* 'C. B.': 'C. B. in the year before her death' is how Ellen would have labelled the picture if that were the case. Both cartes de visite are in the Brontë Society's possession (Seton-Gordon Collection SG 109 and 109a).

The wishful identification of Charlotte Brontë as the subject seems to have arisen from the discovery in 1984 of a glass negative of the carte in the archives of the photographer Sir Emery Walker (see Susan R. Foister's article 'The Brontë Portraits', *BST* 18:5 (1985) for the details of this discovery). It was labelled 'from a carte-de-visite of Charlotte Brontë, taken within a year of her death', following the suggestion of 'Within a year of C. B.'s death' on the reverse of the image it duplicated. Walker had been commissioned to make the negative for the firm of Smith, Elder in 1918, long after anyone at the firm knew Charlotte Brontë personally and twenty-one years after Ellen Nussey's death. Presumably the photograph was in Smith's archive from his dealings with EN in the three decades during which she was trying to publish her Brontë material.

life, and the birthright of every free-spirited woman, regardless of birth, class or looks. Charlotte Brontë had, in some respects, given her imaginative life over to her readers for them to foster and enjoy; she had found she couldn't live it herself, only write it.

· It was also not a situation that promised well for her writing. In the change of tempo and focus, she had all but given up her work. Nicholls told George Smith about an evening, late in 1854, when he and Charlotte had been sitting together by the fire in the dining room, as the wind howled round the house in truly wuthering fashion, when she suddenly said, 'If you had not been with me I must have been writing now.' Did she mean this regretfully, or simply as an introduction to what she did next, which was to go upstairs – 'run' as Nicholls recalled – and fetch 'the beginning of her New Tale'? More for the pleasure it might give herself, one feels, than to hear or solicit her husband's criticisms, she read him a pencilled manuscript of about 7,000 words, the fragment known as 'Emma', at the end of which Nicholls ventured to say, 'The Critics will accuse you of repetition, as you have again introduced a school.' 'O I shall alter that,' she replied unconcernedly. 'I always begin two or three times before I can please myself.' It's an interesting insight into how Charlotte Brontë composed her novels, expecting 'always' to go through several false starts and diversions, and a sad last glimpse at her as a writer, for no more work got done on 'Emma'.

'Emma' is narrated by a childless widow called Mrs Chalfont, whose relation to the story is never revealed and whose usefulness as a device runs out almost immediately. A man called Ellin also appears (the same name as in Charlotte's 'two brothers' fragment of 1853), a deliberately enigmatic character, who might have been intended to act as a sort of amateur detective within a 'puzzle' plot. The tone is light and satirical, quite like Thackeray, in fact, and the school plot that Nicholls felt might be repetitive sounds more like the seminary at the beginning of *Vanity Fair* than anything out of Charlotte's own experience. 'Emma' herself never appears.

With the recession of her writer-self, everything in the familiar home changed. There were other momentous changes too, as Charlotte tried to convey to Ellen in an oblique letter that hints at her newly acquired knowledge of sex:

during the last 6 weeks – the colour of my thoughts is a good deal changed: I know more of the realities of life than I once did. I think many false ideas are propagated – perhaps unintentionally. I think those married women who indiscriminately urge their acquaintance to marry – much to blame. For my part – I can only say with deeper sincerity and fuller significance – what I always said in theory – Wait God's will. Indeed – indeed Nell – it is a solemn and strange and perilous thing for a woman to become a wife. Man's lot is far – far different.

By the end of 1854, Charlotte's London friendships had all but dried up; there were no more letters from Williams, none from Smith. Life concentrated in and around the Parsonage, and Charlotte's days were taken up with parish matters, teas, visiting, organising. Ellen visited once in the autumn of 1854, but the old intimacy was hard to re-establish under the new order, and Ellen liked Mr Nicholls no better than she had before, indeed rather worse.

Charlotte had come to admire Nicholls's friend Sutcliffe Sowden and was hoping that he and Ellen might start to admire each other too. A marriage between Ellen and her husband's best friend would have been perfect from Charlotte's point of view, like the end of a comedy – a drawing-together of allegiances, and protection perhaps against Charlotte and Ellen drifting apart. But Charlotte was above outright matchmaking, and her hints came to nothing. Ellen, meanwhile, cannot have been pleased to receive letters from Charlotte including what 'Arthur' felt on various subjects that had only recently become his business, such as the behaviour of Joe and Amelia Taylor, and her own situation. '[Arthur] often says he wishes you were well settled in life,' Charlotte wrote on 11 October, not very sensitively. In the next letter from the Parsonage, it became clear that Nicholls didn't just feel empowered to intrude his opinion but was actually reading Charlotte's letter over her shoulder, and not much liking what he saw. Nicholls was impatient to go out on a walk and his wife's lingering over the writing desk provoked him to say something that must have been on his mind for a while. Charlotte's letter captures the essence of the conversation that started up as she wrote:

Arthur has just been glancing over this note – He thinks I have written too freely about Amelia &c. Men don't seem to understand making letters a vehicle of communication – they always seem to think us incautious. I'm sure I don't think I have said anything rash – however you must *burn* [three underlines] it when read. Arthur says such letters as mine never ought to be kept – they are dangerous as lucifer matches – so be sure to follow a recommendation he has just given 'fire them' – or 'there will be no more'. Such is his resolve. I can't help laughing – this seems to me so funny, Arthur however says he is quite serious and looks it, I assure you – he is bending over the desk with his eyes full of concern. I am now desired 'to have done with it –' so with his kind regards and mine – Goodbye dear Ellen.

'Fire them' was less a recommendation than an order, from a man who certainly seems every inch the conventional Victorian husband on this occasion, as Charlotte seems the wife. Her protestations that she found it all terribly funny sit rather oddly with the insistence that her husband is serious, and must have confused Ellen (or bored her), because ten days later Charlotte had to send a much more explicit restatement:

Dear Ellen – Arthur complains that you do not distinctly promise to burn my letters as you receive them. He says you must give him a plain pledge to that effect – or he will read every line I write and elect himself censor of our correspondence.

He says women are most rash in letter-writing – they think only of the trustworthiness of their immediate friend – and do not look to contingencies – a letter may fall into any hand. You must give the promise – I believe – at least he says so, with his best regards – or else you will get such notes as he writes to Mr Sowden – plain, brief statements of facts without the adornment of a single flourish.

Ellen did as was requested – almost. Sensing trouble ahead, she made a copy of the pledge she addressed sardonically 'To the Revd. The Magister':*

---

* I am assuming that the surviving text – at Texas University – is a copy made and kept by EN, because of the later pencil notes on it in her hand.

My dear Mr Nicholls

> As you seem to hold in great horror the ardentia verba of feminine epis-
> tles, I pledge myself to the destruction of Charlotte's epistles henceforth,
> if You, pledge *your*self to *no* censorship in the matter communicated[.]

This seems to have satisfied Nicholls, who passed on his thanks via Charlotte. 'We may now write any dangerous stuff we please to each other,'
Charlotte reported; 'it is not "old friends" he mistrusts, but the chances of
war – the accidental passing of letters into hands and under eyes for which
they were never written.' It seems fairly certain that what Nicholls feared
was less the general impropriety of private correspondence falling into the
wrong hands than the fact that the correspondence in question was Currer
Bell's. Having a much better sense of her local celebrity than either Patrick or Charlotte, Nicholls may have understood better than they the
need to protect his wife's privacy. That this had hardly occurred to Charlotte before is borne out by her comment to Ellen 'Strange chances do fall
out certainly. As to my own notes I never thought of attaching importance to them, or considering their fate – till Arthur seemed to reflect on
both so seriously.'

After Charlotte's death, Nicholls resisted all attempts at publicity,
and agreed to the commissioning of Mrs Gaskell's biography only
under duress. He preserved many of Charlotte's manuscripts and
mementoes as an act of private homage to a woman he remained
intensely devoted to, but very few personal letters survive that were
written *to* Charlotte and only one of hers to him (the preservation of
which seems accidental), and we have to assume that either she
destroyed them herself, or that her widower did, in line with his stated
policy. Since her correspondents included Thackeray, W. S. Williams,
Elizabeth Gaskell and Harriet Martineau, this is a cause for deep regret
to posterity, however understandable and even admirable it was from
Nicholls's point of view.

Very few letters of Charlotte Brontë would have come down to us if
Ellen Nussey had kept her side of the bargain, but she didn't. On her
copy of the promise she wrote later, in pencil, 'Mr N continued his
censorship so the pledge was void.' This was obviously a self-justifying
manoeuvre, since no censorship by Charlotte's husband is evident in
anything she sent subsequently, and after his sudden laying down of

the law, he doesn't seem to have mentioned the matter again. How misplaced his trust had been came to light only in the decades following Charlotte's death, when Ellen became very keen to publicise and publish her correspondence from the increasingly famous and revered author. Censorship then really did take place, but of a retroactive kind, and by Ellen, who made many deletions and adjustments to anything that might have shown herself in a bad light. In Charlotte's second letter about the 'pledge', for instance, Ellen substituted the words 'Arthur wishes you would burn my letters' for 'Arthur thanks you for the promise', and suppressed the passage 'we may now write any dangerous stuff we please', to make it look as if Nicholls really had invalidated the agreement. '[H]e never did give the pledge,' Ellen wrote in pencil as a footnote.*

Sir James Kay-Shuttleworth invited himself to visit Haworth in the winter of 1854 and had a scheme in mind for the Nichollses, a living near Gawthorpe worth £200 a year. Nicholls could not accept, out of deference to the needs of Patrick Brontë, a matter 'of course' in Charlotte's eyes, but they did not want to dissuade Sir James entirely. Charlotte had a pipe-dream of her own, which was that Sutcliffe Sowden might benefit from this lucrative position. Partly to keep this possibility open, and partly because of the social pressure that always came to bear on invitations from the Kay-Shuttleworths, Charlotte and Arthur agreed to go to Gawthorpe in the new year. This was despite the fact that Charlotte had been putting off all her other friends' invitations for months and would much rather have gone to the Gaskells at Plymouth Grove – or to Brookroyd, if it hadn't been for a typhus outbreak in the area. It had been a hard Christmas: Tabby was so ill with diarrhoea that she was moved to her great-niece's house to be nursed, and Charlotte had been anxiously seeking advice and medicine on her behalf from the local surgeon, Amos Ingham.

Within a few days of her return from Gawthorpe, Charlotte herself began to feel sick. 'Don't conjecture – dear Nell,' she wrote to Ellen, clearly thinking she could be pregnant, 'for it is too soon yet – though

---

* I am indebted, as so often, to Margaret Smith's footnotes and editorial matter for the information here about the letters. See *LCB* 3, 299 n3, and *LCB* 1, 43–52, for her detailed accounts of EN's concealments.

I certainly never before felt as I have done lately. But keep the matter wholly to yourself – for I can come to no decided opinion at present.' She added that she had been feeling very well until this turn of events: 'I am rather mortified to lose my good looks and grow thin as I am doing.'

The terrible symptoms that Charlotte suffered in the last three months of her life have led people, very naturally, to think that the cause of her death was the thing she had been fearing so long, consumption, but that doesn't seem to have been the case. That Charlotte really was pregnant in the early months of 1855 is clear from letters such as hers to Ellen, above, and from the evidence of Mrs Gaskell's *Life*, which puts the matter politely but explicitly by giving the doctor's opinion that there was 'a natural cause' for the sickness that time would cure, and later by mentioning 'the baby that was coming'. The severity of Charlotte's physical distress, though, did not seem to match 'morning sickness' as it is normally understood, and so consumption has often crept back into people's speculations about Charlotte Brontë's death as an extra factor. Mrs Gaskell's linking of Charlotte's last illness with a lingering cold, contracted 'by a long walk over damp ground in thin shoes', encourages this idea, as if 'morning sickness' alone was not enough. The coughing up of blood also confuses the issue, though, in Charlotte's case, the blood almost certainly came from the stomach, not the lungs.

It is only very recently, with the publicity given to the condition called hyperemesis gravidarum by one famous contemporary sufferer, Catherine, Duchess of Cambridge (Kate Middleton), that the cause of Charlotte Brontë's death can be fully appreciated. 'HG', as it is sometimes known, is an extreme reaction to the hormones of pregnancy that affects around 0.5–2.0 per cent of pregnant women, with varying degrees of severity and for varying lengths of time (some sufferers endure the symptoms for the whole forty weeks; more often the condition improves after the first trimester). Unlike the commonly experienced symptoms of ordinary morning sickness – nausea, vomiting and sensitivity to light, smells and sounds – the HG sufferer experiences a violent and ceaseless disruption of stomach and senses. One very vivid recent account in a newspaper, by Sarah Button, describes what it can be like. Three days after her pregnancy was confirmed, she relates, nausea kicked in 'so aggressively that it was as if I'd run head-first into a brick wall . . . at four weeks pregnant, I felt as if I'd been poisoned.' Button describes how, even with all the assistance that modern medicine allows (drugs and a drip are required constantly to prevent renal failure, dehydration and collapse of the major organs due to malnutrition), she was sick fifty times in one day and brought up blood from the traumatised stomach lining: 'It was as if someone had taken over my body. I couldn't imagine ever feeling normal again.' Her case was so severe that by week nine choices narrowed to a potentially harmful course of steroids or a termination: Button anxiously chose the steroids and in due course gave birth to a healthy baby, but was incapacitated by sickness right up to the end of the pregnancy.

Charlotte Brontë's sufferings, in an age with so little knowledge of this condition and with so few weapons to fight it, can be contemplated only with the deepest pity. The vomiting that everyone hoped and expected would subside in time got worse, and the patient weaker. 'She, who was ever patient in illness, tried hard to bear up and bear on. But the dreadful sickness increased and increased, till the very sight of food occasioned nausea,' Gaskell wrote in the account she drew up later, based on the witness of Arthur Nicholls, Reverend Brontë and Martha Brown. At the time, Gaskell knew nothing of Charlotte's condition or plight and later bitterly lamented that she had not been able to help; indeed there is a suggestion, in what she said later in a letter to Catherine Winkworth, that she understood Charlotte's life could have been saved – perhaps by a termination of the pregnancy: 'I do fancy that if I had come, I could have induced her – even though they had all felt angry with me at first – to do what was so absolutely necessary for her very life.' But, while Charlotte was bedridden and writhing in agony day and night, there was no one on hand in Haworth able or willing to say this.

Martha tried to cheer her mistress with the thought of the child, but it was hard for Charlotte to rally. 'I dare say I shall be glad sometime,' she told the faithful servant, 'but I am so ill – so weary.' She was hardly eating a thing, and being sick constantly. Arthur had to send notes of apology that his wife was currently unable to attend to business, although at the beginning of February they still assumed the trouble would pass in time. Dr MacTurk, the senior physician at Bradford

Infirmary (the best available local doctor), was of the opinion that 'in a few weeks she will be well again.' But in a few weeks she was worse. 'Let me speak the plain truth,' Charlotte scratched in a message to Amelia Taylor, 'my sufferings are very great – my nights indescribable – sickness with scarcely a reprieve – I strain until what I vomit is mixed with blood.'

From her sickbed, Charlotte wrote only a handful more letters. One, to Ellen, asked her to find out more about their mutual friend Mary Hewitt's problematic pregnancy – 'how long she was ill and in what way' – while to Amelia Taylor (the mother of baby Tim) she begged for any remedies she could recommend, 'anything that will do good'. In each case, she gave touching accounts of her husband's care of her, and her grateful love. 'No kinder better husband than mine it seems to me can there be in the world,' she told Laetitia Wheelwright. 'I do not want now for kind companionship in health and the tenderest nursing in sickness', while in her letter to Ellen she called him 'the best earthly comfort that ever woman had'. There could be no greater tribute to the flowering of her love for her 'dear boy' Arthur.

In the middle of this awful ordeal, and during a winter of unusually severe cold, Charlotte had to report to Ellen 'Our poor old Tabby is *dead* and *buried*.' Much to her sorrow and agitation she was too ill to attend the funeral of their beloved old friend, although perhaps she could have watched from the bedroom window as Tabby was buried within sight of the house. Charlotte must have by this time feared for her own survival, for on the same day that Tabby died, 17 February 1855, she made her will:

> In case I die without issue I give and bequeath to my husband all my property to be his absolutely and entirely; but in case I leave issue I bequeath to my husband the interest of my property during his lifetime, and at his death I desire that the principal should go to my surviving Child, or Children, should there be more than one child, share and share alike.

Thus she overturned the cautious provision made in her marriage settlement, which kept her assets out of Nicholls's hands. It was a sign of trust in her husband, now that Charlotte felt secure in his willingness to care for her father in the event of Charlotte predeceasing them both.

In the early weeks of March, with a slight improvement in the weather, Charlotte seemed to be improving slightly too. She took some beef tea, 'spoonsful of wine & water – a mouthful of light pudding'. All in all, though, as Martha remarked, 'a wren would have starved on what she ate.' In the last note she ever wrote, in the feeblest pencilled script, Charlotte characteristically asked after everyone else's health, commiserated with everyone else's troubles, expressed relief at Papa being well. She had not strength to do more. 'I am reduced to greater weakness – the skeleton emaciation is the same &c. &c. &c. I cannot talk – even to my dear patient constant Arthur I can say but few words at once.' About a week before she died, there was a change: 'a low wandering delirium came on', in which the ravaged patient begged for food 'and even for stimulants', as Mrs Gaskell was told. She came to briefly to the sound of prayers being said, and, seeing her husband's stricken face, said, 'Oh! I am not going to die, am I? He will not separate us, we have been so happy.'

Patrick Brontë wrote to Ellen on Friday, 30 March, warning her that the doctors had given up hope of Charlotte's recovery, 'and we only to [*sic*] look forward to the solemn event, with prayer to God, that he will give us grace and Strength sufficient unto our day.' Ellen set off at once from Brookroyd when she received this, but got to Haworth too late: Charlotte had died in the early morning of 31 March, three weeks short of her thirty-ninth birthday. Martha Brown and her sister Tabitha were the only ones present at the death, Arthur Nicholls having gone to take a rest in an adjacent room. Tabitha at first thought the bereaved father was behaving in a strangely calm and controlled way, turning to leave the room with dry eyes and in silence, but came across him in his bedroom soon after, kneeling by his bed, 'crying in agonized tones, "My poor Charlotte! My dear Charlotte!"' The local doctor, Amos Ingham, signed the death certificate. The cause he cited, 'phthisis', usually indicated the wasting caused by tuberculosis, but applied as accurately to the wasting that three months of dehydration and starvation had wreaked on Charlotte's already feeble frame.

Patrick Brontë did not come out of his study when Ellen Nussey arrived, but sent a message asking her to stay for the interment, which took place on 4 April, Sutcliffe Sowden taking the service only eight months after he had officiated at the Nichollses' wedding. Ellen and

Martha put flowers and evergreens in the coffin with their friend's ravaged corpse, and undoubtedly dressed her with special care, perhaps in
one of her London outfits. One of the townsfolk who thronged to the
church for the funeral and to see Mrs Nicholls laid in the vault with her
mother, aunt, brother and three sisters noticed that a violet ribbon was
trapped in the coffin lid.*

* This tiny detail, so small it seems likely to be true, has come down in the family of
the composer Robin Walker, whose great-great-grandfather saw it. See Betty Emma-
line Walker, _The Green Lanes: A Westmorland Childhood_ (York, 1998), pp. 149–50.

Coda

'Currer Bell is dead!' lamented the *Daily News*, in an obituary penned by Harriet Martineau; 'a pang will be felt in the midst of the strongest interests of the day, through the length and breadth of the land.' Martineau was unequivocal about Currer Bell's achievement: her works would, she was sure, 'hold their place in the literature of our country'. Still, she forefronted the biographical facts that already dominated public opinion about the writer: the isolation, emotional and physical hardships of her upbringing and the loss of her family one by one. It was Charlotte Brontë, as much as Currer Bell, who was on her way to becoming 'for ever known'.

Elizabeth Gaskell had been abroad that winter and only heard the news from John Greenwood, the Haworth stationer. She wrote at once to Patrick Brontë, in stunned surprise, and he replied, 'My Daughter, is indeed, dead . . . The marriage that took place, seem'd to hold forth, long, and bright prospects of happiness, but in the inscrutable providence of God, all our hopes have ended in disappointment, and our joy, in mourning.' In their shared bereavement, Patrick Brontë had drawn much closer to Arthur Nicholls, who continued to care for and support the frail old man as a sacred duty to his late wife. When Patrick rewrote his will after Charlotte's death, he left small bequests to his brother Hugh and to Martha Brown but all the rest of his estate went to Arthur Bell Nicholls, no longer the despised seducer but 'my beloved and esteemed son-in-law'.

Even while she was trying to take in the news of Charlotte's death, Elizabeth Gaskell was asking John Greenwood for every detail he could remember about Miss Brontë, 'EVERY particular', already thinking that she might write some sort of memorial. By May she had mentioned such a possibility to George Smith, to whom she had applied for a copy of Richmond's portrait, although she imagined having to wait until 'no one is living whom such a publication would hurt.'

Her surprise was great, then, when she had a letter from Patrick Brontë, in June 1855, suggesting that she write a biographical appreciation of Charlotte, 'long or short . . . just as you may deem expedient & proper', and she accepted right away. A number of crudely inaccurate pieces of journalism had appeared immediately after Charlotte's death, which Patrick Brontë had been inclined to laugh off and Arthur Nicholls thought deserved no response at all. Ellen Nussey, however, had persuaded Patrick that similar 'attacks' would continue unless they oversaw an official biography, setting out the facts of Charlotte's life and defending her (and her sisters) against criticisms of coarseness. Ellen had suggested Mrs Gaskell as being the ideal candidate; what none of them seems to have realised (as Juliet Barker has pointed out) is that the most offensive article, in *Sharpe's London Magazine*, had drawn heavily on gossip generated by Janet Kay-Shuttleworth, which Elizabeth Gaskell herself had helped to spread.

Gaskell went over to Haworth that July with Catherine Winkworth, to discuss the memorial and to meet Mr Nicholls for the first time, something she had avoided doing during Charlotte's lifetime. It was a difficult day: feeling the reality of Charlotte's death and seeing her grave were hard enough, but she also had to try to convey to the two bereaved men what she hoped to do – write a full-length book, not an article or monograph, and concentrate not on the works but on 'her wild sad life, and beautiful character that grew out of it'. When Nicholls brought down some of Charlotte's letters, both he and Patrick Brontë wept sadly over them. Nicholls probably wished he had already destroyed the papers that were now about to be handed over to the biographer, as her quick eye appreciated: 'his feeling was against it's [*sic*] being written, but he yielded to Mr Brontë's impetuous wish.'

Gaskell set about her task with energy and deep interest. Ellen Nussey's horde of around 500 letters was the most fascinating resource, thrilling the biographer with their narrative power and revelations of character, wit and pathos. Gaskell's daughters were set to copying large swathes of the material, as their mother kept up copious correspondences with Charlotte's friends and associates and travelled to many of the places connected with her subject, including Cowan Bridge, Roe Head, Oakwell Hall, even the Chapter Coffee House. By the spring of 1856 only one major source remained unexplored – the Heger family.

Gaskell travelled to Brussels in the spring of 1856 to find that the Hegers did indeed know all about Currer Bell's fame, and identity. Madame Heger, who had read a pirated French translation of *Villette*, refused to see the biographer; Monsieur was, however, the soul of politeness, showed Gaskell some of Charlotte and Emily's *devoirs*, explained his teaching methods, described their school careers – and showed or read her some of Charlotte's letters. Towards the end of their interview, he asked if she could find out from the family what had happened to his replies to Charlotte. '[H]e is sure she would keep them,' Mrs Gaskell told Ellen, 'as they contained advice about her character, studies, mode of life.' What else they contained we shall never know, but Heger's concern at knowing their whereabouts at this sensitive juncture is very interesting – it may even have been the only reason he agreed to meet Gaskell at all. Presumably, Mrs Gaskell returned a negative answer from Mr Nicholls, for nothing more was said about Heger's letters, and she had already intuited enough about the story to decide to hide it from her readers. In the rue d'Isabelle, both Monsieur and Madame must have breathed a sigh of relief.

Patrick Brontë died in June 1861, at the age of eighty-four. He had lived to see his family made famous by the publication of Elizabeth Gaskell's bestselling *Life of Charlotte Brontë* in 1857, and in the last years of his life would often be waylaid on the short walk from the Parsonage to the door of the church by people who wanted to shake the hand of 'the father of the Brontës'. The church was packed for his funeral, where Arthur Bell Nicholls, the chief mourner, was so deeply affected that he had to be supported by his friends.

Nicholls had expected to be appointed perpetual curate in his father-in-law's place, but the church trustees did not elect him and, with short notice, he found himself required to move out of the Parsonage and the town. In some upset and confusion, he returned to Banagher to live with his remaining family there, gave up his ministry and turned to farming. In 1863 he married his cousin Mary Anna Bell (the charming girl whom Charlotte had met on honeymoon), his junior by eleven years. They had no children and led a very quiet life together in a house at the top of the hill above the town filled with relics from Haworth: the Richmond portrait hung in the sitting room, Brontë first editions lined the bookshelves, Brontë watercolours and sketches covered the walls, and a glass case contained some choice items of memorabilia. A substantial link with the old days was kept through Nicholls's retention of Martha Brown as an employee: like Reverend Brontë, she had become devoted to Nicholls over time and was remembered in Banagher for her quaint Yorkshire accent and excellent sponge cake.

Only a few weeks after Nicholls's departure for Ireland, and the accompanying sale of effects from the Parsonage, a young American friend of Elizabeth Gaskell, Charles Hale, made the pilgrimage to Haworth to see for himself the sites so memorably described in his friend's biography. Making his way up Haworth main street, he met locals who already had Brontë anecdotes in place for tourists, and in the Black Bull was served his supper on a tray that, the publican's wife assured him, had previously belonged to Charlotte. Hale got into conversation with a young man who was surrounded by tracings, plans and saucers of india ink, busy transferring his day's observations on to an immense sheet of paper. He was a surveyor for the railway company planning to open a branch line from Keighley to Haworth, 'so that future worshippers will find their pilgrimage easier'.

Hale's visit came at a strange turning point in the Brontës' fame and the village's life. On the one hand, a new broom was in operation: Reverend Brontë was dead, Mr Nicholls was gone, and the new incumbent, John Wade, was busy having the Parsonage thoroughly refitted, in ways that would have made it almost unrecognisable to the former family.* He was also about to knock down and rebuild the church. On the other hand, there was a growing sense of the value of what was being swept away. Locals who had picked up items at the house clearance, like the tray in service at the Black Bull, found, when Hale and his like turned up, that they were in possession of precious relics. Disappointed that he had so nearly missed the sale of effects at which he could have acquired books, pictures and intimate possessions of the Brontës, Hale had to content himself with soaking up as much of the atmosphere as he could, interviewing and photographing locals who remembered the family, and coming away from the Parsonage with some substantial items from the builders' rubbish pile, Mr Brontë's old bell-pull and half a sash window from Charlotte's room.†

---

* He was building a large extension on the lane side, to create a commodious dining room and office on the ground floor with a master bedroom above, a bath and indoor water closet (along with plumbing to the kitchen), all remarkable innovations.

† He later had the glass panes from this incorporated into picture frames (Miller, *The Brontë Myth*, 100). His photographs haven't been traced.

Ellen Nussey was well aware of the value of her letters from Charlotte, and, as the years went by and the fame of the Brontës grew, hoped to profit from them both financially and by association. Once Patrick Brontë was dead, she wrote to Constantin Heger, asking his 'advice' about possible translation of her material into French, and whether he would collaborate with her on an edition. He didn't rise to the threat of exposure implicit in her letter, but cautioned her not to do anything of which her friend would have disapproved, despite the undoubted interest of the subject, 'even after Mrs Gaskell's detailed biography':

> Could I, without the consent of my friend, publish his intimate letters
> – that is to say, his confidences? Has he not allowed me to see more of
> himself than he would wish to show to the first comer? . . . I make no
> unconscionable claim, Madam, to settle this question for you. I know
> that you have too much delicacy for me to be able to suppose that your
> reason and your heart have need of help in this.

These considerations were easily overridden in Ellen's mind by the need to tell 'the truth' about Charlotte, and to have her own position as best friend to genius adequately recognised. In the 1870s she allowed Thomas Wemyss Reid extensive use of the letters for his biography of Charlotte, and in the next decade made an attempt to publish an edition in collaboration with the antiquarian Joseph Horsfall Turner, but fell out with him at a late stage in the production, causing all but a few copies of the book to be destroyed. The next person to court her for her Brontë manuscripts was the journalist Clement King Shorter, later editor of *The Illustrated London News*, who first visited Ellen in 1889 and won her trust. It was Shorter who warned her that copyright law would prevent her printing the letters she owned (news that increased her already very sour feelings towards Nicholls, whom she abused freely in her correspondence); this intelligence undoubtedly influenced her decision to sell a large number of the letters via Shorter to his associate T. J. Wise, ostensibly a highly reputable collector and antiquarian, but actually a shameless forger of literary manuscripts and high-class con-man. Wise promised to keep the Charlotte Brontë letters together as a collection, to be donated at some future date to the nation. In fact, he started selling them off piecemeal almost as soon as he got his hands on them, much to Ellen's understandable horror.

Shorter travelled to Banagher in the spring of 1895 and managed to persuade Arthur Nicholls (then in his seventies) not only to give him access to many of the treasured manuscripts he had kept to himself for forty years and sell some to Wise, but to sell him the copyright on any material that he was to handle for publication, including copyright (and therefore veto) on any of Charlotte's letters to Ellen Nussey that Ellen might seek to publish. Whether or not Nicholls quite understood the extent of the powers he was handing over (he had been confused about the difference between 'copyright' and 'permissions' when Mrs Gaskell's biography was in production), the result of his sudden change of policy was that Clement Shorter and his heirs maintained control over the Brontë literary estate well into the 1970s.

Interested parties such as Nicholls and Ellen Nussey (not to mention Monsieur Heger in Brussels) must have been amazed when a 'Brontë Society' was formed in 1893, one of the first ever associations of its kind, which two years later opened a small museum of manuscripts and relics in a room over the Yorkshire Penny Bank at the top of Haworth's Main Street. When Nicholls died in 1906, at the ripe age of eighty-seven, his widow sold some items from his remarkable collection straight to the Society, and much of the rest of the material was disposed of in two large auction sales, one in 1907 and one in 1916 after her death. In the meantime, Haworth had become such a draw for tourists that the Parsonage became difficult for any parson to live in quietly, and in 1927 the Ecclesiastical Commission put the building up for sale. It was bought by a local worthy, Sir James Roberts, specifically so that he could donate it to the Brontë Society, and the following year the Brontë Parsonage Museum opened, then as now one of the most hauntingly atmospheric writers' house museums in the world.

For all his talk of respecting the wishes and privacy of a dead friend, Constantin Heger proved an unpredictable respecter of them himself. What he felt in 1856 on perusing Charlotte's agonised love-notes and carefully extracting anodyne passages for Elizabeth Gaskell's use is impossible to say, but once that had been done, he may have thought there was no good reason – and perhaps some danger – in keeping the originals.

His wife obviously took a different view: the danger in 'those letters' might lie in their *not* being available as evidence, hence her removal of the fragments from the bin and reconstruction jigsaw-wise. Madame Heger is said to have kept her actions secret (exactly as Madame Beck would have done), showing the letters to her daughter Louise only after the latter had attended a lecture in Brussels, in about 1868,[*] explicitly connecting their family with the characters in *Villette* and criticising their treatment of the Brontë sisters. Louise said that the letters were at that time kept by her mother in a compartment of her jewel box, flat, one imagines, as the intricate mending with gummed strips and thread shows no signs of having been disturbed.

Louise, who was just a toddler when the Brontë sisters arrived at the Pensionnat in 1842 and who lived until 1933, acquired the letters at her mother's death in 1890, but kept them secret in turn. She said that when she told her father about them, he was surprised to discover that they still existed and he tried to throw them away again, but, like her mother, she managed to thwart him. Like many details and dates in Louise's account, this is hard to square with the other evidence. Why would Monsieur Heger ever have thrown the letters away in anger, if he seemed happy to show them and quote them to Elizabeth Gaskell in 1856?

And other evidence indicates that the letters were not kept strictly secret, nor did Monsieur think them destroyed in the 1860s. In 1869 Thomas Westwood, an employee of an Anglo-Belgian railway company who had lived in Brussels for twenty years and whose wife and wife's cousin were former pupils and friends of the Hegers, told a correspondent that *Villette* was 'truer than the biography' and that 'the one true love of [Charlotte Brontë's] life was M. Paul Emanuel.' Westwood himself was in possession of one of Charlotte's school essays, presumably given to him by a member of the family. 'M. Paul Emanuel has quite a bundle of them,' he said. Westwood makes it clear to his correspondent, whose curiosity had been piqued, that Constantin Heger had ceased to be very secretive or discreet about his association with the famous authoress and had 'told the whole story' to Westwood's wife's cousin: his drawing out of Charlotte's talent, her growing obsession with him, 'an enforced parting' when the violence of her feelings became understood, and her despairing letters to him afterwards. 'He told the story,' Westwood said,

---

[*] Louise said she was twenty-nine at the time, and she was born in 1839 (M. H. Spielmann, *The Inner History of the Brontë–Heger Letters*). On the whole, in her account to Spielmann, her dates and calculations are not very accurate.

'and, I am sorry to say, he showed the letters also. He is a finished speci-
men of a Jesuit, but with all that a worthy & warm-hearted man.'

Westwood had been given one of the *devoirs* (he didn't say which
one) and another of them – Charlotte's essay, 'L'Amour Filial' – was
given to Heger's colleague at the Athénée, Charles-Henri Randolphe,
in August 1876. By 1894 someone called Tamar possessed Charlotte's
gift to Constantin, *Ashburnham Church on the Valley-Land*★ (it was sold
on to a collector), and 'E. Nys' owned 'The Spell' (and was probably
the person who had it expensively bound) – it is now in the British
Library. The family seem indeed to have been handing their manuscripts
out fairly freely, and in 1894, four years after Madame Heger's death,
and presumably at Monsieur Heger's instigation, they began to release
Brontë *devoirs* for publication in magazines. And yet, when Clement
Shorter went to Brussels in 1895 on the trail of manuscript material, he
was not granted an interview, and his inquiries were answered on a calling card by Claire Heger, the second-youngest daughter: 'Doctor Heger
regrets not possessing any letters whatever of Charlotte Brontë, having
given them to friends of England a number of years ago.'

Among Brontë memorabilia given by the Hegers, before 1890, to
another ex-pupil called Marion Douglas were Emily's and Charlotte's
gifts to Madame on departure from the Pensionnat in 1842, *The North
Wind* and *Watermill*, also two less explicable items, a photograph of
Patrick Brontë and a lock of Charlotte Brontë's hair.† The photograph
could have been sent at any time after the early 1860s – they were sold
as souvenirs in Haworth, even before Patrick Brontë's death – but the
lock of hair would be hard to account for, unless given or sent to Monsieur Heger by Charlotte herself. In *Shirley*, Caroline Helstone relates
how she took such a keepsake from Robert Moore:

> He was sitting near the table . . . on the temples were many such round
> curls. I thought he could spare me one: I knew I should like to have it,
> and I asked for it. He said, on condition that he might have his choice of
> a tress from my head; so he got one of my long locks of hair, and I got

★ It is on display now at the Parsonage Museum.
† See *Art of the Brontës*, 385; notes to *North Wind* and *Watermill*. Other items in this
stash of Brontëana included 'a Brontë seal' and a sampler sewn by the Hegers' English
nanny, Martha Trotman.

one of his short ones. I keep his, but, I dare say, he has lost mine. It was my doing, and one of those silly deeds it distresses the heart and sets the face on fire to think of: one of those small but sharp recollections that return, lacerating your self-respect like tiny penknives, and forcing from your lips, as you sit alone, sudden, insane-sounding interjections.

Could this reflect what happened in real life? So much in Charlotte's novels is confessed or exposed under the veil of fiction.

In her *Life of Charlotte Brontë*, Elizabeth Gaskell related how, in her presence, someone once challenged Charlotte about the scene in *Jane Eyre* when the heroine 'hears Rochester's voice crying out to her in a great crisis of her life, he being many, many miles distant at the time. I do not know what incident was in Miss Brontë's recollection when she replied, in a low voice, drawing in her breath, "But it is a true thing; it really happened."' It was the loss of her sisters, Gaskell imagined, that Charlotte was thinking of, the 'cries, and sobs, and wailings' of the wind around the sepulchral Parsonage that appeared 'as of the dearly-beloved vainly striving to force their way to her', in the manner of Cathy's ghost at the windows of Wuthering Heights. True though this might have been to the intensity of Charlotte's bereavement, a different cause probably stood behind that most striking and thrilling passage in *Jane Eyre*, one that, when she was writing the book, with her sisters still at her side, was overpoweringly alive to her: the calling of her soul to that of her Master.

The wavering line between fact and fiction seems to disappear altogether here, as does the distinction between what inspires a novel and how novels in turn affect life. In the late 1880s, Constantin Heger sat in his study in the rue d'Isabelle and wrote a charming letter to a former English pupil called Meta Mossman, to whom he felt he should apologise for the long delay in answering one of hers. He and his wife kept up many such friendships and correspondences; they liked to think of their past favourites as extended family, even when they had grown into women, wives, matrons. He hastens to reassure his young friend that, contrary to the evidence, she has not been forgotten by him:

> although it is true that I have not written, I have nevertheless answered you frequently and at length, and this is how. Letters and the post are not, luckily, the only means of communication, or the best, between people

who are really fond of one another: I am not referring to the telephone, which allows one to speak, to have conversation, from a distance. I have something better than that. I have only to think of you to see you. I often give myself the pleasure when my duties are over, when the light fades. I postpone lighting the gas lamp in my library, I sit down, smoking my cigar, and with a hearty will I evoke your image – and you come (without wishing to, I dare say) but I see you, I talk with you – you, with that little air, affectionate undoubtedly, but independent and resolute, firmly determined not to allow any opinion without being previously convinced, demanding to be convinced before allowing yourself to submit – in fact, just as I knew you, my dear [Meta], and as I have esteemed and loved you.

Here is the letter that Charlotte Brontë waited for all those miserable months in 1844 and 1845, the one she would have given almost anything to be handed by the Haworth postman; not the infrequent, testy notes that Heger sent so reluctantly, but an expansive, loving, intimate communication, wrapping the recipient in close and exclusive attention. He thinks of Meta Mossman as he sits smoking his cigar in the gloaming and works a form of magic for her, far away in England: *I see you, I talk with you – with a hearty will I evoke your image*.

In thinking it over you will have no difficulty in admitting that you yourself have experienced a hundred times that which I tell you about communication between two distant hearts, instantaneous, without paper, without pen, or words, or messenger, etc., a hundred times without noticing it, without its having attracted your attention, without anything extraordinary.

The question remains, was this the only time that worldly, wily Constantin Heger proposed a sort of emotional telepathy with one of his former favourites? Had he suggested something of the sort to Charlotte before they parted? Perhaps she felt she had 'reached' him this way, when she said that Rochester's call to Jane *really happened*. Was it his habit to attempt such mental communion across long distances and adverse circumstances?

Or had he simply been reading *Jane Eyre*?

Select Bibliography

Unless otherwise stated, references are to the Oxford World's Classics editions of the Brontë novels, in their most recent paperback issues.

Charlotte Brontë

Jane Eyre, edited by Margaret Smith, with an introduction and revised notes by Sally Shuttleworth (Oxford 2008)

Shirley, edited by Herbert Rosengarten and Margaret Smith, with an introduction and notes by Janet Gezari (Oxford, 2008)

Villette, edited by Margaret Smith, with an introduction and revised notes by Sally Shuttleworth (Oxford, 2008)

The Professor, edited by Margaret Smith and Herbert Rosengarten, with an introduction by Margaret Smith (Oxford, 2008)

Emily Brontë

Wuthering Heights, text edited by Ian Jack, with an introduction and additional notes by Helen Small (Oxford, 2009)

Anne Brontë

Agnes Grey, edited by Robert Inglesfield and Hilda Marsden, with an introduction and additional notes by Sally Shuttleworth (Oxford, 2010)

The Tenant of Wildfell Hall, edited by Herbert Rosengarten, with an introduction and additional notes by Josephine McDonagh (Oxford, 2008)

A Literary Friendship: Letters to Lady Alwyne Compton 1869–1881, from Thomas Westwood (London, 1914)

Adamson, Alan H., *Mr Charlotte Brontë: The Life of Arthur Bell Nicholls* (Montreal, 2008)

Alexander, Christine, *The Early Writings of Charlotte Brontë* (Oxford, 1983)

—, and Sellars, Jane, *The Art of the Brontës* (Cambridge, 1995)

—, and Smith, Margaret (eds.), *The Oxford Companion to the Brontës* (Oxford, 2006)

Allott, Miriam (ed.), *The Brontës: The Critical Heritage* (London, 1974)

Anon., 'Two Brussels Schoolfellows of Charlotte Brontë', *BST*, 5:23 (1913)

Anon., 'The Recently Discovered Letters from Charlotte Brontë to Professor Constantin Heger', *BST*, 5:24 (1914)

Anon., 'The Reverend Arthur Bell Nicholls', *BST*, 15:79 (1969)

Atkins, William, *The Moor: Lives, Landscape, Literature* (London, 2014)

Barker, Juliet R. V., 'Subdued Expectations: Charlotte Brontë's Marriage Settlement', *BST*, 19:1–2 (1986)

—, 'The Brontë Portraits: A Mystery Solved', *BST*, 20:1 (1990)

Barnard, Robert, 'Dickens and the Brontës', *BST*, 25:2 (2000)

Barrett, Sarah, *A Room of Their Own: 80 Years of the Brontë Parsonage Museum 1928–2008* (Kendal, 2008)

Bellamy, Joan, *'More precious than rubies': Mary Taylor, Friend of Charlotte Brontë, Strong-minded Woman* (Beverley, 2002)

Bentley, Phyllis, *The Brontës and Their World* (London, 1969)

Bostridge, Mark, 'Charlotte Brontë and George Richmond', BST, 17:86 (1976)

—, *Florence Nightingale: The Woman and Her Legend* (London, 2008)

Brontë, Patrick, *Cottage Poems* (Halifax, 1811)

—, *The Rural Minstrel: A Miscellany of Descriptive Poems* (Halifax, 1813)

—, *The Cottage in the Wood; or, The Art of Becoming Rich and Happy* (Bradford, 1815)

Chadwick, Ellis H., *In the Footsteps of the Brontës* (London, 1914)

—, 'A Gift from M. le Professeur Constantin Heger to Charlotte Brontë', *The Nineteenth Century and After* (April 1917)

Chapman, Maria Weston (ed.), *Harriet Martineau's Autobiography* (3 vols.; London, third edition, 1887)

Chapple, J. A. V., assisted by John Geoffrey Sharps, *Elizabeth Gaskell: A Portrait in Letters* (Manchester, 2007)

Chapple, J. A. V., and Shelston, Alan (eds.), *Further Letters of Mrs Gaskell* (Manchester, 2003)

Chitham, Edward (ed.), *The Poems of Anne Brontë: A New Text and Commentary* (London, 1979)

—, and Winnifrith, T. J., *Brontë Facts and Brontë Problems* (London, 1983)

Clark, Cumberland, *Charles Dickens and the Yorkshire Schools* (London, 1918)

Cochrane, Margaret and Robert, *My Dear Boy: The Life of Arthur Bell Nicholls, B.A., Husband of Charlotte Brontë* (Beverley, 1999)

Davies, Stevie, *Emily Brontë: Heretic* (London, 1994)

Depage, Henri, *La Vie d'Antoine Depage 1862–1925* (Brussels, 1956)

Dinsdale, Ann, *Old Haworth* (Keighley, 1999)

—, *The Brontës at Haworth* (London, 2006)

Easson, Angus, 'Two Suppressed Opinions in Mrs. Gaskell's *Life of Charlotte Brontë*', *BST*, 16:4 (1974).

Feaver, William, *The Art of John Martin* (Oxford, 1975)

Fermi, Sarah, 'The Brontës at the Clergy Daughters' School: When Did They Leave?', *BST*, 21:6 (1996)

—, 'Mellaney Hayne: Charlotte Brontë's School Friend', *BST*, 27:3 (2002)

Foister, S. R., 'The Brontë Portraits', *BST*, 18:5 (1985)

Frank, Katherine, *A Chainless Soul: A Life of Emily Brontë* (Boston, 1990)

Fraser, Rebecca, *The Brontës: Charlotte Brontë and Her Family* (New York, 1988)

Gérin, Winifred, *Charlotte Brontë* (Oxford, 1967)

—, *Emily Brontë* (Oxford, 1971)

— (ed.), Charlotte Brontë, *Five Novelettes*, transcribed from the original manuscripts and edited by Winifred Gérin (London, 1971)

Gordon, Lyndall, *Charlotte Brontë: A Passionate Life* (London, 1994)

Hargreaves, G. D., 'The Publishing of *Poems by Currer, Ellis and Acton Bell*', *BST*, 15:79 (1969)

Hatfield, C. W., 'Charlotte Brontë and Hartley Coleridge, 1840' (includes 'Ashworth'), *BST*, 10:1 (1940)

Holgate, Ivy, 'The Structure of *Shirley*', *BST*, 14:2 (1962)

Hook, Ruth, 'The Father of the Family', *BST*, 17:2 (1977)

Hopewell, D. G., 'Cowan Bridge', *BST*, 6:31 (1921)

Ingham, Patricia, *The Brontës* (Authors in Context) (Oxford, 2006)

Kay, Brian, and Knowles, James, 'Where *Jane Eyre* and *Mary Barton* were Born', *BST*, 15:2 (1967)

Kellett, Jocelyn, *Haworth Parsonage: The Home of the Brontës* (Keighley, 1977)

Lane, Margaret, *The Brontë Story* (London, 1953)

Lever, Sir T., 'Charlotte Brontë and George Smith: An Extract from the late Sir Tresham Lever's Unpublished Biography of George Smith', *BST*, 17:87 (1977)

Leyland, Francis A., *The Brontë Family, with Special Reference to Patrick Branwell Brontë* (2 vols.; London, 1886)

Liddington, Jill, 'Anne Lister and Emily Brontë 1838–1839: Landscape with Figures', *BST*, 26:1 (2001)

Lock, John, and Dixon, Canon W. T., *A Man of Sorrow: The Life, Letters and Times of the Rev. Patrick Brontë* (London, 1965)

Lonoff, Sue, 'An Unpublished Memoir by Paul Heger', *BST*, 20:6 (1992)

—— (ed.), *Charlotte Brontë and Emily Brontë: The Belgian Essays* (Yale, 1996)

Macdonald, Frederika, 'The Brontës at Brussels', *Woman at Home* (July 1894)

——, *The Secret of Charlotte Brontë* (London, 1914)

MacEwan, Helen, *The Brontës in Brussels* (London, 2014)

Miller, Lucasta, *The Brontë Myth* (London, 2001)

Morden, Barbara C., *John Martin: Apocalypse Now!* (Newcastle, 2010)

Oram, Eanne, 'Brief for Miss Branwell', *BST*, 14:4 (1964)

Palmer, Geoffrey, *Dear Martha: The Letters of Arthur Bell Nicholls to Martha Brown (1862–1878)*, described and transcribed by Geoffrey Palmer (Keighley, 2004)

Ratchford, Fannie Elizabeth, *The Brontës' Web of Childhood* (New York, 1941)

Ray, Gordon N. (ed.), *The Letters and Private Papers of William Makepeace Thackeray*, collected and edited by Gordon N. Ray (4 vols.; London, 1946)

Robinson, Mary, *Emily Brontë* (1883)

Ruijssenaars, Eric, *Charlotte Brontë's Promised Land: The Pensionnat Heger and Other Brontë Places in Brussels* (Keighley, 2000)

——, *The Pensionnat Revisited: More Light Shed on the Brussels of the Brontës* (Leiden, 2003)

Seaward, Mark R. D., 'Charlotte Brontë's Napoleonic Relic', *BST*, 17:3 (1978)

Shorter, Clement K., *The Brontës, Life and Letters: being an attempt to present a full and final record of the lives of the three sisters, Charlotte, Emily and Anne Brontë from the biographies of Mrs Gaskell and others, and from numerous hitherto unpublished manuscripts and letters* (2 vols.; London, 1908)

Shuttleworth, Sally, *Charlotte Brontë and Victorian Psychology* (Cambridge, 1996)

Smith, Margaret, 'Newly Acquired Brontë Letters, Transcriptions and Notes', *BST*, 21:7 (1996)

Spielmann, M. H., *The Inner History of the Brontë–Heger Letters* (London, 1919)

Stevens, Joan (ed.), *Mary Taylor, Friend of Charlotte Brontë: Letters from New Zealand and Elsewhere* (Auckland, 1972)

Stirling, A. M. W., *The Richmond Papers* (London, 1926)

Stoneman, Patsy, *Brontë Transformations: The Cultural Dissemination of Jane Eyre and Wuthering Heights* (Hemel Hempstead, 1996)

—, *Charlotte Brontë* (Tavistock, 2013)

Taylor, Mary, *The First Duty of Women: A Series of Articles Reprinted from the Victoria Magazine 1865 to 1870* (London, 1870)

—, *Miss Miles: A Tale of Yorkshire Life Sixty Years Ago*, with an introduction by Janet H. Murray (Oxford, 1990)

Thompson, E. P., *The Making of the English Working Class* (Harmondsworth, 1991)

Thormählen, Marianne (ed.), *The Brontës in Context* (Cambridge, 2012)

Uglow, Jenny, *Elizabeth Gaskell: A Habit of Stories* (London, 1993)

Weir, Edith M., 'Cowan Bridge: New Light from Old Documents', *BST*, 11:56 (1946)

—, 'New Brontë Material Comes to Light', *BST*, 11:4 (1949)

—, 'The Hegers and a Yorkshire Family', *BST*, 14:3 (1963)

Whitbread, Helena (ed.), *No Priest but Love: Journals of Anne Lister 1824–1826* (London, 1992)

Whitehead, Barbara, *Charlotte Brontë and Her 'dearest Nell': The Story of a Friendship* (Otley, 1993)

Whitworth, Alan, *Thornton Through Time* (Stroud, 2011)

Wise, T. J., and Symington, J. A. (eds.), *The Miscellaneous and Unpublished Writings of Charlotte and Patrick Branwell Brontë* (2 vols.; Oxford, 1936, 1938)

Wood, Steven, *Haworth, Oxenhope & Stanbury from Old Photographs* (Stroud, 2011). *Vol. 1: Domestic & Social Life*; *Vol. 2: Trade & Industry*

—, *Haworth, 'A strange uncivilized little place'* (Stroud, 2012)

—, *Haworth, Oxenhope & Stanbury from Old Maps* (Stroud, 2014)

Yates, W. W., *The Father of the Brontës, His Life and Work at Dewsbury and Hartshead* (Leeds, 1897)

Abbreviations

AB   Anne Brontë
ABN   Arthur Bell Nicholls
BB   (Patrick) Branwell Brontë
CB   Charlotte Brontë (later Nicholls)
CH   Constantin Heger
ECG   Elizabeth Cleghorn Gaskell
EJB   Emily Jane Brontë
EN   Ellen Nussey
GS   George Smith
MB   Maria Brontë (née Branwell)
MW   Margaret Wooler
PB   Reverend Patrick Brontë
WSW   William Smith Williams

Art of the Brontës	Christine Alexander and Jane Sellars, *The Art of the Brontës* (Cambridge, 1995)
Barker	Juliet Barker, *The Brontës* (London, 1994)
BPM	Brontë Parsonage Museum, Haworth
Brontëana	*Brontëana. The Rev. Patrick Brontë, A.B., His Collected Works and Life: The Works, and the Brontës of Ireland*, ed. J. Horsfall Turner (Bingley, 1898)
BS	*Brontë Studies*
BST	*Brontë Society Transactions*
Critical Heritage	*The Brontës: The Critical Heritage*, ed. Miriam Allott (London, 1974)
ECG Letters	*The Letters of Mrs Gaskell*, eds. J. A. V. Chapple and Arthur Pollard (Manchester, 1997)
EJB Poems	*The Poems of Emily Brontë*, eds. Derek Roper with Edward Chitham (Oxford, 1995)
EN Reminiscences	Ellen Nussey, 'Reminiscences of Charlotte Brontë by

"A Schoolfellow"', *Scribner's Monthly*, May 1871, reprinted as an appendix in *LCB* 1, 589–610

EWCB *An Edition of the Early Writings of Charlotte Brontë*, ed. Christine Alexander (Oxford, 1987–91). *Vol. 1: 1826–32; Vol. 2 (Part 1): 1833–4; Vol. 2 (Part 2): 1834–5*

Interviews *The Brontës: Interviews and Recollections*, ed. Harold Orel (Iowa City, 1997)

LCB *The Letters of Charlotte Brontë, with a Selection of Letters by Family and Friends*, ed. Margaret Smith (Oxford, 1995–2004). *Vol. 1: 1829–47; Vol. 2: 1848–51; Vol. 3: 1852–55*

Life Elizabeth Cleghorn Gaskell, *The Life of Charlotte Brontë*, ed. Angus Easson (Oxford, 1996)

Lonoff *Charlotte Brontë and Emily Brontë: The Belgian Essays*, ed. Sue Lonoff (Yale, 1996)

LPB *The Letters of the Reverend Patrick Brontë*, ed. Dudley Green (Stroud, 2005)

PCB *The Poems of Charlotte Brontë: A New Text and Commentary*, ed. Victor A. Neufeldt (New York and London, 1985)

SHB *The Brontës: Their Lives, Friendships & Correspondence* (The Shakespeare Head Brontë), eds. Thomas J. Wise and J. Alexander Symington (4 vols.; Oxford, 1932)

TGA *The Brontës: Tales of Glass Town, Angria and Gondal*, ed. Christine Alexander (Oxford, 2010)

Notes

Volumes cited in short form can be found in the bibliography.

Epigraphs

there's a fire and fury raging in that little woman: William Makepeace Thackeray to
Mary Holmes, 25 February 1852, *The Letters and Private Papers of William
Makepeace Thackeray*, collected and edited by Gordon N. Ray (4 vols.;
London, 1946), 3, 12.

a tiny, delicate, little person: Anne Thackeray Ritchie, 'My Witches' Cauldron',
Macmillans' Magazine, February 1891: extract reprinted in *LCB* 2, 754–5.

talented people: CB to EN, 14 April 1846, *LCB* 1, 463.

Prologue: 1 September 1843

p. 1   *I should inevitably fall*: CB to EJB, 2 September 1843, *LCB* 1, 329.

p. 2   *great honest eyes*: the description is William Makepeace Thackeray's in
        'The Last Sketch', *The Cornhill Magazine*, Vol. 1 (April 1860), quoted in
        Interviews, 109.

p. 2   *[I]t is an imbecility*: CB to EN, ?April 1843, *LCB* 1, 315.

p. 2   *No inhabitant of Brussels*: *The Professor*, 138.

p. 3   *Romanism . . . pervaded every arrangement . . . sensual indulgence . . . reared
        in slavery*: *Villette*, 127.

p. 3   *I felt as if*: CB to EJB, 2 September 1843, *LCB* 1, 329.

p. 4   *[B]ut I was determined to confess . . . I actually did confess*: CB to EJB,
        2 September 1843, *LCB* 1, 330.

p. 4   *consciousness of faculties unexercised*: CB to EN, 7 August 1841, *LCB* 1, 266.

p. 5   *the mere relief*: *Villette*, 162.

p. 5   *I saw her for an instant*: CB to EJB, 1 October 1843, *LCB* 1, 331.

1   Becoming Brontë   1777–1820

p. 6   *My father's name*: PB to ECG, 20 June 1855, *LPB*, 233.

p. 7   *A neat Irish cabin*: PB, *Cottage Poems*, 73.

p. 7   *owned four books*: Lock and Dixon, *A Man of Sorrow*, 4.

p. 8   *insidious, And Malignant enemies*: PB to Hugh Brontë, 20 November 1843, *LPB*, 155.

p. 8   *but . . . of all kinds of tyranny*: PB to the editor of *The Leeds Intelligencer*, 22 July 1843, *LPB*, 143.

p. 9   *very genteelly*: Henry Kirke White to his mother, 26 October 1805, *LPB*, 318.

p. 9   *Nelson's Bronte*: see Jane Grey Nelson, 'Sicily and the Brontë Name', *BST*, 16:1 (1971), and Stephen Whitehead, 'The Dukedom of Bronte and the Name "Brontë"', *BS*, 25:1 (2000).

p. 10   *assumed to be the hero's kin*: see CB to WSW, ?5 November 1849, *LCB* 2, 279.

p. 10   *to live & rot in old England*: PB to the Reverend John Campbell, 12 November 1808, *LPB*, 24.

p. 10   *considerable sums*: PB's will, dated 20 June 1855, is printed in *LPB*, 372.

p. 11   *violated both the dictates . . . peace & contentment . . . The Lady I mentioned*: all from PB to the Reverend John Campbell, 12 November 1808, *LPB*, 24.

p. 11   *He is said*: these stories about PB in Dewsbury come from W. W. Yates, *The Father of the Brontës*.

p. 12   *clever and good-hearted*: Yates, 38.

p. 12   *reported peculiarities*: Yates, 22.

p. 12   *from morning till noon*: *Cottage Poems*, xiv.

p. 12   *To Miss Fennell*: this first edition of *Cottage Poems* is in the Henry W. and Albert A. Berg Collection of New York Public Library.

p. 13   *Cartwright was ready and waiting*: the attack was reported vividly in *The Leeds Mercury*, 45:243 (18 April 1812). See also E. P. Thompson, *The Making of the English Working Class*, 638, and Barker, 45–7. Other information about Rawfolds Mill was accessed from the Yorkshire Archaeological Society website (April 2014), https://www.yas.org.uk.

p. 14   *the group who helped Cartwright*: there were only four of them: Hammond Roberson, who reportedly arrived on the scene on horseback, waving his sword around angrily, two other local manufacturers called

Cockhill and Dixon – a master-dyer and chemical works manager respectively – and 'a local *bon-vivant* named Clough' (E. P. Thompson, *Making of the English Working Class*, 638).

p. 14   *the ink has faded*: see Barker, 46 and 844 n61.

p. 14   *Neither of these stories*: Juliet Barker points out (Barker, 47) that there was no need to give Luddites secret burials.

p. 15   *For some years now*: MB to PB, 18 September 1812, *SHB* 1, 13.

p. 15   *I thank God*: MB to PB, 18 September 1812, *SHB* 1, 13.

p. 16   *nobly-shaped head . . . in his youth*: *Life*, 34.

p. 16   *not pretty*: *Life*, 37.

p. 16   *possessing more than ordinary talents*: *Life*, 40.

p. 16   *there is a rectitude*: CB to EN, ?16 February 1850, *LCB* 2, 347.

p. 16   *If you knew what were my feelings*: MB to PB, 26 August 1812, *SHB* 1, 9.

p. 16   *your arm to assist me . . . when I work . . . I have now written a pretty long letter*: MB to PB, 5 September 1812, *SHB* 1, 11.

p. 17   *a pretty correct notion*: MB to PB, 5 September 1812, *SHB* 1, 11.

p. 17   *And even I begin to think*: MB to PB, 18 September 1812, *SHB* 1, 13–14.

p. 17   *the anticipation*: MB to PB, 21 October 1812, *SHB* 1, 19.

p. 18   *Real love is ever apt to suspect . . . I am certain*: MB to PB, 5 December 1812, *SHB* 1, 22–3.

p. 18   *a pathos of apprehension*: EN Reminiscences, *LCB* 1, 608.

p. 18   *a very few articles*: *SHB* 1, 21. Five years after Maria's death her copy of *The Imitation of Christ* was given to her daughter Charlotte and is now in the Pierpont Morgan Library in New York City.

p. 18   *no record of Maria ever going back*: Elizabeth Gaskell heard that Maria Brontë's friends in Cornwall had 'disowned her at her marriage' (*LCB* 2, 447), a claim which, like many things from the same source, Janet Kay-Shuttleworth, turned out to be distorted or exaggerated.

p. 19   *on the same day and hour*: *SHB* 1, 30.

p. 19   *constant friendly intercourse*: *SHB* 1, 37.

p. 20   *she kissed me and was much affected*: extracts from Elizabeth Firth's diary, *LPB*, 337.

p. 20   *beloved sister*: the copy of *Cottage Poems* inscribed by PB to Elizabeth Branwell is in BPM.

p. 21   *M. E. and C. Brontë to tea*: *LPB*, 340.

p. 21   *Came home in safety*: *LPB*, 340.

p. 21   *We sat up expecting the Radicals*: *LPB*, 341.

p. 21   *by his prophecies*: C. C. Moore Smith's note to Elizabeth Firth's diary, *SHB* 1, 45n.

p. 22   *The sensual novelist*: Patrick Brontë, *The Cottage in the Wood*, 3.

2   An Uncivilised Little Place   *1820–25*

p. 24   *The footprint of Haworth Parsonage*: the shape of the building in 1853 is shown very clearly on the map of Haworth made by the Board of Health assessors that year, a copy of which is in the Keighley Local Services Archive (see plate section). Jocelyn Kellett, in *Haworth Parsonage: The Home of the Brontës* (Keighley, 1977), includes fascinating floorplans showing CB's alterations to the house in the 1850s and John Wade's more extensive changes in the 1860s. More information about the Parsonage, including the detail about the outside stairs, can be found in Sarah Barrett, *A Room of Their Own: 80 Years of the Brontë Parsonage Museum 1928–2008* (Kendal, 2008).

p. 24   *hundreds of thousands of pounds*: ECG to ?John Forster, after 29 September 1853, *LCB* 3, 198.

p. 25   *A strange uncivilized little place*: CB to WSW, 24 August 1849, *LCB* 2, 240.

p. 25   *the language, the manners, the very dwellings*: CB's preface to the 1850 edition of *Wuthering Heights*.

p. 25   *Brutal tendencies*: the opinion of Benjamin Binns, son of PB's tailor, as reported in 'The Brontës and the Brontë Country: A Chat with One Who Knew Them', *The Bradford Observer*, 17 February 1894.

p. 26   *the old hill spirit . . . I believe many of the Yorkshiremen . . . kept themselves very close*: *Life*, 42.

p. 27   *Grandisonian*: the comparison with Samuel Richardson's hero, the epitome of fastidious politeness, was the opinion of BB's friend Francis Grundy, as recalled in 1879; see *Interviews*, 46.

p. 27   *indeed he was cautious*: 'The Brontës and the Brontë Country: A Chat with One Who Knew Them', *The Bradford Observer*, 17 February 1894.

p. 27   *arguments needlessly complicated*: see for instance *LPB*, 140–41, 163, 166, 169.

p. 27   *you have such a method*: *SHB* 1, 15.

p. 27   *I caught a glare*: ECG to ?John Forster, ?after 29 September 1853, *LCB* 3, 199.

p. 28　*volcanic . . . in rapid succession . . . either the make*: passages omitted from the third edition of *Life*, as are the stories about the hearthrug, the boots and the chairs; see *Life*, 471–2.

p. 28　*treasured up in her drawers . . . cut into shreds*: *Life*, 471.

p. 28　*in the fashion of that day*: *SHB* 1, 49–50.

p. 29　*Charlotte certainly passed it on . . . Ellen herself added the detail*: EN Reminiscences, *LCB* 1, 607–8.

p. 29　*They have their humors and their faults*: *LPB*, 71. PB's variations are interesting: in the first of the two quoted quatrains, he has substituted 'failings' for 'foibles', and, in the second, 'To clamor, rage and boast,/ For wives their duties best discharge' for 'Whate'er proud reason boast;/For those their duties best discharge'.

p. 30　*a stranger in a strange land . . . left nearly quite alone*: *SHB* 1, 58.

p. 30　*an internal cancer*: *Life*, 43.

p. 30　*almost every day*: *SHB* 1, 58.

p. 30　*an affectionate, agonising something . . . She was cold and silent*: *SHB* 1, 59.

p. 30　*The mother was not very anxious . . . as it was done in Cornwall*: *Life*, 43.

p. 31　*spiritless . . . toddling wee things*: *Life*, 43.

p. 31　*her constitution was enfeebled*: *SHB* 1, 59.

p. 31　*oh God my poor children!*: related by ECG in a letter to Catherine Winkworth, 25 August 1850, *LCB* 2, 447.

p. 31　*During many years*: *SHB* 1, 59.

p. 32　*all the dear faces*: related in Marion Harland, *Charlotte Brontë at Home* (New York and London, 1899), 28.

p. 32　*[she] tried hard*: *Life*, 46.

p. 32　*unknown, unloved . . . The longing of her childhood*: *Shirley*, 271.

p. 32　*The offspring nestled to the parent*: *Shirley*, 362.

p. 33　*just before the Miss Brontës became famous*: *SHB* 1, 38.

p. 33　*I heard before I left*: quoted in C. M. Edgerley, 'Elizabeth Branwell: The "small, antiquated lady"', *BST*, 9:2 (1937).

p. 34　*whether they be married or single*: this and all the other quotes in the paragraph are from PB to Mary Burder, 28 July 1823, *SHB* 1, 62–3.

p. 35　*one whom I cannot think . . . Happily for me*: Mary Burder to PB, 8 August 1823, *SHB* 1, 65.

p. 35　*many keen sarcasms*: *SHB* 1, 66.

p. 35　*Once more let me ask you*: *SHB* 1, 68.

p. 36　*A story she told*: EN relates it in EN Reminiscences, *LCB* 1, 607.

p. 37   *a little mother . . . superhuman in goodness and cleverness*: EN Reminiscences, *LCB* 1, 593.

p. 37   *the leading topics of the day*: *Life*, 48.

p. 37   *Would you not be happier*: *Jane Eyre*, 58.

p. 37   *as soon as they could read and write . . . signs of rising talent*: *Life*, 47.

p. 37   *I began with the youngest*: *Life*, 48.

p. 38   *the* really *necessitous clergy*: 'Cowan Bridge: New Light from Old Documents', *BST*, 11:56 (1946). The prospectus put forward a remarkably progressive position on female education:

   'This civilized island is blessed with various laudable institutions for the promotion of· Classical and Scientific Learning, and Clergymen can send their sons to the University where ample scope is afforded for those Bright talents which are so frequently found in an humble sphere of life. But hitherto no colleges, no liberal institutions of learning for their daughters where they can reap those blessings their Brethren enjoy, and it by no means unfrequently happens that we may see these pious girls busy – perhaps in a Dairy or employed in some menial occupation in a kitchen.'

p. 39   *the Use of Globes*: details of the curriculum are given in 'Cowan Bridge School: An Old Prospectus Re-examined', *BST*, 12:63 (1953).

p. 39   *reading 'little', writing 'pretty well'*: Cowan Bridge School admission register, quoted in *SHB* 1, 69n.

p. 40   *It is because they love us*: William Carus Wilson, *The Children's Friend for the Year 1836*, Vol. XIII (BPM).

p. 40   *Look there!*: *Child's First Tales, Chiefly in Words of One Syllable for the Use of Infant Schools and Little Children in General*, Vol. 1, 1836.

p. 40   *a passion of resentment*: *Jane Eyre*, 35–6.

p. 41   *the diet, the discipline, the system of tuition*: CB to MW, 28 August 1848, *LCB* 2, 106.

p. 42   *a second Dotheboys' Hall*: W. W. Carus Wilson Jr to *The Halifax Guardian*, 18 July 1857, *SHB* 4, 309.

p. 42   *a bright, clever, happy little girl*: Anna Andrews, former temporary superintendent of Cowan Bridge School, quoted in a letter from W. W. Carus Wilson Jr to *The Leeds Mercury*, 16 May 1857, *SHB* 4, 298. She has often been identified with 'Miss Scatcherd' in *Jane Eyre*, though Sarah Fermi and Judith Smith have done much to clear her name in their article 'The Real Miss Andrews: Teacher, Mother, Abolitionist', *BST*, 25: 2 (2000).

p. 42 *the fury of which [Helen] was incapable*: Jane Eyre, 74.

p. 42 *One former pupil*: unidentified, but quoted by ABN in his letter to *The Halifax Guardian*, 6 June 1857; see 'The Cowan Bridge Controversy', *SHB* 4, 302.

p. 42 *Mrs Gaskell heard numerous stories*: and had to suppress some of them for the third edition of her biography; see the explanatory notes by Angus Easson in *Life*, 474–9.

p. 43 *Another ex-pupil*: reported by ABN in a letter to *The Halifax Guardian*, 15 July 1857, *SHB* 4, 311.

p. 43 *naturally very delicate . . . is it fair to trace*: W. W. Carus Wilson Jr to the *Daily News*, 24 April 1857, *SHB* 4, 297.

p. 43 *an excellent and eminently useful clergyman . . . so delicate that there were doubts . . . They all inherited consumption*: quoted by W. W. Carus Wilson Jr, *SHB* 4, 298.

p. 43 *manhandled sadistically*: *Life*, 58.

p. 44 *My career was a very quiet one*: CB to WSW, ?5 November 1849, *LCB* 2, 279.

p. 44 *for the sake of greater quiet . . . Of the two younger ones*: *Life*, 61.

p. 44 *How far young and delicate children*: Anna Andrews quoted by W. W. Carus Wilson Jr in a letter to *The Leeds Mercury*, 28 May 1857, *SHB* 4, 301.

p. 44 *My little family had escaped*: PB, 'Sermon on the Eruption', *Brontëana*, 212.

p. 45 *black moory substance*: PB's account to *The Leeds Intelligencer*, 9 September 1824, *LPB*, 51.

p. 45 *The torrent was seen coming down the glen*: quoted in William Atkins, *The Moor*, 176.

p. 45 *cowering 'in a Porch'*: the porch mentioned is thought to have been that of Ponden Hall; see Mrs H. Rhodes to J. Erskine Stuart, quoted in Barker, 859 n63.

p. 45 *onward rolls the dark, resistless tide*: *Brontëana*, 207.

p. 46 *I suffered to see my sisters perishing*: CB to WSW, ?5 November 1849, *LCB* 2, 279.

p. 47 *the rigid & lengthened corpse*: 'My compliments to the weather', 'Roe Head Journal', *TGA*, 172.

p. 47 *And, to this moment, I can feel*: BB, 'Calm and clear the day, declining', *Works of Patrick Branwell Brontë: An Edition. Vol. 3: 1837–1848*, ed. Victor A. Neufeldt (New York and London, 1999), 414.

p. 47   *another of my little girls . . . in the end . . . one elderly woman*: PB to Mr Marriner, 10 November 1824, *LPB*, 54.

p. 48   *frequently espoused her cause*: PB to ECG, 30 July 1855, *LPB*, 239.

p. 48   *a hungry, good-natured, ordinary girl*: *Life*, 61.

p. 48   *racy and pungent gossip*: *Jane Eyre*, 78.

p. 48   *it has been suggested*: by Sarah Fermi; see 'Mellaney Hayne: "Charlotte Brontë's School Friend"', *BS*, 27:3 (2002).

p. 48   *by dying young*: *Jane Eyre*, 81.

p. 48   *If people were always kind and obedient*: *Jane Eyre*, 57.

3   The Genii of the Parsonage   1825–31

p. 50   *very quaint in appearance*: EN's opinion, *LCB* 1, 125 n5.

p. 50   *fairishes . . . It wur the factories*: *Life*, 63.

p. 50   *a sort of vegetable glue*: *LCB* 1, 331.

p. 50   *O Dear, O Dear, O Dear*: EJB Diary Paper, 24 November 1834, *SHB* 1, 124.

p. 50   *a bit of a tyke*: Ellis H. Chadwick, *In the Footsteps of the Brontës*, 68.

p. 50   *kindly and conscientious*: *Life*, 49.

p. 51   *there old Brontë*: 'The Brontës and the Brontë Country: A Chat with One Who Knew Them', *The Bradford Observer*, 17 February 1894.

p. 51   *stood around like aliens*: Ellis H. Chadwick (*In the Footsteps of the Brontës*, 87) reports a local Haworth story about the Brontë children being invited to a birthday party where 'Their shyness was painful to behold; they were awkward and silent the whole evening, and evidently greatly relieved when it was time to return home.'

p. 51   *[They] had no idea of ordinary games*: Ellis H. Chadwick, *In the Footsteps of the Brontës*, 87.

p. 52   *a sort of idol*: Benjamin Binns's opinion, 'The Brontës and the Brontë Country: A Chat with One Who Knew Them', *The Bradford Observer*, 17 February 1894.

p. 53   *[she] would tell us the authors*: 'Mary Taylor's Narrative', from a letter to ECG, 18 January 1856, quoted in *SHB* 1, 90.

p. 53   *One black day*: CB to Hartley Coleridge, 10 December 1840, *LCB* 1, 240.

p. 53   *One night, about the time*: CB, 'First Volume of Tales of the Islanders' (30 June 1829), *EWCB* 1, 21–2.

p. 54   *[I had] a band of Turkish musicians*: BB, 'Introduction to the History of the Young Men', 15 December 1830, *The Miscellaneous and Unpublished Writings of Charlotte and Patrick Branwell Brontë* (2 vols.; Oxford, 1936, 1938), 1, 63.

p. 54   *it was night and we were in bed*: CB, 'The History of the Year' (12 March 1829), *TGA*, 3–4.

p. 56   *Thus having made everything ready*: CB, 'Two Romantic Tales', Chapter 2, 'The Voyage of Discovery' (April 1829), *TGA*, 6–7.

p. 56   *Of College I am tired*: PCB, 27, poem dated 'February 1830'.

p. 57   *I am in the kitchen*: 'The History of the Year' (12 March 1829), *TGA*, 3.

p. 57   *We take 2 and see three newspapers*: 'The History of the Year' (12 March 1829), *TGA*, 3.

p. 58   *O those 3 months*: 'Tales of the Islanders', Vol. 2, Chapter 1, *TGA*, 18–19.

p. 58   *several Martin prints*: see *Art of the Brontës*, 21 and notes.

p. 59   *list of painters*: BPM, Bonnell 80.

p. 59   *His vision is uncommonly acute . . . His mind approaches*: 'Anecdotes of the Duke of Wellington', 30 September 1829, *EWCB* 1, 90.

p. 60   *an immense amount of manuscript*: *Life*, 64.

p. 60   *The total length of the Brontë juvenilia*: estimated by Fannie Ratchford in her ground-breaking study *The Brontës' Web of Childhood* in 1941 and Christine Alexander, among others.

p. 60   *a truly prodigious length*: my calculation, based on the approximate length of 'The Spell' in its printed form in *TGA* (84 printed pages at roughly 400 words per page, i.e., 33,600 words), the number of minuscule manuscript pages – 24 – it takes up in the whole booklet (BL Add. MS 34255), and the total number of pages in the manuscript (44).

p. 60   *Making in the whole*: *EWCB* 1, 214.

p. 61   *I began this book*: 'The Adventures of Mon Edouard de Crack', *EWCB* 1, 134.

p. 61   *I wrote this in 4 hours*: preface to 'Albion and Marina', *TGA*, 55.

p. 61   *I wrote this in half an hour*: see Victor A. Neufeldt's textual note, *PCB*, 397.

p. 61   *little works of fiction*: PB to ECG, 30 July 1855, *LPB*, 239.

p. 61   *All that is written in this book*: *SHB* 1, 81.

p. 61   *making subject matter*: Christine Alexander, 'Note on the Text', *TGA*, xliv.

p. 62   *fall into a decline*: PB to Elizabeth Franks, 28 April 1831, *LPB*, 77.

p. 63   *[she] would nurse me*: EN Reminiscences, *LCB* 1, 594.

p. 63   *None can tell*: *PCB*, 75.

p. 63   *the strangest train of thought*: CB, 'Strange Events, by Lord Charles Wellesley', *EWCB* 1, 257.

4   Among Schoolgirls   1831–5

p. 64   *her dress was changed . . . so short-sighted . . . [She] spoke with a strong Irish accent*: 'Mary Taylor's Narrative', from a letter to ECG, 18 January 1856, *SHB* 1, 89.

p. 65   *there was a silent . . . A faint quivering smile*: EN Reminiscences, *LCB* 1, 589.

p. 65   *She was first in everything*: EN Reminiscences, *LCB* 1, 590.

p. 66   *would be kneeling*: EN Reminiscences, *LCB* 1, 591.

p. 66   *We made her try*: 'Mary Taylor's Narrative', from a letter to ECG, 18 January 1856, *SHB* 1, 90.

p. 66   *For years she had not tasted*: EN Reminiscences, *LCB* 1, 590.

p. 66   *She made poetry and drawing*: 'Mary Taylor's Narrative', from a letter to ECG, 18 January 1856, *SHB* 1, 90.

p. 67   *little old woman*: 'Mary Taylor's Narrative', from a letter to ECG, 18 January 1856, *SHB* 1, 89.

p. 67   *She knew the names*: 'Mary Taylor's Narrative', from a letter to ECG, 18 January 1856, *SHB* 1, 90–91.

p. 67   *a lady abbess*: EN, quoted in Clement K. Shorter, *Charlotte Brontë and Her Circle* (London, 1896), 261–2.

p. 67   *delighted to listen to her*: EN Reminiscences, *LCB* 1, 595.

p. 68   *She took all our proceedings*: *SHB* 1, 90.

p. 68   *The whole family*: *SHB* 1, 91.

p. 68   *No one wrote in it*: *SHB* 1, 90.

p. 68   *Her love for them . . . weep and suffer . . . superhuman in goodness and cleverness*: EN Reminiscences, *LCB* 1, 593.

p. 69   *wonders of talent and kindness . . . [T]hey had forgotten what they used to care for*: 'Mary Taylor's Narrative', from a letter to ECG, 18 January 1856, *SHB* 1, 91.

p. 69   *Methought the well-loved dead*: *Villette*, 160 (Chapter 15, 'The Long Vacation').

p. 69   *coaxed out of yielding mammas*: EN Reminiscences, *LCB* 1, 592.

p. 70   *naturally a social, hospitable man*: *Shirley*, 126.

p. 70   *There's no decent way*: Mary Taylor, *Miss Miles*, 28.

p. 71   *very familiar with all the sublimest passages*: EN Reminiscences, *LCB* 1, 595.

p. 71   *I should for once like . . . [Charlotte] evidently was longing*: EN Reminiscences, *LCB* 1, 595.

p. 71   *nothing appearing in view . . . there was always a* lingering *delight*: EN Reminiscences, *LCB* 1, 598.

p. 71   *[A]fter dinner I sew till tea-time*: CB to EN, 21 July 1832, *LCB* 1, 114.

p. 73   *His form was that*: T. J. Wise and J. A. Symington (eds.), *The Miscellaneous and Unpublished Writings of Charlotte and Patrick Branwell Brontë*, 2, 369.

p. 73   *I've some people*: T. J. Wise and J. A. Symington (eds.), *The Miscellaneous and Unpublished Writings of Charlotte and Patrick Branwell Brontë*, 2, 11–12.

p. 73   *he was* then *. . . in wild ecstasy . . . she trembled*: EN Reminiscences, *LCB* 1, 596.

p. 74   *wild and uncultivated . . . as if climbing . . . she probably had been pretty*: EN Reminiscences, *LCB* 1, 596–7.

p. 74   *She talked a great deal*: EN Reminiscences, *LCB* 1, 597.

p. 75   *which she sometimes presented*: EN Reminiscences, *LCB* 1, 597.

p. 75   *with great gusto . . . I tried to hear as little as I could*: EN to T. Wemyss Reid, 3 November 1876, MS Berg Collection.

p. 75   *As a teacher*: Benjamin Binns's recollection in 'The Brontës and the Brontë Country: A Chat with One Who Knew Them', *The Bradford Observer*, 17 February 1894.

p. 75   *rapid and impulsive . . . Tha' willn't, tha' old Irish —' . . . some book which was not the Prayer-book . . . sharp rap with his knuckles*: Benjamin Binns's recollection in 'The Brontës and the Brontë Country: A Chat with One Who Knew Them', *The Bradford Observer*, 17 February 1894.

p. 76   *as motionless as a statue . . . His discourses were characterised*: Benjamin Binns's recollection in 'The Brontës and the Brontë Country: A Chat with One Who Knew Them', *The Bradford Observer*, 17 February 1894.

p. 76   *like twins*: EN Reminiscences, *LCB* 1, 598.

p. 76   *I fed Rainbow, Diamond, Snowflake Jasper*: the first paragraph of this transcription of EJB's Diary Paper (which is in the Brontë Society's collection at BPM) is my own, as the published ones vary, and I'm not happy with the frequent reading of the seventh word as 'pheasant' or 'pheasants', and the eighth as 'alias', in an opened but unclosed paren-thesis. I think that the illegible word that looks like 'pheasants' could be a fifth name in the list of animals fed. All the way through the paper, EJB writes what should be an upper case 'p' as lower case, i.e. 'Sir Robert peel', 'papa' (at the beginning of a sentence as well as mid-sentence). A facsimile of the first page can be seen in Ann Dinsdale's *The Brontës at Haworth*, 46. The second paragraph is Juliet Barker's transcription from Barker, 221.

p. 77   *Anne and I say*: EJB's Diary Paper.

p. 78   *I once thought that he might get into the Merchantile line*: PB to John Driver, 23 February 1838, *LPB*, 115.

p. 78   *I have not one mental qualification*: BB to Francis H. Grundy, 9 June 1842, *Interviews*, 51.

p. 79   *a picture or cut of any kind*: 'Mary Taylor's Narrative', from a letter to ECG, 18 January 1856, *SHB* 1, 90.

p. 79   St Martin's Parsonage, Birmingham: the picture, probably copied from an engraving, is in 'The Roe Head Album' (BPM) and is dated May 1832; see *Art of the Brontës*, 200–201.

p. 79   *a frenzy of productivity*: see *SHB* 1, 77.

p. 79   *so strong was this intention*: Francis A. Leyland, *The Brontë Family*, 1, 127.

p. 80   *tiny adjustments*: see *Art of the Brontës*, 243–4, for Alexander and Sellars' notes on the original and Charlotte's copy.

p. 80   *Branwell's paintings*: both *Terror* and *Queen Esther* are in the collection at BPM.

p. 81   *Miss Brontë brought down*: ECG to unknown, end of September 1853, *ECG Letters*, 249.

p. 81   *upholding the great frame of canvas*: *Life*, 106.

p. 82   *a crude photograph*: a reproduction of it can be seen as Figure 5 in Juliet Barker's article 'The Brontë Portraits: A Mystery Solved', *BST*, 20:1 (1990).

p. 82   *a shocking daub*: the visitor was John Elliot Cairnes, and his letter of 11 October 1858, to William Nesbitt, is quoted at length in *BST*, 18:4 (1984).

p. 82   *the girls were so plain*: John Elliot Cairnes, as above, *BST*, 18:4 (1984).

p. 83   *a large protruding tooth*: 'The Brontës and the Brontë Country: A Chat with One Who Knew Them', *The Bradford Observer*, 17 February 1894.

p. 83   *many teeth gone*: ECG to Catherine Winkworth, 25 August 1850, *LCB* 2, 447.

p. 83   *extremely insignificant*: Frederika Macdonald, 'The Brontës at Brussels', *Woman at Home* (July 1894), 287.

p. 83   *not pleasant*: Anne Thackeray Ritchie to Reginald J. Smith, 18 October 1906, *Interviews*, 160.

p. 83   *doomed to be an old maid*: CB to EN, 4 August 1839, *LCB* 1, 198.

p. 83   *Nature had favoured him with a fairer outside*: CB to WSW, 6 October 1848, *LCB* 2, 124.

p. 83   *I have, in my day*: CB to WSW, 11 March 1848, *LCB* 2, 41.

p. 84   *elaborate pencil-drawings*: *Villette*, 166.

p. 84   *We are all about to divide*: CB to EN, 2 July 1835, *LCB* 1, 139.

p. 84   *Where am I to present my drawing?*: draft letter by BB, quoted in Barker, 226.

p. 84   *It is my design*: PB to Elizabeth Franks, 6 July 1835, *LPB*, 100.

p. 85   *I should have to take the step*: CB to EN, 2 July 1835, *LCB* 1, 139.

p. 85   *just a scrap*: postscript, CB to EN, ?August/September 1836, *LCB* 1, 151.

p. 86   *Duty – Necessity*: CB to EN, 2 July 1835, *LCB* 1, 140.

5   The Double Life   1835–7

p. 88   *at twilight, in the schoolroom*: CB, 'Prefatory Note', 'Selections from Poems by Ellis Bell' (1850), *LCB* 2, 753.

p. 88   *Where wilt thou go, my harassed heart*: *EJB Poems*, 69.

p. 88   *Nobody knew what ailed her . . . The change from her own home*: CB, 'Prefatory Note', 'Selections from Poems by Ellis Bell', *LCB* 2, 753.

p. 89   *queer and non-compliant*: according to Mary Robinson, in *Emily Brontë*, 56–7.

p. 89   *studied alone*: CB, 'Prefatory Note', 'Selections from Poems by Ellis Bell', *LCB* 2, 753.

p. 89   *another lovingly detailed portrait*: EJB's portraits of Grasper, Keeper and Nero are all at BPM, and reproduced in *Art of the Brontës*, plates v, iii and vi.

p. 89   *for the purpose of acquiring information*: from his sponsors' letter to the Three Graces Lodge in Haworth, quoted in Barker, 245.

p. 90   *Read now at least . . . CONDEMN NOT UNHEARD*: BB to the editor of *Blackwood's Magazine*, 8 April 1836, *SHB* 1, 135.

p. 91   *An ocean with a thousand Isles*: 'We wove a web in childhood', *PCB*, 165.

p. 91   *I now heard the far clatter*: PCB, 169.

p. 92   *boring me with their vulgar familiar trash*: 'The Roe Head Journal', *TGA*, 163.

p. 92   *red-in-the-face with impatience*: CB to BB, 1 May 1843, *LCB* 1, 317.

p. 92   *like venom . . . things that nobody else cares for*: CB to EN, 26 September 1836, *LCB* 1, 152.

p. 92   *I strive to conceal*: CB to EN, ?October 1836, *LCB* 1, 153.

p. 93   *I felt as if I could have written gloriously*: 'The Roe Head Journal', *TGA*, 163.

p. 93   *into a kind of lethargy . . . The thought came over me*: 'The Roe Head Journal', *TGA*, 162.

p. 93   *full & liquid*: 'The Roe Head Journal', *TGA*, 163.

p. 93   *Huddersfield & the hills beyond it*: 'The Roe Head Journal', *TGA*, 162–3.

p. 94   *staring, gaping . . . Hang their astonishment! . . . What in all this*: 'The Roe Head Journal', *TGA*, 165.

p. 94   *Men and women who feel all kinds of suffering*: Alethea Hayter, *Opium and the Romantic Imagination* (London, 1968), 40.

p. 94   *after reading De Quincey*: reported by Francis H. Grundy in 1879, see *Interviews*, 48.

p. 95   *had never, to her knowledge*: *Life*, 441.

p. 95   *so exactly . . . [think] intently on it*: *Life*, 441.

p. 95   *The stream of thought*: this and all following quotes in this paragraph are from 'The Roe Head Journal', *TGA*, 163–5.

p. 96   *a feeling like a heavy weight*: 'The Roe Head Journal', *TGA*, 165.

p. 97   *Oh, dreadful is the check*: 'The Prisoner: A Fragment', *EJB Poems*, 182.

p. 97   *I have had enough*: 'The Roe Head Journal', *TGA*, 165.

p. 97   *Don't deceive yourself*: CB to EN, 10 May 1836, *LCB* 1, 144.

p. 97   *I have some qualities*: CB to EN, ?October 1836, *LCB* 1, 153.

p. 98   *If I could always live with you*: CB to EN, 5 and 6 December 1836, *LCB* 1, 156.

p. 98   *I know not how to pray*: CB to EN, 5 and 6 December 1836, *LCB* 1, 156.

p. 98   *I keep trying to do right*: CB to EN, ?October/November 1836, *LCB* 1, 154.

p. 99   *it seems as if some fatality*: CB to EN, 29 December 1836, *LCB* 1, 159.

p. 99   *I will not tell you all I think*: CB to EN, 26 September 1836, *LCB* 1, 151.

p. 99   *Charles Thunder*: CB to EN, ?August/September 1836, *LCB* 1, 151.

p. 99   *I wish I could live with you always*: CB to EN, 26 September 1836, *LCB* I, 152.

p. 99   *I lived on its contents for days*: 'The Roe Head Journal', *TGA*, 173.

p. 99   *Is she alone in the cold earth . . . I can't abide to think*: 'The Roe Head Journal', *TGA*, 166.

p. 100   *There is a voice*: 'The Roe Head Journal', *TGA*, 166.

p. 100   *crude rhapsody*: CB to Robert Southey, 16 March 1837, *LCB* I, 168.

p. 100   *to be for ever known . . . throne of light & glory*: CB's letter presumably containing these phrases is missing, but Southey quotes them back at her in his reply of 12 March 1837, *LCB* I, 166.

p. 100   *She didn't withhold her name or gender*: deducible from Southey's address 'To Miss Charlotte Brontë, Haworth, Bradford', *LCB* I, 167, textual note.

p. 101   *ordinary uses . . . flat & unprofitable*: also quoted back to CB by Southey, 12 March 1837, *LCB* I, 166.

p. 101   *Is it pride which actuates you*: BB to the Editor of *Blackwood's Magazine*, 9 January 1837, *SHB* I, 151.

p. 101   *secluded hills*: BB to William Wordsworth, 19 January 1837, *SHB* I, 151.

p. 101   *flighty . . . disgusted . . . for it contained*: Robert Southey to Caroline Bowles, 27 March 1837, quoted in *LCB* I, 171 n1.

p. 102   *bear the same stamp . . . You live in a visionary world*: Robert Southey to CB, 12 March 1837, *LCB* I, 166.

p. 102   *Many volumes of poems . . . the more likely you will be to deserve . . . every young man . . . You will say*: Robert Southey to CB, 12 March 1837, *LCB* I, 166–7.

p. 102   *It is not because I have forgotten*: Robert Southey to CB, 12 March 1837, *LCB* I, 167.

p. 103   *I felt a painful heat . . . You do not forbid me to write*: CB to Robert Southey, 16 March 1837, *LCB* I, 168.

p. 103   *You kindly allow me . . . My Father is a clergyman*: CB to Robert Southey, 16 March 1837, *LCB* I, 169.

p. 104   *Let me now request*: Robert Southey to CB, 22 March 1837, *LCB* I, 170.

p. 104   *Take care of over-excitement*: Robert Southey to CB, 22 March 1837, *LCB* I, 170.

p. 104   *Southey's Advice*: Robert Southey to CB, 22 March 1837, *LCB* I, 170, textual note.

6   Labour in Vain   1837–41

p. 105   *many remarkable discussions . . . rushed to the front crying . . . a herring in one hand*: these details are from 'The Brontës and the Brontë Country: A Chat with One Who Knew Them', *The Bradford Observer*, 17 February 1894.

p. 106   *mad mechanics*: CB, 'Stancliffe's Hotel', quoted in Christine Alexander, *The Early Writings of Charlotte Brontë*, 178.

p. 106   *I cannot tell you what agony*: CB to EN, 9 June 1838, *LCB* I, 179.

p. 106   *one or two rather plain truths*: CB to EN, 4 January 1838, *LCB* I, 174.

p. 107   *She had but one idea*: 'Mina Laury', *TGA*, 192. That Charlotte dated the manuscript '17 January 1838' – Anne's eighteenth birthday – might mean it was finished as a present to her convalescent sister.

p. 108   *she would turn sick*: *Life*, 132.

p. 109   *I knew I was in a small room*: *Jane Eyre*, 338.

p. 109   *in a constant flow of good-humour . . . They are making such a noise . . . Mary is playing on the piano*: CB to EN, 9 June 1838, *LCB* I, 179.

p. 109   *driven into matrimony*: Mary Taylor, *The First Duty of Women: A Series of Articles Reprinted from the 'Victoria Magazine' 1865 to 1870*.

p. 110   *a man called Jack Sharp*: for more on this, see Gérin, *Emily Brontë*, 76–80, and Katherine Frank, *A Chainless Soul*, 122.

p. 110   *Gentleman Jack . . . You do not know what is said*: Helena Whitbread, *No Priest but Love*, 127.

p. 110   *Elizabeth Patchett surely did too*: Jill Liddington, in *BST*, 26:1 (2001), says very plausibly that the women at Law Hill 'must have talked about the Shibden couple, albeit obliquely'.

p. 111   *desperate little dunces . . . she is requested*: CB to EN, 15 April 1839, *LCB* I, 189.

p. 111   *it was one struggle*: CB to EN, 24 January 1840, *LCB* I, 210.

p. 112   *that dreary Gin-horse round*: CB to EN, 12 March 1839, *LCB* I, 187.

p. 112   *obliquely referred to*: Henry Nussey's diary, Nussey Collections, BL Egerton 3268A, entry for 7 March 1839.

p. 112   *On Tuesday last*: Henry Nussey's diary, Nussey Collections, BL Egerton 3268A, entry for 28 February 1839.

p. 112   *I have no personal repugnance . . . [Your future wife's] character . . . take a worthy man . . . You do not know me*: CB to Henry Nussey, 5 March 1839, *LCB* I, 185.

p. 113 *Received an unfavourable report*: Henry Nussey's diary, Nussey Collections, BL Egerton 3268A, entry for 8 March 1839.

p. 113 *I felt that though I esteemed Henry . . . I was aware*: CB to EN, 12 March 1839, *LCB* 1, 187–8.

p. 113 *ten to one*: CB to EN, 12 March 1839, *LCB* 1, 187.

p. 113 *after the manner of his Countrymen . . . at home you know Ellen . . . [W]ell thought I*: CB to EN, 4 August 1839, *LCB* 1, 198.

p. 114 *an opening . . . as Clerk . . . open a wider field . . . and in time*: PB to John Driver Esqr., 23 February 1838, *LPB*, 116.

p. 115 *sisterly ways*: Margaret Hartley's recollection, as reported in W. W. Yates, 'The Brontë Family: A Suggestion. Two Years in the Life of Branwell Brontë', *Dewsbury Reporter*, 25 November 1893, quoted in *Art of the Brontës*, 330: 'I recollect his sister Charlotte coming, and remember her sisterly ways. She stayed a day, and I believe that was her only visit. They left the house together, and he saw her off by the Keighley coach.'

p. 116 *very like what a frank, wealthy, Conservative gentleman*: CB to EJB, 8 June 1839, *LCB* 1, 191.

p. 116 *I used to think*: CB to EJB, 8 June 1839, *LCB* 1, 191.

p. 116 *[She] does not know my character*: CB to EN, 30 June 1839, *LCB* 1, 194.

p. 116 *the greatest possible quantity of labour*: CB to EJB, 8 June 1839, *LCB* 1, 191.

p. 116 *mental liberty*: CB to EJB, ?July 1839, *LCB* 1, 195.

p. 116 *look on and listen*: CB to EJB, 8 June 1839, *LCB* 1, 191.

p. 116 *to my astonishment*: CB to EN, 30 June 1839, *LCB* 1, 193.

p. 117 *extraordinarily benevolent people . . . certainly on one occasion*: SHB 1, 177.

p. 117 *had no gifts . . . in a very morbid condition . . . if she was invited to walk*: SHB 1, 177.

p. 117 *I love 'ou*: *Life*, 136.

p. 118 *brave defeat . . . doubters*: EN Reminiscences, *LCB* 1, 605.

p. 118 *[S]he was quite overpowered*: EN Reminiscences, *LCB* 1, 606.

p. 119 *No doubt it is terrible*: 'Caroline Vernon', *TGA*, 266–7.

p. 119 *The young lady's feelings*: 'Caroline Vernon', *TGA*, 275.

p. 119 *But how do I wish him to regard me? . . . I wonder whether I love him? . . . I'm very wicked*: 'Caroline Vernon', *TGA*, 290.

p. 119 *She did not want him to love her in return*: 'Caroline Vernon', *TGA*, 303.

p. 120 *standing for upwards of a quarter of a year . . . No, be assured*: 'Caroline Vernon', *TGA*, 271.

p. 120 *a very similar idea*: 'Gerald Emerald extended his hand – which at the moment of writing still remains in that position', Vladimir Nabokov, *Pale Fire* (Harmondsworth, 1962), 211.

p. 121 *A Rowland for your Oliver*: *PCB*, 271.

p. 121 *The Major . . . swashing and martial*: see EN's notes to Anne Brontë's letter of 4 October 1847, *LCB* 1, 545 n6.

p. 122 *the great spirits of the walking party . . . very thirsty*: EN's note to CB's letter of 17 March 1840, *SHB* 1, 201.

p. 122 *became alarming for the length of time required*: EN's note to CB's letter of 17 March 1840, *SHB* 1, 201.

p. 122 *one of her best drawings*: the drawing, in BPM, is not signed, nor is the sitter identified, but Juliet Barker has made a convincing case for it being the portrait of William Weightman by CB that EN refers to in her annotations of CB's letters: 'I recall the taking of Mr Weightman's portrait by Charlotte' (*SHB* 1, 201n); see Juliet R. V. Barker, 'A Possible Portrait of William Weightman', *BST*, 19:4 (1987). However, Barker's assumption that the pencil drawing was one of two pictures of Weightman by CB, one painted and one drawn, seems to me unlikely. CB's references to 'the painting of Miss Celia Amelia Weightman's portrait' in her letter to EN of 17 March 1840 (*LCB* 1, 211) could easily refer to a work by some other member of her family (Anne or Branwell would be likely candidates), painting Weightman at the same time as CB drew him.

p. 122 *He sits opposite to Anne*: CB to EN, 20 January 1842, *LCB* 1, 279.

p. 122 *the evident wandering instability*: CB to EN, end of June 1840, *LCB* 1, 222.

p. 122 *thorough male-flirt . . . perfectly conscious*: CB to EN, 14 July 1840, *LCB* 1, 223–4.

p. 123 *She thought you a fine-looking girl*: CB to EN, 17 March 1840, *LCB* 1, 211.

p. 123 *Several young gentlemen*: CB to Hartley Coleridge (draft), December 1840, *LCB* 1, 237.

p. 123 *standing alone*: 'her nature stood alone', CB, 'Biographical Notice of Ellis and Acton Bell' (1850), *LCB* 2, 746.

p. 123 *making him frantic in action . . . unresisting endurance*: EN, quoted by Wise and Symington in *SHB* 2, 274–5.

p. 123 *[Charlotte] dared not speak to interfere*: this and the other quotes in this paragraph are from *Life*, 214–15.

p. 124 *as if it came from thy Grandmother . . . have the romantic folly*: CB to EN, 20 November 1840, *LCB* 1, 232–3.

p. 124 *Did you not once say to me . . . On one hand don't accept . . . not quite in earnest*: CB to EN, 20 November 1840, *LCB* 1, 234.

p. 125 *instantly conceived a sort of contempt . . . the contempt, the remorse*: CB to EN, 20 November 1840, *LCB* 1, 234.

p. 126 *We are such odd animals . . . supplanted by a stranger . . . Human feelings are queer things . . . excited Aunt's wrath*: CB to EN, 21 December 1839, *LCB* 1, 206.

p. 126 *variable nature . . . strong turn for active life*: CB to EN, ?28 December 1839, *LCB* 1, 207.

p. 126 *A most calm, sedate, sober, abstemious . . . as to the young ones!*: BB to John Brown, 13 March 1840, *SHB* 1, 198–9.

p. 126 *visibly the worst for drink*: Timothy Cockerill, 'A Brontë at Broughton-in-Furness', *BST*, 15:1 (1966).

p. 126 *a strong case . . . [Branwell] left Mr Postlethwaites*: see Barker, 334–5.

p. 127 *merit enough to commend*: a draft letter from Hartley Coleridge to BB, [n.d.]; see *LCB* 1, 238 n1.

p. 128 *demi-semi novelette*: this and all the other quotes in this paragraph are from CB to Hartley Coleridge, 10 December 1840, *LCB* 1, 239–41.

p. 129 *It is no easy thing*: 'Farewell to Angria', *TGA*, 314. Manuscript at BPM, Bonnell 125. The date of this item is not easy to guess at. Christine Alexander places it with the 'Roe Head' fragments, 'about 1839' (*TGA*, 557, note to page 314), while Keith C. Odom has suggested a much later date, around 1850 ('Dating Charlotte Brontë's *Villette*: A Reappraisal', *Papers of the Bibliographical Society of America*, 82:3 (1998)). On the reverse of the paper, and clearly predating 'Farewell to Angria' because the writing is torn through, is a list of names and addresses, including 'Mr. Squeers/Dotheboys-Hall/Greta-Bridge/Yorkshire' (see note to p. 41). Dickens's *Nicholas Nickleby* was first published as a serial in 1838–9.

p. 129 *I wish [the Misses Wooler] or somebody else*: CB to EN, 20 August 1840, *LCB* 1, 226.

p. 129 *it is indeed a hard thing*: CB to Henry Nussey, 9 May 1841, *LCB* 1, 255.

p. 130 *the heavy duty*: CB to EN, 7 August 1841, *LCB* 1, 266.

p. 130 *Of pleasing exterior*: CB to WSW, 3 July 1849, *LCB* 2, 226.

p. 130 *sitting apart from the rest of the family . . . who desired to escape notice*: *Interviews*, 44.

p. 131   *seemed to be qualified*: Francis A. Leyland's recollection, *Interviews*, 40.

p. 131   *some topic that he was acquainted with*: William Heaton's recollection, *Interviews*, 40.

p. 131   *almost involuntarily*, Francis A. Leyland's recollection, *Interviews*, 41.

p. 131   *dramatise . . . stir Miss Brontë up*: EN Reminiscences, *LCB* 1, 609.

p. 131   *a remarkably taciturn, still, thoughtful nature*: CB to WSW, 31 July 1848, *LCB* 2, 94.

p. 132   *I shall never forget*: William Heaton's recollection, *Interviews*, 40–41.

p. 132   *it looks like getting on*: CB repeating back EJB's remark, CB to EJB, ?2 April 1841, *LCB* 1, 251.

p. 132   *nightmare . . . malignant yet cold debauchery . . . lost . . . to all I really liked*: BB to Francis H. Grundy, 22 May 1842, *SHB* 1, 263.

p. 133   *distantly courteous . . . distant and distrait . . . the reverse of attractive*: Francis H. Grundy, 'The Decline and Fall of Branwell Brontë' (1879), quoted in *Interviews*, 46–7.

p. 133   *A scheme is at present in agitation . . . I guess that at the time appointed*: EJB Diary Paper, 30 July 1841, *LCB* 1, 262.

p. 134   *nothing definite is settled about it yet*: AB Diary Paper, 30 July 1841, *LCB* 1, 264.

p. 134   *an eligible situation*: CB to EN, 19 July 1841, *LCB* 1, 260.

p. 134   *The sentence containing this suggestion*: in the same letter of 19 July 1841. Margaret Smith's conjectural reading of the deleted sentence is 'Can events be so turned as that you shall be included as an associate in our projects?'; see *LCB* 1, 261 and 262 n9.

p. 134   *those who had already mastered the elements*: 'Captain Henry Hastings', Gérin (ed.), *Five Novelettes*, 243.

p. 135   *I hardly know*: CB to EN, 7 August 1841, *LCB* 1, 266.

p. 135   *estrangement from one's real character*: CB to EN, 7 August 1841, *LCB* 1, 266.

7   *In a Strange Land*   1842

p. 136   *simple earnest tone . . . These are the daughters*: *Life*, 171.

p. 136   *solely frequented by men*: *Life*, 285.

p. 137   *Above my head*: *Villette*, 48.

p. 137   *she seemed to think . . . I don't remember*: *Life*, 172.

p. 137   *not a beautiful, scarcely a picturesque object*: *Professor*, 47.

p. 137 *Oo somay noo a prazong?*: this and the other phrases following, copied from *Surenne's New French Manual*, 1840, are in PB's 'MS Notebook of French Phrases' at BPM. '[They] must be fully mastered, and ready – semper,' he wrote on the first page. The notebook is usually on display in the museum.

p. 138 *a letter to the press*: *LPB*, 139.

p. 139 *higher than the Pensionnat's chimneys*: see *Life*, 173.

p. 140 *famous for their yield*: see Ruijssenaars, *The Pensionnat Revisited*, 38.

p. 140 *£23.10s*: PB, 'MS Notebook of French Phrases', BPM.

p. 141 *the difference in Country & religion*: CB to EN, May 1842, *LCB* 1, 284.

p. 141 *of precisely the same cast of mind . . . there are 3 teachers . . . no less than seven masters*: CB to EN, May 1842, *LCB* 1, 284.

p. 141 *always an immense favourite*: Frederika Macdonald, 'The Brontës at Brussels', *Woman at Home* (July 1894), 286.

p. 142 *Wappers's epic painting*: *Episode des journées de septembre 1830 sur la place de l'Hôtel de Ville de Bruxelles* now hangs in the entrance hall of the Musée des Beaux Arts in Brussels.

p. 143 *There is one individual*: CB to EN, May 1842, *LCB* 1, 284.

p. 144 *less disagreeable than some of the others*: 'moins désagréable qu'aut autres', Louise de Bassompierre's reminiscence, in 'Two Brussels Schoolfellows of Charlotte Brontë', *BST*, 5:23 (1913). Mademoiselle de Bassompierre was still alive in 1913, and two of CB's other schoolfriends, Laetitia and Frances Wheelwright, died in 1911 and 1912 respectively.

p. 144 *a diminutive, short-sighted, retiring personage*: 'Two Brussels Schoolfellows of Charlotte Brontë', *BST*, 5:23 (1913).

p. 144 *an unsociable, unattractive, unsympathetic disposition . . . as God made her*: 'Two Brussels Schoolfellows of Charlotte Brontë', *BST*, 5:23 (1913).

p. 144 *Emily, though so much the taller*: *Life*, 189.

p. 144 *addressing the wall*: see *Life*, 173.

p. 145 *garroted silence*: one of the Jenkins's sons described the task of walking CB home as 'a purgatorial process . . . from her invincible taciturnity', Thomas Westwood to Lady Alwyne Compton, 21 November 1869, *A Literary Friendship: Letters to Lady Alwyne Compton 1869–1881, from Thomas Westwood*, 3.

p. 145 *If the national character of the Belgians*: CB to EN, ?July 1842, *LCB* 1, 289.

p. 145 *deformity of person*: *The Professor*, 84.

p. 145   *'British English' girl*: *The Professor*, 86.

p. 145   *attuned to the same key*: Frederika Macdonald, 'The Brontës at Brussels', *Woman at Home* (July 1894), 283. ECG also describes Heger's teaching methods at length in *Life*, Chapter 11.

p. 146   *don't draw well together at all*: CB to EN, May 1842, *LCB* 1, 285.

p. 146   *the valuable points of [Emily's] character*: CB to EN, ?July 1842, *LCB* 1, 289.

p. 146   *absolutely* repelled *people*: ECG to Maria Martineau, *c.* 19 August 1855, J. A. V. Chapple and Alan Shelston (eds.), *Further Letters*, 138, reporting a letter to her from ABN, now lost. Arthur Nicholls didn't meet Emily until 1845 and the remark is likely to be coloured by his own later feelings about Emily (and hers for him), but must have been based on a third party's recollections or opinion – possibly Charlotte's.

p. 146   *the newly acquired qualities*: Mary Taylor to EN, 16 February 1843, *LCB* 1, 309.

p. 146   *Imagine Emily*: Mary Taylor to EN, 16 February 1843, *LCB* 1, 309.

p. 146   *choose a time*: Lonoff, 142.

p. 147   *fear and threats*: EJB argues that all God's creatures – human and animal alike – have a divine spark, but those inclined to sinfulness need to be threatened unremittingly with damnation in order to retain and nurture it, the inclination to disobey being so strong. Those who let the divine spark die out face 'a moral chaos without light and without order, a hideous transfiguration of the image in which they were created' (Lonoff, 156), a premonition of the harsh moralism of *Wuthering Heights*.

p. 147   *unusual in a man . . . She should have been a man . . . rendered her obtuse . . . egotistical and exacting*: *Life*, 177.

p. 148   *What importance should be given*: CH's note on 'Le Nid' (Sue Lonoff's translation), Lonoff, 42.

p. 148   *& that sets all things straight*: CB to EN, May 1842, *LCB* 1, 285.

p. 149   *she smiled, at first incredulously*: *The Professor*, 103.

p. 149   *sullen tempers are shewn*: *The Professor*, 100.

p. 149   *glories chiefly*: *The Professor*, 101.

p. 149   *large languid eyes . . . allowed himself*: Zoë Heger to 'K', April 1884, Edith M. Weir, 'New Brontë Material Comes to Light', *BST*, 11:59 (1949).

p. 149   *we do not separate*: Zoë Heger to 'K', 9 January 1889, Edith M. Weir, 'New Brontë Material Comes to Light', *BST*, 11:59 (1949).

p. 150 *One day when summoned to the bed*: 'I gave, at first, Attention close', *PCB*, 334.

p. 150 *a thrilling clasp . . . another heart*: 'Frances', *PCB*, 306. This poem was included in *Poems by Currer, Ellis and Acton Bell* (1846).

p. 150 *some part of each day*: CB to EN, ?July 1842, *LCB* 1, 289.

p. 151 *I am going to shut my eyes . . . well; not only in health . . . [I]f you can't see*: Mary Taylor to EN, shortly before 24 September 1842, *LCB* 1, 293.

p. 151 *the same suffering and conflict ensued . . . Once more she seemed sinking*: CB, 'Prefatory Note', 'Selections from Poems by Ellis Bell', *LCB* 2, 753.

p. 153 *nothing to listen to . . . nothing to look at*: BB to Francis H. Grundy, 22 May 1842, *SHB* 1, 264.

p. 153 *one of my dearest friends*: BB to Francis H. Grundy, 25 October 1842, *SHB* 1, 272–3.

p. 153 *expressed his entire dependence*: PB, 'A Funeral Sermon for the late Rev. William Weightman, M.A.', *Brontëana*, 259.

p. 154 *I'll weep no more thine early doom*: AB, 'I will not mourn thee, lovely one' (December 1842), Edward Chitham (ed.), *The Poems of Anne Brontë: A New Text and Commentary* (London, 1979), 88.

p. 154 *watching – nursing – cherishing her . . . I hastened to Kokleberg*: CB to EN, 10 November 1842, *LCB* 1, 302.

p. 154 *Every trivial accident*: Mary Taylor to EN, 30 October and 1 November 1842, *LCB* 1, 296.

p. 155 *most spirited and beautiful*: Genevieve Wigfall reporting her sight of Brontë relics to EN, 10 December 1889, quoted in *Art of the Brontës*, 385.

p. 155 *as near as convenient*: Elizabeth Branwell's will, *SHB* 1, 277.

p. 155 *such agonising suffering . . . the guide and director . . . gloomy visions*: BB to Francis H. Grundy, 29 October 1842, *SHB* 1, 273.

p. 156 *any day a small share-holder . . . every paragraph & every advertisement*: CB to MW, 23 April 1845, *LCB* 1, 390.

p. 157 *love of work and their perseverance . . . almost fatherly affection . . . and our distress*: CH to PB, 5 November 1842, Margaret Smith's translation, *LCB* 1, 300.

p. 158 *the best teacher we have in Belgium . . . and to gain the assurance and aplomb . . . This is not a question*: CH to PB, 5 November 1842, Margaret Smith's translation, *LCB* 1, 300.

p. 158 *selfish folly . . . a total withdrawal . . . irresistible*: CB to EN, 14 October 1846, *LCB* 1, 503.

p. 159 *quiet simple statement of her wish*: *Life*, 197.

p. 159 *I had no accident*: CB to EN, 30 January 1843, *LCB* 1, 308.

p. 159 *pretty much as she has since described it*: *Life*, 197.

p. 159 *Down the sable flood we glided*: *Villette*, 51.

8   The Black Swan   1843

p. 160 *extremely difficult to manage . . . Instead of showing anger*: Frederika Macdonald, 'The Brontës at Brussels', *Woman at Home* (July 1894), 286.

p. 160 *was known to be very clever*: Frederika Macdonald, 'The Brontës at Brussels', *Woman at Home* (July 1894), 287.

p. 161 *I surrender my unfortunate head . . . she likes me well enough*: CB to Mary Dixon, early 1843, *LCB* 1, 313.

p. 161 *an ugly woman*: Mary Taylor to ECG, 30 July 1857, *Interviews*, 114: 'It must upset most people's notions of beauty to be told that the portrait at the beginning [of *The Life of Charlotte Brontë*] is that of an ugly woman. I do not altogether like the idea of publishing a flattered likeness. I had rather the mouth and eyes had been nearer together, and shown the veritable square face and large disproportionate nose . . .'

p. 161 *A small chalk, ink and wash drawing*: in BPM.

p. 162 *disinterred your portrait . . . I was comforted . . . If it were a little slenderer*: CB to Mary Dixon, 16 October 1843, *LCB* 1, 336.

p. 162 *[S]he seems content at least*: Mary Taylor to EN, 16 February 1843, *LCB* 1, 310.

p. 163 *M. Emanuel was not a man to write books*: *Villette*, 381.

p. 163 *nothing but masking and mummery*: CB to EN, 6 March 1843, *LCB* 1, 311.

p. 163 *I had learned to read*: 'I gave, at first, Attention close', *PCB*, 335.

p. 163 *they get on with wonderful rapidity*: CB to EN, 6 March 1843, *LCB* 1, 311.

p. 164 *I believe that all true poetry . . . I believe that genius*: Lonoff, 244–6.

p. 164 *Without study, no art*: Lonoff, 248–9.

p. 164 *His eyes pierced through the quartz*: Thomas Westwood to Lady Alwyne Compton, 21 February 1870, *A Literary Friendship: Letters to Lady Alwyne Compton 1869–1881, from Thomas Westwood*, 15.

p. 165 *I will not and ought not to intrude*: CB to EN, 6 March 1843, *LCB* 1, 311.

p. 165 *if I could always*: CB to EN, 6 March 1843, *LCB* 1, 311.

p. 166 *These people are wiser than I am . . . Not that it is a crime to marry*: CB to EN, ?April 1843, *LCB* 1, 315.

p. 167   *I am convinced she does not like me*: CB to EJB, 29 May 1843, *LCB* 1, 320.

p. 168   *the people here are no go . . . the phlegm that thickens their blood . . . the black Swan . . . not quite an exception*: CB to BB, 1 May 1843, *LCB* 1, 316–17.

p. 168   *misanthropic and sour . . . as fanatically as ever*: CB to BB, 1 May 1843, *LCB* 1, 316–17.

p. 168   *I was surprised*: CB to BB, 1 May 1843, *LCB* 1, 316–17.

p. 168   *these times, so critical and dangerous*: PB to the Reverend John Sinclair, 4 August 1843, *LPB*, 148.

p. 169   *the Ominous and Dangerous Vagaries of the Times . . . a restless disposition for change*: PB to the editor of *The Halifax Guardian*, 29 July 1843, *LPB*, 144.

p. 169   *with hanging head and lolling tongue . . . nobly stern . . . telling no one*: *Life*, 214.

p. 170   *[O]ne wearies from day to day*: CB to BB, 1 May 1843, *LCB* 1, 317.

p. 170   *mighty distance & reserve*: CB to EN, ?late June 1843, *LCB* 1, 325.

p. 170   *Je tiens ce morceau*: the relic and its inscribed paper wrapper are at BPM (BS, 20a), 'Fragment from the Coffin of Napoléon Bonaparte'.

p. 171   *extreme whiteness and beauty*: Frederika Macdonald, 'The Brontës at Brussels', *Woman at Home* (July 1894), 287.

p. 171   *wild Jäger chorus*: *Villette*, 454.

p. 172   *It is the first time in my life . . . Alas I can hardly write*: CB to EN, 6 August 1843, *LCB* 1, 327.

p. 172   *I know you*: CB to EN, ?late June 1843, *LCB* 1, 325.

p. 172   *I flee the world*: Lonoff, 196. Sue Lonoff, the editor of the Belgian essays, judges that 'La But de la Vie', which carries a date – 24 August – but no year, was more likely to have been written in 1842 than in 1843, but I incline to think the opposite. Thematically it fits exactly with the utter solitude and depression that CB underwent in August 1843. See 'Comments', Lonoff, 200–203.

p. 173   *Time – from 30 to 50 years ago . . . Mem. To be set about with proper spirit*: BPM, Bonnell 118.

p. 174   *There was once a large house called Gateshead*: BPM, Bonnell 118.

p. 174   *[She] never now speaks to me*: CB to EJB, 2 September 1843, *LCB* 1, 329.

p. 175   *When people are by themselves . . . They do not go . . . It was a funny position . . . I felt precisely*: CB to EJB, 2 September 1843, *LCB* 1, 329–30.

p. 175   *The solitude and the stillness*: *Villette*, 160.

p. 176   *the mere outline of my experience*: *Villette*, 161.

p. 176 *pouring out of some portion*: *Villette*, 162.

p. 176 *They are at their idolatrous 'Messe' . . . I have an idea*: CB to EJB, 1 October 1843, *LCB* 1, 331.

p. 176 *single out one or two of these slanderers*: PB to ?Mr Joseph Greenwood, 4 October 1843, *LPB*, 152.

p. 177 *and they have ascribed*: PB to ?Mr Joseph Greenwood, 4 October 1843, *LPB*, 152.

p. 177 *to be retained – semper*: *LPB*, 177.

p. 177 *Should any timid, over-scrupulous person*: PB to the editor of *The Leeds Intelligencer*, 30 January 1841, *LPB*, 125.

p. 177 *fallen into habits of intemperance . . . by C.B. herself . . . remedied the evil*: EN in notes (now at BPM) to her own *The Story of the Brontës: Their Home, Haunts, Friends and Works* (1885–9), quoted in *LCB* 1, 504 n4.

p. 178 *vehemence . . . I could not at that time*: CB to EN, 13 October 1843, *LCB* 1, 334.

p. 178 *Brussels – Saturday morning*: written by CB upside down on the inside back cover of *Russell's General Atlas of Modern Geography* (1836), Pierpont Morgan Library, Printed Books Collection, RB1, 129886.

p. 179 *wholesome discipline*: *Jane Eyre*, 162.

p. 179 *faithfully; without softening one defect*: *Jane Eyre*, 161.

p. 179 *'You,' I said, 'a favourite with Mr Rochester?*: *Jane Eyre*, 160–61.

p. 180 *Do not be indignant at my presumption*: CB, 'Lettre d'un pauvre Peintre à un grand Seigneur' (Sue Lonoff's translation), Lonoff, 360.

p. 180 *I did not think*: CB to EN, 23 January 1844, *LCB* 1, 341.

p. 180 *I suffered much before I left Brussels*: CB to EN, 23 January 1844, *LCB* 1, 341.

p. 181 *I have talked, face to face*: *Jane Eyre*, 252.

p. 181 *he gently raised his hand*: *Villette*, 487.

p. 181 *Je me vengerai!*: M. H. Spielmann, *The Inner History of the Brontë–Heger Letters*, 3.

9   Long-looked-for Tidings   1844–5

p. 183 *as my eyes, are very weak*: PB to George Taylor Esqr., 29 February 1844, *LPB*, 169.

p. 183 *[T]here are times now*: CB to EN, 23 January 1844, *LCB* 1, 341.

p. 184 *My dear little Victoire*: CB to Victoire Dubois, 18 May 1844, *LCB* 1, 346.

p. 184 *if it is only for a moment . . . Oh it is certain*: CB to CH, 24 July 1844 (Margaret Smith's translation), *LCB* 1, 359.

p. 184 *I look on your letters . . . I shall wait patiently . . . a letter which was hardly rational*: CB to CH, 24 July 1844 (Margaret Smith's translation), *LCB* 1, 357.

p. 184 *a record of romantic love*: Frederika Macdonald, *The Secret of Charlotte Brontë*, 41.

p. 185 *But all the same*: CB to CH, 24 July 1844 (Margaret Smith's translation), *LCB* 1, 357.

p. 185 *chatting*: 'when I pronounce the French words I seem to be chatting with you', CB to CH, 24 July 1844 (Margaret Smith's translation), *LCB* 1, 358.

p. 185 *for I am quite convinced*: CB to CH, 24 July 1844 (Margaret Smith's translation), *LCB* 1, 357.

p. 185 *I fear nothing so much as idleness*: CB to CH, 24 July 1844 (Margaret Smith's translation), *LCB* 1, 358.

p. 186 *This weakness of sight*: CB to CH, 24 July 1844 (Margaret Smith's translation), *LCB* 1, 358.

p. 186 *I am not going to write a long letter*: CB to CH, 24 October 1844 (Margaret Smith's translation), *LCB* 1, 370.

p. 187 *from all parts*: *Slater's Royal National Commercial Directory and Topography of the Counties of Chester, Cumberland, Durham, Lancaster, Northumberland, Westmoreland and York* (Manchester, 1848) includes the following entry: 'POST OFFICE, Haworth, William Hartley, *Post Master.* – Letters from all parts arrive (from BRADFORD) daily, Sunday excepted, at twelve noon, and are despatched thereto at three in the afternoon.' I am grateful to Steven Wood for providing this information.

p. 187 *in 'Passing Events'*: when the Duchess of Zamorna is incredulous at getting no message from her husband, for whom she is pining. '"And – and –" continued the Duchess, throwing off restraint & writhing with impatience as she spoke, "Have you no letter for me, Mr. Warner? do you bring me no message, no word of his welfare & no inquiry after mine?"', Gérin (ed.), *Five Novelettes*, 57.

p. 187 *long-looked-for tidings*: *Jane Eyre*, 399.

p. 187 *My hour of torment was the post-hour*: *Villette*, 267–8.

p. 187 *I did my utmost*: CB to CH, 8 January 1845 (Margaret Smith's translation), *LCB* 1, 379.

p. 187 *I said to myself . . . But when one does not complain*: CB to CH, 8 January 1845 (Margaret Smith's translation), *LCB* 1, 379.

p. 188 *all I know – is that I cannot*: CB to CH, 8 January 1845 (Margaret Smith's translation), *LCB* 1, 379.

p. 189 *self-suppression*: Mary Taylor articulated her views on the subject very strikingly in an exchange between young Maria Bell and her elderly spinster friend Miss Everard in *Miss Miles*: "'is it not a very wretched position to have to please unreasonable people – to fawn and flatter in order to get something given – especially if you think you have a right to it all the time, and owe no obligation at all?" "I think it the worst curse we women have to bear," the old lady said, and Maria looked up surprised. "We go to the borders of falsehood, we keep our opinion secret, when we should speak out; and all to keep friends with the wrong-doer, because he is the bread-giver. We get a great deal of praise for doing so, but the world would be better if we had not to do it"' (*Miss Miles*, 328).

p. 189 *[S]he thought that there must be some possibility*: Mary Taylor to ECG, January 1856, quoted in *SHB* 2, 26.

p. 189 *selfish old man . . . gloomy anger*: quoted in Bellamy, '*More precious than rubies*', 3.

p. 190 *The Misses Brontë's Establishment*: a copy of the prospectus is in BPM; a reproduction of it appears in the plate section.

p. 191 *retired situation*: CB to EN, ?c. 22 August 1844, *LCB* 1, 364.

p. 191 *those girls were all off to the Misses Cockills*: as reported by CB to EN, ?10 August 1844, *LCB* 1, 363.

p. 191 *donations to keep it afloat*: see PB's correspondence with the National Society and notes on 'the Haworth Case' in the section of *LPB* titled 'Mainly Education'.

p. 191 *Every one wishes us well*: CB to EN, ?2 October 1844, *LCB* 1, 368.

p. 192 *We have no present intention*: CB to EN, ?2 October 1844, *LCB* 1, 368.

p. 192 *occasional home . . . silently aware . . . distressing rumours*: *Life*, 218.

p. 192 *toujours malade*: CB to CH, 24 October 1844, *LCB* 1, 369.

p. 192 *This lady*: BB to Francis H. Grundy, October 1845, *SHB* 2, 64.

p. 193 *ill . . . he is so very often*: CB to EN, 31 July 1845, *LCB* 1, 412.

p. 193 *proceedings which he characterised . . . on pain of exposure*: CB to EN, 31 July 1845, *LCB* 1, 412.

p. 194 *Mr Robinson even bought his wife a necklace*: Juliet Barker has pointed out this detail.

p. 194 *spoke freely*: contained in a dossier of evidence, much of it hearsay, which the publisher George Smith drew up after the publication of ECG's *Life* in 1857 in connection with Lady Scott's (Mrs Robinson's) threats of libel: '[PB's] conversations with his son, who frequently spoke freely with him, left no doubt as to the nature of the intimacy', George Smith, 'Recollections of a Long and Busy Life', National Library of Scotland, MS 23191–2, quoted in Barker, 458 and 925 n55.

p. 194 *diabolical seducer*: PB to ECG, 2 April 1857, *LPB*, 252.

p. 194 *romantic domestic treachery*: *The Professor*, 157.

p. 195 *a name which can't have failed to strike a chord*: in her essay on Napoleon for Monsieur Heger (Lonoff, 278), Charlotte compares Wellington's glory to 'one of the ancient oaks that shade the mansion of his fathers on the banks of the Shannon'.

p. 195 *appears a respectable young man*: CB to Mrs Rand, 26 May 1845, *LCB* 1, 393.

p. 195 *[H]e must be like all the other curates . . . I pronounced a few sentences*: CB to EN, ?18 June 1845, *LCB* 1, 399.

p. 195 *a very funny but feeling description*: *Shirley*, Chapter 1.

p. 196 *a tall cabinet decorated with heads of the twelve apostles*: the cabinet is now at BPM. The Eyre brasses and connections between North Lees Hall and CB's 'Thornfield' and the history of the Vicarage are discussed in M. F. H. Hulbert, *Jane Eyre and Hathersage* [n.d.] and *Discovering Hathersage Old Vicarage* (1985), both published by Hathersage Parochial Church Council.

p. 196 *I am quite contented for myself*: EJB Diary Paper, [31] July 1845, *LCB* 1, 408.

p. 196 *a work on the First Wars . . . The Gondals still flo[u]rish . . . our first long Journey*: EJB Diary Paper, [31] July 1845, *LCB* 1, 408.

p. 197 *hers was naturally*: CB, 'Biographical Notice of Ellis and Acton Bell' (1850), *LCB* 2, 745.

p. 197 *[Charlotte] is now sitting sewing in the Dining-Room*: AB Diary Paper, 31 July 1845, *LCB* 1, 410–11.

p. 197 *My hopes ebb low . . . It is only absolute want of means*: CB to EN, 18 August 1845, *LCB* 1, 418.

p. 198 *In procuring it*: *Life*, 227.

p. 198 *He gave a start of surprise*: CB to EN, 31 July 1845, *LCB* 1, 412.

p. 198 *sounded like music in my ears . . . Every word was most precious to me*: CB to CH, 18 November 1845, *LCB* 1, 435.

p. 198 *a brief translation of some French verses*: CB to WSW, 15 December 1847, *LCB* 1, 576 and 577 n6.

p. 199 *I have no other way*: BB to J. B. Leyland, ?25 November 1845, *LCB* 1, 439.

p. 199 '*I gave, at first, Attention close*': *PCB*, 333. The poem, called originally 'At first I did attention give' (*PCB*, 274), became one Charlotte wrote and rewrote – and then, in her novels, published and republished. Having been incorporated into 'The Master' (*The Professor*), and that novel having failed to find a publisher, it was modified once more for inclusion in *Jane Eyre*. It appears there in part, incongruously enough, as the song Rochester sings to his fiancée in the idyll between his proposal and their calamitous wedding day. But there Brontë changes all the pronouns from male to female, and the ending from one of anguished separation to love triumphant.

p. 200 *ornamented and redundant . . . work his way through life*: CB, 'Preface', *The Professor*, 3.

p. 201 *as good as I can write*: CB to WSW, 14 December 1847, *LCB* 1, 574.

p. 201 *whose verdure*: *The Professor*, 215.

p. 201 *Come to England and see*: *The Professor*, 197–8.

p. 202 *in her eyes . . . almost triumphant . . . I am glad you have been forced to discover*: *The Professor*, 114.

p. 203 *The summer and autumn have seemed very long*: CB to CH, 18 November 1845 (Margaret Smith's translation), *LCB* 1, 435–6.

p. 204 *I wish I could write to you . . . Farewell my dear Master*: CB to CH, 18 November 1845 (Margaret Smith's translation), *LCB* 1, 435.

p. 204 *What happened to the letters*: documented by M. H. Spielmann in *The Inner History of the Brontë–Heger Letters*, using information from Louise Heger.

p. 205 *deprecate anything leading to the publication*: ECG to GS, 1 August 1856, *ECG Letters*, 400–401.

p. 205 *I am in a fever*: CB to CH, 18 November 1845 (Margaret Smith's translation), *LCB* 1, 437.

p. 205 *the address of a cobbler*: the pencilled words are barely legible. Margaret Smith comments in her notes to this letter (*LCB* 1, 438 n15) 'they may refer to a M. Talairier or Talavrier, shoemaker ("cordonnier") in the Rue des Trois Têtes off the Montagne de la Cour in Brussels, and to someone else, possibly another tradesman, in the Rue de la Caserne.'

p. 205 *and he asked her therefore*: SHB 1, 289.

p. 206 *She said [it] with the sincerity of manner*: SHB 1, 289, apparently quoting from a letter of Laetitia Wheelwright.

p. 206 *put away, out of sight*: Villette, 294.

p. 206 *old Jew broker . . . In all this I had a dreary something*: Villette, 295.

p. 206 *I was not only going to hide a treasure*: Villette, 296.

10   Walking Invisible   1845–6

p. 207 *hence it ensued*: CB, 'Biographical Notice of Ellis and Acton Bell' (1850), LCB 2, 742.

p. 207 *Riches I hold in light esteem*: EJB Poems, 120.

p. 207 *[The poems] stirred my heart like the sound of a trumpet*: CB to WSW, ?early September 1848, LCB 2, 119.

p. 207 *not common effusions . . . To my ear*: CB, 'Biographical Notice of Ellis and Acton Bell' (1850), LCB 2, 742.

p. 208 *no woman that ever lived*: CB to WSW, ?early September 1848, LCB 2, 119.

p. 208 *one, on the recesses of whose mind . . . it took hours*: CB, 'Biographical Notice of Ellis and Acton Bell' (1850), LCB 2, 742.

p. 208 *We had very early cherished*: CB, 'Biographical Notice of Ellis and Acton Bell' (1850), LCB 2, 743.

p. 209 *The bringing out of our little book*: CB, 'Biographical Notice of Ellis and Acton Bell' (1850), LCB 2, 743.

p. 209 Chambers' Edinburgh Journal: I am indebted to Margaret Smith's notes in LCB 2, 46 n6, for this information.

p. 209 *civil and sensible reply*: CB, 'Biographical Notice of Ellis and Acton Bell' (1850), LCB 2, 743.

p. 209 *a Collection of short poems*: CB to Messrs Aylott and Jones, 28 January 1846, LCB 1, 445.

p. 209 *If you object*: CB to Messrs Aylott and Jones, 28 January 1846, LCB 1, 445.

p. 209 *exclusively of a religious character . . . but I presume*: CB to Messrs Aylott and Jones, 31 January 1846, LCB 1, 449.

p. 209 *yielded some harmless pleasure*: CB, 'Biographical Notice of Ellis and Acton Bell' (1850), LCB 2, 742.

p. 210 *dictated by a sort of conscientious scruple . . . we had noticed*: CB, 'Biographical Notice of Ellis and Acton Bell' (1850), LCB 2, 743.

p. 210 *three persons – relatives*: CB to Messrs Aylott and Jones, 6 February 1846, *LCB* I, 451.

p. 211 *Eden sunshine . . . sank to dregs*: 'Frances', *PCB*, 306.

p. 211 *to linger o'er the past . . . He says: 'She loved me more than life*: 'Gilbert', *PCB*, 280–81.

p. 212 *And we might meet*: 'Frances', *PCB*, 308. Victor Neufeldt points out in his notes (*PCB*, 446) that the origins of this poem were Angrian, 'perhaps an expression of Mary [Percy]'s despair over the loss of Zamorna'. However, 'the final version of the poem was undoubtedly shaped by Charlotte's feelings about Heger.'

p. 212 *employed it as was to be expected . . . [It] was very forced work . . . a hopeless being . . . it is scarcely possible*: CB to EN, 3 March 1846, *LCB* I, 495.

p. 213 *we shall be most thankful*: CB to Eliza Jane Kingston, 8 May 1846, *LCB* I, 472.

p. 213 *three distinct and unconnected tales . . . a work of 3 vols.*: CB to Messrs Aylott and Jones, 6 April 1846, *LCB* I, 461.

p. 213 *light literature*: Aylott's daughter, Mrs Martyn, said her father 'was rather old-fashioned and had very narrow views regarding light literature', *SHB* 2, 80.

p. 214 *Tom Winnifrith and Edward Chitham*: Winnifrith suggested it first, in *Brontë Facts and Brontë Problems* (1983), and Chitham has written at length on the subject in *The Birth of Wuthering Heights: Emily Brontë at Work* (Basingstoke, 1998).

p. 214 *because he's more myself than I am*: EJB, *Wuthering Heights*, 71.

p. 214 *my love for Heathcliff*: EJB, *Wuthering Heights*, 73.

p. 215 *heaven did not seem to be my home*: EJB, *Wuthering Heights*, 71.

p. 215 *If the auditor of her work*: CB, 'Editor's Preface to the New Edition of *Wuthering Heights*' (1850), *LCB* 2, 749.

p. 215 *carefully copied from the life*: AB, 'Preface to the Second Edition', *The Tenant of Wildfell Hall* (Oxford, 1992), xxxviii.

p. 216 *incapacitated from deceiving and injuring others*: AB, *Agnes Grey*, 124.

p. 216 *as vain, as selfish, and as heartless*: AB, *Agnes Grey*, 111.

p. 216 *it is foolish to wish for beauty . . . instinctive dislike*: AB, *Agnes Grey*, 122.

p. 216 *Yes! at least, they could not deprive me*: AB, *Agnes Grey*, 129–30.

p. 217 *I sometimes thought they contributed . . . much different to anybody else*: *Life*, 229.

p. 217 *The sisters retained the old habit . . . At this time*: *Life*, 247.

p. 217 *I never interfer'd with them*: PB to ECG, 20 June 1855, *LPB*, 234.

p. 217 *admitted to Elizabeth Gaskell*: see *Life*, 247.

p. 218 *once told her sisters that they were wrong*: ECG, quoting Harriet Martineau, *Life*, 247.

p. 218 *possessed . . . with the feeling . . . great and stirring interest*: ECG, quoting Harriet Martineau, *Life*, 247.

p. 218 *how can we be more comfortable . . . He refuses to make an effort*: CB to EN, 14 April 1846, *LCB* 1, 463.

p. 218 *the inability to make my family aware*: BB to J. B. Leyland, ?28 April 1846, *LCB* 1, 467.

p. 218 *never knew . . . what his sisters had done*: CB to WSW, 2 October 1848, *LCB* 2, 123.

p. 219 *if we rarely taste the fulness of joy*: *The Professor*, 133.

p. 219 *a little mistake*: CB to Messrs Aylott and Jones, 28 March 1846, *LCB* 1, 459.

p. 219 *had all been opened*: CB to Messrs Aylott and Jones, 7 May 1846, *LCB* 1, 470.

p. 220 *upon their own merits*: unsigned review, *Critic*, 4 July 1846, *Critical Heritage*, 59.

p. 220 *be in truth but one master spirit*: unsigned notice, *Dublin University Magazine*, October 1846, *Critical Heritage*, 63.

p. 220 *a fine quaint spirit*: unsigned notice, *Athenaeum*, 4 July 1846, *Critical Heritage*, 61.

p. 220 *the presence of more genius*: unsigned review, *Critic*, 4 July 1846, *Critical Heritage*, 60.

p. 220 *rhymes . . . never alludes to them*: CB to WSW, ?early September 1848, *LCB* 2, 119.

p. 221 *a dreadful state of health . . . the account which [Allison] gave*: BB to J. B. Leyland, June 1846, *LCB* 1, 475.

p. 221 *in bitter tears and prayers . . . worn . . . out in attendance*: BB to J. B. Leyland, June 1846, *LCB* 1, 476.

p. 222 *my angel Edmund*: see Margaret Smith's note 6, CB to EN, 17 June 1846, *LCB* 1, 479. The account books are in the Robinson Papers at BPM.

p. 222 *What I shall do I know not*: BB to J. B. Leyland, June 1846, *LCB* 1, 476.

p. 222 *an image he drew*: a pen and ink sketch, enclosed with this letter to Leyland (Brotherton Collection) and reproduced in *SHB* 2, 97.

p. 222 *pretext to throw all about him . . . [he] declares now*: CB to EN, 17 June 1846, *LCB* 1, 477–8.

p. 223 *The right path*: CB to EN, 10 July 1846, *LCB* 1, 482–3.

p. 223 *Miss Brontë . . . was going to be married*: CB to EN, 10 July 1846, *LCB* 1, 483.

p. 223 *though others had*: *Life*, 238.

p. 223 *I scarcely need say*: CB to EN, 10 July 1846, *LCB* 1, 483.

p. 224 *as she expressed in a letter to Ellen*: CB to EN, 29 June 1847, *LCB* 1, 532.

p. 224 *a pencil-drawing exists*: Pierpont Morgan Library, Bonnell Collection, MA 2696. See also 'Sketch of Mr Nicholls', *Art of the Brontës*, 281.

p. 224 *search out an operator*: CB to EN, 9 August 1846, *LCB* 1, 491.

p. 225 *numerous similar streets*: *Life*, 242. For more about the lodgings see Brian Kay and James Knowles, 'Where *Jane Eyre* and *Mary Barton* were Born', *BST*, 15:2 (1967).

p. 225 *hints about how to manage . . . For ourselves I could contrive*: CB to EN, 21 August 1846, *LCB* 1, 493.

p. 225 *feeling of strangeness*: CB to EN, 21 August 1846, *LCB* 1, 492.

p. 226 *Belladonna, a virulent poison*: *BST*, 15:2 (1967).

p. 226 *He is very patient*: CB to EN, 31 August 1846, *LCB* 1, 496.

11   That Intensely Interesting Novel   1846–8

p. 227 *it was not every day*: *Life*, 245–6.

p. 227 *something more imaginative and poetical*: CB, 'Preface', *The Professor*, 3.

p. 228 *to go all lengths*: *Jane Eyre*, 12.

p. 228 *Nobody knows how many rebellions*: *Jane Eyre*, 109.

p. 228 *it seemed as if my tongue*: *Jane Eyre*, 27.

p. 228 *Ere I had finished this reply*: *Jane Eyre*, 37.

p. 229 *At eighteen most people wish to please*: *Jane Eyre*, 91.

p. 229 *I sometimes regretted*: *Jane Eyre*, 98.

p. 230 *I have but a field or two to traverse . . . every nerve I have is unstrung*: *Jane Eyre*, 244.

p. 230 *There was every article of furniture*: *Jane Eyre*, 228.

p. 230 *I stopped: I could not trust myself*: *Jane Eyre*, 384.

p. 231 *I sometimes have a queer feeling*: *Jane Eyre*, 252.

p. 231 *It is not agreeable*: CB to EN, 13 December 1846, *LCB* 1, 507.

p. 231 *it is said*: John Greenwood told this dramatic story in his notebooks, with Anne discovering the fire and failing to rouse Branwell to the danger. Emily is the heroine of the hour, behaving very much as Jane Eyre does in the novel: 'she tore the blazing bedding from the bed and threw it into the middle of the room – the safest place. Rushing down-stairs into the kitchen, she seized a large can, which happened to be full of water at the time. Dashing upstairs she threw the water on the blazing pile and quenched it at once', Albert H. Preston, 'John Green-wood and the Brontës', *BST*, 12:1 (1951).

p. 231   *after he became an inebriate*: EN to J. A. Erskine Stuart, 24 February 1894, transcripts of letters to Dr J. A. Erskine Stuart, BPM.

p. 231   *dragging his way home*: 'The Brontës and the Brontë Country: A Chat with One Who Knew Them', *The Bradford Observer*, 17 February 1894.

p. 232   *a new lifes battle*: BB to J. B. Leyland, 24 January 1847, *LCB* 1, 512.

p. 232   *in more than competence . . . live at leisure*: BB to J. B. Leyland, 24 January 1847, *LCB* 1, 512.

p. 232   *ghastly dying eye*: BB to J. B. Leyland, 24 January 1847, *LCB* 1, 514.

p. 232   *cost what it may*: BB to J. B. Leyland, 24 January 1847, *LCB* 1, 512.

p. 233   *Sir My Relatives, Ellis and Acton Bell and myself*: CB to Thomas De Quincey, 16 June 1847, *LCB* 1, 529–30.

p. 234   *Florence Nightingale*: in the early 1860s, Nightingale asked Milnes if she could borrow the book (*Poems by Currer, Ellis and Acton Bell*) that he had read aloud to her in 1846, so that she could transcribe some of the poems into a notebook of favourites. See Mark Bostridge, *Florence Nightingale: The Woman and Her Legend* (London, 2008), 106 and 415–16.

p. 235   *Gentlemen I beg to submit*: CB to Messrs Smith, Elder & Co., 15 July 1847, *LCB* 1, 533.

p. 235   *This was not calculated . . . evinced great literary power . . . [the writer] could produce a book*: George Smith, 'Charlotte Brontë', *Interviews*, 87.

p. 235   *it declined, indeed, to publish that tale*: CB, 'Biographical Notice of Ellis and Acton Bell' (1850), *LCB* 2, 744.

p. 235   *accustom the public*: CB to Messrs Smith, Elder & Co., 7 August 1847, *LCB* 1, 535.

p. 236   *Presently the servant came*: *Interviews*, 90.

p. 236   *may suit the public taste*: CB to Messrs Smith, Elder & Co., 12 September 1847, *LCB* 1, 539.

p. 237   *one hundred pounds is a small sum*: CB to Messrs Smith, Elder & Co., 12 September 1847, *LCB* 1, 540.

p. 237   *to walk invisible*: 'What author would be without the advantage of being able to walk invisible? One is thereby enabled to keep such a quiet mind.' CB to WSW, 4 January 1848, *LCB* 2, 4.

p. 237 *as to choice of subject or style*: CB to Messrs Smith, Elder & Co., 12 September 1847, *LCB* 1, 540.

p. 238 *One of the freshest and most genuine books*: Howitt's Journal of Literature and Popular Progress, 20 November 1847, see *LCB* 1, 565 n2.

p. 238 *very clever and striking*: The Manchester Examiner and Times, 16 November 1847, see *LCB* 1, 565 n4.

p. 238 *like the Cartoons of Raphael . . . true, bold, well-defined*: Era, 14 November 1847, see *LCB* 1, 564 n1.

p. 238 *This is not merely a work*: Atlas, 23 October 1847, *Critical Heritage*, 67.

p. 238 *psychological intuition . . . It reads like a page*: Fraser's Magazine, December 1847, *Critical Heritage*, 86.

p. 238 *that intensely interesting novel*: Queen Victoria's diary, 13 May 1858, *Critical Heritage*, 389.

p. 238 *lost (or won if you like)*: William Makepeace Thackeray to WSW, 23 October 1847, *Critical Heritage*, 70.

p. 238 *true, sound, and original . . . Whatever faults . . . as an analysis of a single mind*: The Examiner, 27 November 1847, *Critical Heritage*, 76–7.

p. 239 *There are moments*: CB to WSW, 11 December 1847, *LCB* 1, 571.

p. 239 *heaven knows*: CB to EN, ?29 October or early November 1847, *LCB* 1, 556.

p. 239 *but his suspicions*: Life, 263.

p. 239 *Papa I've been writing a book . . . Children, Charlotte has been writing a book*: ECG to Catherine Winkworth, 25 August 1850, *LCB* 2, 448–9. ECG had just heard this anecdote from CB when they met at Briery Close, and reports to Catherine Winkworth, 'I think I can remember the exact words.' In the version she put into her biography of Brontë seven years later, there are significant tidyings and augmentations, but she still says, 'I wrote down her words the day after I heard them; and I am pretty sure they are quite accurate' (*Life*, 263).

p. 240 *though clever in their kind*: PB to ECG, 20 June 1855, *LPB*, 234.

p. 240 *abominable paganism*: 'abominably pagan' is what the reviewer (Elizabeth Rigby) in Quarterly Review for December 1848 thought of Wuthering Heights, *Critical Heritage*, 111.

p. 240 *of limited experience*: Britannia, 15 January 1848, *Critical Heritage*, 224.

p. 240 *wants but the practised skill*: Douglas Jerrold's Weekly Newspaper, 15 January 1848, *Critical Heritage*, 228.

p. 240 *all the emotions . . . talent of no common order*: *Critical Heritage*, 243–4.

p. 240 *left no painful impression*: *Atlas*, 22 January 1848, *Critical Heritage*, 233.

p. 241 *brothers of the weaving order*: J. G. Lockhart to Elizabeth Rigby, 13 November 1848, quoted in *LCB* 1, 562 n5.

p. 241 *social regenerator . . . comes before the great ones . . . the very master of that working corps*: CB, 'Preface', *Jane Eyre*, 4.

p. 242 very, very *sorry*: CB to WSW, 28 January 1848, *LCB* 2, 22.

p. 243 *I feel that your cup of life*: CB to WSW, 22 June 1848, *LCB* 2, 79.

p. 243 *as good as I can write*: CB to WSW, 14 December 1847, *LCB* 1, 574.

p. 243 *It is my wish to do my best*: CB to WSW, 18 December 1847, *LCB* 1, 579.

p. 243 *He saw my heart's woe*: *PCB*, 340. The poem was not published until 1915.

p. 245 *[It] is with difficulty one can prevail on her*: CB to EN, 7 October 1847, *LCB* 1, 547.

p. 245 *The motives which dictated this choice*: CB, 'Biographical Notice of Ellis and Acton Bell' (1850), *LCB* 2, 745.

p. 245 *great pleasure in making arrangements . . . I would not hurry its completion . . . much depends*: T. C. Newby to EJB, 15 February 1848, *LCB* 2, 26.

p. 246 *unromantic as Monday morning . . . real, cool, and solid*: *Shirley*, 5.

p. 246 *with respect to a proposed story*: Ivy Holgate, 'The Structure of Shirley', *BST*, 14:2 (1962).

p. 246 *which at that time*: Harry Speight was the 'chronicler of old Bingley', interviewed in 1898, Ivy Holgate, 'The Structure of Shirley', *BST*, 14:2 (1962).

p. 247 *do such men sway the public mind*: CB to WSW, 28 February 1848, *LCB* 2, 35.

p. 247 *I wish I had written it in a cool moment*: CB to WSW, 11 March 1848, *LCB* 2, 41.

p. 247 *their rational and justifiable efforts for liberty*: CB to WSW, 29 March 1848, *LCB* 2, 45.

p. 247 *[E]arthquakes roll lower than the ocean*: CB to WSW, 29 March 1848, *LCB* 2, 45.

p. 248 *I have still no doubt*: CB to MW, 31 March 1848, *LCB* 2, 48.

p. 248 *I believe that 'the people'*: *Shirley*, 275.

p. 248 *old maids*: *Shirley*, 329.

p. 249 *a lover feminine can say nothing . . . Take the matter as you find it*: *Shirley*, 89–90.

p. 250 *in some region of the southern hemisphere*: *Shirley*, 128.

p. 250   *I remember once*: *Shirley*, 230.

p. 250   *If . . . the authorship of other works of fiction has been attributed to me*: 'Note to the Third Edition', 13 April 1848, *Jane Eyre*, 6.

p. 250   *insanely bent*: CB to WSW, 13 March 1848, *LCB* 2, 42.

p. 250   *your great world – your London . . . a glimpse of what I might call* loathsome: CB to WSW, 15 February 1848, *LCB* 2, 27.

p. 251   *capricious*: 'The visit strikes me as an odd whim: I consider it quite a caprice, prompted probably by curiosity', CB to EN, 26 June 1848, *LCB* 2, 81.

p. 251   *quite a* fureur: *SHB* 2, 228.

p. 251   *was as though Charlotte Brontë herself was present*: *SHB* 2, 228.

p. 251   *we do not subscribe*: CB to EN, 26 June 1848, *LCB* 2, 81.

p. 252   *Dear John*: BB to John Brown, 'Sunday noon', Brotherton MS 19c Brontë, B.4/22.

p. 252   *There is a phase of insanity . . . The sole aim and desire of the being thus possessed*: CB to WSW, 4 January 1848, *LCB* 2, 3.

p. 253   *no domestic demon*: Francis H. Grundy, 'The Decline and Fall of Branwell Brontë', *Interviews*, 57.

p. 253   *the cheeks yellow and hollow*: Francis H. Grundy, 'The Decline and Fall of Branwell Brontë', *Interviews*, 56.

p. 254   *We washed ourselves . . . we went in*: CB to Mary Taylor, 4 September 1848, *LCB* 2, 112.

p. 255   *shuffling scamp*: CB to Mary Taylor, 4 September 1848, *LCB* 2, 111.

p. 255   *a pale, mild, stooping man of fifty . . . a long, nervous shaking of hands*: CB to Mary Taylor, 4 September 1848, *LCB* 2, 112.

p. 255   *[Y]ou must go to the Italian opera . . . [To] all the rest of the world*: CB to Mary Taylor, 4 September 1848, *LCB* 2, 113.

p. 255   *The desire to see some of the personages*: CB to Mary Taylor, 4 September 1848, *LCB* 2, 113.

p. 256   *They must have thought us queer, quizzical looking beings*: CB to Mary Taylor, 4 September 1848, *LCB* 2, 113–14.

p. 256   *You know I am not accustomed*: *Life*, 287.

p. 257   *a couple of odd-looking country-women . . . to see their elegant, handsome son*: CB to Mary Taylor, 4 September 1848, *LCB* 2, 114.

p. 257   *A more jaded wretch than I looked*: CB to Mary Taylor, 4 September 1848, *LCB* 2, 115.

12   Across the Abyss   1848–9

p. 258   *intolerable mental wretchedness*: BB to J. B. Leyland, ?17 June 1848, *LCB* 2, 77.

p. 258   *infatuated slave*: CB to EN, 18 August 1848, *LCB* 2, 194.

p. 258   *latterly consumptive*: CB to Laetitia Wheelwright, 15 March 1849, *LCB* 2, 190.

p. 259   *a constitution still so strong*: BB to J. B. Leyland, 24 January 1847, *LCB* 1, 513.

p. 259   *and . . . catch hold to the door side*: C. Holmes Cautley, 'Old Haworth Folk Who Knew the Brontës' (1910), *Interviews*, 207.

p. 259   *the first . . . that she had ever attended*: 'the crisis was hastened by the awe and trouble of the death-scene – the first I had ever witnessed', CB to WSW, 2 October 1848, *LCB* 2, 122.

p. 259   *the bar of eternity*: see 'Extracts from a Funeral Sermon for the late Rev. William Weightman', Appendix XIII, *LPB* 364.

p. 260   *the depth and tenderness . . . Oh, John, I am dying! . . . In all my past life*: Francis A. Leyland, *The Brontë Family* (1886), *LCB* 2, 278–9.

p. 260   *How unusual that word . . . painful, mournful joy*: CB to WSW, 6 October 1848, *LCB* 2, 124.

p. 260   *My Son! My Son! . . . My poor Father*: CB to WSW, 2 October 1848, *LCB* 2, 122.

p. 260   *impressions experienced*: CB to WSW, 25 June 1849, *LCB* 2, 224.

p. 261   *I do not weep from a sense of bereavement*: CB to WSW, 2 October 1848, *LCB* 2, 122.

p. 261   *When I looked on the noble face*: CB to WSW, 6 October 1848, *LCB* 2, 124.

p. 261   *The final separation*: CB to EN, 9 October 1848, *LCB* 2, 126.

p. 261   *I feel much more uneasy*: CB to EN, 29 October 1848, *LCB* 2, 130.

p. 261   *Emily's cold and cough . . . Her reserved nature*: CB to EN, 29 October 1848, *LCB* 2, 130.

p. 262   *[M]y sister Emily*: CB to WSW, 2 November 1848, *LCB* 2, 132.

p. 262   *you must look on*: CB to WSW, 2 November 1848, *LCB* 2, 132.

p. 262   *I have again and again*: CB to WSW, 7 December 1848, *LCB* 2, 148.

p. 262   *When she is ill . . . I think a certain harshness*: CB to WSW, 2 November 1848, *LCB* 2, 132–3.

p. 262   *forced, total neglect*: CB to EN, *c.* 29 January 1849, *LCB* 2, 173.

p. 262 *Stern selfishness*: 'Her conduct was the very essence of stern selfishness', a passage deleted by ECG from her manuscript; see Angus Easson, 'Two Suppressed Opinions in Mrs Gaskell's *Life of Charlotte Brontë*', *BST*, 16:4 (1974).

p. 262 *has never consented*: CB to WSW, 9 December 1848, *LCB* 2, 151.

p. 263 *The weather that autumn*: recorded by a local man, William Shackleton of Keighley: W. Shackleton, 'Meterological Journal 1844–50', Cliffe Castle Museum, Keighley.

p. 263 *comparative inferiority*: unsigned review of *Poems by Currer, Ellis and Acton Bell* (1848), *Spectator*, 11 November 1848, *Critical Heritage*, 65.

p. 263 *blind . . . as any bat*: CB to WSW, 16 November 1848, *LCB* 2, 140.

p. 263 *Jane Eyre fever*: identified by 'E. P.' [Edwin Percy Whipple] in *North American Review*, October 1848; see *Critical Heritage*, 97.

p. 264 *seems to take a morose satisfaction*: *Critical Heritage*, 247.

p. 264 *Acton Bell succeeded in depicting profligacy*: *Critical Heritage*, 262.

p. 264 *As I sat between them*: CB to WSW, 22 November 1848, *LCB* 2, 142.

p. 264 *the marks of more than one mind . . . Strange patch-work*: CB to WSW, 22 November 1848, *LCB* 2, 143.

p. 264 *[S]he is very ill . . . God only knows*: CB to EN, 23 November 1848, *LCB* 2, 145.

p. 265 *the first glance at her face*: CB to WSW, 25 June 1849, *LCB* 2, 225.

p. 265 *dying all the time*: reported by ECG in her letter to ?John Forster, ?after 29 September 1853, *LCB* 3, 200.

p. 265 *the conflict of the strangely strong spirit*: CB to WSW, 25 December 1848, *LCB* 2, 159.

p. 265 *If you will send for a doctor*: *Life*, 293.

p. 265 *in the arms of those who loved her*: CB to ?WSW, 20 December 1848, *LCB* 2, 155.

p. 266 *Emily suffers no more*: CB to EN, 23 December 1848, *LCB* 2, 157.

p. 266 *calm and sustained . . . sweetly pretty and flushed . . . My dear little Anne*: all reminiscences by EN, in her typescript copy of 'The Story of the Brontës', Hatfield Papers, BPM.

p. 266 *A dreadful darkness closes in*: Edward Chitham (ed.), *The Poems of Anne Brontë: A New Text and Commentary*, 163.

p. 267 *unused any of us*: CB to WSW, ?13 January 1849, *LCB* 2, 168.

p. 267 *like train oil*: CB to EN, 10 January 1849, *LCB* 2, 166.

p. 267 *It is well known*: Thomas John Graham, *Modern Domestic Medicine* (1826), 247.

p. 267 *[L]ife has become very void*: CB to WSW, 2 January 1849, *LCB* 2, 165.

p. 267 *When we lost Emily*: CB to WSW, ?13 January 1849, *LCB* 2, 168.

p. 268 *merely photographed from the life*: CB to WSW, 2 February 1849, *LCB* 2, 181.

p. 268 *sanguine hopes*: CB to EN, *c.* 29 January 1849, *LCB* 2, 173.

p. 268 *[T]here have been hours*: CB to Laetitia Wheelwright, 15 March 1849, *LCB* 2, 190–91.

p. 269 *consequently obliged*: CB to EN, 29 March 1849, *LCB* 2, 194.

p. 269 *we creep rather than walk*: CB to EN, 1 May 1849, *LCB* 2, 205.

p. 269 *in a semi-lethargic state*: CB to MW, 16 May 1849, *LCB* 2, 210.

p. 269 *dreary mockery . . . Oh – if it would please God*: CB to EN, *c.* 12 & 14 May 1849, *LCB* 2, 209.

p. 269 *the pious courage and fortitude*: EN's reminiscence, reported by ECG in *Life*, 307.

p. 270 *baby fashion . . . nervously angry . . . I am not hurt*: EN's notes to her type-script copy of 'The Story of the Brontës', Hatfield Papers, BPM.

p. 270 *deeply assured*: CB to WSW, 4 June 1849, *LCB* 2, 216.

p. 270 *Take courage, Charlotte . . . The door to the room*: *Life*, 309–10.

p. 270 *burst forth in agonised strength*: EN's notes to 'The Story of the Brontës', Hatfield Papers, BPM.

p. 270 *Anne, from her childhood . . . wise – perfect – merciful . . . Why life is so blank*: CB to WSW, 4 June 1849, *LCB* 2, 216.

p. 271 *but half consoles . . . Anne had had enough*: CB to WSW, 13 June 1849, *LCB* 2, 220.

p. 271 *There must be Heaven or we must despair*: CB to WSW, 13 June 1849, *LCB* 2, 220.

p. 272 *in strange ecstasy*: CB to EN, 23 June 1849, *LCB* 2, 222.

p. 272 *may look wistfully round*: CB to WSW, 25 June 1849, *LCB* 2, 224.

p. 272 *I left Papa soon*: CB to EN, 23 June 1849, *LCB* 2, 222–3.

13   Conquering the Big Babylon   1849–51

p. 273 *his anxiety harasses me*: CB to EN, 14 July 1849, *LCB* 2, 230.

p. 273 *spirit . . . strong enough*: CB to WSW, 4 June 1849, *LCB* 2, 216.

p. 273 *two persons whom it would not suit*: CB to WSW, 26 July 1849, *LCB* 2, 232.

p. 274 *Lonely as I am*: CB to WSW, 3 July 1849, *LCB* 2, 227.

p. 274 *hereafter I look for no great earthly comfort*: CB to WSW, 26 July 1849, *LCB* 2, 232.

p. 274 *what Emily Brontë would have been*: *Life*, 315.

p. 274 *the most prominent and peculiar*: CB to WSW, 21 August 1849, *LCB* 2, 237.

p. 275 *Men of England!*: *Shirley*, 330.

p. 275 *What on earth is the matter with you?*: *Shirley*, 162.

p. 275 *I feel weaker than formerly*: *Shirley*, 163.

p. 275 *I read the leading articles*: *Shirley*, 276.

p. 276 necessary *occupation*: quoted in Mark Bostridge, *Florence Nightingale: The Woman and Her Legend* (London, 2008), 145.

p. 276 *what are they to do*: Lynn McDonald (ed.), *Collected Works of Florence Nightingale* (16 vols.; Ontario, 2012–12), 7, 494.

p. 276 *may well have been uppermost*: Mark Bostridge, *Florence Nightingale: The Woman and Her Legend* (London, 2008), 145.

p. 276 *[W]hat were the faults of that devoir?*: *Shirley*, 410.

p. 277 *over our nerves like fingers . . .* Where is *the other world?*: *Shirley*, 356.

p. 277 *a woman pretty nearly unsexed*: James Lorimer, unsigned review, *North British Review*, August 1849, *Critical Heritage*, 116.

p. 277 *To such critics I would say*: CB to WSW, 16 August 1849, *LCB* 2, 235.

p. 278 *scarce supportable*: CB to WSW, 16 August 1849, *LCB* 2, 236.

p. 278 *Jane Eyre, in spite of some grand things . . . There is throughout it a murmuring*: Elizabeth Rigby, unsigned review, *Quarterly Review*, December 1848, *Critical Heritage*, 110 and 109–10.

p. 278 *too odiously and abominably pagan*: *Critical Heritage*, 111.

p. 279 *What we deeply feel is our own*: CB to WSW, ?31 August 1849, *LCB* 2, 246.

p. 279 *moral Jacobinism . . . Never was there a better hater . . . To say that* Jane Eyre *is positively immoral*: unsigned review, *Christian Remembrancer*, April 1848, *Critical Heritage*, 90–91.

p. 280 *masculine, inured to suffering . . . fiery judgment on society . . . they have not the same means*: Eugène Forçade, *Revue des deux mondes*, 31 October 1848, *Critical Heritage*, 101–2.

p. 280 *However this is not to be yet*: CB to WSW, ?c. 15 September 1849, *LCB* 2, 254.

p. 281 *fairly broke down*: CB to EN, ?24 September 1849, *LCB* 2, 263.

p. 281 *Were my Sisters now alive*: CB to WSW, 1 November 1849, *LCB* 2, 272.

p. 281 *gossiping inquisitiveness*: CB to WSW, ?1 October 1849, *LCB* 2, 266.

p. 281 *read all over the district . . . I met sometimes*: CB to WSW, 1 November 1849, *LCB* 2, 272.

p. 282 *Why can [the Press] not be content*: CB to James Taylor, 6 November 1849, *LCB* 2, 280.

p. 282 *the grand function of woman*: G. H. Lewes in *The Edinburgh Review*, January 1850, *Critical Heritage*, 161.

p. 282 *I can be on my guard against my enemies*: CB to G. H. Lewes, ?c. 10 January 1850, *LCB* 2, 330.

p. 282 *I certainly don't think*: Elizabeth Barrett Browning to Mary Russell Mitford, 18 February 1850, Frederic G. Kenyon (ed.), *The Letters of Elizabeth Barrett Browning* (2 vols.; London, 1897), 1, 435.

p. 282 *The hand was a cramped and nervous one*: *Harriet Martineau's Autobiography*, ed. Chapman, 2, 326.

p. 283 *addressed her reply*: *Harriet Martineau's Autobiography*, ed. Chapman, 2, 327.

p. 283 *She said I was not to answer it . . . [S]he is a good – she is a great woman*: CB to WSW, ?17 November 1849, *LCB* 2, 286–7.

p. 283 *to care about literature . . . lost sight of whatever was prominent*: CB to G. H. Lewes, 1 November 1849, *LCB* 2, 275.

p. 283 *almost formed the resolution*: CB to WSW, 19 November 1849, *LCB* 2, 290.

p. 284 *big Babylon*: CB to EN, ?5 December 1849, *LCB* 2, 299.

p. 284 *[K]indness is a potent heart-winner*: CB to EN, 26 November 1849, *LCB* 2, 298.

p. 284 *[he] too is really most gentlemanly . . . the little man . . . the Helstone order of men . . . He tries to be very kind*: CB to EN, 26 November 1849, *LCB* 2, 298.

p. 285 *in a chilly fashion . . . Boys! I have been dining with 'Jane Eyre'*: George Smith, 'Recollections of a Long and Busy Life', National Library of Scotland MSS 23191–2, quoted by Margaret Smith in *LCB* 2, 300 n8.

p. 285 *He is a very tall man*: CB to PB, 5 December 1849, *LCB* 2, 301.

p. 286 *whether a tall moustached man . . . in came a neat little woman . . . [S]he was so pleasant*: '"Innocent and Un-Londony": Impressions of Charlotte Brontë', *BST*, 19:1–2 (1986).

p. 286 *ideas, images, pleasant feelings*: CB to WSW, 19 December 1849, *LCB* 2, 312.

p. 286 *I think I should scarcely like to live in London*: CB to MW, 14 February 1850, *LCB* 2, 344.

p. 287 *a little lady in a black silk gown . . . But I had time for a good look at her . . . She has a very sweet voice*: ECG to Catherine Winkworth, 25 August 1850, *LCB* 2, 447.

p. 287 *At 19 I should have been thankful*: ECG to Catherine Winkworth, 25 August 1850, *LCB* 2, 448.

p. 288 *[Their works] appeared at last*: CB, 'Biographical Notice of Ellis and Acton Bell' (1850), *LCB* 2, 744.

p. 289 *Never in all her life*: CB, 'Biographical Notice of Ellis and Acton Bell' (1850), *LCB* 2, 746.

p. 289 *An interpreter ought always*: CB, 'Biographical Notice of Ellis and Acton Bell' (1850), *LCB* 2, 746.

p. 289 *[she was] long-suffering, self-denying*: CB, 'Biographical Notice of Ellis and Acton Bell' (1850), *LCB* 2, 746.

p. 289 *thankful to subside*: CB to Elizabeth Smith, 25 May 1850, *LCB* 2, 406.

p. 290 *other and less agreeable arrangements*: quoted by Margaret Smith in *LCB* 2, 414 n1.

p. 290 *all five were remarkable*: CB to EN, 12 June 1850, *LCB* 2, 415.

p. 290 *full of authoresses . . . the charming* CURRER BELL *. . . 'Rochester' airs*: 'Vivian' [G. H. Lewes], 'A Flight of Authoresses', *Leader*, 15 June 1850, quoted in *LCB* 2, 425 n3.

p. 290 *[Emily's] eyes, her features*: CB to EN, 12 June 1850, *LCB* 2, 414.

p. 291 *in every lineament*: CB to EN, 12 June 1850, *LCB* 2, 415.

p. 291 *I was moved to speak to him*: CB to EN, 12 June 1850, *LCB* 2, 414.

p. 291 *the trembling little frame . . . An impetuous honesty . . . New to the London world*: William Makepeace Thackeray, 'The Last Sketch', *The Cornhill Magazine*, April 1860, *Interviews*, 109.

p. 292 *I indulged Miss Brontë*: George Smith, 'Charlotte Brontë', *The Cornhill Magazine*, December 1900, *Interviews*, 93.

p. 292 *chief incidents*: CB to EN, 12 June 1850, *LCB* 2, 414.

p. 292 *a somewhat difficult guest . . . Strangers used to say . . . For my own part*: George Smith, 'Charlotte Brontë', *The Cornhill Magazine*, December 1900, *Interviews*, 95–6.

p. 292 *buoyant animal spirits*: CB to EN, 21 June 1850, *LCB* 2, 419.

p. 293 *I believe that George and I understand each other very well*: CB to EN, 21 June 1850, *LCB* 2, 419.

p. 293 *No, I never was in the least bit in love*: GS to Mrs Humphry Ward, 18 August 1898, 'Charlotte Brontë and George Smith: An Extract from the late Sir Tresham Lever's Unpublished Biography of George Smith', *BST*, 17:87 (1977).

p. 294 *She was very small*: George Smith, 'Charlotte Brontë', *The Cornhill Magazine*, December 1900, *Interviews*, 92.

p. 294 *we all sat silent and expectant . . . in mittens, in silence, in seriousness . . . To say that we little girls . . . Every one waited*: Anne Thackeray Ritchie, *Chapters from Some Memoirs* (1894), extract in *LCB* 2, 754–5.

p. 295 *I do and I don't*: related by George Smith, 'Charlotte Brontë', *The Cornhill Magazine*, December 1900, *Interviews*, 98.

p. 295 *She would make you a very nice wife . . . Oh! you know whom I mean*: George Smith, 'Charlotte Brontë', *The Cornhill Magazine*, December 1900, *Interviews*, 98.

p. 296 *uneasily and perpetually conscious . . . the possession of genius*: George Smith, 'Charlotte Brontë', *The Cornhill Magazine*, December 1900, *Interviews*, 92.

p. 296 *I never remember the time . . . Was it weak*: *Villette*, 483 and 484.

p. 296 *some early hip trouble . . . not remarkable in appearance*: John Richmond to Reginald Smith, 30 December 1909, BPM, SG 102.

p. 296 *brown merino wool*: A. M. W. Stirling, *The Richmond Papers* (London, 1926), 60.

p. 297 *Richmond said*: reported by William Cory in 1867, who had the story from his old schoolfriends Montagu and Arthur Butler, *Interviews*, 204.

p. 297 *an expression difficult for a society portraitist to flatter*: for a discussion of how George Richmond idealised sitters, see Mark Bostridge, 'Charlotte Brontë and George Richmond', *BST*, 17:86 (1976).

p. 297 *general impression of chin*: Anne Thackeray Ritchie to Reginald J. Smith, 18 October 1906, *Interviews*, 160.

p. 297 *illuminating features*: A. M. W. Stirling, *The Richmond Papers* (London, 1926), 60.

p. 297 *half in apology*: A. M. W. Stirling, *The Richmond Papers* (London, 1926), 60.

p. 297 *one citing Anne and the other Emily*: for CB saying that the likeness reminded her of Anne, see Stirling, *The Richmond Papers* (1926), 60. William Cory reported CB as having said 'it is so like my sister Emily' (*Interviews*, 204), though it must be borne in mind that he had his information at third hand.

p. 298 *she had met Dickens*: reported by John Stores Smith in 'Personal Reminiscences: A Day with Charlotte Brontë' (1868), *Interviews*, 168.

p. 298 *and never would*: 'Dickens had not read *Jane Eyre* and said he never would as he disapproved of the whole school. He had not read *Wuthering Heights*', Jerome Meckier, 'Some Household Words: Two New Accounts of Dickens's Conversation', *The Dickensian*, 71:1:375 (January 1975).

p. 299 *meet, work, talk and walk together . . . She appears exhaustless*: CB to EN, 18 December 1850, *LCB* 2, 535.

p. 299 *[S]he looked up at me . . . I saw at once*: *Life*, 372.

p. 299 *this did not prevent her*: *Harriet Martineau's Autobiography*, ed. Chapman, 2, 350.

p. 299 *a death-blow to [Martineau's] future usefulness*: CB to James Taylor, 24 March 1851, *LCB* 2, 589.

p. 300 *some hours as happy*: CB to WSW, 20 July 1850, *LCB* 2, 427.

p. 300 *somehow about to be married to somebody*: CB to EN, 15 July 1850, *LCB* 2, 425.

p. 301 *each moment he came near me*: CB to EN, 9 April 1851, *LCB* 2, 600.

p. 301 *significant eulogy . . . I have told him nothing*: CB to EN, 5 May 1851, *LCB* 2, 611.

p. 302 *out of patience*: CB to EN, 5 May 1851, *LCB* 2, 611.

p. 302 *second-rate . . . something of the gentleman . . . one passing glimpse*: CB to EN, 23 April 1851, *LCB* 2, 609.

p. 302 *good – mild and uncontentious*: CB to EN, ?28 July 1851, *LCB* 2, 671.

p. 303 *proper, steady-going, clerical faults . . . finding himself invited to tea . . . could make strange havoc*: *Shirley*, 531.

p. 303 *he sat alone – clapping his hands*: CB to EN, ?28 January 1850, *LCB* 2, 337.

p. 303 *One reviewer*: an anonymous one, in *Fraser's Magazine*, December 1849; see *Critical Heritage*, 152–5.

p. 303 *at once the most highflown*: unsigned review, *The Times*, 7 December 1849, *Critical Heritage*, 151.

p. 303 *as Adam's son*: CB, 'Preface', *The Professor*, 3.

p. 304 *my feelings towards it . . . You may allege*: CB to GS, 5 February 1851, *LCB* 2, 572.

p. 305 *tremble on her hostess's arm*: as related by Elizabeth Smith to ECG and used in *Life*, 381.

p. 306 *thirty thousand souls . . . not one loud noise*: CB to PB, 7 June 1851, *LCB* 2, 631.

p. 306 *The brightest colours blaze on all sides*: CB to PB, 31 May 1851, *LCB* 2, 625.

p. 306 *Whatever human industry has created*: CB to PB, 7 June 1851, *LCB* 2, 630–31.

p. 306 *not much in my way*: CB to ECG, ?14 June 1851, *LCB* 2, 639.

p. 306 *a mixture of a Genii Palace*: CB to EN, 2 June 1851, *LCB* 2, 628.

p. 307 *Thackeray should have one*: see CB to GS, 1 July 1851, *LCB* 2, 655.

p. 307 *he has not merely a double*: CB to PB, 17 June 1851, *LCB* 2, 640–41.

p. 308 *strangely suggestive*: CB to EN, 2 June 1851, *LCB* 2, 628.

p. 308 *very remarkable . . . the presence of an intellect*: 'A Phrenological Estimate of the Talents and Dispositions of a Lady', *LCB* 2, 658.

p. 308 *Her attachments are strong and enduring . . . Her sense of truth and justice*: 'A Phrenological Estimate of the Talents and Dispositions of a Lady', *LCB* 2, 657.

p. 308 *She is sensitive*: 'A Phrenological Estimate of the Talents and Dispositions of a Lady', *LCB* 2, 658.

p. 309 *Before I received your last*: CB to GS, 8 July 1851, *LCB* 2, 663.

p. 309 *Can I help wishing you well . . . You do not know*: CB to GS, 22 September 1851, *LCB* 2, 699.

14   *The Curate's Wife*   1851–5

p. 311 *quite out of Manchester Smoke*: CB to GS, 1 July 1851, *LCB* 2, 655.

p. 311 *a fond but bashful suitor*: CB to ECG, 22 May 1852, *LCB* 3, 48.

p. 312 *What is it you say*: CB to GS, 22 September 1851, *LCB* 2, 700.

p. 313 *calm sleep*: the next year, CB looked back on EN's latest visit, saying 'I do miss my dear bed-fellow. No more of that calm sleep.' CB to EN, ?26 October 1852, *LCB* 3, 73.

p. 313 *I am not sure myself*: CB to EN, 4 May 1852, *LCB* 3, 44.

p. 313 *we find it difficult to disconnect*: unsigned review, *The Examiner*, 5 February 1853, *Critical Heritage*, 175.

p. 313 *A sorrowful indifference*: *Villette*, 156.

p. 313 *[I]s there nothing more for me in life? . . . I believe in some blending*: *Villette*, 361.

p. 314 *I cannot write books handling the topics of the day*: CB to GS, 30 October 1852, *LCB* 3, 75.

p. 315 *trudges*: CB to EN, 6 June 1852, *LCB* 3, 51.

p. 315 *The Sea is very grand . . . [H]ad Mr. Nicholls been there*: CB to PB, 2 June 1852, *LCB* 3, 47–8.

p. 315 *not that I am likely*: CB to GS, 30 October 1852, *LCB* 3, 75.

p. 316 *If the witholding of the author's name*: CB to GS, 30 October 1852, *LCB* 3, 74.

p. 317 *it amuses me*: William Makepeace Thackeray to Lucy Baxter, 11 March ?1853, MS Berg, tipped in to H. B. Forman's copy of *Villette* (1853). The letter, with minor punctuation changes, appears in *The Letters and Private Papers of William Makepeace Thackeray*, collected and edited by Gordon N. Ray (4 vols.; London, 1946), 3, 233.

p. 318 *it is now a very different matter*: CB to EN, ?9 December 1852, *LCB* 3, 91.

p. 318 *dim misgivings*: CB to EN, 15 December 1852, *LCB* 3, 92.

p. 318 *with little sympathy*: CB to EN, 15 December 1852, *LCB* 3, 93.

p. 318 *vaguely felt . . . the meaning*: CB to EN, 15 December 1852, *LCB* 3, 93.

p. 318 *like lightning it flashed on me*: CB to EN, 15 December 1852, *LCB* 3, 93.

p. 319 *one ordinarily so statue-like*: CB to EN, 15 December 1852, *LCB* 3, 93.

p. 319 *a strange shock . . . I could only entreat him*: CB to EN, 15 December 1852, *LCB* 3, 93.

p. 319 *Agitation and Anger*: CB to EN, 15 December 1852, *LCB* 3, 93.

p. 319 *rush to the brain . . . almost be to kill him at once*: CB to EN, 26 July 1852, *LCB* 3, 58.

p. 320 *turbulence of feeling . . . He just treats him*: CB to EN, 18 December 1852, *LCB* 3, 94.

p. 320 *bitter against him . . . They don't understand*: CB to EN, 2 January 1853, *LCB* 3, 101.

p. 320 *He is very discreet*: PB to the Reverend W. J. Bullock, 31 January 1853, *LPB*, 215.

p. 320 *a rude, and dissenting population . . . has nearly approached*: testimonial of Reverend J. Burnet, vicar of Bradford, 'Romance in the Parsonage: New Nicholls Letters', *The Daily Telegraph*, 10 January 1936.

p. 321 *rather the real . . . Mrs S[mith] and her daughters*: CB to EN, 19 January 1853, *LCB* 3, 108.

p. 321 *There was a poor girl*: George Smith, 'Charlotte Brontë', *The Cornhill Magazine*, December 1900, *Interviews*, 92–3.

p. 321 *to make my heart swell*: CB to EN, 15 February 1853, *LCB* 3, 123.

p. 321 *It must be read continuously*: unsigned review, *Literary Gazette*, 5 February 1853, *Critical Heritage*, 180.

p. 321 *In Passion and Power*: unsigned review, *Leader*, 12 February 1853, *Critical Heritage*, 184.

p. 321 *Currer Bell might have called*: unsigned review, *Spectator*, 12 February 1853, *Critical Heritage*, 181.

p. 322 *any possible translation of it*: The title page of *Villette* contains a note unusual for the date: 'The Author of this work reserves the right of translating it'.

p. 322 *You see how much the ladies think . . . now . . . vowed*: CB to WSW, 23 March 1853, *LCB* 3, 138.

p. 322 *either the kind or the degree*: Harriet Martineau recalling, for ECG, what she wrote to CB in 1853, *Life*, 425.

p. 322 *I know what love is*: CB to Harriet Martineau, ?February 1853, *LCB* 3, 118.

p. 323 *the writer's mind contains nothing but hunger*: Matthew Arnold to Mrs Forster, 14 April 1853, quoted in *Critical Heritage*, 201.

p. 323 *a still more wonderful book than* Jane Eyre *. . .* Villette *–* Villette: George Eliot to Mrs Bray, 15 February and 12 March 1853, *Critical Heritage*, 192.

p. 323 *dangerous designs . . . His conduct might have been excus'd*: PB to CB, January 1853, *LPB*, 212.

p. 323 *I see people cheating one another . . . Ah! My dear Mistress*: PB to CB, January 1853, *LPB*, 213–14.

p. 324 *some doubts have occurred to me*: ABN to the Society for the Propagation of the Gospel, quoted in 'Romance in the Parsonage: New Nicholls Letters', *The Daily Telegraph*, 10 January 1936.

p. 324 *that dark gloom of his*: CB to EN, 4 March 1853, *LCB* 3, 130.

p. 324 *flaysome*: CB to EN, 4 March 1853, *LCB* 3, 129.

p. 324 *I own I respect him for this . . . I pity him inexpressibly*: CB to EN, 6 April 1853, *LCB* 3, 149.

p. 325 *[He] stood before my eyes*: CB to EN, 16 May 1853, *LCB* 3, 165.

p. 325 *unmanly driveller . . . Compassion or relenting*: CB to EN, 16 May 1853, *LCB* 3, 166.

p. 325 *never will forget or forgive . . . I am afraid*: CB to EN, 19 May 1853, *LCB* 3, 167.

p. 326 *remembering his long grief*: CB to EN, 27 May 1853, *LCB* 3, 168–9.

p. 326   *implacable*: CB to EN, 27 May 1853, *LCB* 3, 169.

p. 326   *weak and bewildered*: CB to EN, ?13 June 1853, *LCB* 3, 175.

p. 326   *strangely arrested . . . it seemed as if a thick curtain*: CB to ECG, 18 June 1853, *LCB* 3, 177.

p. 327   *very miserable*: 'He wrote to her very miserably; wrote six times, and then she answered him, a letter exhorting him to heroic submission to his lot, &c.', Catherine Winkworth to Emma Shaen, 8 May 1854, *LCB* 3, 258.

p. 327   *bearing her position . . . enduring to the end . . . You talk wonderful nonsense*: Mary Taylor to EN, 24 February to 3 March 1854, *LCB* 3, 228.

p. 328   *when you turn with distaste*: CB to GS, 3 July 1853, *LCB* 3, 181.

p. 328   *not going to write again*: ECG to John Forster, 3 May 1853, *LCB* 3, 160.

p. 328   *Do you . . . find it easy*: CB to ECG, 9 July 1853, *LCB* 3, 182.

p. 328   *Papa and Mamma*: CB to MW, 30 August 1853, *LCB* 3, 189.

p. 329   *piping & wailing and sobbing . . . (fancy it! only they two left)*: ECG to ?John Forster, ?after 29 September 1853, *LCB* 3, 197.

p. 330   *just as regularly as he puts on his watch*: ECG to ?John Forster, ?after 29 September 1853, *LCB* 3, 199.

p. 330   *Before tea we had a long, delicious walk*: ECG to ?John Forster, ?after 29 September 1853, *LCB* 3, 197–8.

p. 330   *wild tales of the ungovernable families*: ECG to ?John Forster, ?after 29 September 1853, *LCB* 3, 198.

p. 330   *Tabby says*: ECG to ?John Forster, ?after 29 September 1853, *LCB* 3, 200.

p. 331   *a strong-built, somewhat hard-featured man . . . sadly broken*: Richard Monckton Milnes to ECG, 30 January 1854, *LCB* 3, 223.

p. 332   *My dear Sir*: CB to GS, 10 December 1853, *LCB* 3, 213.

p. 332   *These courtesies*: CB to ?WSW, 6 December 1853, *LCB* 3, 212.

p. 332   *afterwards wrote more at length*: George Smith, 'Charlotte Brontë', *The Cornhill Magazine*, December 1900, *Interviews*, 102.

p. 332   *really fine . . . She said 'Father I am not a young girl[']*: ECG to John Forster, ?17 May 1854, *LCB* 3, 261.

p. 333   *I must marry a curate . . . another man in this house . . . if he wished to kill his daughter?*: ECG to John Forster, ?17 May 1854, *LCB* 3, 261–2.

p. 333   *for Mr. Nicholls has in all things proved himself*: CB to EN, 11 April 1854, *LCB* 3, 240.

p. 333   *[I]t has cost me a good deal . . . I cannot conceal from myself . . . such a character*

... *do the fickleness*: Catherine Winkworth to Emma Shaen, 8 May 1854, *LCB* 3, 257.

p. 334 *I am still very calm ... Providence offers me this destiny*: CB to EN, 11 April 1854, *LCB* 3, 240.

p. 334 *a marriage settlement*: for a transcription and discussion of the settlement see Juliet R. V. Barker, 'Subdued Expectations: Charlotte Brontë's Marriage Settlement', *BST*, 19:1–2 (1986). The original is in BPM.

p. 335 *like a snowdrop*: reported by ECG, *Life*, 450.

p. 336 *surpassed anything I remember*: CB to Catherine Wooler, 18 July 1854, *LCB* 3, 278.

p. 336 *a pretty lady-like girl*: CB to MW, 10 July 1854, *LCB* 3, 276.

p. 336 *like a gentleman's country-seat*: CB to MW, 10 July 1854, *LCB* 3, 276.

p. 336 *the passages look desolate and bare ... quiet, kind and well-bred*: CB to MW, 10 July 1854, *LCB* 3, 276.

p. 336 *English order and repose*: CB to MW, 18 July 1854, *LCB* 3, 278.

p. 337 *It seems [Mrs. Bell] was brought up in London*: CB to MW, 10 July 1854, *LCB* 3, 276.

p. 337 *I must say I like my new relations ... I pray to be enabled*: CB to MW, 10 July 1854, *LCB* 3, 276.

p. 337 *such a wild, iron-bound coast*: CB to Catherine Winkworth, 27 July 1854, *LCB* 3, 279.

p. 337 *take the matter in my own way ... I did not want to talk*: CB to Catherine Winkworth, 27 July 1854, *LCB* 3, 279–80.

p. 338 *seemed to go mad – reared, plunged ... I saw and felt her kick ... I had my thoughts about the moment*: CB to Catherine Winkworth, 27 July 1854, *LCB* 3, 280.

p. 338 *Papa has not been well ... longing,* longing intensely: CB to EN, ?28 July 1854, *LCB* 3, 282.

p. 338 *The wish for his continued life*: CB to MW, 22 August 1854, *LCB* 3, 286–7.

p. 338 *Each time I see Mr. Nicholls*: CB to MW, 22 August 1854, *LCB* 3, 287.

p. 339 *one of the greatest curses*: CB to MW, 6 December 1854, *LCB* 3, 305.

p. 339 *[M]y husband flourishes*: CB to EN, 7 September 1854, *LCB* 3, 288.

p. 340 *I am afraid there is not any portrait*: EN to T. Wemyss Reid, 24 November 1876, MS Berg Collection.

p. 340 *I did not expect perfection*: CB to MW, 22 August 1854, *LCB* 3, 286.

p. 340 *settled and content*: CB to EN, 21 November 1854, *LCB* 3, 303.

p. 340 *May God make me thankful for it!*: CB to MW, 15 November 1854, *LCB* 3, 301.

p. 341 *If you had not been with me . . . The Critics will accuse you . . . O I shall alter that . . . I always begin two or three*: ABN to GS, 11 October 1859, John Murray archive, quoted in appendix, 'Emma', *The Professor*, 225–6.

p. 342 *during the last 6 weeks*: CB to EN, 9 August 1854, *LCB* 3, 283–4.

p. 342 *[Arthur] often says*: CB to EN, 11 October 1854, *LCB* 3, 293.

p. 343 *Arthur has just been glancing over this note*: CB to EN, ?20 October 1854, *LCB* 3, 295.

p. 343 *Dear Ellen – Arthur complains*: CB to EN, 31 October 1854, *LCB* 3, 296–7.

p. 344 *My dear Mr Nicholls*: EN to ABN, November 1854, *LCB* 3, 297.

p. 344 *Strange chances do fall out*: CB to EN, 7 November 1854, *LCB* 3, 298.

p. 344 *Mr N continued his censorship*: EN pencil note on EN to ABN, November 1854, *LCB* 3, 297.

p. 345 *Arthur wishes you would burn my letters . . . [H]e never did give the pledge*: *LCB* 3, 299 n3.

p. 345 *Don't conjecture – dear Nell*: CB to EN, 19 January 1855, *LCB* 3, 319.

p. 346 *a natural cause . . . the baby that was coming*: *Life*, 454.

p. 346 *a long walk over damp ground*: *Life*, 454.

p. 347 *so aggressively . . . It was as if someone had taken over*: Sarah Button, 'Pregnancy Sickness Nearly Killed Me', *Guardian Weekend*, 11 October 2014.

p. 347 *She, who was ever patient*: *Life*, 454.

p. 347 *I do fancy that if I had come*: ECG to John Greenwood, 12 April 1855, *ECG Letters*, 337.

p. 347 *I dare say I shall be glad sometime*: *Life*, 454.

p. 348 *in a few weeks she will be well again*: ABN to EN, 1 February 1855, *LCB* 3, 323.

p. 348 *Let me speak the plain truth*: CB to Amelia Taylor, ?late February 1855, *LCB* 3, 327.

p. 348 *how long she was ill and in what way*: CB to EN, on or after 21 February 1855, *LCB* 3, 326.

p. 348 *anything that will do good*: CB to Amelia Taylor, ?late February 1855, *LCB* 3, 327.

p. 348 *No kinder better husband*: CB to Laetitia Wheelwright, 15 February 1855, *LCB* 3, 325.

p. 348   *the best earthly comfort*: CB to EN, on or after 21 February 1855, *LCB* 3, 326.

p. 348   *Our poor old Tabby*: CB to EN, on or after 21 February 1855, *LCB* 3, 326.

p. 348   *In case I die without issue*: 'Last Will and Testament of Charlotte Nicholls', copy in Pierpont Morgan Library, New York, MA 2695.

p. 349   *spoonsful of wine & water*: CB to EN, ?early March 1855, *LCB* 3, 328.

p. 349   *a wren would have starved*: *Life*, 454.

p. 349   *I am reduced to greater weakness*: CB to EN, ?early March 1855, *LCB* 3, 328.

p. 349   *a low wandering delirium . . . and even for stimulants*: *Life*, 455.

p. 349   *Oh! I am not going to die, am I?*: *Life*, 455.

p. 349   *and we only to look forward to*: PB to EN, 30 March 1855, *LCB* 3, 330.

p. 349   *crying in agonized tones*: John Lock and Canon W. T. Dixon, *A Man of Sorrow*, 477.

Coda

p. 351   '*Currer Bell is dead! . . . a pang will be felt . . . hold their place*: Harriet Martineau, obituary of Charlotte Brontë, *Daily News*, April 1855, *Critical Heritage*, 301 and 305.

p. 351   *My Daughter, is indeed, dead*: PB to ECG, 5 April 1855, *LPB*, 227.

p. 351   *my beloved and esteemed son-in-law*: 'Patrick Brontë's Will', 20 June 1855, Appendix XVI, *LPB*, 372.

p. 351   EVERY *particular*: ECG to John Greenwood, 4 April 1855, *ECG Letters*, 336.

p. 351   *no one is living*: ECG to GS, 31 May 1855, *ECG Letters*, 345.

p. 351   *long or short . . . just as you may deem*: PB to ECG, 16 June 1855, *LPB*, 232.

p. 352   *as Juliet Barker has pointed out*: Barker, 780–81.

p. 352   *the wild sad life and beautiful character*: ECG to GS, 4 June 1855, *ECG Letters*, 347.

p. 352   *his feeling was against it's being written*: ECG to EN, 24 July 1855, *ECG Letters*, 361.

p. 352   *a pirated French translation of* Villette: probably the 1855 translation which descendants of the Hegers brought to Haworth on a visit in 1953; see *LCB* 3, 85 n1.

p. 353   *[H]e is sure she would keep them*: 'I promised M. Héger [*sic*] to ask to see his letters to her; he is sure she would keep them, as they contained advice about her character, studies, mode of life. I doubt much if Mr Nicholls has not destroyed them.' ECG to EN, 9 July 1856, *ECG Letters*, 394.

p. 353 *people who wanted to shake the hand*: according to the obituary of Mary Anna Nicholls, *The Times*, 2 March 1915.

p. 354 *quaint Yorkshire accent and excellent sponge cake*: 'Reminiscences of a Relation of Arthur Bell Nicholls', *BST*, 15:79 (1969).

p. 354 *so that future worshippers*: 'An American Visitor at Haworth, 1861', *BST*, 15:2 (1967).

p. 355 *even after Mrs Gaskell's detailed biography . . . Could I, without the consent*: CH to EN, 7 September 1863, *SHB* 4, 249–50. The translation is by the editors of *SHB*: Heger's original letter, in French, is on pp. 247–9.

p. 356 *'copyright' and 'permissions'*: ABN had been manoeuvred into transferring copyright on 'the materials of the biography' to GS and ECG, though he was not happy about it: 'it seems to be taken for granted that I am to do so, tho' why it should, I know not, as I never entered into any arrangement with Mrs Gaskell', ABN to GS, 3 December 1856, quoted in Barker, 795.

p. 357 *truer than the biography . . . the one true love of [Charlotte Brontë's] life*: Thomas Westwood to Lady Alwyne Compton, 21 February 1870, *A Literary Friendship: Letters to Lady Alwyne Compton 1869–1881, from Thomas Westwood*, 15.

p. 357 *M. Paul Emanuel has quite a bundle of them*: Thomas Westwood to Lady Alwyne Compton, 21 November 1869, *A Literary Friendship: Letters to Lady Alwyne Compton 1869–1881, from Thomas Westwood*, 11.

p. 357 *told the whole story . . . He told the story . . . and, I am sorry to say*: Thomas Westwood to Lady Alwyne Compton, 21 February 1870, *A Literary Friendship: Letters to Lady Alwyne Compton 1869–1881, from Thomas Westwood*, 16.

p. 358 *they began to release*: see, for instance, the publication of EJB's 'Filial Love' in *Woman at Home* (September 1894), 'reproduced in facsimile from manuscript in possession of the Héger [*sic*] family in Brussels'.

p. 358 *Doctor Heger regrets*: carte-de-visite of Mademoiselle C. Heger, Berg Collection, NYPL, Brontë C. 247123b (my translation). The card's original envelope is pasted inside Clement Shorter's copy of *Villette*, also in the Berg Collection, and marked 'From Paul Emanuel's Daughter'.

p. 358 *He was sitting near the table*: Shirley, 194.

p. 359 *hears Rochester's voice*: Life, 337.

p. 359 *cries, and sobs, and wailings . . . as of the dearly-beloved*: Life, 337.

p. 359 *Meta Mossman*: she, her sister, mother and aunt were all former pupils at the Pensionnat Heger and were a Yorkshire family, related to the Taylors. See Edith M. Weir, 'The Hegers and a Yorkshire Family', BST, 14:3 (1963).

p. 359 *although it is true . . . In thinking it over*: CH to 'L' [Meta Mossman], Letter V, Edith M. Weir, 'New Brontë Material Comes to Light', BST, 11:4 (1949).

Acknowledgements

The Brontë Parsonage Museum, Haworth, houses the largest and most important collection of Brontëana in the world and has been my frequent destination during the writing of this book. I would like to thank all the staff of the museum and library for their kindness and help, but especially the Collections Manager, Ann Dinsdale, whose expertise and lively interest in my subject has made every visit to the Parsonage Library a great pleasure. I would also like to thank Sarah Laycock for her unfailingly prompt and efficient answers to many queries and Linda Proctor-Mackley and Jenna Holmes for help along the way.

For the use of copyright materials and illustrations, and kind permission to quote from manuscripts in their collections, I would like to thank the Brontë Society, British Library, Brotherton Library, University of Leeds, City Archive of Brussels, Keighley Local Studies Library, National Portrait Gallery, New York Public Library, Pierpont Morgan Library and Royal Library of Belgium. Many individual members of staff at libraries, galleries and other institutions have generously given me their time, attention and professional expertise during the research for this book, and I would particularly like to thank Maria Molestina and the staff of the Manuscript Reading Room, Pierpont Morgan Library, New York City; Isaac Gewirtz, Lyndsi Barnes and Joshua McKeon of the Henry W. and Albert A. Berg Collection of New York Public Library; Elizabeth Denlinger of the Pforzheimer Collection, New York Public Library; Katie Thornton and Lucy Arnold of the Brotherton Library, University of Leeds; Rebekah Lunt and Fran Baker of the John Rylands Library, Manchester; Kirsty Gaskin of Cliffe Castle Museum, Keighley; Caroline Brown of Keighley Local Studies Library; Timothy Engels of Brown University Library; the staff of the Upper Reading Room of the Bodleian Library, Oxford; Dr David Smith of St Anne's College Library, Oxford; and the staff of the Manuscript Room at the British

Library. I am also very grateful to the staff of the Heinz Archive of the National Portrait Gallery, and especially to Tim Moreton, who in September 2013 arranged a private viewing for me of George Richmond's portrait of Charlotte Brontë, not at that date on display in the gallery.

My debts to the many Brontë scholars and biographers who have preceded me will be clear from the book's notes and bibliography, but I would like to pay particular tribute here to the fine biographies of Charlotte Brontë by Lyndall Gordon, Rebecca Fraser and the late Winifred Gérin, and to Lucasta Miller's seminal study of Brontë reception, *The Brontë Myth*. Dr Juliet Barker's magisterial work, *The Brontës*, which drew together a wealth of primary and secondary material about the family and their times and established a base of facts about them of unmatchable value and solidity, has been an invaluable resource, and I am also very grateful for Dr Barker's responses to my queries during the writing of this book. Christine Alexander's extensive research into, and editing of, the Brontë juvenilia has been of inestimable value to me, not least for her expertise in deciphering and interpreting the minuscule handwriting used by the Brontë siblings in their earliest writings. I would also like to express my appreciation of the work of Christine Alexander and Jane Sellars in their fine edition of *The Art of the Brontës* and that of Victor A. Neufeldt in *The Poems of Charlotte Brontë*, Sue Lonoff in *The Belgian Essays* and, in various other critical and editorial capacities, Herbert Rosengarten, Edward Chitham, Patsy Stoneman, Tom Winnifrith, Sally Shuttleworth, Dinah Birch, Dudley Green, Stevie Davies, Marianne Thormählen and Janet Gezari.

But my greatest debt is to the scholarship of Margaret Smith, whose three-volume edition of *The Letters of Charlotte Brontë*, published between 1994 and 2004, has opened out to readers the full scope and significance of Charlotte Brontë's correspondence. Smith published many items for the first time, corrected attributions, dates and readings, and set all of the letters in a context of impeccably researched annotation and commentary. Her edition has been the essential tool in my biography, as the fullest and most suggestive source to date of Charlotte Brontë's behaviour and private opinions, and I am very grateful for her generous permission to quote from her work.

For their various contributions of information, encouragement and hospitality I would like to thank Janet Allen, Jay Barksdale, Kate Clanchy, Sarah Fermi, Lyndall Gordon, Sir John and Lady Sue Harman, Alexandra Harris, Selina Hastings, Elliot Kendall, Deborah Lutz, Lucasta Miller, Patsy Stoneman, Marion Taylor and Robin Walker. Mark Bostridge has generously shared his ideas and opinions on the Brontës with me for the past three years, and I am very grateful to him for all our conversations on the subject, and for his ready provision of leads and information. In Belgium, the members of the Brontë Brussels Group, led by Helen MacEwan, proved most convivial and knowledgeable company on two visits, in 2012 and 2015, and I have found their website and blogs of constant use in my research. Helen has also given much friendly help and advice, especially about illustrations, for which I am very grateful. In Haworth, Marian Reynolds at Cherry Tree Cottage and Brenda Taylor and Carol at Ponden Guest House were welcoming hosts, while Steven Wood was extremely generous with his time and assistance, especially over maps and local history sources. He was the best possible guide to changes in the area over the past two hundred years, and walking Haworth moor with him in the autumn of 2014 was pivotally important to my research as well as a great pleasure.

I would like to thank Carolyn Dinshaw and Marget Long for being such charming companions at North Lees Hall in the summer of 2014. I would also like to thank the staff of Hollybank School, Mirfield (the site of Roe Head School), the staff of Red House Gomersal, and Jocelyn Hill, John Williams and Janet Allen at Elizabeth Gaskell's House, Manchester.

At Viking Penguin I would like to thank a superb team, led by my editor Venetia Butterfield, with assistance from Hermione Thompson and Isabel Wall. Donna Poppy's meticulous reading at the copy-editing stage saved me from making many mistakes, and I am very grateful for her strenuous efforts on behalf of achieving a clean text. Julia Murday, Celeste Ward-Best, Amelia Fairney, Samantha Fanaken and Samantha Halstead have dealt with marketing and publicity with effortless professionalism, and Keith Taylor has guided the whole project expertly through production with the help of Emma Brown, Sara Granger and Claire Mason.

I was very fortunate to be awarded a grant from The Authors' Foundation during the writing of this book and would like to express my gratitude to the assessors of the award and to its administrators, The Society of Authors.

Lastly, I would like to thank Zoë Waldie, my agent, for her invaluable friendship, kindness and support, her assistant Lexie Hamblin at Rogers, Coleridge and White, and also Hannah Westland, whose infectious enthusiasm for this project at its inception was extremely important to me and who has remained a most affectionate well-wisher throughout.

Paul Strohm has been the most patient of partners during the writing of this book, and it is dedicated to him with love and gratitude.

Index

Abbotsford, Roxburghshire, 300
'Acton Bell' (pseudonym) *see* Brontë, Anne
Albert, Prince Consort, 306
Alexander, Christine, 61, 95n, 377
Allison, William, 221
Alnwick, Northumberland, 118
Andrews, Anna (teacher at Cowan Bridge), 42, 43, 374
Arblay, Frances d' (Fanny Burney): *The Wanderer*, 209n
Arnold, Matthew, 323
Athenaeum (magazine), 220, 238
Athénée Royal (school, Brussels), 140, 180, 205–6
Atkins, William, 45
Atkinson, Frances (*née* Walker), 20, 62, 69
Atkinson, Thomas, 19–20, 62, 69
Atlas (magazine), 238, 240
Aubigné, Jean-Henri Merle d', 307
Austen, Jane: *Pride and Prejudice*, 147; *Emma*, 322
Aykroyd, Tabitha ('Tabby'): taken on as servant, 47; character, 50; oversees Brontë children, 54, 57, 76–7, 123, 197; accident, 125–6; ailing, 262; relates stories to Elizabeth Gaskell, 330; confronts Patrick Brontë over his treatment of CB, 333; illness and death, 345, 348
Aylott and Jones (publishers), 209–10, 213–14, 217, 219, 400

Baer, Ann, 117n
Ball, Mr and Mrs, 225

Banagher, County Offaly, Ireland, 195, 336–7, 353–4; Banagher Royal Free School, 337 and n
Barbier, Auguste, 161, 198; 'L'Idole', 198
Barker, Juliet, 82n, 84n, 126, 193n, 265n, 352, 386, 396
Barrett Browning, Elizabeth, 282
Bassompierre, Louise de, 144, 389
Belgium, 135, 142
Bell, Dr Allan, 337
Bell, Harriette, 336–7 and n
Bell, Joseph, 336
Bell, Mary Anna (*later* Nicholls), 336, 353
Belmontet, Louis, 161, 198
Benson, A. C., 117
Bewick, Thomas, 58
Binns, Benjamin, 76, 83, 231
Birstall, West Yorkshire, 73, 85, 107
Blackwood's Magazine, 57, 90, 101, 127, 152
Blake Hall, Mirfield, 111, 122
Blakeway, Elizabeth, 328, 332
Blanche, Mademoiselle (teacher, Brussels), 141, 167, 174
Bolster, Violet, 224
Bolton Abbey, North Yorkshire, 83
Bonaparte, Napoleon, 143–4, 161; relic of coffin, 170
Bowles, Caroline, 101
Bradford, West Yorkshire, 20, 36, 106, 114–15
Bradley, John, 78, 83
Bradley, Reverend James, 195
Branwell family of Penzance, 15, 190
Branwell, Anne (*née* Carne, CB's maternal grandmother), 15

Branwell, Charlotte (*née* Branwell, CB's aunt), 15, 18–19

Branwell, Elizabeth (CB's aunt): life in Penzance, 15, 74; in Thornton, 20; in Haworth to nurse sister, 31, 33; moves to Haworth, 35–6; as mother-substitute to Brontë children, 36, 89; character and habits, 20–21, 50–51, 74–5, 121–2, 125–6; finances and estate, 35, 62, 114, 156, 157n; as housekeeper, 50, 121–2, 125–6; teaches nieces, 52; appearance, 74; relations with brother-in-law, 74; helps set Branwell up in business, 114; suggests holiday in Liverpool, 118; offers to support school plan, 134; lends money to nieces for education abroad, 135; illness and death, 154–5; burial, 155; will, 156–7, 190; leaves money to nieces, 156

Branwell, Joseph, 15, 18–19

Branwell, Richard, 15

Branwell, Thomas (CB's maternal grandfather), 14–15

Bretton, Dr John Graham (*Villette*), 206, 304, 308, 309, 315–16

Brewster, Sir David, 306 and n

Bridlington, Yorkshire, 118, 134

Briery Close, Ambleside, 287

Britannia (magazine), 240

British and Continental Mercury (newspaper), 138

British Library, 204, 358

British Museum, London, 137

Brontë Parsonage Museum, 61n, 108n, 155n, 169, 335n, 356, 358n

Brontë Society, 356

Brontë, Anne (CB's sister): birth and childhood, 22, 24, 31, 36; quizzed by father, 37; imaginative life, 37, 54–5, 61, 87; and bog burst, 45; home life with sisters, 57, 71–2,

76–7; caricatured by CB in 'The Young Men's Magazine', 73; 'like twins' with Emily, 76, 196; and Gondal saga, 76, 196, 197; Diary Papers, 77, 134, 190, 197, 250; in portraits by CB, 80–81; depicted in *The Brontë Sisters* by Branwell, 81–2; appearance, 81–2, 133; attitudes to love and marriage, 87; at Roe Head School, 89; leaves Roe Head, 107; takes up governess post at Blake Hall, 111; social awkwardness, 111; stammer, 111, 132; conduct as governess, 111; feelings towards animals, 111, 269; feelings for William Weightman, 122, 153–4; introversion, 131–2; post at Thorp Green, 153, 157, 169, 192; inherits money from aunt, 156–7; aware of Emily's writing, 190; and school plan, 192; secret understanding of Branwell's situation, 192, 193; resigns post at Thorp Green, 193; and Branwell's decline, 194, 197, 244–5; trip to York with Emily, 196; writing 'Passages in the Life of an Individual' (*Agnes Grey*), 197, 199; poems, 208, 210; pseudonym 'Acton Bell', 209, 221, 233; controversy over 'brothers Bell', 220, 241, 250, 253–4, 263–4; *Poems* published, 219–21; model for Mary Rivers in *Jane Eyre*, 230; publication of *Agnes Grey*, 234; dealings with Thomas Newby, 237, 240, 257; affected by brother's decline, 252; in London with CB, 254–7; illness, 266–7, 268; fortitude in final days, 269–70; death and burial, 269–70; grave, 315

WORKS:

poems: 'I will not mourn thee, lovely one', 153–4; 'A dreadful darkness closes in', 266–7

prose: *Agnes Grey*, 111, 197, 214, 215–17, 237, 239, 240–41, 244, 250; *The Tenant of Wildfell Hall*, 244, 253, 277–8

Brontë, Charlotte:

BIOGRAPHY/PERSONAL LIFE: birth and christening, 20; childhood, 30–31; mother's death, 32–3; memories of mother, 32–3; leaves home for Bradford, 36; childhood games and activities, 37, 51, 53–4; at Cowan Bridge School, 38, 39–40; dislike of school regime, 40–41, 43–4; sent back to Cowan Bridge, 47–8; at Roe Head School as pupil, 64–9, 71; dreams of dead sisters, 69; visits Red House in Gomersal, 70; tutors sisters at home, 71, 75; superintendent of new Sunday School, 75; depicted in *The Brontë Sisters* by Branwell, 81–2; exhibits drawings at Fine Arts exhibition, 83; takes post at Roe Head, 85–6; mental distress at Roe Head, 91–4, 97–9, 106–7; religious doubts, 97; decreasing control over Glass Town saga, 99; sends poems to Southey, 100–101; replies to Southey's letter, 103–4; quarrels with Margaret Wooler, 106–7; returns to work at Heald's House, 108; mental breakdown at Heald's House, 108; marriage proposal from Henry Nussey, 112–13; marriage proposal from David Pryce, 113–14; visits Branwell's studio in Bradford, 115; governess to Sidgwick family, 115; holiday with Ellen at Easton and Bridlington, 118; sees the sea, 118; responds to William Weightman's Valentines, 121; sends writing to Hartley Coleridge, 127–8; governess to White family, 129–30; plans to establish own school, 134–5, 179, 183, 190–91; inspired by Mary Taylor to travel abroad, 135; journey to Brussels in 1842, 136; early months at Pensionnat Heger, 143–50; separate lessons from Constantin Heger, 145; offered a part-time teaching post at Pensionnat, 150; in Brussels, summer 1842, 150–52; called home by aunt's death, 154–5; returns to Brussels in 1843, 158–9; learning German, 161; attends Mardi Gras carnival with Constantin Heger, 163; gives English lessons to Constantin Heger, 163; despondency and loneliness in Brussels, 165, 170, 172–3, 176; essay read at speech day, 171 and n; planning novel or story, 173; goes to confession, 175–6; gives in notice, 178; leaves Pensionnat, 180–81; offered post at Manchester school, 183; corresponds with Constantin Heger, 184–9, 202–4; produces school prospectus, 190–91; solicits business for school, 191; abandons school scheme, 191; holiday with Ellen Nussey in Hathersage, 193, 195–6; thinks of going to Paris, 197; publishes translations from the French, 198–9; writing novel ('The Master'), 199–200; discovers Emily's poems, 207; plans to publish poems with sisters, 208–9;

BIOGRAPHY/PERSONAL LIFE (*cont.*):
proposes jointly authored novel to
Aylott and Jones, 213–14; *Poems*
published, 219–21; goes to
Manchester with Emily, 224;
accompanies father to Manchester
for eye operation, 225–6; begins
Jane Eyre, 226; sends *Poems* to
admired authors, 233; *Jane Eyre*
accepted by Smith, Elder & Co.,
236; *Jane Eyre* published, 238; CB
reveals authorship to father,
239–40; begins new novel, 245–6;
Jane Eyre adapted for the stage,
250–51; anonymity threatened,
251; travels to London with Anne,
254; reveals identity to Smith,
254–5; visits the Opera, 256; and
Branwell's death, 260–61; Emily's
illness and death, 261–5; takes
Anne to Scarborough, 268–71;
Anne's death and burial, 270; in
Filey with Ellen, 271–2; and
bereavement of siblings, 274, 277,
312–13, 316; *Shirley* published,
281; 'frenzy' around identity of
'Currer Bell', 281–2; visits Smiths
in London in 1849, 283–6; visits
London in summer of 1850,
289–98; trip to Scotland, 1850,
300; James Taylor proposes,
300–302; writing *Villette*, 304, 317;
visits London in summer of 1851,
305–9; visits phrenologist, 308;
visits the Gaskells in Manchester,
311; revisits Scarborough and
Filey, 314–15; Arthur Nicholls
proposes, 318–20; visits London in
January 1853, 321; falls out with
Ellen Nussey, 326–8; secures
father's consent to marriage,
332–3; claims to be giving up
writing, 328; wedding, 335;
honeymoon in Wales and Ireland,
335–8; accident in Gap of Dunloe,
338; pregnancy, 345–9; illness and
death, 346–9; burial, 349–50

CHARACTERISTICS AND PERSONALITY: dutiful
nature, 1, 85–6, 147–8, 176, 223;
physical appearance and manner, 2,
64–5, 81–2, 83, 133, 144, 160–61,
162, 256–7, 296, 392; social isolation,
27, 36, 51, 68, 71, 105, 116, 144–5,
190; questioning of authority, 30,
48–9, 68, 202, 228, 229; intellectual
distinction, 65–6, 70–71, 108, 143,
163; conscience, 68; love for siblings,
68–9, 129, 190; self-consciousness,
74, 115, 144, 167, 290, 292, 295, 296;
as teacher, 75, 77, 92, 158, 160–61,
163, 184; household skills and duties,
76, 125–6, 183, 189–90, 339;
self-suppression, 92, 93, 104, 194,
203; anger, 93–4, 116–17, 194, 279;
imaginative flights and occasional
extrovertism, 113–14, 131, 163; as
governess, 115–18, 130; sensitivity
to criticism, 303
alter egos and pseudonyms, 59;
'Charles Townshend', 72, 127–8,
233, 237, 241, 277, 280–81;
'Charles Thunder', 99; 'Currer
Bell', 209–10, 209n, 238, 242–3,
250, 251, 254–5, 281–2, 289; 'Miss
Brown', 255, 256; 'Miss Fraser',
308

HEALTH: frailness, 40, 43, 64–5, 66, 326;
short sight, 65, 66, 318; diet, 66,
125; trance-like states, 91–2, 93–6,
230; nervous disorders and
depression, 108–9, 116–17, 172–3,
183, 203–4; fears of blindness, 186;
teeth, 226

LITERARY, ARTISTIC AND INTELLECTUAL LIFE:
knowledge of French language, 52,
134–5, 143, 185, 198; interest in
visual arts, 58–9, 66, 78–9, 137; as
poet, 59, 91, 100–101, 121, 150, 163,
164, 198–9, 208–12, 243–4; as artist,
79, 80–81, 83–4, 155; portraits of
Anne Brontë, 80–81; ambition to
write and publish, 100–101, 104, 179,
185–6, 198–9, 200, 208; view of
Emily Brontë's writing, 207–8, 215,
216, 263 and n, 288–9; view of Anne
Brontë's writing, 208, 216–17, 288–9
dealings with publishers, 226, 233;
Chambers, 209; Aylott and Jones,
209–10, 213–14, 217, 219–20;
Henry Colburn, 220; Smith, Elder
& Co., 235–8, 243, 253, 267–8, 303;
writing methods, 217, 227–8, 341;
controversy over 'brothers Bell',
220, 241, 250, 253–4, 263–4
early imaginative games and writing,
53–6, 59–60, 61–2, 72–3; minuscule texts, 59–60, 173; imaginary
world, 128–9, 168, 173; sophistications and continuations of Glass
Town saga, 72–3, 91–2, 94,
99–100, 128, 173, 229
translations: from French, 161,
198–199, 211; from German, 161
and n

OPINIONS AND IDEAS: religious views and
faith, 3–4, 98, 140, 145, 176, 307–8,
251–2, 261, 311; hero-worship of
Wellington, 55, 59, 67, 144, 161,
195, 292; politics, 66–7, 246–9;
love and marriage, 87, 112–14,
124–5, 166, 194, 195, 223, 327–8,
332–3, 341–2; children, 117, 311,
329; finances and attitude to
money, 134, 151, 156–7, 166, 183,
191, 212, 219, 231, 237, 257 and n,
318, 332–3, 334, 348–9; Belgians,
145, 149, 168, 180; genius, 164,
180; class politics, 201–2, 248–9;
sexual politics, 202, 228, 248–9,
275–6, 282; heroines, 217–18, 229;
revolutionary sensibility, 246–9,
279–80; women and writing,
328–9; parenthood, 329; war, 339

PORTRAITS OF: *The Brontë Sisters*, 81–2,
340; portrait by Mary Dixon,
161–2; portrait by George
Richmond, 161, 296–8, 340, 351,
353; possible self-portrait, 178–9;
photograph mistaken for one of
CB, 339–40 and n

RELATIONSHIPS: with father, 30, 38, 183–4,
260, 301–2, 323–4, 334–5, 338; with
brother, 72–3, 74, 127, 132, 192, 194,
197–8, 200, 212, 218–19, 222, 231,
252, 260–61; with Ellen Nussey,
85–6, 90–91, 97–9, 118, 195–6, 251;
with William Weightman, 122–3;
with Constantin Heger, 143, 147,
149, 150, 160, 162–3, 164–7, 168,
170, 178, 184, 188–9, 198–9, 211–12,
243–4; gifts from Heger, 168, 170,
180; letters to Heger, 183n, 184–9,
198, 199, 204–6, 356–8; letters from
Heger, 184, 185, 202–3, 206, 353;
with Zoë Heger, 155, 165, 166–8,
170–71, 178, 200, 205; with George
Smith, 292–6, 308–10, 328, 331–2;
ungracious over George Smith's
engagement, 332; with Arthur Bell
Nicholls, 223–4; draws portrait of
Nicholls, 224, 315, 318–20, 324–5,
326, 332–4, 337, 340, 348–9

WORKS:
Angrian stories and writing: 'Farewell
to Angria', 41n, 129, 387; 'History
of the Year', 56–7, 59, 76;

WORKS (*cont.*):

'The Young Men's Magazine', 59, 68; 'The Green Dwarf', 72; 'High Life in Verdopolis', 72, 173; 'Arthuriana', 72; 'The Bridal', 72; 'Roe Head Journal', 92, 93, 96; 'Stancliffe's Hotel', 106; 'Mina Laury', 107; 'Caroline Vernon', 118–20, 128, 143; 'Ashworth', 118n, 127, 128, 143, 200; 'Henry Hastings', 128, 134, 143; 'The Spell', 173, 200, 358; 'Scrap Book', 173; 'Passing Events', 187

art works: *St Martin's Parsonage, Birmingham*, 79; *The Atheist Viewing the Dead Body of His Wife*, 80; *Bolton Priory*, 83; *Kirkstall Abbey*, 83; *William Weightman*, 122; *Watermill*, 152, 155 and n, 358 and n; *Ashburnham Church on the Valley-Land*, 358 and n

critical writing: 'A Word to *The Quarterly*', 279; 'Biographical Notice of Ellis and Acton Bell', 288–9

French *devoirs*, 143 and n; 'L'Ingratitude', 143n, 146; 'Le Nid', 147–8; 'L'Immensité de Dieu', 148; 'La Mort de Napoléon', 161; 'La Chute des Feuilles', 164; 'Le But de la Vie', 172; 'Letter d'un pauvre Peintre à un grand Seigneur', 179–80

poems: 'We wove a web in childhood', 91–2; 'I gave, at first, Attention close', 150, 163, 181, 199, 398; 'Pilate's Wife's Dream', 210; 'Mementos', 210; 'Frances', 211–12; 'Gilbert', 211–12; 'He saw my heart's woe', 243–4

published works *see under individual titles: Jane Eyre, Poems, The Professor, Shirley, Villette*

unfinished stories: 'The Story of Willie Ellin', 328, 341; 'Emma', 341

Brontë, Elizabeth (CB's sister), 19, 20, 36, 54; school in Wakefield, 38; at Cowan Bridge School, 38–9, 44, 46; illness and death, 46, 259 and n, 263, 271; funeral, 47

Brontë, Emily Jane (CB's sister): birth and childhood, 21, 36; imaginative life, 37, 54–5, 61, 87; quizzed by father, 37–8; at Cowan Bridge School, 43, 44, 46, 47; and bog burst, 45; housekeeping duties, 57, 89, 125–6, 183, 197; home life with sisters, 71–2, 197; caricatured by CB in 'The Young Men's Magazine', 73; appearance, 76, 81–2, 83, 88, 110, 133, 144, 290; relationship with Anne, 76, 132, 196; and Gondal saga, 76, 196, 197, 208; Diary Papers, 76–7, 133–4, 196, 250; poor spelling, 77; depicted in *The Brontë Sisters* by Branwell, 81–2; depicted in remaining fragment of *The Gun Group*, 82 and n; goes to school at Roe Head, 84–5, 87; attitudes to love and marriage, 87; homesickness, 88–9, 146, 151; poetry, 88, 190, 197, 207–9, 245; formidable character and anti-social tendencies, 89, 110, 123–4, 131, 144, 147, 189, 208, 262; love of animals, 89, 110, 169; paintings and drawings, 89, 152, 155 and n, 358 and n; pursuing study at home, 89; post at Law Hill, 110–11; as teacher, 110, 152; inspiration for, and composition of, *Wuthering Heights*, 110, 199; immune to Weightman's charm, 121; nicknamed 'The Major', 121; violently disciplines Keeper, 123–4; on Branwell's questionable success, 132; and school plan, 133–4, 152, 192;

travels to Brussels, 136; at the
Pensionnat Heger, 141, 144, 146–7,
155; intellectual distinction, 144, 147;
antipathy to Constantin Heger, 146;
teaching music at Pensionnat, 150,
152; attitude to religion, 151; spends
summer in Brussels in 1842, 151–2;
called home by aunt's death, 154;
inherits money from aunt, 156;
finances, 156–7, 234; bitten by dog,
169; and Branwell's decline, 194, 196;
visits York with Anne, 196; anger at
CB's discovery of poems, 208; insists
on anonymity, 208; pseudonym
'Ellis Bell', 209 and n, 221, 233;
controversy over 'brothers Bell', 220,
241, 250, 253–4, 263–4; *Poems*
published, 219–20; scornful of
publication, 220; accompanies CB to
Manchester, 224; model for Diana
Rivers in *Jane Eyre*, 230; rescues
Branwell from burning bed, 231,
402–3; publication of *Wuthering
Heights*, 234, 240; dealings with
Newby, 237, 240, 257; planning
another novel, 245; model for
Shirley Keeldar in *Shirley*, 248,
274–5; illness and death, 261–5, 267,
269, 271

WORKS:

essays (French *devoirs*), 146–7, 390
poems: 'The Bluebell', 88; 'A little
while, a little while', 88; 'Loud
without the wind was roaring', 88;
'The Old Stoic', 207; 'The
Prisoner', 234
prose: *Wuthering Heights*, 25, 110, 214
and n, 215–16, 231, 234, 237, 239,
240, 263–4, 277, 288

Brontë, Maria (CB's sister), 19, 31, 36,
37–8, 54, 57; school in Wakefield, 38;

at Cowan Bridge School, 38–9, 43;
illness at school, 43, 46; death, 46, 259
and n, 271; paragon character, 48, 51
Brontë, Maria (*née* Branwell, CB's mother):
family background and youth, 14–15;
letters, 15–18; essay, 16; appearance,
16; character, 16–17; engagement to
Patrick Brontë, 17–18; possessions
lost in shipwreck, 18; wedding,
18–19; moves to Thornton, 19;
friendship with Elizabeth Firth,
19–20, 21; births of children 21–2;
relations with Patrick Brontë, 27,
28–30; dress cut up, 28–9; last illness,
30–32; death, 32, 259n
Brontë, Patrick (CB's father): background
and youth, 6–10; family name, 6,
9–10; religious views, 8, 25; family
relations, 8, 10, 190; career as
teacher, 8; at Cambridge University,
9–10; and money, 9, 47, 85, 140, 156,
199; Irishness, 9, 11–12; takes Holy
Orders, 10; curacies, 10, 11, 19, 20,
22; relationship with Mary Burder,
10–11, 34–5; poetry, 11, 12–13, 22,
90; feelings for Jane Fennell, 12–13;
political sympathies, 14, 57–8, 105,
168–9; manner and appearance, 16,
26–9, 76, 133, 177; proposes to Maria
Branwell, 17; wedding, 18–19; move
to Thornton, 19; anxieties about
insurrection, 8, 21; guns, 21, 28, 330;
move to Haworth, 23; social
isolation, 26–7; habits, 26, 36, 51,
191–2, 225, 268–9, 273–4; letters to
newspapers, 27, 169, 177; strong
opinions and reported eccentricities,
28–30, 35, 53, 75; sensibility, 30, 33,
225–6; proposes to Elizabeth Firth,
33; proposes to Isabella Dury, 33–4;
tests children with mask, 37–8;
experiences 'extraordinary disruption' of bog

Brontë, Patrick (*cont.*):

burst, 44–5; tutors son, 52, 78; health, 62, 108; relations with sister-in-law, 74, 156; in the pulpit, 76; ambitions for his son, 78, 84–5, 114, 192; contentions with local Nonconformists and Dissenters, 90, 105, 168–9, 182, 191; speaks at 1837 hustings, 105; sets Branwell up in business, 114; accompanies Charlotte and Emily to Brussels, 136; home-made phrasebook, 137–8; visits Waterloo, 138; deteriorating eyesight, 176, 183, 213, 224–5, 318, 326; consumption of alcohol, 176–7, 182; support of church school, 182, 191; disgust at Robinson affair, 194; unaware of daughters' literary activity, 217, 219, 239; operation for cataracts, 226; told of publication of *Jane Eyre*, 239–40; pride in CB's achievements, 240; concern for son, 251–2; grief for son, 260; and daughter Anne's illness, 266; and James Taylor's interest in CB, 300, 301–2; and Arthur Nicholls's interest in CB, 323–6, 334; and CB's illness and death, 349–50; fondness for Arthur Nicholls, 351; will, 351; death and funeral, 353; *Winter-Evening Thoughts* (poems), 12; *Cottage Poems* (poems), 12–13, 20, 22; *The Maid of Killarney* (prose), 22; *The Cottage in the Wood* (prose), 22, 251; 'The Phenomenon' (poem), 45

Brontë, Patrick Branwell (CB's brother): birth and childhood, 21, 24; imaginative life, 37, 54, 55; quizzed by father, 37–8; precocity, 52, 78; education, 38, 52, 77–8; and bog burst, 45; and deaths of sisters Maria and Elizabeth, 47; social isolation, 51 and n; toys, 54–5; contributions to Glass Town and Angrian sagas, 59, 61, 72–3, 90, 99, 128, 200; appearance and manner, 73–4, 75–6, 83, 131; caricatured as 'Wiggins' by CB, 73; thinks Rydings 'Paradise', 73–4; teaches at Sunday School, 75–6; perceived Irishness, 76, 105; lack of religious zeal, 78; trains in art, 78–9, 84; applies to Royal Academy of Art, 84 and n; career as professional artist, 89, 114–15; Freemason, 89; ambition to be writer, 90, 100–101, 127, 152; opium-taking, 94–5, 192, 198, 253; writes to *Blackwood's Magazine*, 90, 101, 152; writes to Wordsworth, 101 and n; burnt in effigy after defending father at hustings, 105; moves to Bradford studio, 114–15; friendship with William Weightman, 120, 153; misleads Mary Taylor, 125; tutor to Postlethwaite family, 126–7; dissolute behaviour, 126, 132, 192, 218, 222, 231–2, 245; possibly fathers illegitimate child, 127; writes to Hartley Coleridge, 127; dismissed from job in Broughton, 127; takes job at Sowerby Bridge railway station, 130–31; sensibility, 132; transfers to Luddenden Foot, 132; publishes poems as 'Northangerland', 132, 152, 199; dismissed from job at Luddenden Foot, 152; unemployed at home, 153; distressed by aunt's death, 155–6; takes up post as tutor to Edmund Robinson, 157; liaison with Lydia Robinson, 192–4, 196, 199; writing novel, 199; unaware of sisters' literary activity, 218; hears news of Edmund Robinson's death, 221–2; debts, 231; sets bed on fire, 231;

increasing depression and psychotic symptoms, 232, 251, 252–3; last illness and death, 259–60

WORKS:

art works: *Terror*, 80; *Queen Esther*, 80; *The Brontë Sisters*, 81–2, 297; *The Gun Group*, 82 and n, 297; portraits commissioned in Bradford, 115; *A Parody* (caricature), 232 and n

poems: 'At dead of midnight – drearily', 127; translations of Odes of Horace, 127; 'Heaven and Earth', 132; 'Morley Hall', 218 and n; 'Penmaenmawr', 336

prose: 'And the Weary are at Rest' (novel), 199; 'The Wool is Rising' (story), 200

Brookroyd, Birstall (home of Nussey family), 107, 251, 281, 300

Broughton-in-Furness, Lancashire (now Cumbria), 126, 127, 130

Brown, John (sexton): sponsors Branwell Brontë into Freemasons, 89; friendship with Branwell Brontë, 90, 120, 126–7, 196; anecdotes about Branwell Brontë, 132n; Arthur Nicholls's landlord, 213, 320; letter from Branwell Brontë, 252; and Branwell Brontë's death, 260; disapproval of Arthur Nicholls, 320

Brown, Martha (Brontë family servant): loyalty, 82; joins household, 125; and Brontë memorabilia, 162 and n; as servant, 197, 281; information given to Elizabeth Gaskell, 265, 347; initial antipathy to Arthur Nicholls, 320; and CB's last illness and death, 347, 349–50; in Patrick Brontë's will, 351; moves to Banagher, 353–4

Brown, Tabitha, 259, 349

Brunty, Alice, or Eleanor (*née* McClory, CB's paternal grandmother), 6, 10

Brunty, Hugh (CB's paternal grandfather): alternative spellings of name, 6; family background, 6; domestic life, 7

Brunty, Hugh (Patrick Brontë's brother), 10

Brunty, William (Patrick Brontë's brother), 8

Brussels, Belgium, 135, 136, 138–9, 151–2

Buckworth, Reverend John, 11, 30–31

Burder, Mary, 10–11, 13, 25n, 34–5

Burdett-Coutts, Angela, 256, 312

Burns, Helen (*Jane Eyre*), 37, 42, 44, 48, 228, 236 and n

Burns, Robert, 7, 90

Butterfield, Francis, 246 and n

Button, Sarah, 346–7

Byron, George Gordon, 6th Baron, 53, 59, 161

Cairnes, John Elliot, 380

Carroll, Lewis *see* Dodgson, Charles

Cartwright, William, 13–14

Catherine, Duchess of Cambridge (Kate Middleton), 346

Chambers' Edinburgh Journal, 209

Chapel Royal, Brussels, 138, 141

Chapelle, Monsieur (teacher, Brussels), 158, 163, 180

Chapter Coffee House, London, 136, 158, 254, 256

Chartism, 105, 106, 168, 246, 249

Châteaubriand, René, Vicomte de, 145, 148

Chatterton, Thomas, 136

Chénier, André, 198

Chitham, Edward, 214, 400

cholera, 2, 142, 153, 154

Christian Remembrancer (periodical), 279

Clayton, A. B., 80

Clergy Daughters' School, Cowan Bridge: establishment and situation, 38–9; trustees, 38, 209n; curriculum, regime and fees, 39–41, 42–4, 47, 374; identification with Lowood School in *Jane Eyre*, 41–2, 48, 282; food, 42–3; blamed for CB's ill-health, 43; typhus outbreak, 45

Cockill, Elizabeth, and sisters, 191

Colburn, Henry, 220

Coleridge, Hartley, 127–8, 185, 198, 233

Coleridge, Samuel Taylor, 93

consumption (tuberculosis), 43, 46, 62, 258–9, 266–7, 273, 288, 346, 349

Conwy, Wales, 335

Cook, Ann, 94

Corn Laws and political unrest, 21

Crimean War, 339

Crimsworth, William (*The Professor*), 137, 141, 145, 149, 194, 200, 201, 202

Critic (magazine), 220, 238

Crosby, Dr, 258

Cuba House, Banagher, 336–7 and n

'Currer Bell' (pseudonym) *see* Brontë, Charlotte

Currer, Miss, 209n

Daily News, 322, 351

De Quincey, Thomas, 94, 127, 233; *Confessions of an English Opium-Eater*, 94

De Renzy, Reverend George, 335

Delavigne, Casimir Jean-François, 145

Desart, Earl and Countess of, 256

Dewsbury (West Yorkshire), 11, 12, 107

Dickens, Charles: and *Jane Eyre*, 41, 298, 414; as possible model to CB, 268, 321; opportunities to meet, 280, 285, 290, 298; as a social commentator, 307, 321; *Nicholas Nickleby*, 41 and n, 298, 387; *David Copperfield*, 298; *Sketches by Boz*, 321; *Oliver Twist*, 321; *Barnaby Rudge*, 321

Dixon family of Brussels, 2, 3, 161, 162

Dixon, Mary, 161, 162, 172

Dodgson, Charles (Lewis Carroll), 234n

Douglas Jerrold's Weekly (periodical), 240

Douglas, Marion, 358

Drumballyroney, County Down, 8, 10, 77

Dublin University Magazine, 220

Dunloe, Gap of, 338

Dury family, 115

Dury, Isabella, 33–4

Dury, Reverend Theodore, 33 and n, 38

Earl of Liverpool (steamship), 159

Earnley, Sussex, 112

Earnshaw, Catherine (*Wuthering Heights*), 214–15, 231, 359

Eastlake, Lady *see* Elizabeth Rigby

Easton, Yorkshire, 118

Edinburgh Review (periodical), 282

Edinburgh, 293–4, 300

Eliot, George (Mary Ann Evans), 323

Elliott, Ebenezer, 246

'Ellis Bell' (pseudonym) *see* Brontë, Emily

Emanuel, Paul (*Villette*), 4, 163, 181, 305, 322

Engels, Friedrich: *Condition of the Working Class in England*, 201

Enoch, Frederick, 220–21

Evans, Ann (teacher at Cowan Bridge), 44

Evans, Mary Ann *see* Eliot, George, 323

Examiner (periodical), 238, 313

Eyre family of Hathersage, 196

Eyre, Jane (*Jane Eyre*), 42, 58, 116, 165, 179, 181, 217, 228, 333

Eyton, Reverend John, 11, 38

Factory Bill 1843, 168

Félix, Eliza *see* 'Rachel'

Fennell family, 17

Fennell, Jane (*née* Branwell, first Mrs John Fennell), 14, 16

Fennell, Jane *see* Morgan, Jane

Fennell, John, 11, 16, 18–19, 33 and n, 190

Firth, Elizabeth *see* Franks, Elizabeth

Firth, John Scholefield, 19, 20, 30, 33 and n

'Flossy' (spaniel), 123, 169, 264, 272, 323

Foister, Susan R., 340n

Fonblanque, Albany, 238, 239

Forbes, Dr John, 285

Forçade, Eugène, 280

Forster, John, 298, 329

Franks, Elizabeth (*née* Firth), 19, 20, 21, 22, 31, 33, 44, 62, 70

Fraser's Magazine, 238, 303

Garrs, Nancy, 21, 28, 32, 44–5, 47, 50

Garrs, Sarah, 21, 29, 44–5, 47, 50, 259n

Gaskell family, 311

Gaskell, Elizabeth Cleghorn: research for, and writing of, *The Life of Charlotte Brontë*, 6, 26, 41–4, 136, 147, 180n, 192, 198, 351–3, 404; impressions of Patrick Brontë, 16, 27–30, 66, 330, 352; and criticisms of *Life*, 43; first access to Brontë juvenilia, 59–60; shown Branwell's portrait of CB and sisters, 81; and opium, 95–6; and CB's letters to Heger, 186, 205, 353, 356–7; fascination with CB, 239, 286–7, 288; view of CB's feelings for Arthur Nicholls, 223; second thoughts about Emily Brontë, 262; writes to CB about *Shirley*, 283; meets CB, 287; friendship with CB, 311; has CB to stay in Manchester, 311–12; visits Haworth in 1853, 329–31; schemes to further CB's romance, 331; thoughts on CB's pregnancy and illness, 346–7; hears of CB's death, 351; *Life of Charlotte Brontë*, 27–8, 42, 95, 287–8, 353, 359; *Mary Barton*, 268, 307, 311; *Ruth*, 307; *Cranford*, 328

Gaskell, William, 311, 312

Gawthorpe Hall, Lancashire, 286–7, 345

Gérin, Winifred, 171n; *Charlotte Brontë*, 171

Gomersal, West Yorkshire, 70, 85, 154

Gore, Catherine, 285

Graham, Dr Thomas John: *Modern Domestic Medicine*, 108 and n, 267

Grant, Reverend Joseph, 190, 195, 335

Great Barr, Birmingham, 232

Great Exhibition, Crystal Palace, 306

Greene, Thomas, 29

Greenwood family of Springhead, 26

Greenwood, John, 82, 217, 351, 402

Greta Bridge, Yorkshire, 41, 127

Grimshaw, Reverend William, 22, 25

Grundy, Francis, 41n, 78, 133, 152, 153, 155, 192, 252–3

Hale, Charles, 354

Halifax Guardian (newspaper), 132, 169, 199

Halifax, West Yorkshire, 110, 217, 258

Hardshaw, Reverend Andrew, 7–8

Hartley, Margaret (Isaac Kirby's niece), 115, 385

Hartshead-cum-Clifton, Yorkshire, 11, 13, 19

Hathersage, Derbyshire, 196, 198

Haworth Parsonage, 23–4, 134, 176

Haworth Temperance Society, 177, 246n

Haworth, West Yorkshire, 22, 24, 25, 105, 212 and n; Haworth Moor, 26, 71, 329–30; bog burst, 44–5; 1837 election, 105, 168; day school opens, 182; post office, 187, 219, 395; pub (The Black Bull), 90, 105, 153, 253, 354

Hayne, Mellaney, 47–8

Hayter, Alethea, 94

Heald's Hall, Liversedge, Yorkshire, 41

Heald's House (school), Dewsbury Moor, 107, 108, 134

Heathcliff (*Wuthering Heights*), 110, 214–15, 214n, 218, 231

Heaton family of Ponden Hall, 26

Heaton, William, 132

Hebden Bridge, West Yorkshire, 201n

Heger family, 150, 155n, 165, 172, 176, 179; possession of Brontë papers and memorabilia, 173 and n, 204–5, 304, 358 and n

Heger, Claire, 358

Heger, Constantin Georges Romain:
object of CB's affection, 3, 163,
166, 177, 188–9, 313; used as a
model in CB's fiction, 4, 163,
231–2, 248, 276, 285, 304–5, 308,
322, 357; encourages wife to accept
Brontë sisters as pupils, 136;
background, 141–2; characteristics
and manner, 142–3, 145, 148–9,
162–3; gives separate lessons to
Brontë sisters, 145; teaching
methods and literary taste, 145–6,
147–9, 161; and Emily Brontë,
146–7; advice to CB, 148, 164–5,
200; behaviour towards favoured
pupils, 149–50, 158, 359–60; writes
to Patrick Brontë, 155, 157–8;
feelings for CB, 158, 163, 164–5,
178, 181, 184; reprimands CB's
pupils, 160; takes English lessons
from CB, 163; chill in relations,
167; CB describes as 'the black
Swan', 168; gifts to CB, 168,
170–71, 180; encourages CB's plan
to set up a school, 179; sorrow at
parting, 181; letters to CB, 184,
185, 202–3, 353; letters from CB,
183n, 184–9, 198, 199, 203–6,
356–8; and Elizabeth Gaskell, 205,
352–3; CB's ideal reader, 211; and
Ellen Nussey's letters from CB, 355

Heger, Louise, 204–5, 357 and n

Heger, Zoë Claire (*née* Parent): accepts
Brontë sisters as pupils, 136;
background and family life, 139–40,
142, 165; as proprietress of
Pensionnat, 140–41; care of charges,
149–50; offers Brontë sisters a
second term, 150; goodwill towards
Brontës, 151, 158, 167; growing
wariness concerning CB, 166–8,
170, 181, 205; surveillance tech-

niques, 167; appearance, 171;
accompanies CB to Ostend, 181;
used as model in CB's fiction, 194,
200–201, 250, 304; and fate of CB's
letters, 204–5, 352–3, 356–7; reads
Villette, 352; death, 358

Helstone, Caroline (*Shirley*), 32–3, 248–9,
277, 358

Henri, Frances (*The Professor*), 149, 150,
201, 202, 228

Herschel, Sir John, 239, 247

Hodgson, Reverend William, 113

Hogg, James: *The Private Memoirs and
Confessions of a Justified Sinner*, 90

Horsfall, William, 13

Huddersfield, West Yorkshire, 11, 21, 70,
93

Hudson, George, 156

Hugo, Victor, 145

Hunsworth Mill, 70, 109, 135

Hunt, Leigh, 239, 242, 257

hyperemesis gravidarum (illness of
pregnancy), 346–7

Ingham family of Blake Hall, 111

Ingham, Dr Amos, 345, 349

Irish insurgence, 8, 21

Jane Eyre (CB): autobiographical elements,
37, 40–41, 44, 48, 108–109, 118n,
130, 181, 187, 230–31, 252, 268,
359–60; originality of, 48–9, 202,
227–30, 247; suggested illustrations,
83; inspiration and composition,
174, 196, 217, 226, 227–8, 234–5,
236n; self-portrait in, 179; publication, 236–8; critical reception,
238–9, 263–4, 277–80; dedication of
second edition to Thackeray, 241–2;
third edition, 250; 'A Word to *The
Quarterly*', 279

Jenkins family (Brussels), 139, 144–5

Jenkins, Reverend Evan, 138

Johnson, Samuel, 136

Kavanagh, Julia, 291

Kay-Shuttleworth, Lady Janet, 27, 286–7, 352

Kay-Shuttleworth, Sir James, 286–7, 345

Keeldar, Shirley (*Shirley*), 275; modelled on Emily Brontë, 248, 274

'Keeper' (mastiff), 89, 123–4, 169, 265 and n, 272, 313

Keighley Mechanics Institute, 78–9, 79n, 121

Keighley, West Yorkshire, 26, 29, 39, 57, 168, 182n, 190, 212, 236, 254

Kellett, Jocelyn, 372

Kilkee, County Clare, 337

Kingston, Eliza, 156, 157n, 190

Kingston, Jane (*née* Branwell), 156

Kirby family of Bradford, 114–15; *see also* Hartley, Margaret

Kirk Smeaton, West Yorkshire, 324, 328, 331

Kirke White, Henry, 9

Kirkstall Abbey, 17, 83

Koekelberg, Brussels, 144, 154

La Fontaine, Jean de, 143

La Trobe, James, 106

Lamartine, Alphonse de, 145, 148

Lascelles, Viscount, 256

Law Hill (school, Halifax), 110–11

Law, William, 161–62

Lawton, Marianna, 110

Lebel, Joachim-Joseph, 170, 171

Leeds Intelligencer (newspaper), 133, 169, 177

Leeds Mercury (newspaper), 45, 246

Leeds, West Yorkshire, 83, 106, 158, 247

Leopold I, King of Belgium, 5

Lewes, George Henry, 238, 255, 282, 283, 290 and n, 321

Leyland, Francis, 79, 131

Leyland, Joseph Bentley, 115, 199, 218, 222, 232, 258

Liddington, Jill, 384

Lister, Anne, 110–11, 123

Lister, Miss (pupil at Roe Head), 92, 93, 94

Literary Gazette (periodical), 238, 321

Liverpool, 118, 196

Lockhart, J. G., 233, 241, 278, 298

London, 136, 250

Lowood School (*Jane Eyre*), 41–2, 48, 228, 268, 298

Luddism, 13–14, 67, 246

Macdonald, Frederika, 160 and n, 185; 'The Brontës at Brussels', 160n, 171n

Macready, William, 284–5

MacTurk, Dr, 347

'The Master' (CB) *see The Professor*

Magdalene College, Cambridge, 112

Manchester, 21, 183, 201, 224, 225 and n, 311

Marie, Mademoiselle (teacher, Brussels), 141

Martin, John, 58–9, 115; *Belshazzar's Feast*, 58; *Joshua Commanding the Sun to Stand Still*, 58; *The Deluge*, 58; *St Paul Preaching at Athens*, 58; *Queen Esther*, 80

Martineau, Harriet: recalls CB's view of heroines in fiction, 217; intrigued by the identity of 'Currer Bell', 282–3; meets CB, 285–6; invites CB to Ambleside, 298–9; criticises *Villette*, 322; obituary of CB, 351; *Illustrations of Political Economy*, 282; *Deerbrook*, 282; *Letters on the Laws of Man's Nature and Development*, 299

Martineau, James, 152

Marx, Karl, 116

Methodism, 8–9, 11, 15, 25

Middleton, Kate *see* Catherine, Duchess of Cambridge

Miller, Lucasta, 354n

Millevoye, Charles Hubert, 198; 'La Chute des Feuilles', 164

Milnes, Richard Monckton, 127, 234, 331

Mirabeau, Honoré Gabriel Riqueti, comte de, 145

Mitford, Mary Russell, 282

Montgomery, Robert, 80

Moore, Louis (*Shirley*), 4, 248, 275, 276

Moore, Robert (*Shirley*), 249, 276, 358

Moore, Thomas: *Life of Byron*, 155

Morgan, Jane (*née* Fennell), 12, 14, 16, 18–19

Morgan, Lady, 256, 285

Morgan, William, 11, 13, 14, 18–19, 33 and n, 114–15, 260

Morpeth, Lord, 105

Mossman, Meta, 359–60, 423

Nabokov, Vladimir, 120; *Pale Fire*, 120

National Gallery, London, 137, 257, 285

National School Society, 75, 191

Nelson, Rear-Admiral Horatio, Duke of Bronte, 9–10

Neufeldt, Victor, 400

New Zealand, 135, 189, 328

Newby, Thomas: offers to publish Ellis and Acton Bell's novels, 234, 237; publication goes ahead, 239; bad business practices, 240–41, 253, 255; advises Emily on second book, 245; CB and Anne confront, 257

Newman, John Henry, 307

Nicholls, Alan, 336

Nicholls, Arthur Bell: curatorship of CB material, 82, 344, 356, 422; arrives in Haworth, 194–5; character and demeanour, 195, 224, 302–3, 334, 337; as curate and Sunday School teacher, 213, 320, 325, 353; feelings for CB, 223–4, 302, 319, 320, 333, 325; portrait of by CB, 224; conducts Emily's funeral service, 265; difficult relations with Patrick Brontë, 269, 320, 323, 325, 326; caricatured in *Shirley*, 302–3; proposes to CB, 318–20; plans to emigrate, 320–21, 324; in Kirk Smeaton, 324, 327; difficulty containing his sorrow, 325–6; appearance and manner, 331; renewed courtship of CB, 331; offered posts by Vicar of Leeds, 331; marries CB, 335; takes CB on honeymoon to Ireland, 335; married happiness, 339; devotion to Patrick Brontë, 339, 351, 353; gives opinion of 'Emma' (CB), 341; strictures over CB's letter-writing, 342–4; offered living by Sir James Kay-Shuttleworth, 345; CB's pregnancy and death, 347, 349–50; against writing of memoir, 352; and Elizabeth Gaskell, 352, 353, 356; return to Banagher, 353; remarries, 353; death, 356

Nightingale, Florence, 234, 275–6 and ns, 312, 403

North American Review (periodical), 263

North British Review (periodical), 277

North Lees Hall, Derbyshire, 196, 397

Noyer, Marie-Josephine, 142; death 142

Nussey family, 107, 112, 223

Nussey, Ellen: reminiscences of CB and her family, 18, 29, 36, 66, 73–5; meets CB, 65; at Roe Head School, 65–71; and CB's letters, 65, 90, 344–5, 355; entertains CB at Rydings, 73–4; visits to Haworth, 74–5, 121, 166, 266, 312–13, 316, 342; impressions of Patrick Brontë, 74, 177; social sensitivities, 85–6, 107; feminine inertia, 87, 151; protective of CB's memory, 90, 352; object of CB's affection, 97–9; suggests seaside holiday, 118; interest in William Weightman, 121, 122–3; holiday with CB in Hathersage, 195; on family black sheep, 231; suspects CB's authorship of *Jane Eyre*, 251; in Scarborough and Filey with Anne Brontë and CB, 269–71; falls out with CB, 326–8; attends CB's wedding, 335; images of, 339–40 and n; relations with Arthur Nicholls, 342–5, 355

Nussey, George, 85, 107, 223

Nussey, Reverend Henry: acquaintance with CB, 112, 113; first curacy, 112; proposes to CB, 112–13; as model for St John Rivers in *Jane Eyre*, 113; marries, 195

Nys, E., 173n, 358

Oakwell Hall, Birstall, 191, 352

opium, 94–6, 253

Ostend, 137

Outhwaite family, 20 and n

Outhwaite, Frances, 20, 22, 269

Outhwaite, John, 20, 177, 224

Oxenhope, West Yorkshire, 182, 195

Oxford Movement, 307

Patchett, Elizabeth, 110

Peel, Sir Robert, 58, 67, 76

Pensionnat Heger (school, Brussels), 1, 136, 139–140, 141, 165, 200

Penzance, Cornwall, 14–15, 74, 156, 267

Peterloo Massacre, 21, 106

pets belonging to the Brontë family, 89, 176, 197; *see also* 'Keeper', 'Flossy'

Peveril Castle, Derbyshire, 196

Poems by Currer, Ellis and Acton Bell (CB, EJB and AB), 209–12, 219–21, 241, 245, 246 and n; sales, 220, 233–4, 234n; critical reception, 220–21

Postlethwaite family of Broughton-in-Furness, 126, 127

Proctor, Adelaide, 295

Professor, The (CB, first titled 'The Master'), 5, 145, 149, 150, 163, 174, 181, 199, 200–201, 214, 218, 226, 234, 235; 236, 243, 245, 249, 303–4

Proust, Marcel, 230

Pryce, Reverend David, 113–14, 131, 290

Quarterly Review, 278–9

Quillinan, Edward, 101

railways, 118, 130–31, 132, 136, 152–3, 156, 198, 234, 236, 254, 354

'Rachel' (stage name of Eliza Félix), 309

Rand, Ebenezer, 182, 190, 191

Rand, Sarah (*née* Bacon), 182, 191, 195

Randolphe, Charles-Henri, 358

Ratchford, Fannie, 377

Rawfolds Mill, 13–14, 67

Redhead, Reverend Samuel, 23

Redman, Joseph, 89, 335

Regent's Park Zoological Gardens, London, 289

Reid, Sir Thomas Wemyss, 340, 355

Revue des deux mondes (periodical), 280

Richardson, Samuel, 128; *Sir Charles Grandison*, 128

Richmond, George, 161, 296–8, 413

Rigby, Elizabeth (Lady Eastlake), 241, 278, 279

Rivers, St John (*Jane Eyre*), 113

Roberson, Reverend Hammond, 14, 19, 20, 41, 248, 370

Robinson family of Thorp Green, 134, 153, 157, 169, 197, 258, 269

Robinson, Edmund, 157, 193n

Robinson, Edmund, Sr, 192, 193, 194, 221; will, 221 and n, 222 and n

Robinson, Lydia (later Lady Scott), 192–4, 196, 199, 221–2, 232, 258, 260, 397

Robinson, Lydia Mary, 222n

Robinson, William, 114

Rochester, Edward (*Jane Eyre*), 4, 118n, 179, 181, 187, 229–31, 359–60

Roe Head School, Mirfield, 62–7, 85, 87–8, 98–9

Rogers, Samuel, 286

Royal Academy of Art, 84 and n, 257, 289

Royal Northern Society for the Encouragement of the Fine Arts, 83

Rue d'Isabelle, Brussels, 139 and n, 140

Ruskin, John, 242, 285, 296; *Modern Painters*, 285

Russell, William Howard, 339

Russell's General Atlas of Modern Geography, 178

Rydal, Cumberland, 127

Rydings, Birstall (Nussey family home), 73–4

St John's College, Cambridge, 9, 78

St-Josse-ten-Noode, Brussels, 2, 154, 174

St Michael's Church, Haworth, 24, 25, 182, 259; Sunday School built, 75

St Paul's Cathedral, London, 137

Saint-Pierre, Bernadin de, 148, 171

SS-Michel-et-Gudule, Cathedral of (Brussels), 3–4, 139, 175

Sand, George, 321

Scarborough, East Yorkshire, 169, 194, 267, 269–71

Schiller, Friedrich, 161 and n; 'Der Taucher', 161n

Scott, Lady (first wife of Sir Edward Scott), 232, 258

Scott, Lady (second wife of Sir Edward Scott) *see* Lydia Robinson

Scott, Sir Edward, 258

Scott, Sir Walter, 57, 59, 161, 196, 300; *Peveril of the Peak*, 196; *Marmion*, 263

sexuality, 110–11, 123

Shaen, Emma, 329

Shannon (river), 195, 397

Sharp, Jack, 110

Sharpe's London Magazine (periodical), 352

Shaw, William, 41

Shibden Hall, Halifax, 110

Shirley (CB, first titled 'Hollow's Mill'), 4, 14, 32–3, 70, 109, 195, 245–50, 257, 267–8, 274–7, 281; real-life models, 248; publication, 281; reception, 281–3, 303

Shorter, Clement King, 355, 356, 358

Sidgwick family of Stonegappe, 115–16, 117 and n, 130

Sidgwick, John Benson, 115–16, 118 and n

Silverdale, Lancashire, 46

Simeon, Charles, 9, 11, 25

Slade, Mrs, 130

Smith family, 256, 257, 284

Smith, Elizabeth, 257, 284, 293, 315, 318, 321

Smith, George: reads manuscript of *The Professor*, 235; acceptance and publication of *Jane Eyre*, 236–8, 253; meets CB, 253–5; CB's host in London, 255–7, 284–5, 289–92, 305; intimacy with CB, 292–4, 300, 301, 308–10; appraisals of CB, 293–4, 295–6; as 'Dr John' in *Villette*, 304, 309, 315–16; marries, 328, 332

Smith, Reverend James, 182 and n, 183, 190, 195

Snowe, Lucy (*Villette*), 5, 163, 175, 176, 181, 206, 296, 304–5, 322

Society for the Propagation of the Gospel, 320

Sophie, Mademoiselle (teacher, Brussels), 141, 167, 180

Southey, Robert, 100, 101, 185, 198; reply to CB's first letter, 102–3; reply to CB's second letter, 104, 164, 282

Sowden, Reverend Sutcliffe, 324, 333; officiates at CB's wedding, 335, 342, 343, 345; officiates at CB's funeral, 349

Spectator (magazine), 322

Spielmann, Marion H., 357n, 398

Stanley, Beatrice E., 212n

Sterne, Lawrence, 120

Stonegappe, Lothersdale, North Yorkshire, 115, 118, 129

Stowe, Harriet Beecher, 314; *Uncle Tom's Cabin*, 314 and n

Stuart, J. A. Erskine, 231

Taylor family of Red House, Gomersal, 70, 135, 231, 248, 250

Taylor family of Stanbury, 26, 183

Taylor, Amelia (*née* Ringrose), 329, 348

Taylor, James, 237, 268, 282, 284; proposes to CB, 300–302; in Bombay, 313

Taylor, John, 166

Taylor, Joseph, 131, 135, 136–7 and n, 166, 186, 187, 251, 329, 334

Taylor, Martha: at Roe Head School, 69; visits Haworth, 109; at school in Brussels, 135, 144; death and burial, 154, 161, 291

Taylor, Mary: at Roe Head School, 64–5, 70–71; opinions of CB, 64, 66, 161, 187, 189, 327–8, 392; personality and characteristics, 65, 67–8, 70–71, 151; opinions, 66–7, 70, 109, 151, 396; at home, 70; visits Haworth, 109, 121, 125; attracted to Branwell Brontë, 125; travels in Europe, 135, 151; on journey to Brussels with CB, 136–7; at school in Koekelberg, 144; on Emily Brontë, 146; nurses dying sister Martha, 154; plans to move to Germany, 154; criticises Patrick Brontë, 189; emigration to New Zealand, 189; defends CB's right to choose marriage, 327; *Miss Miles*, 109, 396; essays, 109

Taylor, William Henry, 162, 251

Teale, Dr, 266

Tennyson, Alfred, 1st Baron, 233, 247

Thackeray, Anne, 294–5, 297

Thackeray, William Makepeace: admired by CB as 'social regenerator', 241–2; responds to CB's dedication of *Jane Eyre* second edition, 242; keen to meet 'Currer Bell', 255; meets CB, 285; account of conversation with CB, 291–2; impressions of CB, 291–2; entertains CB to dinner,
294–5; lectures, 305; opinion of *Villette*, 317; *Vanity Fair*, 238, 255, 268, 278; *Henry Esmond*, 307

Thompson, John, 115

Thornfield (*Jane Eyre*), 230, 397

Thornton, West Yorkshire, 19

Thornton, Henry, 9

Thorp Green, North Yorkshire, 153, 155, 169, 192, 193, 197, 210, 221, 222

Tighe, Reverend Thomas, 8

Times (newspaper), 303, 339

Todmorden, West Yorkshire, 190

Tone, Wolfe, 8

Trinity College, Dublin, 182, 195

Trollope, Anthony, 285

Trotman, Martha, 150, 358n

Turner, J. M. W., 83

Turner, Joseph Horsfall, 355

Upperwood House, Apperley Bridge, 130, 135

Victoria, Queen, 5, 238

Villette (CB), 4, 5, 69, 95, 109, 137, 159, 163, 171n, 175, 180–81, 187, 206; inception and composition, 303, 313–14, 315–17; reception, 318, 321–3

Vincent, Reverend Osman Parke, 124

Voltaire, 52, 143

Wade, Reverend John, 354 and n

Walker, Amelia, 20n

Walker, Anne, 110

Walker, Sir Emery, 340n

Walker, John, 110

Walker, Robin, 350

Wappers, Egide Charles Gustave, *Épisode des journées de septembre 1830 sur la place de l'Hôtel de Ville de Bruxelles*, 142

Ward, Mrs Humphry, 293

Waterclough Hall, Halifax, 110

Waterloo, Battle of, 20, 138; battlefield, 138

Weightman, William: arrives in Haworth, 120; writes Valentines for Brontë sisters, 120–21; sits for portrait by CB, 122, 386; 'male-flirt', 122–3; friend to Branwell Brontë, 153; illness and death, 153; funeral, 153; possible model for Weston in *Agnes Grey*, 216

Wellington, Arthur Wellesley, 1st Duke of, 20, 55, 58, 144, 161, 171, 195, 292, 297

Wesley, John, 8–9, 25

Westall, Richard, 155

Westminster Abbey, London, 137

Westwood, Thomas, 357–8

Wethersfield, Essex, 10–11, 34

Wheelhouse, Dr, 265

Wheelwright family of Brussels, 144, 152, 172

Wheelwright, Frances, 144, 389

Wheelwright, Laetitia, 205–6, 268, 348, 389

Wheelwright, Dr Thomas, 144

White family of Upperwood House, 129–130, 135, 191

Wilberforce, William, 9

William IV, King: coronation, 69

Williams, William Smith: CB advises about his daughters' careers, 130; reads and praises *The Professor*, 235; first reader of *Jane Eyre*, 236; dealings with CB in role as editor, 238, 243, 268, 279, 281, 304, 314; friendship with CB, 242–3, 342; attends dramatisation of *Jane Eyre*, 250–51; meets CB, 255; socialises with CB in London, 256–7; concern for Emily Brontë during illness, 262; suggests companion for CB, 273; CB compares to 'easy down or warm fur', 284; at Mrs Smith's ball, 290; gives CB his opinion of James Taylor, 313; CB snubs in letter, 332

Wilson, William Carus, 39, 40, 43; *Child's First Tales*, 40, 281

Wilson, William, 224–5, 226

Winkworth, Catherine, 327, 329, 333–4, 347

Winnifrith, Tom, 214, 400

Wise, Thomas J., 355

Wiseman, Cardinal, 286, 307

Wood, William, 265

Woodhouse Grove School, Apperley Bridge, 11, 14

Wooler family, 64, 107–8, 115, 134

Wooler, Catherine, 69, 134, 141

Wooler, Margaret: as head of Roe Head School, 64–5, 88; character, 67, 92; as role model, 67, 134; and Emily Brontë, 89; disagreement with CB and breach, 106–7; moves school to Heald's House, 107; affection for CB, 108; sympathy with CB's distress, 108; asks CB to take over running of Heald's House School, 134; model for Mrs Pryor in *Shirley*, 248; attends Anne Brontë's funeral, 270; visited by CB in Hornsea, 329; gives CB away at wedding, 335

Wooler, Marianne, 85, 134

Wordsworth, William, 100, 101, 127, 128, 233

Worsnop, Thomas, 246n

Wuthering Heights (film, William Wyler, 1939), 214n

York and North Midland Railway Company, 156

York, Yorkshire, 196

Zamorna, Duke of (Arthur Augustus Adrian Wellesley, Marquis of Douro, King of Angria), 59, 72–3, 80, 91, 106, 107, 115, 118, 119–20, 229

CLAIRE HARMAN

SYLVIA TOWNSEND WARNER

The poet Sylvia Townsend Warner rose to sudden fame with the publication of her classic feminist novel Lolly Willowes in 1926, but never became a conventional member of London literary life, pursuing instead a long writing career in her own individualistic manner. Cheerfully defying social norms of the day, Warner lived in an openly homosexual relationship with the poet Valentine Ackland for almost forty years. Together, they were committed members of the Communist party and travelled twice to Spain during the Civil War, but Warner paid for her outspokenness with years of neglect, and channelled much of her emotional and intellectual energy into letters, poems and heart-breaking diaries that remained unpublished during her lifetime. In this enthralling and enlightening biography, Claire Harman tells the story of Warner's remarkable life and restores her to her rightful place as one of Britain's most unique and brilliant writers.

'As passionate and truthful, elegant and enchanting as its subject' *George D Painter*

'One of the most shamefully under-read great British authors of the past 100 years' *Sarah Waters*

'Harman skilfully weaves Sylvia's stories and letters into the biography, and the brilliance of the samples on display constantly takes you aback... Outstanding' *Sunday Times*

CLAIRE TOMALIN

CHARLES DICKENS: A LIFE

Charles Dickens was a phenomenon. His novels are read the world over and he enriched the English language. He mocked power and greed while speaking up for ordinary people. His public readings brought adoring crowds, and he was seen as a cheerful family man. Yet there was a darker Dickens whose demons drove him to reject his wife, fail his children, break with friends and conduct a secret love affair in his last years. In *Charles Dickens: A Life*, Claire Tomalin gives us the best account yet of the man, his works, his times and, most of all, his extraordinary genius.

'Tomalin has captured Dickens, in sun and shadow, with all the full-hearted exuberance, generosity and keen wit that he merits' Boyd Tonkin, *Independent*

'Powerful and remarkable. It is a celebration of a great genius. No question: you put Tomalin's book down knowing that you have met a living author' Miriam Margolyes, *The Times*

'Tomalin brings this energetic, complicated, life-affirming, monstrous man so vividly to life that, when he drops dead, it is like a light going out' Jeremy Paxman, *Country Life*

CLAIRE TOMALIN

THOMAS HARDY: THE TIME-TORN MAN

Paradox ruled Thomas Hardy's life. His birth was almost his death; he became one of the great Victorian novelists and reinvented himself as one of the twentieth-century's greatest poets; he was an unhappy husband and a desolate widower; he wrote bitter attacks on the English class system yet prized the friendship of aristocrats.

In the hands of Whitbread Award-winning biographer Claire Tomalin, Thomas Hardy the novelist, poet, neglectful husband and mourning lover all come vividly alive.

'Another triumph for a biographer who goes from strength to strength' Melvyn Bragg, *Guardian, Books of the Year*

'Tomalin provides an object lesson in how to write a life' *Economist*

'A moving story, and Tomalin tells it vividly, with as great a fund of sympathy and sense, as can be imagined' *Daily Telegraph*

He just wanted a decent book to read ...

Not too much to ask, is it? It was in 1935 when Allen Lane, Managing Director of Bodley Head Publishers, stood on a platform at Exeter railway station looking for something good to read on his journey back to London. His choice was limited to popular magazines and poor-quality paperbacks – the same choice faced every day by the vast majority of readers, few of whom could afford hardbacks. Lane's disappointment and subsequent anger at the range of books generally available led him to found a company – and change the world.

'We believed in the existence in this country of a vast reading public for intelligent books at a low price, and staked everything on it'
Sir Allen Lane, 1902–1970, founder of Penguin Books

The quality paperback had arrived – and not just in bookshops. Lane was adamant that his Penguins should appear in chain stores and tobacconists, and should cost no more than a packet of cigarettes.

Reading habits (and cigarette prices) have changed since 1935, but Penguin still believes in publishing the best books for everybody to enjoy. We still believe that good design costs no more than bad design, and we still believe that quality books published passionately and responsibly make the world a better place.

So wherever you see the little bird – whether it's on a piece of prize-winning literary fiction or a celebrity autobiography, political tour de force or historical masterpiece, a serial-killer thriller, reference book, world classic or a piece of pure escapism – you can bet that it represents the very best that the genre has to offer.

Whatever you like to read – trust Penguin.